Architecture of the Last Colony

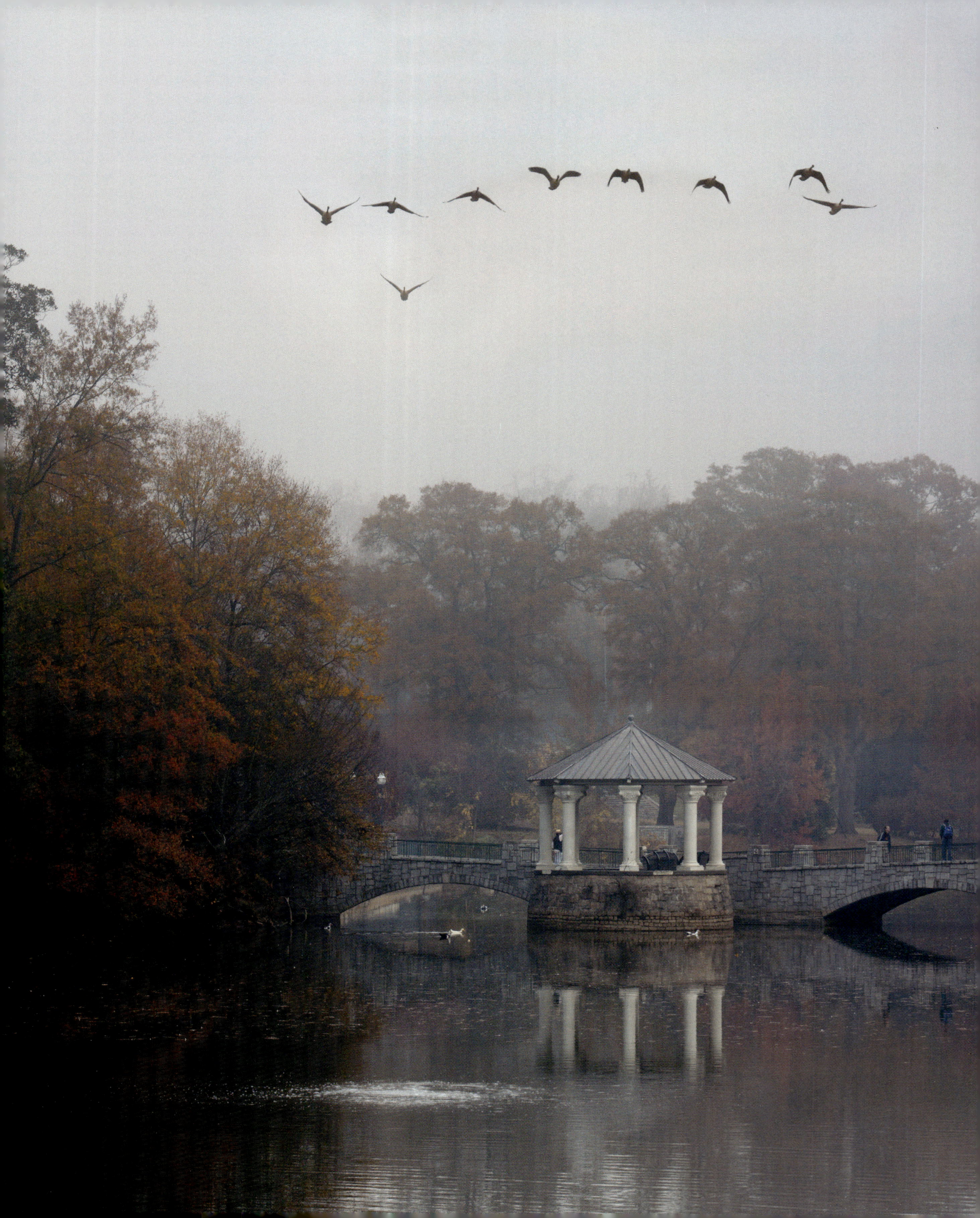

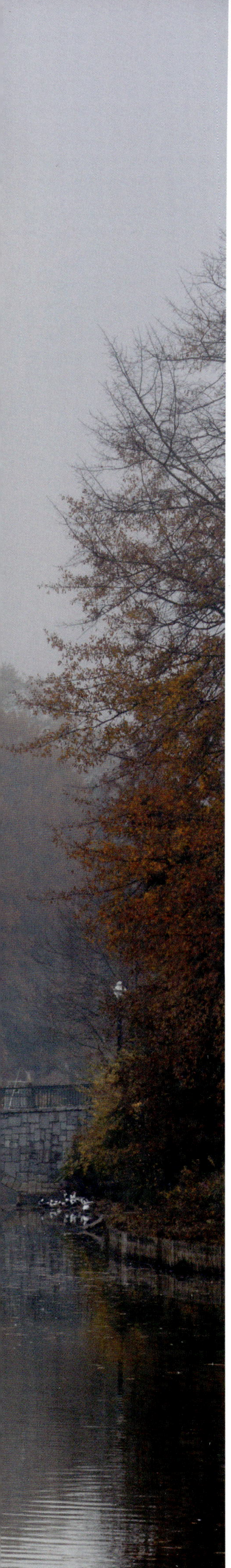

Architecture of the Last Colony

Georgia's Historic Places, 1733–2000

Edited by Mark C. McDonald

The Georgia Trust for Historic Preservation ✦ *Atlanta, Georgia*

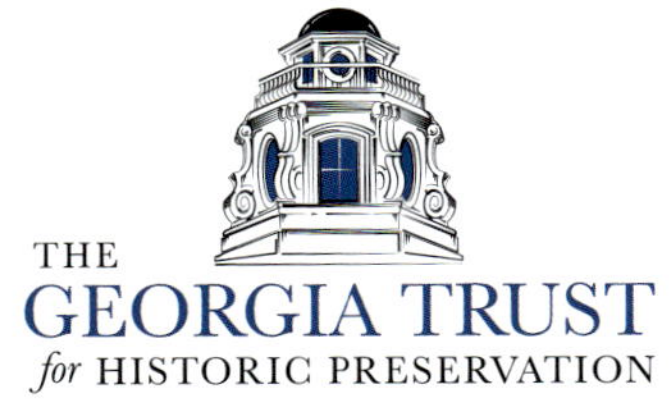

1516 Peachtree Street NW
Atlanta, Georgia 30309

www.georgiatrust.org

Designed by Louise OFarrell

Set in Adobe Jenson Pro
Printed and bound by Martin Book Management

The paper in this book meets the guidelines for permanence and durability of the Committee on Production Guidelines for Book Longevity of the Council on Library Resources.

Printed in the United States of America

27 26 25 24 23 C 5 4 3 2 1

Library of Congress Control Number: 2023940478
ISBN 9780820362960 (hardcover)

The Board of Trustees of the Georgia Trust for Historic Preservation expresses its gratitude to the following patrons who provided funds in support of the publication of this book:

The Watson-Brown Foundation

Mr. and Mrs. William Woodson Douglas III
The Knox Foundation
Mildred Miller Fort Foundation, Inc.
Mary Lane Morrison Foundation in Memory of Howard Jackson Morrison Jr.

Juliet and John Allan
The Beehive Foundation
Elizabeth and Sheffield Hale
State Mutual Insurance

Anonymous
Tina and Paul Blackney
Greta and Stephen Covington
Garbutt Construction Company
Paula and Larry Knox
Sherry and John Lundeen
Marilyn M. McMullan and John F. McMullan
Katrina and Floyd Newton
Carey and Bill Peard
Rebecca and Mark Riley
Melody and Joe Thomas
Tom B. Wight

Mary B. and W. Murray Air
Kathy and Norris Broyles
Candace L. Carlson
Charles F. Crisp
Patty and Todd Deveau
Eileen and Bo DuBose
Pat and Joe Edwards
Jenny Wheatley Fletcher
Sandy and Tom Gay
Kathy and Pete Hendricks
Caroline Howell
Pamela and Neville Isdell
Heather and Joshua King
MCAF (Material Culture & Arts Foundation)
Carmie and Mark McDonald in Honor of Carl Gable
Betsy and Sandy Morehouse
Patrick Parker
Susan and Ted Pound
Grace and Bill Quinn
In Memory of Stephen A. Reichert
Therese and Brian Rhodes
Peggy and John Shepard
Anita M. Shippen
David Austin Smith
Dean and Bronson Smith in Memory of Larry Singleton
Lyniece Talmadge
Pamela Dorminy-Uros and Nick Uros
In Memory of Charlotte R. and John Waters
Jeane Yancey in Memory of Patrick Henry Yancey Jr.

Tiffany and Blake Alewine
Judge and Mrs. H. Scott Allen
Anonymous
William T. Baker
Mickey Betts and Richard Wilson
Teri and Mose Bond
Davis Samuel Butner
Laura and Jim Bynum
M. Rebecca Carr
Ben Carter and Joe Watkins
Sally and Archie Davis
Mindy and Mike Egan
Newton M. Galloway
Alicia and Bryan Haltermann in Honor of Mary Bryan Haltermann
Historic Rural Churches of Georgia
Christopher A. D. Howard and Carey Pickard III
Katherine and David Johnson
Jeane and Walter Jones in Honor of Mark C. McDonald
Kelly Jordan
Leeann and Jeff Kole in Memory of Kaye Robinson Kole
Christine Davis Lambert in Memory of Roy Lambert
Kathy and Richard Lee
Nell and Guy Long
Dell F. and R. Bruce MacGregor
Sue Mann in Memory of Roy W. Mann
Laura Thomson McCarty
Diane and W. Henry Parkman
Suzanne and Mac Peden
Ray, Ellis & LaBrie Consulting
Betty Rayburn in Honor of Mark C. McDonald
Riddle Architecture, P.C.
Frances A. Root
Vickie Chung Rusek and Stasio French Rusek
Jane and Jim Sibley in Honor of Barbara and Les Callahan
Roger J. Smith
Lisa and Mason White
Mr. and Mrs. Ridley McLean Williams
Mr. and Mrs. W. Cole Woodruff
Alan M. Youngblood
Camille W. Yow
Zion Church Restoration Inc., Talbotton, Georgia

The Georgia Trust apologizes to any donors who contributed to this publication after September 1, 2022, and are not listed.

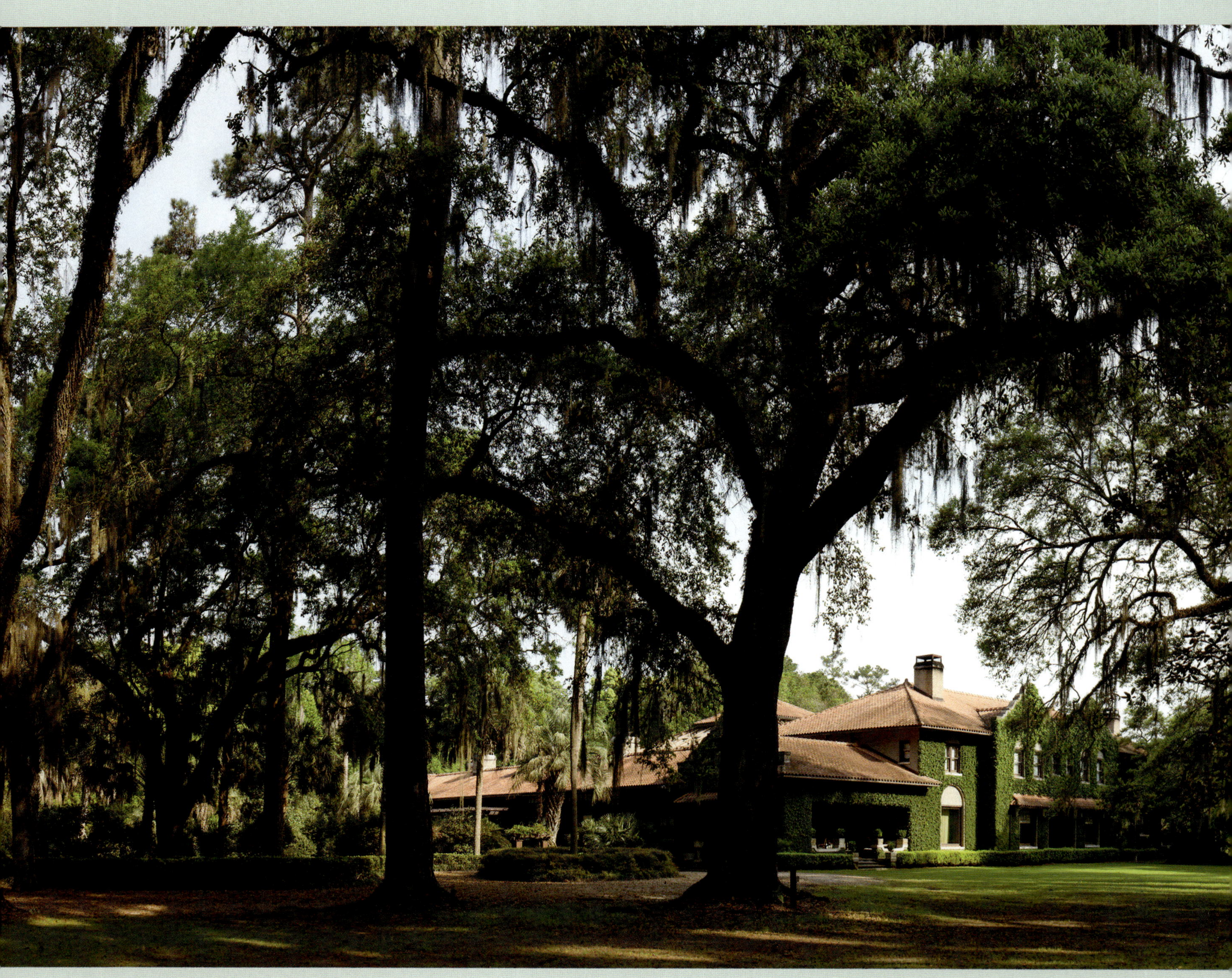

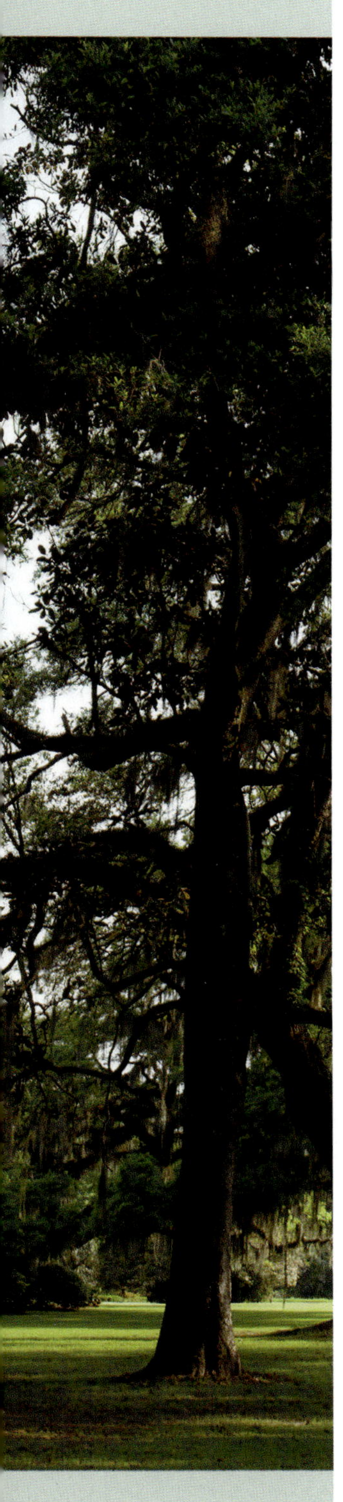

CONTENTS

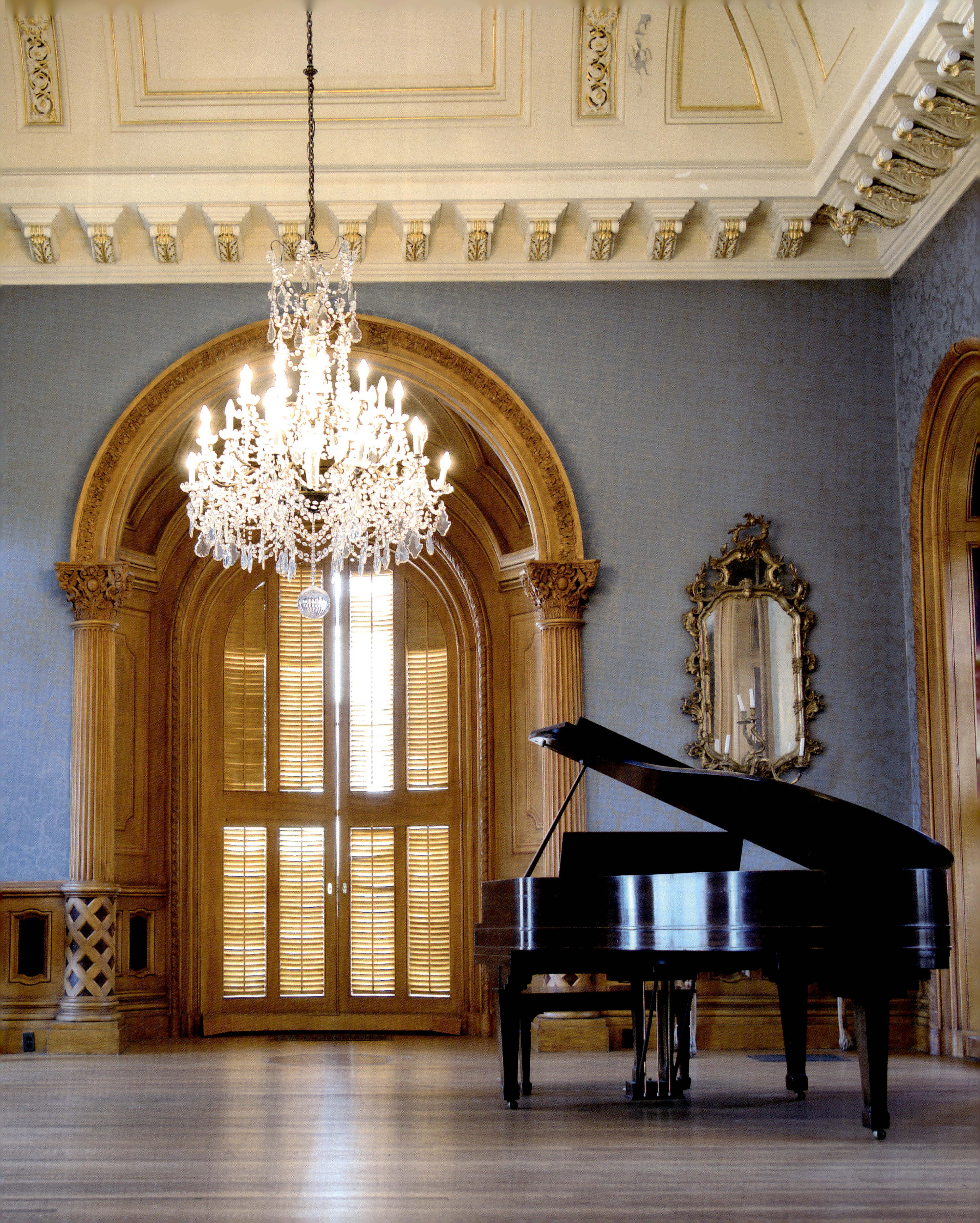

PREFACE

Alexis de Tocqueville, in his *Democracy in America*, published in 1835, provided many insights into the nascent culture of our nation. Concerning the spirit in which the Americans cultivate the arts, he wrote, "They will habitually prefer the useful to the beautiful, and they will require that the beautiful be useful."

Peter Gordon's 1734 perspective view of Savannah, which is the earliest known image of colonial Georgia, shows the urban plan of the European settlement cut out of the virgin pine forest. The squares and building lots are neatly arranged on the sandy soil of coastal Georgia, almost completely devoid of the shade of the thousands of trees that surround it. This is Georgia's origin story, and it clearly reveals the objectives of James Oglethorpe and his fellow settlers. As Tocqueville observed, utility took precedence over beauty; the need for shelter, security, food, and water came first. The Savannah we know today, verdant, ordered, sophisticated, and, above all, beautiful, is a veritable miracle.

The rest of Georgia's story is a less mythologized yet more complex narrative. It is a story of the white man's expansion into lands which had been occupied by Indigenous people for hundreds of years, of the importation of enslaved Africans, and of the constant clearing of land for the building of farmsteads, cities, railroads, skyscrapers, subdivisions, factories, airports, shopping malls, and other man-made structures.

In the late eighteenth century, physical location was the dominant factor in determining architectural development. The necessity for transportation by water required Savannah to be established on the coast at the mouth of the Savannah River and Augusta to be founded up the same waterway, east of the land still controlled by Indigenous people. In 1790, Creek Indian deal maker Alexander McGillivray traveled to New York to finalize negotiations for cession of Native land east of the Oconee River, thus opening this fertile woodland to white settlement. Much of the distinguished agriculturally based architecture of the early nineteenth century was created in this area.

The slow but certain removal of Indigenous people continued to control settlement patterns until the 1830s, when the Cherokee were unlawfully and forcibly displaced. Despite the consequent availability to white settlement of millions of acres of valuable land, Georgia grew slowly, as agricultural and economic foundations developed. River locations were still much advantaged, as passable roads hardly existed and railroads were yet to be developed. Only after the invention of the cotton gin by Eli Whitney on a plantation near Savannah did widespread cotton production create the economic sea change that led to increased settlement in middle Georgia. Soon the woodlands would be cleared for vast fields of white and construction of grand antebellum Greek Revival mansions and vastly

Facing: Johnston-Felton-Hay House, Macon

more Plantation Plain–style houses. Many of these agricultural landscapes and houses yet survive, in remarkably good condition.

The city of Atlanta, originally known as Terminus, because it was established at the end of the Western and Atlantic Railroad, did not depend on a seaport or river landing. Atlanta owes its existence to the industrial age, and it has been in a constant state of dynamism. Inhabited by approximately ten thousand people when Sherman captured it in 1865, Atlanta rebuilt from its ashes and seems to reinvent itself every other decade. It began as wooded foothills of the Appalachian Mountains, and its tree canopy may be its most admirable and best-preserved quality. Between the trees is city of beautiful neighborhoods hanging on against all odds. These neighborhoods possess distinguished houses from the Victorian era and from the prosperous decades before the stock-market crash of 1929, as well as a collection of influential modern buildings.

The challenges to preservation in Georgia sit at two extremes of the spectrum. In many of the state's rural areas, the threat to historic resources is abandonment and neglect. While many residents admire the architecture of Sparta, Washington, Thomaston, Eatonton, Bainbridge, and scores of other small cities, the high-paying jobs—and thus the privately provided resources that traditionally have been so crucial to preservation initiatives—remain, as they did one hundred years ago, in urban areas.

In Georgia's larger cities, most notably Atlanta, the preservationists' task is quite opposite, as the challenges of constant development differ markedly from those posed by abandonment and neglect. The pressures of development make any building—even a landmark—that sits on valuable land a target for demolition. The new building is all too frequently out of scale and a product of inferior design and materials. When historic buildings are saved in Atlanta, it is frequently because of sound public policy, sympathetic owners, and use of tax incentives for rehabilitation.

This volume differs significantly from other studies of Georgia's built environment. All the buildings and places featured herein are extant, as the authors wish to inspire readers to visit the sites for themselves. As the Georgia Trust for Historic Preservation is interested in protecting the full panoply of historic structures and places, this book is intended to cover the wide diversity of places that make up our built environment. Historic houses, commercial and institutional buildings, industrial sites, urban plans, historic landscapes, art environments, and other resources are all addressed. In addition, the authors have included, where appropriate, sidebar features that tell the stories of notable preservation victories and that we hope demonstrate the creative solutions that preservationists have employed to ensure that these significant resources will be preserved for the benefit of future generations.

While this book is dedicated to the committed, hardworking, and talented people—professionals and volunteers alike—who have given countless hours for the noble cause of historic preservation, it is expressly published for the edification of the generations yet to come.

ACKNOWLEDGMENTS

FOR A STATEWIDE historic preservation organization to survive for fifty years is an accomplishment to be recognized; for it to thrive is testament to the dedication and generosity of the citizens of Georgia. The publication of this volume is an auspicious act of celebration for this anniversary.

The Georgia Trust for Historic Preservation wishes to thank its members, staff, and trustees for their support of the publication of this survey of some of the noteworthy buildings that define our state's landscape and enrich our countryside, towns, and cities.

The Georgia Trust also recognizes and expresses its gratitude to the authors and photographers who generously donated their time and talents to bring this volume to life. It was a challenge to choose from the abundance of significant buildings and landscapes in the last and largest of the original thirteen colonies.

Our publication partners at the University of Georgia Press played a key role in the creation of this book. We thank them for their encouragement and professionalism in seeing this volume through every stage of its development and publication.

This book was not only a tremendous undertaking by our writers and photographers; it also required a substantial financial commitment. As usual, the Georgia Trust membership willingly embraced the concept of the book, and our board of trustees expresses its gratitude to the patrons that provided the funds to bring this vision to fruition. It is our hope that this volume will be an inspirational and helpful guide to those who seek to understand and preserve Georgia's rich architectural heritage.

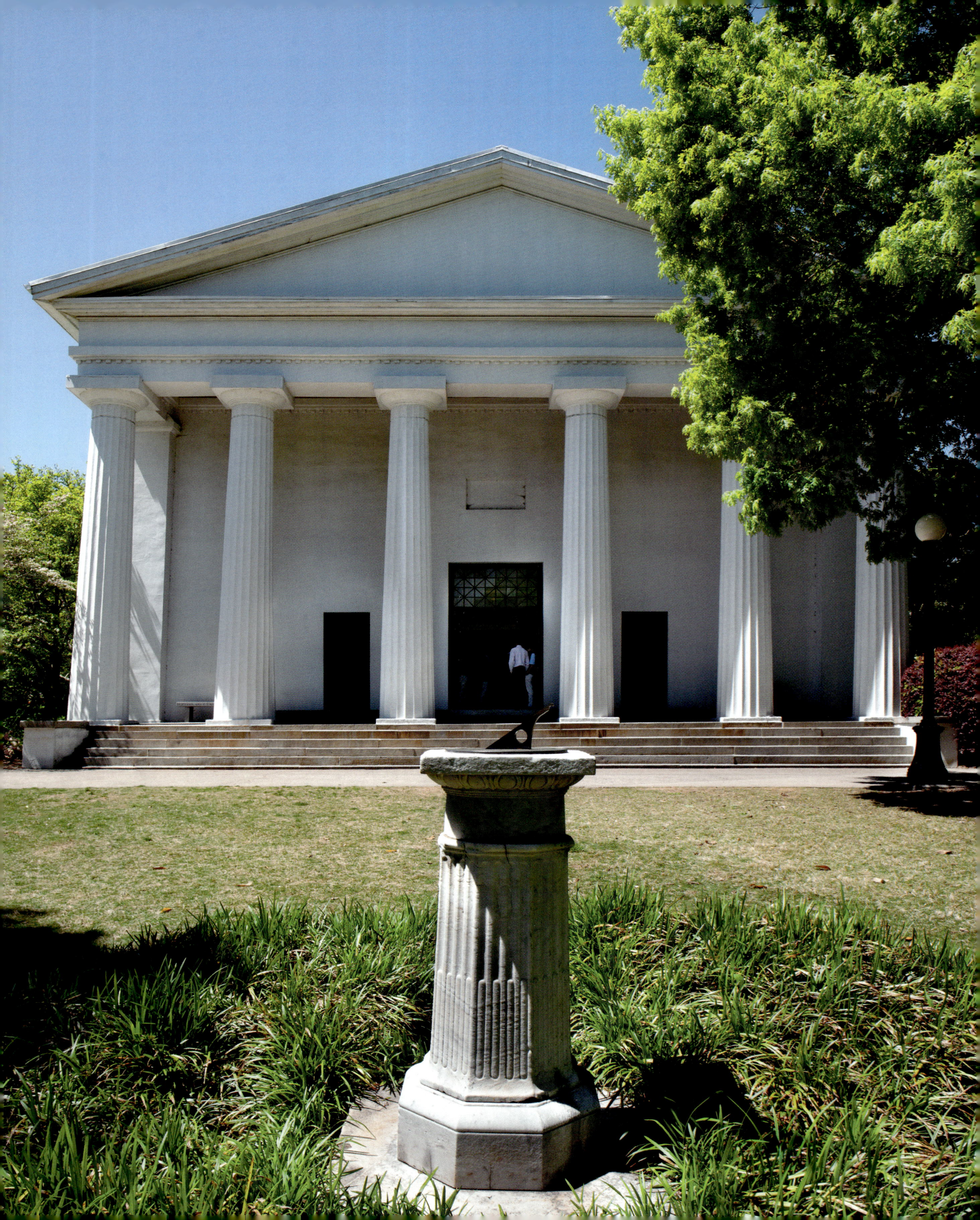

INTRODUCTION

A Half Century of Preservation

MARK C. MCDONALD

Although it was the last-established colony, Georgia was one of the first states to engage in organized efforts to preserve historic sites. In 1951 the Georgia Historical Commission was established by the Georgia General Assembly and placed under the supervision of the office of the secretary of state. Advocates for the passage of this act came largely from local historical societies, who were looking for the state's assistance and coordination. C. E. Gregory, a retired newspaper editor from the *Atlanta Journal*, became the commission's first executive secretary, and in 1960, his daughter, Mary Gregory Jewett, who had formerly served as its staff historian, was named director. In 1966 the passage of the National Historic Preservation Act required the establishment of state historic preservation offices (SHPOs) in every state of the union. Mary Gregory Jewett was named Georgia's first state historic preservation officer in 1969.

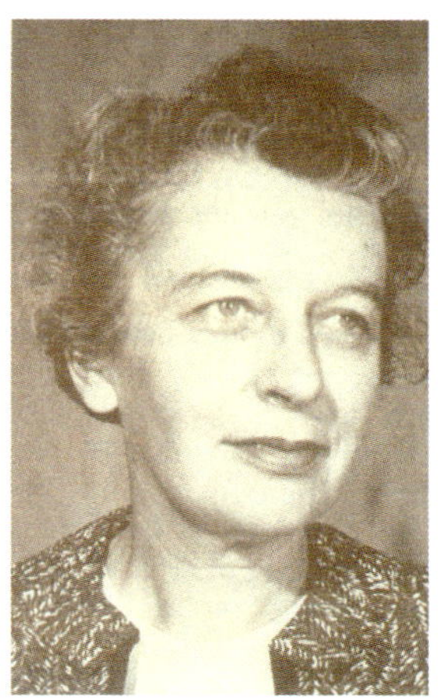

Mary Gregory Jewett

The National Historic Preservation Act of 1966 created the national preservation program that we know today. It established the National Register of Historic Places, required that environmental review of all federal undertakings, including transportation projects, consider potential effects on historic resources, and provided funding to promote historic preservation in the fifty states.

Local historical societies who had worked to establish the Georgia Historical Commission began to develop an interest in the preservation of historic places in their communities. The Historic Savannah Foundation was established in 1955 by a group of seven women in response to the demolition of Savannah's beloved City Market building, formerly located in Ellis Square, and threats to the Isaiah Davenport House. Historic Savannah, under the leadership of Leopold Adler and others, began a highly successful revolving fund program in 1959, when it saved the 1850 Marshall Row building. Historic Savannah continues its real estate–based preservation programs, having now saved approximately four hundred historic buildings through preservation easements and covenants.

Facing: University of Georgia Chapel, Athens

The 1960s were a rich decade for activism in America, including for community heritage citizen-led involvement. Thomasville Landmarks (1964), Historic Macon (formerly Middle Georgia Historical Society and Macon Heritage, 1964), Historic Augusta (1965), Historic Columbus (1966), and Athens-Clarke Heritage Foundation (1967) all came into being in this decade, and all continue their strong advocacy efforts today. The Sumter Trust was established in 1972 and is still active in preservation in Americus and in the county. Many of these organizations functioned for years without the benefit of full-time staff and were led by idealistic, dedicated, and hard-working volunteers.

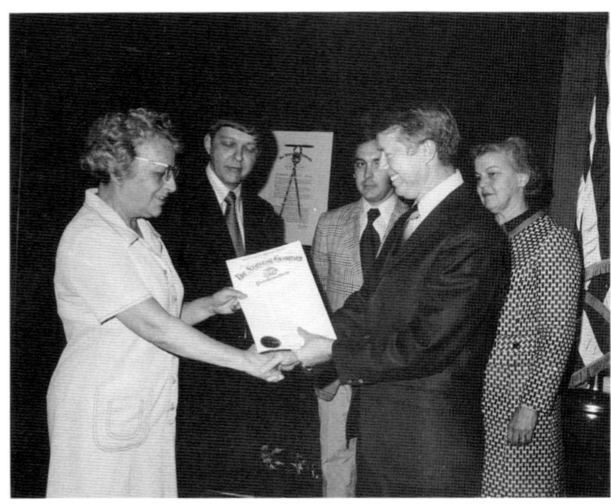

Governor Jimmy Carter presenting a proclamation of support to Georgia Trust members, mid-1970s

In 1973 Governor Jimmy Carter reorganized state government and transferred the responsibilities of the Georgia Historical Commission to the newly formed Department of Natural Resources, Office of Planning and Research, Historic Preservation Section. David Sherman was named section chief and state historic preservation officer.

Georgia has continued to be a national leader in preservation education. There are few, if any, states that offer as many graduate programs in historic preservation. The University of Georgia (UGA) began offering classes in the field in its landscape architecture program in 1973 and established a master's of historic preservation degree in 1982. In 1983, UGA began to offer a joint JD-MHP program with the School of Law.

The Savannah College of Art and Design began offering classes in Savannah in 1978 and initiated its undergraduate degree in 1979 and its master's in 1995. Georgia State University first offered its heritage preservation program in 1983 within the Department of History. In addition, the Georgia Institute of Technology offers coursework in historic preservation as part of its renowned School of Architecture.

The growth of the historic preservation movement has created great demand for the skilled craftsmen and technicians needed to perform the complex and demanding restoration work on historic buildings. In 2008, after encouragement by the Historic Savannah Foundation, the Savannah Technical College began offering an associate degree in historic preservation, a historic preservation and restoration diploma, and a technical certificate of credit.

While cities and counties were incorporating local organizations to address preservation needs, Georgia lacked a nonprofit organization to advocate on the statewide level for progressive preservation policies and coordinate activities among local groups. Leadership from local organizations began to explore the feasibility of establishing a stronger voice for the growing movement.

The Georgia Trust for Historic Preservation was formed by a group of these individuals who were passionate about preserving the state's historic built environment and saw a need for a nonprofit organization that could focus on a statewide effort to preserve it. The organization grew out of a series of statewide annual conferences held between 1969 and 1973 that attracted Georgians interested in history, architecture, landscaping, environmental design, and community development. From the enthusiasm of these early conferences came the effort

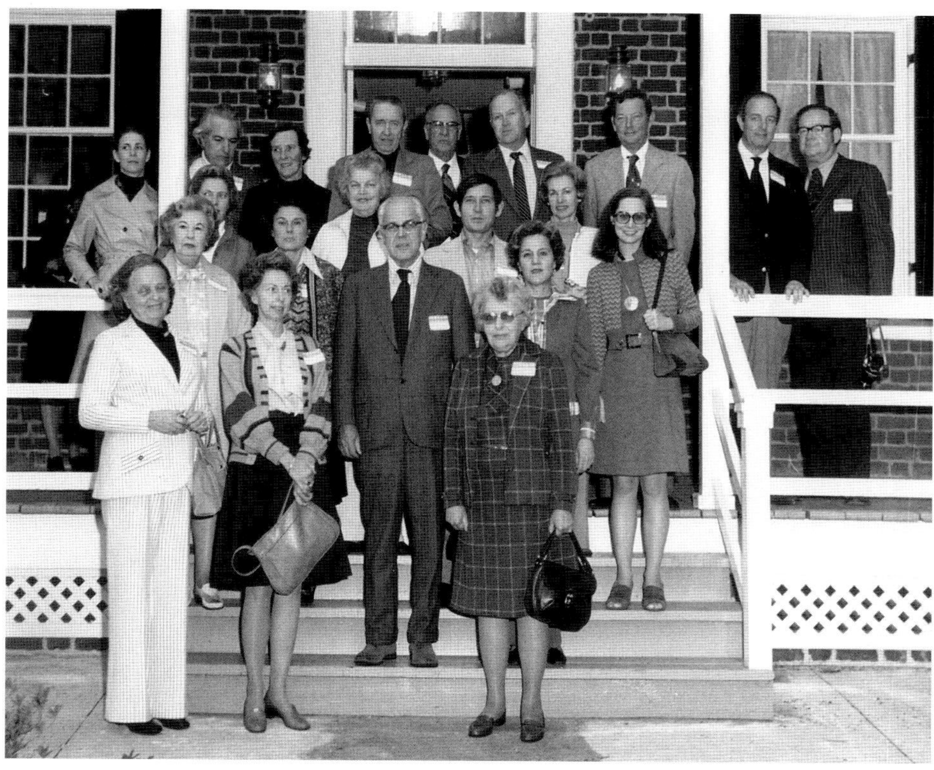

Georgia Trust for Historic Preservation founding trustees

to form the Trust. Through those five formative years, the energy was growing, and the Georgia Historical Commission transitioned into the Department of Natural Resources with Governor Carter's reorganization of state government. Ultimately, at the 1973 conference in Macon, the creation of the Georgia Trust for Historic Preservation was announced. The theme of the conference that year was "Preservation—Our Trust."

The organization's first president was Mary Gregory Jewett of Atlanta, who had been a major force in the founding of the Trust. The first chairman was Atlanta resident and connoisseur and collector of Georgia decorative arts William W. Griffin, who secured the Trust's charter from the State of Georgia. The first vice president was Marguerite Williams of Thomasville, whose longtime commitment to preservation would lead to her receiving the National Trust for Historic Preservation's highest honor, the Louise du Pont Crowninshield Award, in 1997. Other members of the founding board of trustees were Louise Allen, Louise "Bib" Hay Anderson, Elizabeth "Betty" Hay Curtis, Turner Bryson, William Bush, Gardell Christainsen, Clifford Clarke, Edward DeZurko, Beverly DuBose Jr., Walter Hartridge, Paul Hawkins, Clason Kyle, Lewis Larson Jr., W. Frank McCall Jr., William Mitchell Jr., Mary Morrison, Edward Neal, Hubert Owens, Ann Singer, Phinizy Spalding, Gail Talmadge, and Barry Wright.

During its charter year, the young fledgling organization grew to over one thousand members, due to a successful membership drive led by Marguerite Williams of Thomasville. In late 1974 the Trust opened its first office, in the First National Bank Building on Decatur's historic square, and hired its first employee, Janet Pecha.

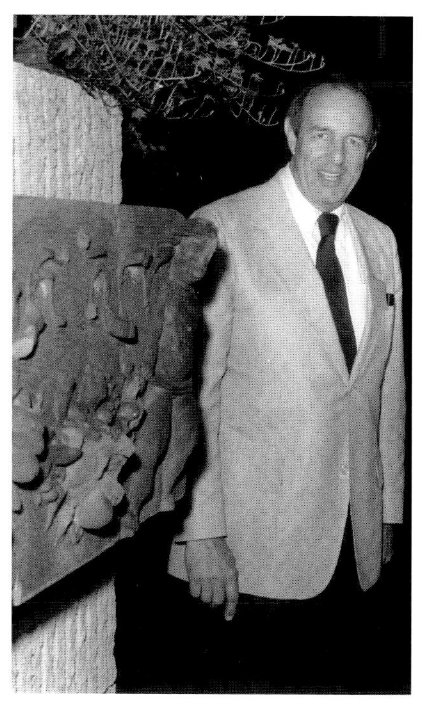

William Griffin

In 1975 the Trust moved to 9 Baltimore Place, in the historic Baltimore Block near downtown Atlanta. The 1885 structure was Atlanta's first row-house group, but by the time the Trust moved in it had evolved into mixed-use spaces.

In 1977 a major opportunity was presented to the young organization. Macon's Johnston-Felton-Hay House, which was completed on the eve of the Civil War, had long been recognized as one of Georgia's most important antebellum buildings. In 1973 it was designated as a National Historic Landmark. The house was first opened to the public in 1964 by the P. L. Hay Foundation.

The Hay House, as it was widely known, attracted many tourists, who were treated to a tour of the elegant interior of the building by the Hay family's former butler, Chester Davis. Income from tours was insufficient to maintain the house, however, and its elaborate exterior was showing signs of deterioration,

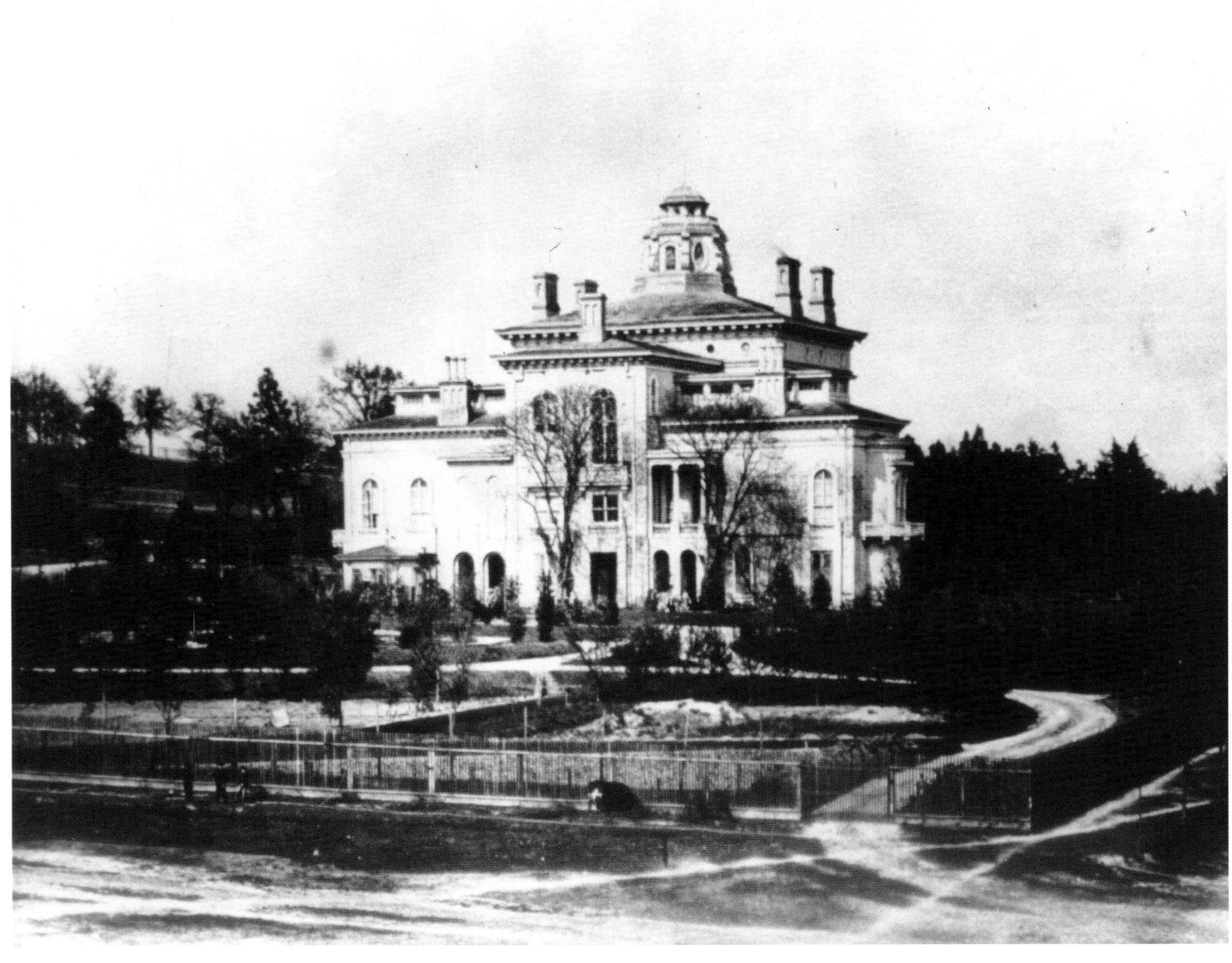
Hay House, Macon, ca. 1860

with rotting wood and peeling paint. The house's aging electrical and mechanical systems presented additional problems. In early April 1977, acting on behalf of the Hay family, Macon mayor Buckner Melton approached Georgia Trust president Edward Neal of Columbus about a gift of the property to the new organization. Neal wrote the executive committee of the offer of the house, its contents and "liquid capital of $84,500." He asked them to study the proposal in preparation for their meeting a few days later at the Trust's annual statewide conference in Rome. At that meeting, with mostly positive assessments, suggesting that the gift would "give the Trust a project" and would "make the Trust more visible," Marguerite Williams's motion to accept Hay House was unanimously adopted. At the subsequent board meeting, with little additional discussion, the board of trustees also voted unanimously to accept the property as the Trust's first museum site. The announcement of the acquisition of Hay House was the lead story in the National Trust's monthly *Preservation News*.

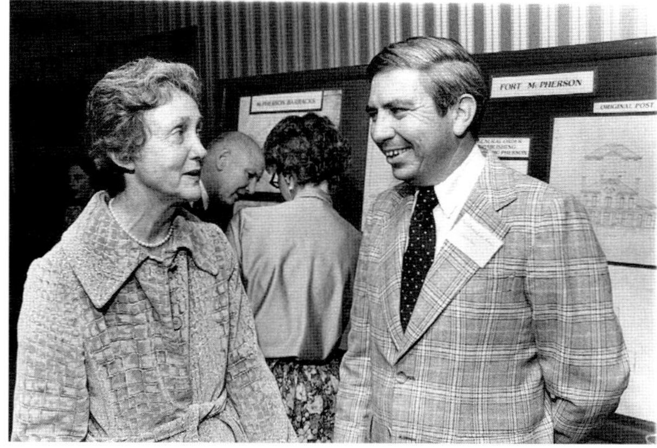

Mrs. William Griffin and Ed Neal

Although the transfer was not effective until the end of December, trustees, led by Bradley Hale, pressed ahead with the exploration of the site, fundraising, and consideration of management. Fran LaFarge became the first director, the position funded in part through a federal grant to the City of Macon. LaFarge engaged Maryel Battin, a leader in the Macon preservation community. Battin worked with interns to catalogue the thousands of objects that came with the house. By 1978 the first board of Hay House was appointed, as a standing committee of the Georgia Trust. Chaired by Nancy Anderson, the fourteen-member committee included three Hay family members and, among others, Phil Walden, founder of Capricorn Records. Mayor Melton served from the start as chairman of the fundraising committee and raised over $350,000 for work on the building.

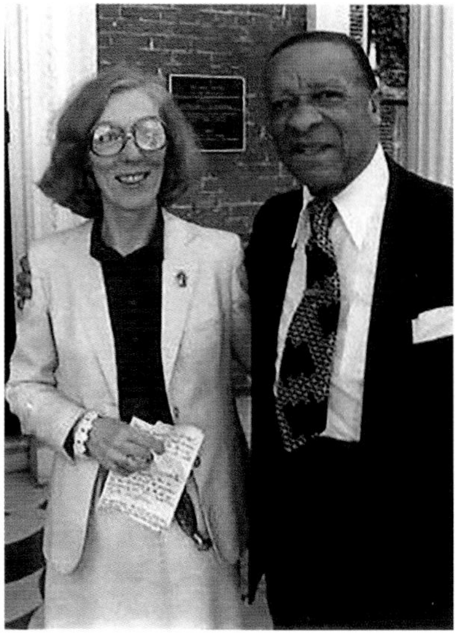

Fran LaFarge and Chester Davis

In March of 1978 the Trust held a public grand opening program on a Sunday, and over three thousand people toured the house. The energetic committee and its members, bolstered by other locals, continued to raise funds for the next two years. By summer of 1978 the house had been the subject of articles in the new magazine *Southern Accents* and countless newspapers and was soon to be featured in books such as *Landmark Houses of Georgia* by Savannah photographer Van Jones Martin and Atlanta author William R. Mitchell Jr.

The Georgia Trust commissioned Atlanta architect Norman Askins to work on a use plan for the basement, which called for a tearoom and a bar in the wine-cellar area. The director developed lesson plans and school-group tour programs, while architectural interns from Georgia Tech went to work drawing and measuring the building to Historic American Buildings Survey (HABS) standards. A search of the attic revealed over fifty original 1855 drawings, most in tatters, by the architects T. Thomas and Son of New York. Research with the Felton family turned up amazing documents and photographs that assisted in rewriting the site's history and preparing for restoration. Board and staff began an oral-history project to collect information from surviving Felton family who had lived in the house, Chester Davis, and the Hay sisters, now Betty Curtis and Bib Anderson.

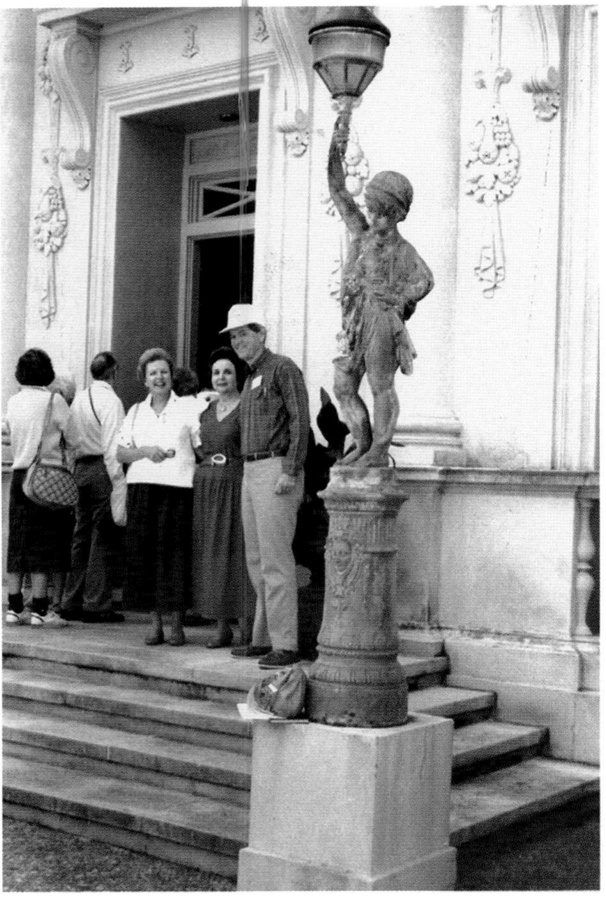

An early Georgia Trust "Ramble"

Social events were prominent among the early fundraisers for the building and remain so today. Rental income was key to cash flow during this time, as it is today. A portion of the house was rented to the Junior League as offices, and rental events began in 1981 with the first wedding bookings and the first Christmas decorating displays.

The Georgia Trust offered its first Ramble in 1974, to Oglethorpe County and Lexington, and in 1975 it sponsored more Rambles, one to Inman Park in Atlanta, another to Columbus, and a third to Jarrell Plantation and Old Clinton in Jones County. These have remained one of the Trust's most popular events for its members.

In 1978 the Georgia Trust began its preservation awards program. Minette Bickel was hired as the Trust's first executive director. True to its founding purposes, the Trust began its advocacy efforts, and in 1979 the Georgia Historic Preservation Act was passed, the enabling legislation that gave local governments the authority to establish local historic districts and historic preservation commissions to oversee design criteria and prevent demolitions in these designated areas.

In 1979 the Trust moved to Unit 11 of the Baltimore Block. In 1981 Greg Paxton, a young preservationist working at the Historic Charleston Foundation, accepted the position of executive director and took the helm as lead staff member of the Trust. Gloria Tinsley, longtime membership director and executive secretary, proved to be a key person in the development of the organization, until her retirement in 2009.

In this period the National Trust for Historic Preservation established the National Main Street program, which became a highly effective means toward revitalizing America's downtown commercial districts. Georgia was one of the first states to enroll in the program, and the Trust was a key player in this effort. In 1981 the Trust raised $100,000, half of which was donated by Marguerite Williams. By 1982 Mary Lowe had been hired as the first design consultant for the Main Street Georgia program.

A few years later, Baltimore Block was sold to a developer for rehabilitation, and the Georgia Trust began a search for a new headquarters. Rhodes Hall, the

Right: Minette Bickel, Bradley Hale
Far Right: Greg Paxton, Gloria Tinsley

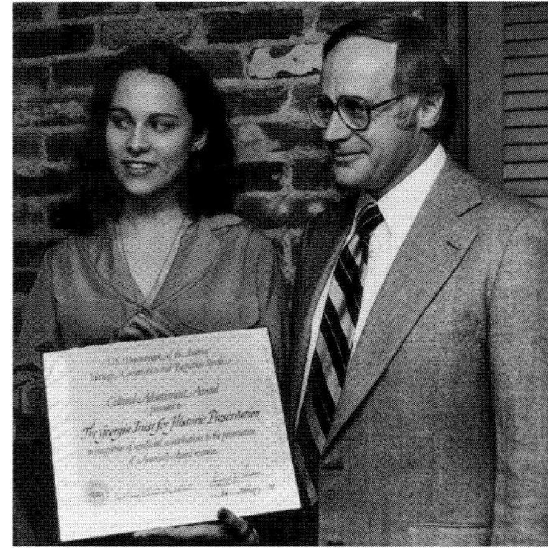

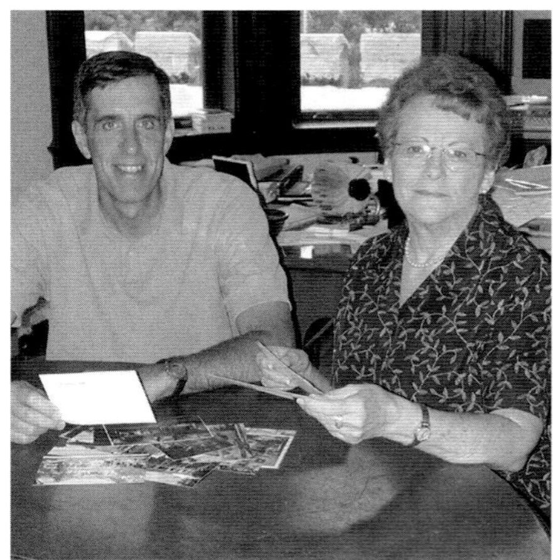

historic home of Amos G. Rhodes, founder of the Rhodes Furniture Company, was languishing on Peachtree Street in Midtown Atlanta. The home was built in 1902–4 and is a rare example of Romanesque Revival residential architecture that survived years of Atlanta's progress and commercialization. Rhodes chose prominent Georgia architect Willis F. Denny II (1877–1905), known for his use of Stone Mountain granite, to design the home. The interior detailing and features represent the finest Victorian style of the period and include rich colors, exquisite woodwork, picturesque murals, ornate ceilings, and intricate parquet floors. The home also contains the most modern technologies of its time, including radiator heat on the first floor, an alarm system, and a call system for the servants. Electricity was featured on a grand scale throughout the home, with over three hundred light bulbs used in the ceilings and sconces to give the castle a warm glow. Notoriously frugal, Rhodes nevertheless spared no expense on the public areas of the home, desiring to impress his friends and high-society Atlanta with this crowning jewel of his achievement. Amos and Amanda Rhodes named their elaborate home Le Reve.

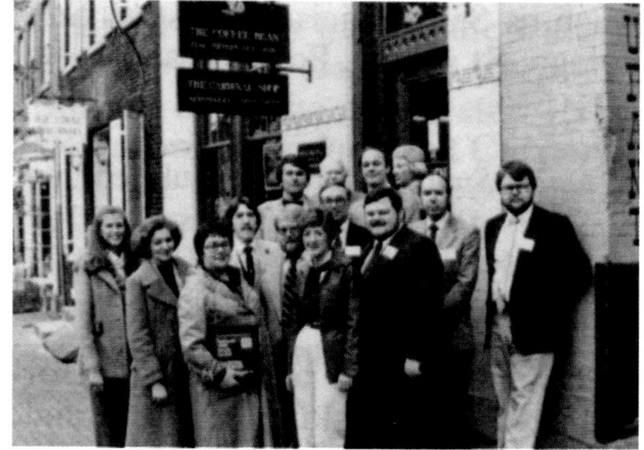

National Main Street program participants

Upon the death of Amos Rhodes, the mansion was left to the Rhodes' children, who then deeded the building to the State of Georgia in 1929, with the restriction that it must be used for historical and educational purposes, thus ensuring its continued preservation. It served as the state archives from 1930 to 1965, until a new archives building was constructed on Capitol Avenue. After the archives were relocated from Rhodes Hall, the building was used for storage and occasional meetings and events, but it began to deteriorate significantly, which caused great distress to both the Rhodes descendants and preservationists.

In 1980 the State conducted a major study of the building to determine the scope of work needed and to propose possible uses. In 1982 the Georgia Trust approached the State of Georgia for Trust headquarters about leasing the building to the Georgia Trust, an arrangement that would satisfy the restriction placed upon the building in the 1929 deed.

In 1983 the State leased the building to the Georgia Trust to serve as its headquarters. With the long-term lease, the Trust was also given the responsibility of restoring and maintaining the building, which was no small task. Taking advantage of the condition of the building, in 1984, the Georgia Trust launched "The Haunted Castle" which proved to be a highly successful Halloween fundraiser that continued until 1992. In 1986 efforts to establish a capital campaign for the restoration of Rhodes Hall began in earnest.

Also in that year, the Joint Legislative Study Commission on Economic Development through Historic Preservation was created by the General Assembly. The commission's recommendation for funding for regional historic preservation planners and increased funding for the statewide historic preservation office, as well as $101,000 for Rhodes Hall and $40,00 for Hay House, was passed by the Georgia General Assembly. In 1987 the Georgia Trust established Georgians for Preservation Action (GAPA) as a statewide advocacy organization to address national and state preservation issues.

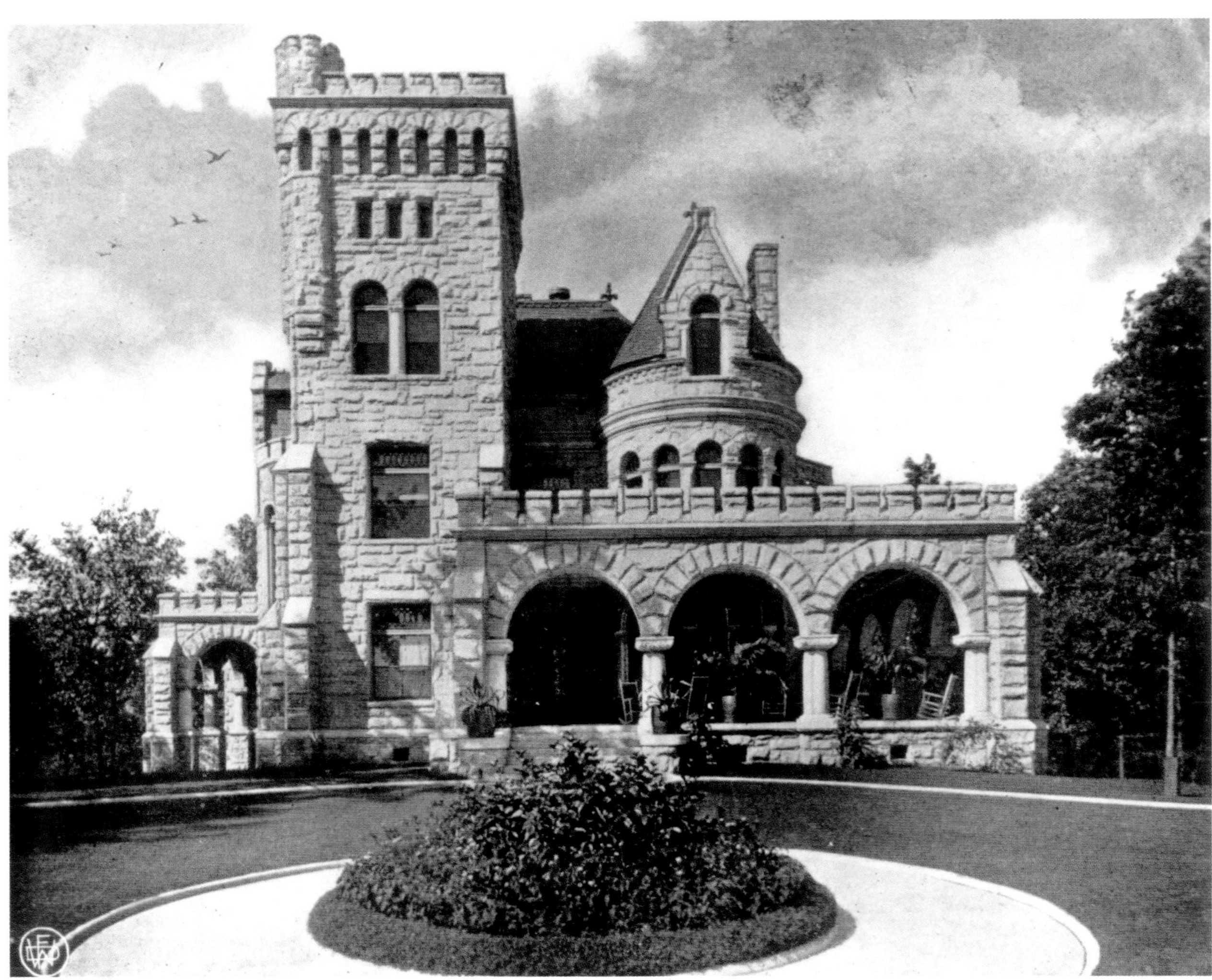

Rhodes Hall, Atlanta, ca. 1904

In 1990 the Georgia Trust was presented with another major challenge when the McDaniel-Tichenor House in Monroe, Georgia, along with significant financial assets, was bequeathed to it by Emily Burney Tichenor, widow of Henry McDaniel Tichenor. This impressive Italianate house had been the home of Governor Henry Dickerson McDaniel, who served as the fifty-second governor of Georgia, from 1883 to 1886. During his administration, construction began on the new state capitol in Atlanta. The house had been a family home of the Tichenor family and required extensive rehabilitation before it could be opened to the public. Over the next sixteen years, the Trust, along with advocates in Monroe, invested substantial effort and financial resources in restoring the house, cataloging the thousands of pieces of furniture and decoration that came with it, and establishing an archive of the numerous photographs, letters, and other papers. In the end, challenges presented themselves that made it more feasible for the house to be operated by a local group whose sole responsibility would be to manage and operate the house as a museum and special-events facility. Consequently, in 2006 the Georgia Trust board of trustees decided to deed the house to McDaniel-Tichenor House Inc., a local group that has successfully operated the McDaniel-Tichenor House ever since.

Also in 1990, the Georgia Trust began a capital campaign to continue restoration of Rhodes Hall and Hay House and to establish an endowment fund, begin a heritage-education program, and create a revolving fund for endangered properties. A heritage-education program to teach a new generation of Georgians about historic preservation and a revolving fund to buy and resell important threatened properties had long been seen by members as key to the Trust's mission. This capital campaign exceeded its goal and raised over $3 million.

Following the successful capital campaign, Rhodes Hall was returned to its original grandeur, through replastering and painting walls, repairing and refinishing floors, restoring and refinishing woodwork, and repairing and maintaining fixtures and features throughout. In 1991 the mahogany staircase, hand-carved handrail, and leaded glass windows were reinstalled with funds provided by the Frank Sheffield Foundation. These important features had been removed by the state Department of Archives and History in 1965 and replaced with a simple staircase, handrail, and plain glass windows. A pink silk damask wall covering was carefully matched by textile manufacturer Scalamandré and reinstalled in the front parlor.

Tommy Jones served as director of restoration at the Georgia Trust during the pivotal years 1986–95, while both Hay House and Rhodes Hall restoration efforts were initiated. Under the supervision of Greg Paxton and Tommy Jones, work began on converting the offices of the Georgia Department of Archives and History into a museum and headquarters of the Georgia Trust. Several talented craftsmen, including Jens Christiansen, Carston Jenson, and Michael Purser, were invaluable in restoring the leaded glass windows, staircase, woodwork, and floors of Rhodes Hall.

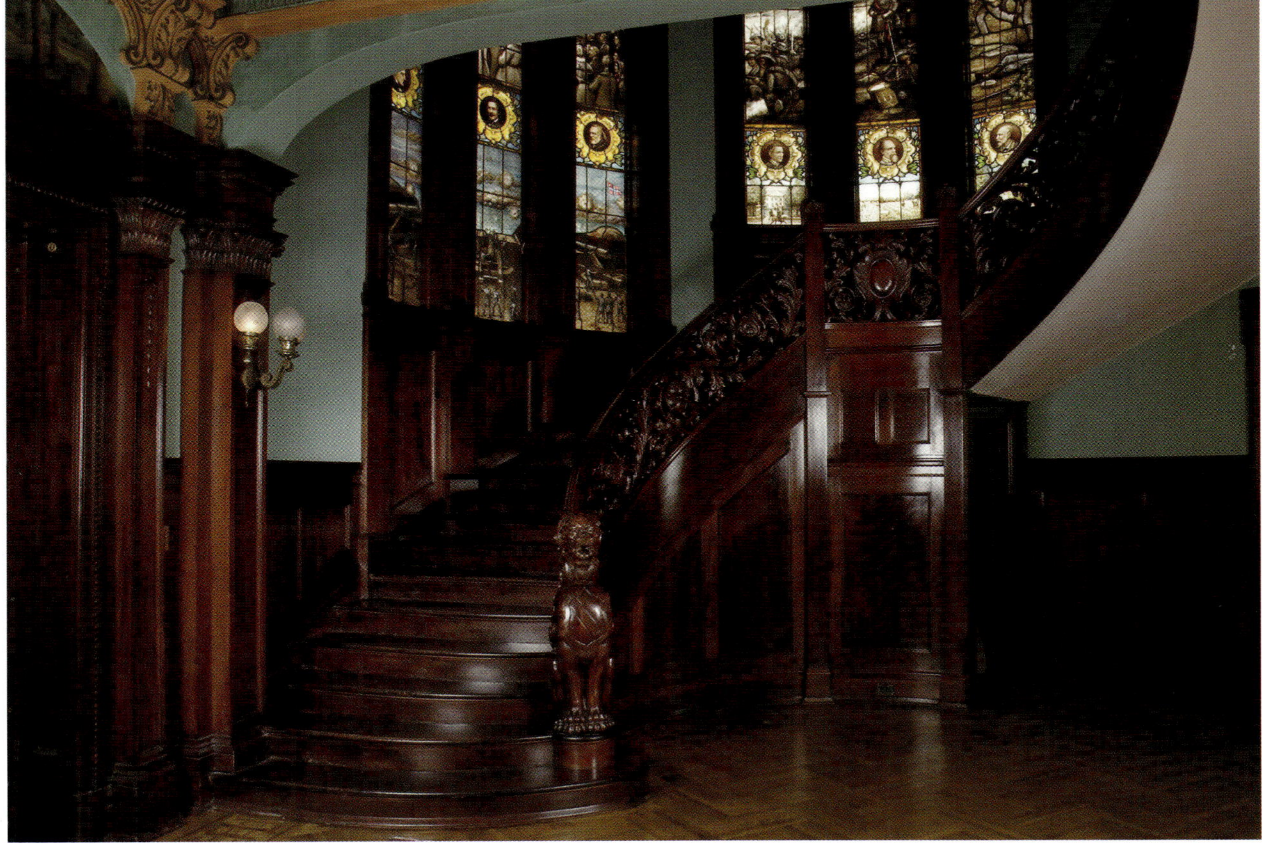

Rhodes Hall staircase

At Hay House, investigation had begun under the site's first executive directors, Fran LaFarge (1978–82) and Bruce Sherwood (1983–87), but most of the substantial work was initiated under the direction of Sandy Barrow (1987–90) and Marilyn Ashmore (1990–99). Rehabilitation of the electrical system was begun, and on the 1905 Felton wing, the ground floor loggia was enclosed for new bathrooms and a director's office, changes which were critical for improved visitor services. Restoration of the Music Room was followed by that of the Marble Hall and the Walnut Hall with their original Johnston marbleized and grained finishes from the 1860s. Initial research had shown the extent of decorative finishes in the house, particularly in the entrance hall, where the marbleized trompe l'oeil decoration of the walls remained intact under layers of early twentieth-century paint. The discovery of the original paint and consequent conservation in these spaces, by International Fine Arts Consulting (IFACS), put the Trust on the map, as these rare original faux finishes were celebrated in magazines, in books such as the National Trust's *America Restored*, and in scholarly programs.

Tommy Jones worked closely with Hay House board members and the Washington Library to research, document, and begin the daunting task of restoration of what had been the Hay family's home and transforming it into a museum that recognized the long occupancy of the Johnston, Felton, and Hay families, each of whom had left their mark on the house. In 1993 the Trust published Jones's short history of the house, *The Johnstons, Feltons, and Hays: 100 Years in the Palace of the South*. The assistance of Bonnie Dowling, Ann Corn Felton, and Tom Wight was particularly helpful through these years, along with that of many others.

In 1993, a spring event, the Secret Gardens Tour, now called Spring Stroll, began as a ticketed promenade of private Macon gardens. A thriving corps of docents and interns staffed the site in the 1990s, including several who later became officers and leading board members of Hay House. Throughout the 1990s, state and federal grants, alongside private donations, funded more work on the grounds and in main-level rooms.

Promises to begin a heritage-education program were fulfilled in 1991 when the Georgia Trust began its award-winning program Talking Walls, which operated in communities throughout the state. It helped educators incorporate local historic resources into lesson plans that meet the curriculum at all grade levels. Partnering with school systems and local organizations, the Talking Walls workshops provided heritage resource guides for teachers that included historical documents, maps, photographs, information about local historic sites, and other materials related to the community's cultural traditions and history. Since its inception, Talking Walls has reached a network of over 2,200 teachers in 70 school systems in 63 counties of Georgia. It is estimated that the program has influenced more than one million students across the state.

The year 1991 also saw the initiation of the Georgia Trust statewide Revolving Fund program. In that year, the Trust purchased and sold the highly significant Terrell-Stone House in Sparta. This building features Jeffersonian Classical details and is a rare example of the Federal style in Georgia. Plans to return the

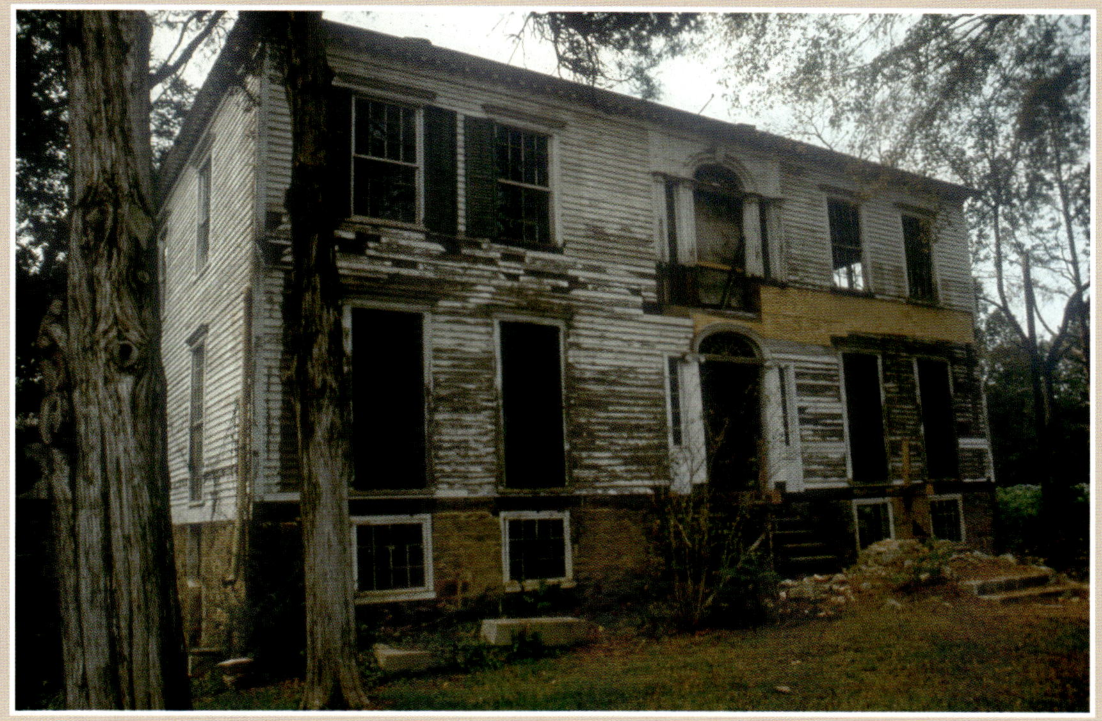

Terrell-Stone House,
Sparta, before and after

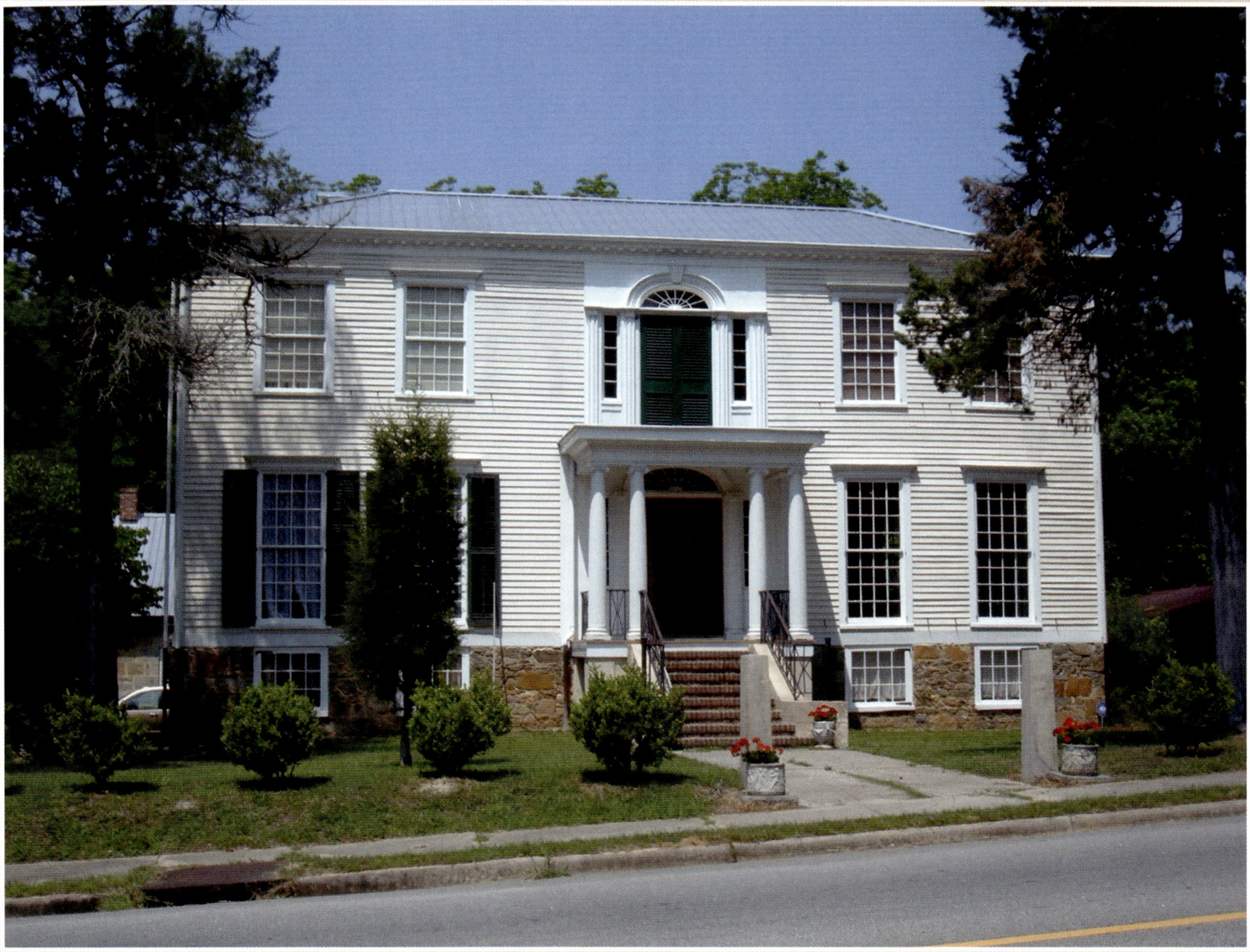

house to its 1820 appearance were developed by the Trust. It was rehabilitated according to these plans and is protected by a conservation easement. Board chair Janice Biggers of Columbus provided leadership, aided by her personal experience working the Historic Columbus Foundation Revolving Fund.

Preservation activities continued at a feverish pitch throughout the 1990s. In 1993 the Commission for the Preservation of the Capitol was established. Advocacy efforts continued to be successful, and in 1994 the General Assembly funded the Georgia Heritage 2000 grants and in 1995 increased funding to $270,000 annually. In 1996, when Atlanta took center stage as host of the Summer Olympics, the Georgia Trust leased Rhodes Hall to the Turkish Olympic delegation for the summer and received a substantial financial windfall. Also in that year, the General Assembly provided a $350,000 appropriation for deferred maintenance needs at Rhodes Hall, which financed roofing and other exterior repairs and third-floor central air conditioning and heating.

A key staff member at the Trust from 1994 to 2001 was Greta Terrell Covington. Covington assumed several important roles at the Trust during her tenure, including development director, director of preservation, and director of external affairs, and she led GAPA during these years. Mose Bond, originally from Dalton but now serving as an executive for Trust Company Bank in Atlanta, served as board chair from 1992 to 1994 and was also key to the Georgia Trust's success.

The Trust's application in 1997 for a federal grant of $557,000, funded through the Intermodal Surface Transportation Efficiency Act (ISTEA), was successful and these monies were later combined with funds raised in the successful Hay House Capital Campaign of 2004, chaired by Bradley Hale and William Matthews and led by Tom Wight, which eventually raised $7.5 million. All these funds enabled a restoration of the roof and cupola, as well as work on other interior spaces, including the Reception Room, where discoveries of earlier finishes were made.

One of the Georgia Trust's most successful endeavors was the publication of *J. Neel Reid: Architect of Hentz, Reid and Adler and the Georgia School of Classicists*, by William R. Mitchell Jr., in 1997. Proceeds from this book now fund the J. Neel Reid Prize, awarded annually by the Trust. In October 1998, the Georgia Trust received the prestigious Trustees Award for Organizational Excellence at the National Trust for Historic Preservation conference that was held in Savannah. At the end of a very busy year and decade, the Trust, in cooperation with Georgia Public Broadcasting, produced a one-hour documentary titled *A Georgia Trust*, which premiered on December 16, 1998.

In 1998, the board of trustees named the Trust's volunteer of the year award in honor of Camille Yow. Yow was the recipient of the Trust's first volunteer of the year award, given in 1979. She served as a member of the board of trustees from 1979 to 1985 and over a twenty-year period created, chaired, or otherwise worked on over forty special events that attracted more than 200,000 patrons and raised $2.5 million in support of the mission of the Trust. Yow's signature event, Salute to American Craft, was particularly financially beneficial and underscored preservation's link with craftsmanship.

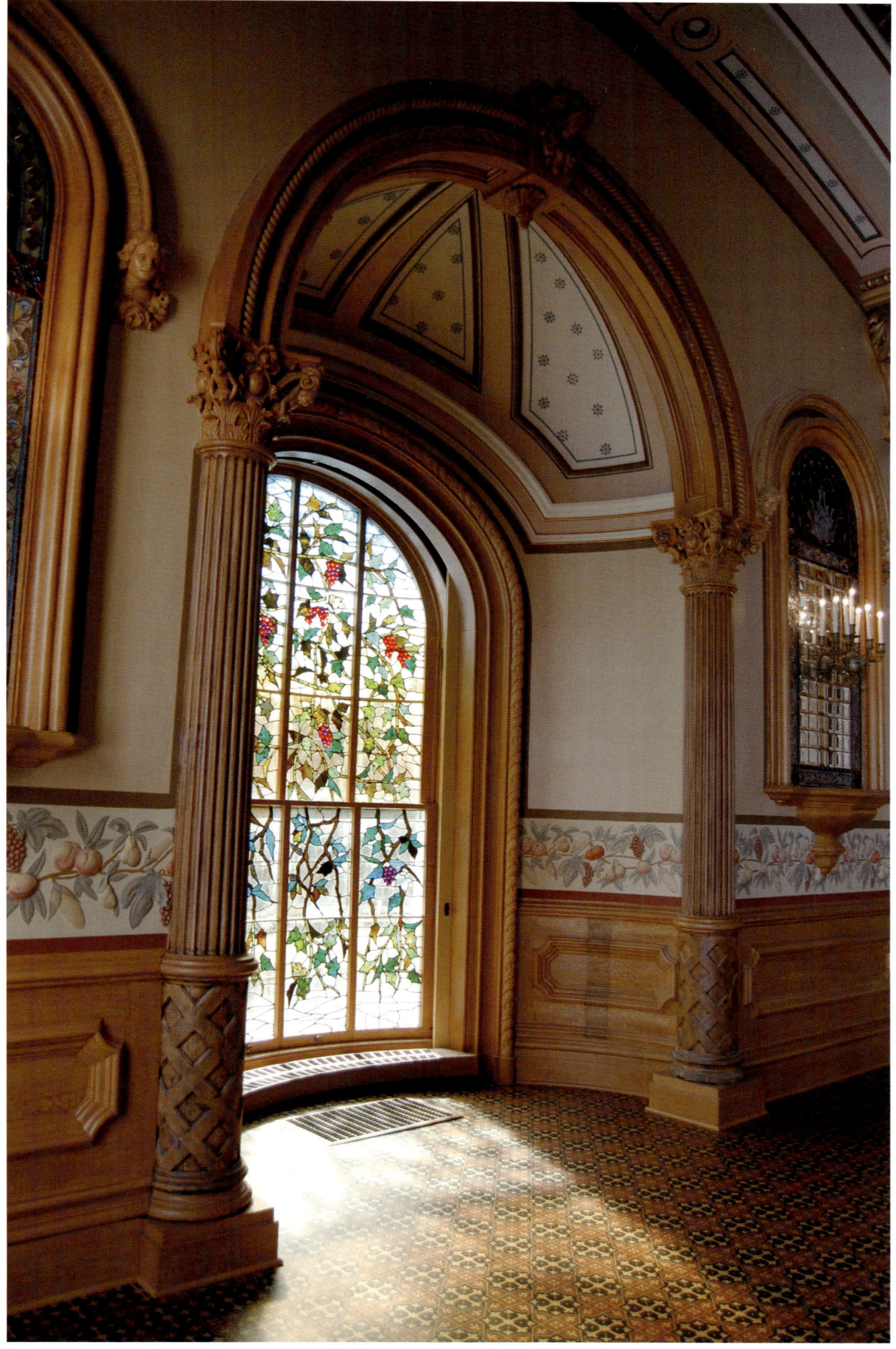

Hay House restoration

Sheffield Hale was the first recipient of the Camille Yow Volunteer of the Year award, in 1998. Hale followed a distinguished family tradition of service to the Trust. His grandfather Frank Sheffield anonymously funded the restoration of the carved mahogany staircase and leaded glass windows at Rhodes Hall, and his father Bradley served as board chair from 1978 to 1981, a period of enormous growth in terms of membership, revenue, and prestige for the Trust. Sheffield Hale offered extraordinary service and expertise on legal matters to the Trust, including on real estate, leasing of Rhodes Hall to the Turkish Olympic delegation during the 1996 summer Olympic games, publishing agreements for the Neel Reid book, and many other matters. He served as board chair from 2000 to 2002.

The Trust's Revolving Fund continued its high level of activity throughout the 1990s. Nine historic buildings were acquired and resold during the decade. Notable projects included the Camak House in Athens, which is an important Greek Revival brick mansion located on a large parcel of land in the Pulaski Street neighborhood. The Georgia Railroad was chartered in this house in 1834. Among others, the Cabaniss House, a circa 1820 house built in the Neo-Palladian style in Jones County, and the early twentieth-century Bon Air Hotel in Bainbridge were also saved by the Revolving Fund.

The first decade of the new millennium began with promise for America and for the Georgia Trust. By 2001, sales of the Neel Reid book were so favorable that the Trust was able to award its first Neel Reid Prize, to Cara Cummins, a young architect who chose to travel to Rome, Italy, for her research. In 2005 a second edition of the book was published.

The September 11, 2001, attacks shocked America, and a resulting economic downturn adversely affected the Georgia Trust and many other nonprofit organizations. Preservationists across the state, led by GAPA, advocated for a tax credit to encourage investment in Georgia's large and small cities. In 2002, the General Assembly passed legislation creating a 25 percent state income-tax credit for the rehabilitation of historic buildings. This new law placed a $5,000 cap on state tax for owner-occupied historic homes and income-producing structures. A preferential property tax for rehabilitated historic structures was also passed.

Advocacy efforts did not stop there, and a bill to produce a preservation automobile license plate was passed in 2005. The proceeds from the sale of the car tags were dedicated to enhancing the grant program offered by the Georgia State Historic Preservation Office.

In 2006 one of the Trust's key programs, Places in Peril, kicked off when the organization named ten sites to a list of historic places threatened by deterioration, neglect, or development pressure. The Trust conducted a very successful fund drive that garnered a $100,000 grant from the National Trust Partners in the Field program. Proceeds from this campaign were used to establish both a Georgia Trust field officer to offer direct assistance to Places in Peril listings and a grant program for badly needed bricks-and-mortar funding.

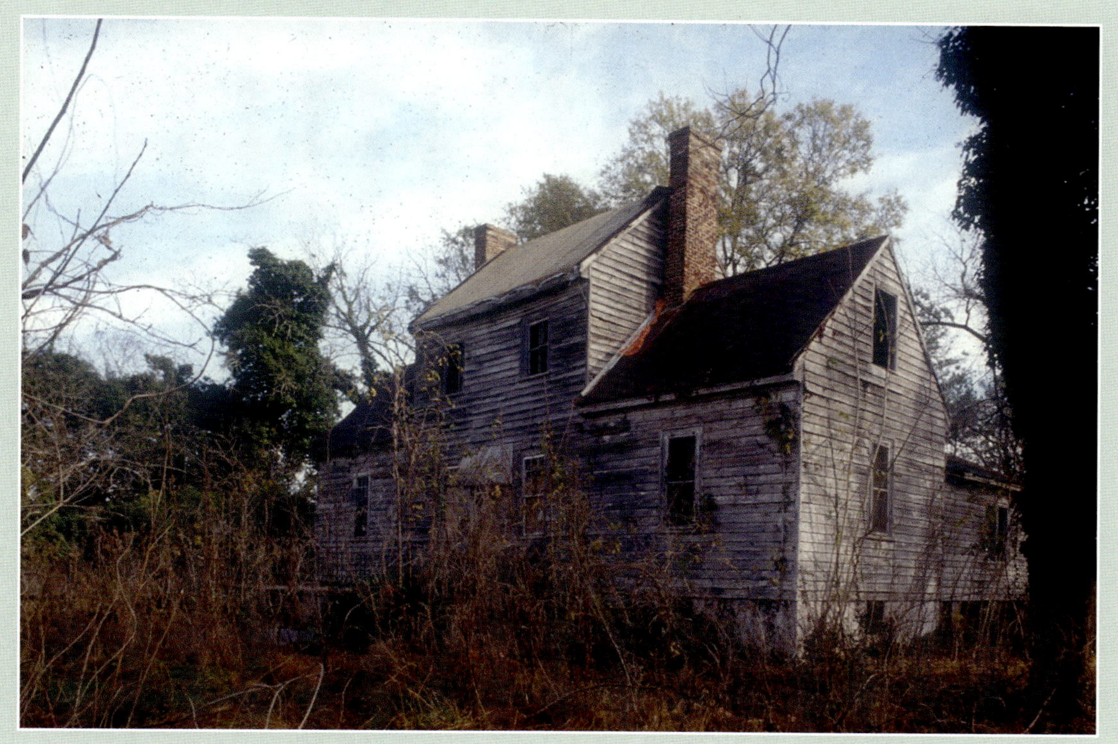

Cabaniss House, Jones County, before and after

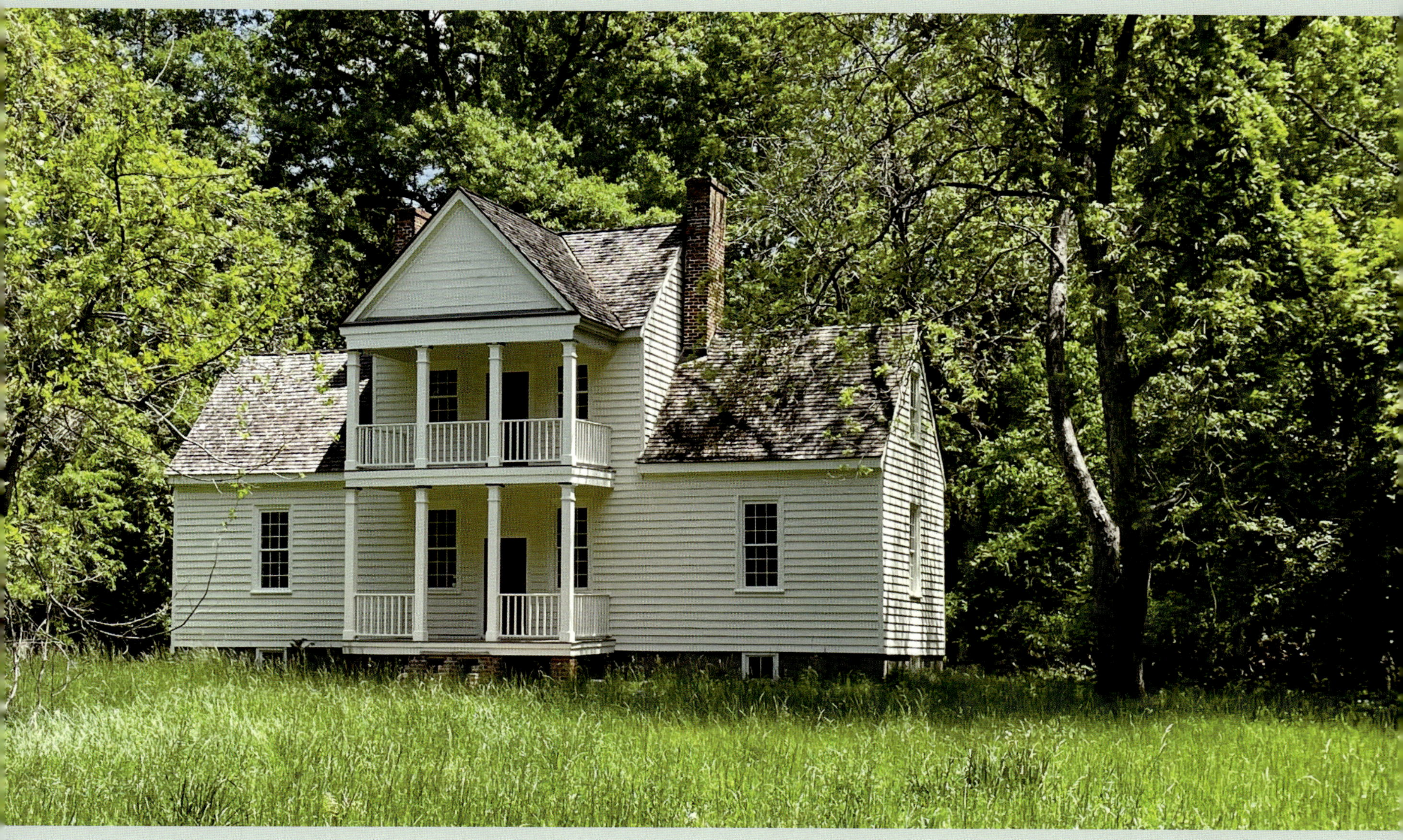

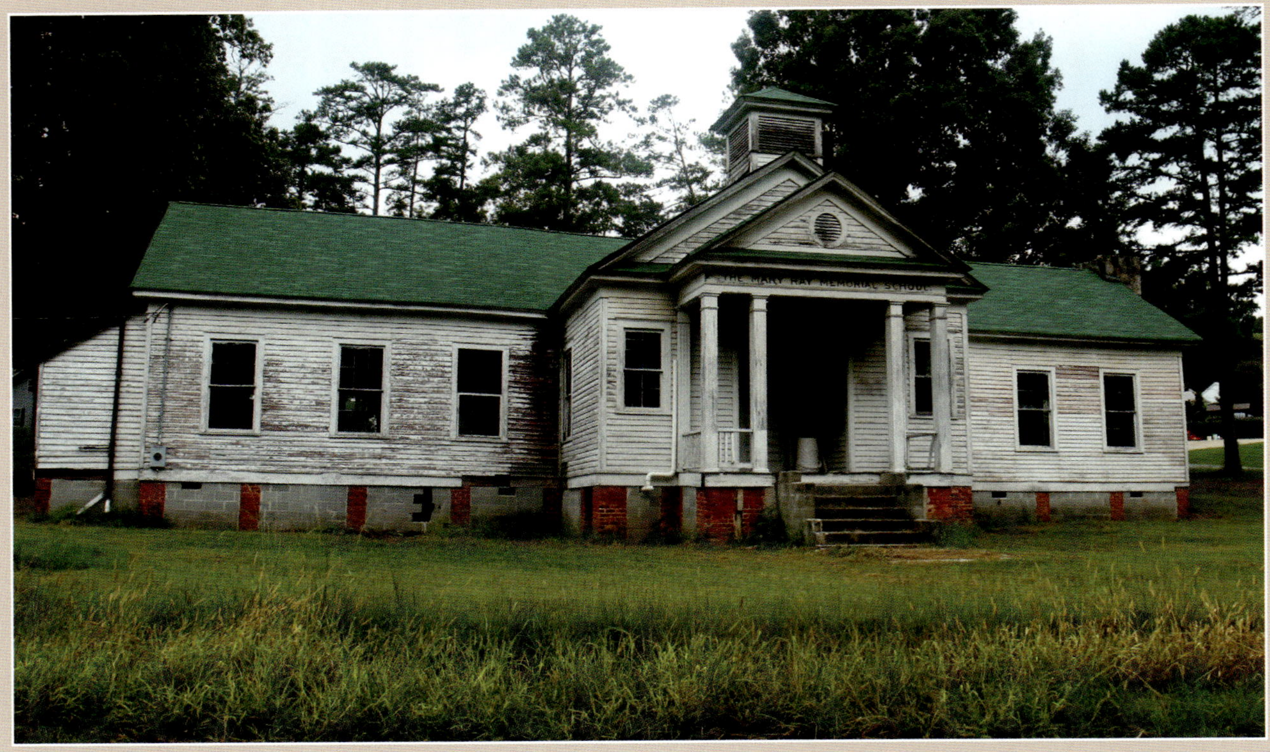

Mary Ray Memorial School, Coweta County, before and after

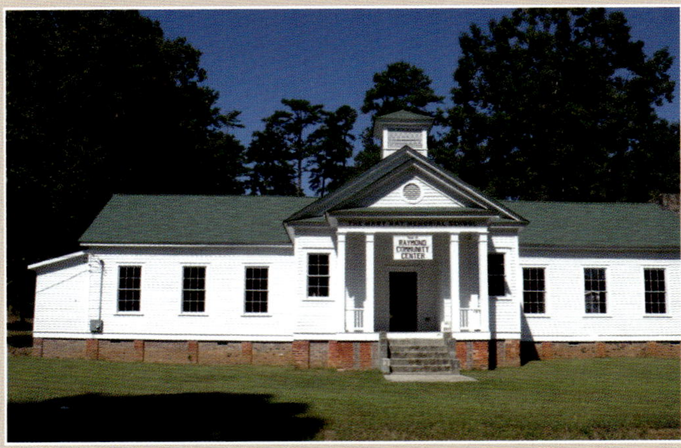

In 2007 longtime Georgia Trust president and chief executive officer (CEO) Greg Paxton resigned to accept a position as executive director of Maine Preservation. Paxton's twenty-seven-year tenure witnessed the Trust grow from small beginnings into one of the largest and most effective preservation organizations in the country. He received many awards for his work, including the Governor's Award in the Humanities.

A national search for Paxton's replacement was initiated, and in April 2008 Mark C. McDonald was selected by the board of trustees to be the next president and CEO. McDonald had twenty-two years of experience leading preservation nonprofits, including ten years as executive director of Historic Savannah

Foundation, where he had invigorated that organization and rebuilt its finances. McDonald, a former practicing attorney, had a special interest in using real estate transactions to save historic buildings.

In the summer of 2008, the Trust again proved successful in its legislative advocacy, when HB 851 passed the General Assembly. This bill greatly improved the Georgia state income-tax credit by raising the credit caps on individual owner-occupied projects from $5,000 to $100,000 and on income-producing rehabilitation projects from $5,000 to $300,000. Governor Sonny Perdue threatened a veto, so a highly energized effort was undertaken by GAPA to demonstrate grassroots support and persuade the governor to sign the bill into law, an effort that was eventually successful.

The Georgia Trust Revolving Fund remained active in the 2000s, despite the 2008 financial crisis. A total of fifteen buildings were acquired and saved by the Trust in the decade. Due in part to a sagging real estate market, the Trust was able to encourage owners to donate, in whole or in part, assets to the Revolving Fund. Another large hotel building, the Colquitt in Moultrie, was partially donated to the Trust in 2003 and resold to Hal and Patricia Carter, who successfully rehabilitated it into apartments on Courthouse Square in Moultrie. This project underscored the Trust's commitment to Main Street revitalization.

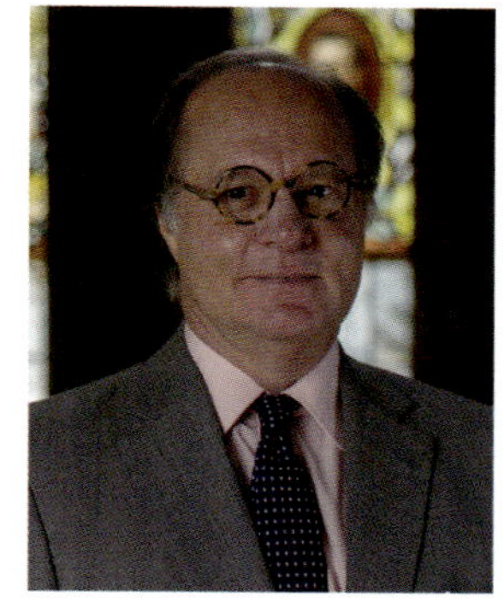

Mark C. McDonald

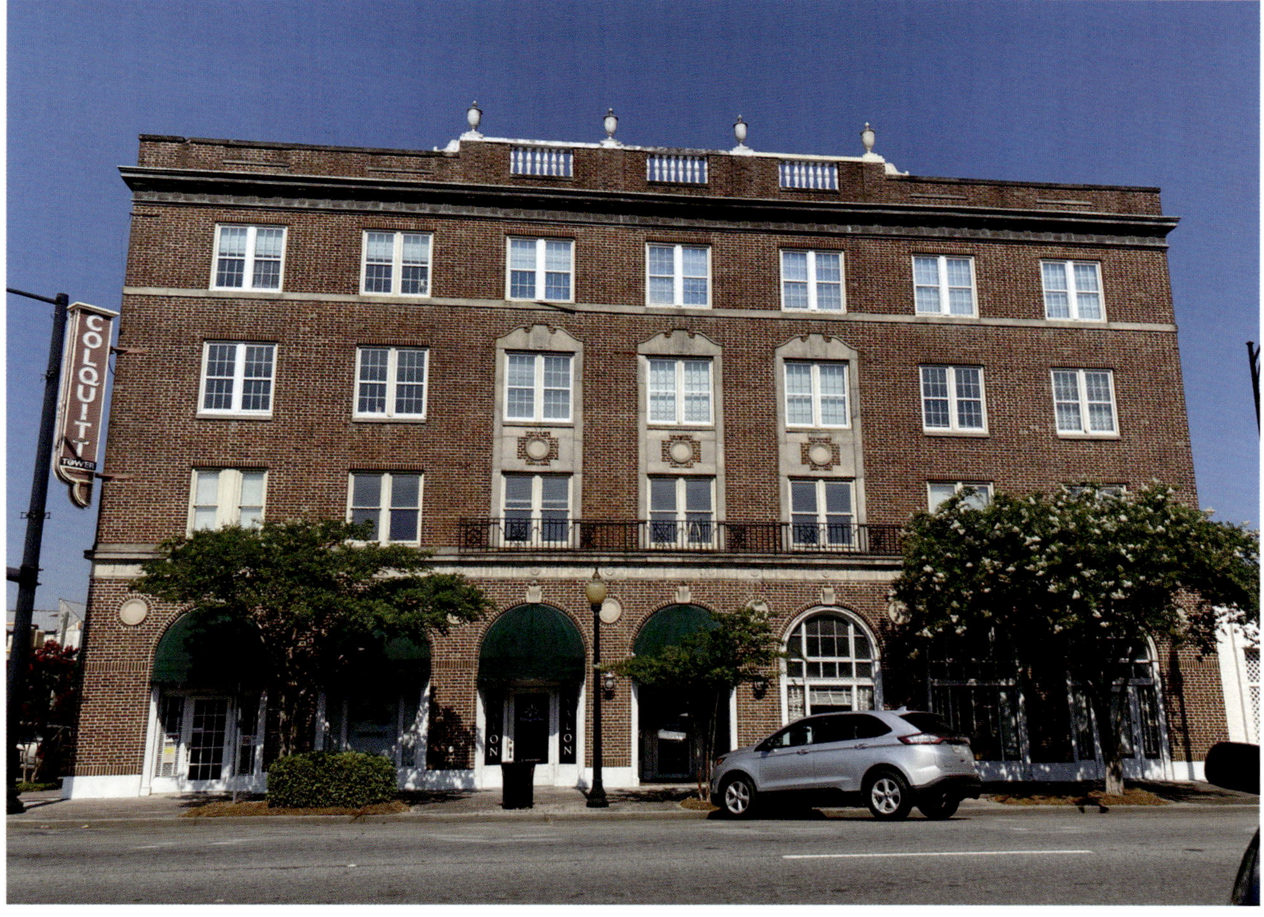

Colquitt Hotel, Moultrie

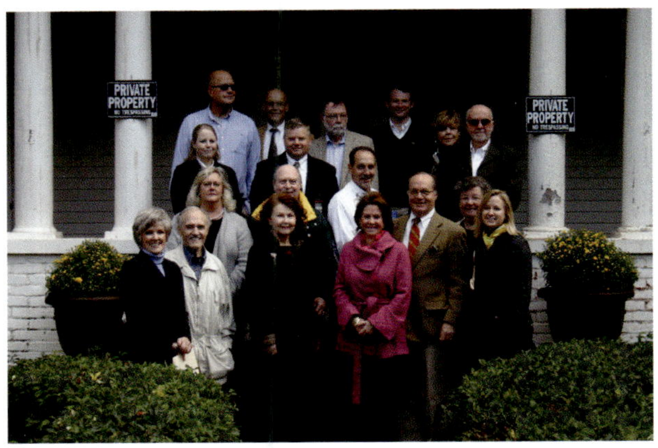

Forsyth citizens who saved houses from Walmart construction

Another key project was the preservation of three nineteenth-century houses in Forsyth. These had been acquired by Walmart and were planned for demolition in order to satisfy zoning requirements for a superstore imposed by the city. Encouraged by Forsyth citizens and its mayor, the Trust contacted Walmart's real estate department and after extensive negotiations were able to convince the corporation to donate the three homes and $50,000 to the Revolving Fund. The city accepted the protections of the Trust's conservation easement and designated the houses as part of a required buffer strip. All three homes were sold to and successfully rehabilitated by Veronica and Percell Kelley.

In 2008–9, Georgia's Department of Natural Resources awarded Rhodes Hall $650,000 in proceeds from a bond issue to make the building accessible to all. Greatly needed elevator and accessible bathrooms were installed, and the Trust supplemented these funds with a grant from the Woodward Foundation to repair and refinish the oak parquet floors on the parlor floor. These and second-story floors were expertly refinished without sanding by Michael Purser, nationally known historic-floors expert.

The completion of the highly successful $7.5 million capital campaign for Hay House meant that much needed work to the National Historic Landmark in Macon could proceed. Under the leadership of Director Katey Brown and the restoration committee, work began on the ground level, where floors were refinished, plaster restored, and the original faux oak graining was reinstalled. A gallery space was created in the ground-floor summer parlor and dining room.

Hay House's remarkable dining room on the first floor contained fascinating original features in a state of considerable decay. After extensive study and analysis, the restoration team began exploratory demolition that uncovered new and exciting information. A decorative paint scheme far more colorful and complex than anticipated was revealed, and a multicolored Renaissance Revival floor

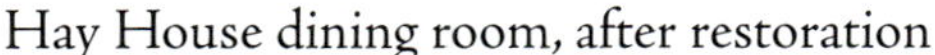

Hay House dining room, after restoration

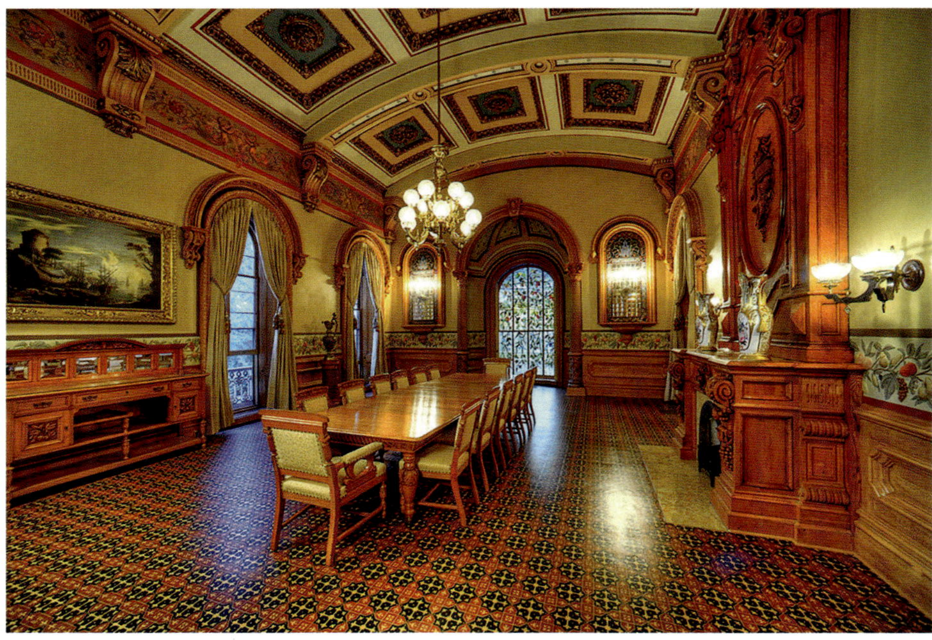

cloth was discovered under cabinetry added in the late nineteenth century. After approval of a change in the restoration master plan, these findings were implemented in a breathtaking and transformative restoration of the dining room by Geoffrey Steward and the IFACS team. In addition, Hay family–period wallpaper was reinstalled in the grand double parlors, and furnishings were sent to a conservator for restoration.

The second decade of the twenty-first century was a time of growth and accomplishment for the Trust and positioned the organization at the forefront of leadership in national preservation circles. Under the direction of board chair Kimbrough Taylor, the Georgia Trust established a sustainability task force in 2010 composed of over twenty leaders in the field of energy efficiency, sustainability experts, and historic-preservation practitioners. The task force held several meetings with the goal of uniting the laudable interests of the sustainability and preservation movements. The Trust developed a comprehensive presentation that was given on numerous occasions throughout the state, and finally, after years of work, in 2013 the Georgia Trust and Southface Energy Institute launched the Earthcraft Sustainable Preservation program. It was the first in the country to offer certification of rehabilitation projects that are pursued with environmentally sustainable methods and results. In 2021 the Trust debuted its Georgia Trust Green program, which emphasized the rehabilitation of historic homes in a manner designed to save energy costs and reduce greenhouse gases.

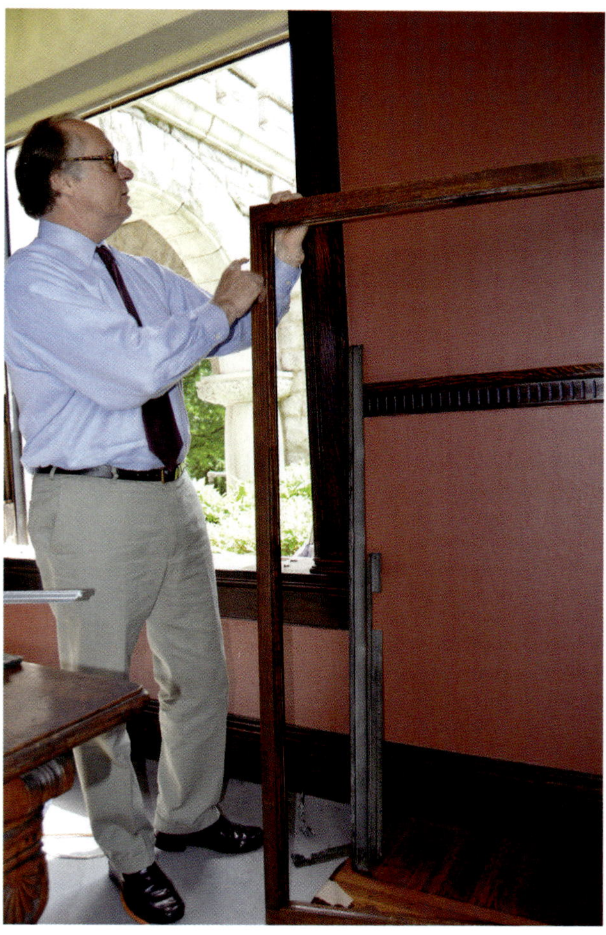

Rhodes Hall, green rehabilitation

In concert with the Earthcraft Sustainable Preservation, the Trust began to explore the sustainable rehabilitation of Rhodes Hall. In 2011, the Kendeda Fund awarded the Georgia Trust $130,000 from its Grants to Green program. This led the Trust to initiate a capital campaign, and in 2012 "Rhodes Hall: From Historic to Sustainable" was approved by the board of trustees with a goal of $1.7 million. Thanks to a $700,000 grant from the Lettie Pate Evans Foundation and other generous gifts, $2.2 million was eventually raised, with the excess going toward the establishment of an endowment for the maintenance of the headquarters of the Georgia Trust.

In 2013–14 rehabilitation was begun under the leadership of committee chairs and architects Gene Surber and Arthur Clement. Rhodes Hall's rehabilitation made the building environmentally efficient through the installation of a ductless HVAC system, improved insulation, repairs to the windows, roof, and porch ceilings, and installation of LED fixtures and Energy Star appliances. Rhodes Hall's utility bills diminished by 25 percent, while the building was made much more comfortable. The Georgia Trust received the Atlanta Better Buildings Award for water conservation and the Southface Award for Excellence following this remarkable transformation. The upper floors continue as offices for the Trust, while the main floor is used for museum and event space.

A preservation story gained widespread news coverage in 2012, when the National Park Service ruled the Dobbins Mining Landscape, near Cartersville, eligible for the National Register of Historic Places. This nineteenth-century manganese mine, owned by the prominent Rollins family, had been slated by the Georgia Department of Transportation as on the route for a major highway connecting I-75 to Rome, Georgia. This would have destroyed the mining features and the scenic beauty of the mountain landscape. Advocacy by the Rollins family attorney Henry Parkman and by the Georgia Trust prevailed, and the eligibility decision by the Keeper of the National Register invoked Section 106 and 4(f) processes and prevented the highway plans from proceeding. The 2012 Places in Peril listing was a key factor in this preservation victory.

During this same busy time, the Trust's advocacy efforts continued. In the legislative session of 2012, the SHPO was unfortunately scheduled for zero funding and faced the elimination of its nationally recognized Georgia African American Historic Preservation Network (GAAHPN). The Trust put its GAPA network into high gear, and after extensive community activism and work by Trust personnel, SHPO's funding was reinstated at a workable level. Former state senator and preservationist George Hooks of Americus volunteered his services to the Trust as leader of the advocacy program, and in 2015 a new round of enhancements to the state tax credit passed the General Assembly. This legislation removed the $300,000 credit cap on commercial projects and created the potential for projects with up to $5 million in state tax credits.

After 2012, restoration of the Green Parlor at Hay House to its 1860s appearance marked the end of the principal main-level work, and emphasis shifted upstairs to the second-floor bedrooms and hall. With the restoration committee's approval, Jonathan Poston engaged the well-known team of architectural historians Carl Lounsbury and Willie Graham and paint conservator Susan Buck, all of Williamsburg, to begin analysis of the bedroom floor. The Secret Room on the stair landing was restored in 2013, followed by the Hay Bedroom and Bath. Master plan revisions for the remaining bedrooms allowed the restoration of the hall to the Johnston 1860s look.

Hay House Green Parlor, after restoration

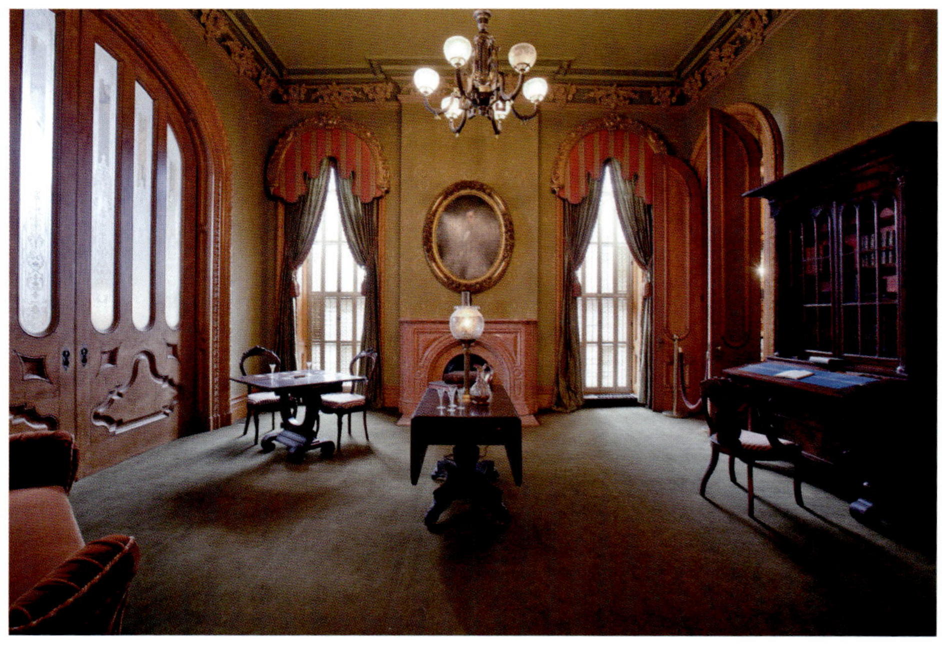

In 2019–20, progress was made on restoring bedrooms to the 1912 Felton era. The interest of Maconites in Hay House has never waned. Hay House and the Georgia Trust have proven that an American house museum can indeed be a success in the twenty-first century.

In 2015 the board of trustees approved an additional capital campaign for the badly needed rehabilitation of the Rhodes Hall landscape. Highly respected landscape architect Edward Daugherty was recruited to chair the landscape committee, and after a selection process the firm of Tunnell and Tunnell was selected to design a new scheme that would improve safety and security of the site, solve drainage problems, and enhance entrance to the building and improve its appearance. The new capital campaign raised over $1 million, thanks in large part to a gift of $500,000 by Dean DuBose Smith made in memory of her mother, Duffie Woodruff DuBose, longtime trustee and supporter of the Georgia Trust. In 2017 the landscape project was completed, with all the goals of the undertaking accomplished. In addition, a landscape endowment fund was created.

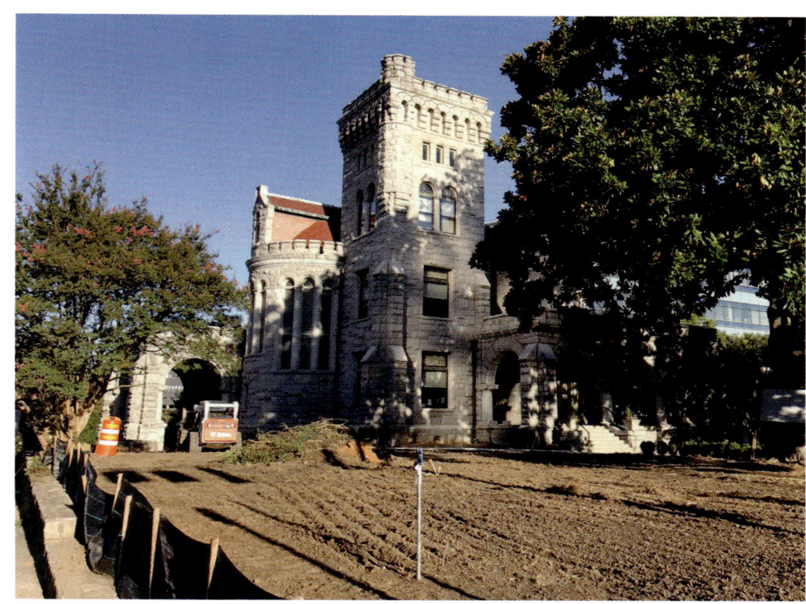

Rhodes Hall landscape, during construction

In 2017 the Trust initiated its first major membership campaign in several years, called Forward 44 to celebrate forty-four years of its existence. The goal was to rebuild the preservation department, whose staff had been reduced following the 2008 financial crisis. This highly successful effort enabled the Trust to double its staff dedicated to implementing the preservation programs of the Trust.

Indeed, Revolving Fund activities have increased substantially since 2010. As of publication of this book, the Trust has protected seventy-seven buildings through historic-preservation conservation easements. Efforts in the highly significant antebellum city of Sparta were a special focus of the fund. A three-fifths interest in the Sayre-Alford House, an important early Greek Revival building, was left to the Trust in the will of Mrs. Bobby West Alford, and the Trust negotiated a partial purchase of the remainder. After the first sale of the building proved unsuccessful, the Trust sold the home to Ben Carter and Joe Watkins, who rehabilitated not only this house but an adjacent property as well. Work with Robert and Suzy Currey proved very productive, and a nineteenth-century railroad warehouse was acquired and rehabilitated. With the encouragement of the Curreys and other Sparta citizens, especially Mayor Sistie Hudson, several more Sparta houses were acquired, sold, and rehabilitated. After a devastating fire at the Hancock County Courthouse, the Trust assisted in an award-winning reconstruction of this beautiful Victorian public building.

Another key property donated to the Trust was the Maxwell-Stokely House in Crawford, Oglethorpe County. This antebellum Plantation Plain–style house was enlarged in the Victorian period by the ancestors of former Georgia Trust board chairman Nathaniel Hansford. The beautiful residence was given to the Trust by Nathaniel and Frances Hansford in 2016 and sold in 2017 with a conservation easement.

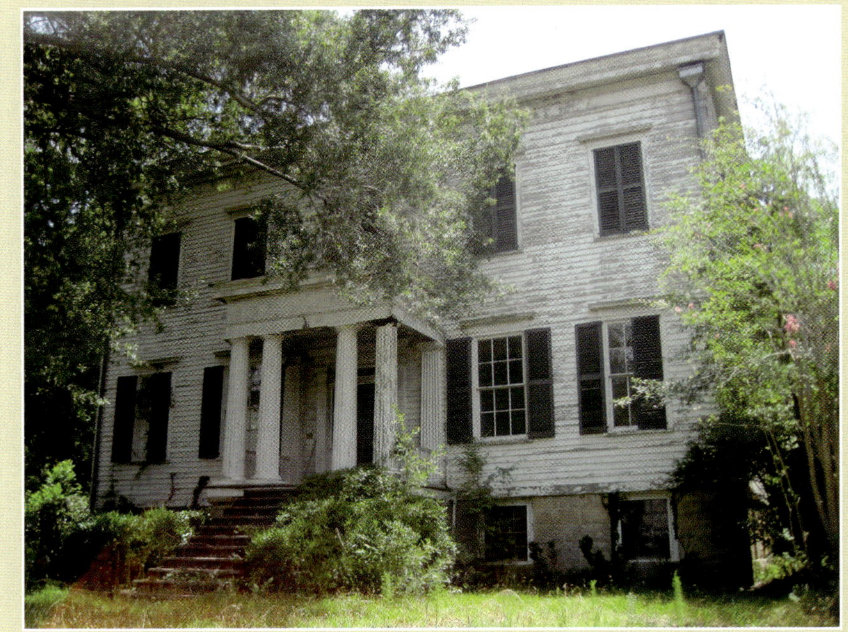

Sayre-Alford House, Sparta, before and after

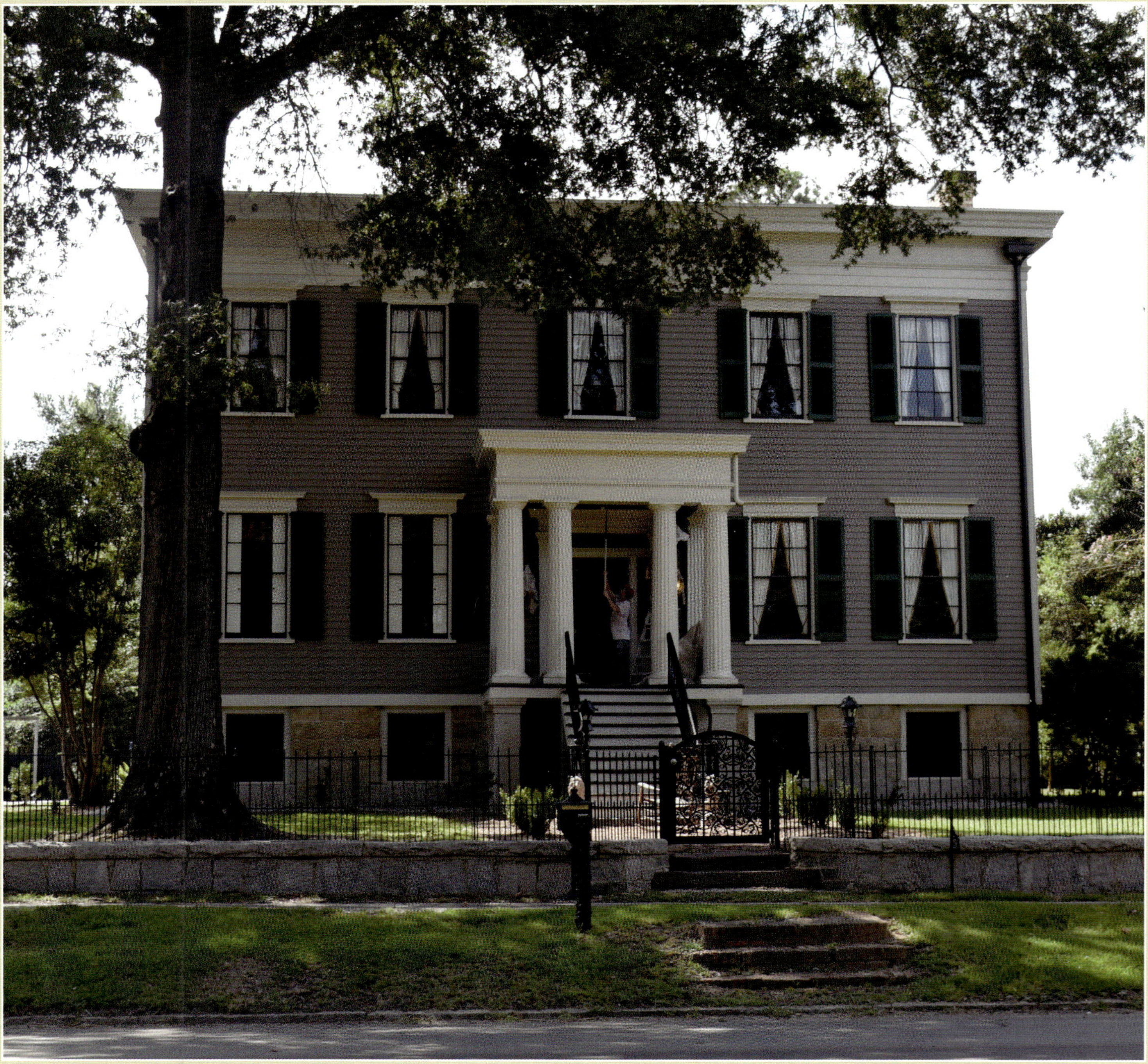

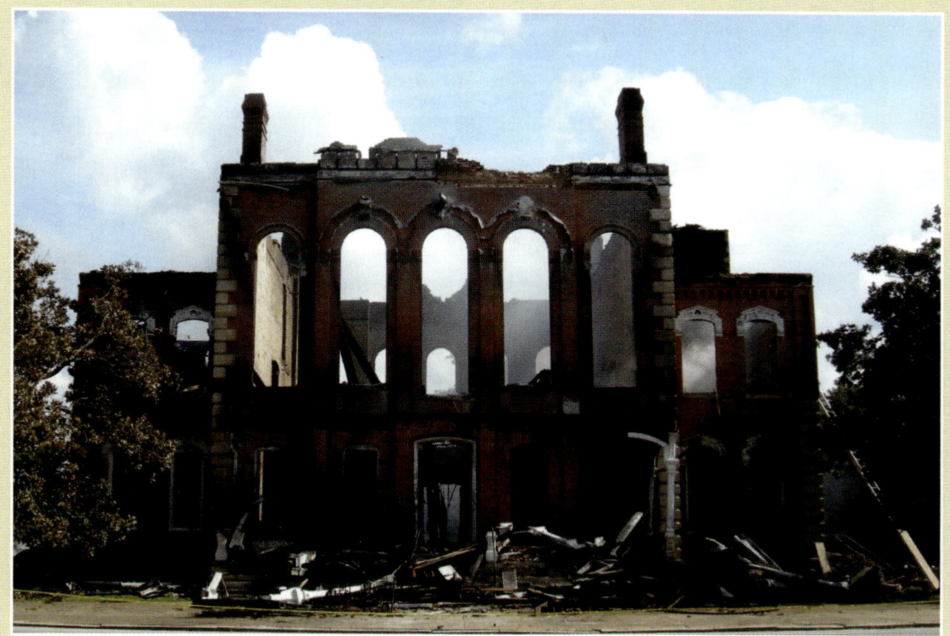

Hancock County Courthouse, after the fire and reconstruction

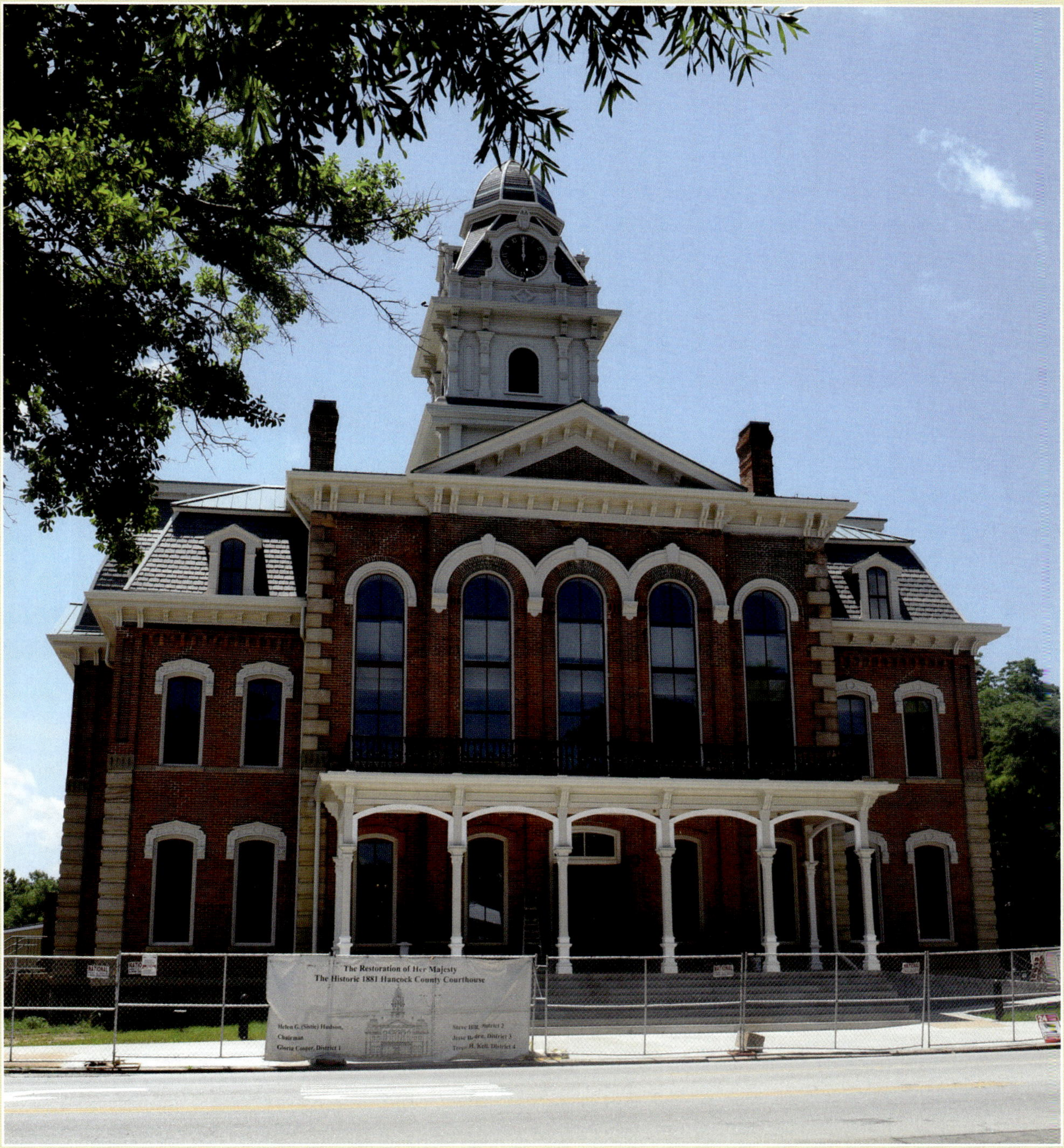

In 2017, the Georgia Trust formalized and added to its existing series of educational offerings under a new rubric, the Historic Preservation Institute. This undertaking was funded by the DuBose Family Foundation and included the Historic Preservation Leadership course, Revolving Fund workshops, Capital Campaign Training for Preservation Nonprofits, and classes focusing on energy efficiency for historic buildings.

With the encouragement of board chairman Bill Peard, the Georgia Trust began to focus preservation work on the west side of Atlanta, where the Beltline project was transforming neighborhoods, sometimes at risk of the loss of affordable housing and displacement of longtime owners. Trust staff identified and acquired two historic houses and a vacant lot from the family of Edward Johnson, a retired Tuskegee Airmen ground instructor and first African American licensed master electrician in Atlanta. The Trust's stated goals were to rehabilitate the historic buildings with energy-efficient features and then sell them as affordable housing, focusing on reinforcing the occupancy of longtime residents of the neighborhood. The Trust decided to donate the vacant lot to Habitat for Humanity and completed the green rehabilitation of both houses and sold them successively to buyers who met the income requirements.

Another noteworthy accomplishment from the early 2020s was the acquisition of Zion Episcopal Church in Talbotton from the Episcopal Diocese of Atlanta. This abandoned wooden Gothic Revival building is thought to be one of the most important buildings of its type in the United States. The Trust conveyed the church to Zion Restoration Inc., a nonprofit organization that quickly restored the building.

In addition, the Trust received as a donation the Weaver-Dallas House in Thomaston from Dr. Mary Williams. This 1820s Federal-style home had been in the same family since the 1830s. After a national marketing campaign, multiple offers were received before the Trust sold it subject to a conservation easement.

As many will remember, the worldwide COVID-19 pandemic had a dramatic effect on the lives of Americans, and nonprofit organizations were not immune. At the Georgia Trust, special events, including the 2020 Gala, two Rambles, and various others, were cancelled. Others continued but with strict social distancing and vaccination mandates in place. Pandemic assistance grants were critical to the Trust's well-being, but the remarkable and inspiring occurrence was the substantial increase in giving by the Trust membership. This strong financial support bolstered the spirits and morale of the trustees and staff. Sales of Revolving Fund properties increased during this time, due to a desire by many to have a second home outside the crowded cities.

In early 2018, the Georgia Trust board of trustees adopted a three-year strategic plan to cover the 2018–20 period. This document included plans for the celebration of the organization's fiftieth anniversary in 2023, one item of which was the publication of this book on Georgia architecture and preservation.

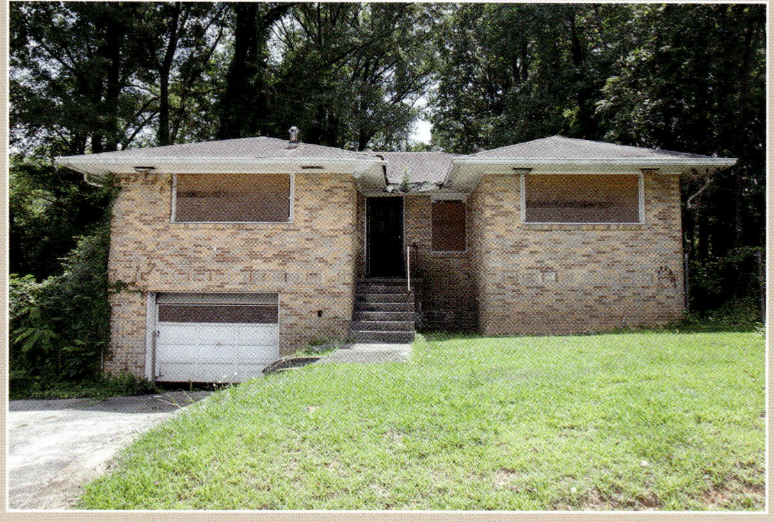

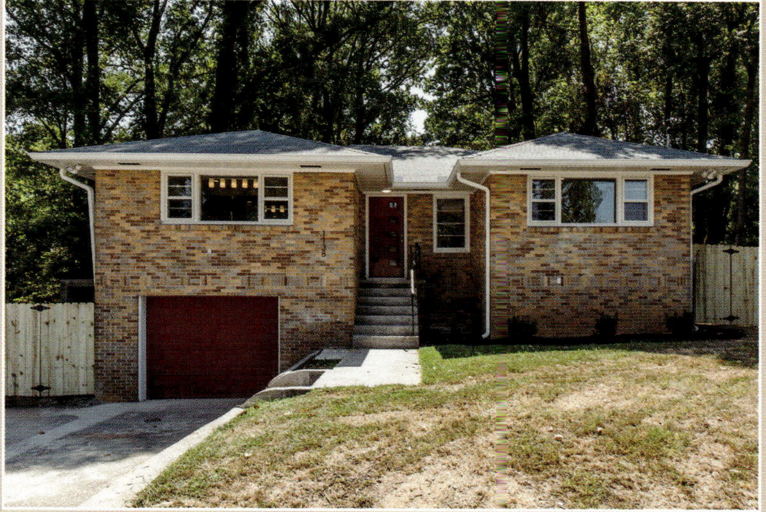

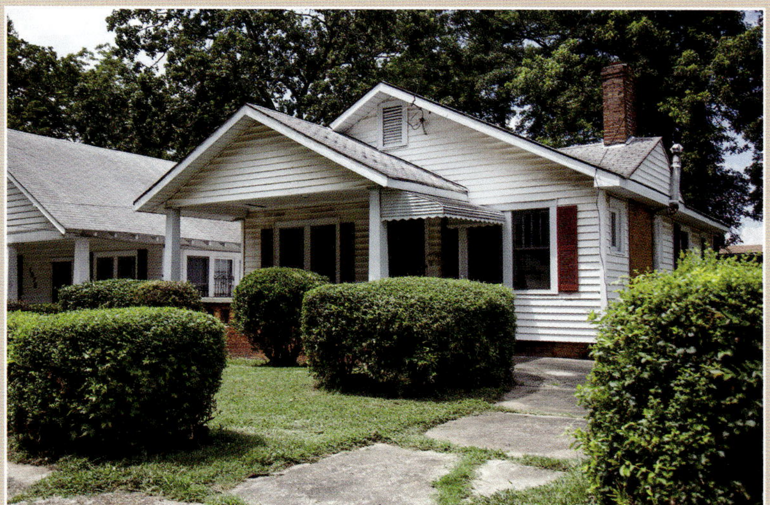

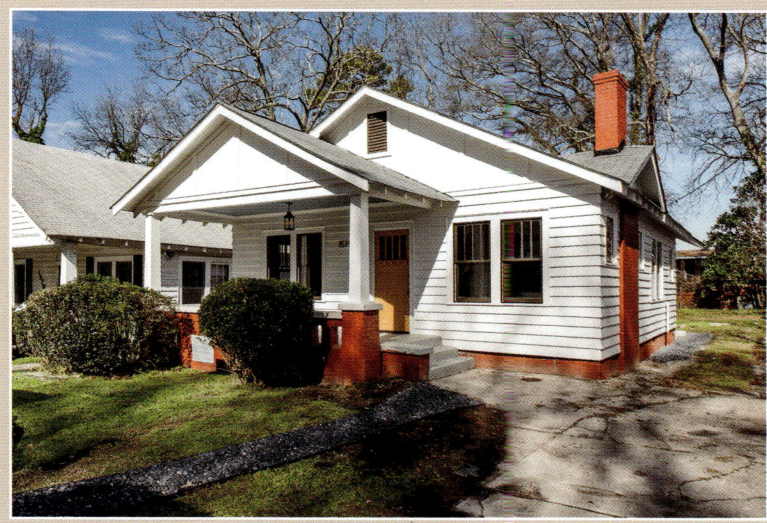

West Atlanta Preservation Initiative Houses, before and after

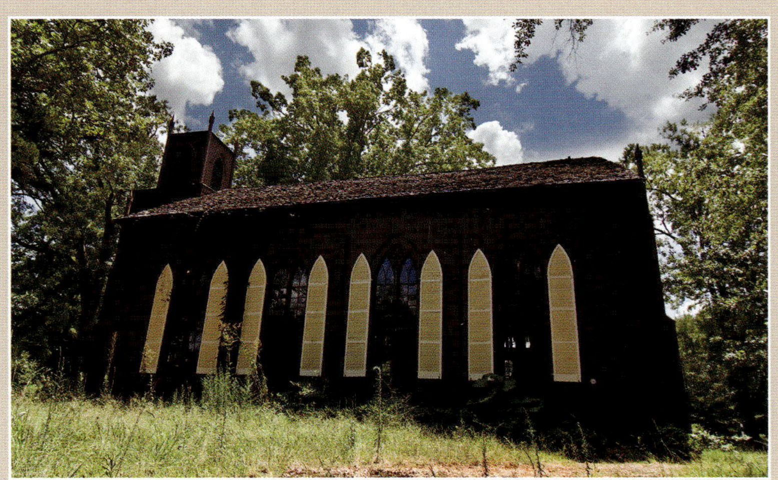

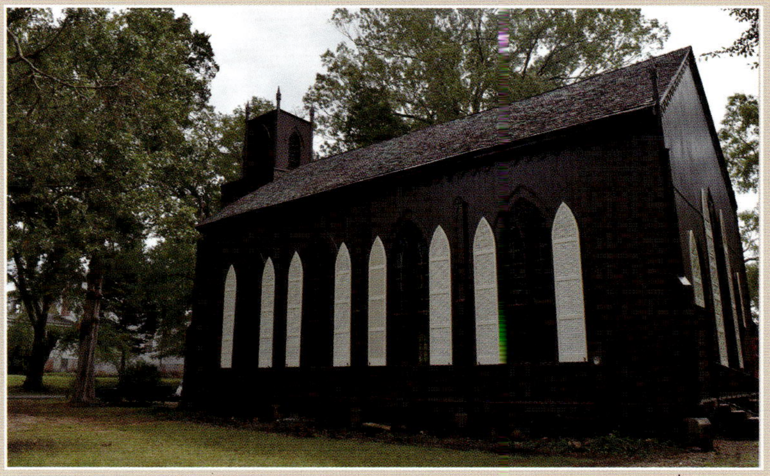

Zion Episcopal Church, Talbotton, before and after

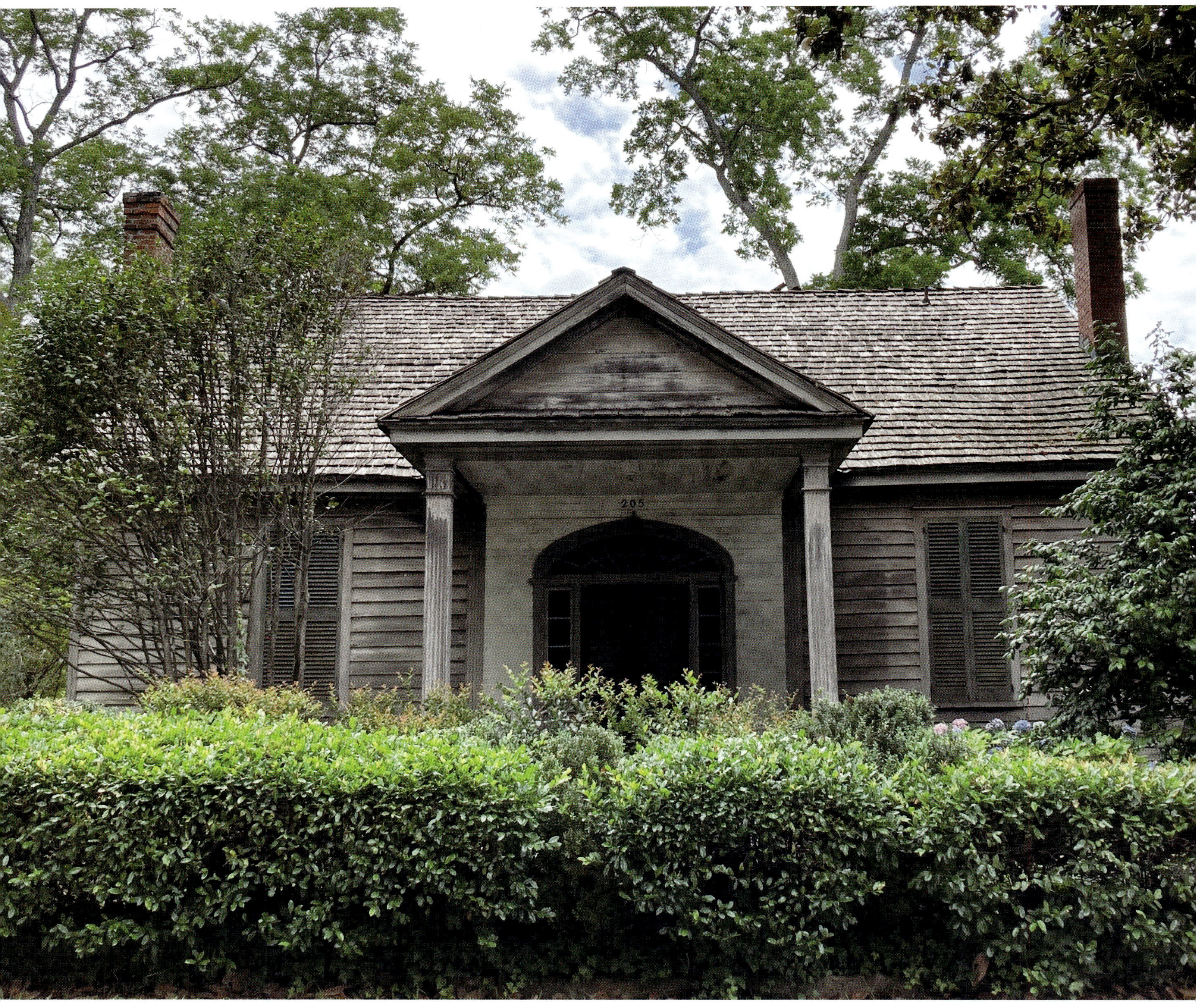

Weaver-Dallas House, Thomaston

Fifty years is a relatively brief period in the fullness of time, but the leadership of the Trust will attest that each fiscal year has seemed daunting. The challenges brought by a mainstream disposable culture that sees virtually everything, from a plastic drinking straw to an entire streetscape, as fodder for the landfill make the work of historic preservation difficult, at best.

The leadership of the Georgia Trust, however, has never been daunted in their quest to make the heritage of Georgia relevant to its present and its future. While the Trust has been the beneficiary of some very dedicated and talented employees, the success of the organization is ultimately attributable to strong leadership from the community. From its founding in 1973, when it was operated by volunteers, and throughout its history, the board of trustees has provided the continuity, vision, financial support, and management that have ensured the faithful execution of its mission and adherence to a value system that upholds our built environment as vital and necessary to the improvement, edification, and preservation of our culture.

Georgia Trust for Historic Preservation Board Chairs

1973–1977	William W. Griffin, Atlanta
1977–1978	Edward W. Neal, Columbus
1978–1981	William Bradley Hale, Atlanta
1981–1984	John C. Hagler III, Augusta
1984–1986	E. Roy Lambert, Madison
1986–1988	Archie H. Davis, Atlanta
1988–1990	Hugh K. Rickenbaker Jr., Atlanta
1990–1992	Janice Persons Biggers, Columbus
1992–1994	W. Moses Bond, Atlanta
1994–1996	T. Marion Slaton, Atlanta
1996–1998	Pat Edwards, Barnesville
1998–2000	C. Dexter Jordan Jr., Columbus
2000–2002	F. Sheffield Hale, Atlanta
2002–2004	Tom B. Wight, Macon
2004–2006	Raymond R. Christman, Atlanta
2006–2009	Michael L. Starr, Atlanta
2009–2011	G. Kimbrough Taylor, Atlanta
2011–2013	V. Nathaniel Hansford, Lexington
2013–2015	Ira D. Levy, Rome
2015–2017	William B. Peard, Atlanta
2017–2019	Georgia Schley Ritchie, Atlanta
2019–2021	David A. Smith, Decatur
2021–2023	Norris A. Broyles III, Atlanta
2023–present	Tiffany B. Alewine, Flowery Branch & Savannah

State of Georgia Historic Preservation Department Heads

1969–1974	Mary Gregory Jewett
1974–1975	Jackson O'Neal Lamb
1975–1978	David Sherman
1978–1994	Elizabeth A. Lyon
1994–1998	Mark Edwards
1998–2009	W. Ray Luce
2009–2022	David Crass
2022–present	Jennifer Dixon

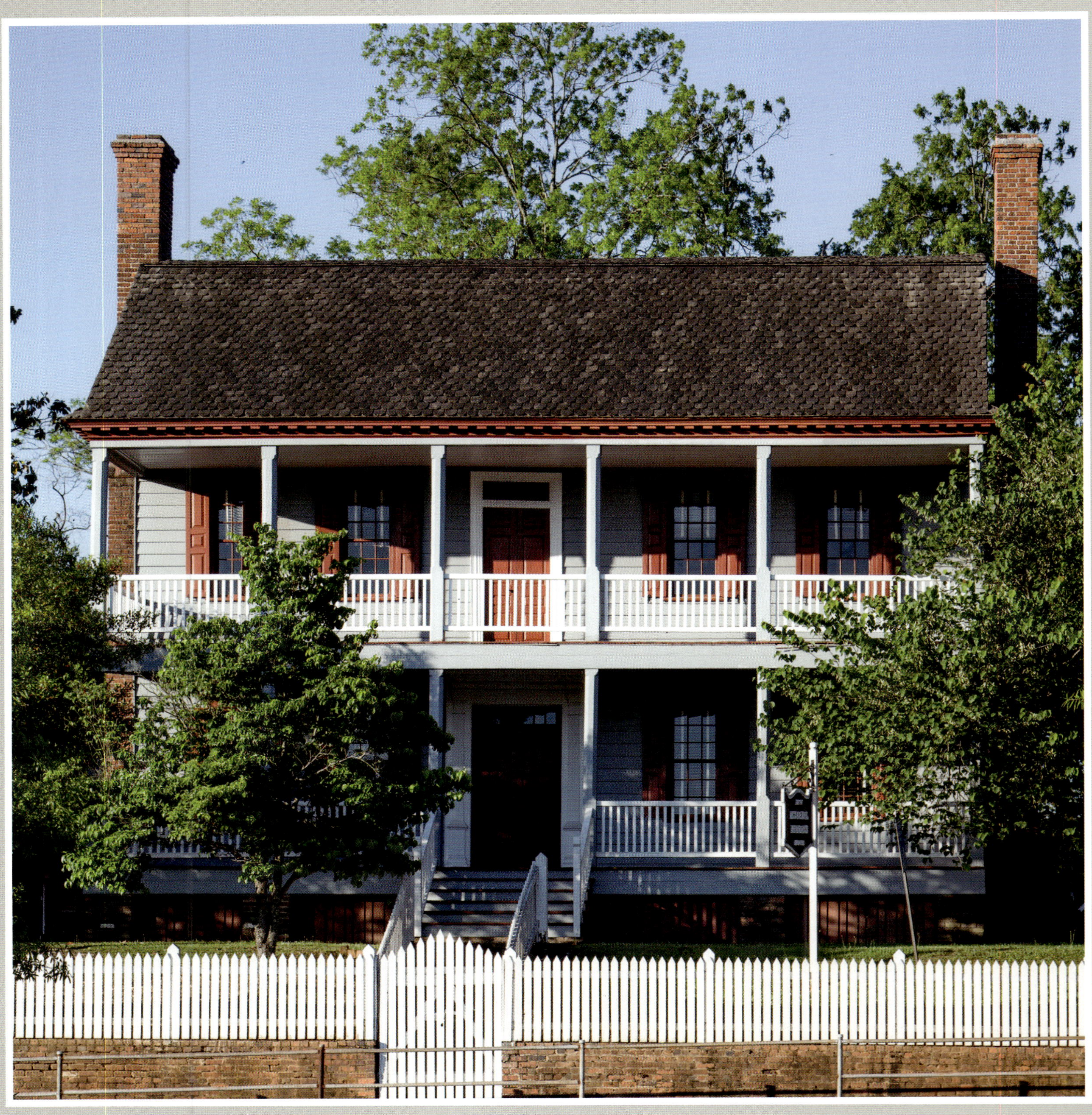

I. Eighteenth-Century Georgia Architecture in a Modern World

CARL I. GABLE

Friends and Enemies

A VARIETY OF VISIONARY MOTIVES prompted the eighteenth-century founders and promoters of the new province of Georgia. For some, the province offered freedom from imprisonment for debt. For others, freedom from slavery or demon rum—both prohibited in the early years. The most compelling reason for carving a new colony out of the western territory of South Carolina, however, was simply defense.

The older colony had begun life at Charleston in 1670. By 1733 its citizens perceived the land west and south of the Savannah River as a haven for their enemies, current and potential. Spanish forts and missions probed northward from Florida; French military scouts and traders infiltrated from the French territories to the west along the Mississippi River. And the communities of Creek (Muscogee) and Cherokee Indians who were settled and hunting throughout the territory were a regular and increasing source of friction and conflict. A new province beyond the Savannah River represented for South Carolinians a highly desirable buffer between themselves and all the potential invaders who lurked in the backcountry.

Of course, a Cassandra amid the South Carolinians and the new Georgia settlers would have known that their most dangerous enemies did not lie to the south and west but in their own midst. Their greatest threat would come from their British rulers and those who remained loyal to them in the war of revolution that awaited just four decades hence.

Building on Sand

Little survives of the architecture Georgia created before 1800, during its first sixty-seven years. Of the approximately 15,800 houses in the state in 1800, few

Facing: Ezekiel Harris House, Augusta

remain: just eight in and near Savannah, a few in Augusta, and a curious rock house in McDuffie County's lost town of Wrightsboro, plus one church in Midway and another in Ebenezer. All the rest, except for fragments here and there (and a few with provenance too unsettled to assess), have been wiped out through more than two centuries of intervening wars, fires, hurricanes, redevelopment, and changing tastes and priorities. Yet this small inventory of houses and churches offers modern Georgians important windows onto the remarkably diverse backgrounds, cultures, and aspirations brought by the pioneering settlers.

Georgia, the last and westernmost of the British colonies in North America, attracted a surprising procession of groups and individuals seeking economic opportunity and religious freedom. Many arrived directly from European countries, including settlements of Scots at Joseph's Town and New Inverness, French at Highgate, Germans at Hampstead, and Austrian Protestants at Ebenezer.

Other groups migrated from the older American colonies, such as settlers from the Dorchester, Massachusetts, area who first stopped to create new communities in Connecticut and South Carolina and then sent some of their congregation onward to present-day Midway, Georgia, between Savannah and Brunswick. Some Quaker families who settled first in Pennsylvania and then in adjacent mid-Atlantic colonies followed a similar path, pausing first in North Carolina and then moving still further south to found Wrightsboro, Georgia.

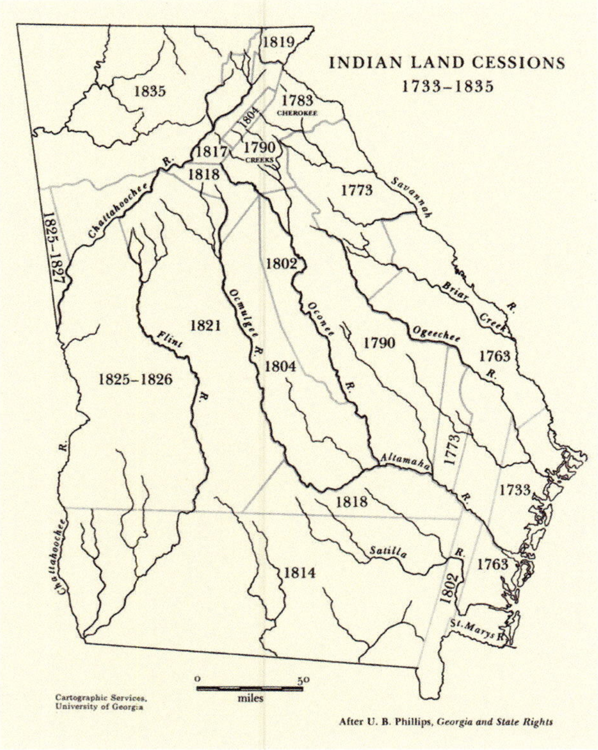

There are two ways of looking at the original expanse of colonial Georgia. The British king's initial twenty-one-year charter to Gen. James Oglethorpe and his fellow trustees encompassed broadly all the territory above Florida and below North Carolina and westward from South Carolina to the Pacific Ocean. Obviously there were other claimants to much of that land, including the French along the Mississippi River and the Spanish to the west beyond that. The Spanish also made noisy complaints from Florida.

For Oglethorpe and his successors, however, the problems caused by European claimants seemed remote when compared to a more immediate matter: the new colonial territory was already occupied by thousands of Indigenous people. Therefore, despite the king's contrary view, as a practical matter Georgia was no larger than the area around Savannah that fifty chiefs of the Lower Creek nation ceded to Oglethorpe and the trustees in an initial 1733 treaty. A series of additional treaty cessions would follow in later years, and the expansion of colonial Georgia traces the pattern of these treaties. First the boundaries were pushed down the Atlantic coast to Saint Marys and up the Savannah River to Augusta and beyond (1763). Further negotiations moved the lines still more north and west (1773), with more additions to come after the turn of the century. This progressive expansion of the colony is reflected in Georgia's surviving eighteenth-century buildings.

Indian Land Cessions, 1733–1835

Pioneering Georgia

Wild Heron Plantation lies fifteen miles south of Savannah on the Little Ogeechee River. The house tells us a great deal about the first decades of colonial Georgia architecture by virtue of what it is *not*. In particular, it bears no resemblance to the grand brick plantation houses that were being built in the same period around Charleston, little more than one hundred miles up the Atlantic coast. There was no need here for the builder to consult the treatise of the Italian architect Andrea Palladio to ensure the proper dimensions for Corinthian columns, nor even the simplified English pattern books to source lesser embellishments.

What the builder at Wild Heron needed was an understanding of the Georgia climate, of the need to elevate the house on brick piers in order to allow breezes to circulate under it, and of the need to place the three chimneys outside the perimeter of the house instead of in the interior as in the cooler colonies to the north. Ventilation and airflow was also a prime concern in the placement of the doors and windows and the full-width porches in front and back. Dormer windows set in a spraddle roof also aid air circulation, while opening the upper half-floor to light.

The result was a plain and simple one-and-a-half story cottage answering local needs and recognizing the economic realities of a colony that was but twenty years old, not eighty-three years like neighboring South Carolina. This plain elevated cottage style, wood-framed with clapboard siding, appeared often as Georgia expanded in settlements up the Savannah River toward Augusta and beyond.

Who built the house at Wild Heron? The question calls for reflection. Francis Harris acquired the land in 1756 by way of a royal grant directly from King George II. Harris had arrived in Georgia about 1739 as an accountant charged with helping to straighten out the colony's tangled financial records. His talents and training propelled him swiftly to a place among the colony's political and business leaders. By 1744 he and James Habersham had formed the first Georgia firm focused on direct export and import of agricultural products and other trade goods. Both men were members of the Governor's Council, and Habersham was its president; Harris became the first Speaker of the colony's House of Commons.

The house at Wild Heron was built by David Cutler Braddock, not Harris, but Harris bought the house from him in 1755, shortly after it was completed. Braddock was a sea captain who may have done business with the Habersham & Harris trading company. (Habersham once affirmed to the Governor's Council that Braddock was "an excellent seaman.") In fact, Captain Braddock may have built the house for Harris's account, not for himself. Such a maneuver might have avoided some of the restrictions on property transfer that prevailed in the mid-eighteenth century. Regardless of whether Braddock or Harris was financially responsible for building Wild Heron, there is no doubt that it was Harris's wife who named it. Wild Heron had been the name of her estate in Hampshire, England, which she sold when she and Harris married and moved to Georgia in 1750.

Wild Heron Plantation raises two fundamental and related issues about historic preservation, in Georgia and more generally. The first is the role of slavery for 113 years of Georgia's history. Today, many are surprised to learn that the idealistic founders banned slavery in the colony, just as they banned the sale of whiskey and the concentration of land under a few dominant owners. Unfortunately, in the face of severe economic adversity in the early years, expedience soon deposed idealism. Slavery, touted as a remedy for the colony's economic decline, was legalized by 1751. The trustees surrendered their charter from the king the following year, and Georgia was converted to a crown colony in 1755. Wild Heron was well situated to benefit financially from the new rules. Large tracts of land were added to the property, so there was low wetland suitable for rice production as well as higher elevations for expanding the increasingly important cotton crop. Enslaved workers, ultimately more than 125 of them, were deemed key to success in both crops.

Wild Heron was passed down through successive Harris generations for almost two centuries. Then, in 1935, the house, in dilapidated condition, was acquired and refurbished by Shelby Myrick of Savannah, who added several basement rooms, installed modern amenities, and altered some interior finishes.

A property such as Wild Heron is not preserved as a symbol of its troubled past, and certainly not as a monument to it. What Wild Heron offers each new generation is a reminder of the past, of its struggles and failures sacrifices and compromises—the sacrifices of the Harris family in forging the colony of Georgia and providing leadership in the American Revolution and the sacrifices of generations of the harshly enslaved in their lives at Wild Heron and of their descendants thereafter in a segregated society.

The second lesson from Wild Heron, and all of the other historic buildings discussed here, is that their continued survival in the modern world cannot be assumed. These properties are a part of their broad community, and they will prosper only as long as they retain the respect, love, and protection of their people. With that support they can continue as vibrant elements of our lives, now and into the future.

On March 12, 1734, in the second year of Georgia's existence—and long before either David Cutler Braddock or Francis Harris of Wild Heron Plantation ever set eyes on the colony—thirty-seven newly arrived families milled about the dock at Savannah. They had reached the final leg of a long journey. Very few of the new arrivals spoke English, so the air must have been filled with German chatter as the group and the two ministers who led them peered around, hoping for an early reading on whether they had made a grave mistake by trading the certain dangers of their Austrian homeland for the unknown risks on the frontier of the New World.

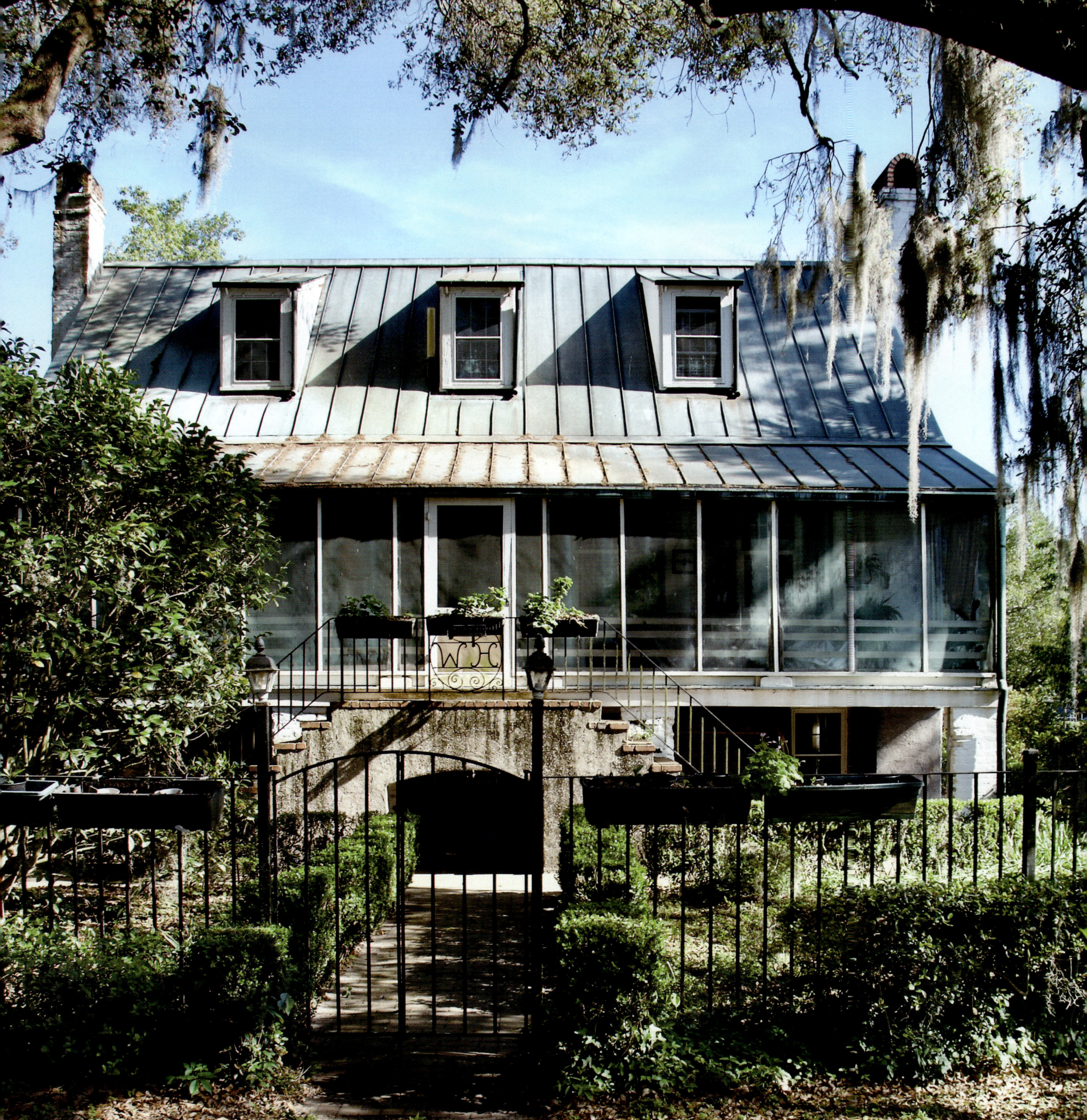

Wild Heron, near Savannah

The English colony was scarcely a year old, but the latest immigrants—who had been expelled from Salzburg in present-day Austria because of their religious beliefs—were not the first non-English European settlers in Georgia. In addition to groups of Scots and French, there was already a band of German speakers. Those earlier settlements were located near Savannah and southward. Their primary mission was to buffer Georgia from its greatest military threat, the Spanish soldiers who were fortified 150 miles to the south at Saint Augustine. Oglethorpe had different plans for the Salzburgers. Their home was to be Ebenezer, a new town he planned for them thirty miles upstream on the Savannah River, set back six miles from the bank. For Oglethorpe, Ebenezer's role was to buffer Savannah from the Indians, whose lands began only a few miles away.

Despite the settlers' best efforts, siting Ebenezer six miles from the river quickly proved impractical. The land was low and unsuitable for farming, and the distance from the river made trade and communication with Savannah difficult. After three years they moved the settlement, creating New Ebenezer on more promising land fronting directly on the river. The community soon achieved stability, with an economy based on small farms, silk production, and trade with the Indians.

In 1769 the townspeople were able to complete construction of their magnificent Jerusalem Church, despite the interruptions of the First Cherokee War, 1758–61, and the broader hostilities of the French and Indian War. Jerusalem Church still thrives today, the oldest active church building in Georgia and the oldest Lutheran church in continuous use in the United States. Its survival is all the more remarkable because New Ebenezer, the once prosperous community around it, has become another lost town of Georgia. Much of it was destroyed in successive battles between British and patriot forces during the American Revolution. Thereafter the diminished town struggled, hanging on until finally disappearing about 1855. Yet the spirit of the community seems still vital, embodied in Jerusalem Church and its serene, sheltering graveyard.

The church is an enduring reflection of the vision and industry of the early congregation. The exterior walls are of brick handmade near the site from local clay and laid in the English bond pattern. Flemish bond, more common in the American colonies, would have been more economical and perhaps have provided a more elegant finish, but English bond requires less skill in workmanship and supervision, which may have been the deciding factor on the Georgia frontier, where brickwork of any type was not common. The structure's 69-foot length is only 15 percent greater than its width. The strength of the masonry walls permits the two-story height needed to accommodate a gallery and two complete rows of windows circling all four walls. The upper windows are half the size of the lower ones, and a few still display some of the original glass panes. All of the window and door openings are supported by segmental relieving arches set in brick.

The interior worship space is bathed in the uniform white of its plaster walls and painted wood surfaces; the room is warmed by the rich brown stain of the gallery rail and the elegant, scrolled walnut endcaps of the pews. The chamfered columns with Doric capitals, which support the gallery, draw attention to the unsettling anomaly: the gallery was installed to segregate the enslaved in attendance at worship services. The Georgia colony's original prohibition of slavery, rum, and concentrated landholdings was one of the attractions that brought the Salzburgers to Georgia, and they gave the colonial proprietors their strong political support to maintenance of the proscriptions. The opposition was overwhelming, however, and with time slavery and plantations arrived in Ebenezer just as they did in the rest of Georgia. And rum was probably already there.

Ebenezer, however, never settled comfortably into the new plantation-centered economy that enveloped it and by the mid-nineteenth century could be numbered among Georgia's lost towns. But Jerusalem Church was never lost and today continues the traditions that the original Reverends Johann Martin Bolzius and Israel Christian Gronau brought to the Georgia frontier so long ago.

Jerusalem Lutheran Church, near Rincon

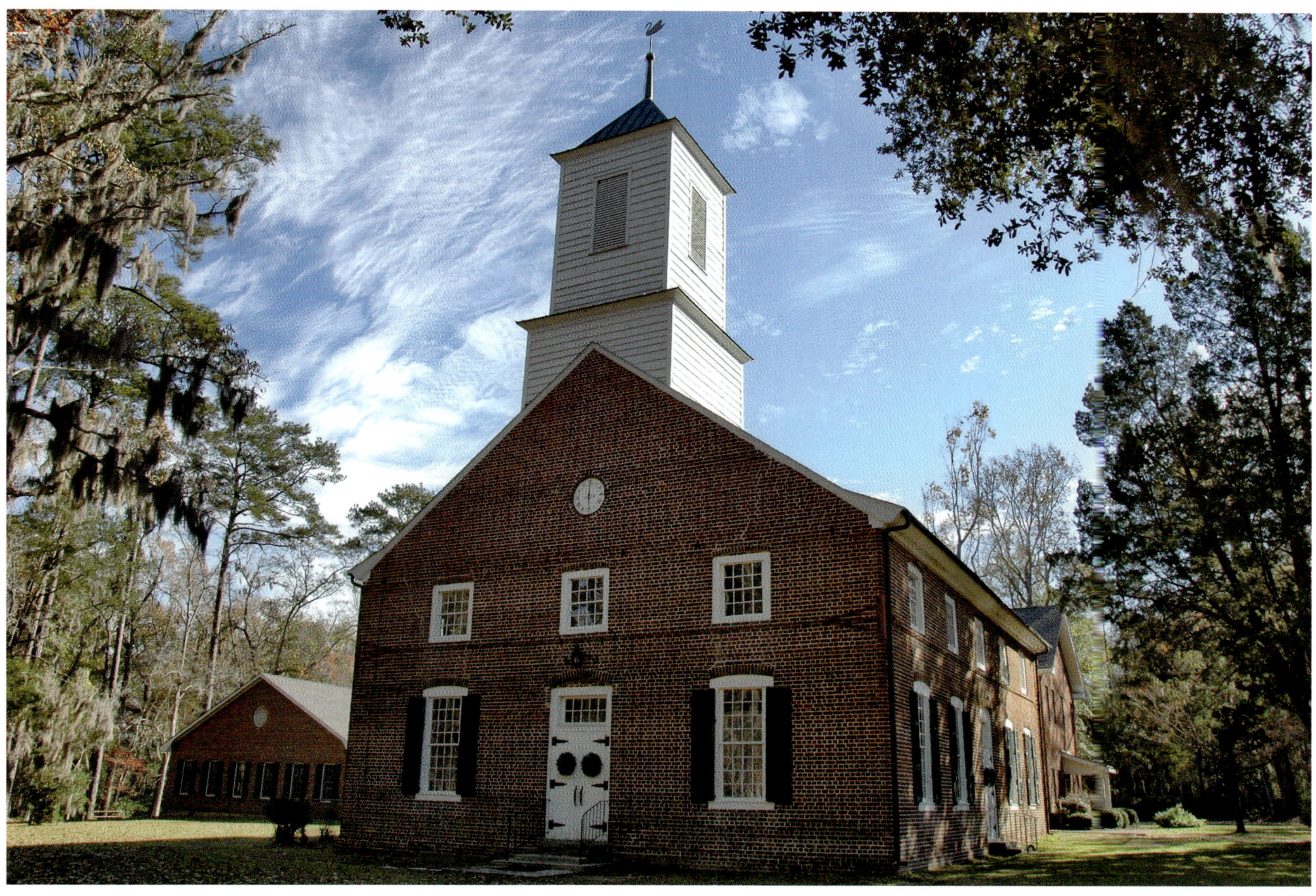

The Thomas Ansley House, also known as the Rock House, is a lost house in a lost township. Even the memory of it would probably be lost if the eighteenth-century Quaker pioneer Thomas Ansley had not chosen to build his house with walls of rugged fieldstone two feet thick, instead of the usual wood or brick. Because of Ansley's foresight, this historic treasure in McDuffie County, thirty-five miles west of Augusta and the Savannah River, though empty now and periodically assaulted by vandals, still faces the world defiantly, as mysterious as some stele left in the wilderness by alien visitors.

Today, almost 250 years after it was built, the Rock House has two lessons to teach. The first is the desperate saga of its origin and early years; the second is the message it offers about the ability of a modern community, through vision, patience, and determination, to seize its history and preserve it for the future.

Thomas Ansley was born in Freehold, New Jersey, where he and Rebecca Cox married in 1760. Although there is no documentary evidence that either of them was of the Quaker faith, the newlyweds immediately joined with a group of local Quakers who planned to travel down the Great Wagon Road from Philadelphia and resettle in the backcountry of western North Carolina. The North Carolina move soon proved to be a mistake, as the political establishment there swiftly adopted legislation and policies marginalizing the new arrivals.

Fortuitously, or so it seemed at the time, the colony of Georgia had obtained a large new cession of land from its Indian neighbors in 1763, tripling the colony's uncontested land and extending it far up the Savannah River, past the Indian trading center and military outpost at Augusta. The Quaker leadership in North Carolina seized the opportunity and petitioned James Wright, Georgia's royal governor, for a land grant to establish their own township in the newly available territory.

The plan fit wonderfully with the governor's own goals. On the one hand, he was able to plant a buffer settlement of industrious and grateful newcomers thirty-five miles into the interior of former Indian territory. On the other, the governor somehow managed to end up with personal ownership of more than 3,000 acres of the 12,000 acres that his colonial government earmarked for the Quakers in 1767. (The notorious Yazoo land fraud lay more than a quarter century ahead, but maybe a tendency for loose play with Indian land was emerging already.) In recognition of the governor's assistance, the new township was named Wrightsborough, later simplified as Wrightsboro.

Soon Thomas Ansley and his family were back on the Great Wagon Road, which was gaining a reputation as the most-traveled road in America, despite its primitive condition. Now the Ansleys followed it onward to Augusta. Arriving among Wrightsboro's earliest settlers and landowners, the Ansleys joined their neighbors in creating a new town for the second time in less than ten years.

The naturalist William Bartram reported, after a 1773 visit, that the fledgling township was thriving, with about twenty houses already built. Moreover, several competing traders were offering retail goods with prices matching those in Augusta. Perhaps Bartram did not notice that a combination of early crop failures

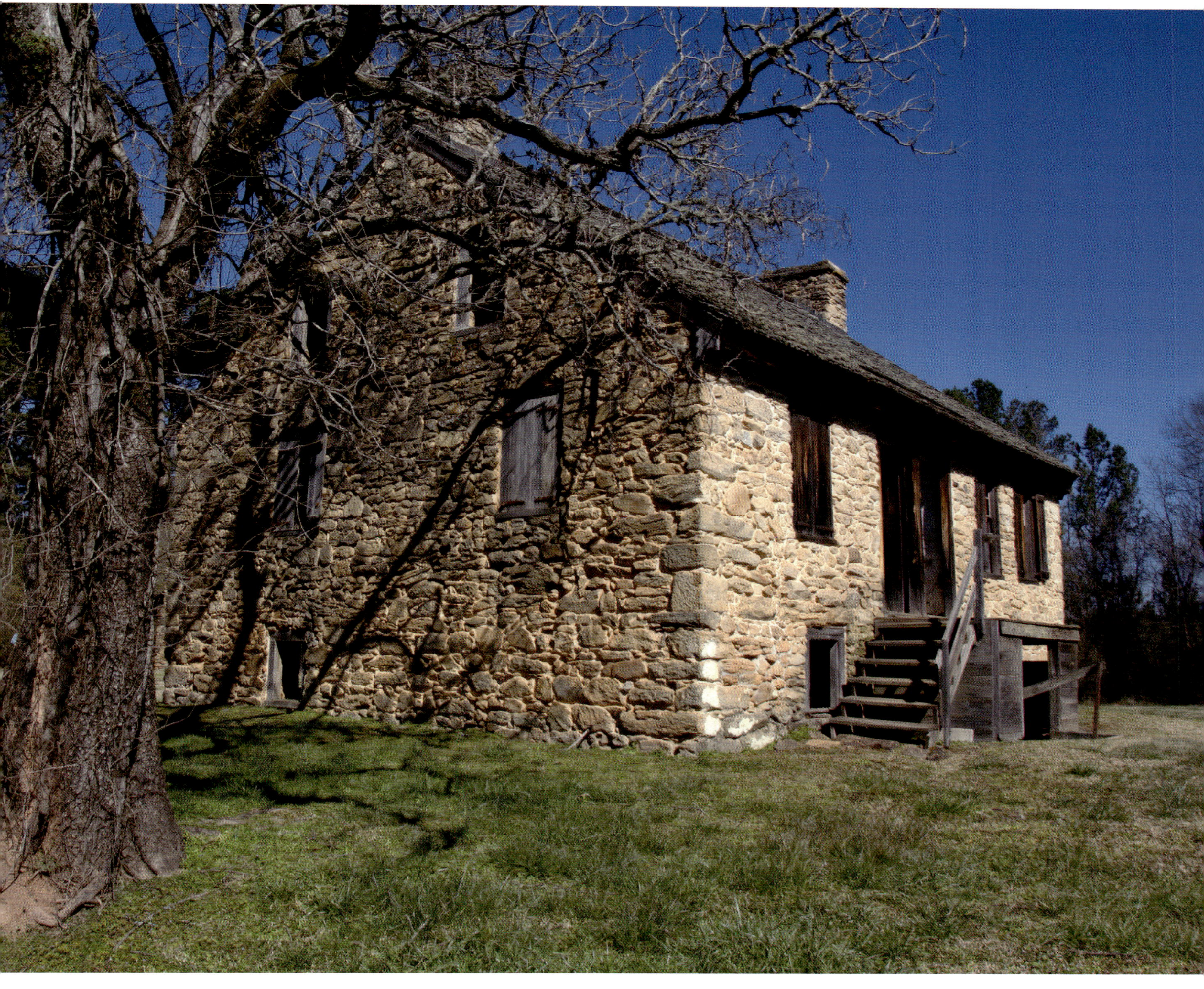

Thomas Ansley House, near Thomson

and Indian harassment had already driven almost a third of the Wrightsboro settlers back to Augusta or downriver to Savannah. The Revolutionary period proved worse, beginning with the Second Cherokee War in 1775 and followed by successive onslaughts of patriots against suspected loyalists and retaliatory massacres of patriots by loyalists. A war zone is a treacherous neighborhood for anyone, but it offered a special challenge to a community of Quakers dedicated to pacifism.

The 1783 Treaty of Paris at last brought an end to most hostilities. Thomas Ansley and his wife, with a burgeoning family that would grow to six boys and two girls, could return to planning their future. Ansley acquired 2,400 acres of land five miles outside of town and set about building a new one-and-a-half-story house with a full daylight basement and large attic. Recent dendrochronology testing has revealed a circa-1795 construction date. The basement, with a compacted clay floor, was directly accessible by an outside door; interior stairs at the center of the house connected the four rooms of the principal floor with both basement and attic. The two front rooms each had doors to the exterior, where they were served by a common stoop. In light of his decade-long experience of life in the midst of war, it can be no surprise that Ansley chose to build his new home of stone. After all, building houses of stone was a tradition in the Delaware Valley region where the Ansleys grew up, reflecting the region's own Anglo-Germanic traditions.

The early postwar years brought growth for Wrightsboro but problems for its Quakers, who felt that the special nature of the town was changing with the influx of so many non-Quakers. After 1774, when the Society of Friends mandated that enslaved people held by Quakers must be freed, they also began to feel themselves at a commercial disadvantage, as enslaved labor became a greater factor in the economy. The invention of the cotton gin in 1793 on Mulberry Grove plantation near Savannah, though a revolutionary labor saver itself, led to rapid expansion of labor-intensive cotton production. Moreover, a persuasive Quaker abolitionist crusaded through Georgia and South Carolina warning that enslaved people there would soon rise in a massacre of their masters as deadly as the one in Santo Domingo in 1791. A number of Wrightsboro Quakers seized on the crusader's advice and left for new "free" settlements north of the Ohio River; others migrated further west. Thomas Ansley, for age or other reasons,

Thomas Ansley House, near Thomson, interior

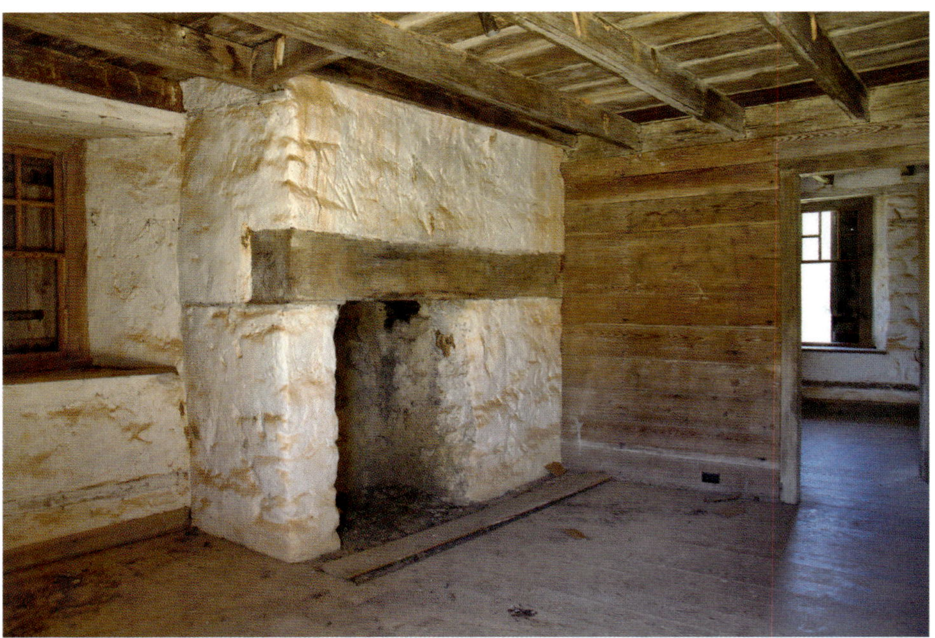

remained in the Georgia township he and others had pioneered in the wilderness. Ansley died in 1809, and his descendants continued to own and reside at the Rock House until 1839.

After the original church burned in 1810, the replacement—because of the exodus of so many Quakers—reopened as an interdenominational congregation and later, in 1837, affiliated with the Methodist denomination. The town of Wrightsboro surrendered its charter; the church, one of the last indicia of community, disbanded in 1966. Its fate may have been sealed in the early nineteenth century, when the town refused to allow the proposed new rail line from Augusta to present-day Atlanta to run its tracks through Wrightsboro. That choice ensured that in the coming century the industrial, agricultural, and commercial development of the region would be centered elsewhere.

The Rock House survives, but its life for the last one hundred years has not been easy. The community support that the it needs and deserves has begun to coalesce. Jimmy Carter, thirty-ninth president of the United States, no doubt applauds the effort; after all, Ann Ansley, his great-great grandmother, was a child of the Rock House.

The story of Meadow Garden, known as the home of George Walton, weaves together all the threads that make architectural history fascinating. First, there is the patron of the property: George Walton is one of the foundational figures in Georgia history and a prominent figure in the birth of the country. His titles abounded: president of Georgia's pre-Revolutionary Council of Safety, colonel in the militia, governor, delegate to the Continental Congress, Georgia chief justice, U.S. senator. By the time he was twenty-six years old he had ensured that his name would be remembered in history as long as his country survived. That was his age when he signed the Declaration of Independence, one of three signers from Georgia and one of the youngest of all the fifty-six. Add that he was orphaned in Virginia while still an infant, apprenticed as a carpenter, and already a leading trial lawyer in Georgia by the time the American Revolution began, and you see an accomplished and formidable personality.

Yet, from afar we see some shadows in Walton's later career that make it difficult to determine whether his full portrait has been captured. Like numerous other leaders in the Revolution, Walton faced challenges in recovering from debts accumulated during the war. Dodging creditors was a constant worry. For example, although he referred to himself as "George Walton of Meadow Garden" from the time of his home's construction in 1791–92, his name never appeared in its chain of title deeds. His nephew Thomas Watkins was the first owner of record, followed by two other associates who held it in trust for Walton's son.

Walton also got entangled in some vicious political feuds. At one point his political alliance with General Lachlan McIntosh in their dispute with Button Gwinnett, another signer of the Declaration of Independence, led to both McIntosh and Walton being expelled from the Georgia legislature and indicted for several alleged criminal offenses. Then things got worse: Gwinnett and McIntosh shot each other in a duel. Gwinnett died of his wound; McIntosh

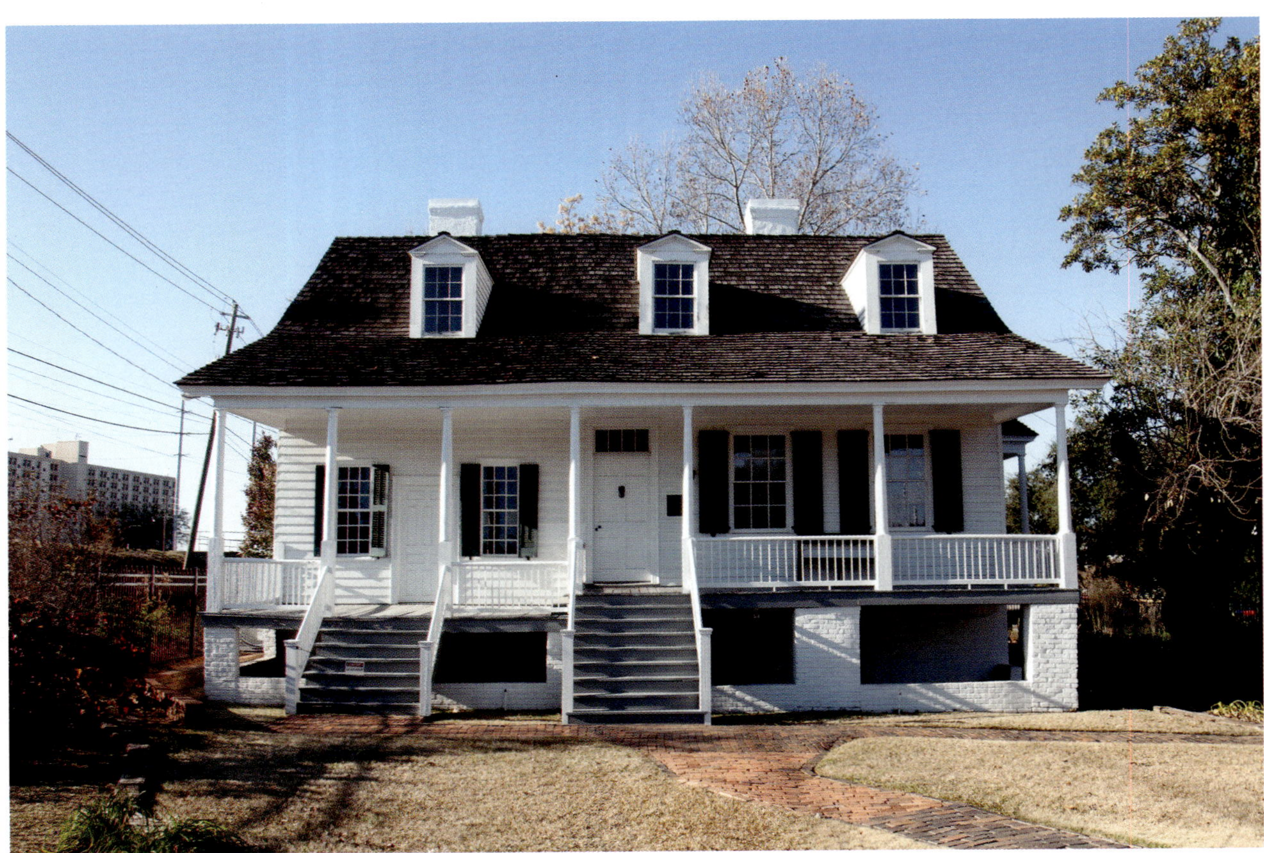

George Walton House, Augusta, before rehabilitation

survived and was acquitted of murder. Walton, in the meanwhile, was censured for supporting McIntosh in the affair. Finally, Walton had an awkward connection with the notorious Yazoo land fraud rigged by Governor George Mathews and some cronies in the state legislature. Walton, as a member of the legislature, voted in favor of the corrupt land sale, but any further involvement is uncertain. Walton was a man of exceptional achievement whom we have yet to know in full.

Meadow Garden was built in two stages on a 100-acre parcel of land. The original story-and-a-half wood-frame structure atop brick piers was commissioned by Walton in 1791. It has similarities to the Wild Heron Plantation house discussed above, but use of the form in the Sand Hills area around Augusta has led to examples there being dubbed "sand hill cottages."

Walton died in 1804, and in 1835 a very similar, three-bay structure was added, adjoining the original one, the two parts separated by a new hallway that leads to a second front door. The floor of the hallway and the added rooms also rest on recycled brick piers, but these are about two steps higher than the piers under the original cottage. The result is a house with two adjacent front doors, the threshold of one being about two steps higher than the other. The old and new segments of the house were also distinguished by the distinctly different inclines of their roofs and the presence of two dormer windows on the addition. The balustraded porch of the original segment was extended across the facade of the addition, which unified the two parts to some degree, but the eccentricity of the differing rooflines and floor levels remained.

Research Leads to Accurate Restoration at Home of One of the Nation's Founders

The national society of the Daughters of the American Revolution purchased Meadow Garden in 1900, and at some point in the twentieth century the original roofline was altered to match the addition, with a dormer window added as well. The result was an effective unification of the roofline of the two segments, but this resulted in the loss of any clear sense of the historic home as it looked when George Walton built it and lived there, and of the vicissitudes of its evolving life thereafter.

The Georgia chapter of the Daughters of the American Revolution assumed ownership of Meadow Garden in 1960, and in 2018 they launched a study into how, as good stewards, they should preserve the property and present its story to future generations. After intense structural and archival study by Greg Jacobs of Landmark Preservation, the chapter launched a courageous and ambitious plan in 2018 to return Meadow Garden to the period following the first addition but before the roof of the original segment had been altered to match the new. Now the Walton family's Meadow Garden has reemerged as a study of life and change in Georgia through several generations of the early American republic. Further ongoing research has revealed twentieth-century changes to the interior of Meadow Garden, and it is anticipated that continued restoration will lead to a more accurate interior, one that reflects George Walton's residency.

This architectural research, the restoration, and the DAR's work received a Preservation Award for Excellence in Stewardship from the Georgia Trust for Historic Preservation in 2020.

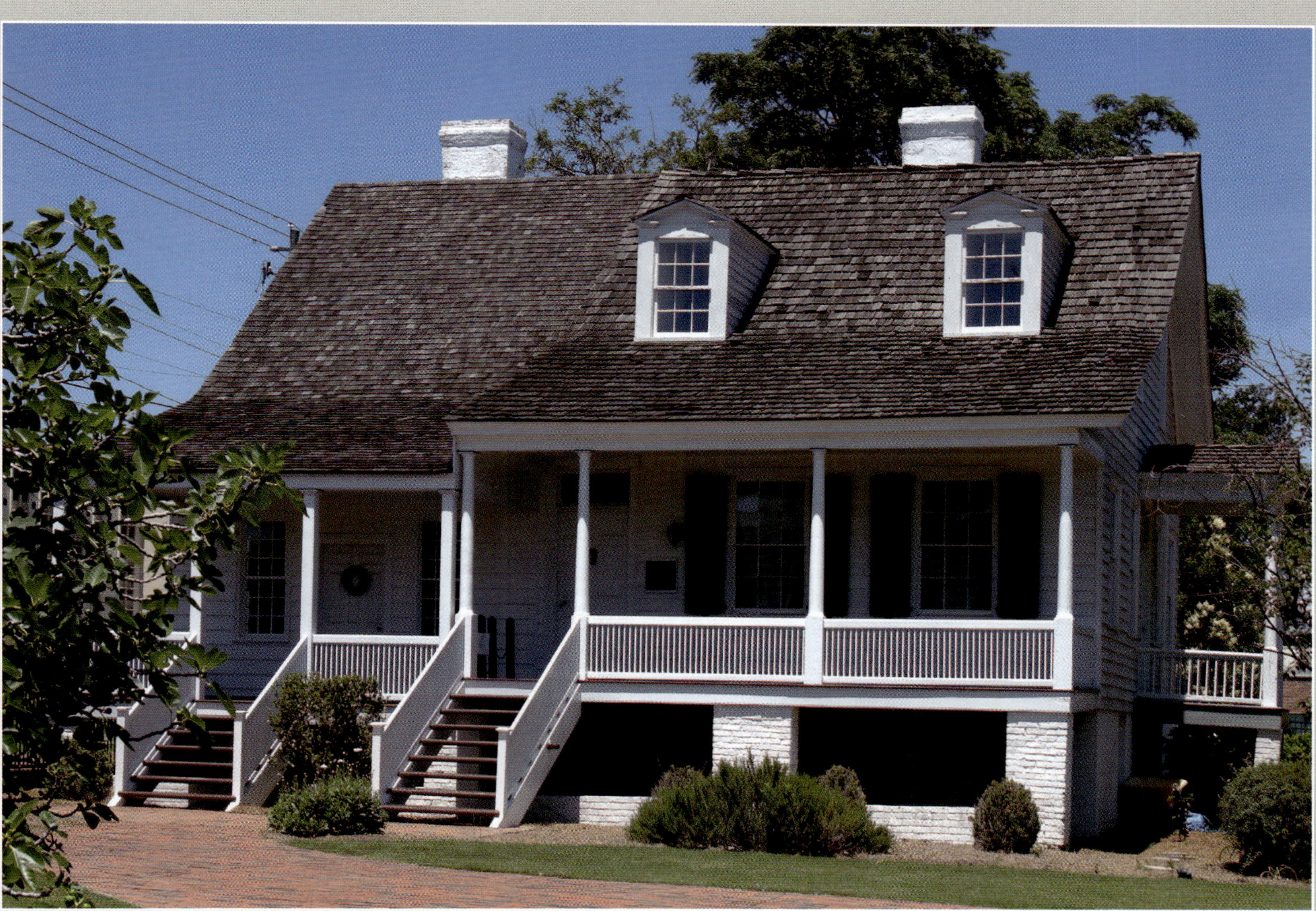

George Walton House, Augusta, after rehabilitation

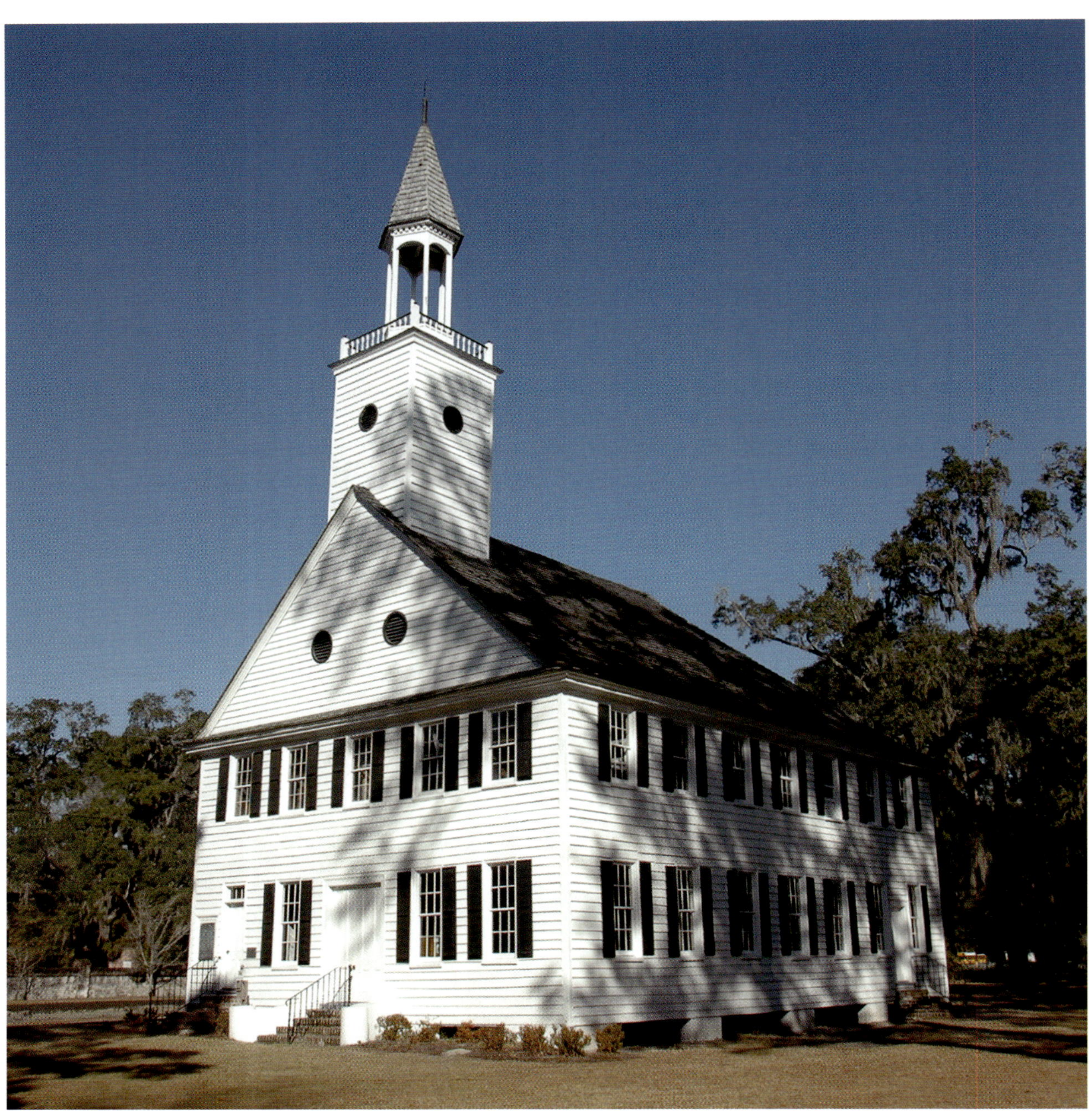

Midway Congregational Church, Midway

In 1778, during the American Revolution, British invaders from Florida turned the area around Midway, twenty-seven miles south of Savannah, into a war zone. The original Midway Congregational Church did not survive. The British force, after first failing to rendezvous with the second arm of a planned sea-and-land pincer attack, failed to pin down the outnumbered Revolutionary forces for a decisive battle. It may have been frustration that led them to torch the log church that the settlers had built soon after they founded Midway in 1752.

The congregation was able to complete a grander replacement structure in 1792, after peace had returned. The beaded wood clapboard building is laid out in a south-north rectangle with the length one-and-a-half times the width. The south end, with the principal entrance, is gabled, with a hipped roof at the opposite end. Double rows of windows bring light to the main floor of the sanctuary and to the large U-shaped gallery for enslaved workers on the upper level. The boxed pews are original, but the orientation of the sanctuary was altered in 1849 by moving the pulpit from the long east wall to its present position centered on the shorter north wall. The gallery was enlarged at the same time.

Overall, the calm and largely undecorated appearance of the church both inside and out is suggestive of unadorned Congregational churches in New England. The correlation is not a matter of chance, because the settlement at Midway traces to New England in a direct line.

The Midway story begins with the great migration of Puritans to New England in 1630. A number had originated in the area around Dorchester in southern England, and Dorchester is the name they gave their new home in the Massachusetts Bay Colony. Their nomadic journey had only begun. Five years later, religious and political disagreements prompted half of them to join a recent settlement in present-day Connecticut. They promptly renamed that town Dorchester also (although it was changed to Windsor a few years later). Their migration was still not ended. In 1696 descendants of the Connecticut settlers were on the move again, this time to the new colony of Carolina—which was itself just twenty-six years old—to found a new town eighteen miles northwest of present-day Charleston, South Carolina. Their New England minister, a recent Harvard graduate, led the transition. The new settlement, of course, was named Dorchester. The New Englanders soon built this Dorchester IV into a prosperous farming and trading community that became, briefly, the third largest town of South Carolina. Yet circumstances dictated one last move, from South Carolina to Georgia, in 1752, prompted by both the greater availability of fertile land and the prospect of reduced friction with the established Church of England (unaware that the Church of England would become the established church of Georgia just a few years later). The new Georgia town was named Midway, not Dorchester.

The Puritan heritage of the community ensured more than its denomination and the architecture of its church. It also placed the Midway residents among Georgia's most outspoken supporters of Massachusetts in the struggles leading to the American Revolution. That two of Georgia's three signers of the Declaration of Independence were from Midway was not entirely coincidence, nor was the 1777 decision to rename Saint John's Parish as Liberty County.

The historic Midway Congregational Church and its New England affiliations benefited Midway in another notable way. Three pastors who filled the pulpit at Midway proved to be progenitors of distinguished American families; one was the father of Samuel F. B. Morse, the leading American portrait painter who invented the telegraph; another the father of educator and author Oliver Wendell Holmes and grandfather of U.S. chief justice Oliver Wendell Holmes Jr.; and the third the grandfather of Ellen Louise Axson, who was First Lady of the United States as the wife of President Woodrow Wilson. The classic, elegant church at Midway is intertwined with the earliest settlement history of four American states—Massachusetts, Connecticut, South Carolina, and Georgia—and with the war to achieve national independence.

For most of its two centuries of existence, the Ezekiel Harris House had a mistaken identity—which on balance was probably a good thing. The story was that the house was built before the Revolution, possibly even as early as 1750, by an Indian trader named Robert Mackay and that it became known to his Indian clientele as the White House. In fact, as research in the mid-1970s confirmed, the land was bought by Ezekiel Harris, a tobacco merchant, in 1794, and the house was built soon thereafter.

The mistaken conviction that the house was Robert Mackay's historic pre-Revolutionary Indian trading post was an advantage because it led the Richmond County Historical Society to purchase the property in 1847 for preservation. Then in 1956 ownership passed to the Georgia Historical Commission, a state agency with even more ambitious plans for restoration. Most of the nineteenth-century additions and alterations were carefully reversed, and the exterior color was returned to its original blue-gray with dark red trim. Alas, the commission seems to have suffered a serious case of "buyer's remorse" when their research uncovered that they had not bought and restored Mackay's 1770s White House trading post, as they had intended. Instead, they owned the house

Ezekiel Harris House, Augusta

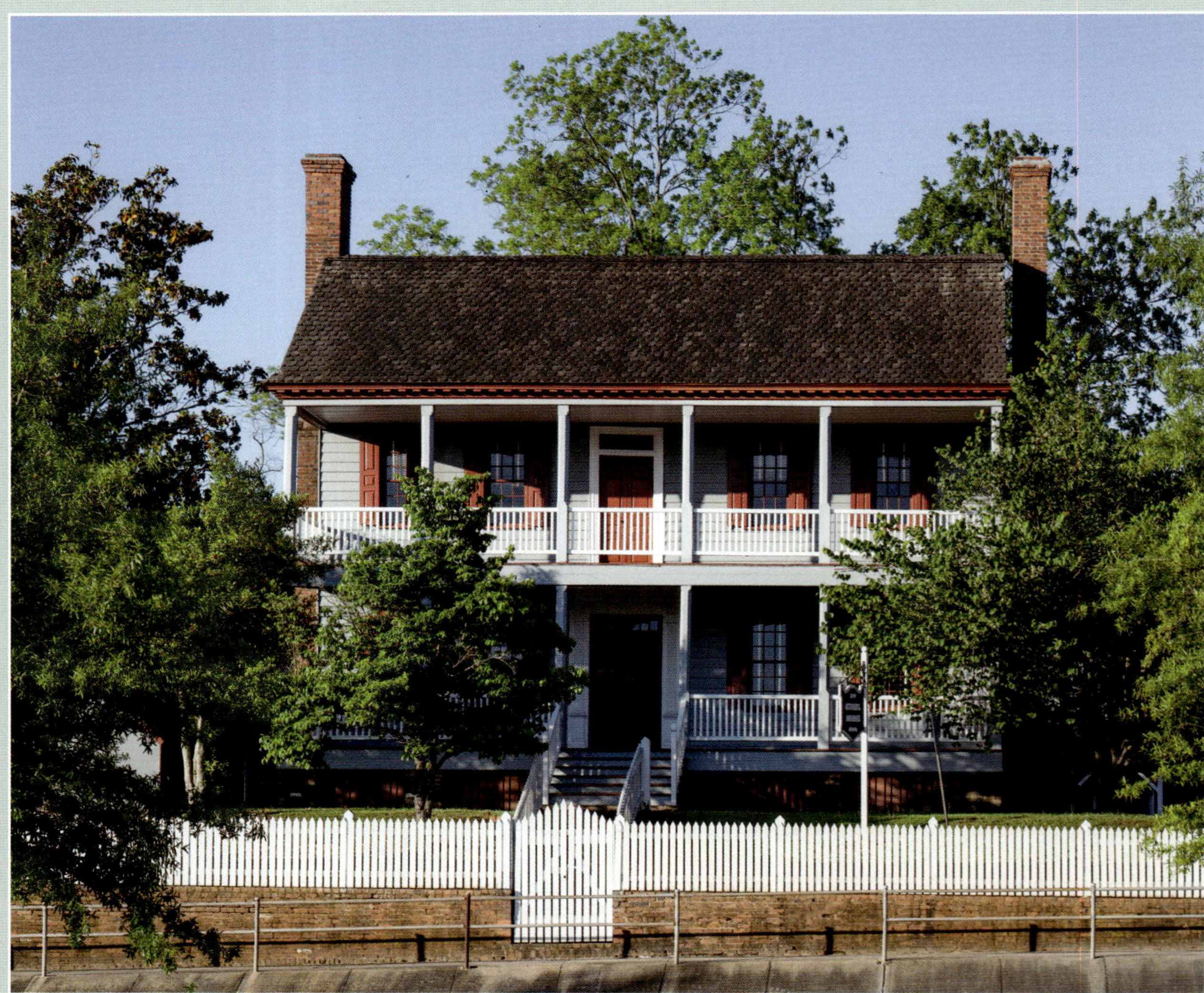

of a lesser-known tobacco merchant built about twenty years later. Their pain was compounded by knowing that they had used furniture and furnishings from the earlier, pre-Revolutionary period in their preservation program.

The commission's impulse was to close the property, but local supporters stepped in and the house has been operated by the Augusta Museum of History since 2004. The result is much more impressive than a re-created trading post would ever have been.

The house is a two-story wood-frame structure with beaded siding. The gambrel roof extends over double porches on each facade; the one in front runs the length of the building, but the one in the rear is enclosed at each end. One of the two end chimneys is laid in Flemish bond. Finally, the house shows touches of decorative elements drawn from English pattern books, confirming that in the final decade of the century aspirational homebuilders in Augusta as well as Savannah were looking for stylistic leads beyond the borders of their state. The result at Harris House is transitional, edging away from Colonial simplicity but not so advanced as Savannah in the move toward Federal style. Especially notable at the Harris House is the magnificently detailed double doorway at the front entrance, opening into an arched hallway leading through the house. The design suggests a pattern from William Salmon's *Palladio Londonensis* (London 1743).

Savannah Lost and Found

About six or seven o'clock in the early evening of November 26, 1796, a light north-northeast breeze dancing across Market Square in Savannah lifted an errant ember that had escaped an oven at Gromet's Bakery and dropped it on a flammable roof nearby. By about one the next morning approximately two-thirds of all the buildings in Georgia's largest city were destroyed. It is said to have been the most devastating fire of any American city up to that time. All of the economic recovery that Savannah had experienced in the thirteen years since the American Revolution was wiped out in a space of eight hours. Most of the luxurious houses that had begun to dot the city as it returned to prosperity were built of wood, except for their brick chimneys. In the devastation on the morning following the Great Fire of 1796, hundreds of bare brick chimneys rose from the dismal landscape like a grim Stonehenge.

Thus, with few exceptions, the finest homes and churches built in Georgia in the eighteenth century did not survive to the next one. And the century that followed was not much kinder to the survivors. After the 1796 fire, the determined and resilient Savannahians made rapid progress in rebuilding their city—and in enacting new building regulations designed to prevent a recurrence of the tragedy. But twenty-four years later, the Great Fire of 1820, beginning in City Market, repeated on the same scale all the destruction of the earlier fire. With such a bad start, maybe the marvel is that even six Savannah buildings remain as part of our lives more than two hundred years later.

When he built his wood-frame house in Savannah sometime between 1760 and 1767, Christian Camphor could have had no idea that it would one day be the oldest urban residence in Georgia. He would be even more surprised to see that the modest saltbox house he built—three rooms, with a ladder leading to more space in the attic—has levitated. Now the entire structure perches atop another floor, all-brick, which was built beneath it in 1871. Camphor would also be curious about the second-floor balcony, which was probably added when the original cottage was jacked up.

So, on the one hand, the change to the house is quite radical, but on the whole Georgia's earliest surviving urban residence—the only one predating the Revolution—still preserves a sense of its original character 250 years later. It also shows, when compared with its contemporaneous country cousin, Wild Heron, that Savannah in its third decade had not yet developed a distinctive urban architecture. We can be grateful that the Camphor House lay just beyond the reach of the Great Fire of 1796, so that we can make such comparisons today.

Christian Camphor House, Savannah

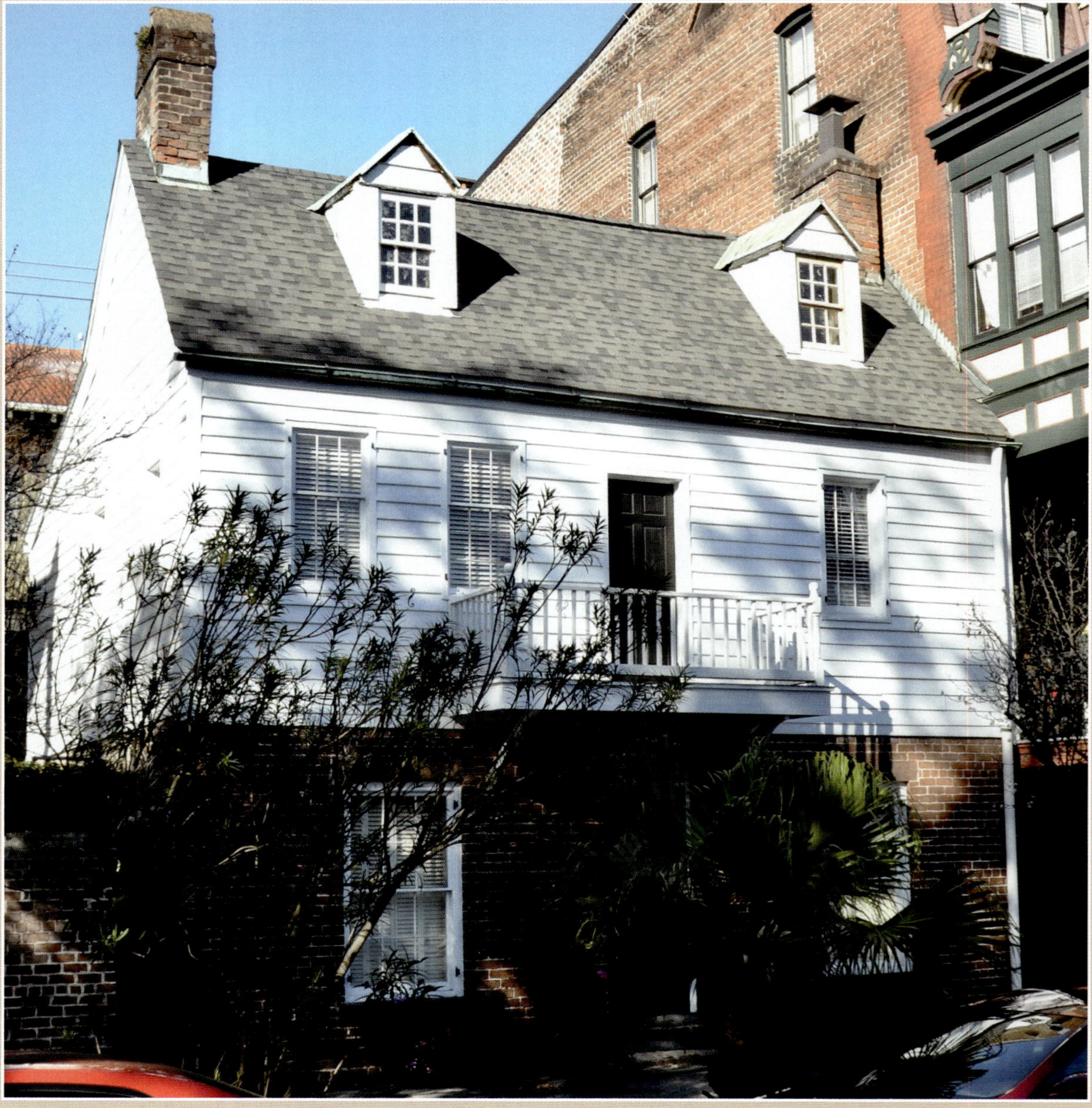

The James Habersham Jr. House leads us onto the new architectural stage of post-Revolutionary Savannah, but we immediately encounter a problem in looking to the house as a guide to the period: although the Habersham House escaped the Great Fire of 1796, it did not escape much else. James Habersham Jr. died in 1799, just ten years after the house was built. By 1812 the house had already changed hands and was enlarged and remodeled as a bank. Later the house was home to lawyers' offices, a bookstore, the Georgian Tea Room, an antiques dealer and, most recently, The Olde Pink House, a busy restaurant and tavern. The frequent changes in use brought a succession of alterations to the structure, sometimes major ones, both inside and out. So it takes some effort to reimagine what the house looked like when Habersham and his family moved in.

The house began life as a two-story rectangular brick structure with a gable roof. The exterior walls, finished in stucco, are decorated with quoins at the corners, and over the front entrance a Palladian-style window brings light to the landing of the stairway inside. The vertical impact of the quoins is balanced by

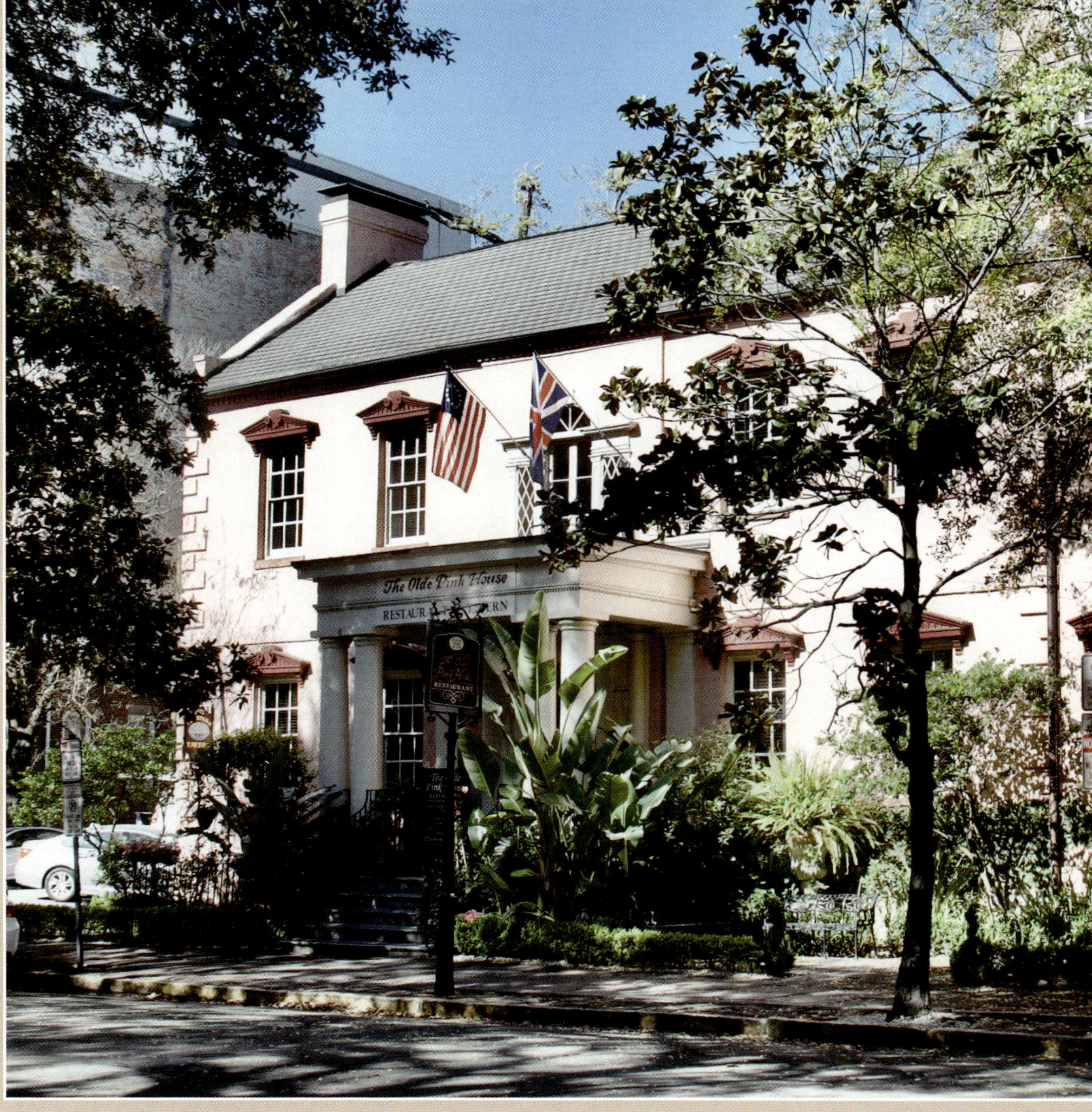

James Habersham House (Pink House Restaurant), Savannah

the horizontal dentils of the cornice beneath the eaves and a stringcourse crossing the facade between the stories.

Clearly, Savannah architecture had come a long way since Christian Camphor built his small three-room saltbox cottage twenty-nine years earlier and eight blocks away. Camphor needed shelter; Habersham was seeking more. He wanted commodious living and working spaces but, like other prosperous businessmen and political leaders, he also wanted an elegant home for entertaining and impressing his peers, and he wanted a home that would display his taste and awareness of stylish trends beyond the insular bounds of Savannah and Georgia—the Palladian window, for example, and the decorative quoins at the corner, plus the fancy cornice and stringcourse. Perhaps they had already passed a little out of fashion in London, but in Savannah in 1789 they carried a clear message: This is a magnificent modern mansion. At last, as the century moved toward its final decade, Georgia was developing an urban architecture, now often guided by an experienced amateur architect or a pioneering professional.

Alterations to the Habersham House began early in the next century. First, the bank that took over in 1812 added a large wing onto the north end of the house to accommodate its staff and operations. By 1820 a large front portico was added in the fashionable new Greek Revival style. Along the way, another wing was added at the rear. Then, about mid-century, an owner decided to freshen the facade by installing broken-top pediments over each window.

After its post–Civil War challenges, and with the normal wear of time, the building moved into decline as its 150th anniversary came and went. Fortunately, a well-known Savannah antiques dealer and architectural preservationist, James A. Williams, stepped forward to acquire and renovate the Habersham House, which subsequently became a Savannah tourist landmark as the Pink House restaurant.

Apart from his business activities, Jim Williams was well-known in Savannah for two reasons. First, he might be called a "serial" preservationist of significant Savannah architecture. Of the seven eighteenth-century Savannah houses identified and discussed here, Williams restored at least three: the Oddingsells House, the Hampton Lillibridge House, and the Habersham House. The second reason for Williams's renown is that he was charged with murder, and ultimately acquitted, in the sensational case described in John Berendt's 1994 bestseller *Midnight in the Garden of Good and Evil.*

Savannah's Warren Square was laid out in 1791, as the city's growth surged in the post-Revolutionary period. So it is not surprising that the square and the area around it are home to some of the city's earliest surviving residences. The surprise is that several of the houses are immigrants, born not far away and then moved to their present locations in the 1960s in a program to preserve them and remove them from harm's way.

The elegant George B. Spencer House is not one of the immigrants. Built on its present site by George B. Spencer in the earliest days of the square, it might be regarded as a picture-book example of an early two-and-a-half-story wood-frame

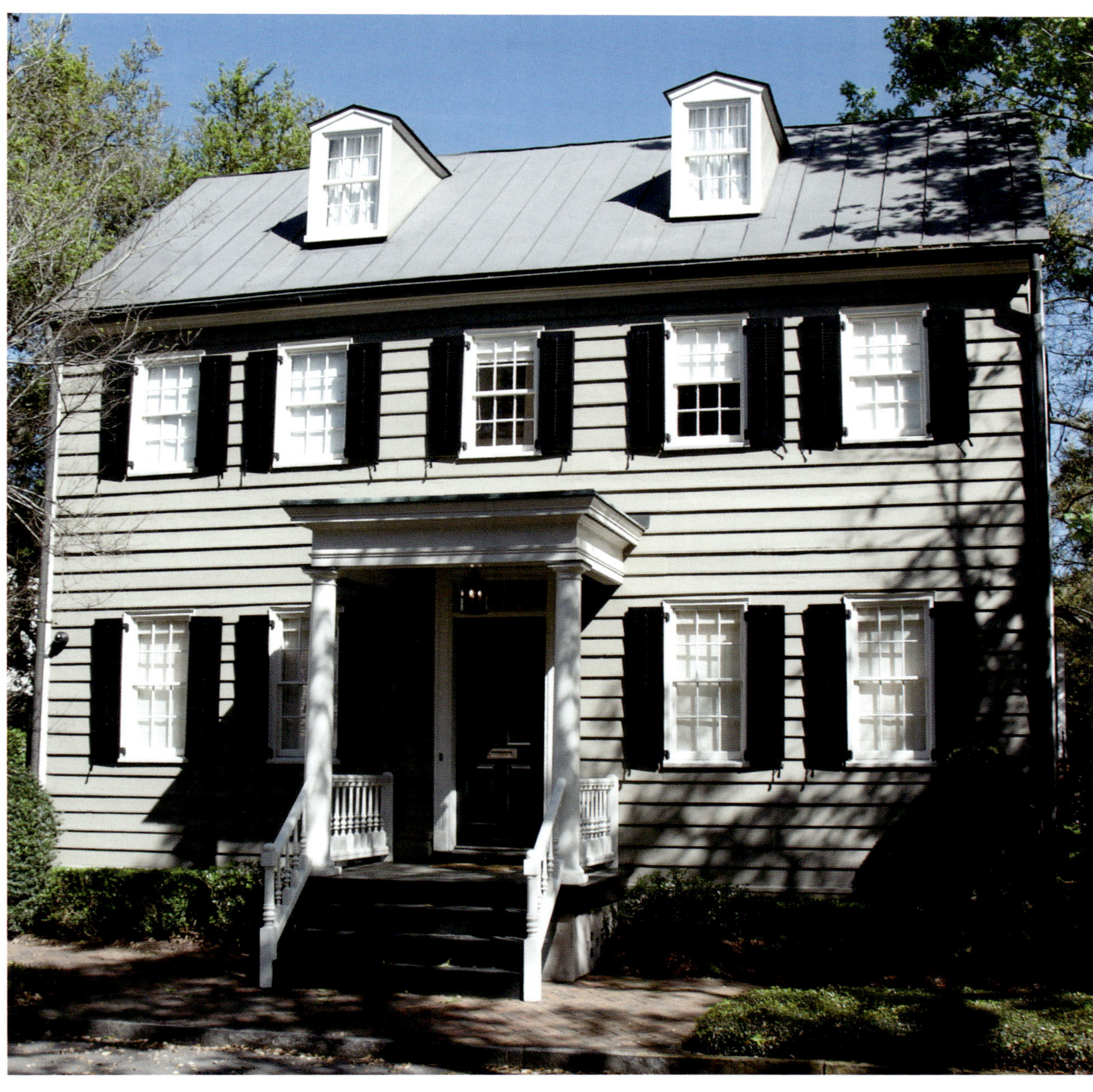

George B. Spencer House, Savannah

house in the new Federal style, except for two anomalies. The first is the portico, added or rebuilt in the 1830s, which is stylistically consistent with the original building but too large for it. A bigger problem in principle, but more tucked away, is a two-story brick addition with a shed roof added to the rear of the house at about the same time that the portico was added in front. The interior, balanced on a central hall, is highlighted by a parlor with a beautifully detailed mantel and overmantel.

In a familiar pattern, by mid-twentieth century the Spencer House had fallen into a nearly derelict state, saved only by timely intervention from Savannah Foundation Inc., which in the 1950s took essential steps to preserve it. Then in 1993 Mills Lane IV, continuing a tradition begun by his parents, Mills B. Lane Jr. and Anne Waring Lane, stepped forward to sponsor a rehabilitation of the property. Thus, through combined efforts Savannah's preservation community rescued one of their city's true architectural gems.

A recent rehabilitation of the John Berrien House, just south of Warren Square, is so dramatic that one is compelled to consider first whether the project crossed the line between reconstruction of an original eighteenth-century mansion and construction of a twenty-first-century replica. The startling answer is that substantially all the house we see now has been there since the 1790s but shrouded for the past century and a half by abuse, neglect, and, ultimately, abandonment.

John Berrien grew up in a prosperous New Jersey family. His ancestors arrived in America in the late 1600s as settlers in New Netherlands, the Dutch colony centered in present-day New York. His father was a judge on New Jersey's supreme court and a trustee of the College of New Jersey (now Princeton University). In 1775, on the eve of the American Revolution, Berrien followed some of his mother's relatives to Georgia, where he joined the Continental Army as a seventeen-year-old second lieutenant. As aide-de-camp to General Lachlan McIntosh, he was with George Washington at Valley Forge in the winter of 1777–78. His family's New Jersey home was Washington's headquarters for a brief period in 1783.

Berrien took on an active political life when he returned to Savannah after the war, including service as a city alderman and as inspector of revenue for the Port of Savannah. In 1791 he bought a house lot on East Broughton Street and began construction of the house soon thereafter. The house was likely complete by 1797, when Berrien sold the property and moved to Louisville, the new state capital, to take up service as state treasurer.

The house Berrien built was a two-story wood-frame structure with beaded clapboard siding set atop a brick daylight basement. A double stair provided entry from the sidewalk to the lower living floor. The interior rooms were arranged around a central hall, with elaborate carved wood mantels and molding on the parlor and bedroom floors. Now, after a sad trip to near destruction, that is the house that has emerged again.

The Berrien House's early life might have seemed charmed. First it narrowly avoided the Great Fire of 1796. Then in 1822 Berrien's son, John Macpherson Berrien, later a U.S. senator from Georgia and attorney general under President Andrew Jackson, managed to acquire the house that his father had sold, bringing it back into the family for the next thirty-seven years. During that period the Berrien House was a regular stop for visiting politicians, including Henry Clay and Daniel Webster.

As that era ended, alterations arrived, in two installments. In 1871 the owner built an internal wall and additional staircase, dividing the structure into two townhouses. His brother-in-law resided upstairs in the one on the corner and operated a pharmacy in its ground floor. In 1916 the two residential floors were chopped into smaller tenement rooms and jacked up about three feet so that the basement could be rebuilt as full-height retail spaces, including a branch bank. The resulting three-story building was then encased in stucco, like icing on a failed cake. Before a hundred more years had passed, the building was an

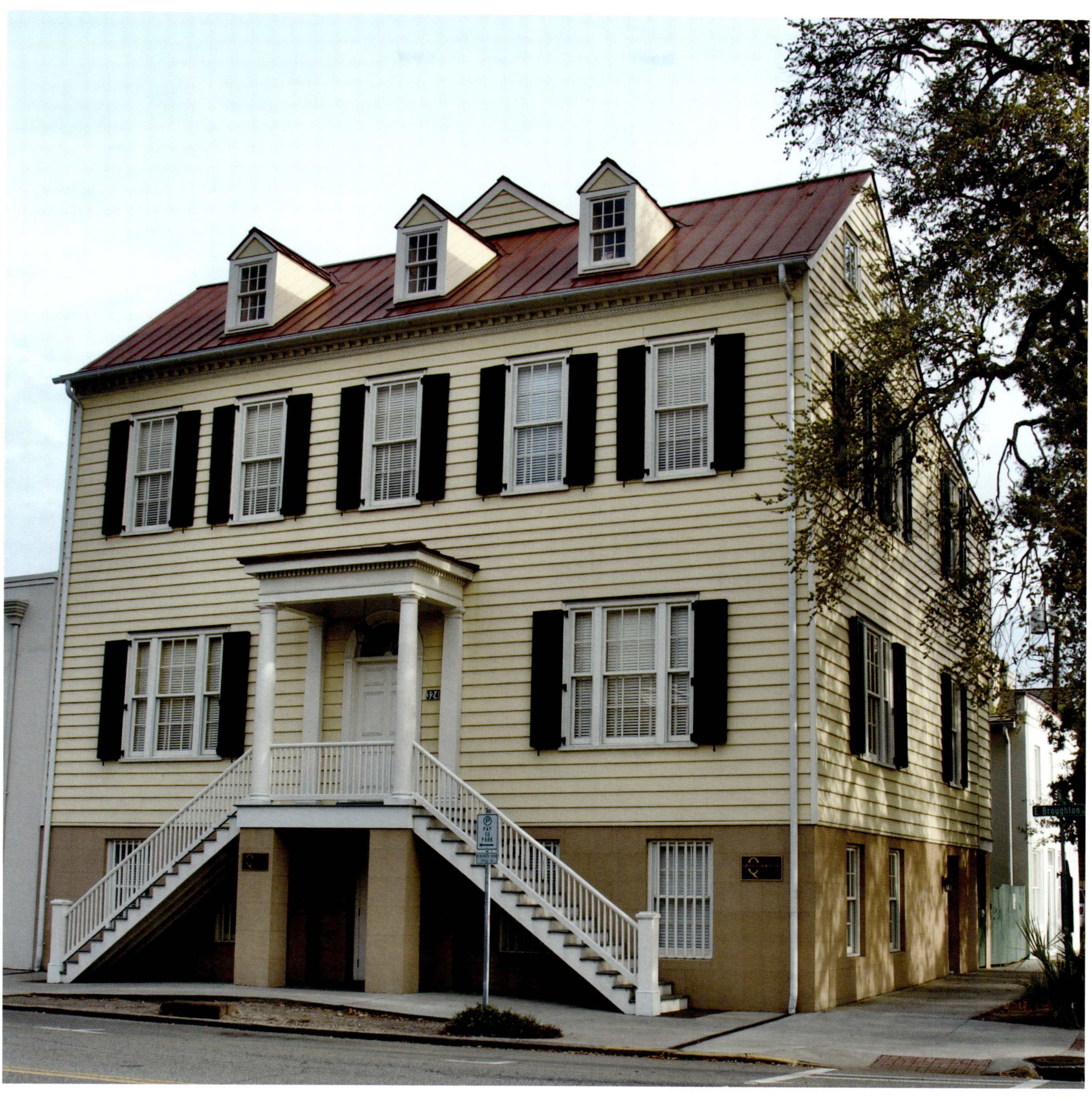

abandoned derelict under threat of foreclosure, and in 2009 it was placed on the Places in Peril list compiled annually by the Georgia Trust. Ultimately there emerged a savior: a direct descendant of Berrien living in New York arrived to bring the Berrien House into the family for the third time and return it to its early glow. The two residential floors were even lowered three feet to their original elevation. An early treasure of Savannah was unmasked.

John Berrien House, Savannah

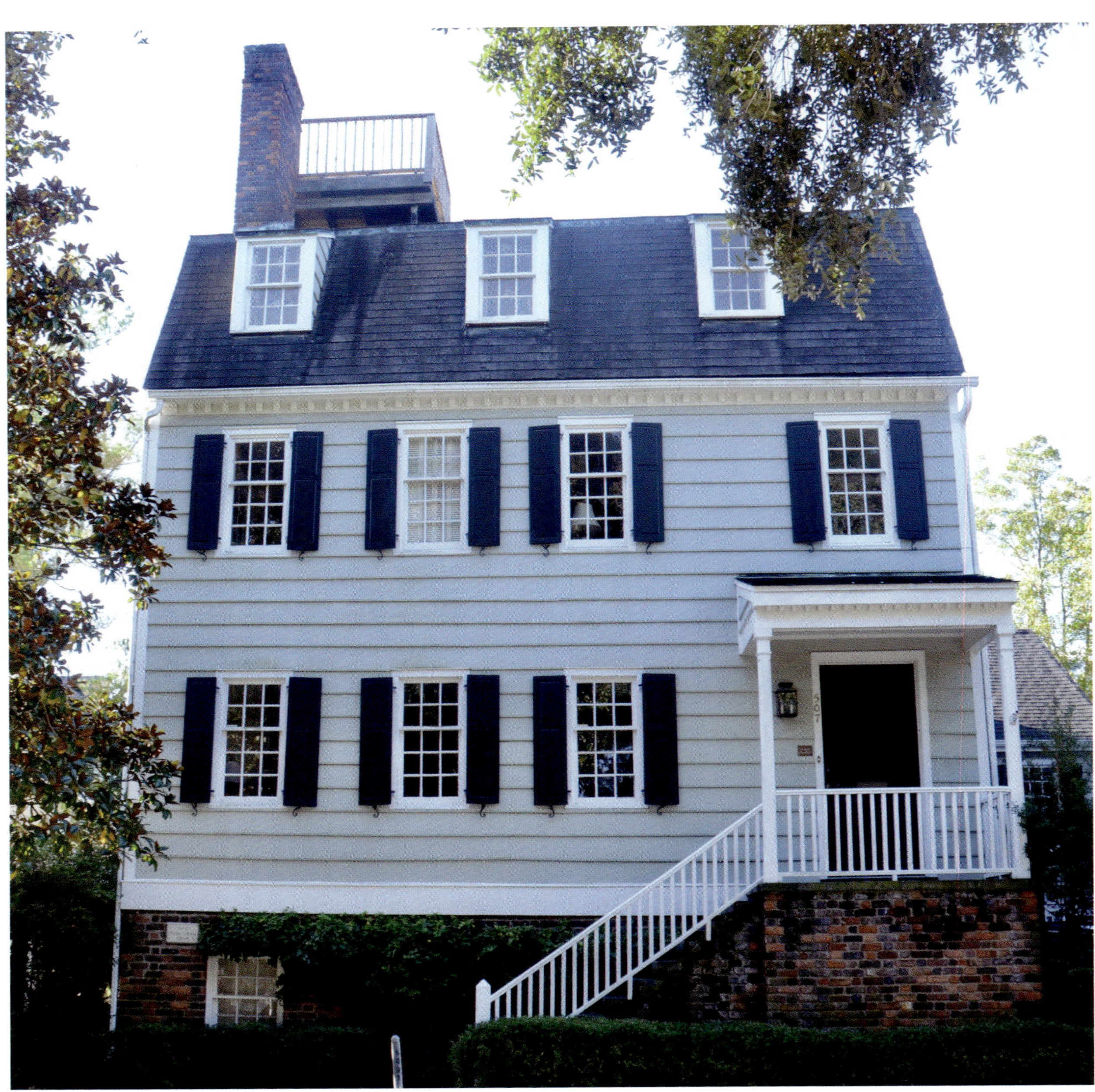

Hampton Lillibridge House, Savannah

Hampton Lillibridge, a prosperous planter from Newport, Rhode Island, built two houses side-by-side on East Bryan Street in the mid-1790s. Each was a two-and-a-half-story wood-frame structure set over a raised basement, and each had a gambrel roof, which was unusual in Georgia but less so in Rhode Island, where Lillibridge grew up. After Lillibridge's death his widow sold the house referred to as No. 1, happily unaware that it would be referred to in the twenty-first century as one of Savannah's most notable haunted residences. After an initial period as a boardinghouse, it passed through multiple owners, often with long intervening periods of standing empty. Finally in 1962, when both of the Lillibridge houses were dilapidated and targeted for razing, James A. Williams, some of whose other contributions to architectural preservation in Savannah have been described above, stepped forward with a plan for moving the houses intact to a new site on East Julian Street, where they could be restored to their handsome original state.

The plan worked perfectly for Lillibridge No. 1, now once again a proud reminder of late eighteenth-century Savannah. Lillibridge No. 2, on the other hand, collapsed while the move was underway and never arrived at its new site. And perhaps Lillibridge No. 1 did not make the four-block move alone. The moving crew reported to Williams that they heard strange, unidentified voices and other noises coming from the house as the transfer was underway; one worker saw a mysterious old man appear behind an upper window. Taking no chances, Williams is said to have arranged for the Episcopal bishop to perform an exorcism at the house to expel any ghosts.

The Mongin House is another of Savannah's peripatetic houses, chased to its present site in 1964 by the ominous shadow of the wrecking ball. The flight of the Mongin House was shorter than most, however, because it moved only from one lot on Warren Square to another one nearby. The wood-frame house with clapboard siding and a gable roof bears a strong resemblance to the earlier John

Mongin House, Savannah

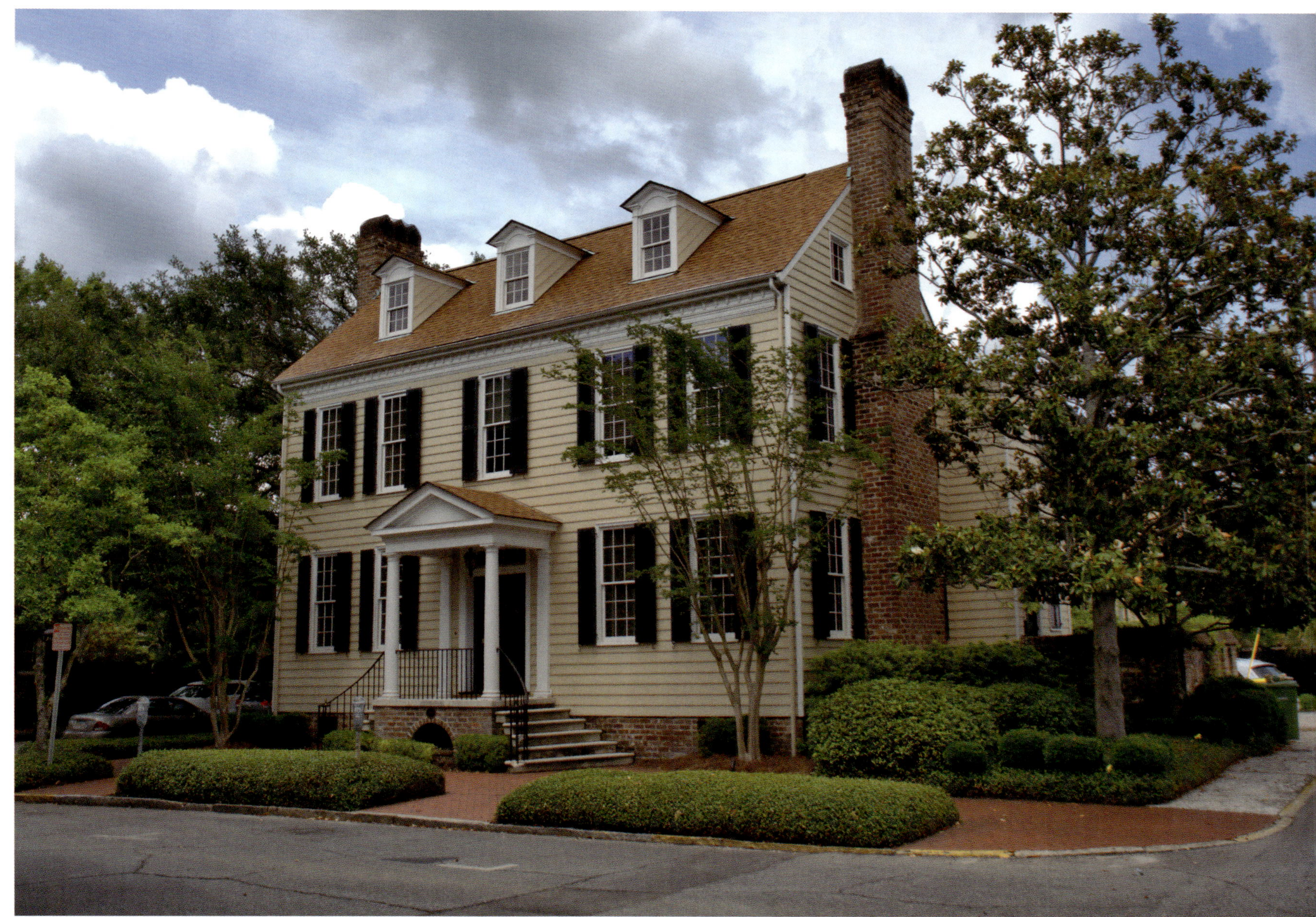

Berrien House, especially considering that the height of its brick basement was reduced when the house was moved to its present site. There are also similarities to the original George B. Spencer House. They all show that the influence of Federal style architecture was firmly established in urban Savannah as the eighteenth century drew to a close.

John David Mongin built a tremendous fortune during his lifetime, but he seems to have had a low profile in Savannah. Beginning in the area around Beaufort and Daufuskie Island, South Carolina, fourteen miles up the coast from Savannah, Mongin assembled a string of plantations extending down to the Great Ogeechee River in Georgia southwest of Savannah, but his family was centered on out-of-state Daufuskie. He did not hold any notable position in politics or the military, traditional roads to name recognition. He did engage in some merchant activities at the Savannah wharves, however—a plantation-supply business in 1778 and agricultural exports after the Revolution. Back on Daufuskie, where he was better known, he was sometimes referred to as "Money Mongin," which might suggest that feelings of respect were mixed with resentment.

The Mongin House had a checkered life after John David Mongin sold it in 1805, including some years as a rectory for Christ Church and service as a hospital during the yellow fever outbreak of 1876. By 1964 commercial interests dictated that the historic house be razed so the land beneath could be put to higher-value use. Two prolific Savannah preservationists had a better vision. Mills B. Lane Jr. and his wife Anne Waring Lane acquired the house, moved it to a less vulnerable spot on the same square, and restored it to its present condition. The Lanes acquired and restored dozens of historic Savannah homes in the 1960s and 1970s. Their son Mills B. Lane IV, himself an architectural historian and publisher, assisted in their remarkable civic work and continued it after them.

The Major Charles Oddingsells House near Washington Square may seem at first surprisingly modest for a man of the major's stature and wealth. It is, after all, a simple one-and-a-half-story wood-frame cottage set on a brick daylight basement. The bell-cast eaves, designed to divert rainwater away from the foundations, are intriguing, but otherwise the house is more reminiscent of the pre-Revolutionary Wild Heron Plantation house or the Christian Camphor House than it is of more contemporaneous structures like the Hampton Lillibridge or Mongin houses. The anomaly may be explained by the fact that Oddingsells was primarily a plantation owner based on Skidaway Island about fifteen miles away. The new home he built in Savannah was intended primarily as an in-town second home.

The Oddingsells House brings us again to the inspired work of Savannah's most prolific historic preservationists, the Lane family—Mills B. Lane Jr., his wife Anne Waring Lane, and their son, Mills B. Lane IV—whose impact on historic Savannah has already been noted. Oddingsells House and four others on the same block were among the dozens of houses the Lanes acquired and restored in the 1960s and 1970s, including three of the city's seven surviving eighteenth-century homes.

Choosing Our Past

We build our future on what we treasure, preserve, and utilize from our past. Civilization is not born every morning when we wake up. The present and future are built on the past, and we each have a role in ensuring that they are built on the beauty, hope, and aspirations of that past, and not on its conflict, oppression, and cynicism. This is a responsibility of every generation.

Of course we cannot congeal the past, like a specimen suspended in amber. There is always a great collective and unconscious evolutionary process of reshaping to serve the future. That is what we are seeing when we examine these examples of earlier Georgia life—the past morphing into the future.

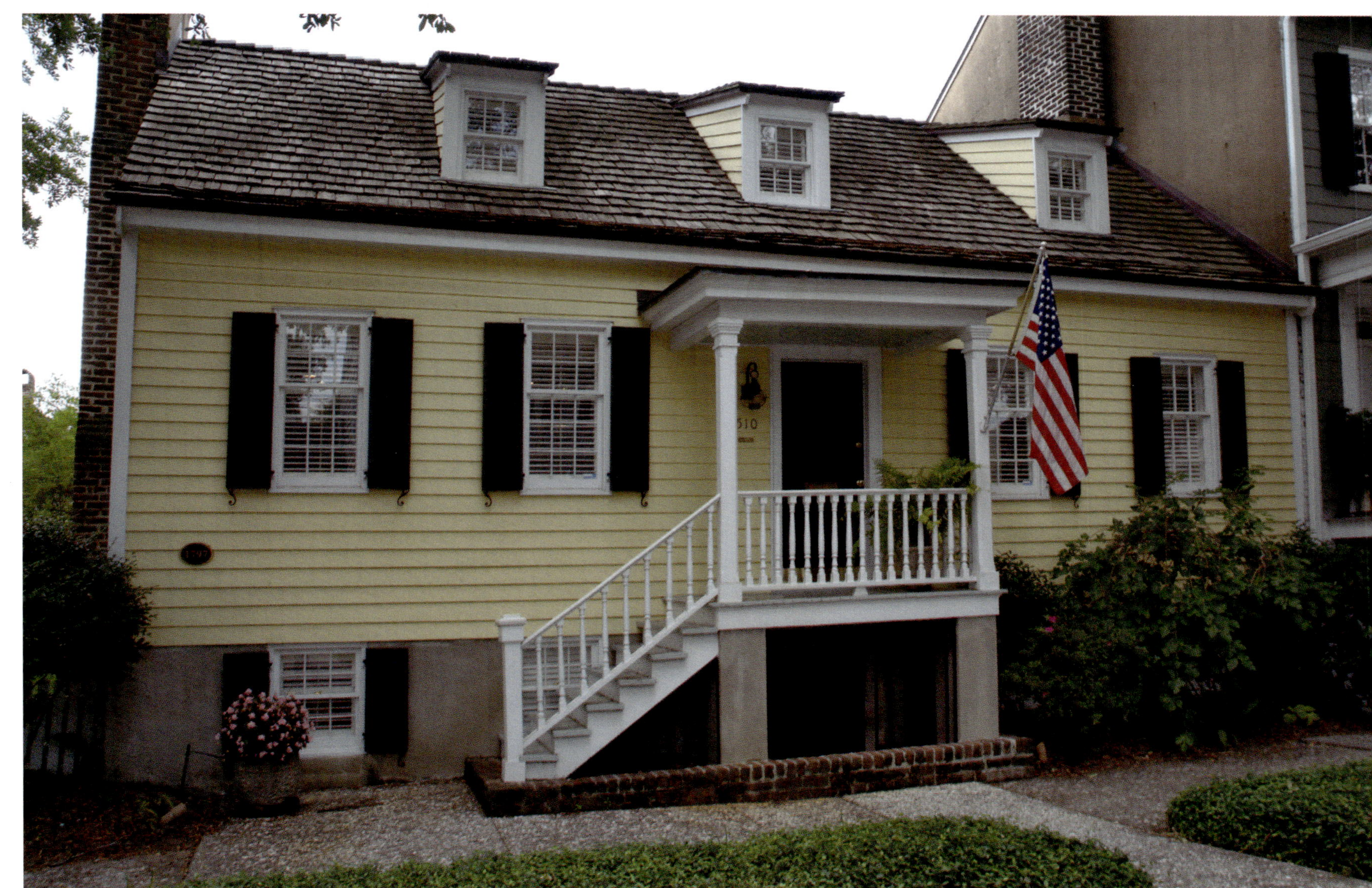

Oddingsells House, Savannah

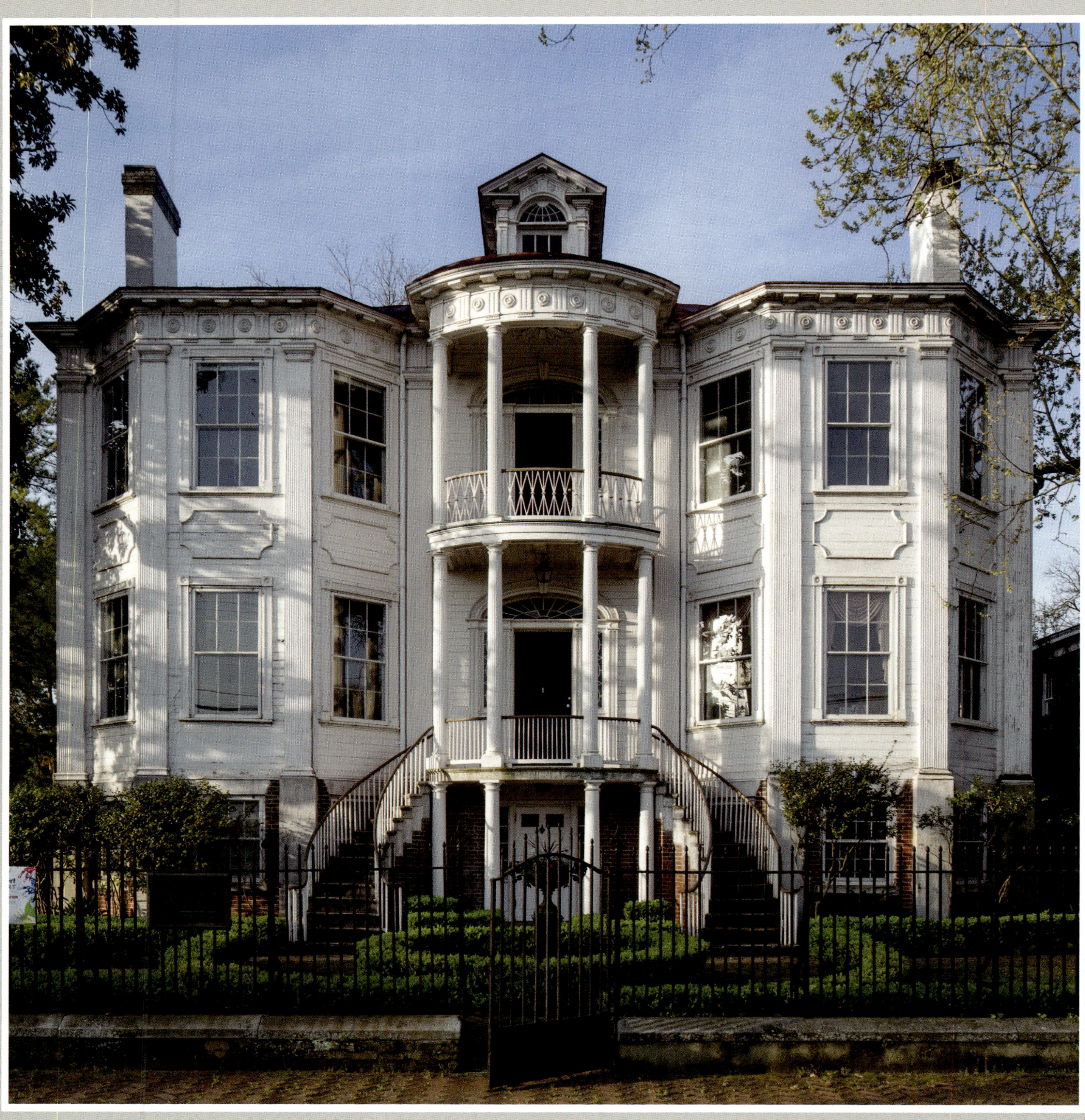

II. The Antebellum Era, 1800–1865

JOSEPH SMITH

At the beginning of the nineteenth century the state of Georgia was geographically limited to twenty-four counties arrayed along the Atlantic seacoast and up the Savannah River. To the west, the Oconee River and part of the Altamaha formed a boundary with the lands of the Muscogee (Creek) and Cherokee peoples, with Spanish Florida south of the Saint Marys River. The state's economic basis at the time was primarily agricultural, with rice, indigo, and Sea Island cotton cultivated on the coast and tobacco and corn grown in the Piedmont. Roughly fifty years earlier, Georgia had abandoned its founding precepts of pecuniary moderation and self-improvement, adopting lucrative plantation agriculture along with its reliance on African enslavement to produce the bulk of its most profitable export crops.

For four decades following the American Revolution, Georgia's upcountry counties experienced an influx of slaveholding white migrants originating primarily in Virginia and the Carolinas. Rapid population growth in counties away from the coast reordered political power in the state toward the interests of the newcomers and created immense pressure for further territorial cessions from Georgia's Native American peoples. Despite valiant, sustained resistance by the Muscogee and Cherokee, the entirety of their tribal lands within the boundaries of the state was opened to white settlement before 1840, with the tribes forcibly removed to the Indian Territory west of the Mississippi.

Confiscated Native American lands were distributed in a series of eight land lotteries conducted by the state between 1805 and 1833. Those eligible to enter the lottery were white families with at least one child, widows with children, and single white males residing in the state for at least a year. Native Americans were prohibited from participation, ensuring neither the Cherokee nor the Muscogee could legally retain claim to their ancestral lands. Free Blacks were also excluded, denying them the opportunities for economic self-determination and political power inherent in land ownership.

Facing: Nicholas Ware House, Augusta

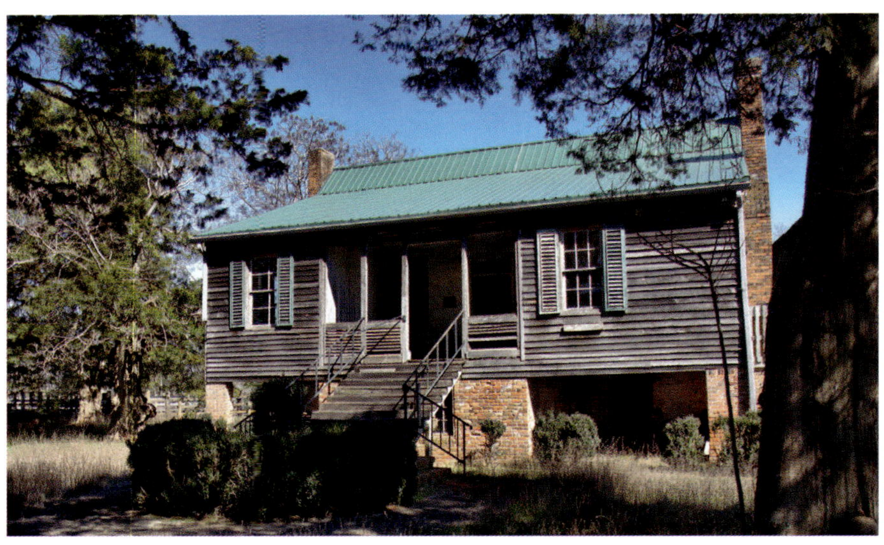

Bowdre-Rees-Knox House, McDuffie County

Cotton had been a fixture of the Georgia landscape since the middle of the eighteenth century, though the conditions for its domination of agricultural production in the state coalesced only at the end of that century. Planters along the Georgia coast traditionally grew a long-staple cotton variety on the high ground of their plantations, but the finishing step of separating seed from fiber, tediously performed by hand, limited the scale of its production. Alternative short-staple "upland" cotton varieties, imported from Asia, could be grown well in Georgia, but their short fibers were inferior to the Sea Island varieties, and seed removal was far more difficult. Planters had little incentive to work with it.

The invention of a reliable mechanical cotton "engine" in the 1790s revised long-held concepts about cotton production by substituting a quick mechanical process for the tedious labor of seed removal. The gin worked effectively on both short- and long-staple varieties, thereby allowing cotton to be profitably grown in areas far from the coast. Upland cotton cultivation in Georgia expanded concurrently with expanding white settlement into the upcountry.

With the economic potential of upland cotton demonstrated, planters acquired and consolidated landholdings, often buying out smaller farmers, to create industrial-scale plantations whose reality was far removed from romantic visions of Tara-like pastoral beauty. By the first decade of the nineteenth century, cotton had become the business of Georgia, and though other crops, like tobacco and corn, continued to be grown, the prerogatives of cotton production and the planter class eclipsed all others in economic, social, and political importance.

Though the popular notion of a uniformly agrarian antebellum Georgia persists, the decades before the Civil War saw burgeoning industrial development in the state. While nonagricultural manufacturing in antebellum Georgia never rivaled the scale nor diversity of that developed in the Northeast and Midwest in the same period, the foundation for Georgia's successful postbellum industrial development was nonetheless laid before the Civil War.

Following the lead set by South Carolina in the early 1830s, Georgia eagerly adopted new railroad technology. No less than four Georgia railroads were chartered in the 1830s, their lines eventually linking the state's major cities. Augusta, Macon, Columbus, and Savannah developed first as regional trade hubs in the era of river commerce, and from this position they further evolved as rail centers, with branch lines reaching out into surrounding plantation districts and smaller cities. By the eve of the Civil War, Georgia had laid more track miles than any other state in the Deep South.

Terminus, the settlement that would become Atlanta, was a new type of Georgia city, its raison d'être derived not from river, road, or ocean access but from being the end point of a planned state railroad connecting Georgia to Chattanooga and beyond to the Midwest. By the 1840s rail lines from Augusta and

Macon interlinked at the town, providing connections to the ports at Charleston and Savannah. More lines arrived in the 1850s, extending rails west and south of the city to West Point and Montgomery. Atlanta grew into Georgia's most important rail hub by 1860, making it a ripe target for United States troops striking at the heart of Confederate supply lines during the Civil War and resulting in its destruction in 1864. Indeed, Atlanta's significance as a transportation hub led to its rapid redevelopment during Reconstruction as Georgia's leading postbellum city.

By necessity, this chapter's treatment of extant antebellum Georgia architecture must be limited in breadth. A fuller survey conveying the sheer variety of the built environment in this period would stretch into hundreds of subject buildings. What follows is a selection of buildings representing the major aesthetic and technological movements of the age, including vernacular and high-style houses; churches; commercial, educational and public buildings; railroad structures; and defensive works.

Slavery

When considering Georgia architecture of the antebellum period, one should keep in mind that, almost without exception, those responsible for the buildings benefited from enslaved labor in ways great and small and, therefore, bear their share of responsibility for the stain of slavery and white supremacy on American history. Just as any accounting of Georgia's antebellum architectural legacy must acknowledge the aesthetic and technological merit of so many historic buildings of the era, it must also acknowledge, frankly and openly, that legacy's culpability in perpetuating the "peculiar institution."

The six decades of the antebellum era saw Georgia evolve economically, demographically, and geographically, propelling it to the first rank of Southern states. In 1860, on the eve of the Civil War, the state's population exceeded one million, six-and-a-half times its size in 1800. In that same period, the number of enslaved people in Georgia grew eightfold. The expansion of plantation agriculture resulted in a concurrent increase in the number of enslaved Africans working those plantations, so that by 1860 almost 44 percent of the state's population, more than 462,000 people, were held in bondage. These numbers are the highest recorded for Georgia in any of the U.S. censuses conducted between 1790 and 1860.

Georgia's enslaved workers did not toil in agriculture alone. Institutional, industrial, and infrastructure advancements of the era were largely built on a foundation of forced labor. Many builders relied upon enslaved laborers and craftsmen to assist in the erection of their work, as did iron foundries, mills, and manufacturers of all stripes. Indeed, every public works and infrastructure project of the antebellum era used enslaved labor to build, maintain, and operate these enterprises. Georgia's railroads preferred to use enslaved workers in the construction of new rail lines, so that, by the 1850s, these companies were among the largest slaveholding and slave-hiring entities in the state.

Georgia's Antebellum Vernaculars and House Types

Vernacular buildings, of which precious few remain, once far outnumbered the high-style showplaces for which the antebellum era is still remembered. While many of Georgia's antebellum elites embraced up-to-date architectural trends, this clamor for fashion was not universal among Georgians. Most buildings of the era were not high style, because most could not afford to build, or simply chose not to build, to that exacting level of finish.

In architectural parlance, the term "vernacular" refers to buildings (or parts of buildings) that demonstrate no discernible stylistic intentions. Vernacular buildings reflect a pragmatic and utilitarian approach to shelter, in large part inherited from previous generations, and they perpetuate the use of local or regionally specific building forms, traditional construction techniques, and locally available materials. Built in both urban and rural settings, Georgia's antebellum vernaculars included dwelling houses of all classes as well as the simple everyday buildings supporting the necessary activities of daily life.

The term "high style" connotes a complete, academic employment of architectural style, but rarely did the financial ability of a building owner allow for such a treatment. More commonly, builders embellished their work by degrees, so that most buildings of the period fall along a continuum between high style and vernacular. In such buildings, stylistic flourishes may be found in the design of porches and porticoes, staircases, fireplace mantels, trims and moldings, and windows and doors. While not high style per se, these buildings are also not purely vernacular.

Georgia housewrights plying their trade in the antebellum period employed standardized layouts and forms with such consistency that these have now been identified and catalogued as particular house types. These early residential types are built around the module of a single room, or "pen," that was multiplied, pushed, and pulled to derive house forms repeated all over the state. Georgia's most common antebellum house types include single and double pens, dogtrots, saddlebags, hall-parlor cottages, central-hall cottages, I-houses, Plantation Plain houses, Georgian cottages, and Georgian houses. Just as houses may be high style, vernacular, or somewhere in between, they also may or may not belong to a particular house type. By identifying and classifying both type and style, modern preservationists are better able to accurately describe historic buildings and understand the evolution of both characteristics through Georgia's history.

The circa-1816 Bowdre-Rees-Knox House, built for the migrant Virginia planter Thomas Bowdre near the Wrightsboro settlement in Columbia (now McDuffie) County, is a well-preserved example of a raised vernacular hall-parlor plantation house. Its Federal-style pine mantels and faux-grained plank wainscot and doors, intact after more than two hundred years, embellish what is otherwise a very simple house. While Thomas Bowdre's house bears little resemblance to the elaborate Greek Revival big houses so ubiquitous by the 1830s, it nonetheless functioned as the center of a plantation of over 1,500 acres.

Like most former plantations, the Bowdre-Rees-Knox House survives today unaccompanied by the numerous outbuildings formerly populating its landscape. Postbellum transitions in plantation agriculture away from centralized organization frequently resulted in outbuildings being relocated, abandoned, or repurposed. Most eventually rotted away from disuse, leaving little trace. Inevitably, our twenty-first century perception of the antebellum plantation is blinkered by the buildings that have survived to the present. In too many cases this is a lone big house picturesquely sited amid well-maintained gardens, lawns and large trees.

The typical working plantation was very different: far hotter, smokier, grittier, and malodorous than the idealized landscapes we see today. Enslaved workers assigned to the "domestic precinct" toiled within the big house and in and around outbuildings whose function related directly to the day-to-day operation of the household: kitchens, smokehouses, storehouses, wells, cisterns, and privies. Although some of these functions might be accommodated within the big house in a raised basement, they were typically consigned to outbuildings. Town houses built by planters and other elites functioned in a similar way.

Quarters housing enslaved workers were often located within sight of the big house, both as a conspicuous display of affluence and as a form of monitoring and

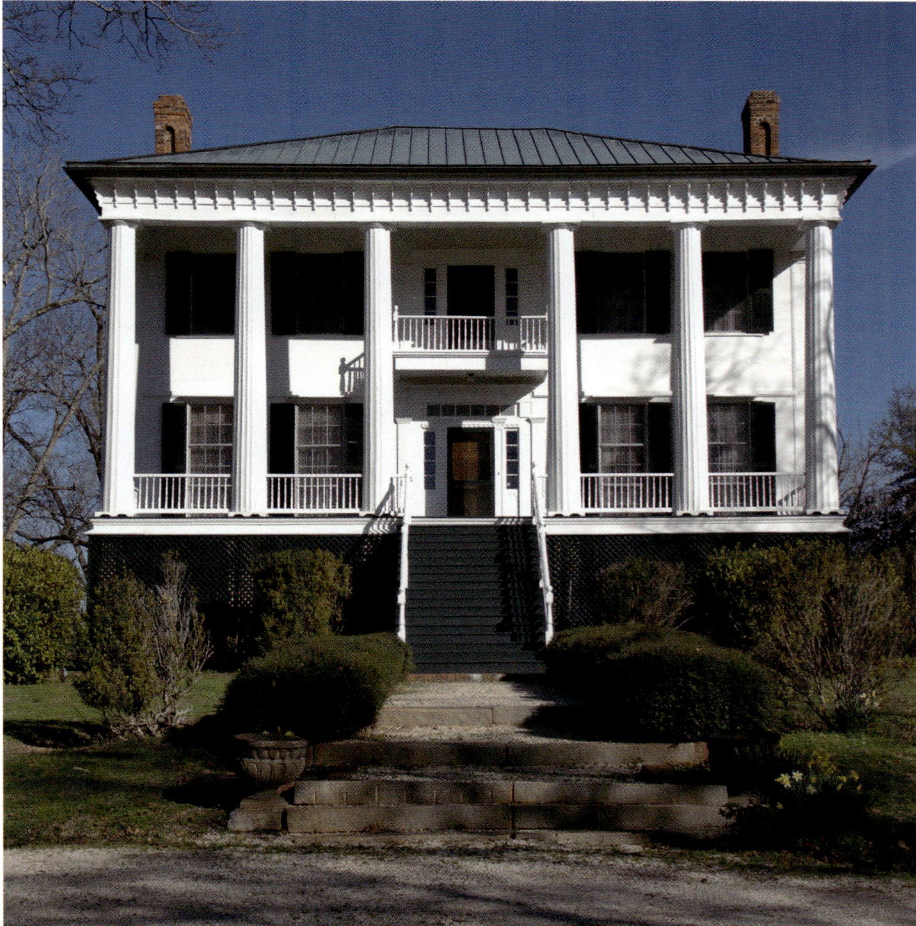

Shoulderbone Plantation, Hancock County

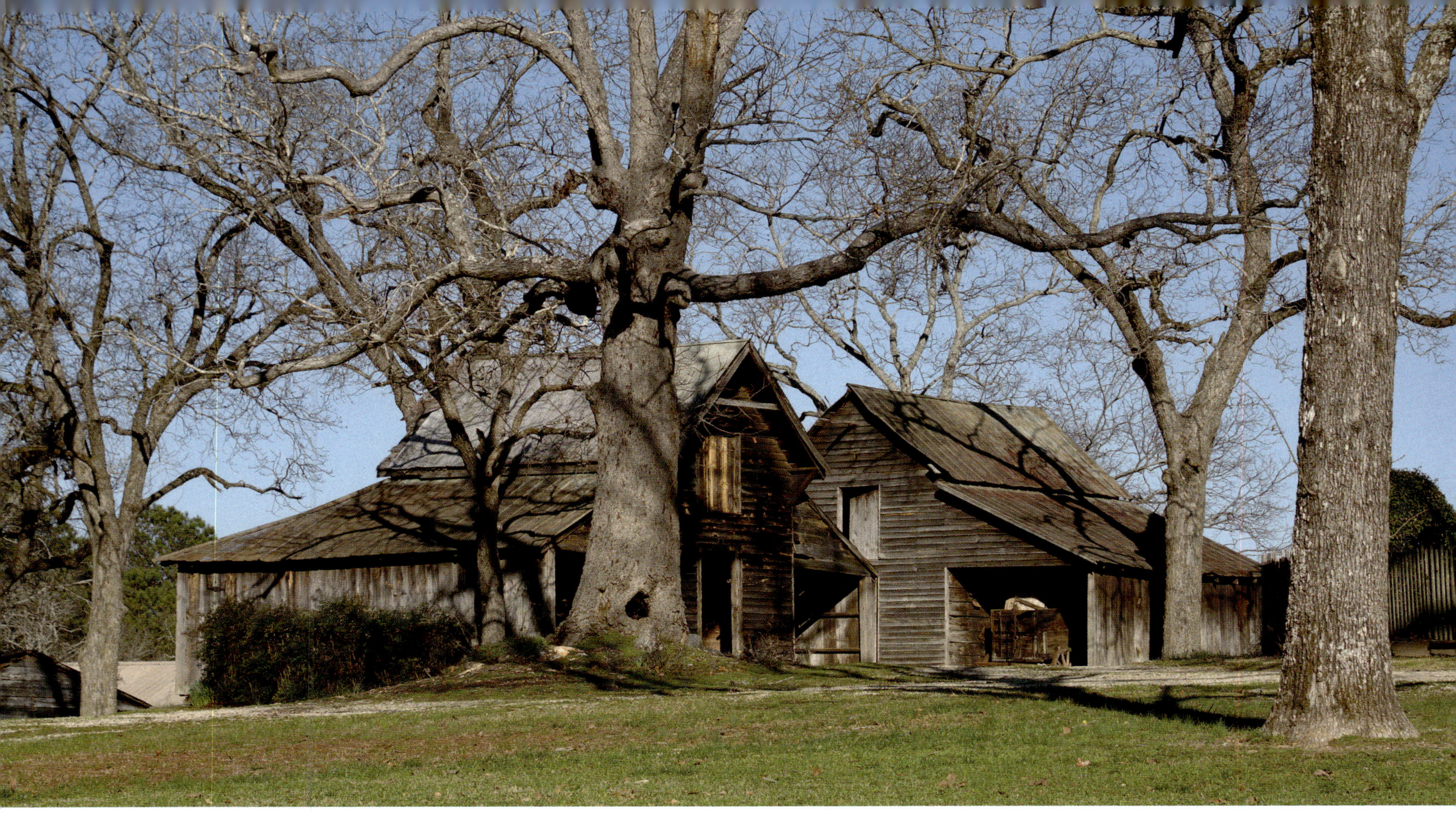

Shoulderbone Plantation Outbuildings, Hancock County

control. Elsewhere among the pastures, fields, and orchards one might find clusters of additional outbuildings related to plantation functions: dwellings, workshops, stables, barns, cribs, pens, mills, gins, coops, and sheds of all varieties.

Because outbuildings typically followed traditional forms and used common materials that barely changed over the course of a century or more, even when they do survive it can be difficult to accurately date them from appearance alone. Science steps in when connoisseurship fails, making dendrochronology, radiocarbon dating, and other types of forensic analysis critically important to the accurate dating of vernacular resources.

The John S. Jackson Plantation, also known as Shoulderbone Plantation, was built circa 1856 near White Plains in Hancock County. Typical of rural Piedmont cotton plantations, the house is neither crude nor particularly sophisticated, certainly grandiose but not exceptionally grand. While the big house is a relatively standard archetype, far rarer is the preservation of five historic outbuildings dating to the 1850s. They include a buggy shed and storage barn, a well house, a corn crib, and a privy. All of these historic wood-framed outbuildings are of utilitarian design, purely functional in configuration. A former kitchen outbuilding was located directly at the rear of the house, but only its foundation remains.

Though exceedingly rare, several antebellum Georgia plantations also retain well-preserved outbuildings from the era. These include Westover in Baldwin County, Birdsville Plantation in Jenkins County, and Hurt-Rives Plantation in Hancock County.

The Federal Style in Georgia

Characterized by its restrained classical motifs, delicate woodwork, and taut, smooth wall surfaces, the American Federal style was largely derived from the Adam style popular in Britain from the 1760s to the 1790s. In the United States, the emergence of the mature Federal idiom dates to the early 1790s in the work of architects and builder-architects like Charles Bulfinch, Samuel McIntire, and Asher Benjamin. Beginning in 1797, Asher Benjamin's prolific publication of pattern books spread his interpretation of the Federal style (and later, the Greek Revival) to a national audience, promoting the penetration of current architectural fashion deep into the country's hinterlands.

In the first three decades of the nineteenth century, Georgians of means embraced the Federal style for their finer buildings. While this was particularly true in larger, older cities like Savannah and Augusta, the wealthy denizens of smaller, newer Piedmont towns like Washington and Milledgeville were equally enthusiastic adopters of the style. The opening of much of the upcountry to white settlement in these decades provided a tabula rasa of sorts for the propagation of the Federal idiom, though in truth, rough vernacular buildings were typically first erected as the land was cleared for agriculture. The development of stable upcountry communities with strong trade ties to the coast eventually allowed elites in these areas to remodel earlier, uncouth buildings or to erect new buildings in the current fashion.

Savannah's Oliver Sturges House (ca. 1813) is an archetypical example of a Federal-style brick row house, similar to that one might find at the time in Charleston, Baltimore, or New York. Formerly one of a pair of matching houses, the Sturges House features Flemish-bond brick and red sandstone jack arches above its windows. Its six-panel entry door, with sidelights and elliptical transom window, is framed by a refined Federal stoop featuring curving wrought ironwork and slender Tuscan columns. Originally a two-story house, a third story was added in 1835 in a matching style.

One of the most interesting Georgia residences in the Federal style was the townhouse commissioned circa 1818 by Nicholas Ware, a wealthy planter and politician from Augusta. Many of the facts of the Ware House's construction are obscured by history, including the identity of its architect-builder. Set upon a high raised basement of Flemish-bond brick, the house is both tall and set close to the street. Its builder embellished the front facade with semioctagonal bays flanking a slender outward-bowing two-story portico. Three stacked Federal-style doorways, the upper two featuring elliptical transom lights and leaded glass sidelights, align along the centerline of the front facade, which is clad entirely in horizontal flat plank siding. Large glass panes in the six-over-six hung sash windows were unmistakably extravagant for the time. The side and rear facades exhibit a far simpler treatment than the front, though the elaborate Doric entablature wraps all sides of the house.

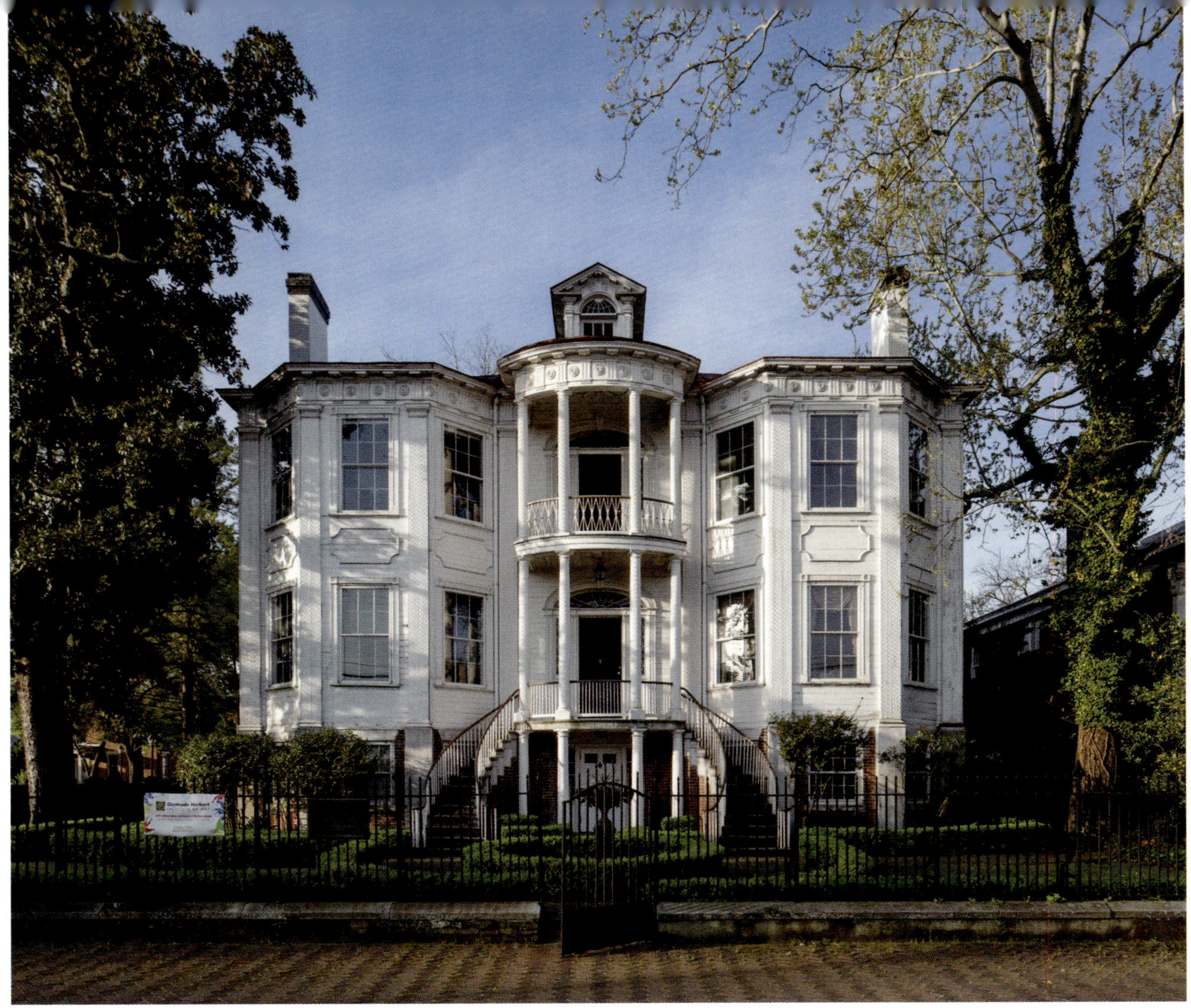

Nicholas Ware House, Augusta

Ware's house is configured as a typical two-story "Georgian House" of four rooms with a central hall, here subdivided on the first floor into a reception hall at the front and a stair hall at the rear. The central hall features a very fine elliptical stair set to one side. The fireplaces on each floor are located on the outside walls of the house, allowing the parlors on the east side of the first floor to open to each other for dancing and other entertainments. A beautiful leaded-glass elliptical transom window hovers above four pocketing panel doors at the common parlor opening, allowing light to be shared between rooms.

A lawyer by training, Ware served as mayor of Augusta before being elected to the U.S. Senate, where he served from 1821 until his death at age forty-eight in September 1824. Ware's widow Susan sold many of the house's contents at executor's sales held in January 1825, and in April and May 1825 the house itself was advertised for sale in the *Augusta Chronicle* and other newspapers in the region. The buyer is unknown, but in subsequent years a series of wealthy and prominent Augustans owned and occupied the house, including the textile-mill magnate William C. Sibley, who made it his home from 1871 to 1909.

As the fashionable residential areas of Augusta migrated away from the city center, the Ware House suffered a period of decline that saw it threatened with demolition. In 1937 Olivia Herbert, a wealthy New Yorker and winter Augusta resident, purchased and renovated the house before donating it to the Augusta Art Club. Renamed the Gertrude Herbert Institute of Art in honor of Herbert's deceased daughter, the organization still operates the Ware House as a gallery and art studio open to the public.

Other fine Federal style houses of note in Georgia include the beautifully restored Isaiah Davenport House (ca. 1820) in Savannah, the Terrell-Stone House in Sparta (ca. 1821), and the Dr. Kilpatrick House in Augusta (ca. 1800).

A fascinating feature of antebellum Cherokee and Muscogee material culture is the degree to which these tribes internalized Euro-American building traditions, and, on occasion, its architectural fashions, as part of their own lexicons. In the eighteenth and nineteenth centuries, both the Muskogee and Cherokee people maintained longstanding, often-fractious relationships with white traders, missionaries, and government agents, allowing the regular exchange of goods, services, and information across treaty lines.

Between 1823 and 1825, William McIntosh, chief of the Coweta band of the Muscogee, built an inn at Indian Springs which is substantially similar in form and finish to those built by white settlers in the Georgia upcountry. Likewise, the reconstructed and relocated buildings at the Cherokee capital, New Echota, exhibit a vernacular vocabulary of hewn-log and braced-frame construction shared by Native Americans and white settlers at the time. Most extravagantly, the high-style Vann House, built in the heart of the Cherokee Nation near New Echota, reflects both Georgian and Federal-style influences, though the source of its design is unknown.

The genesis of the current Vann House is somewhat murky. In the customary telling, the house was built circa 1804 for James Vann, a prominent Cherokee chief who was the most successful entrepreneur and planter of his day in the Cherokee Nation. At the time of his murder in 1809, Vann's business operations included plantations, ferries, taverns, campgrounds, and toll franchises along Federal Road traversing Cherokee territory. While much of the historic interpretation at the Vann House site today reflects James Vann's story, new evidence uncovered in the late 2000s shifts responsibility for the construction of the house to his favorite son, Joseph Vann. As the primary inheritor of his father's estate, Joseph was widely known as "Rich Joe" Vann.

In 1819, the journals of the Moravian missionaries at nearby Springplace record that Joseph Vann had undertaken construction of a "large brick house." Vann retained the brothers James and John McCartney as framers and finish carpenters for the project and contracted separately with Robert Howell, a mason and plasterer, to complete the building's brick shell. Despite some setbacks, the work was reported complete by 1824.

A lawsuit filed in March 1825 in Kingston, Tennessee, offers a glimpse into the vicissitudes of the house's construction. John McCartney sued Joseph Vann for payment of expenses incurred in building the house and two other structures on Vann's plantation. Vann claimed that McCartney's stair construction was defective and that the house had a leaky roof, requiring Howell to replaster the interior. The records are unclear whether Vann and McCartney reached a settlement, but they do include detailed inventories of materials, expenses, and labor for the construction of the house. The correlation between these materials lists and the Vann House as it survives to the present provides strong evidence that it was Joseph Vann rather than his father who commissioned the house.

The Vann House features unusual and idiosyncratic interior details and a distinctive polychrome paint scheme. The carpentry, especially the mantels and parlor overmantel, reflect an awareness of the architectural fashion of the era, but in both composition and detail there are deviations from the "academic" form. The hanging staircase, stabilized with additional structure, remains a feat of architectural derring-do and is used even today by visitors. The four-color interior paint scheme of clay red, yellow ochre, pale blue, and mossy green used natural pigments to mirror the colors of field and forest, earth and sky.

The great irony of Joseph Vann's life is that his identification as Cherokee, regardless of his wealth, status, or education, ultimately came to be viewed by the state and federal governments as disqualifying for land ownership. Vann's plantation, along with the remaining lands of his countrymen, was parceled up in the 1832 land lottery and eventually forced into sale. In March 1835, after participating in active resistance to removal actions, Vann and his family left Georgia for the Indian Territory, traveling the Trail of Tears. As a planter, the basis of much of Vann's wealth was human chattel, thereby allowing him to retain his workforce despite his removal. In the Indian Territory, Vann quickly reestablished his elite status, built upon the value and production potential of his enslaved laborers.

For a century after Vann's removal, his former house in Georgia suffered much abuse from subsequent owners, undergoing extensive modifications that significantly altered the function and appearance of the house. By the 1930s, when photographed for the Historic American Buildings Survey, the back of the house was used as the front, the north portico had been removed, and a kitchen ell extended from what had originally been the front of the house. By the 1950s, further travails included a collapsing south porch, missing window glass, and roof leaks that rotted much floor structure. The last private owner sold the house to the Georgia Historical Commission in 1952, and between 1952 and 1958 the architect and historian Henry Chandlee Forman oversaw an extensive repair and reconstruction project to return the Vann House to some semblance of its original appearance. The house and grounds are now a state historic site interpreting the story of the Vann family, their enslaved workers, and their roles within the Cherokee Nation.

An interesting regional variation of the Federal style developed in Georgia in the very late 1810s through the 1820s. Termed "Milledgeville Federal" because of the preponderance of its use in and around the state capital, many examples can still be found across the Georgia Piedmont. Builders in the style embellished their houses with classicized, pedimented porticoes, either one or two stories in height, appended to the front of traditional vernacular house forms, most often central-hall, I-house, or Plantation Plain types.

The showpiece portico attested to the craftsmanship of its builder, whose talents in the arts of design, carpentry, and woodcarving were employed judiciously to achieve the desired effect. The elegance and refinement of tours-de-force entryways convey something of the interiors, where curvilinear staircases

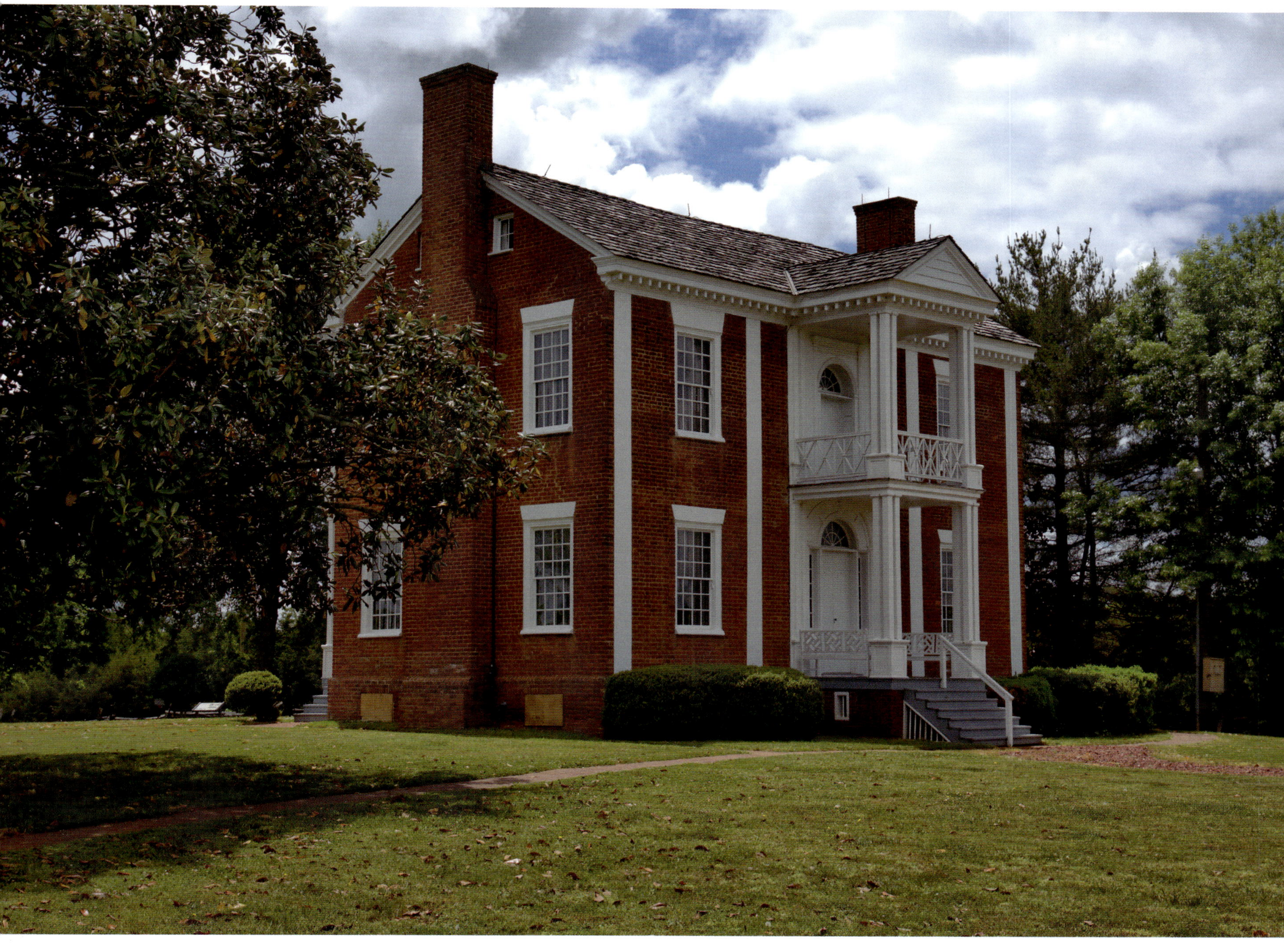

Vann House, Murray County

of sinuous line and elaborately yet daintily carved mantelpieces exhibit woodcarving skills to rival the earlier work of Samuel McIntire in Massachusetts. Elsewhere on such a house one might find a modillioned cornice or a properly articulated frieze, but often even this slight embellishment was omitted in favor of the vernacular. It is in the porticoes, doorways, sidelights, and transoms that the builder's superlative skills were truly expressed.

The builder-architect Daniel Pratt, born in New Hampshire in 1799, emigrated to Savannah in 1819 before moving on to Milledgeville in 1821. As a young man, Pratt apprenticed to a carpenter, and his training in the building trades continued during his time in Savannah. The chronology of his work in Milledgeville indicates he was employed almost immediately, with multiple significant commissions

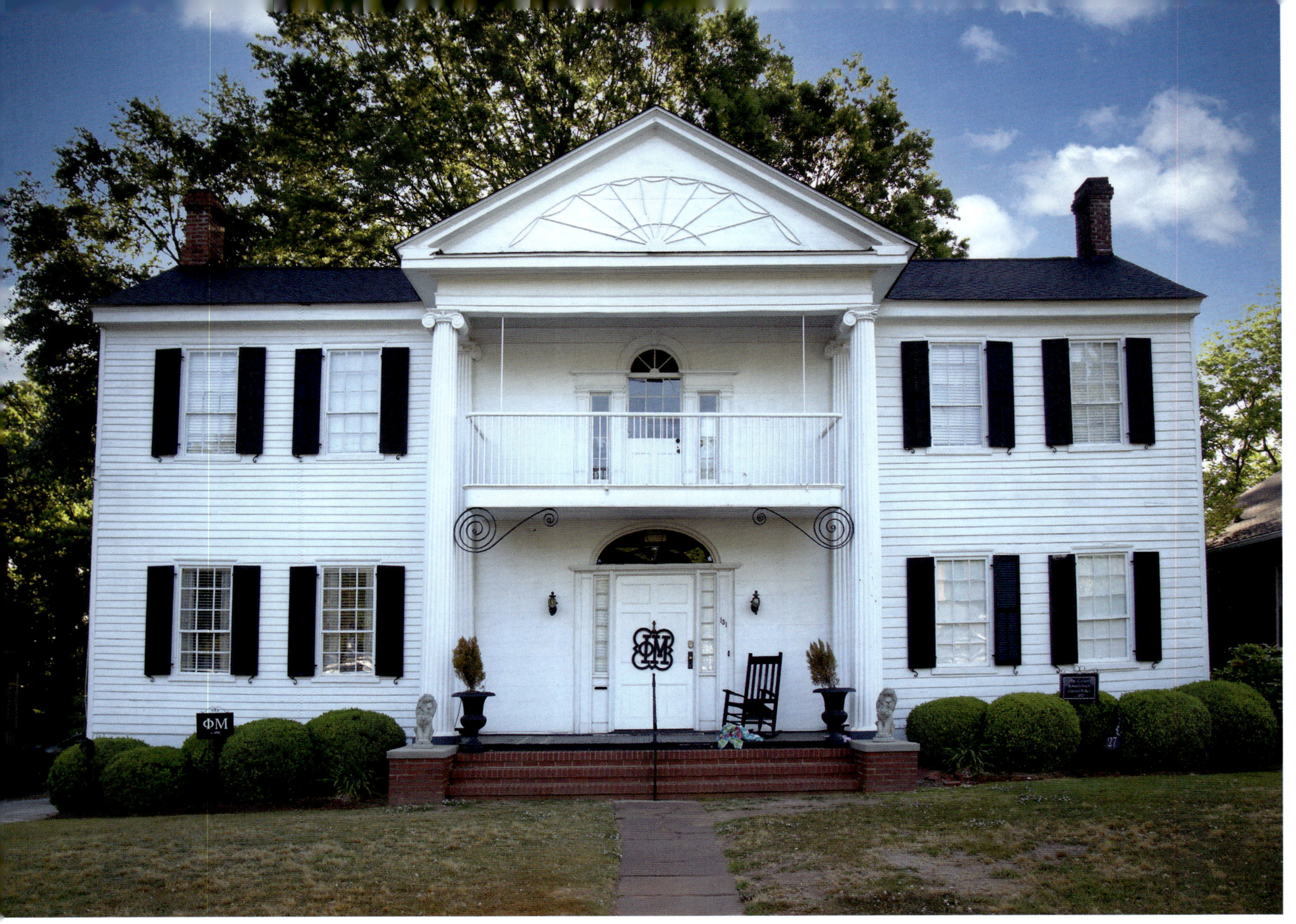

The Cedars, Milledgeville

in the early 1820s. Among those surviving today are "The Cedars" (the Howard-Jarrett-Garrard-Walker House, ca. 1822), the Gordon-Banks House (ca. 1827), later relocated to Newnan, and the Williams-Grantland-Orme-Crawford-Sallee House (ca. 1822). In the early 1830s, Pratt migrated to Alabama, where he established the Daniel Pratt Gin Company outside of Montgomery. His success manufacturing an improved cotton gin brought him great wealth and enabled him to found a company town, prosaically christened "Prattville," in 1839.

The English-born John Marlor was Pratt's contemporary and sometime collaborator, though Marlor was ten years older. In 1820, he arrived in Milledgeville by way of Charleston, where he spent his childhood and apprenticed in the building trades. Marlor's version of Milledgeville Federal was more idiosyncratic and less reliant upon pure symmetry than Pratt's work, as best exemplified by his Brown-Stetson-Sanford House of 1825. In the years after its construction, the house served as a residence, hotel, and well-known local tearoom. In the mid-1960s a campaign mounted by concerned citizens to save the house from demolition marked a turn in favor of preservation in Milledgeville. In 1966, it was moved to its present location, restored, and opened as a house museum.

The Greek Revival in Georgia

In the United States, significant early expressions of what was termed the "Grecian" form of neoclassicism can be found in the work of the expatriate English architect Benjamin Henry Latrobe and his American-born proteges William Strickland and Robert Mills. The itinerant English architect William Jay, practicing briefly in Savannah, was another early adopter of what became known as the Greek Revival, though his influence outside of that city was limited. It was Mills, serving as the superintendent of public buildings in South Carolina in the early 1820s, whose Greek Revival designs for courthouses, jails, and the state asylum provided the template for similar buildings erected in Georgia over the next three decades.

Beginning in the 1820s, and especially after 1830, nationally influential pattern books from architect-builders like Asher Benjamin and Minard Lafever began to feature Greek Revival examples. Such pattern book authors broke down complex architectural concepts into illustrated instructions understandable to the average housewright or carpenter with a rudimentary grasp of geometry. Pattern books were also portable, facilitating the spread of architectural fashion outside of cities into small towns and the countryside alike. The brilliance of Asher Benjamin's work was his adaptation of high-style design to what he termed "the present style of building in the United States of America." His use of the term "present style" referenced not only architectural design, but also American building techniques and materials then in common use, simplifying the practical application of his designs in the field.

Designers and builders in the Greek Revival style employed any of the three ancient Greek architectural orders (and some later permutations) in their work: the Doric, the Ionic, and the Corinthian. Each order not only describes the appearance of architectural elements within the order but also defines a set of proportional relationships between its constituent parts. In principle, a builder adhering to the rules of order would erect a harmonious, well-proportioned building. As applied in the field, however, the widely varying skills of builders and craftsmen and the degree of their adherence to the proportional system of the chosen order resulted in myriad idiosyncratic and free interpretations of the classical language.

In the South, the popularity of the Greek Revival style was particularly pronounced in residential construction, where its democratic allusions, monumentality, and potential for opulence appealed to the antebellum elite. For these "white-columned" residences, builders developed several typical modes by which Greek Revival detailing was applied to traditional two- and four-room house types. Popular in town and country alike, the boxy symmetry of the I-house, central-hall cottage, Georgian cottage, and Georgian house types proved ideal for the application of Grecian elements of varying complexity and grandeur.

The first mode featured a front facade with a heavy Greek entablature supported on a monumental colonnade that often wrapped the sides of the building.

The potential for ostentation of the high-style Greek Revival in this mode was fully exploited in houses like the Cowles-Bond-Woodruff House (1836) in Macon, Glen Mary (ca. 1848) in Hancock County, and Bellevue (1853–55) in LaGrange. All three houses utilize properly proportioned orders in their colonnades and entablatures, in these cases Roman Doric, Greek Doric, and Scamozzi Ionic, respectively.

A second mode followed the classical temple form, with front pediment supported on columns. Exemplary of this mode are Orange Hall (ca. 1838) in Saint Marys, as well as Bulloch Hall (ca. 1839) and Mimosa Hall (ca. 1841) in Roswell. All three of these buildings use vernacular versions of the Greek Doric order, though none employs the proportional system appropriate to the order.

The third mode featured a portico of one or two stories centered on the house's front facade, which could also be one or two stories in height. Builders often crowned such porticoes with pediments, though more rarely an entablature alone would suffice, especially if the portico was one story. Augusta's Montrose (the Reid-Jones-Carpenter House) from 1849 is a significant high-style example of this mode in a one-story house elevated high on a raised basement. The Reid-Green-Lawrence-Eidson House in Eatonton (ca. 1855) is a doppelgänger of Montrose, but rendered in two stories with a lower raised basement. Both houses employ the Corinthian order.

For over two hundred years the work of the English architect William Jay has been synonymous with refinement, taste, and sophistication in the city of Savannah. Jay arrived in Savannah at the end of 1817, after completing his apprenticeship in London. The merchants, planters, and factors of the rapidly growing town were flush with money from the burgeoning cotton trade, and Jay's family and social connections in Savannah positioned him to benefit immediately from those relationships. Before his departure from Savannah around 1825, Jay designed several large residences, a school, a theater, and the Savannah branch of the Bank of the United States. His designs for the William Scarbrough House and the branch bank prominently employed Greek Revival elements—prescient examples of the direction American architecture would take in the next three decades.

In 1818, Jay was retained to design two new houses in Savannah, one for Alexander Telfair, youthful head of a long-prominent coastal Georgia family, and another for the merchant, planter, and steamship entrepreneur William Scarbrough. Jay's first commission in the city, the year before, was a large house for the financier, merchant, and slave trader Richard Richardson. That house, now better known as the Owens-Thomas House, is highly regarded today for its stylistic novelty, technical innovation, and beauty. All of Jay's extant buildings in Georgia exhibit the taut wall surfaces, muted rooflines, and creative subversion of classical rules that were seen in the work of certain English neoclassical architects, particularly John Soane.

Jay's house for William Scarbrough is raised slightly above the street on a rusticated podium, with a front entry framed within a portico featuring a fully

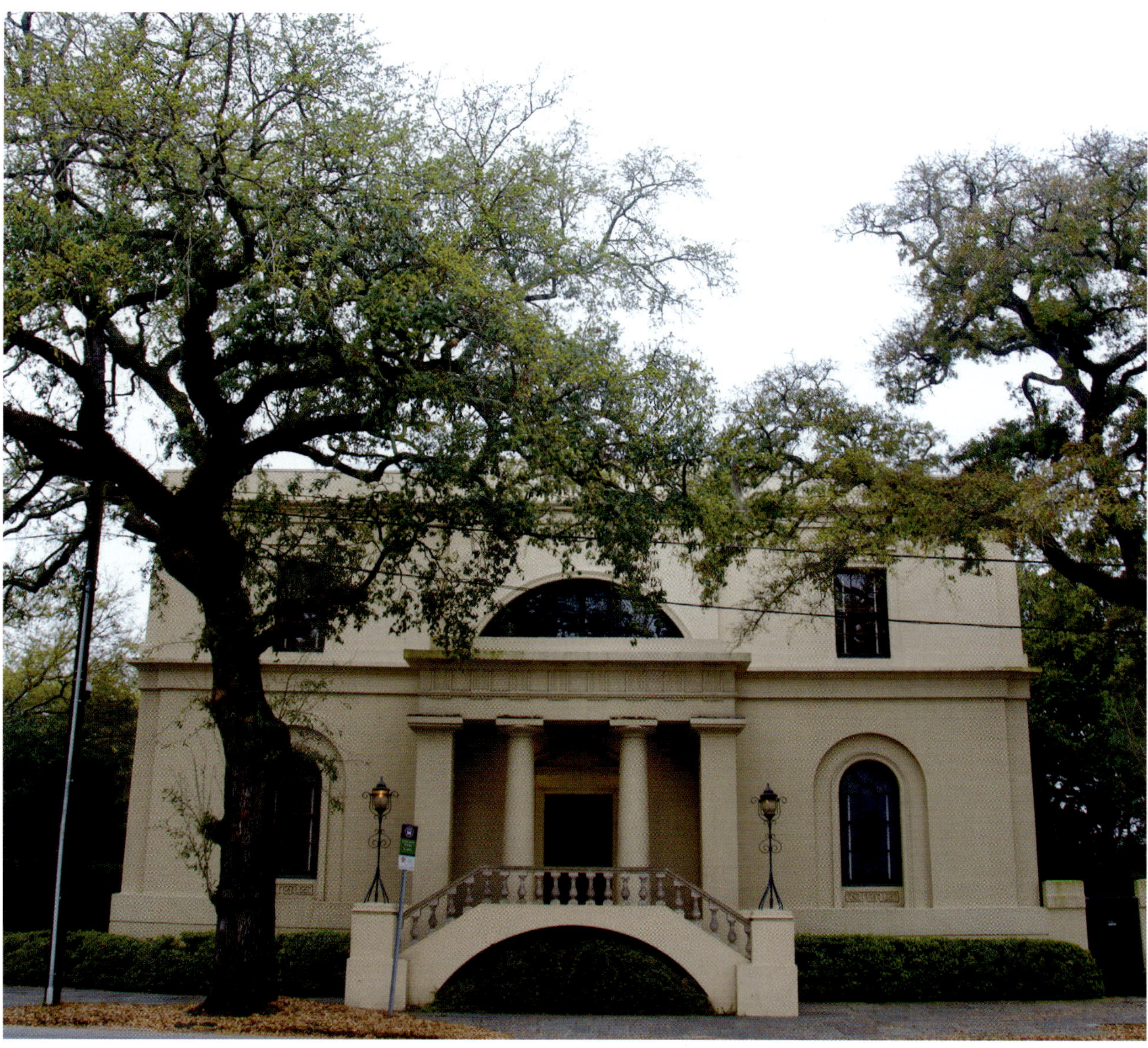

William Scarbrough House, Savannah

detailed Doric entablature supported on two Doric columns in antis, likely the first use of this order on a building in Georgia. The house's street facade is divided roughly into thirds, with a slightly projecting center pavilion matching the width of the centered, projecting portico. A hallmark of Jay's work is the absence of a projecting cornice at the top of the building facade. Rather, the architect extended parapets above the top belt course, with the central pavilion parapet being slightly taller than those on each side.

William Scarbrough and his wife Julia were socially ambitious, and by early 1819 their house was complete enough to host President James Monroe, who was in Savannah for the launch of the first transatlantic steamship, SS *Savannah*. Scarbrough was the chief investor and promoter of the venture, and its eventual financial failure coupled with the loss of the ship led him to financial ruin. In November 1820 Scarbrough lost the house at a marshal's sale.

Robert Isaac, whose wife Lucy was Julia Scarbrough's sister, purchased the house and its contents, allowing members of the Scarbrough family to remain in residence as de facto owners until Julia's death in 1851. In 1835, three years before

Scarbrough's death, his son-in-law Godfrey Barnsley, an English-born cotton factor, assumed management of the rapidly deteriorating and still-incomplete residence. Over the next two years Barnsley spent ten thousand dollars repairing and altering the house for his own purposes. His addition of a third story at the top of the house required the complete removal of the roof and resulted in a significantly changed appearance. In the 1840s Barnsley and his wife and children decamped to a country estate, Woodlands, in Cass (now Bartow) County, with widowed mother-in-law Julia Scarbrough remaining in Savannah.

In 1878, the philanthropist George W. J. DeRenne deeded the house in trust to the Savannah board of education for permanent use as a school for African American children. Christened the West Broad Street School, the house would serve the cause of Black education for the next eighty-four years, until 1962. The Savannah board of education, like most in the South, took little initiative to improve facilities for its Black students, and by the mid-twentieth century the school suffered the physical effects of long-term neglect.

In the years after the Civil War, the West Broad Street neighborhood changed significantly. As early as the 1880s, the large residences that had been its hallmark when Scarbrough built his house were demolished and replaced with small dwellings, warehouses, stables, and workshops. West Broad Street evolved into the commercial heart of Black Savannah during the postbellum nineteenth century. Major institutions of Savannah's Black community, including First African Baptist Church and First Bryan Baptist Church, were located near the school.

Between 1962 and 1972, concerned Savannahians made significant efforts to obtain title to the house and begin much-needed repairs. The Scarbrough House Foundation was organized for that purpose, with an eye toward using the building as a maritime museum. In 1972, the Historic Savannah Foundation acquired the house, and under the supervision of the Pennsylvania architect John Milner, rehabilitation began that year.

Milner's design removed Barnsley's third floor addition, reconstructing a roofline and rooftop lantern for which little original evidence remained. For this work Milner copied a period example in Bath, England, where William Jay had been born. All exterior stucco was removed to expose the house's brick walls, and the interior floors, walls, and ceilings were gutted to framing to expedite structural repairs. Historic plaster and wood lath was removed and discarded. The stair in the atrium was removed, while historic interior features intended for reuse, like paneled doors and wood trims, were removed for safekeeping, restoration, and eventual reinstallation.

In 1996, the Scarbrough House was acquired by the Ships of the Sea Maritime Museum, which immediately undertook another significant rehabilitation to prepare the house for use as a museum. The roof was again reconstructed, this time recreating a roofline patterned on William Jay's original design for the Telfair House. The museum has done an admirable job of interpreting the complex history of the house for its visitors, including an explanation of the years of use as a school. In the years since the last rehabilitation, the house has been well maintained, and its fine decor, interesting displays, and expansive, shady gardens combine to present an aesthetically pleasing experience to the public.

As a popular phenomenon in Georgia, the transition from the Federal style to the Greek Revival occurred between the late 1820s and the middle 1830s, roughly contemporary with the aforementioned style update promoted in popular pattern books. The change in taste developed incrementally, and as a result, many buildings from this period exhibit elements of both styles.

Examples of this transitional styling can be found in the work of the brothers Collin and Henry Rogers, builder-architects practicing in LaGrange and vicinity in the 1830s. Nutwood (ca. 1833), built for the planter Joel Newsom, is archetypical of the Rogers aesthetic, a transitional Greek Revival permutation of the Milledgeville Federal style. Nutwood's basic form is a vernacular I-house, two stories high and one room deep, with a two-story rear ell on the west side. Modern alterations placed a bathroom tower at the back of the house and extended the ell, but they are clearly demarcated from the historic form.

Nutwood, Troup County

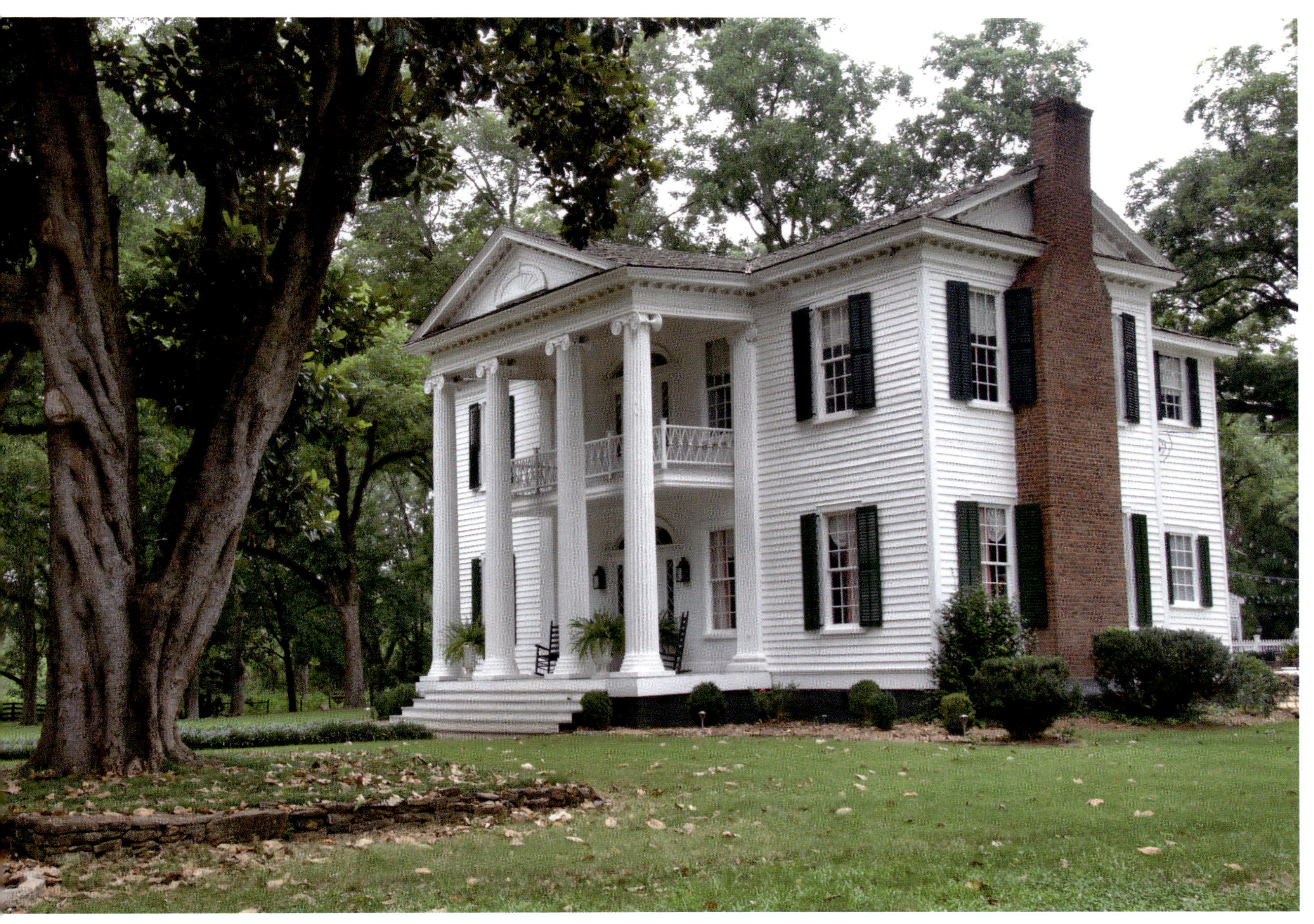

Nutwood's front facade features a monumental Ionic portico with elegantly carved volutes on its columns, thoroughly Greek in treatment. Consistent with its transitional styling, Nutwood's stacked front doorways employ Federal-style elliptical fanlights and reeded casings, and the wide portico balcony is enclosed by delicate sheaves-of-wheat-patterned railings. Like some of Daniel Pratt's work in Milledgeville, the pediment of Nutwood's portico is embellished with a blind elliptical fanlight, also Federal in spirit. A bracketed cornice wraps the otherwise vernacular house. The craftsmanship displayed in houses like Nutwood, and the Nathan Boddie House (ca. 1836), completed the year after Henry Rogers's death, compares favorably to the work of Pratt, Marlor, and others in Milledgeville. The Rogers brothers are known to have employed enslaved workers in their commissions, some of whom they trained as skilled carpenters, masons, and carvers.

Two antebellum outbuildings at Nutwood survive to the present, a smokehouse and a detached kitchen, hinting at the historic appearance of its domestic plantation landscape. In recent years the Nutwood property has been converted into a winery, with a tasting barn near the house. The house is well maintained as a private residence.

In all eras and all places, existing buildings have been modified, whole or in part, to suit the needs of owners. This was equally true in the antebellum era, when older houses, especially vernaculars, were altered to better reflect current tastes, not infrequently as a showy display of an owner's nouveau riche standing. One such example is the Rogers' Henderson-Orr House (1829/1832) in Coweta County, which appended a two-story I-house and portico to an earlier one-story vernacular hall-parlor house, converting the original house into a rear ell.

The English-born builder-architect John Wind likely emigrated to the United States in the mid-1830s, settling in New York. It was there, in 1838, that the Georgia planter Jackson J. Mash encountered him, enticing the young craftsman to emigrate to the vicinity of Thomasville in order to design and build Mash's plantation mansion. Little is known about Wind's origins in Britain or where he received his training, and the lack of concrete information has given rise to much myth. What is known is that, in censuses, advertisements, and surveys from the years between 1835 and his death in 1863, Wind described his vocation as "joiner" (1835), "watch and clockmaker" (1850), "master mechanic" (1860), and "architect" (1860). As with other informally trained building mechanics of the era, Wind's evolution from specialist tradesman to builder-architect was a gradual one.

Though his earlier Greenwood Plantation in Thomasville is perhaps better known to the general public, Wind's design for the big house at Cedar Grove Plantation (later renamed Susina) is the most intact and unmodified example of his work. Cedar Grove was commissioned circa 1841 by James J. Blackshear, brother-in-law of Thomas Jones of Greenwood Plantation. At Cedar Grove, Wind's portico covers the middle three of the house's five bays, with stacked entryways and double doors, sidelights, and transoms. The exaggerated width of these centered elements is reflected in the unequal spacing of the portico's

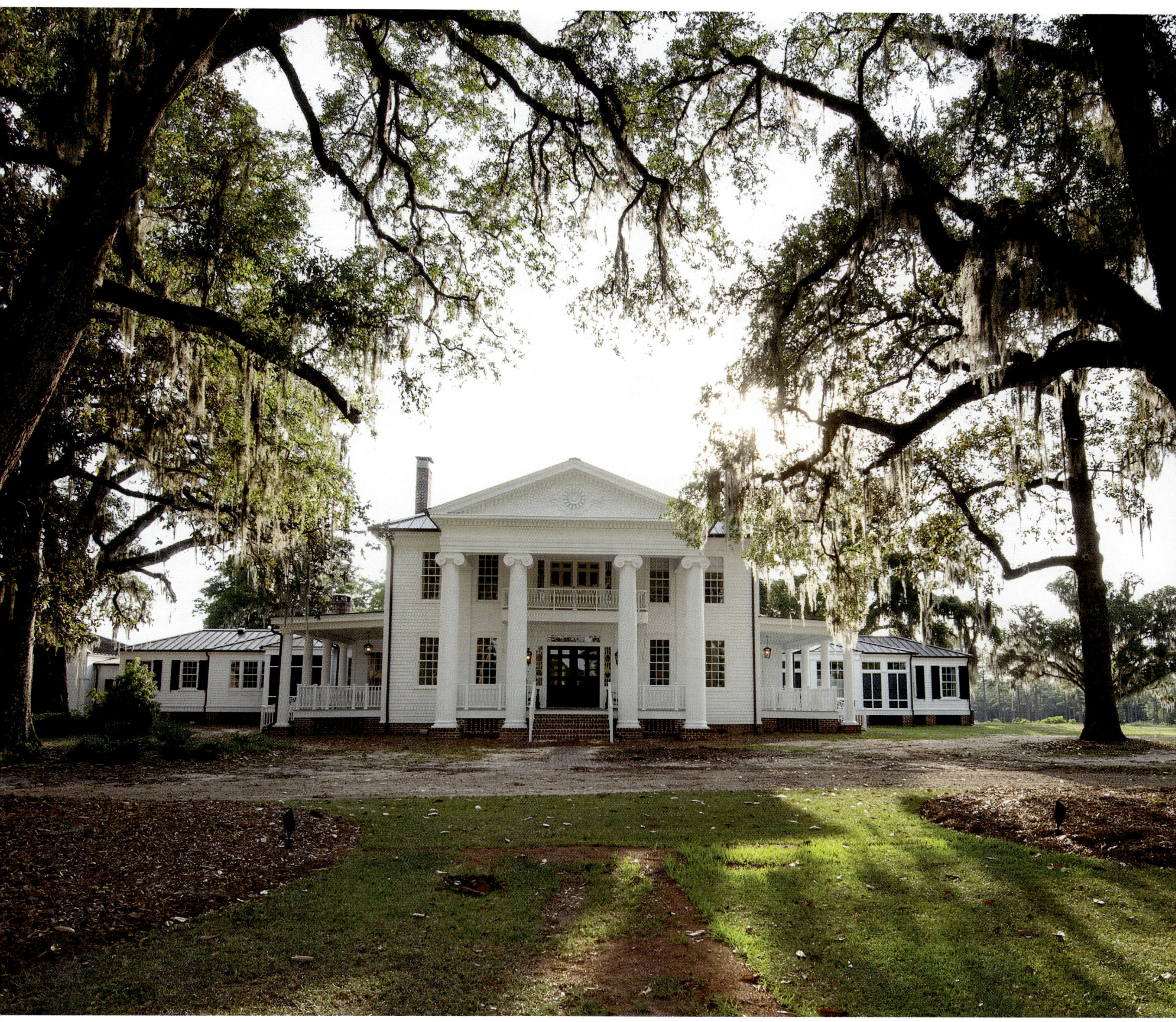

Cedar Grove Plantation (Susina), Grady County

monumental Ionic columns. The stoop and the cantilevered balcony above it nest within the surrounding portico. The carving work in the column capitals and pediments is particularly fine. A photograph from the 1880s shows Cedar Grove with front and rear doors thrown wide open, looking like a grand dogtrot and functioning in the same way.

The Greek Revival residence built by Elam Alexander for Judge Cadwalader (Cadwell) W. Raines in Macon is one of the state's most architecturally intriguing houses in that style. Built circa 1849–50, the house closely follows the "Anglo-Grecian villa" design published in the 1849 pattern book *The Architect* by William H. Ranlett. Perhaps Ranlett should have referred to his design as an "Anglo-Italianate" villa, for it bears more of the hallmarks of that fashionable style than it does of the traditional Greek Revival. Ranlett's contemporaries, A. J. Davis, Richard Upjohn, and Henry Austin foremost among them, had moved strongly in the direction of asymmetrical massings, with eclectic use of towers, balconies, and loggias. These types of "exotic" elements would become the hallmark of eclectic Victorian architecture in the United States after 1840. Ranlett's use of the Italianate in his villa design certainly reflects the move toward broken massing, but it also retains the somewhat more conservative symmetry seen in some expressions of that style.

The Raines House is diagonally cruciform in plan, with its primary entrance located between two arms of the cross. Each arm is two stories, with a continuous Ionic entablature wrapping all sides at the roofline. Monumental pilasters at each outside corner visually support the entablature, with pediments crowning the ends of each arm. This exterior detailing is expertly done, with a precision of line that remains clear even today.

Within the house, the core around which the arms radiate is an octagonal central hall, roughly 19 by 22 feet. This hall, more of a three-story atrium, contains a dramatic continuous spiral staircase rising two stories to a tower projecting above the roofline. Functioning as a great light monitor, with eight windows drawing natural light into the center of the house, the tower illuminates the vertical space below in manner similar to Charles Cluskey's lantern and dome at the Executive Mansion in Milledgeville.

By retaining the Italianate massing of the Ranlett design while dressing it in a Grecian idiom, Alexander created a dynamic new form for the Greek Revival, one unlike any extant in Georgia at the time. Far more accomplished than a typical housewright, he was regarded in his prime as a master builder. While not a professional architect per se, he possessed a keen eye for detail and proportion, and ably adapted the designs found in pattern books for the specific needs of his clients. Though perhaps better known today as the builder of fine houses for Macon's antebellum elite, Alexander was also responsible, wholly or in part, for the erection of many of Macon's first civic and institutional buildings, among them the first Bibb County Courthouse (1829), the Macon & Western Railroad office, later Macon City Hall (1837), the first building of Georgia Female College, later Wesleyan Female College (1839), and the First Presbyterian Church in Macon (1828).

The 1830s and 1840s saw a profusion of Greek Revival church building in Georgia. The style was not associated with any one Christian denomination more than another, so especially in larger cities and towns, one might find Greek Revival–style Baptist, Methodist, Presbyterian, and Episcopal houses of

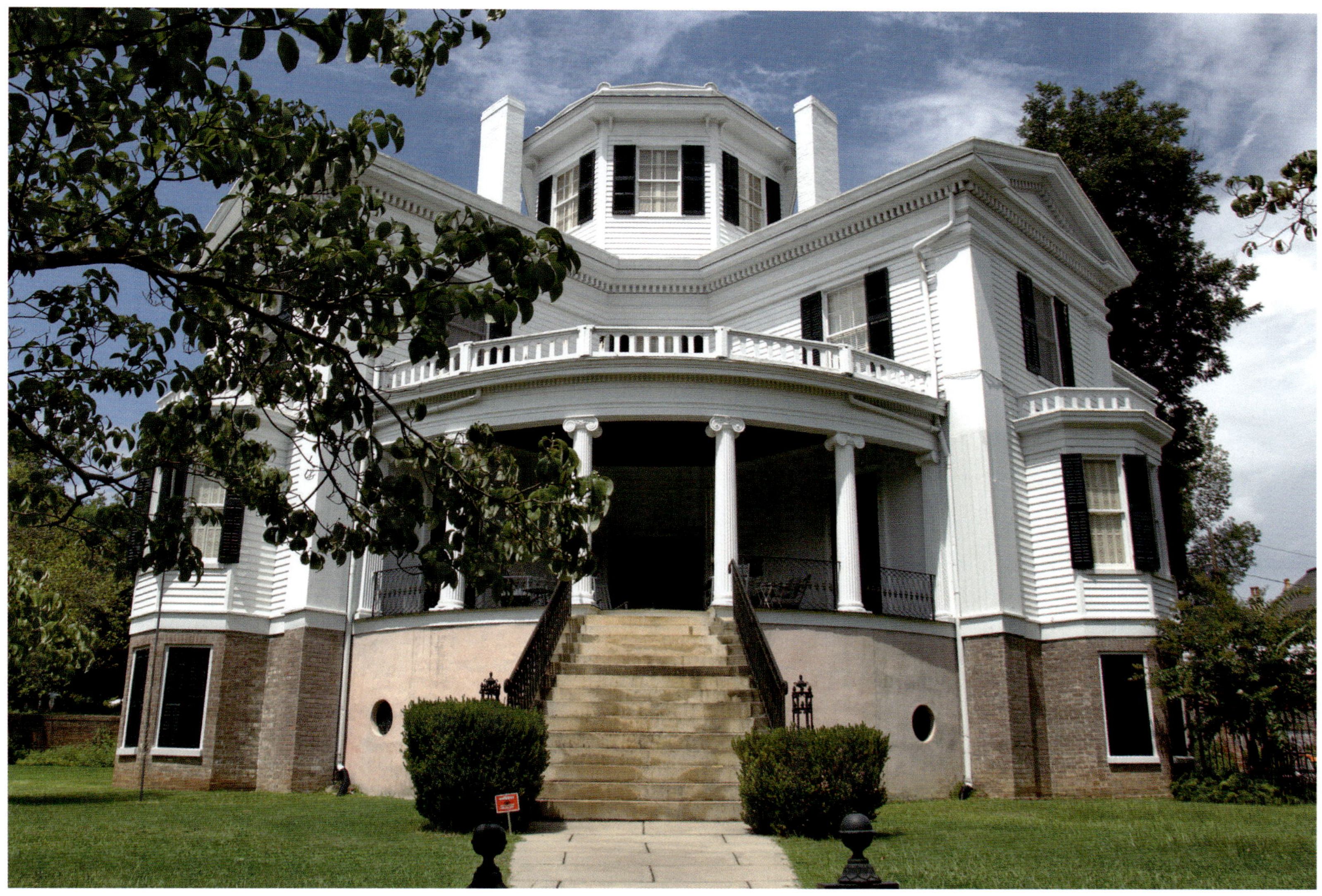

Raines-Miller-Carmichael House, Macon

worship. Savannah's historic district possesses the greatest number of extant antebellum Greek Revival churches of any city in Georgia; these include First Baptist Church (1831–33), Christ Church (1838–41), Trinity Methodist Church (1848–50), and First African Baptist Church (1859–61). The postbellum First Bryan Baptist Church (1873), designed by the Savannah surveyor and civil engineer John B. Hogg (or possibly his colleague John W. Howard), is a stylistic continuation of the antebellum Greek Revival.

Outside of Georgia's cities, a profusion of small Greek Revival wood and masonry churches in far-flung locales attests to the almost universal embrace of the style. Of note is the Madison Presbyterian Church (1841–42), one of several extant antebellum churches in the town of Madison in the center of Georgia's Piedmont region. The church's designer, said to be the local brick mason Daniel Killian, eschewed a projecting classical portico, preferring to show the austere gable end of the structure, which is punctuated with three windows and three doors. A truncated bell tower caps the building's front gable. The *Southern Miscellany* newspaper, celebrating the opening of the church in May 1842, described it as having exterior stucco of a "yellowish color" which is "pleasing to

Madison Presbyterian Church, Madison

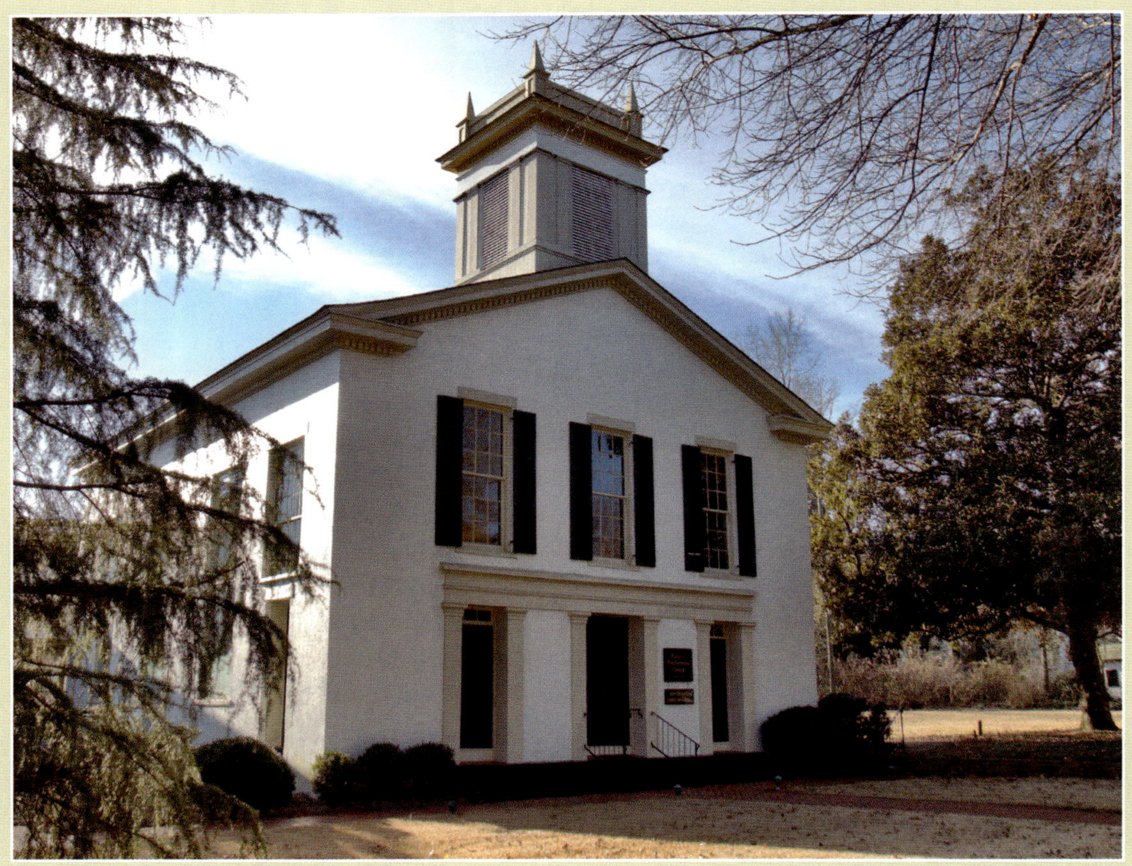

First African Baptist Church, Savannah

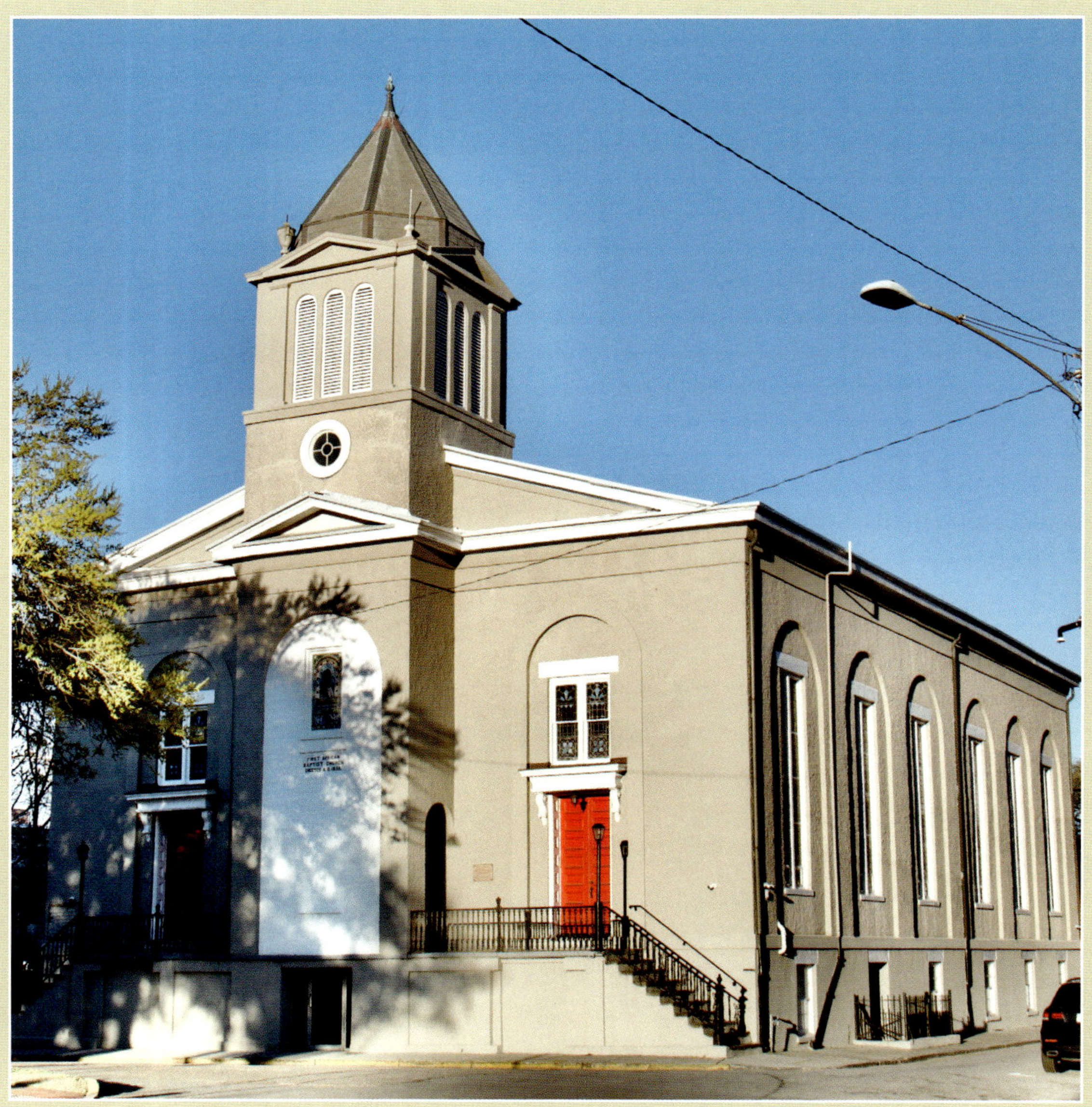

the eye." The stucco remains that color today, still pleasing to the eye, on a building largely unchanged from its opening so many years ago.

First African Baptist Church in Savannah is ambitious yet austere in its employment of the Greek Revival style. The sanctuary was erected in 1859–61 using materials and labor donated by enslaved and free Black craftsmen and laborers in Savannah, members of one of the oldest independent Black Baptist congregations in Georgia. As a work of architecture, First African Baptist embodies the struggle of enslaved and free Blacks in the antebellum era to create independent spaces for assembly, reflection, and spiritual uplift.

The genesis of the First African Baptist congregation dates to 1773, when the enslaved missionary pastor George Liele was first licensed by the Baptists to preach in Georgia. Between 1773 and 1782, Liele converted many free and enslaved Blacks in Savannah and the surrounding plantations to Christianity. After Liele's departure, the congregation coalesced around the charismatic pastorship of Andrew Bryan, who would lead it for the next twenty-four years. Officially organized as First African Baptist Church in 1788, the congregation grew to over two thousand members by the early 1830s.

An intracongregational doctrinal schism in 1832 led to the establishment of First African Baptist Church, separate from the congregation that became known as First Bryan Baptist Church. The departing group, led by Rev. Andrew Cox Marshall, purchased the recently vacated Baptist meeting house on Franklin Square, using the building for the next twenty-seven years. In July 1859 work began on a substantial new building of Savannah gray brick. By March 1860, services were being held in the basement, though the sanctuary was not yet completed. Reports at the time state the new church cost $5,000 to build, with a further $6,000 required to finish it. Most of this expense was borne by the parishioners themselves, through small donations at weekly services.

First African Baptist Church stands as testament to the determination and dedication of its congregants and builders. For more than a year and a half, work crews performed their tasks in the evenings after the end of the workday. No member of the church was wealthy, yet by contributing small sums as able, they collectively effected a great outcome. The completed church, with space to seat seven hundred worshipers, was dedicated in May 1861.

An expansion completed in February 1888 extended the sanctuary rearward by almost 30 feet. The work included the addition of a semioctagonal chancel at the rear of the church featuring two stained-glass windows memorializing the first six pastors of the church. Images of the church from the late nineteenth century show a front with a very different appearance than one sees today. A wood-framed bell tower, added atop the central pavilion in the 1870s, was emphatically vertical, almost exaggeratedly so, made up of stacked box-like sections rising above the brick base and topped with an octagonal spire. In the low-rise Savannah of the late nineteenth century, where church spires were primary architectural landmarks, the tower of First African Baptist was an unapologetic proclamation of its existence and its ambition. Toppled "with a loud crash" in the hurricane of August 1893, the tower was rebuilt in 1925 at a more modest scale.

The Italianate and Gothic Revival in Georgia

The construction of the first American railroads in the late 1820s and early 1830s sparked a revolution in the national culture. The interval for transfer of information between major cities and far-flung locales contracted from weeks to days, and eventually from days to hours. Railroads transformed architecture in Georgia by allowing the rapid movement of people, materials, and information to almost all parts of the state. At the same time, designs in pattern books captured the imagination of affluent Georgians with aspirational tastes. By the 1840s and 1850s, Georgians were able, for the first time, to choose among several popular styles with which to embellish their homes, while the rate at which such idioms went in and out of fashion was significantly shorter than at the beginning of the century.

Of the multitude of eclectic architectures of the age, the Italianate and the Gothic Revival found the greatest purchase among the elites of Georgia's antebellum society. The 1838 publication of *Rural Residences* by the architect Alexander Jackson Davis had an outsize influence in popularizing the Gothic Revival style, especially for its use in picturesque country houses and rural churches. Davis would go on to collaborate with Andrew Jackson Downing, the most significant American landscape architect of the period, in the publication of *Cottage Residences* (1842) and *The Architecture of Country Houses* (1851). In the 1840s and 50s, other architects, including Minard Lafever, Calvert Vaux, D. H. Arnot, and, most significantly, Richard Upjohn, published widely read American pattern books promulgating a menagerie of exotic and picturesque styles, Gothic Revival and Italianate among them. First introduced in Davis's *Rural Residences*, the rustic wooden form of the Gothic Revival, termed Carpenter Gothic, was further popularized by Upjohn in *Upjohn's Rural Architecture* (1852) which specifically illustrated wood-framed Gothic Revival church buildings.

In the 1850s and 1860s, late in the national transition from Greek Revival to the Italianate, more than a few builders in Georgia persisted in their use of the traditional Georgian House building type, even for houses styled in the new fashion. They continued with the fenestration and massing of the Greek Revival while somewhat perfunctorily cladding the main form building with Italianate trappings. The exception to this tendency is most often seen in the treatment of porches and verandas for such houses, where cast-iron filigree was a preferred material. The James Hamilton House, now the Alpha Delta Pi Sorority House in Athens (1857–61), and also the Rankin House (1860–67) in Columbus are archetypical of the phenomenon.

In Savannah, where the configuration of tithing lots was well suited for row-house development, the Italianate idiom supplanted the Greek Revival by the early 1850s. Row houses like the Noble Hardee House (ca. 1860) and trust-lot mansions like John S. Norris's Mercer-Williams House (1860–68), both on Monterey Square, are fine examples of the symmetrical adaptation of the style to brick-and-stucco buildings. Commercial Italianate became so popular that it remained the de facto style for standardized three- and four-story brick commercial buildings until well into the postbellum period.

Rarer in Georgia are examples of residential Italianate in the "Tuscan villa" form, with its picturesque asymmetry, towers, balconettes, loggias, and arched, grouped windows. The Judge Clifford Anderson House (1859) in Macon, is a fine example, though its architectural audacity is somewhat diluted by its use of wood lap siding in lieu of stuccoed brick on the exterior. Perhaps the most elaborate example of a wood-framed Italianate house in Georgia is the postbellum estate West End, now called the Nichols-Hardman Farm, built by Captain James Nichols at the western end of the Nacoochee Valley in 1870.

Though less common in residential use, the Gothic Revival, and especially the Carpenter Gothic, can be found across Georgia. The James Sledge House in Athens (ca. 1860), later owned and restored by the renowned Georgia historian and preservationist Phinizy Spalding, is a high-style example of the story-and-a-half Gothic variant of the Georgian House type. The Sledge House features three very steeply pitched front-facing gables, a hallmark of the type, embellished with decorated barge boards. Its cast-iron filigree porch, though most often associated with Italianate houses, is nonetheless a perfect complement to the eclectic charm of the house.

For obvious reasons of economy, the wood-frame Carpenter Gothic idiom was far more ubiquitous than full-blown Gothic Revival for residences in Georgia, and several fine examples remain. These include the Redmond-Hickman House (1861) in Augusta, the Etheridge-DuBose-Peck House (1853) in Sparta, and the postbellum Wesley O. Connor House (ca. 1869) in Cave Spring.

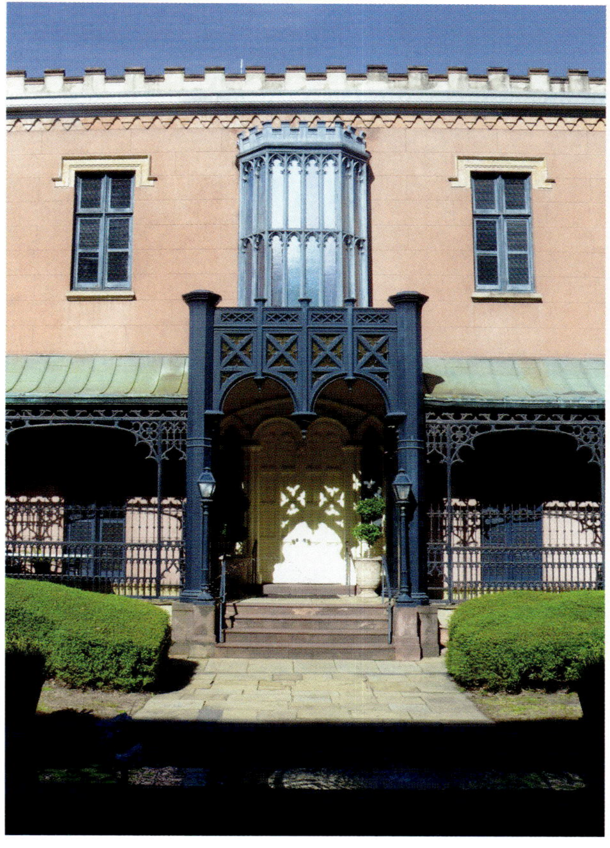

Green-Meldrim House, Savannah, doorway detail

Perhaps the most elaborate example of the residential Gothic Revival in Georgia is the Green-Meldrim House in Savannah, built for the cotton export factor Charles Green. Arriving in Savannah in 1833 from his native Shropshire, England, Green eventually became a partner in the trading firms Andrew Low and Company in Savannah and Isaac, Low and Company in Liverpool. In his role as an export factor, Green played a central role in the international brokerage of cotton from the port of Savannah, and he extracted great wealth from the Southern cotton economy and the system of enslaved labor that underpinned it.

In 1850, Green retained the services of architect John S. Norris to design a large house on a trust lot he had purchased at the northwest corner of Madison Square. Norris arrived in Savannah several years before to work on the U.S. Custom House, and in 1849 he completed a transitional Greek Revival–Italianate house for Green's business partner Andrew Low.

Norris's house for Green is two stories, stucco over brick, with a wraparound cast-iron veranda on its east and south sides. The main mass is crowned in a crenellated Gothic parapet obscuring a low, hipped roof. The stucco is scored to resemble stone and is painted a ruddy pink color. Architectural accents in the facade, including the water table, crenellated parapet, and windowsills and label molds, are carved from buff-color sandstone. A deep two-story rear ell extends from the west side of the house to the back of the lot, originally containing an attached kitchen, carriage house, and quarters for Green's enslaved household staff. Construction on the house began in July 1850 and was largely complete by the beginning of 1854, though Green family records indicate further improvements were made until 1861.

Green's extensive trading connections in the United States and Britain facilitated the importation of exotic marbles, furnishings, and decorative art for the house, resulting in a reported construction cost of $93,000. Certainly no expense was spared in the effusion of molded plasterwork, decorative carvings, and elaborate articulation of floor, wall, and ceiling finishes in the house's interior.

The cast-iron work on the house is notable for the profuse Gothic ornamentation of the veranda and the stout, portcullis-like portico framing the entryway. In an April 1851 article describing the house under construction, the *Savannah Morning Herald* enthusiastically proclaimed, "Its sculptured tracery, its bay and oriel windows, and its elegant outline will give it novel and graceful appearance."

Perhaps the most momentous event in the house's history occurred in the winter of 1864, when General William Tecumseh Sherman was offered its use as his headquarters. Charles Green, for all his personal interest in the perpetuation of the slave economy, was a pragmatic man, and as he was still a citizen of England, he was also ostensibly neutral in the war. Reaching Savannah after his thirty-seven-day March to the Sea, Sherman made use of Green's house from December 22, 1864, until February 1, 1865, and while there he sent his well-known telegraph to President Lincoln presenting "the city of Savannah, with 150 heavy guns and plenty of ammunition, and also about 25,000 bales of cotton" as a Christmas gift.

Also significant in the house's history is the meeting held on January 12, 1865, between Sherman, Secretary of War Edwin M. Stanton, and Black community leaders, mostly Baptist and Methodist pastors from Savannah. This gathering led to Sherman issuing Special Field Order No. 15, which, if it had survived Andrew Johnson's administration, would have reserved a 400,000-acre, 30-mile wide strip of the Sea Islands and mainland, from the south side of Charleston to the Saint Johns River in Florida, to establish landholding among the formerly enslaved. It was a bold vision that, if followed through, would have radically transformed the South's postbellum political landscape.

Located on the southwest trust lot of Madison Square, Saint John's Episcopal Church has anchored the west side of Madison Square with the Green-Meldrim House since the 1850s. Construction of the church, designed by the Buffalo, New York, ecclesiastical architect Calvin N. Otis, began in 1851, and it was consecrated in May 1853, a year before the substantial completion of Green's house. Saint John's purchased the Green-Meldrim House in 1943, ten years after the death of prominent Savannah jurist and politician Peter Meldrim, who had occupied it since 1892. The parish maintains the house to the present, with the

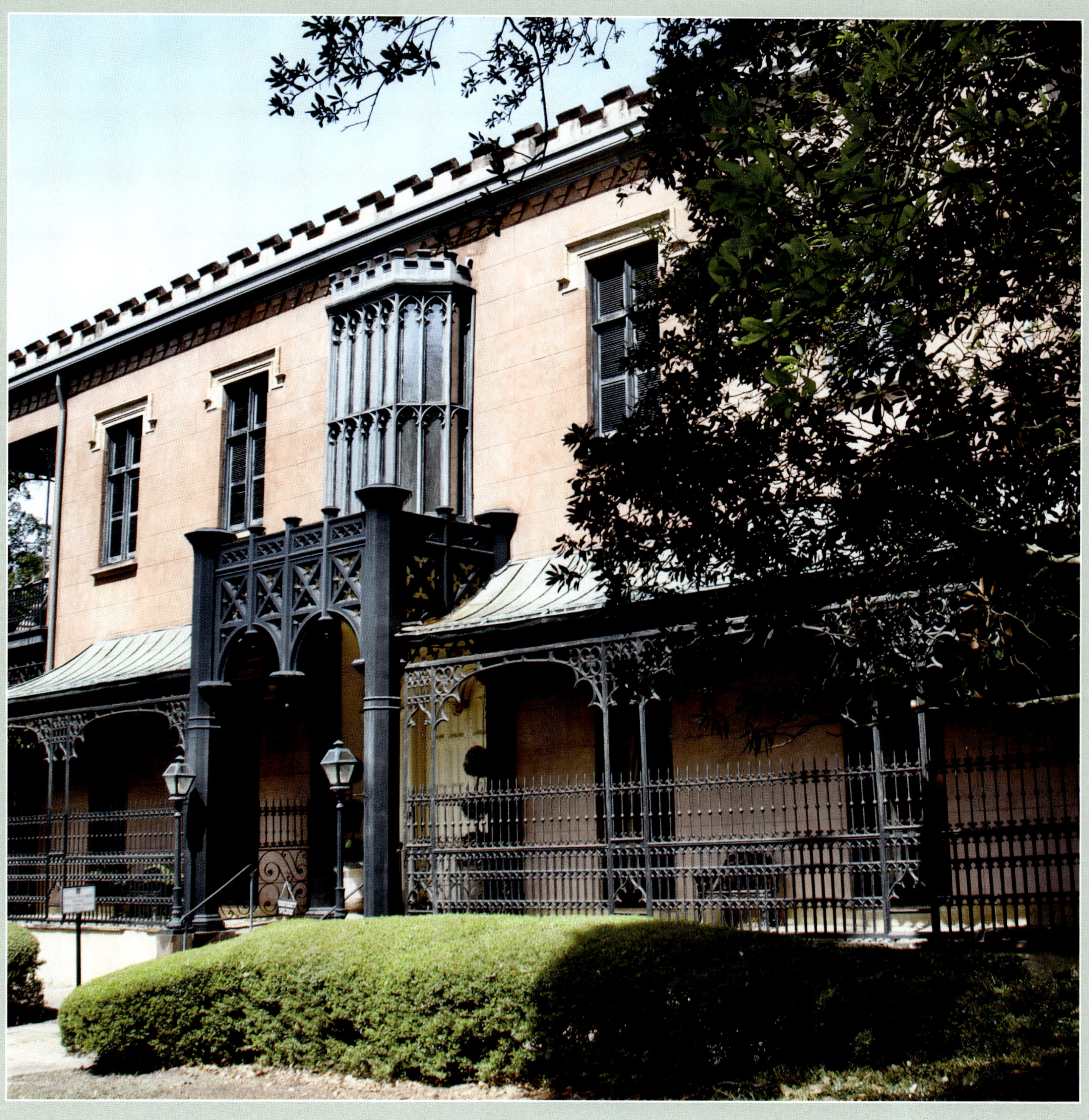

Green-Meldrim House, Savannah

carriage house wing used as the residence for the rector. The main house is open regularly for public tours.

By the late 1850s, Columbus had grown from the frontier settlement it had been thirty years prior to the third-largest city in the state. Its location along the falls of the Chattahoochee River, with rail connections to Macon and Montgomery and steamboat access to the Gulf of Mexico, made it a hub of agricultural, commercial, and industrial activity in the western section of the state and eastern Alabama in the decades leading up to the Civil War. The city attracted a mix of planters, entrepreneurs, professionals, businessmen, and industrialists who erected commercial buildings and residences to reflect their prosperity.

The Italianate mansion Dinglewood was built in 1858–59 for the planter Joel Early Hurt on his suburban estate in Wynnton, then situated a mile east of Columbus proper. The firm of Barringer & Morton, well known locally for both residential and commercial work in the growing city, designed and built the house. Samuel Hatcher, a fellow planter and associate of Hurt, may have assisted in the design. The mansion boasts many features of high-style Italianate: deep roof overhangs, curvilinear brackets; half-round arched windows, an ornate cupola, and candelabra columns along its wraparound veranda. The exterior walls are stuccoed brick now painted a soft pink color.

Dinglewood's main two-story block is organized as a Georgian House type, although here it is supplemented with a one-story range of rooms arrayed across the back of the first floor. The left (west) side of the house contains a grand double parlor with large pocket doors separating the front and back rooms, while a curving mahogany stair dominates the central hall. The rear range consists of three rooms: a dining room on the west, a reception hall behind the central hall, and a bedroom on the east. Both dining room and bedroom feature bay windows overlooking formerly sweeping side yards. These views are now obscured by residences built in the early twentieth century when Dinglewood's property was subdivided. Unusually, a porte cochere is centered at the back of the house, so that visitors entering this way first enter the rear reception hall before moving into either the dining room or the central hall.

The house's interior decor features elaborate ceiling plasterwork, Carrara marble mantles, and gilded mantel and pier mirrors. The scale of the parlor rooms is majestic, with enormous pocketed hung sash windows extending to the floor where they overlook the veranda. One of the most gracious of Southern antebellum architectural features, these portal windows, when fully open, allow for maximum airflow and easy movement between the interior and exterior. A report in the *Columbus Daily Times* from September 1860 reports that Hurt's "splendid mansion" included "all the modern city improvements" including a gas works to convert coal to gas for use in interior lighting. The article further reports the house cost $30,000 to build.

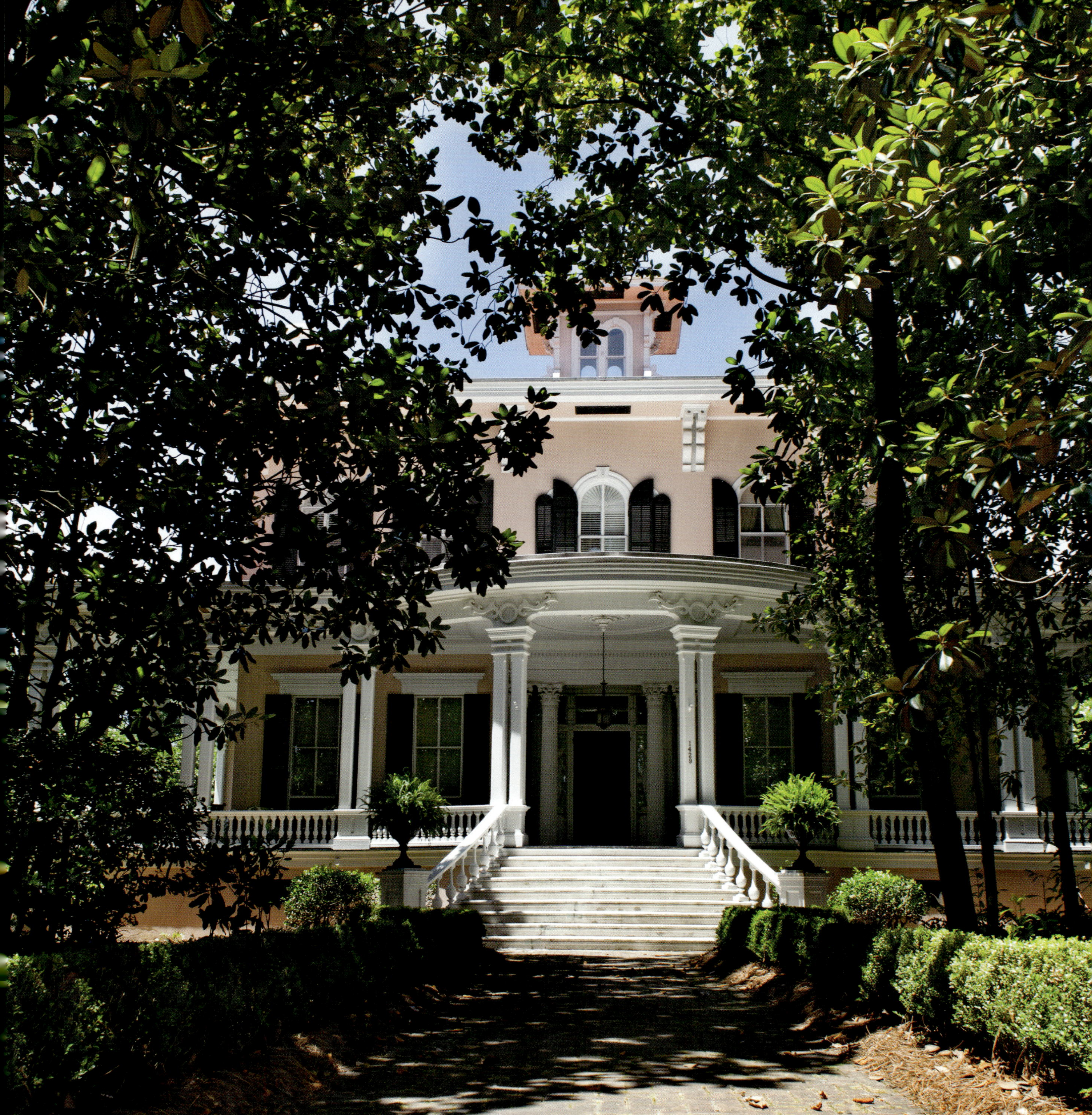

Dinglewood, Columbus

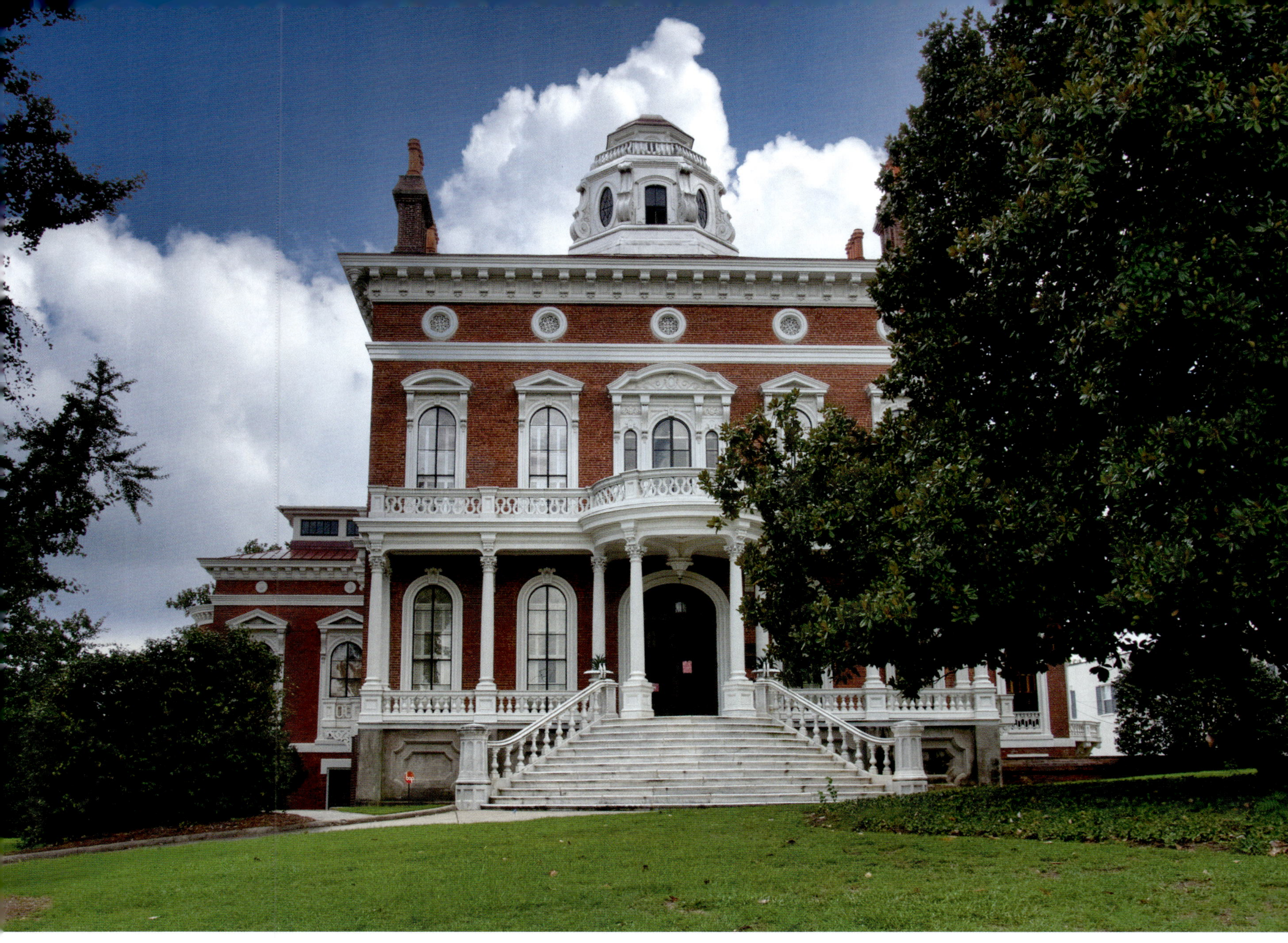

Johnston-Felton-Hay House, Macon

The Johnston-Felton-Hay House (1855–59) is a superlative example of what might be termed the Baroque phase of Italianate in American architecture. Aesthetically, this elaborate palace counts among its kindred the Morse-Libby Mansion (1858–60) in Portland, Maine, and perhaps even The Breakers (1893–95) in Newport, Rhode Island. All three buildings combine romanticized elements of the rural Italian villa with those of the urban palazzo into a particularly Americanized idiom, less formal and academically precise than the Italian Renaissance Revival.

The Johnston-Felton-Hay House was as fashionable a house as existed in America at the time, and to Maconites more accustomed to grand but dated Greek Revival houses, it must have seemed like something from a fever dream. For its design, William Butler Johnston, an extraordinarily successful Macon businessman, sought out the services of the prolific New York architecture firm T. Thomas and Son, well-known as the designers of hotels, banks, and large residences in that city. Johnston traveled often for business and was known to have stayed at New York hotels designed by his future architects, including the mammoth, 1,000-room Saint Nicholas Hotel (1853). In his letters from New York to his new wife Anne, Johnston boasts "Mr. Thomas says that my plan will make one of the best arranged houses he has ever seen and would be a splendid plan for a New York house."

The architecture firm of T. Thomas and Son was comprised of the Welsh-born Thomas and his London-born son Griffith Thomas, with the possible inclusion of another architect son, Thomas Jr. The elder Thomas had arrived in New York around 1833, in his early fifties, with Griffith joining the firm in 1838. Griffith Thomas, thirty-seven years younger than his father, was likely the firm's lead designer by the time of Johnston's commission, and he took over full operation of the practice by 1860. His design for the Emerson-Holmes Building in downtown Macon, employing an inventive Italianate idiom comparable to the Johnston house, was completed in 1859.

In 1851, William Butler Johnston had married Anne Clark Tracy, daughter of a prominent local jurist, the late Judge Edward Tracy. Marrying for the first time at age forty-one, Johnston had already achieved the social status and material wealth to allow the newlyweds to embark upon an extended grand tour of Europe for their honeymoon, departing New York for London in November 1851 and then moving on to Paris, Avignon, Marseilles, Nice, Genoa, Florence, and Rome, with subsequent stops in Germany. They returned to Macon in early 1854 after three years away. Such an opulent lifestyle was new to Johnston, who, though he was counted among Macon's citizens of means, was recorded in the 1850 census as having resided in a boarding house.

While abroad, the Johnstons took in a full complement of fashionable social engagements, but more importantly for the future house in Macon, they saw up-to-date examples of European art, architecture, and technology. While in London in 1852, they visited the Crystal Palace Exhibition in Hyde Park, where they would have seen, as its official title proclaims, "works of industry of all nations." Almost certainly the couple conversed about the house they would build upon their return, and they began to purchase furnishings, artwork, and materials to fill it.

The property upon which the Johnstons built their house was gifted to Anne by her father. The large trapezoidally shaped parcel, totaling 3.8 acres, combined four separate city lots. In the early 1840s Judge Tracy built a wood-frame house there, which was moved to Mulberry Lane prior to construction of the new house. Though situated less prominently than its neighbor the Cowles-Bond-Woodruff House, the new Johnston house, with its crowning octagonal cupola, nonetheless commanded a beautiful prospect of the city.

William Butler Johnston himself appears to have played an outsize role in the design of his new house, decamping to New York in the fall of 1855 to "oversee" the completion of drawings. It is unknown whether such micromanagement was appreciated by his highly competent architect, but Johnston returned to Macon in November of that year, drawings in hand, ready to commence the work. Johnston took free rein in modifying Thomas's design to suit his taste. He engaged the local builder-architect James B. Ayres to execute the work, and it is likely that Ayres's expertise as a designer in his own right facilitated the changes Johnston made to the finished house. Most significantly, Johnston chose to build a brick masonry structure rather than a wood-framed, lap-sided one, with the surface of the brick stuccoed to resemble brownstone. This original finish was replaced before 1876 with red stucco scored with white joints to mimic tight-jointed red finish brick. Remnants of this faux-brick treatment, though heavily eroded, can be seen on the house today.

The house is superlative in myriad ways. It was perhaps the most technologically advanced private residence in the state at the time, with hot and cold running water, indoor bathrooms, gas lighting, and central heat. The kitchen, typically detached or semidetached in more modest dwellings, was incorporated into the capacious basement level, along with ample pantry and storage space. Gas lighting was incorporated into the original construction, a logical extension of Johnston's earlier investment in the Macon Gas Light Company, the first gas utility in the city.

Johnston's association with James B. Ayres likely began in the 1840s with the start of construction on the first water system in Macon, for which Ayres was one of the chief contractors and Johnston eventually an investor. By the 1850s the system supplied water from spring-fed cisterns at the base of College Hill to much of the city. A still extant brick pump house, located near the site of Johnston's future house, was built circa 1854 to provide pressure for the municipal water mains. On the northwest corner of his own property, Johnston eventually built a grotto-like spring house dug into the hill slope, creating a picturesque water feature in his garden. The spring, still flowing today, served as a water source for both the house and the city system. Outflow from the spring was pumped into a 20,000-gallon copper tank in Johnston's attic, providing ample water pressure for plumbing fixtures located on lower levels of the house. It was not until the 1880s that the house was connected to Macon's municipal water system.

At 18,000 square feet, Johnston's house was the largest built in Georgia up to that time. It is organized into a central block of three floors on a raised basement, while symmetrical two-story side wings, also on raised basements, bookend a two-story central rear ell located behind the main house block. A two-story octagonal cupola crowns the hipped roof, and its lower tier is buttressed with oversized inverted consoles. At the roof's edge, a substantial cornice is supported on tightly spaced console brackets.

The front facade is five bays wide, with arched windows framed in stout stone casings with carved keystones. Second-floor windows are capped with pediments on console brackets, while the third-floor features round openings disguised to look like attic vents. Enormous arched entry doors, perhaps designed in homage to those at Rome's Pantheon, convey the illusion of riveted bronze, yet are expertly faux-finished wood. An elaborate balustraded front porch, supported on eight Corinthian columns on plinths, extends across the entirety of

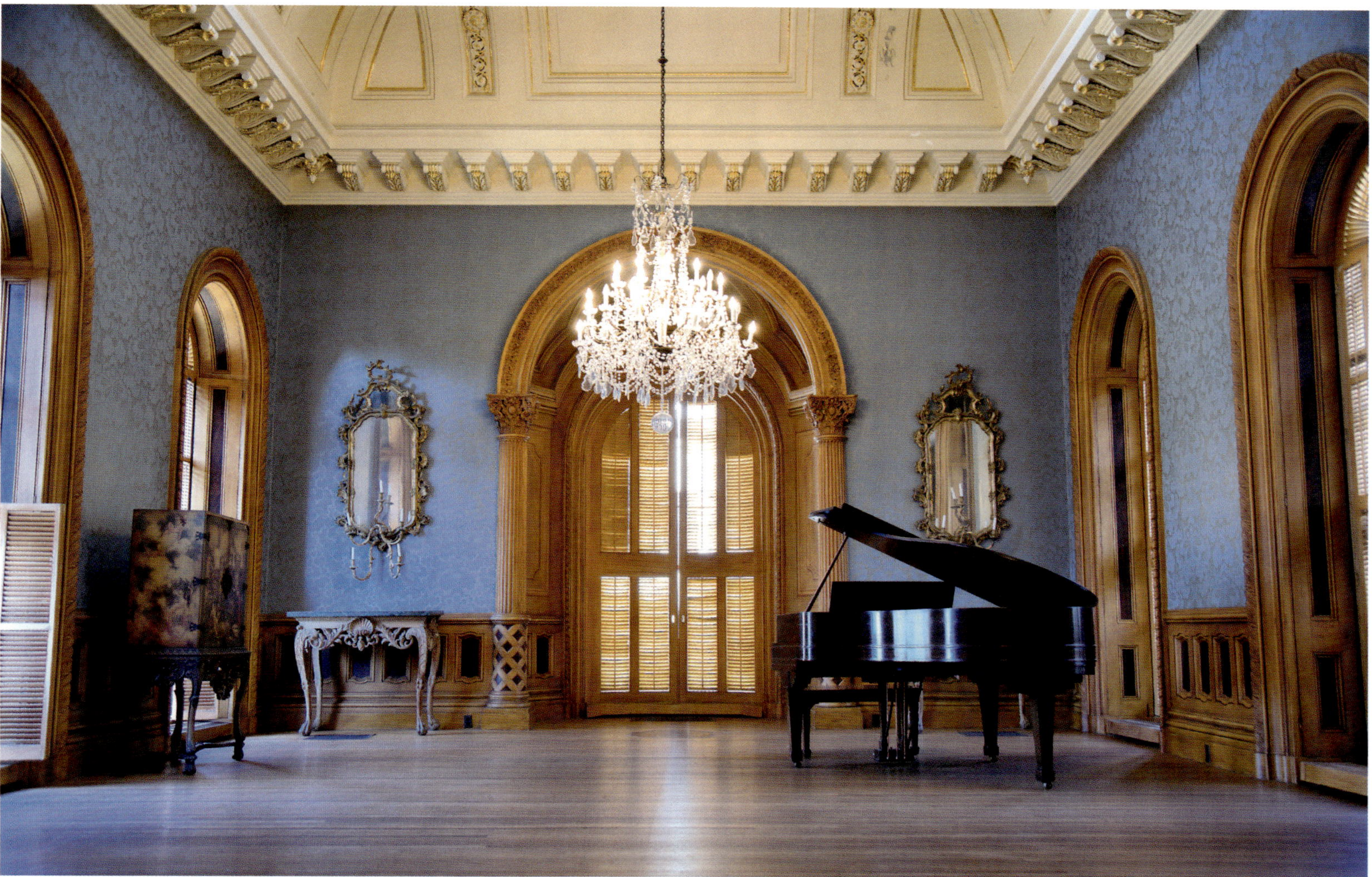

Johnston-Felton-Hay House, Macon

the first-floor facade. Its semicircular middle bay swells outward, and a grand stone stair cascades to the ground.

Monumental in scale, palatial in decor, the twenty-four-room house cost a reputed $100,000 to build and another $100,000 to furnish, exceeding even the sum Charles Green lavished upon his residence in Savannah. No expense was spared in acquiring artwork, furnishings, and craftsmen, both American and European, to embellish practically every interior surface. The roster included Auguste Tripod, a Swiss decorative painter, who created the trompe l'oeil variegated marble walls in the entry hall. It is a curious fact of the age that Johnston could have afforded to adorn his house with real marble panels, yet it was the illusion conveyed in Tripod's work that was the more valued.

The builder-architect James Ayres, like his older colleague Elam Alexander, employed enslaved craftsmen in his building projects, either as his personal property or hired from other slaveholders. While Ayres's use of enslaved labor is unremarkable for the era, that two of these men are today known to us by name is precious and rare. Primus Moore, a plasterer, and Ben Jackson, a carpenter, are known to have assisted in the creation of the Johnston house. Primus Moore's skills were well-regarded locally, and he continued in his trade after Emancipation.

The Johnston daughters, Mary Ellen and Carrie, remained part of the household even after marriage. Several years after William Butler Johnston's death in 1887, Carrie and husband George Duncan were removed to their own house nearby, while Mary Ellen and husband William Felton remained in the family home. Anne Tracy Johnston and her widowed brother-in-law Dr. John Baxter, a frequent business partner of her husband, also resided in the palatial home, until both died in 1896.

In 1901 the two Johnston daughters split the property, with Mary Ellen retaining the southern half, including the house, and Carrie receiving the northern half containing the gardens and spring house, in addition to a cash settlement. Carrie subdivided her half of the property into four lots along Georgia Avenue and three along Cherry Street. The new house eventually built at the corner of Nisbet Place and Georgia Avenue was constructed over Johnston's arcaded spring-house grotto, which is partially extant today in its subbasement.

Between 1901 and 1912 the Feltons undertook a campaign of alterations to make the house more comfortable for their personal use. In addition to significant alterations to the rear, the work included first-time electrification as well as replumbing bathrooms with modern fixtures and piping systems. Interior finishes were remodeled to reflect sensibilities of the day. After the deaths of Mary Ellen and William Felton, both in 1926, the house was purchased by Macon banker and insurance executive Parks Lee Hay. Making interior-design and landscape alterations to suit their tastes, Parks Lee Hay and his wife Maude occupied the house until their deaths in 1957 and 1962, respectively.

Maude Hay's death came during the urban-renewal scourge, when American cities and towns large and small eviscerated their architectural histories while chasing the dream of modernist prosperity. Fortunately, the Hay family, recognizing this existential threat, established the P. L. Hay Foundation to convert the house into a viable house museum and tourist attraction. The Johnston-Felton-Hay House was listed on the National Register in 1971 and declared a National Historic Landmark in 1974. In 1977, the Hay Foundation conveyed title to the property, by then simply known as the Hay House, to the Georgia Trust for Historic Preservation. For forty-four years the Georgia Trust has interpreted, preserved, and restored this one-of-a-kind Georgia landmark.

Also of note is the Slate House (ca. 1855), an antebellum grouping of row houses constructed by James Ayres as rental quarters for craftsmen working on the Johnston House. The row features a slate-clad mansard roofline typical of the Americanized version of the Second Empire style. Whether the roof form is original to the Slate House row or was a later modification is unknown, but, if original, it may be one of the earliest extant examples of that roof form in the United States, predating construction of the Corcoran Gallery (now the Renwick Gallery) in Washington, D.C. (1859), by several years.

In Georgia, the construction of Federal-style and Greek Revival churches was ubiquitous until the 1840s, when ecclesiastical forms of the Gothic Revival first appeared in the state. This is roughly concurrent with the national popularity of

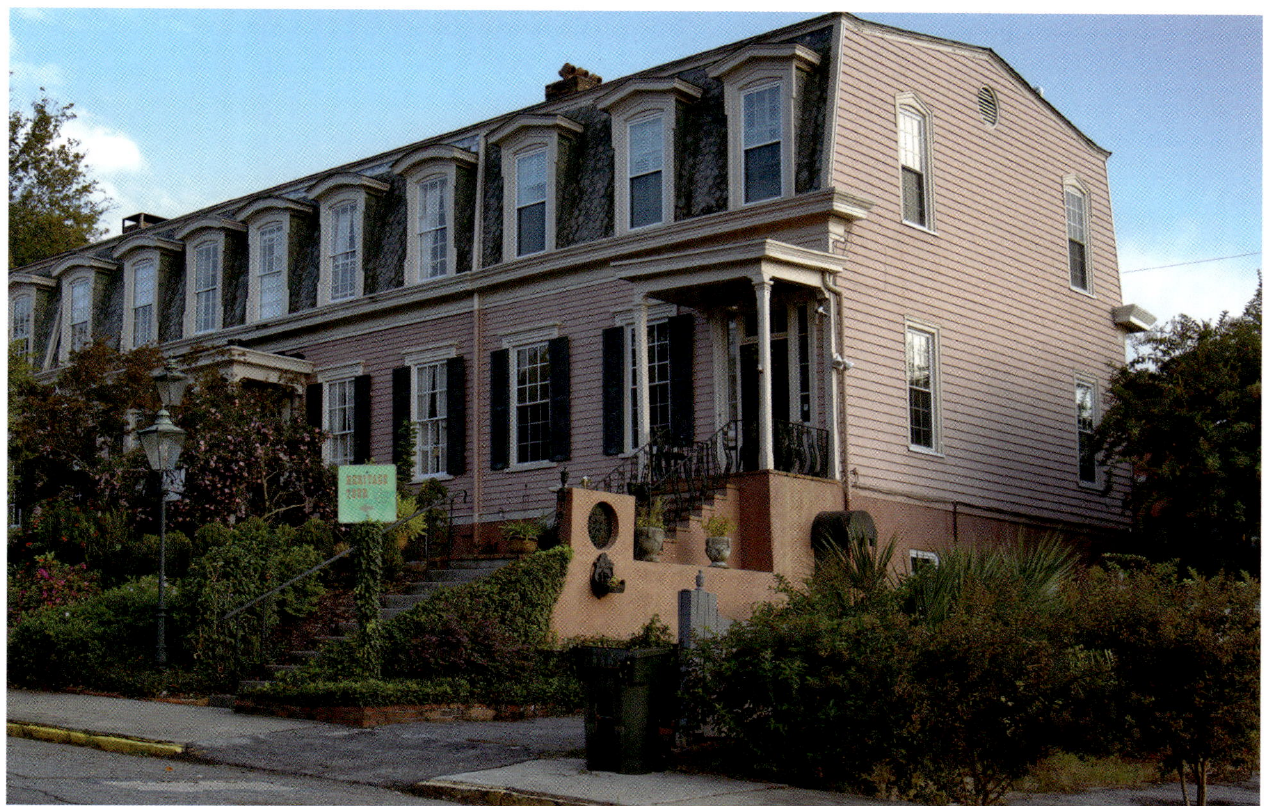

Slate House, Macon

the style, illustrating that builders in Georgia were staying abreast of new architectural trends. The prescient Gothic Revival remodeling of the Old Capitol in Milledgeville in the late 1820s and early 1830s likely influenced the design of Saint Stephen's Episcopal Church (1841–43), the oldest Carpenter Gothic building in Georgia. Damaged by United States troops during Sherman's March to the Sea, Saint Stephen's still graces Statehouse Square adjacent to the Old Capitol. Methodists in Madison built one of the earliest Gothic Revival churches in Georgia in about 1844. The building was later sold to Episcopalians and now serves as the Church of the Advent.

The 1850s saw the construction of numerous Gothic Revival churches, including the Unitarian Universalist Church (1850–51) in Savannah, Christ Church (1851) in Macon, and the previously mentioned Saint John's Church (1851–53) in Savannah. In the postbellum period and into the twentieth century, the Gothic Revival remained popular in Georgia for both Catholic and Protestant churches, as well as at least one synagogue, Congregation Mickve Israel in Savannah, designed by the architect Henry Harrison and built in 1876–78.

A very fine Carpenter Gothic church can be found in Talbotton, thirty-five miles northeast of Columbus. Construction on Zion Episcopal Church began in 1848 under the supervision of the builder James Cottingham with the assistance of the plasterer and brick mason Miranda Fort. Bishop Stephen Elliott, in his 1853 address to the convention of the Episcopal Diocese of Georgia, recounted his travel to Talbotton that year to consecrate the new church, a "very pretty house of worship," as he called it, and he made special note of the "indefatigable

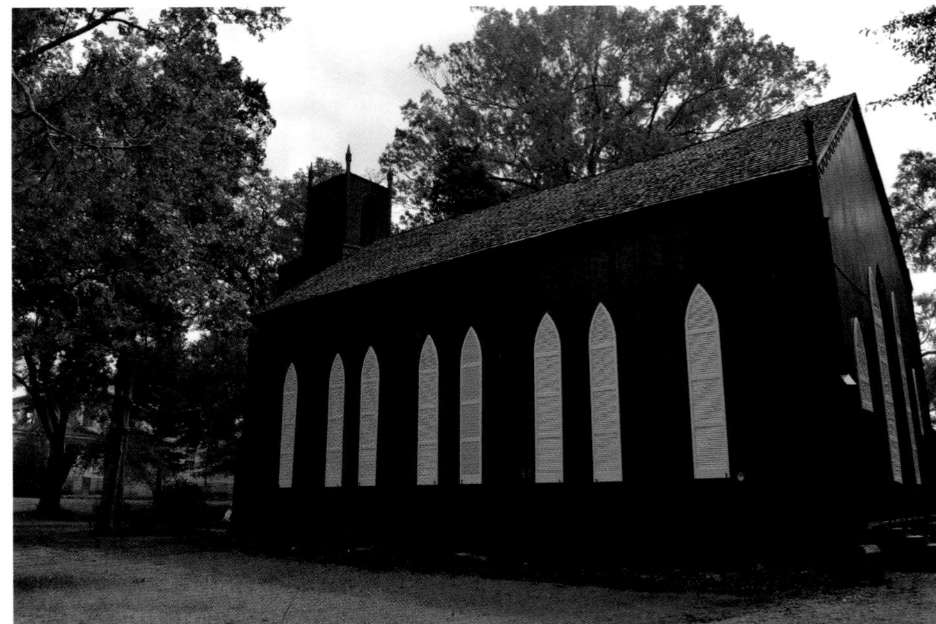

Zion Episcopal Church, Talbotton

exertions" of the founding rector, Rev. Richard Johnson, to raise the funds that made the new building possible. At the 1848 diocesan convention, Johnson reported that he had raised $1,800 by subscription to begin construction of the new church.

Zion Episcopal Church is simple in form, consisting of a rectangular gabled sanctuary with a boxy, stepped tower at its front. The simple, cubic belfry, perched atop the tower, is bluntly capped with a shallow hipped roof not visible from the ground. Rather, each of its corners is fit with an octagonal post extending several feet higher than the roof and terminating in a finial. Crenellated bands near the top of each finial resemble crowns, perhaps an allegorical motif. This feature is repeated above each corner buttress on the body of the sanctuary, rising above the roofline and emphatically pointing skyward.

The church's exterior walls are sided in vertical pine planks fit tightly together without protective wood battens covering the seams. This hints that Zion's builders may have used hidden splines or tongue-and-groove planks to prevent water from seeping into the joints. Photographs indicate that, until at least 1936 and possibly as late as the 1950s, the church's exterior was unpainted, somehow maintaining its integrity after possibly a hundred years of weather exposure. By the 1960s, however, the building's exterior had been painted dark brown, as it remains today. Exterior restoration work undertaken in 2019–20 included caulking the plank seams and repainting the building.

Zion's interior survives in its unpainted form, imbuing it with the warm ambiance of pine, walnut, and cedar, remnants of Georgia's antebellum old-growth forests. A shallow vestibule inside the front door contains a pair of winding stairs leading to the organ loft above and two galleries extending along the sides of the church. The sanctuary is still fitted with its original walnut box pews, while the galleries above are equipped with simple bench-like pews once used by enslaved worshipers attending services. At the chancel, the communion rail features a trefoil shape repeated in the gallery railings and window heads. The walnut altar is paneled to match. Modified scissor trusses, sawn from white cedar, support the roof.

In the gallery above the church entrance is a hand-pumped pipe organ installed in 1850. Designed and built by Henry Pilcher, an English-born maker working primarily in the northeastern United States, the Zion Episcopal Church organ is the oldest surviving example of a Pilcher instrument in the country.

At Zion, there was clearly a desire to create a "correct" Gothic church, yet the idiom was unfamiliar to those tasked with building it. The poignant tension between ambition and ability is reflected in the builders' translation of complex shapes into simpler, flattened forms that could be rendered in the materials locally available. The passage of time has imbued once-common pine and walnut woods with an aura of permanence and profundity. Taken as a whole, Zion Episcopal Church transcends the limitations of its architectural conventions to become a masterpiece of vernacular invention.

Antebellum Public Buildings

In 1785, Georgia was first in the nation to charter a state-supported institution of higher education, the University of Georgia. While the state set aside 40,000 acres to endow this institution, the actual location of the school was not determined until 1801, when 633 acres of a tract selected by John Milledge was transferred to the board of trustees. The new university developed concurrently with a new town, Athens, situated on hilly terrain between the North and Middle branches of the Oconee River. Until the land cession of 1783, the site of Athens was part of the Cherokee territory, traversed by a trading path that eventually became the Federal Road, which connected Athens to Nashville via Chattanooga.

The campus of the University of Georgia that developed over the first half of the nineteenth century is remarkably intact despite a wide disparity in the ages and styles of its constituent buildings. Concentrated in the area now known as North Campus, they include the first permanent structure built for the university, Old College (originally Franklin College), as well as additional classroom and dormitory buildings; professor's residences; the chapel; several iterations of the first libraries; and the homes of the first two literary (or debating) societies at the university. Building styles reflect the changing tastes of the antebellum era, including the anachronistic, simplified Georgian styling of Old College, the Federal style of Demosthenian Hall (1824), and the Greek Revival temple represented by the Chapel (1832–35).

For the first fifteen years of its existence, the University of Georgia was an institution on paper only, as no buildings had been built for its use and no faculty hired to provide instruction. Funding for university operations was to be provided by the sale of lots in the new town, creating an alternatingly symbiotic/parasitic relationship between the two that continues to the present. Throughout the antebellum period the university platted and sold new city lots, both to finance capital projects and to allow for the expansion of the rapidly growing town.

University president Josiah Meigs, a graduate of Yale College, worked with the builder-architect Jett Thomas and the contractor John Billups to determine the configuration and appearance of Franklin College. Meigs patterned the building using Yale's Connecticut Hall (1752) as his model. When completed in 1806, Franklin College joined an assortment of simple log and wood-framed structures commissioned in previous years, including a dwelling for Meigs and a story-and-a-half log classroom building.

Ambitious in scale though subdued in styling, Franklin College loomed large, three stories of Flemish-bond brick perched on a rise overlooking the new town. As a building, it was almost bereft of stylistic affectation, beyond jack-arched lintels above windows and doors and belt courses at each floor. Regardless, the completion of the college in 1806 was met with much jubilation and praise, especially by Meigs himself, who reported in the *Augusta Chronicle* that "better accommodations for students cannot be found in any College in the United States." Certainly in comparison to the wood structures making up the remainder of the University of Georgia, Franklin College was a palace.

In 1908, an ill-considered renovation of the building replaced most of the exterior brick skin, a change that is immediately apparent when comparing brick of the early nineteenth century to that of the twentieth. A later renovation in the 1940s effectively gutted the interior and removed the chimneys, so that in the present day only the foundation and roof are original. Nevertheless, the much-abused building still stands as a reflection of the University's ambitious origins.

After a moribund period resulting from the upheaval of the War of 1812, the 1820s saw a stabilization of the university's fortunes and an increase in the student body. The need for new space resulted the construction of Philosophical Hall (now Waddel Hall) in 1821 to provide facilities for the university library, as well as scientific instruction and storage of necessary equipment. In keeping with the architectural conservatism of Franklin College, builders designed Philosophical Hall in a simplified Federal style, barely identifiable as part of the idiom so fashionable at the time.

In 1823, the construction of New College resulted in Franklin College being rechristened "Old College," the name it retains to this day. Similar in scale and layout to its predecessor, New College perpetuated the architectural simplicity of previous university buildings, barely Federal in stylistic aspiration but differentiated from its predecessors in the use of scored stucco to mimic the look of dressed stone. Destroyed by fire in 1830, the building was reconstructed as originally built. Oriented perpendicularly to Old College, the siting of New College initiated the practice of fronting most new university buildings along a line roughly centered on the axis of College Street. By the 1850s, the expanding campus included new buildings located to the east and south of Old College, including housing for professors and the university president.

Exhibiting greater architectural distinction than its predecessors is Demosthenian Hall, completed in 1824 as the home for the Demosthenian Literary Society, a debating society founded in the earliest days of the university. An 1820 schism in the membership led to the creation of the Phi Kappa Literary Society, whose 1836 building is reposed in permanent opposition to Demosthenian Hall. Built of stuccoed brick, Demosthenian Hall is a fine example of the Federal style, which less than a decade later would be subsumed by the Greek Revival. The hall's simple exterior betrays little of the fine period detail of the interior. The debate hall, occupying the full area of the second floor, is decorated with an effusion of fully realized Federal ornament, including a trapezoidally vaulted plaster ceiling featuring molded plaster swags, elaborate cornicework, and deeply carved striated casings at windows and doors. This is one of the finest extant Federal interiors in the Piedmont, on par with those in Augusta and environs.

Demosthenian Hall, University of Georgia, Athens

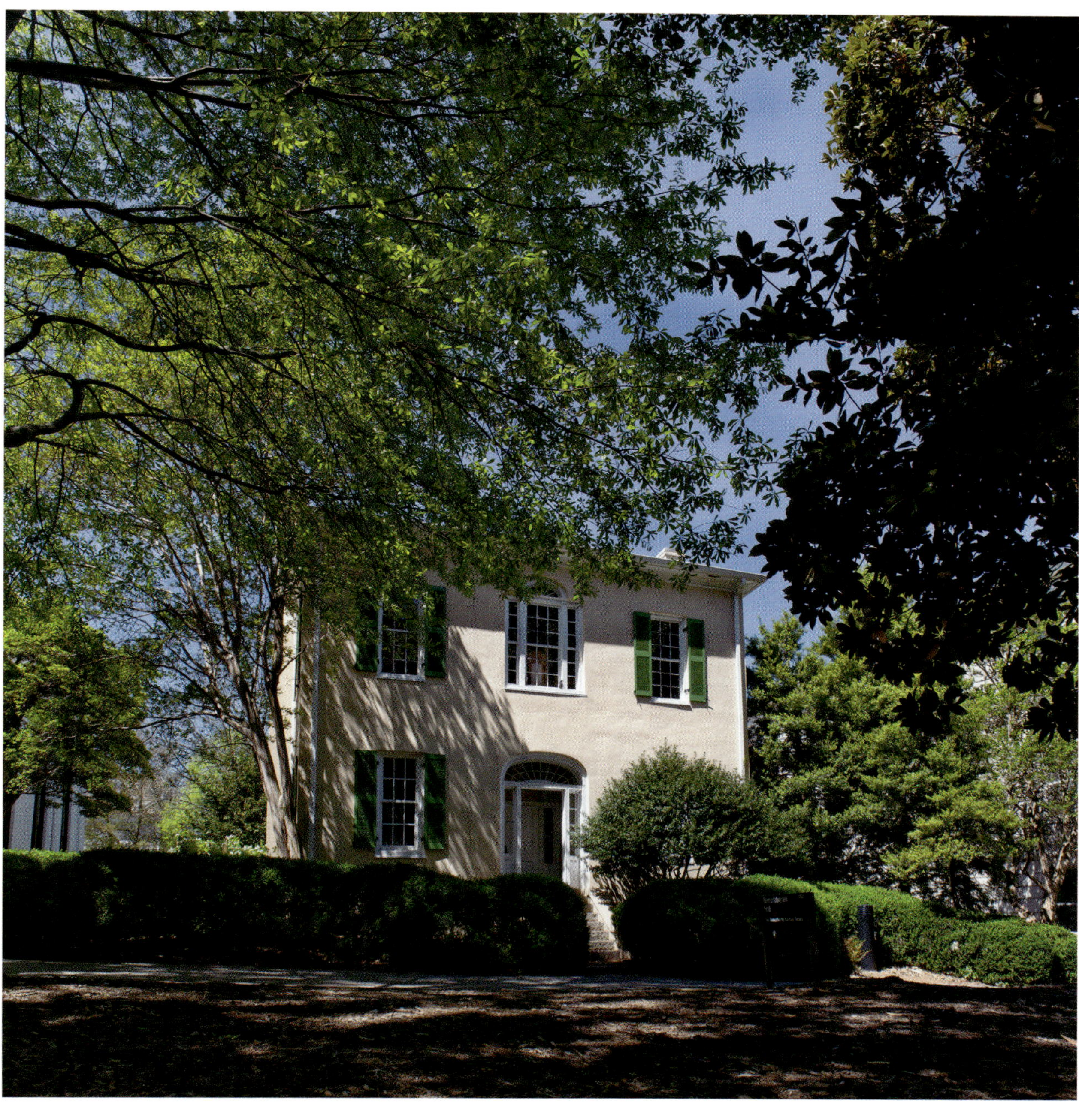

The Greek Revival arrived in Athens with the construction of four new buildings in the style, beginning in the 1830s: Ivy Hall (1831), the Chapel (1832–35), Phi Kappa Hall (1836), and eventually the Library Building (1862). The solid, imposing Chapel replaced a wood-framed building that had burned in 1830. James R. Carlton and Benjamin Towns designed and built the Chapel while Towns was concurrently the architect-builder of the U.S. Mint in Dahlonega. Because fire was such a common hazard in an age when open flame was used for heating in every inhabited building, the new Chapel, resembling a Greek temple of the Doric order, was designed to be as fireproof as possible. The building's shell, including walls, columns, entablature, and the pediment tympanum, is rendered entirely in stuccoed brick. However, in contrast to other, more ambitiously fireproof buildings of the era, the Chapel's floor and roof structure remained conventionally combustible.

Taken as a whole, the Chapel is well-proportioned, but the builders' decision to use brick for elements that would normally be rendered in carved stone or wood imparts the building's classical details with an abstract quality. Nonetheless, the arrival of such a substantial structure in the midst of the expanding campus immediately made it a landmark, and, as such, the zero-mile marker for the city of Athens was relocated to a spot at the base of the front steps.

As originally built, an attractive wood bell tower perched atop the Chapel's portico, but it was removed in 1913 due to structural deterioration. The tradition of ringing the Chapel bell to celebrate gridiron victories was noted as early as 1894 and continues to the present, though the bell is now mounted in a pylon-like wood structure at the rear of the Chapel.

Following its establishment in 1820, the Phi Kappa Literary Society occupied a series of impermanent accommodations, which ended with the 1836 construction of the Phi Kappa Hall. Prominent alumni of the society funded the new structure, which was located directly opposite rival Demosthenian Hall. Architecturally, the temple-like Phi Kappa Hall is vernacular Greek Revival in style. Built of brick laid in a common bond pattern, Phi Kappa's facade features a portico supported by four unfluted stuccoed brick columns. The proportions and details of the columns and the pediment are an idiosyncratic interpretation of the Greek Doric, and its execution in this case exhibits the builder's unfamiliarity with the system of proportions intrinsic to the academic exercise of classical architecture.

The oppositional arrangement of Demosthenian Hall and Phi Kappa Hall, like duelists eying one another across the grounds, was repeated at Emory College (now Oxford College of Emory University) in Oxford, Georgia. There, the Few Literary Society Hall (1850) faces off with its rival Phi Gamma Hall (1851) across the campus quadrangle. Phi Gamma Hall, recently restored, is a fine example the *distyle in antis* Greek temple form. The lightness and refinement of its Ionic pediment and entablature are in marked contrast to the more ponderous solidity of buildings in the Greek Doric order.

The University of Georgia's iconic three-legged cast-iron Arch, representing the three branches of state government and its philosophical pillars (Wisdom,

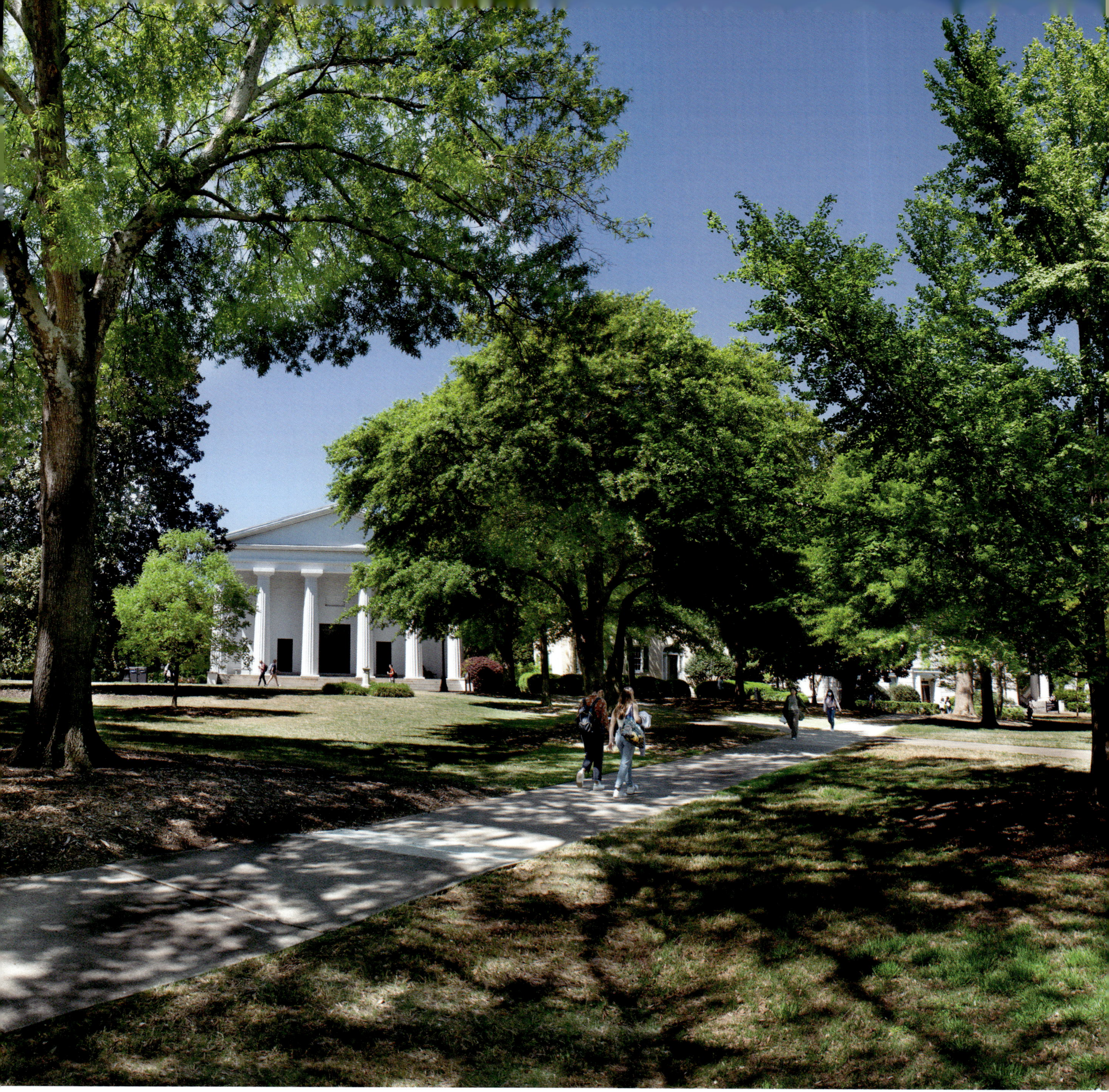

University of Georgia Chapel, Athens

Justice, Moderation) was locally fabricated in 1857. Erected as part of a larger fencing project to prevent the town's cows from grazing on the university's grounds, the Arch was first called "the Gate", in reference to gate panels installed between the columns. In the twentieth century, as the bovine menace abated, the gate panels were removed and "the Arch" was born.

In the year following the 1802 cession of Muscogee lands beyond the Oconee River, political pressure from upcountry politicians pushed the legislature in Louisville to seek a new home. Louisville's association with the Yazoo land fraud of 1795 had proved fatal to its aspirations to become the permanent capital of the state, and in May 1803 a commission was convened to identify a suitable site for a new capital city at the fall line of the Oconee River, about fifty miles west of Louisville. The new city was to be called Milledgeville, in honor of then-governor John Milledge.

The state government's relocation from Louisville took about four years to complete. A contract for the new Capitol building was let out in 1805, with an appropriation of $60,000 for the work. The legislature selected Jett Thomas and John Scott to design and build the new structure. Thomas's work on Franklin College at the University of Georgia, one of the largest brick structures in the state at the time, offered a modicum of proof that Thomas and Scott could complete the work. The new Capitol, far larger than Franklin College, required more than 1.3 million bricks to be manufactured on the banks of the nearby Oconee River.

Delays of several years in the completion of the work resulted in substantial cost overruns. An 1811 arbitration was convened to determine final payment for the builders. As part of this process, Thomas and Scott produced a materials list for the Capitol's construction which strongly suggests they erected a building designed in either a Georgian or Federal style, much like Franklin College in Athens.

The completed building would have appeared far different from the Gothic Revival edifice we see today, which is likely a result of expansion and remodeling performed from 1827 to 1834. This work, undertaken in stages, completely altered the massing and style of the Capitol by stuccoing the brick and building blocky wings on the north and south ends. The Gothic re-styling added pointed arches to windows and doors and crenellated parapets along the roofline. Charles Blaney Cluskey, soon to design the Governor's Mansion in town, added porticoes and granite steps in 1835.

In the United States, the crenellated form of the Gothic Revival, with its castle-fort connotations, was increasingly in vogue. The remodeled Georgia Capitol was in the vanguard of the Gothic Revival style in America and was completed almost twenty years earlier than Louisiana's capitol, the only other state capitol rendered in the style.

Sherman's occupation of Milledgeville in 1864 resulted in significant damage to the building, though it was spared complete destruction. Repairs were performed in 1866, but, two years later the legislature voted to permanently relocate the state capital to Atlanta. In the years after the building was vacated, it served as the Baldwin County Courthouse until 1879, when the new Middle Georgia Military and Agricultural College was founded.

The new college repurposed the Old Capitol building as administrative and classroom space, later developing a pleasant Collegiate Gothic campus surrounding it. Now called Georgia Military College, the school owns the building, and its ongoing stewardship ensured the Old Capitol survived and was repaired

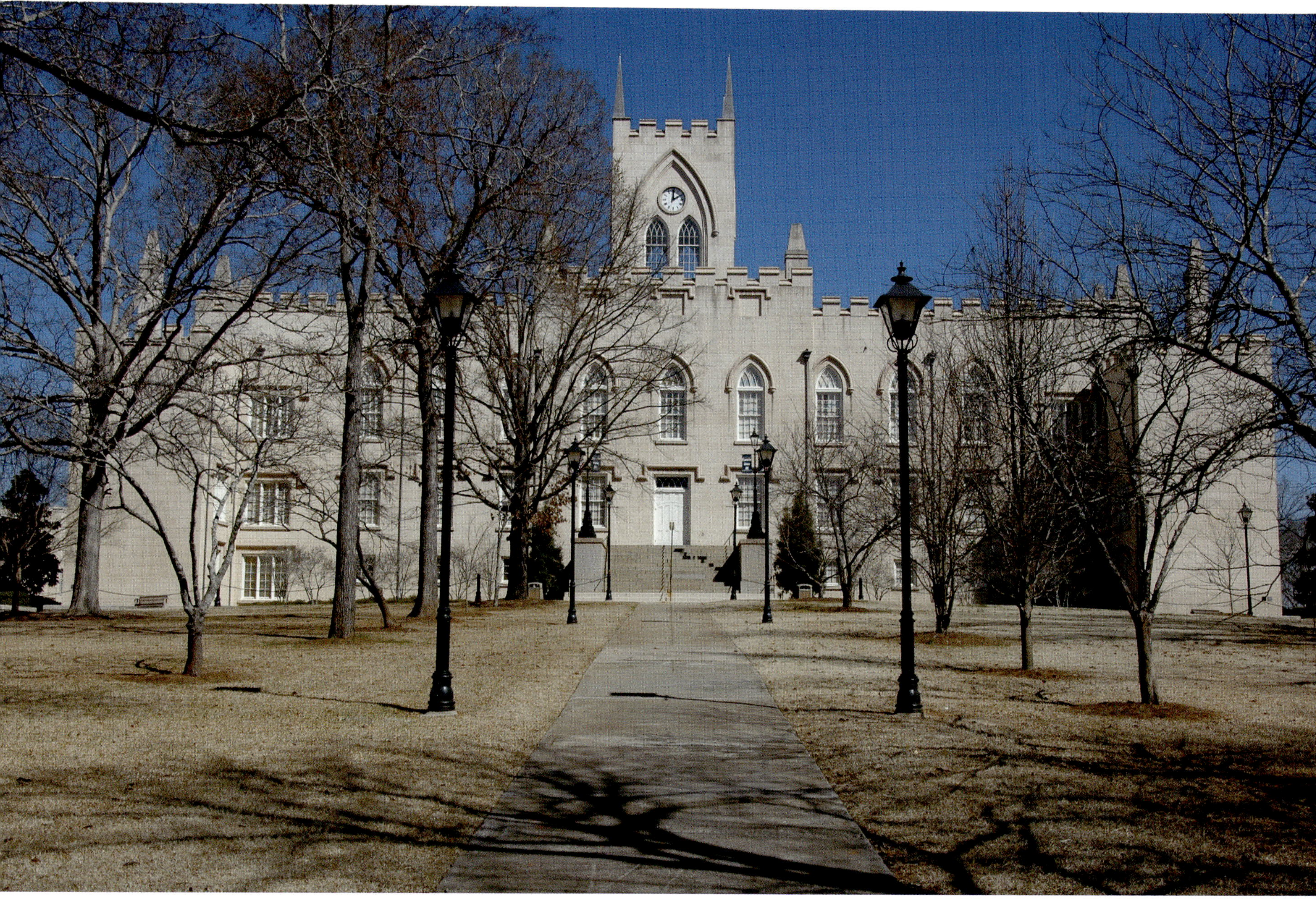

after significant fires in 1894 and 1941. Though much of the building's historic interior was destroyed in the 1941 fire, the Old Capitol was renovated in the late 1990s to recreate much of the original character of the interior, especially the old House of Representatives chamber.

Old State Capitol, Milledgeville

The state legislature granted authorization for construction of a new executive mansion in 1835. Before that time, the governor resided in various frame buildings in Milledgeville, none purpose-built as a home for the sitting executive. Jared Irwin, the first governor to reside in Milledgeville, lived in a log cabin.

In 1837, the legislature solicited separate architectural designs for the new executive mansion from both John Pell and Charles Blaney Cluskey. Though the building committee preferred Pell's design, its cost was disqualifying, resulting in Cluskey's plans being selected for construction. By the building's completion in 1839, the cost of the work exceeded $50,000. This was two-thirds more than initial estimates, but still less than the projected cost of Pell's design.

An Irish immigrant trained in architectural design in the New York firm of Town and Davis, Cluskey relocated to Savannah around 1830, perhaps to assist in the design and construction of Henry McAlpin's lost Hermitage Plantation. In 1835, Cluskey designed and built the Medical College of Georgia in Augusta, establishing his reputation more widely in the state.

The exterior of Cluskey's Governor's Mansion reflects a monumental simplicity. A pedimented Ionic portico projects forward, while a grand cascade of granite steps unfurls below it. Cluskey treated the mansion's windows plainly, their Grecian styling evident only in the raking, smooth-faced granite lintels surrounded by pale pink stucco. A tall, flat stuccoed entablature rests upon wide pilasters at the building's corners and sweeps around the building and the portico. Granite capitals and bases adorn the portico columns and pilasters, which rest on a deep shelflike granite water table. Cluskey's granite elements are as sharp and refined today as the when they were installed.

The mansion's interior design balances the dual public-private functions expected of the building. It served as both the seat of executive power in the state and the private residence of the governor. The state's business, including that of the governor's office, was largely conducted on the main level, while the family's household functions were sequestered mostly on the second floor. Whereas typical Greek Revival mansions of the time featured a bisecting central hallway running front-to-back in the building, Cluskey opted for a sequence of rooms in the middle of his house, controlling access from the front door to the governor's office. Within the raised basement, the large, low-ceilinged dining room hosted both public and private functions, albeit with wildly differing levels of intimacy.

The two-story rotunda breaks the horizontal stratification of public and private. Situated at the center of the house, the rotunda is crowned in a coffered, domed ceiling and flat-ceilinged lantern. Sunlight glints off architectural accents gilded in twenty-three-carat Dahlonega gold. Because the governor's office was located immediately behind it, the space provided a dramatic waiting room for visitors of favor. A continuous cantilevered balcony rings the rotunda at the second floor, serving as a kind of substitute central hallway, with four doorways at each floor connecting to adjacent spaces.

Seven elected governors occupied the mansion between 1839 and 1865, and the last, secession governor Joseph E. Brown, was arrested there by federal troops in 1865. Union general William Tecumseh Sherman set up his temporary headquarters in the mansion as his troops passed through the capital in November 1865, and Sherman himself occupied the dining room for one night.

Vacant after the capital was moved to Atlanta in 1868, the mansion was used as a boarding house for most of the 1870s, after which the state loaned it for use as a barracks by the Middle Georgia Military and Agricultural College. In 1891 the new Georgia Normal and Industrial College, most recently rechristened Georgia College and State University, was deeded the building, which it used for more than fifty years as a dormitory and residence of the president. The college undertook a series of much-needed renovations and repairs in the late

1960s, opening the lower two floors to the public for tours. The entire building was carefully and extensively restored to its antebellum appearance in the early twenty-first century and is open daily for tours.

Antebellum Commerce and Industry

During the 1810s and 1820s, post-Revolutionary American nationalism, coupled with the desire for speedy, safe, and reliable commercial transportation systems, motivated the planning and execution of "internal improvements" across the country. In Georgia, the earliest of these projects included turnpikes, canals, and navigational aids focused on the network of overland and river trade routes between the upcountry and the coast, as well as coastal defensive fortifications on the Savannah River below that city.

As early as the 1810s, entrepreneurs in the Piedmont erected water-powered mills and factories alongside creek and river shoals to produce a variety of products, including timber, flour and grains, thread and yarn, and finished textiles. In locales without a steady source of waterpower, coal- or wood-fired stationary steam engines operated machinery in "steam mills."

Old Governor's Mansion, Milledgeville

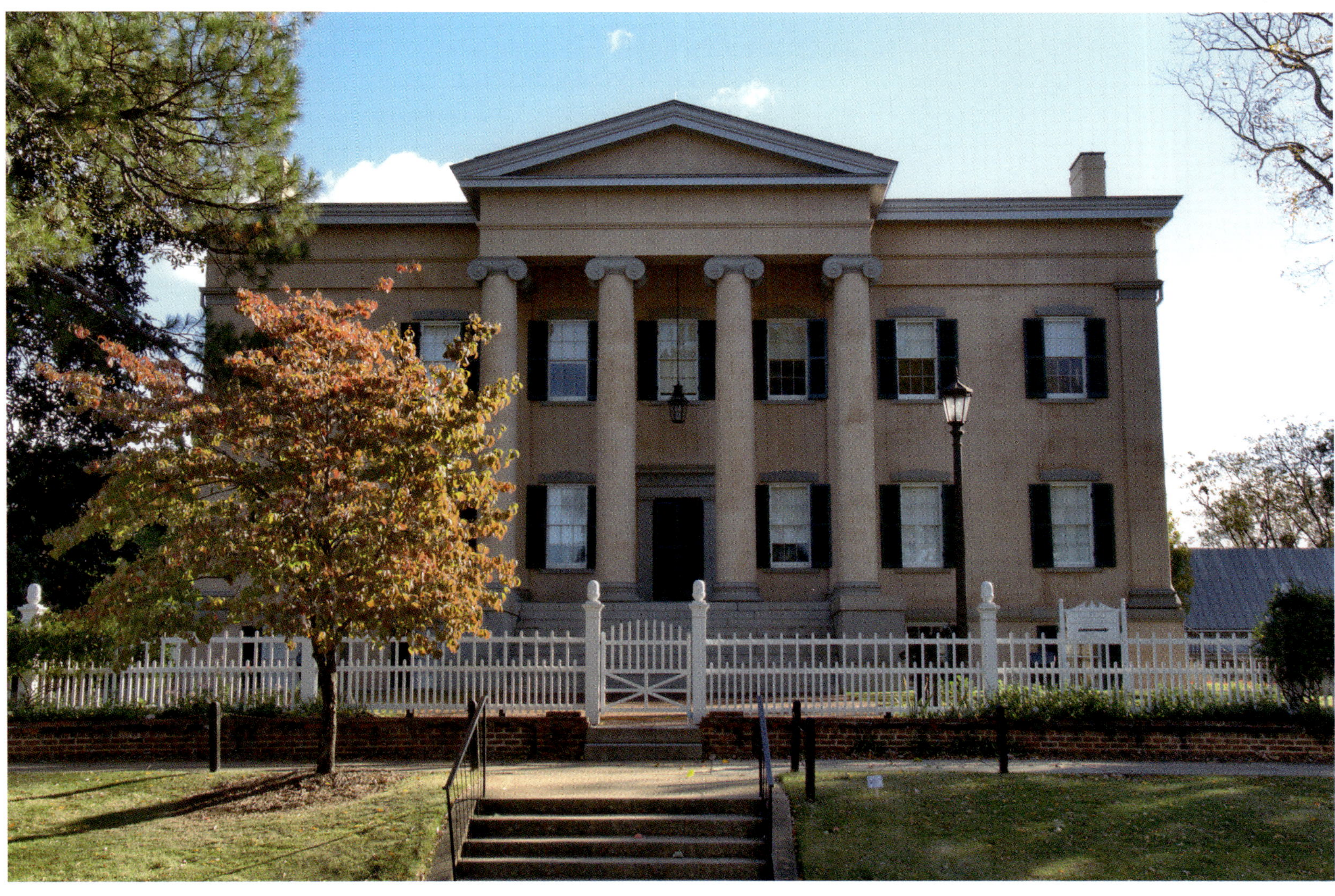

The expansion of railroad systems into much of the state created the need for skilled mechanics and support industries, especially ironworks, to manufacture parts and equipment to keep the trains running. Though an early iron industry had developed in north Georgia in the 1820s and 1830s, the period between 1840 and 1860 saw the establishment of large foundries and rolling mills in Savannah, Macon, Augusta, Columbus, and Atlanta, forming the backbone of antebellum heavy industry in the state. Facilities like the Robert Findlay Iron Works and Schofield's Iron Works in Macon could produce stationary steam engines, machine parts, cast-iron stoves, cookware, and architectural cast ironwork in addition to myriad other cast and forged iron and brass implements and parts.

Augusta, embracing its potential as an industrial and manufacturing center, began construction on the Augusta Canal in 1845 to better regulate water volume from the Savannah River. Surviving the Civil War unscathed, the Augusta Canal system was expanded in the 1870s, growing into the largest, most ambitious, and most successful canal project of its type in the Southeast. The city grew into an industrial powerhouse, with numerous support industries seeded among the giant postbellum textile mills.

Columbus, too, built extensive dams and canals, these on the Chattahoochee River. In 1851 William H. Young established the Eagle Manufacturing Company, a textile mill, along the Columbus riverfront. Powered by water, the Eagle mill was instrumental in developing power canals in Columbus. Though burned during Wilson's Raid in 1865, the Eagle mill, rebuilt and rechristened the Eagle and Phenix Manufacturing Company, eventually grew into the largest such facility in the state, exceeding in production even the water-powered mills of Augusta.

Young was a very successful entrepreneur, with business interests in banking and insurance in addition to textile manufacturing. In 1856 he became president of the reorganized Bank of Columbus, and in that role he was responsible for the erection of one of the most interesting commercial buildings of the antebellum period, the Bank of Columbus.

Ground was broken in August 1860 at a site then known as Hogan's Corner. The proposed three-story Italian Renaissance Revival–style building was unique in Georgia at the time, because its two street facades were fabricated entirely of interlocking cast-iron plates. As early as the 1820s, small commercial buildings in the northeastern United States employed cast-iron posts and lintels in their street-level storefronts, but it was not until 1848 that James Bogardus in New York fabricated the first full cast-iron building facade. In subsequent years, cast iron's reputation for economy and fire-resistance brought national renown to Bogardus and his rival Daniel Badger, who both shipped disassembled facades by rail across the country.

A Columbus newspaper report from March 1861 announced that the cast iron for the building facade had arrived and was "in course of erection." Though the local Columbus Iron Works was capable of producing the facade, its maker remains unknown. Despite the onset of the Civil War, the work was complete enough by October 1861 for the bank to occupy the first-floor. In November

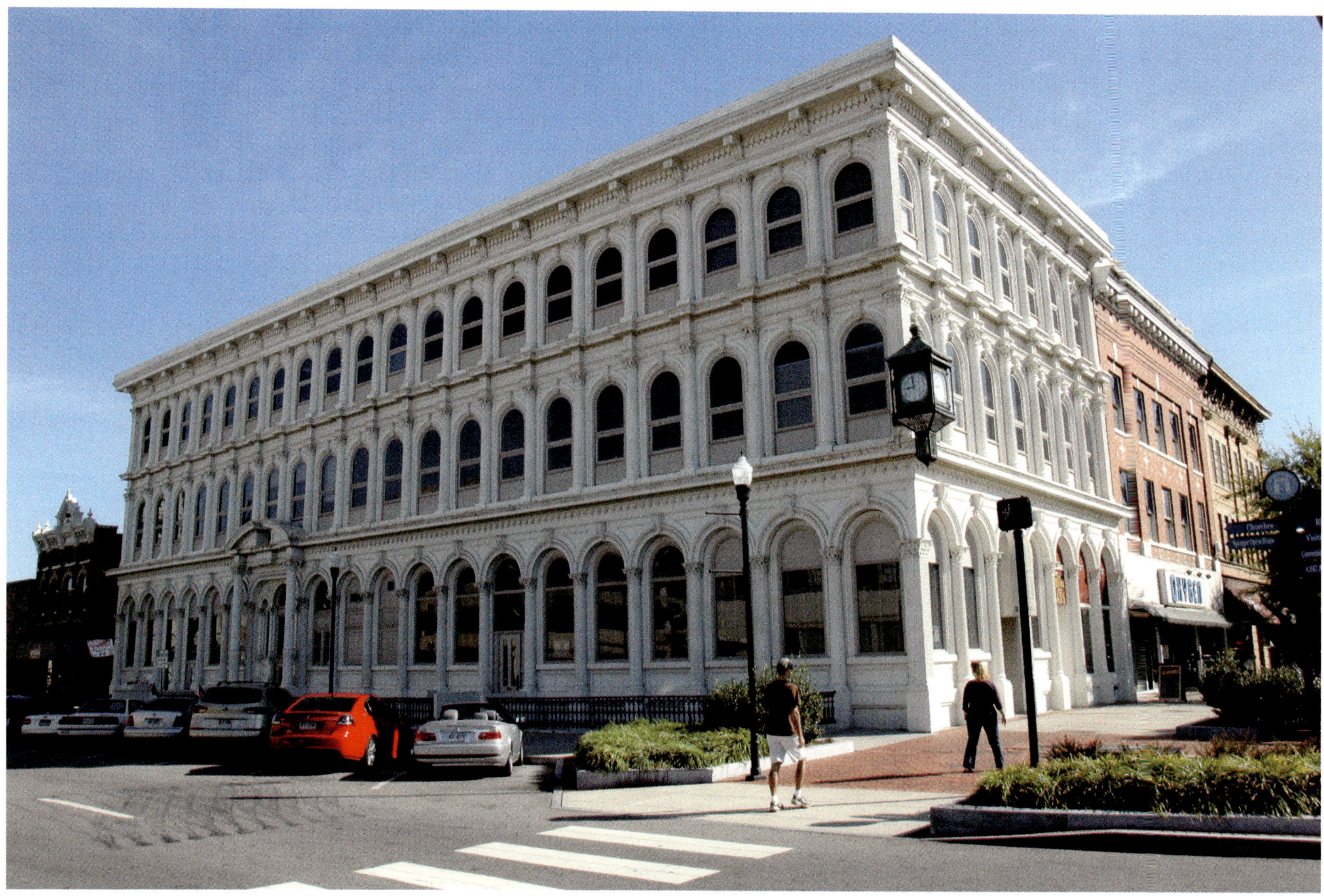

Bank of Columbus, Columbus

1862, the Georgia Home Insurance Company, another business concern associated with William H. Young, relocated its offices to the east side of the new building. Though the brick shell, floor structure, roof, and cast-iron facade were complete by the end of 1862, only the interiors of the basement and first floor were usable during the war. For years, wood shutters and planks covered the window openings at the unfinished second and third floors.

As was common among Southern banks, the fortunes of the Bank of Columbus declined after the war. In May 1869, the Georgia Home Insurance Company purchased the building at auction for $28,000. At the time of the sale, estimators calculated that another $8,000 to $10,000 would be required to finish the building, on top of the $60,000 already expended on its construction. In September 1869, builders installed seventy-five new windows designed in "a combination order corresponding to the architecture of the building," finally completing the structure more than nine years after the groundbreaking. In August 1872 the insurance company modified the northwest corner of the building to become a two-sided entrance, with the cast iron for the alteration manufactured by the Columbus Iron Works.

Until a catastrophic 1957 fire gutted the building, the 1869 windows were intact. The muntin pattern of these arched windows was uniquely suited to the architecture of the building, reflecting a geometry emblematic of both the Italianate and Italian Renaissance Revival styles. The fire caused damage valued at over $1 million, and though the building shell was salvaged and repaired with little impact on the cast-iron facade, the windows installed after the fire and their modern counterparts seen today made no attempt to replicate the historic design.

The most significant surviving railroad building complex from the antebellum period was built by the Central Railroad, later the Central of Georgia Railway, at its terminus in Savannah. The Central complex is located on the west side of the city between West Broad Street (now Martin Luther King Jr. Blvd) and the Savannah-Ogeechee Canal. West Broad formed the western boundary of Savannah's ward system, and the new railroad consolidated two large parcels to the north and south of Louisville Road, providing relatively close access to developed sections of the city. A passenger station, warehouse, and repair shop were built on the site by the mid-1830s, but by the 1850s the Central required expanded and modernized facilities to service its new locomotives and rolling stock. In the twenty years since its founding, the Central Railroad had developed into a regional rail system that rivaled in mileage and volume lines in the northeastern and middle-Atlantic states.

William Morrill Wadley, general superintendent of the Central Railroad, was responsible for making the new Savannah Shops a reality. The new integrated facility was built primarily between 1851 and 1860, with a new passenger station started in 1860 but delayed by the war until 1866, with small modifications made ten years later. The project brought together into one large complex the Central's primary maintenance facility along with an administration building, two freight warehouses, a cotton yard, and the later passenger depot. The Central's maintenance buildings included a roundhouse for repairing engines; a building for fabricating tender frames; a shop for work on passenger coaches; shops for pattern-making blacksmithing, carpentry, upholstery, printing, and painting; sheds for materials storage; and a boiler and engine house to power the machines on the site, featuring a stationary steam engine manufactured by the Robert Findlay Iron Works in Macon. Elevated brick viaducts, still extant, carried the rail lines out of the west side of the facility, across West Boundary Street and the Savannah-Ogeechee Canal, heading toward Macon. Contemporary reports say the cost of the complex exceeded $500,000.

One of the most interesting features of the complex is a tall brick stack and cast-iron water-storage tank, completed in 1855. The stack provided exhaust ventilation for the surrounding shops and the roundhouse through underground tunnels connected to each building. The stack is faceted into sixteen faces, and radiating around its base are a series of sixteen arched openings, through which one may access sixteen wedge-shaped chambers serving as privies and changing rooms for workers.

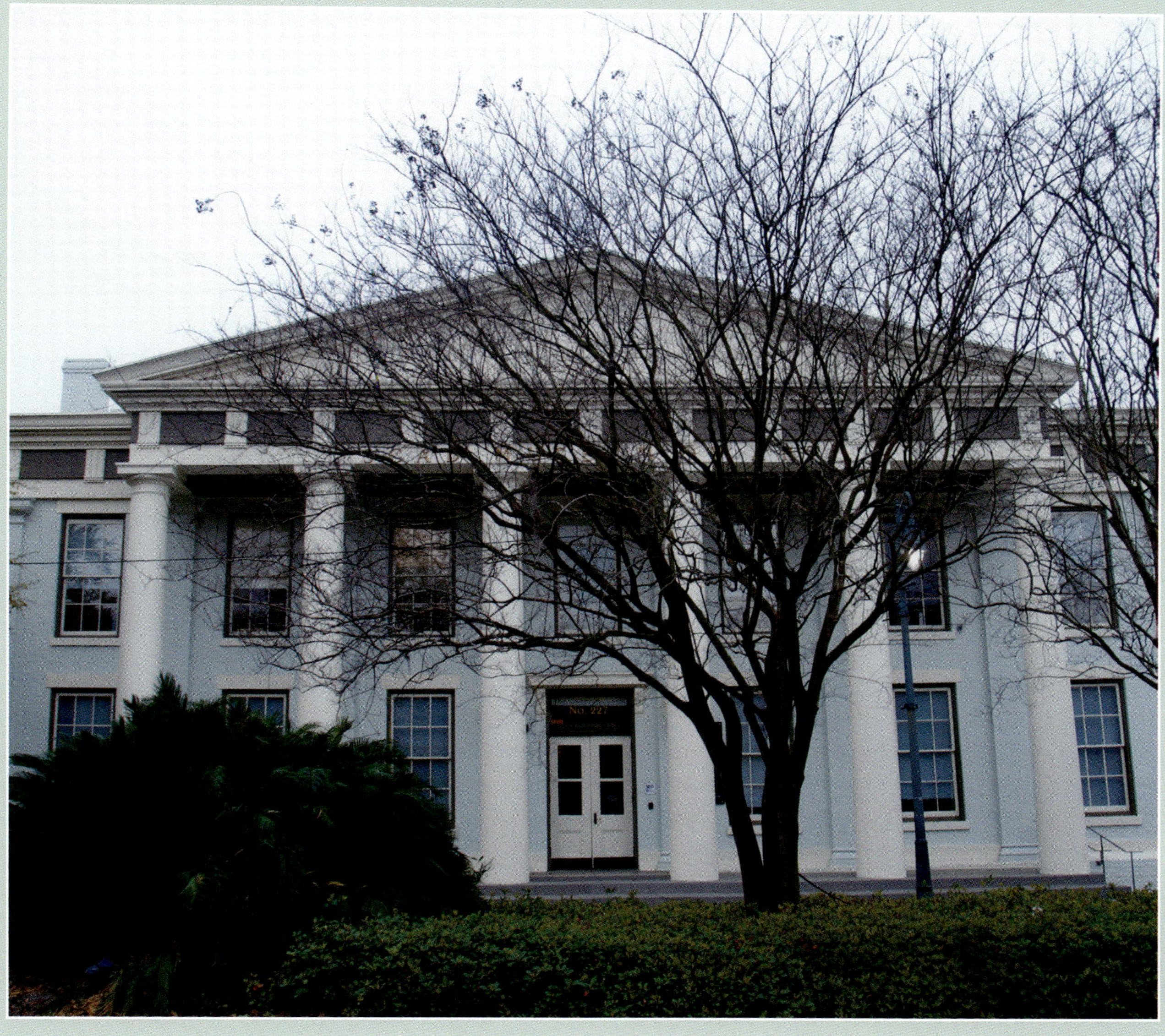

Central of Georgia Gray Building, Savannah

The years after the completion of the Savannah Shops saw changes made to the facility. In the postbellum era, a new office building, the Red Building, was added just to the south of the Gray Building (1856), which had traditionally served as the administrative center. Other buildings were modified and repurposed as needed. A fire in 1923 destroyed the carpentry shop, and a new one was built, immediately making use of the salvageable remnants of the original. In 1926, the roundhouse and turntable were completely rebuilt to accommodate the larger engines of the age, and the roundhouse was converted from a fully round building to an open semicircle. The 1855/1878 machine-shop building, partially extant in 1976 when the Historic American Engineering Record performed a photographic and photogrammetric survey of the property, had collapsed by 1977, leaving only its first-floor perimeter walls standing. The most significant extant antebellum buildings remaining from the Central complex are the Gray Building (1856); the Passenger Terminal (1860–66) with its Train Shed (1861); the Up-Freight House (1853); the Produce Freight House (1859); the Cotton

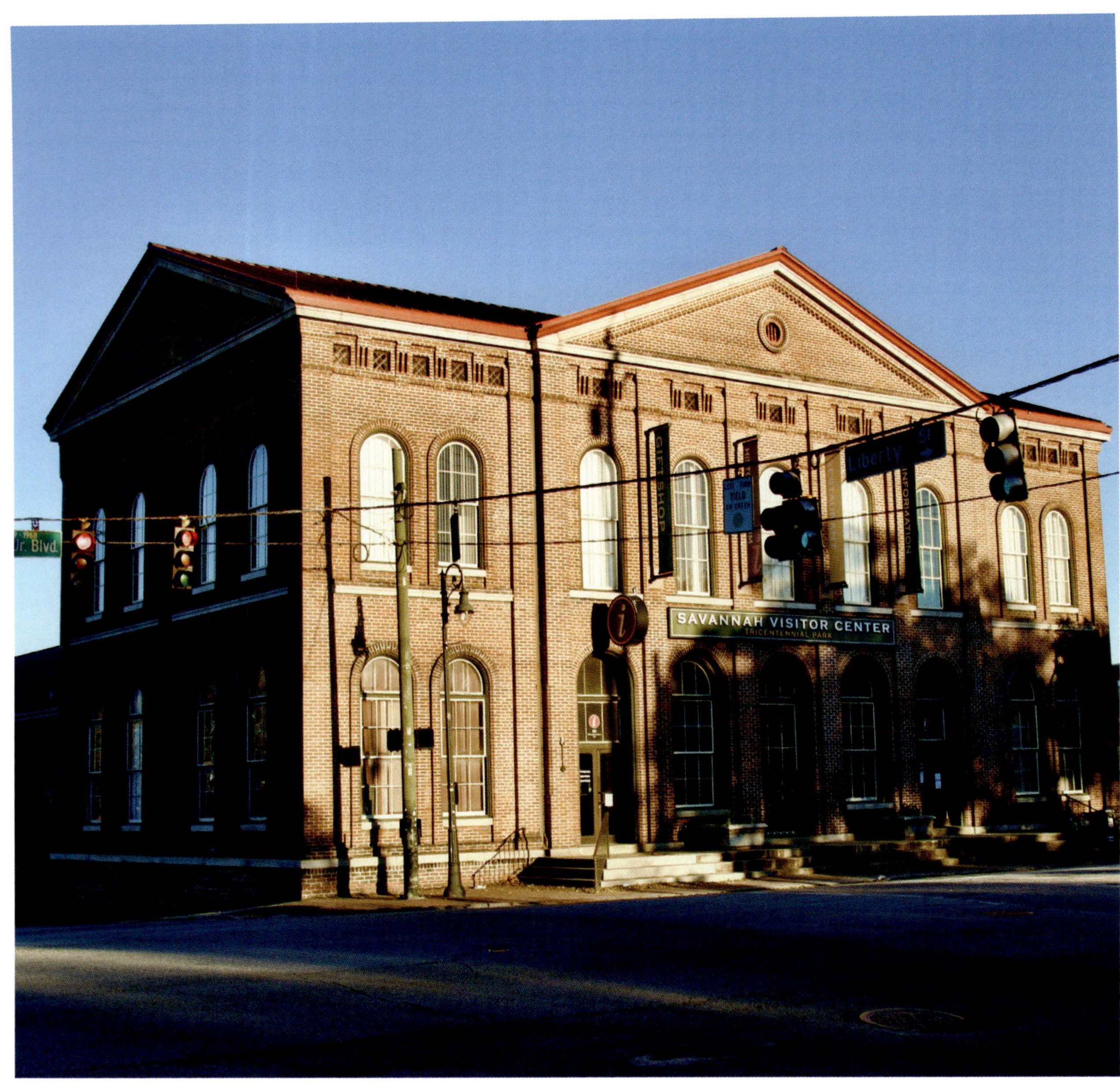

Central of Georgia Passenger Terminal, Savannah

Yard Gates (1856); the Engine and Boiler House (1854); the stack and water tank (1855); and the two sets of viaducts (1853 and 1860).

After decades of decline in railroad traffic, exacerbated by the decimation in cotton production caused by the boll weevil and the development of alternate forms of long-distance transportation, the complex closed in the early 1960s. In the years since its disuse as a working railroad facility, the buildings of the Savannah Repair Shops and Terminal Facilities underwent significant changes, including dilapidation and loss, but also rebirth and reuse. The Gray Building and Red Building were purchased by the Savannah College of Art and Design (SCAD) and adapted for educational use. An award-winning rehabilitation of the Gray Building in 2011 expanded the SCAD Museum of Art by incorporating the 800-foot-long ruin of the 1853 Up-Freight House into a state-of-the-art facility. In 1989 the Coastal Heritage Society opened the Savannah History Museum inside the train shed of the Passenger Terminal. The terminal building itself serves as the Savannah Visitor Center. With the explosion of tourism in Savannah in the last twenty-five years, the Passenger Terminal is one of the most frequently visited historic buildings in the city. The remnants of the Repair Shops are now the Georgia State Railroad Museum and the Savannah Children's Museum, both operated by the Coastal Heritage Society.

Antebellum Defensive Works

Fort Pulaski, located on Cockspur Island just inside the mouth of the Savannah River, was built as part of the Third System of forts ordered by President James Monroe after the War of 1812. The island possesses an unobstructed view of shipping entering or exiting the river, making it strategically ideal for a defensive installation. Preliminary site work for the new fort began in 1828, when assistant engineer Lieutenant Robert E. Lee arrived to take up his first commission, working on drainage canals and earthworks to make the site ready for construction of the fort. Lee served there until 1831.

The land for the fort was purchased by the federal government incrementally between 1830 and 1845 from the State of Georgia and several private owners. Construction began in earnest in 1833. The work was performed by military engineers and personnel, white brick masons, and enslaved carpenters and laborers who had been hired out to the government. All those laboring on the project lived in a ready-built village on the island.

The massive brick walls of Fort Pulaski rest upon a foundation of timber grillage, a kind of interlaced timber platform, set on top of a grid of long timber piles driven into the sand and mud. The walls are 32 feet tall and vary in thickness between 7 and 11 feet. Approximately twenty-five million bricks were laid in an English-bond pattern, creating strong, redundant connections between the multiple brick wythes within the thick walls. The fort is five-sided, with its north and south walls set square to the west wall along the "back" of the fort. The eastern walls, forming the seaward side, are chevron-shaped, with the point facing the sea. Barrel-vaulted casemates occupy four of the five sides, while the long, fifth side at the back of the fort contained barracks.

Savannah gray brick, manufactured at the Hermitage Plantation, was used for the fort's exterior facing, while the brick in the vaults of the casemates is smooth, red brick likely imported from the North. These bricks are fit together with incredible precision, with most of the mortar joints no wider than one-quarter inch. Molded and rubbed bricks form the complex shapes of barrel vaults and cross vaults, with no variation in joint width throughout. Fort Pulaski is, without question, the highest expression of the brick mason's art in Georgia.

A triangular demilune extends westward from the back of the fort and contains tabby magazines where powder and ammunition were stored. The fort and demilune are surrounded by a wet moat fed by the river's tidal flow. By 1840 workers had completed the fort itself, but another seven years was required to bring the demilune and moat into service. An illuminated navigational aid, the

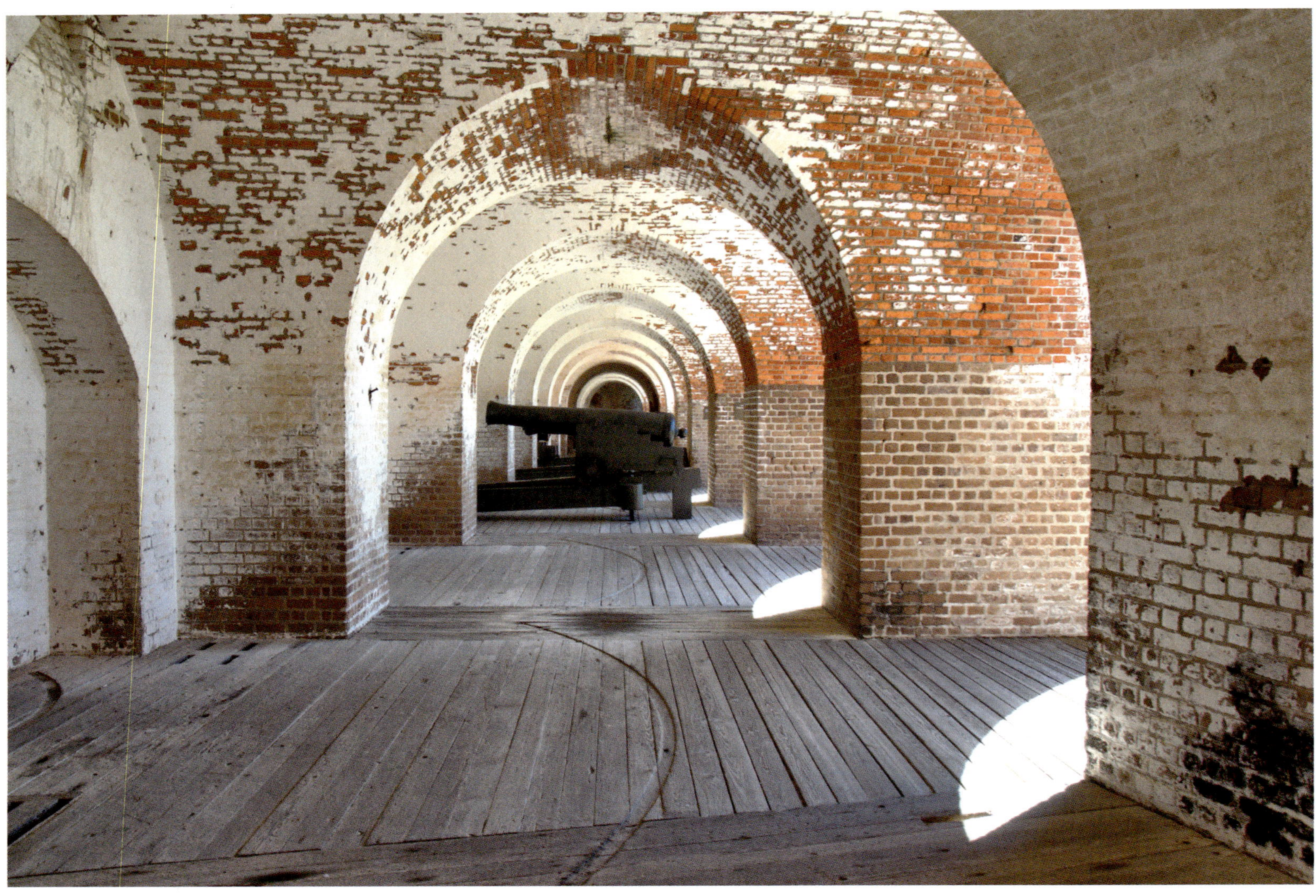

Fort Pulaski National Monument, Cockspur Island

Cockspur Island Lighthouse, was constructed in 1848 off the southeast tip of the island to guide ships into the river's south channel. The lighthouse, designed by the architect John S. Norris, was destroyed by a hurricane in 1854 and rebuilt in 1856 on the same foundation.

In 1861, prior to the outbreak of the Civil War, Fort Pulaski was not garrisoned. Southern outrage over the federal reinforcement of Fort Sumter without notification to the State of South Carolina motivated Georgia governor Joseph E. Brown to order Georgia militia to immediately occupy Fort Pulaski. With Georgia's secession from the Union, the fort was made ready for war, and coastal batteries on nearby Tybee Island were withdrawn to Pulaski.

By the end of that year, United States troops, under the command of General Quincy Gillmore, occupied Tybee Island. Gillmore's men built a line of eleven batteries strung along the northern edge of the island, each aimed at the brick fort in the middle of the river. They hauled guns across the salt marshes to establish batteries where none were thought possible, and even when observers at Pulaski became aware of them, they were assumed to be too far out of range to damage the fort.

On April 10, 1862, a thunderous artillery barrage commenced from the American batteries on Tybee. These positions were supplied with experimental rifled cannon, including Parrott and James rifles, whose efficacy against masonry fortifications was tested for the first time. In the fusillade unleashed that day, the new guns proved that heavier rounds could be sent farther, and with greater accuracy, than from any smooth-bore cannon of the day. Repeated pounding of the same targeted area resulted in the near demolition of the southeast angle of the fort after only thirty hours. Further bombardment on the morning of April 11 breached the southeast wall, exposing the fort's north powder magazine to incoming fire.

Gaining nothing by attempting to forestall the inevitable, Fort Pulaski's commanding officer, Colonel Charles Olmstead, surrendered to General Gillmore in the early afternoon of the eleventh. With this victory, Gillmore had proven unequivocally that no masonry fortification in the world was secure from quick "reduction" if targeted by these new weapons. The fall of Fort Pulaski was cataclysmic for Georgia's largest city. Savannah had lost its connection to the sea, its trade, and its livelihood. The fort's new occupants quickly rebuilt breached sections of its wall, but even today glimpses of the destruction wrought during the siege can be plainly seen on the pockmarked south and southeast walls.

Georgia's extant antebellum buildings reveal a variety of craftsmanship, expertise, and aesthetic sophistication exercised by building mechanics working between 1800 and 1865. In those years, Georgians generally kept apace of national architectural trends while continuing the use of many traditional building materials and forms passed down from previous generations. Thus, the state possesses some unique interpretations of popular styles, with varying levels of architectural "correctness." Though only a fraction of the buildings of the era have survived to the present, Georgia retains a national reputation for the quality of its antebellum architecture.

For much of the twentieth century, the study of this period focused primarily on the dwelling places of the planter class and other elites whose prosperity was buoyed by the cotton plantation economy. The adoption of the National Historic Preservation Act of 1966 and the subsequent development of the secretary of the interior's associated standards facilitated the burgeoning academic study of antebellum vernacular and utilitarian structures, often associated with Black history, by including them in programs like the National Register of Historic Places and in tax-incentive programs. The past forty years of preservation in Georgia has sought to rebalance the story of the antebellum era to better convey the complexities and contradictions of life in that time.

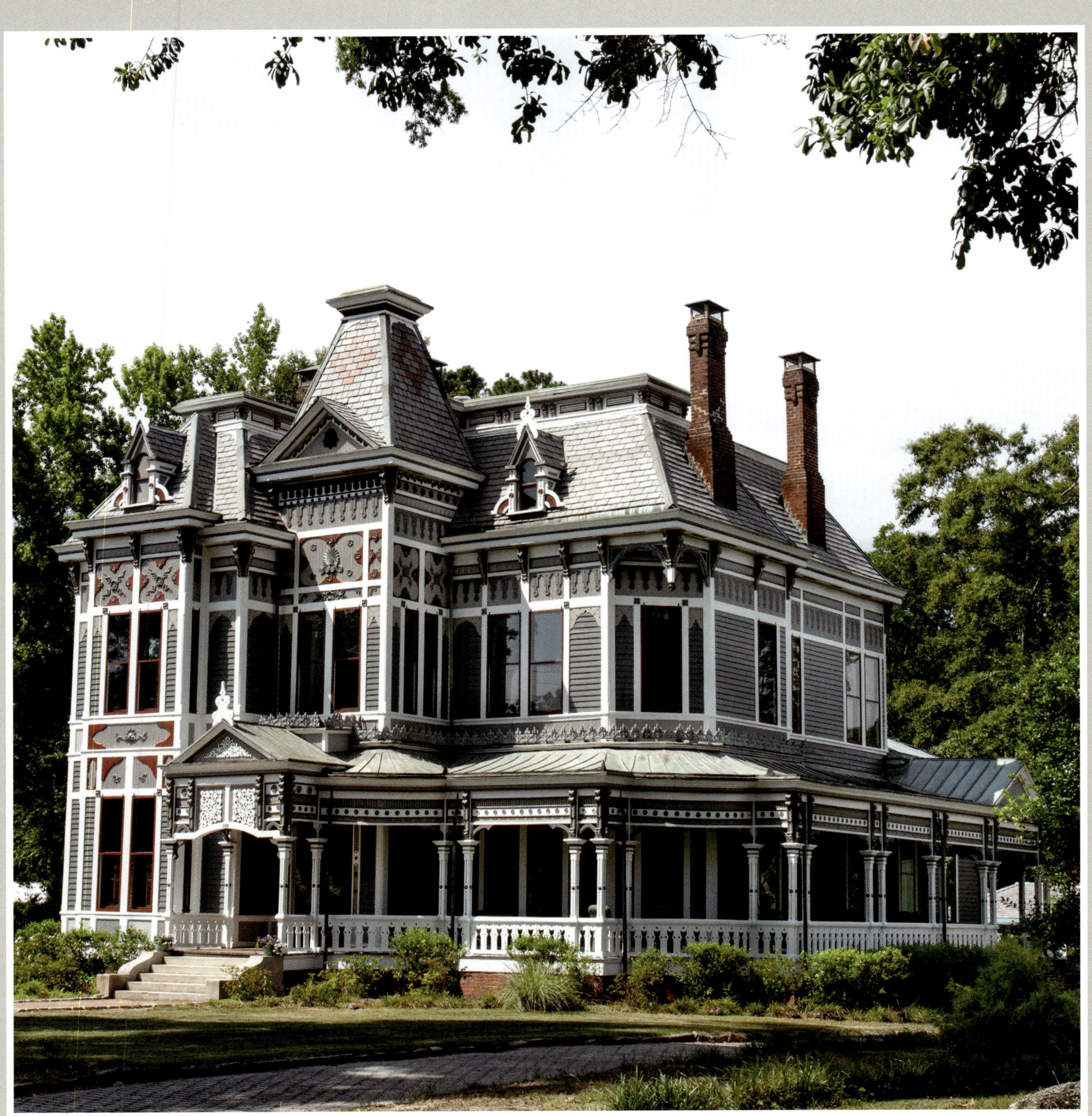

III. The Victorian Era

CARMIE JONES MCDONALD

IT COULD BE SAID THAT the most important physical features of the late nineteenth-century Georgia landscape were the cotton field and the railroad track. The restoration and expansion of the railroads was a driving force in Georgia's economic recovery following the Civil War. In antebellum Georgia, the state had experienced limited success with early industrialization efforts, but the postwar period saw increased urbanization and industrialization related to the production and processing of cotton. The expansion of rail service throughout the state spurred development in previously rural areas and connected Georgia's communities to markets beyond her borders. The new railroad network not only expedited the exportation of cotton, it also enabled Georgia's cities to keep pace with the latest national and international events, technological developments, and architectural trends. Advancement in printing and the circulation of magazines and periodicals exposed middle-class Georgians to literature, fashion, and the allure of exotic locales previously unknown. The combination of increased wealth and information flowing into the state transformed Georgia's built environment in the late nineteenth century.

The field of architecture underwent profound changes in the mid to late nineteenth century with the introduction of formalized architectural education in the United States. Massachusetts Institute of Technology was first to offer a degree in architecture, in 1868, followed by Cornell University, the University of Illinois, Columbia University, and Tuskegee Institute. The American Institute of Architects (AIA) was founded in the 1850s to "promote the scientific and practical perfection of its members" and the first chapter was established in New York in 1867. By 1892, the Southern chapter was established, followed by the Atlanta chapter in 1906. But despite the professionalization of architectural practice at the end of the nineteenth century, the vast majority of buildings in Georgia were still built by carpenters and craftsmen using pattern books and local traditions to guide their work.

Facing: Parrott-Camp-Soucy House, Newnan

Pattern books written in the years following the Civil War were different than those available in the first half of the nineteenth century. The target audiences for the early pattern books were builders and woodworkers in mills that mass produced decorative architectural elements. These books provided instruction rather than inspiration and were not intended to be used as catalogues for design ideas. As their popularity increased, pattern books evolved to include floorplans and elevations that homeowners could use, in consultation with their builders, to select a style of building appropriate to their needs. These house-plan catalogues proved so popular that some architects began to offer complete sets of plans by mail. George Barber, an architect in Knoxville, Tennessee, in the late nineteenth century took this practice one step further, marketing his plans worldwide and even shipping some architectural elements directly to job sites.

At the same time Georgia was experiencing this influx of new ideas, innovations in construction technology were having a significant impact on the forms and styles of buildings being erected. Balloon framing was significantly lighter than earlier timber construction and enabled builders to create the complex forms that are common to Victorian architecture. Similarly, the mass production of decorative elements using machine powered lathes and jigsaws simplified the building process and made it possible for builders to purchase these elements ready-made, rather than having to produce them by hand. The mass production of building materials and the transit network to deliver them resulted in a shift from more regional forms of architecture to a national style that was, ironically, imported from England.

Victorian architecture refers to the architectural styles that were prevalent during the reign of England's Queen Victoria (1837–1901). Victorian architecture is not, therefore, a particular style, but rather a variety of styles that were popular in the late nineteenth century. While a number of styles fall into the category, this chapter will focus on the Second Empire, Stick, Queen Anne, Romanesque Revival, and Folk Victorian styles, as they were most widely used in Georgia. Many of the same factors that drove the development of Victorian styles in England were influential in her thirteenth colony—industrialization, innovation, transportation, and experimentation. The Victorian era represented a new age in Georgia's architectural development. It was exuberant, unrestrained, and sometimes excessive. Because of the eclectic nature of Victorian architecture, it can at times be difficult to distinguish one style from another. It is our hope that this chapter will provide a foundation for your exploration and enjoyment of Georgia's Victorian heritage and a desire to preserve it for generations to follow.

Second Empire

The defining feature of the Second Empire style is its distinctive mansard roof. The style was named for seventeenth-century French architect Jules Mansart, and it features a double-pitched hipped roof, with the lower of the two slopes steeper than that above. Mansard roofs can be characterized by straight, flared, or convex forms and almost always feature dormer windows and slate as the

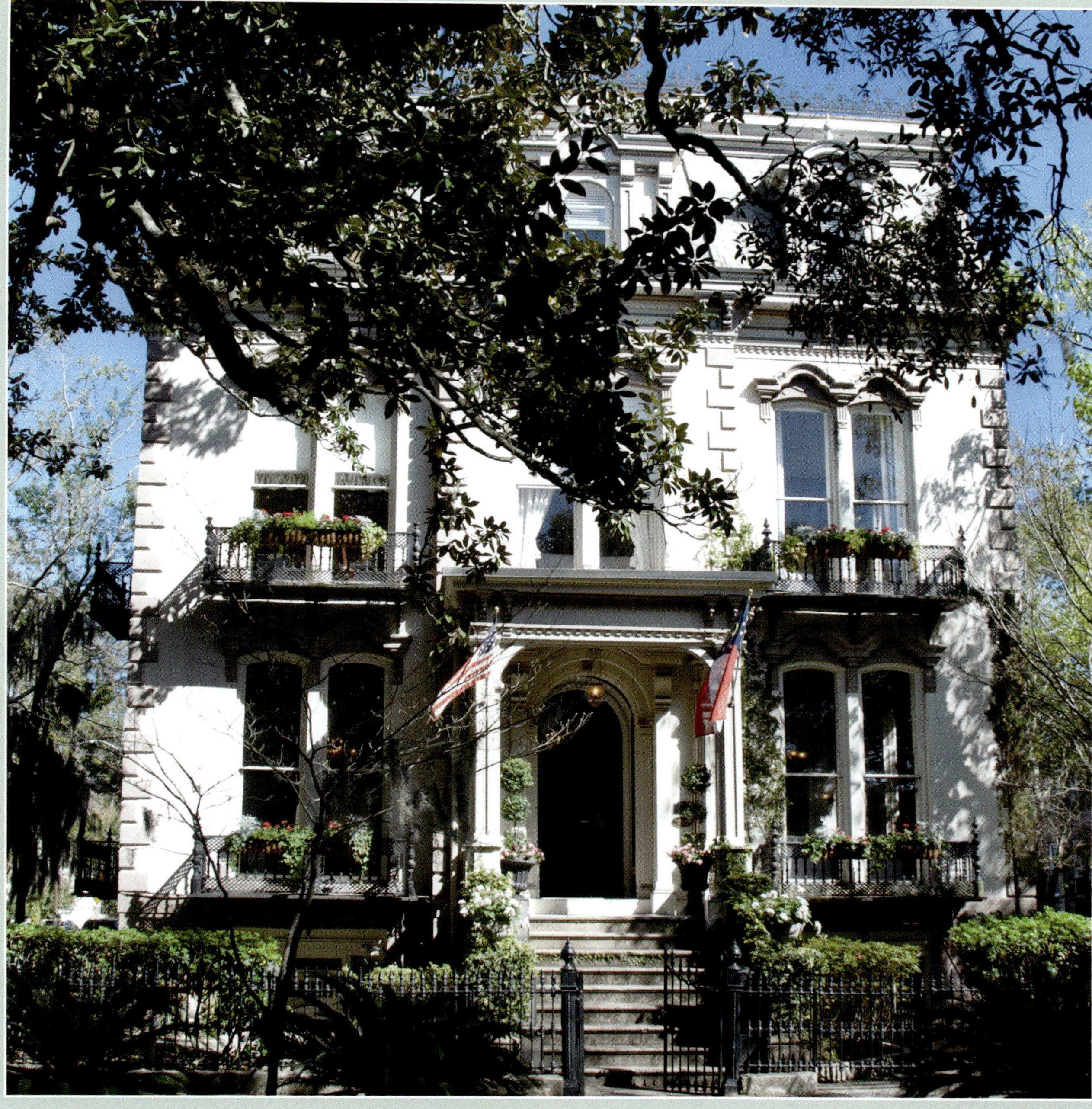

Hamilton-Turner House, Savannah

roofing material. While many Second Empire buildings are square or rectangular, others feature asymmetrical plans with porches, bay windows, and central or offset towers. Second Empire buildings are typically built of brick and are sometimes finished in stucco, while others feature wood siding. High-style examples feature decorative window hoods and elaborate cornice detailing.

The Hamilton-Turner House was built in Savannah in 1873 for wealthy businessman Samuel Pugh Hamilton. It is prominently located on one of Lafayette Square's four trust lots, which were typically reserved for public buildings and grand-scale houses. The building is square in plan and features a projecting central gable with a porch on the first floor. The Hamilton-Turner House exhibits many hallmarks of the Second Empire style, including a mansard roof with dormer windows and decorative metal cresting along the roofline, paired brackets along the cornice, elaborate window hoods, and paired windows and entry doors.

Industrialist George T. Jackson built Enterprise Mill in Augusta in 1877. It was designed by Jones S. Davis, a mill builder from Massachusetts who also worked in Atlanta. This impressive textile mill was constructed following the enlargement of the Augusta Canal in 1872–75. While the functionality of the building was paramount in its design, Davis incorporated elements of the Second Empire style to reflect prevailing tastes. The three-story, rectangular building is of red brick and features two large square towers that divide the facade into three sections. The towers are capped with convex mansard roofs and wooden cupolas. The roofs are clad in metal shingles and feature louvered dormers. Decorative brick corbeling is found in the cornice underneath the mansard roofs. The remainder of the building is more utilitarian in design and is dominated by regularly spaced double-hung wood windows that allowed light and air into the building.

Enterprise Mill, Augusta

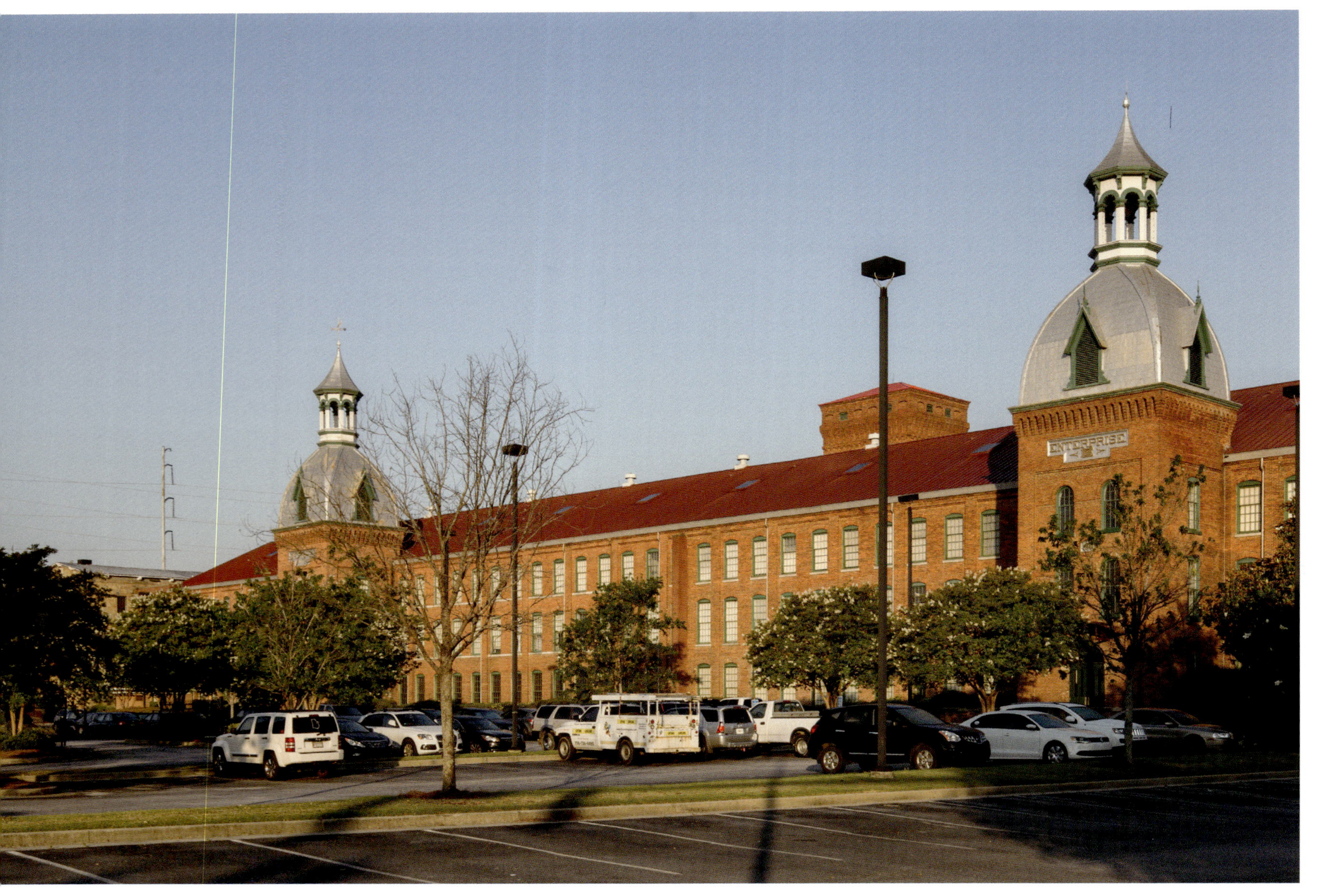

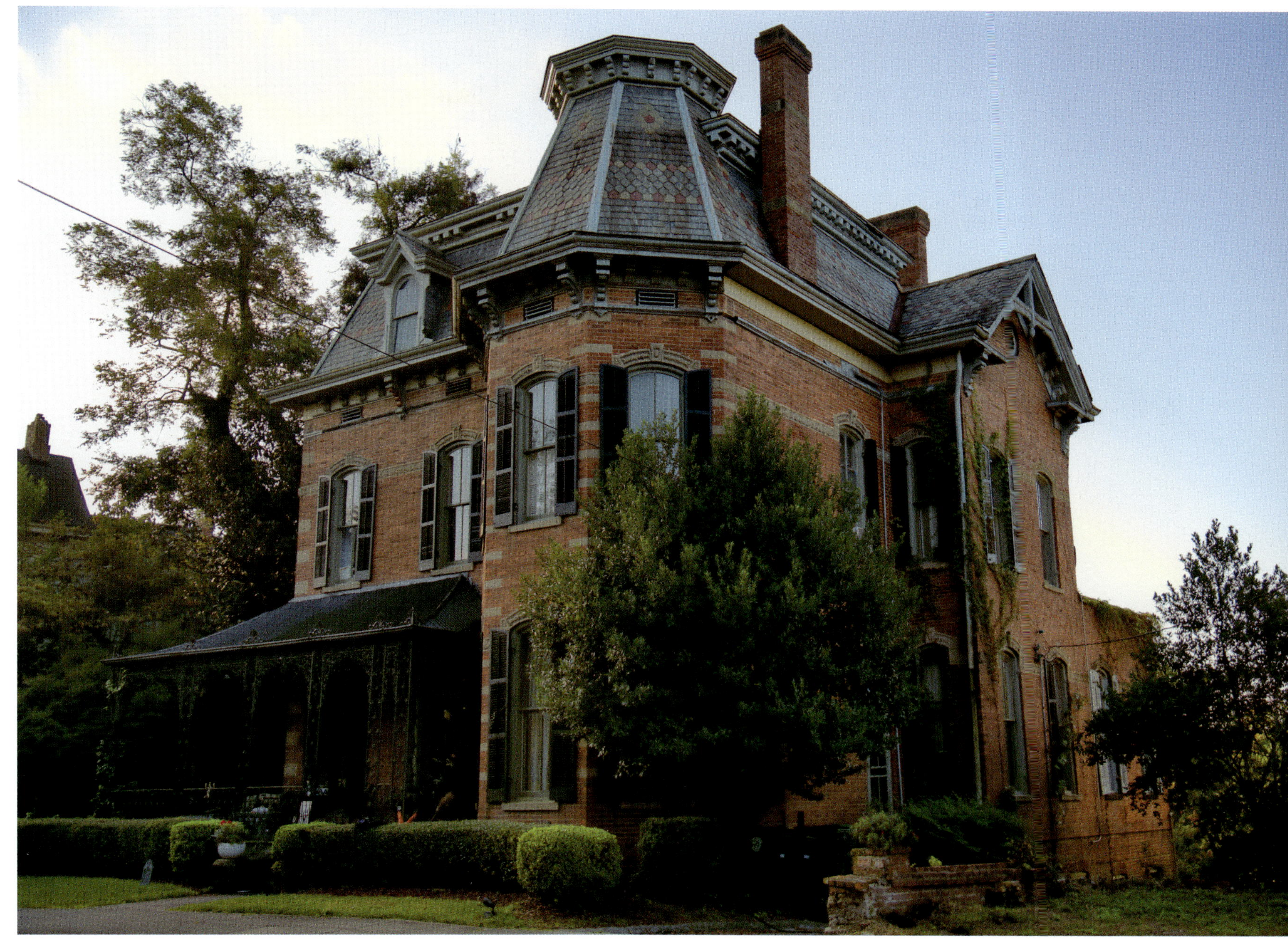

Hatcher-Groover-Schwartz House, Macon

The Hatcher-Groover-Schwartz House was built in Macon in 1880 by businessman Marshall James Hatcher of Marshallville, Georgia. Hatcher owned and operated a dairy on property that is now part of the Ocmulgee National Monument. While the designer of the Hatcher-Groover-Schwartz House is unknown, the building is a fine example of the Second Empire style and stands out among the many classically inspired houses on Macon's fashionable College Hill. It is asymmetrical in plan, with a two-story projection adjacent to the front door. The mansard roof is straight sided with a decorative pattern in its slate sheathing. The building is made of red brick with contrasting stone detailing in the quoins and window surrounds and features a wrought-iron porch with concave roof that extends along half of the primary facade and side of the house. The Hatcher-Groover-Schwartz House is said to be the only example of Second Empire architecture in Macon.

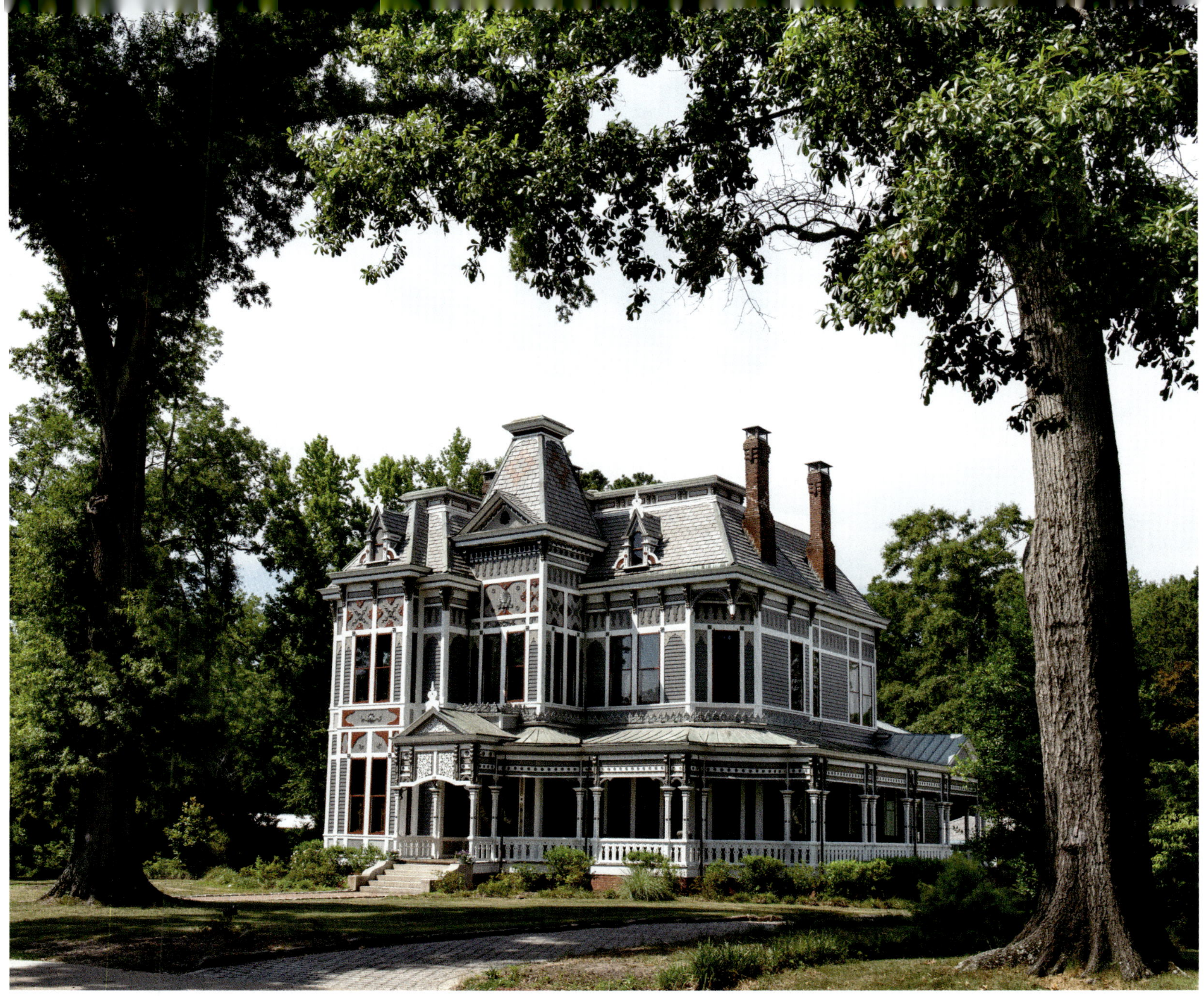

Parrott-Camp-Soucy House, Newnan

Originally built as a single-story dwelling in the 1840, the Parrott-Camp-Soucy House in Newnan was purchased by Judge John S. Bigby as a wedding gift for his daughter, Callie Bigby Parrott. In 1885 it was substantially remodeled to its current appearance. The building exhibits many identifying features of the Second Empire style with regard to both form and decoration. It features a square tower on the front of its asymmetrical facade. The tower, like the rest of the building, has a straight sided mansard roof with patterned slate. The roof features dormer windows and metal cresting along the roofline. The house is constructed of wood and retains historic decorative detailing including a bracketed cornice, elaborate front and side porches, and applied surface ornament. Also characteristic of the Second Empire style are the paired windows and entrance doors.

One of the most striking examples of the Second Empire style in Georgia is the Hancock County Courthouse in Sparta, completed in 1883. The building is situated on one side of the city's central square, atop a slight hill. The opposite side of the square features a tree-lined street that provides a dramatic view of the courthouse and the center of Sparta. The courthouse was designed by Atlanta

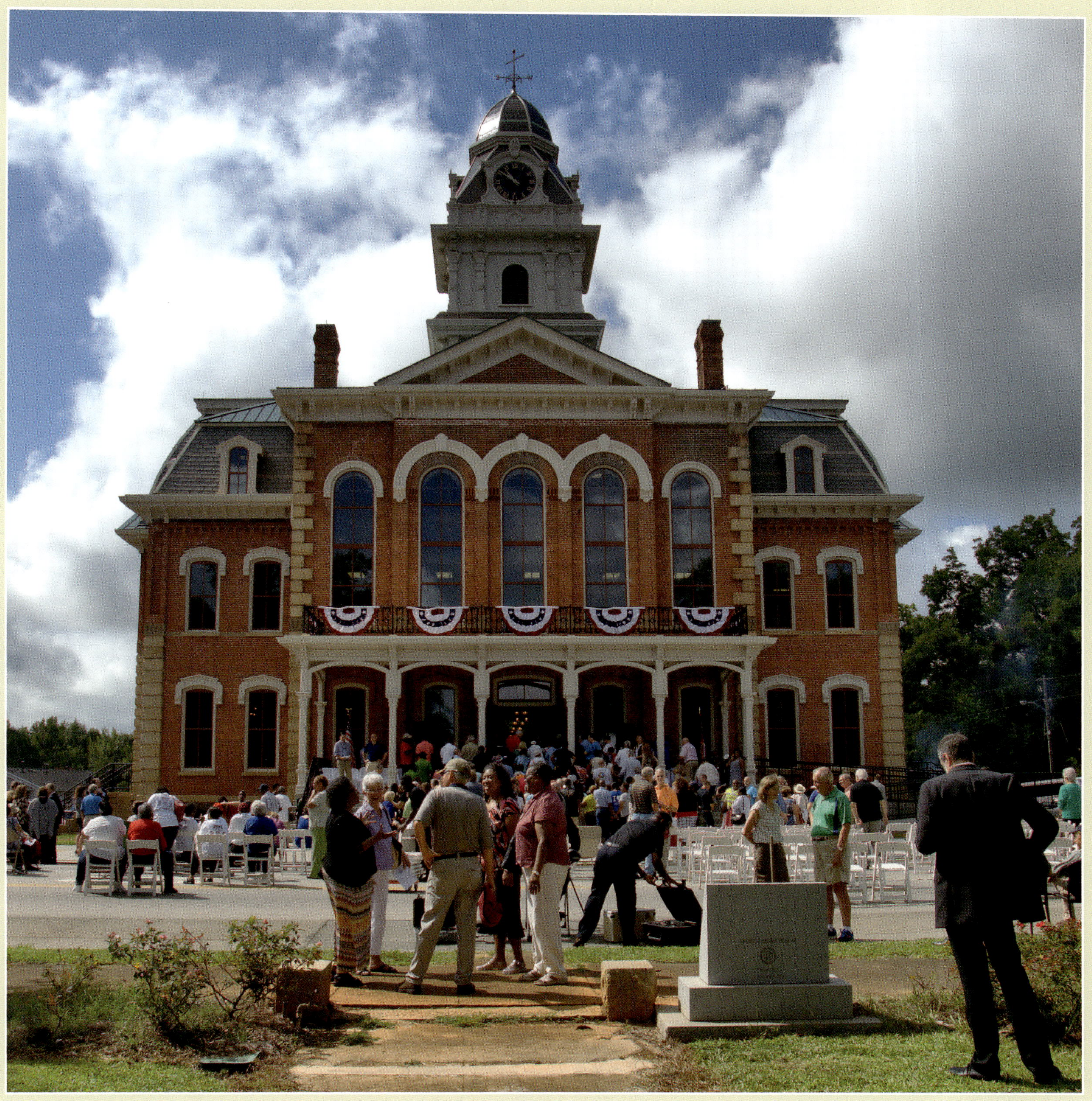

Hancock County Courthouse, Sparta

architects Parkins and Bruce. It is a three-story building, roughly square in plan, with a projecting central section. The central section reads as though it is two stories, as the upper-story courtroom-level windows are double height. The first floor of the central section features a porch with turned supports and arched bracing. The building is constructed of red brick with stone quoins and window surrounds. The courthouse's most notable feature is its large central cupola that sits atop a straight sided mansard roof. The cupola is comprised of three registers and features a clock in its convex roof.

On August 11, 2014, a fire ripped through the courthouse, destroying the famed clock tower and gutting the building, leaving only the exterior brick walls standing. The fire burned for nearly three weeks and reached temperatures hot enough to melt the 800-pound bell in the clock tower. Thanks to the determination and political will of Hancock County Commission chairwoman Sistie Hudson, along with a sound insurance policy purchased through the Association of County Commissioners of Georgia, the reconstruction efforts began within days of the fire. Within a month, steel reinforcements were placed against the exterior walls, which had been determined to be structurally sound. Architectural plans—borrowed by neighboring Walton County in the 1990s—were returned. Its courthouse, in Monroe, was also designed by Parkins and Bruce and is a sister to the Hancock County building.

Stick Style

Stick Style, although not commonly found in Georgia, is finely demonstrated in the Lapham-Patterson House in Thomasville. The style is characterized by steeply pitched gable roofs, often featuring decorative trusses and diagonal or curved support bracing, wooden construction, and decorative stickwork detailing. The style was commonly found in summer cottages in the Northeast in the 1860s and 1870s but was also used for townhouses in urban areas, including San Francisco.

The Lapham-Patterson House was built in 1884–85 as a resort cottage for Chicago businessman C. W. Lapham. Unlike those in the Northeast, Southern resort cottages like the Lapham-Patterson House were built for use in winter when mild temperatures allowed for outdoor activities. The architect-designer of the Lapham-Patterson House is unknown, but the building is individually listed as a National Historic Landmark in recognition of its outstanding architecture. It features a three-story octagonal core flanked by nonmatching, two-story wings, all of which are connected by porches on both the ground and second floors. The central core features a colossal portico and clipped gable roof, while the wings feature front-facing gables. Architectural detailing in the gables is unique to each bay and includes decorative trusses, curved support bracing, and stickwork detailing. The building features clapboard and shingle siding in a variety of patterns, as is typical of Stick Style.

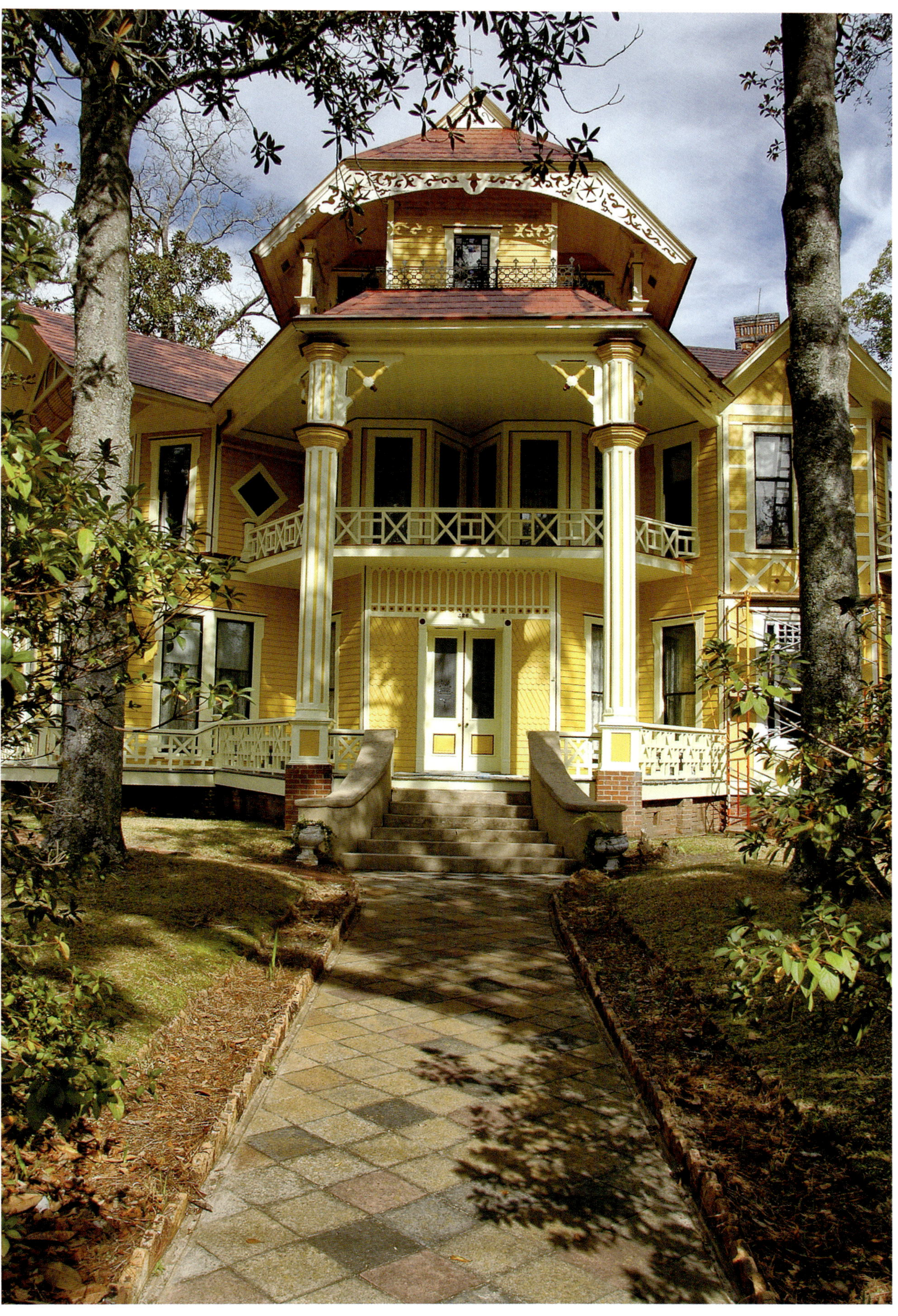

Lapham-Patterson House, Thomasville

Queen Anne

The widespread popularity of the Queen Anne style in Georgia can largely be attributed to the proliferation of architectural pattern books in the late nineteenth century and the expanding railroad network that delivered decorative millwork to communities across the state. Although the style was named for Queen Anne, it does not reflect the architectural influences of her reign (1702–15), but rather demonstrates characteristics of Elizabethan and Jacobean building styles. Hallmarks of the Queen Anne style include asymmetrical building forms with steeply pitched gabled or hipped roofs. Buildings may be constructed of wood or masonry and often feature a combination of materials, which contributes to the decorative appearance associated with the style. Porches are a common feature, as are towers in round or polygonal shapes. Within the Queen Anne style, several subtypes illustrate the diversity of decorative details utilized during the period. These include spindle-work or Eastlake-style decoration that incorporates machine-made elements such as friezes, brackets, and balustrades. Other subtypes feature half-timbered detailing and patterned masonry inspired by medieval buildings.

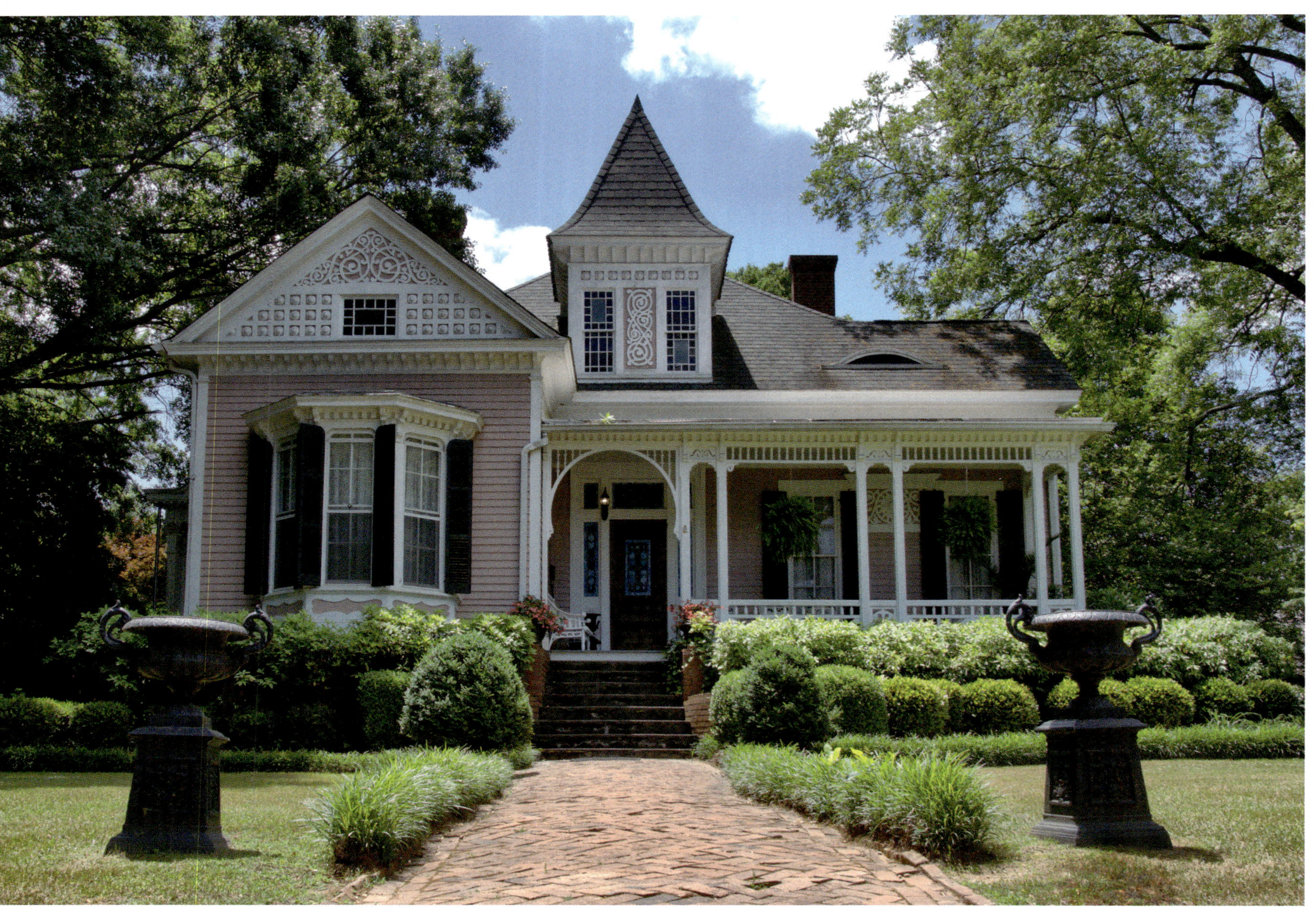

Hill-Harris House, Washington

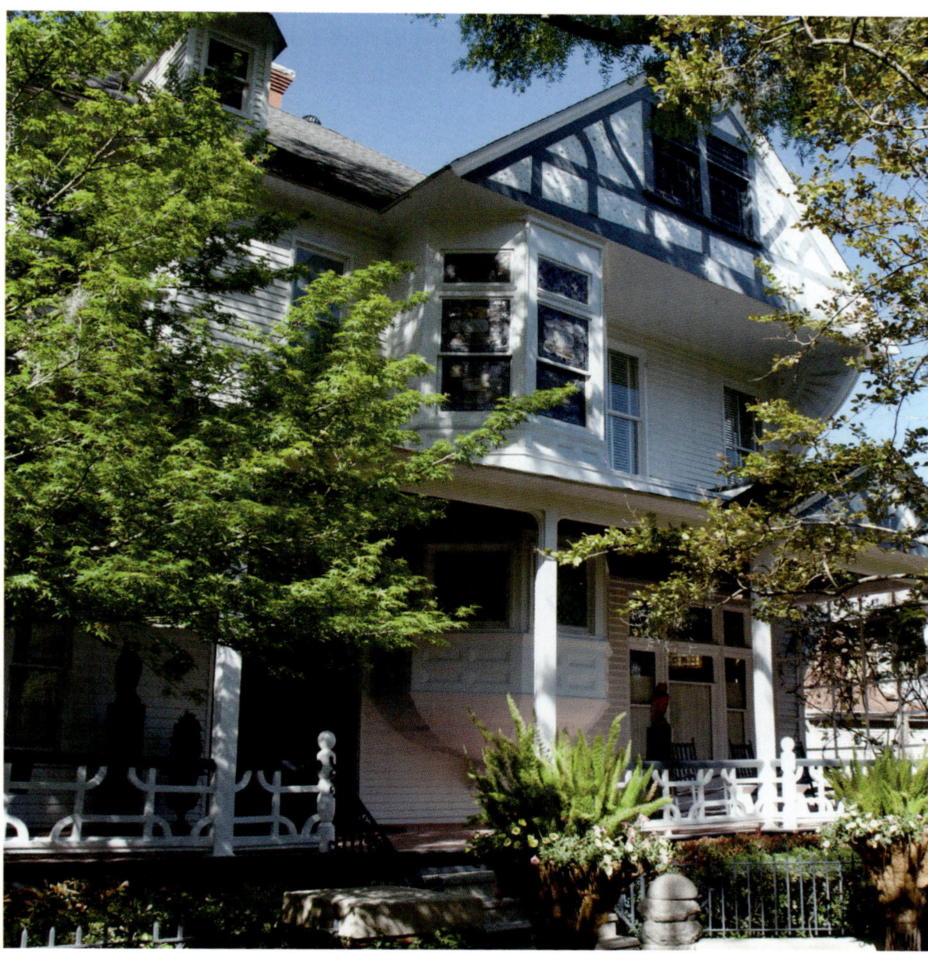

Smithfield Cottage, Savannah

The Hill-Harris House in Washington, Wilkes County, stands as a testament the prosperity of the primarily agricultural area in the decades following the Civil War. The house was built in 1890 and features many decorative details associated with the Queen Anne style. The building is asymmetrical in plan, with an irregular roof shape and multiple gables. The facade has a three-story octagonal tower with an ogee-shaped roof as well as a wrap-around porch on the first floor. The house is constructed of wood and features a variety of decorative elements, including turned porch posts, balustrade, spindle-work frieze, and gable decoration.

The residence now known as Smithfield Cottage was built for J. P. Williams in 1888 in Savannah's Victorian District. The building was designed by prominent architects Fay and Eichberg, who were both from New York but worked extensively in Atlanta and Savannah. Smithfield Cottage is a fine example of the half-timbered subtype of the Queen Anne style. The wood building has an irregularly shaped plan and a complex roofline with multiple gables. The decorative scheme is dominated by the half-timbering found in the gables on the front and side of the building. Other evident hallmarks of the style include oriel and bay windows, solid brackets underneath the eaves, and patterned masonry chimneys. The building was restored by the Savannah College of Art and Design, and many interior architectural features, including mantelpieces, woodwork and stained glass, were retained.

The Augusta Cotton Exchange, built in 1886, is a monument to both the agricultural and industrial history of Victorian-era Georgia. The building was constructed during a time of significant growth in cotton production and manufacturing in Augusta. The city's location on the Savannah River, along with its inland transportation connections, made it a hub for the cotton trade at the end of the nineteenth century, and the Cotton Exchange building was at the geographical and metaphorical center. The large masonry building was designed by Enoch William Brown and built by William Henry Goodrich and is a good example of a commercial building constructed in the Queen Anne style. It is rectangular in plan and features front- and side-facing gables as well as a round turret above the principal entrance. The turret is supported by a cast-iron Corinthian column that was produced at the local foundry of Charles F. Lombard. The red-brick exterior is accented by light-colored stone in the window surrounds, stringcourses, and decorative lattice detailing. The gable end features a Palladian window set within a sunburst motif.

Augusta Cotton Exchange, Augusta

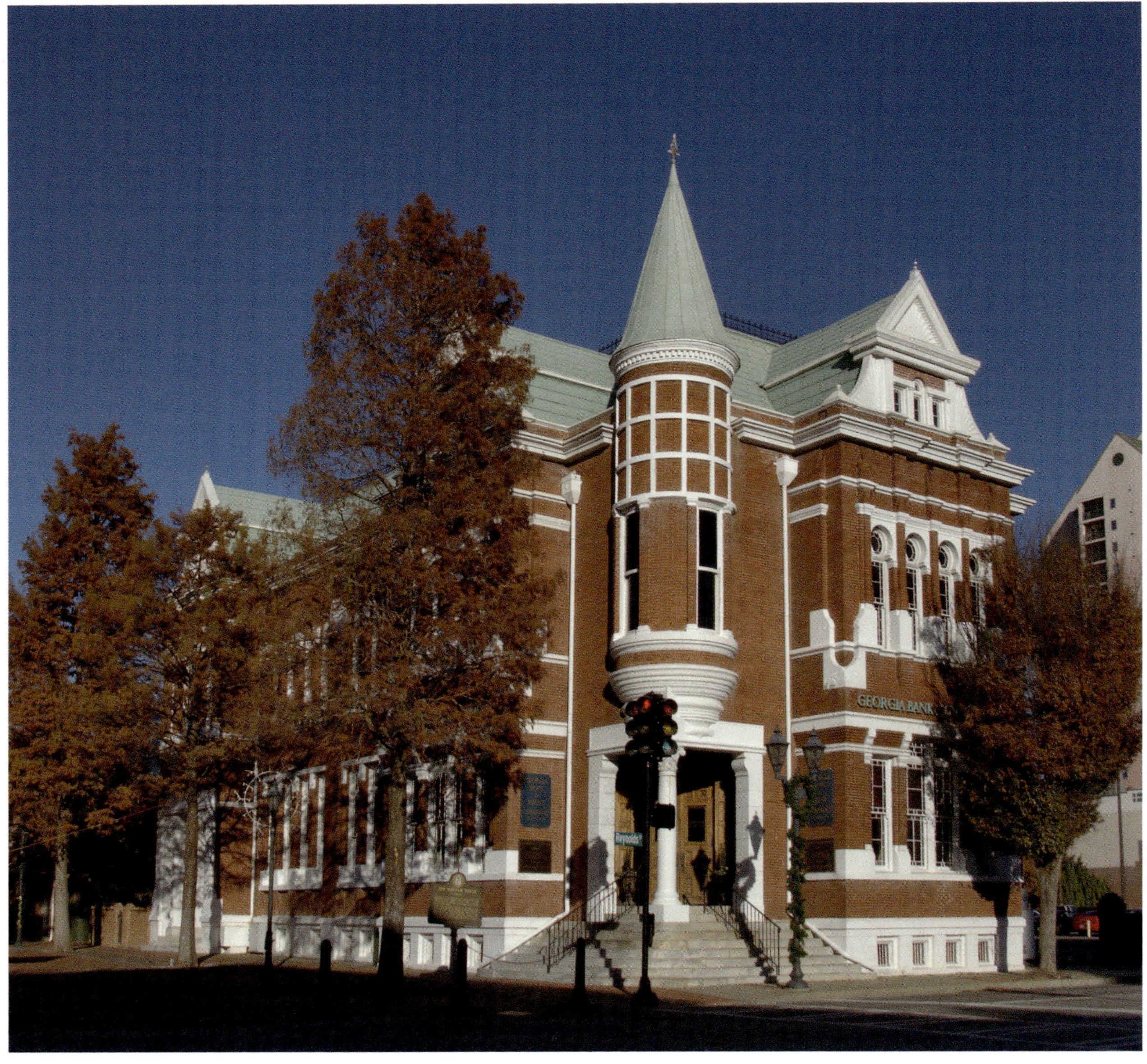

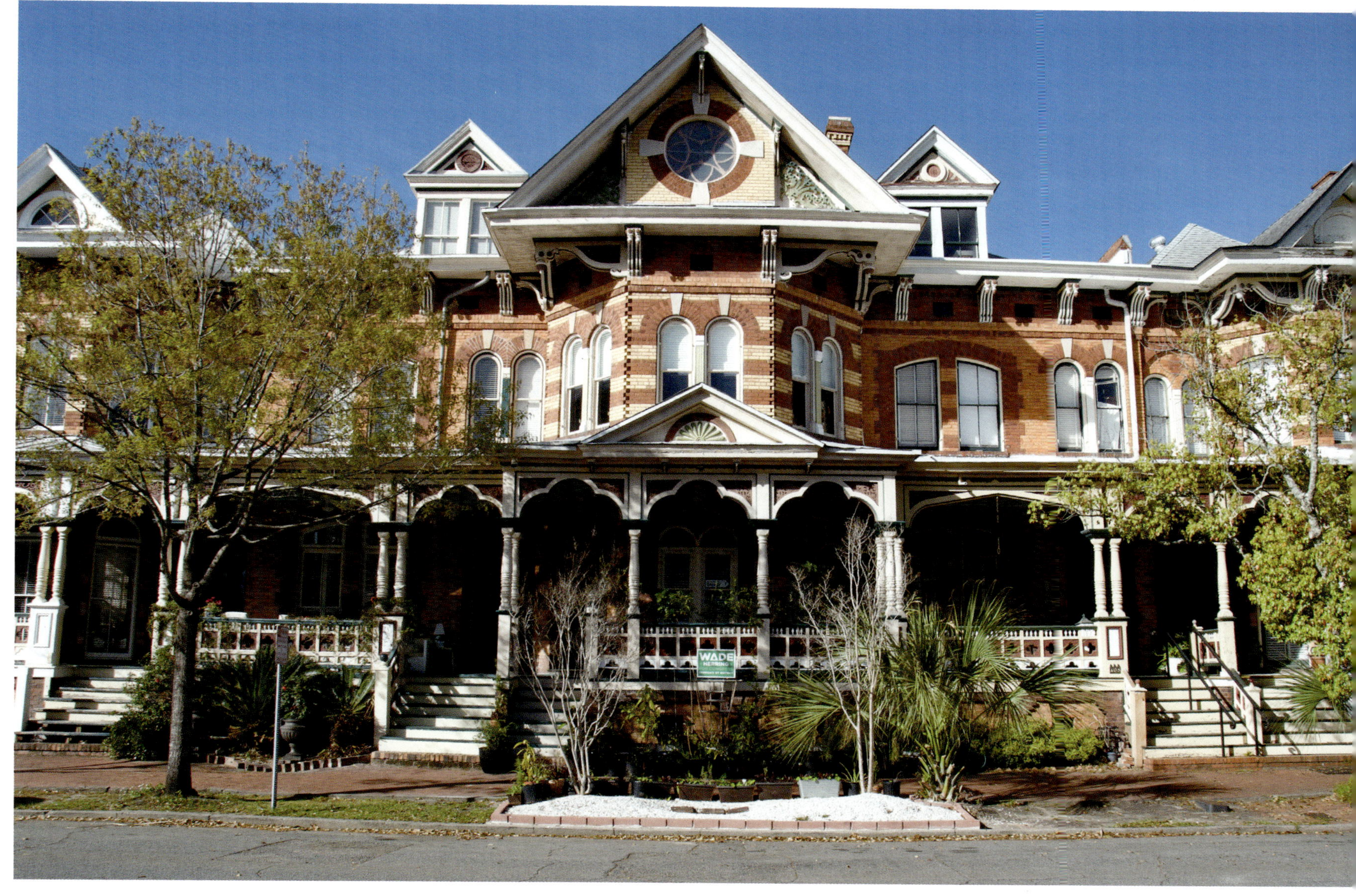

McMillan Row Houses, Savannah

The brothers Thomas and Ronald McMillan built several buildings in Savannah's Victorian District in the 1890s. They were born in North Carolina and relocated to Savannah, where they operated a successful naval-stores business. In addition to his professional success, Thomas McMillan served as an alderman for the City of Savannah and two terms in the state legislature. This row of five attached townhouses at 402–410 East Huntington Street, constructed in 1892, is a unified, single architectural composition noteworthy for its banded polychrome masonry construction. The row features a symmetrical five-part facade with the emphasis on the projecting central unit. The central unit and the two outer units have prominent front-facing gables, while the other two units have dormer windows. The row features a porch across the full width of the facade, with turned columns, Tudor and trefoil-shaped brackets, and a balustrade with quatrefoil and trefoil design. There are large brackets underneath the eaves. The gables on the end units have a sunburst design, while the central gable features a round stained-glass window set within decorative scrollwork. Paired windows are set within rounded and jack arches across the facade of the building.

One of Georgia's most distinguished landmarks, the Jekyll Island Club was established as a winter resort for America's wealthiest families, including the Rockefellers, Vanderbilts, Pulitzers, and Morgans. The Queen Anne–style Club House was designed by Chicago architect Charles A. Alexander and constructed in 1887. It is an L-shaped masonry building that is visually divided into three sections. The primary section is four stories high and features a round tower on the corner. The tower itself is five stories high and features a conical roof, bracketed cornice, and external viewing platforms on the fourth and fifth stories. A rounded corner pavilion on the first floor of the Club House echoes the shape of the tower that rises beside it. Behind the primary section is a lower, three-story section that connects it with the rear four-story section. Like the primary section, the rear section features a rounded pavilion on the first floor. The building's three-part composition is unified by a porch on the first floor that runs the length of the Club House and by a series of contrasting horizontal stringcourses between each of the floors. Porches on the top floors of each section are supported by heavy brackets and feature simple detailing reminiscent of the Stick Style. The original porte cochere on the building's primary section features a series of three rounded "moon gate" arches that are typical of Queen Anne spindle-work detailing.

Jekyll Island Club, Jekyll Island

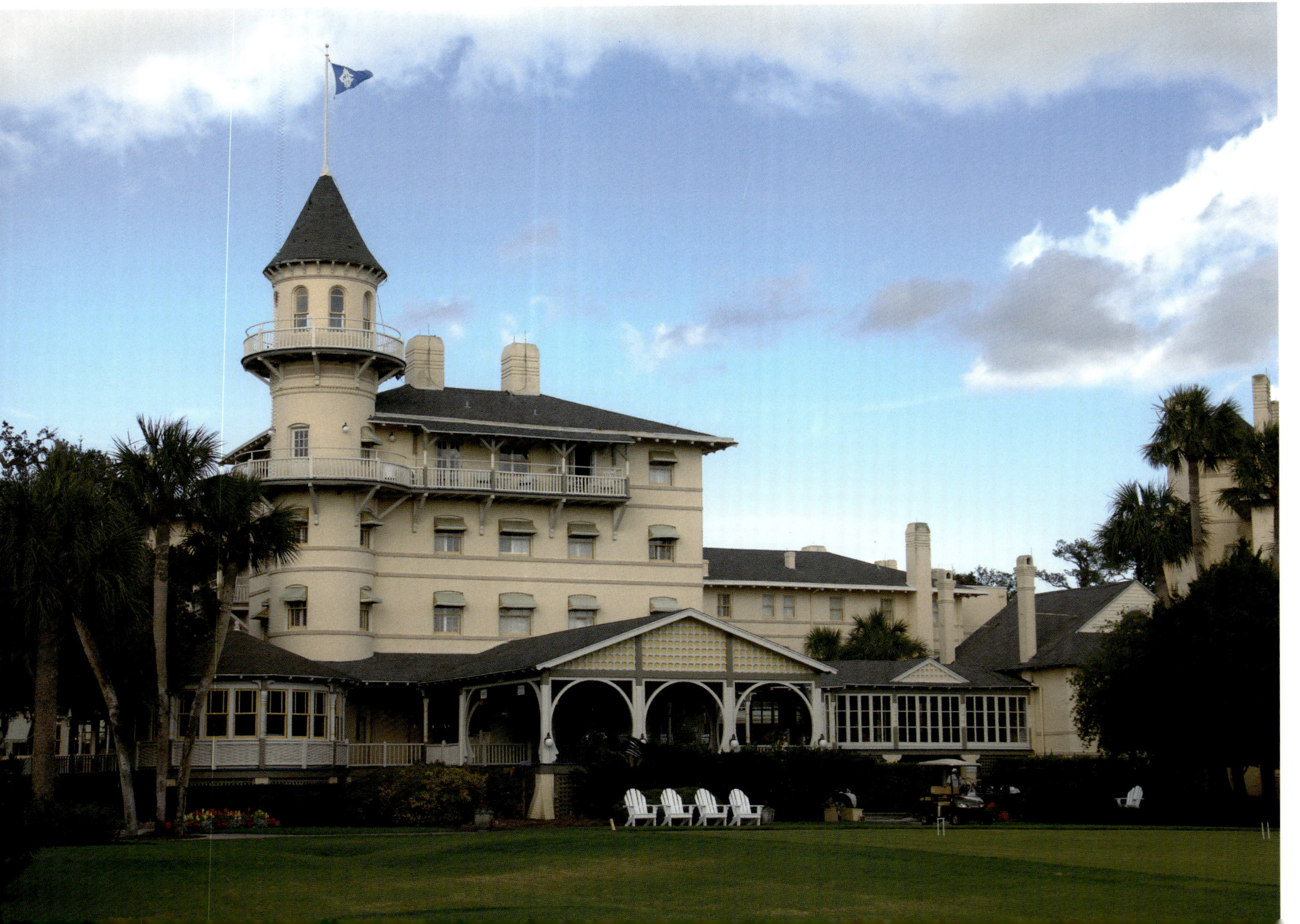

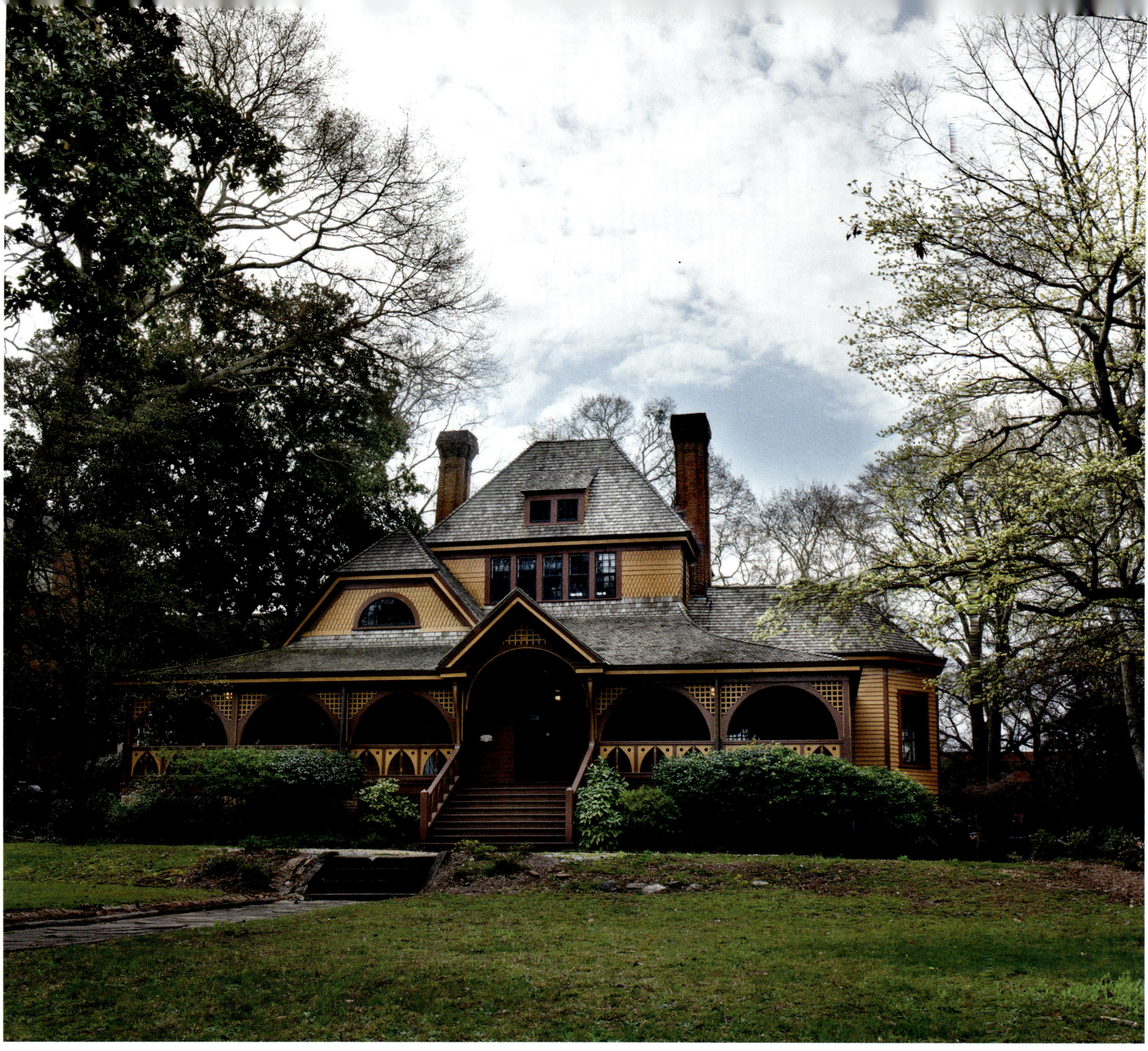

The Wren's Nest, Atlanta

Home to author and *Atlanta Constitution* editor Joel Chandler Harris, the Wren's Nest was built as a simple single-story structure and updated to its current appearance after Harris purchased the property in 1881. At that time, Atlanta's West End was an unincorporated village outside of the city, connected by mule-drawn trolleys. The original house was remodeled by architect George P. Humphreys of the firm Norrman and Humphreys. The two-story frame building includes many Queen Anne features, such as asymmetrical massing and a complex roof form composed of a hipped roof and cross gables. The design is defined by the large porch that runs the width of the building and features wide arched openings framed with lattice. The porch also has an unusual fretwork handrail. The building's interior remains largely unchanged and features many original architectural details, paint colors, and furnishings. The building is individually listed as a National Historic Landmark and serves as a house museum and a center for creative writing.

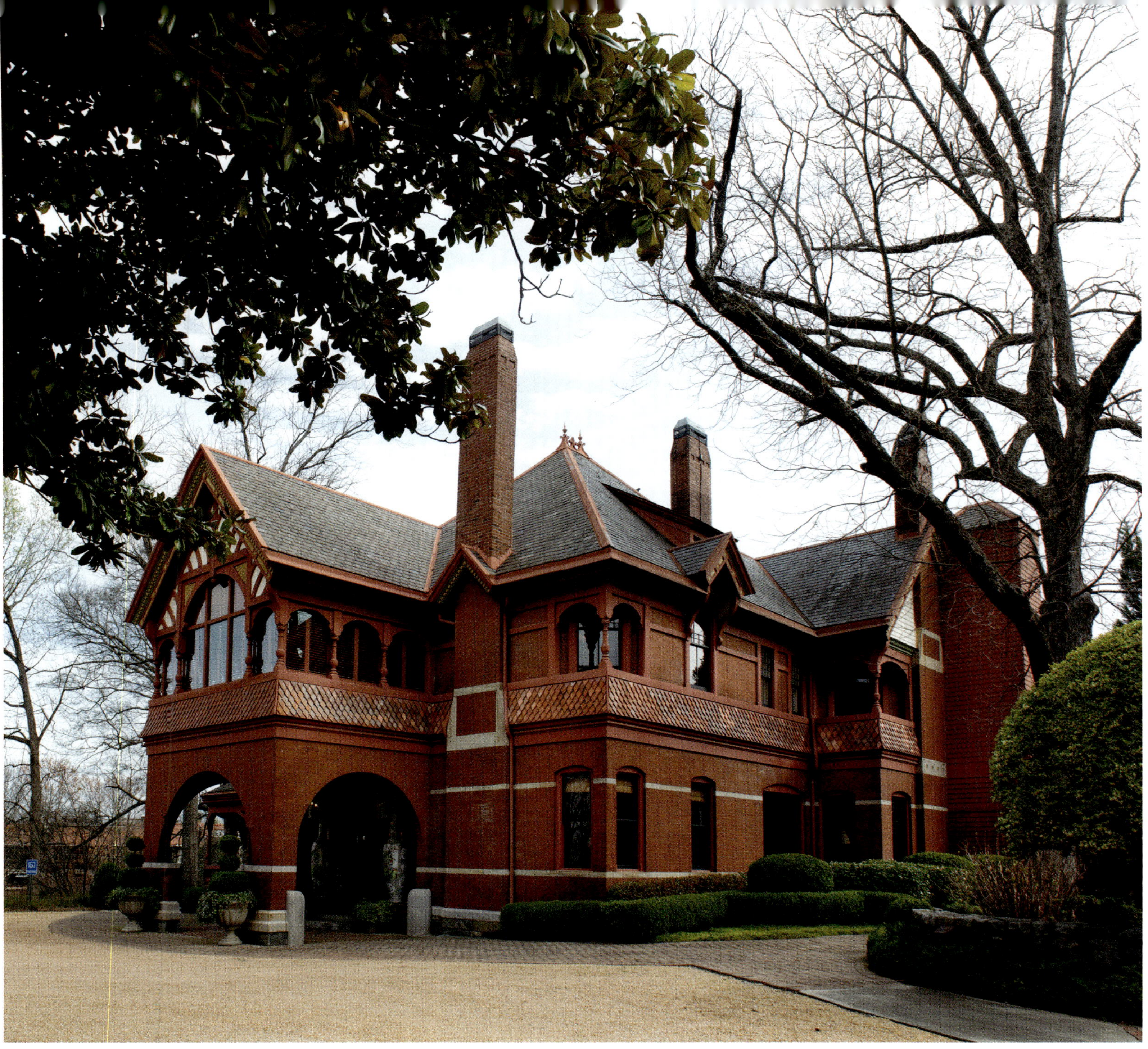

Peters House, Atlanta

Located in the heart of Midtown Atlanta, the Edward C. Peters House stands as a testament the city's development since the late nineteenth century. The area where the Peters House stands was once a 400-acre tract of land just north of downtown. Transportation and trade had a significant impact on the city, and by 1878 the Atlanta Street Railway Company, of which Peters's father, Richard, was cofounder, connected downtown to the northern suburbs, bisecting Peters's property and establishing Peachtree Street as one of the growing city's main thoroughfares. The Peters House was designed by Swedish architect Gottfried L. Norrman in 1883. It is a two-and-a-half-story red-brick building with asymmetrical massing and a cross gabled roof. The building features many hallmarks of the Queen Anne style, including half-timbering in the principal gable and turned porch posts and railings on the west and north sides. The Peters House utilizes multiple masonry materials to provide relief on the exterior walls. These include red brick, terra-cotta "shingles," and contrasting stone stringcourses. The building's interior retains a high degree of integrity with original mantels, paneling, and decorative wall treatments still intact. The building was rehabilitated by the Savannah College of Art and Design in 2007 and serves as a center for literary arts and writing.

Dr. Martin Luther King Jr. is one of Georgia's most distinguished native sons. His birth home is located on Atlanta's Auburn Avenue. This historic corridor was the center of African American life in the city in the late nineteenth and twentieth centuries. The "Sweet Auburn" district was home to many African American businesses, churches, and civic and cultural institutions and reflected the achievements of the community it served, despite the racist policies that kept Atlanta segregated until the mid-twentieth century. Although Sweet Auburn was primarily a commercial area, it also included a residential section, where Martin Luther King Sr. and his wife, along with her family, made their home from 1925 to 1941. Martin Luther King Jr. was born in the house on January 15, 1929.

The Martin Luther King Jr. Birth Home was built in 1895 in the Queen Anne style. The two-story frame house has a hipped roof with cross gables and an asymmetrical building form. Like many Queen Anne–style houses, the building features a large one-story porch that extends along its front and side. The porch has turned supports and delicate fretwork brackets. Other decorative detailing includes a sunburst panel and decorative shingles in the front-facing gable.

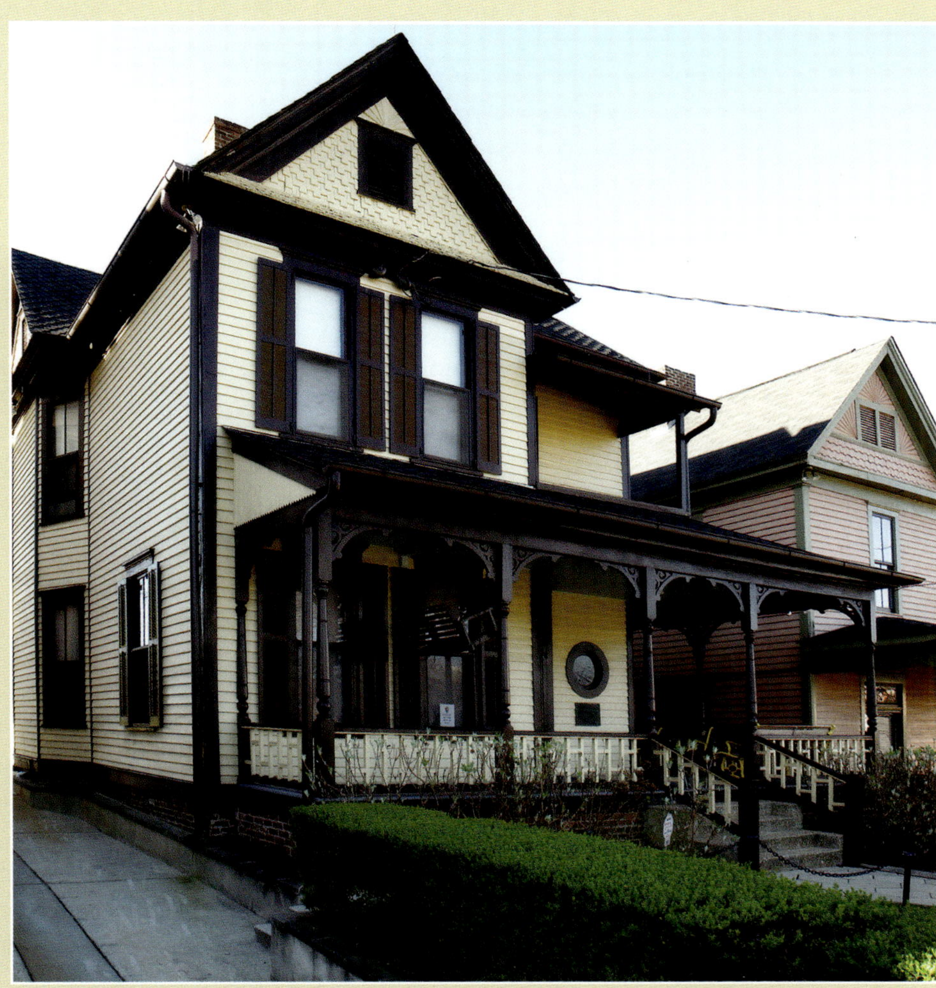

Martin Luther King Jr. Birthplace, Atlanta

Romanesque Revival and Richardsonian Romanesque

The Romanesque Revival arrived in America in the mid-nineteenth century. Like other Victorian styles, it combined elements from earlier architectural periods, but it was primarily identified by use of rounded arches, towers, and decorative masonry work. The style was typically limited to commercial, civic, and religious buildings because of the expense of masonry materials. It was not until the late nineteenth century that the style grew in popularity and began to be seen in residential buildings as well as large-scale public commissions. This Richardsonian Romanesque style was named for American architect Henry Hobson Richardson, whose distinctive work was derived from medieval forms and their elaboration. Richardson was born in Louisiana and educated at Harvard and was the second American to study architecture at the Ecole des Beaux-Arts in Paris. Although Richardson's work was primarily centered in the northeastern United States, his influence can be seen in buildings across Georgia. Richardsonian Romanesque buildings are characterized by solid masonry forms that feature low, rounded arches, towers with conical roofs, and asymmetrical compositions. Decorative detailing is often found in polychrome stonework, column capitals, and decorative plaques that feature floral or geometric patterns based on medieval designs.

Stone Hall, also known as Fountain Hall, was constructed on the campus of Atlanta University in 1882 and served as the university's admissions office until 1929, when it was leased to Morris Brown College. Stone Hall has been recognized as a National Historic Landmark because of its association with African American education in the South in the nineteenth century, but it is also architecturally significant as a transitional Victorian building that features elements of the Queen Anne and Romanesque Revival styles. It was designed by Swedish born architect Gottfried L. Norrman, who was active in the postbellum South. Norrman received many commissions in Atlanta, but few of his buildings are extant, which contributes to the significance of Stone Hall. The three-story brick building features a symmetrical plan and elevations and is defined by a four-story square clocktower that rises from the center of the primary facade. The entrance to the building is recessed behind a large Romanesque Revival arch in the first floor of the tower. While the second and third floors have single rectangular windows, the fourth floor of the tower features a triple arched opening on the front and double arched openings on the sides. The triple arched opening is constructed of contrasting stone that is also seen in window openings and stringcourses throughout the building. Stone Hall also features the decorative brickwork imitative of medieval buildings that is common to the Renaissance Revival style.

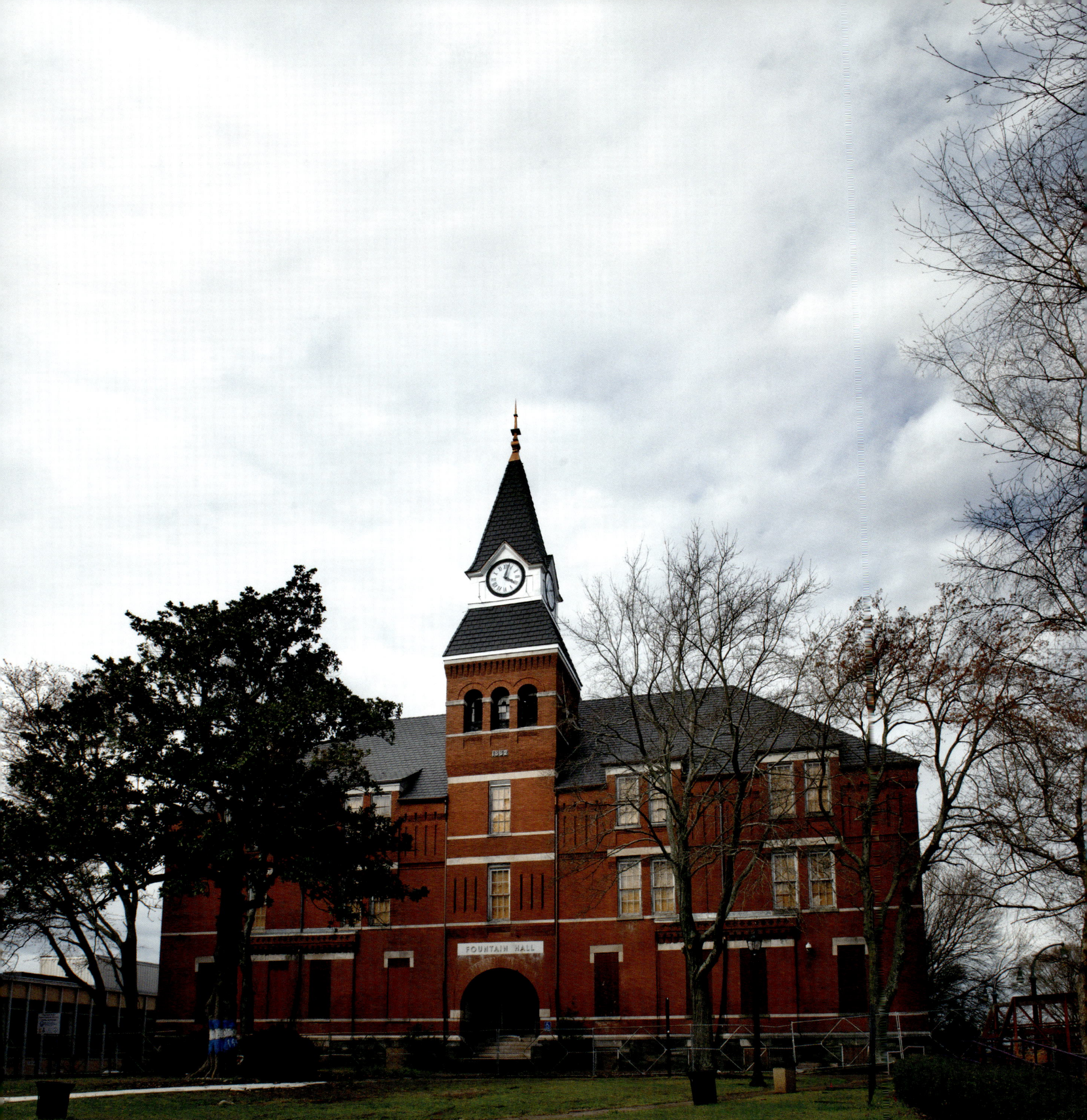

Stone Hall, Atlanta

The Oglethorpe County Courthouse in Lexington was designed circa 1887 by architects Lorenzo G. Wheeler, William H. Parkins, and Hannibal I. Kimball. The Romanesque Revival red-brick and granite building has a balanced, although not strictly symmetrical, facade. The courthouse's primary entrance is marked by a central three-story square clocktower with a conical roof. The two turrets that form the front corners of the tower spring from low granite columns with cushion capitals. The third floor features an open space behind granite arches that spring from corbels and form a central column. The tower is flanked by identical two-story bays that feature wide granite arches on the ground floor and paired arched openings above. On either side of the bays are low square towers with pyramidal roofs and granite stringcourses. The towers feature different fenestration patterns, and the west tower projects slightly from the plane of the facade. The building's west facade features a two-story bay that attaches to the projecting tower, while the east facade features a large stone arch on the ground floor and a triple arched opening above.

Oglethorpe County Courthouse, Lexington

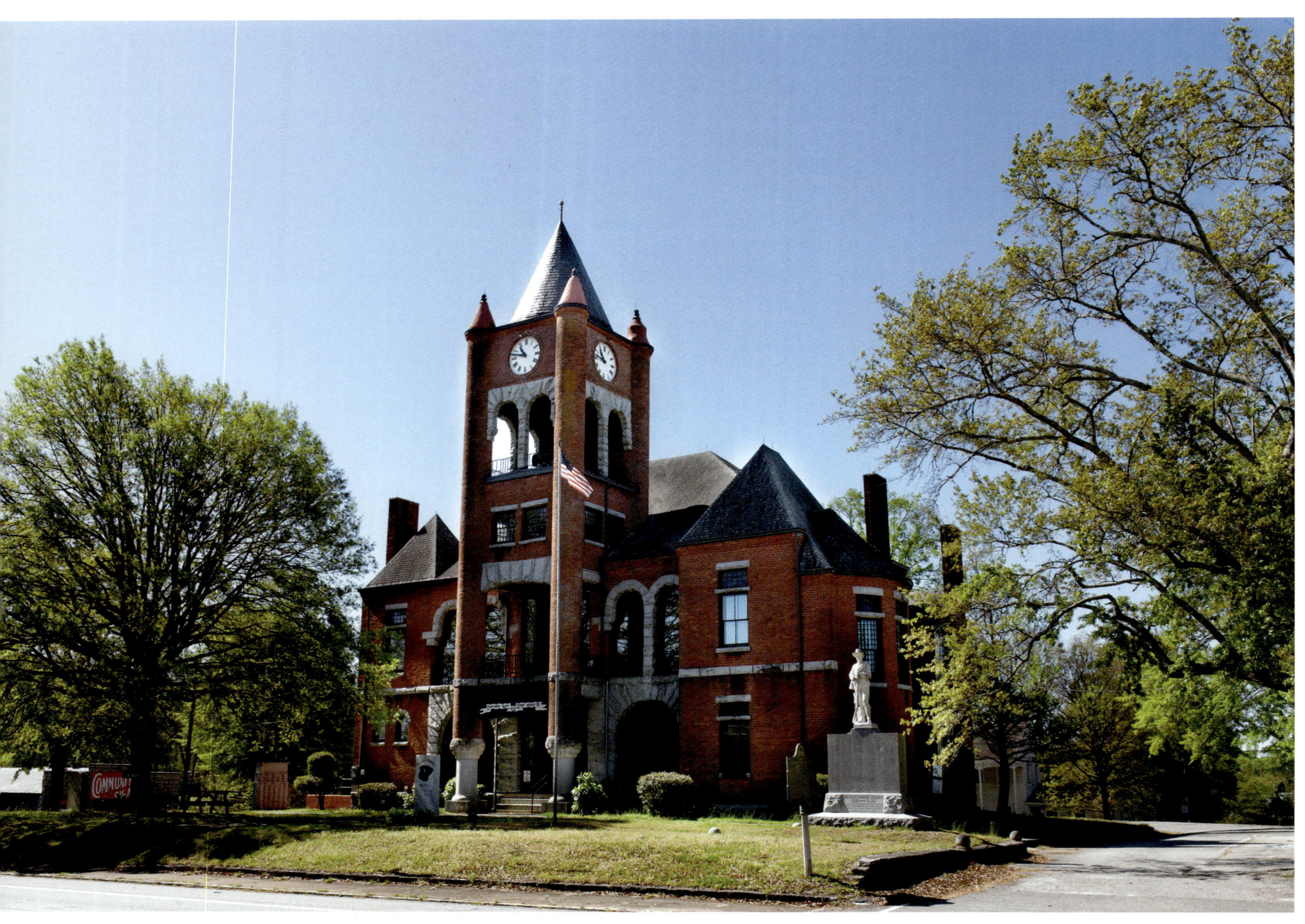

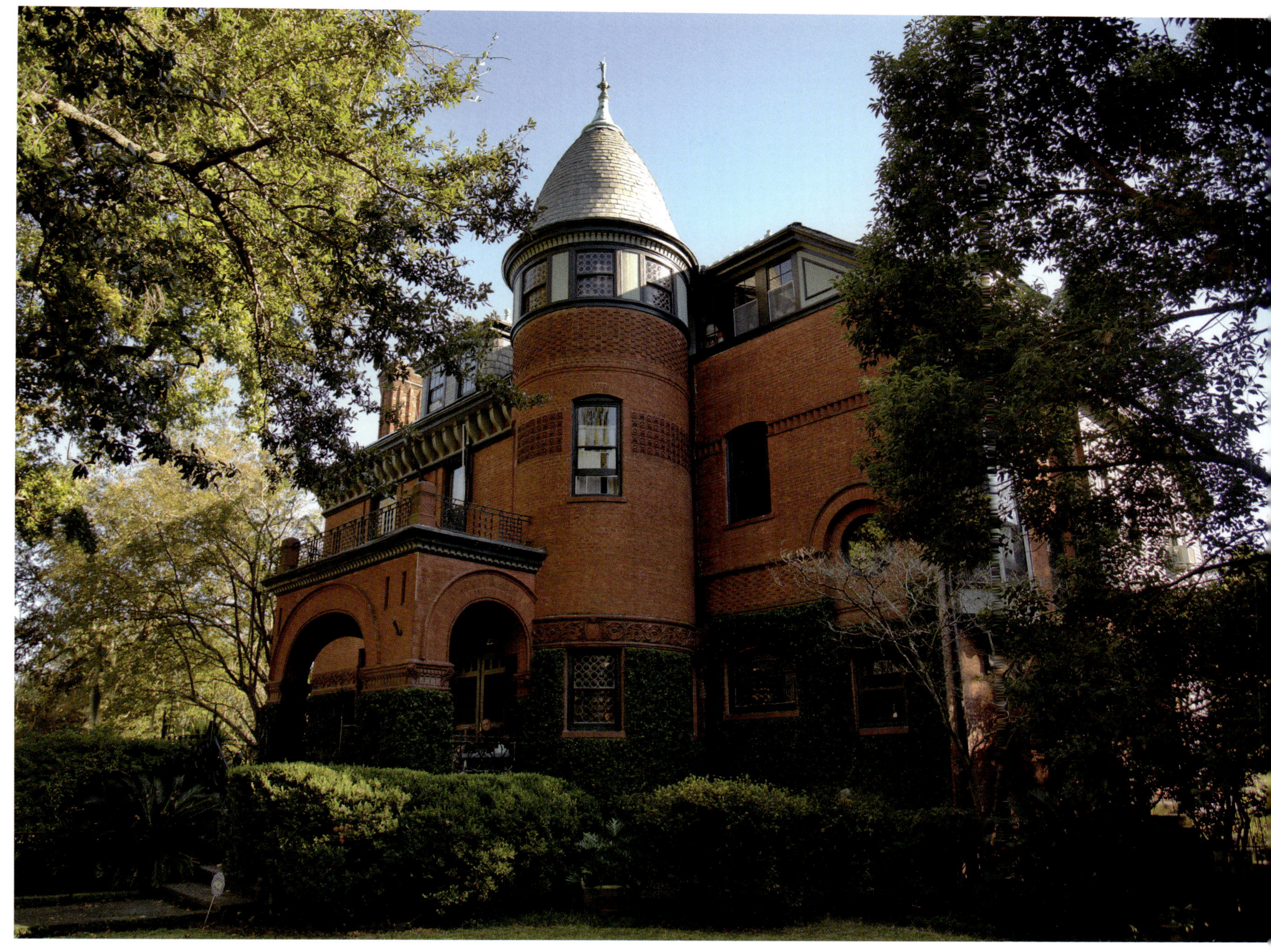

Baldwin-Neely House, Savannah

Located on an expansive lot, the Baldwin-Neely House was designed by prominent Boston architect William Preston in 1887 and was one of many commissions he received in Savannah. The house was built during a period of economic prosperity in Savannah and reflects the status of its original owner, George Johnson Baldwin. Like other houses of the Victorian period, the Baldwin-Neely House features elements of several architectural styles, including Queen Anne and Romanesque Revival. The building's asymmetrical facade is a common feature of both styles, but the masonry construction is more commonly found in Romanesque Revival buildings. The facade of the Baldwin-Neely House features a one-story masonry porch with wide arched openings on three sides. Just behind the porch and slightly off to one side is a three-story round tower with a conical roof. There is a significant amount of decorative masonry work, including terra-cotta ornament on the east-facing chimney.

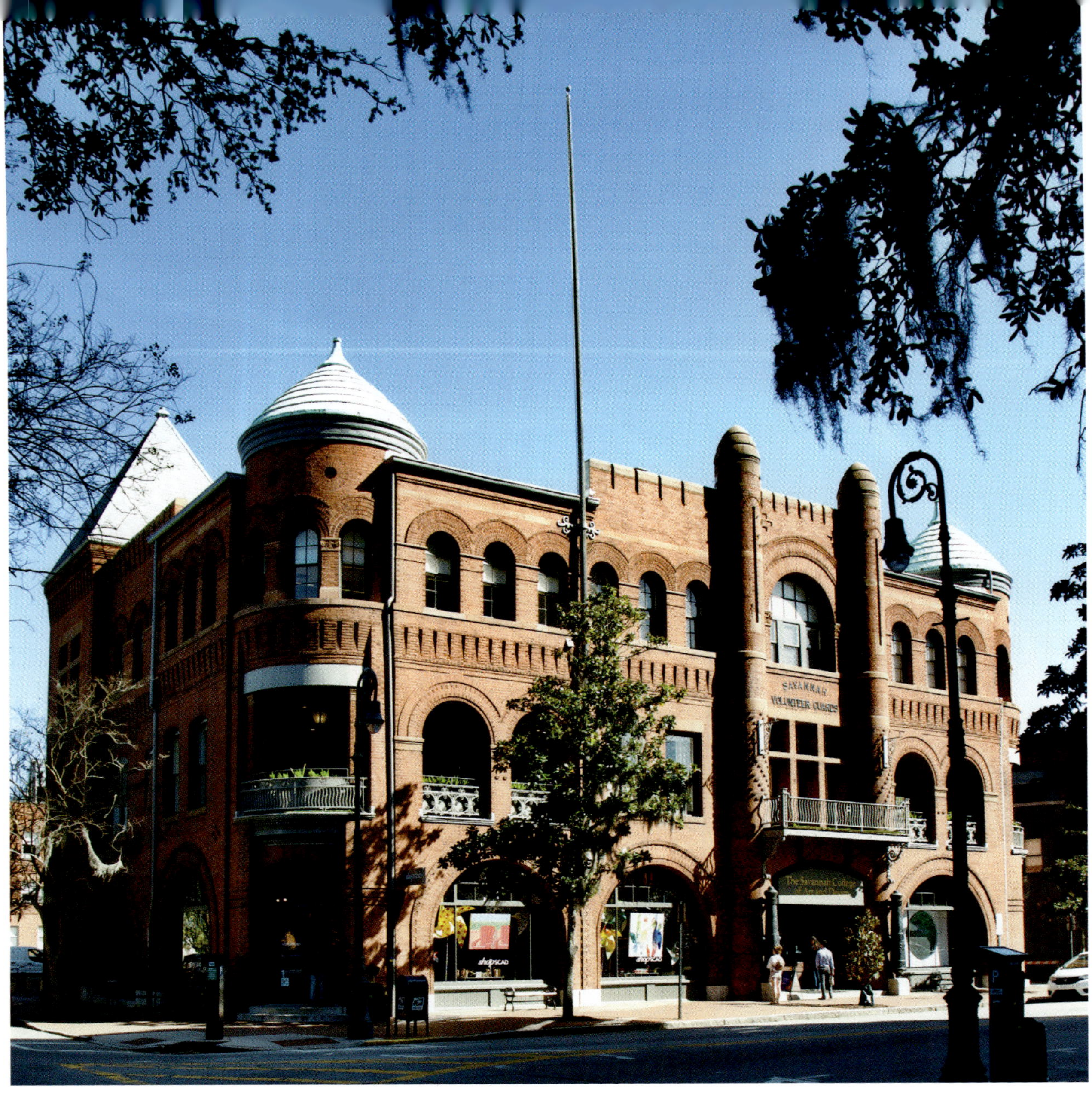

Savannah Guards Armory, Savannah

Also designed by William Preston, the Savannah Volunteer Guards Armory was constructed in 1892. Preston designed many other public buildings in Savannah, including the Savannah Cotton Exchange (1886), the Savannah DeSoto Hotel (1888, demolished 1968), and the Chatham County Courthouse (1889). The Savannah Volunteer Guards Armory is located on Madison Square, and the three-story corner building features asymmetrical facades on Bull and Charlton Streets, with the primary entrance on Bull Street. It is constructed of red brick and features arched door and window openings on both facades. There is a square tower with a pyramidal roof at the northeast corner of the building and round towers with conical roofs on the northwest and southwest corners. The primary entrance on Bull Street is flanked by elongated brick turrets that extend beyond the parapet wall. The ground floor is defined by wide Romanesque arches and an entrance in the northwest corner tower. The second story features recessed porches set behind arched openings along the Bull Street facade. The third story features smaller arched window openings with contrasting stone details. Details such as crenellation, corbeling, and loopholes contribute to the fortresslike appearance of the building.

Americus's famous Windsor Hotel was designed by Gottfried L. Norrman in 1892 and features elements of Queen Anne and Romanesque Revival styles. The hotel was built during an economic boom that followed Reconstruction, and the elaborate building reflects the prosperity and optimism of Americus in the late nineteenth century. Designed to attract winter visitors from the North, the Windsor Hotel featured more than one hundred guest rooms on five floors, as well as a grand open lobby and ballrooms for socializing. The red-brick building has an irregular floorplan and elevations, with multiple square and round towers rising above smaller wings that connect them. The hotel's primary facade is anchored by a five-story square tower that features a three-story arched opening with recessed porches on the second and third floors. The fourth floor of the tower has arched window openings that are echoed in blind arches and windows on the fifth floor. A simple terra-cotta stringcourse separates the third and fourth floors, while a highly decorative frieze separates the fourth and fifth. The primary facade also features a four-story round corner tower with a conical roof. The tower has arched window openings on all four floors and an arched door opening on the ground floor. Although the heyday of the rail travel that first brought guests to the hotel has passed, the Windsor Hotel continues to impress visitors to the city and serves as a reminder of vibrant Victorian Americus.

Windsor Hotel, Americus

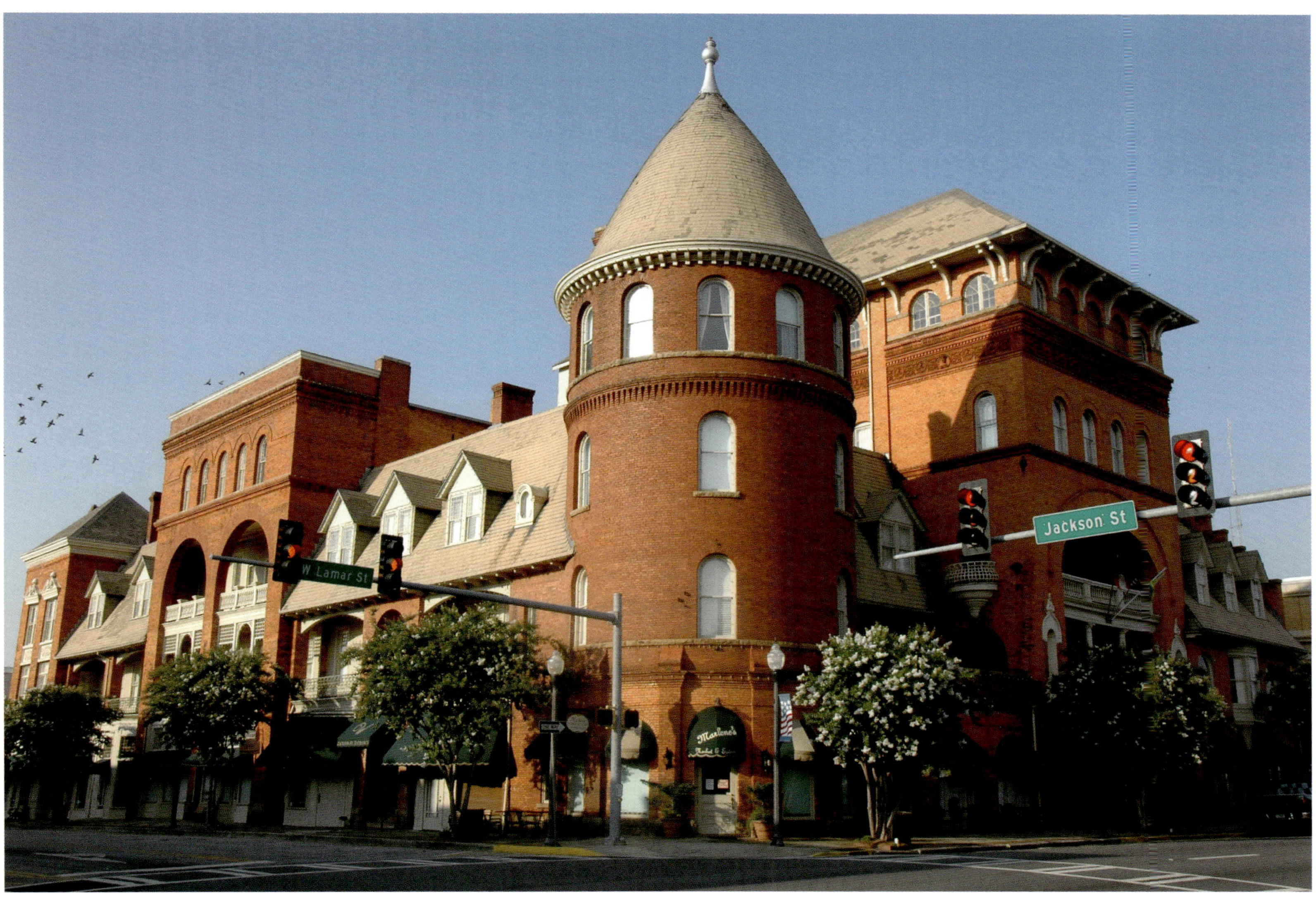

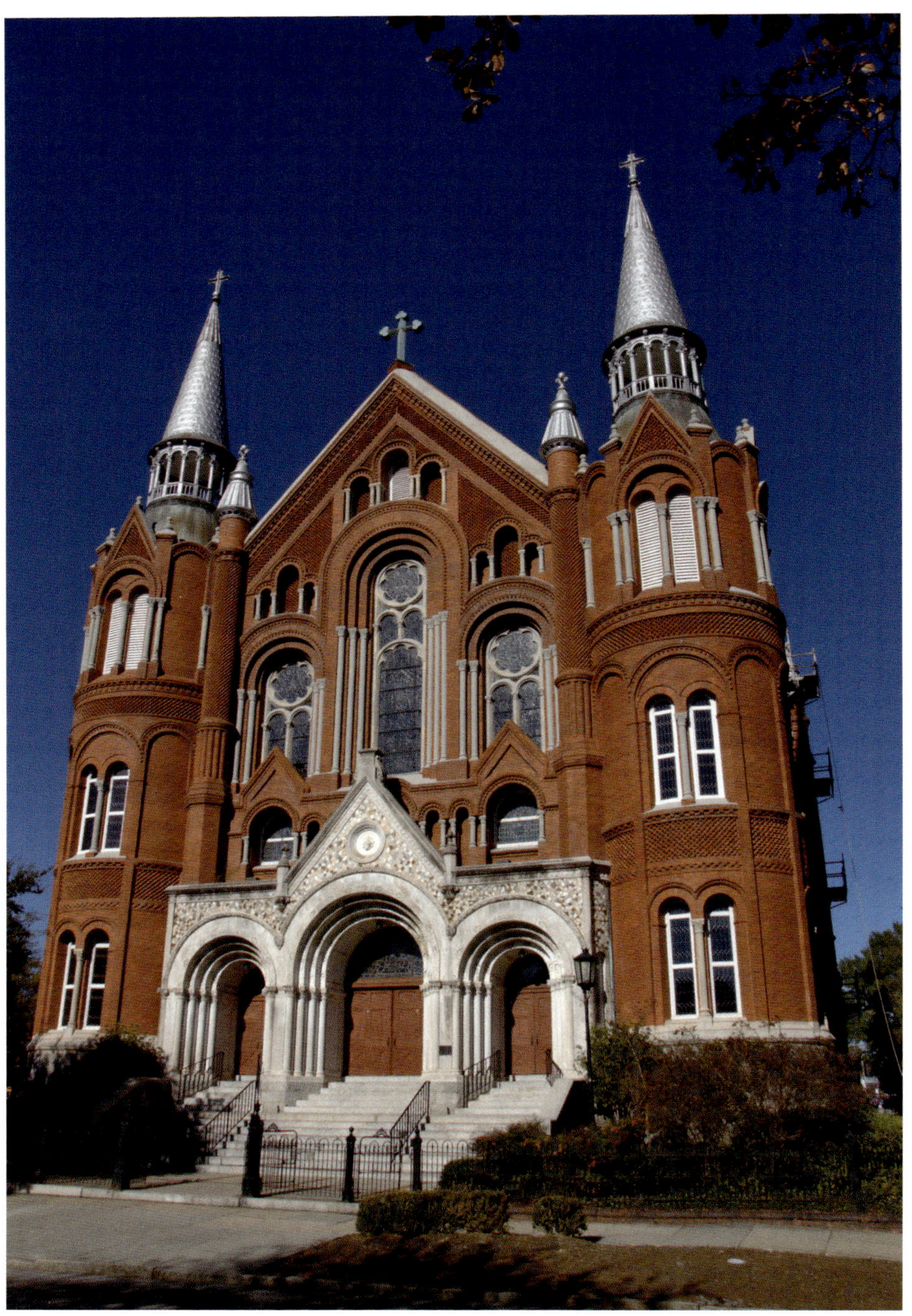

Sacred Heart Catholic Church, Augusta

The Sacred Heart Catholic Church in Augusta is a high Victorian composition that features elements of the Gothic and Romanesque Revival styles. It was designed in 1898 by Cornelius Otten, a Jesuit lay brother who also designed Saint Joseph's Church in Macon. The church features a symmetrical composition, more typical of Gothic Revival than of later Richardsonian Romanesque buildings, and is defined by its massive scale and proliferation of arches. The central portion of the church features a three-part arched entrance porch in contrasting stone on the first level and arched openings on the middle and upper levels. These triple arches spring from slender columns in contrasting stone and feature circular and round-headed rectangular windows. The central portion is flanked by round towers that are vertically divided in three sections. All three sections feature pairs of round-headed arched windows, but each section is uniquely articulated with different brick patterns, column arrangements, and use of materials. The church is said to have fifteen unique brick patterns incorporated in its design. The Sacred Heart Catholic Church, like many other Victorian buildings, is not a pure expression of a particular style. Rather, it illustrates the eclectic nature of the period.

The headquarters of the Georgia Trust for Historic Preservation, Rhodes Hall was designed in 1904 by architect Willis F. Denny for Atlanta furniture magnate A. G. Rhodes. The house was built on Rhodes's 114-acre estate on Peachtree Street, which was then a residential area. Rhodes Hall is a rare example of a Richardsonian Romanesque residential building in Georgia, and it reflects the status of its original owner. It was constructed using locally quarried Stone Mountain granite and features a steeply pitched red-slate roof. The building is

Rhodes Hall, Atlanta

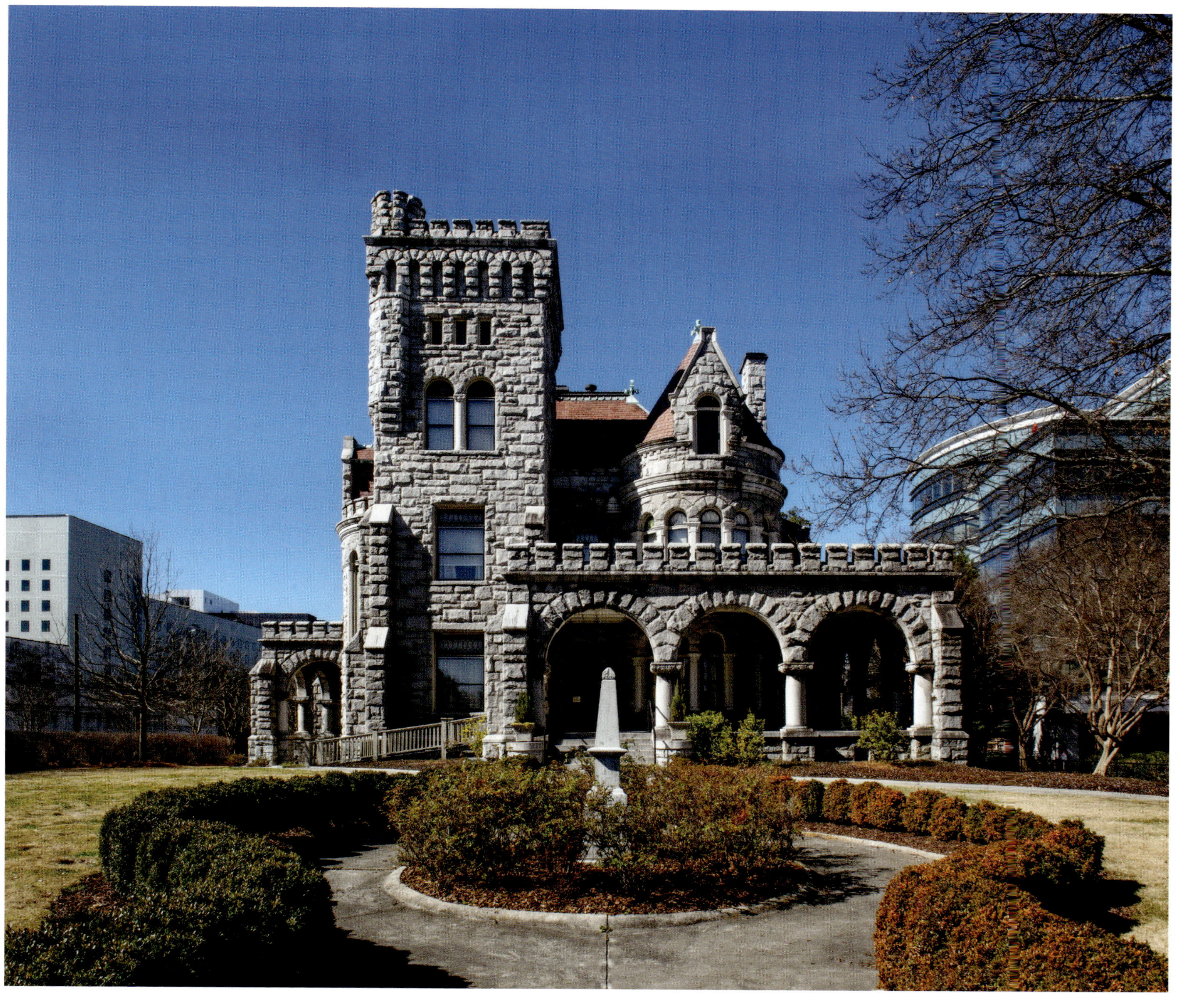

typical of the of the Richardsonian Romanesque style, with asymmetrical facades, square and rounded towers, and front and side porches set behind wide arched openings. The front porch arches spring from low columns with cushion capitals featuring a floral design. Similarly, the porte cochere on the building's south facade features wide arches supported by stone columns. The primary facade is anchored by a four-story square tower with rectangular window openings on the first, second, and fourth floors and paired arched windows on the third floor. The tower features a small turret, crenellation, and corbeling. The primary facade also features a three-story round tower with a conical roof and gabled dormer window. The building's interior is highly intact and features original leaded glass, mural paintings, carved mahogany staircase and fireplace mantels, lighting fixtures, and parquet floors. The building was deeded to the State of Georgia by the Rhodes family following Amos Rhodes's death in 1928. It first served as the home of the Georgia Archives but then was abandoned and sat empty for years. Under the supervision of the Trust, the rehabilitation began in 1990. Original features were restored, and in 2017 energy conservation measures were taken to ensure the long-term sustainability of the building.

Folk Victorian

The Folk Victorian style, like the Queen Anne style that preceded it, flourished as a result of the expanding railroad network and the consequent widespread availability of decorative architectural detailing in the late nineteenth century. The architectural forms of Folk Victorian buildings, however, were often vernacular or "folk" iterations of the high-style Queen Anne forms found in pattern books or architect-designed buildings of the period. Some Folk Victorian buildings were designed in the style, while others were existing buildings that were updated with decorative detailing. Hallmarks of the style include simple, often symmetrical side- or front-gabled forms as well as gable-and-wing examples. Folk Victorian houses are typically constructed of wood, with decorative detailing found on porches and gables and in brackets underneath the eaves.

The King-Tisdell Cottage, built in Savannah in 1896, is named for two of its owners, Sarah King and Robert Tisdell. King and Tisdell were part of a vibrant African American entrepreneurial culture in Savannah in the nineteenth century, and King operated a confectionary from the home. The King-Tisdell Cottage was moved from its original location on Ott Street, but the building retains integrity of design and reflects the ubiquitous Folk Victorian style. The building is a two-story, side-gabled cottage with a raised foundation. Typical of Folk Victorian architecture, the frame building features a symmetrical facade with a front porch that spans the width of the building. The porch is elaborated with turned columns, spindle-work detailing, and a bracketed cornice. Folk Victorian detailing is also used in the bargeboards on the two dormer windows and in the side gable.

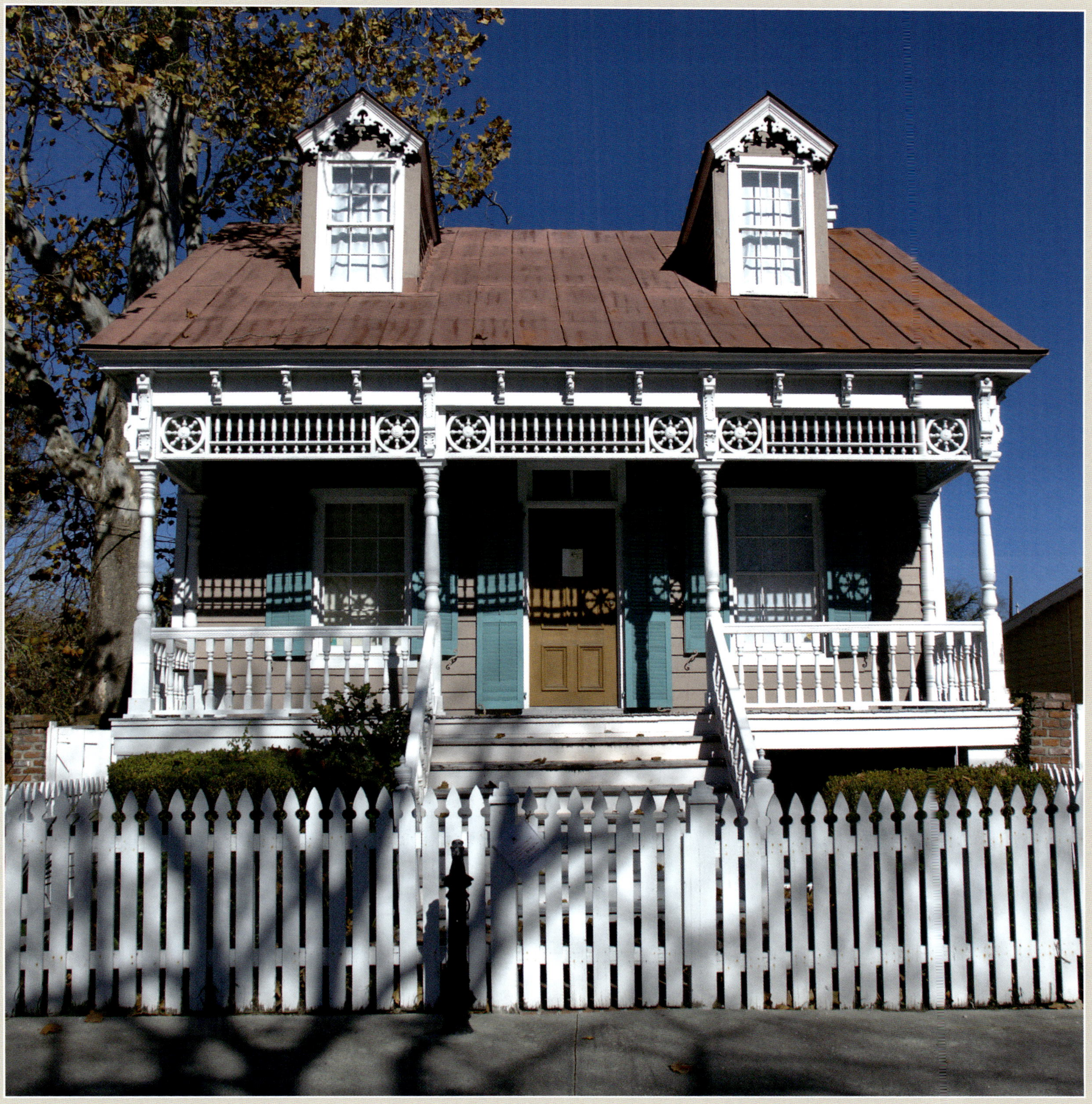

King-Tisdell Cottage, Savannah

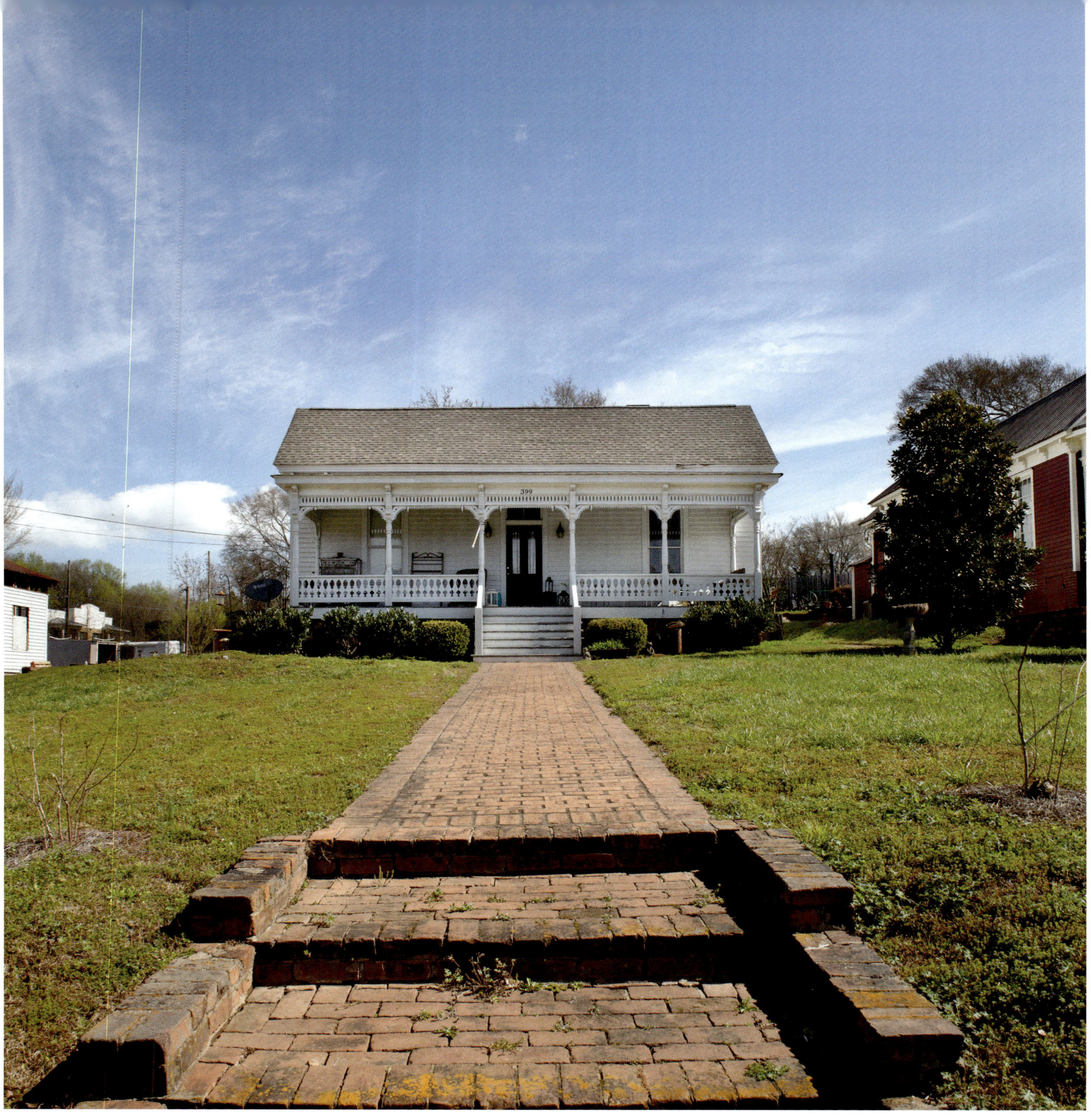

McLeroy House, Madison

The McLeroy House, located just northwest of Madison's town park, is a side-gabled frame building with a symmetrical facade and wide front porch. The porch features Folk Victorian detailing including turned columns, sawn balusters and a spindle-work frieze. The house also features bracketed eaves on the primary facade and in the side gable. This property was purchased by the Georgia Trust Revolving Fund in 2009. It was sold and rehabilitated in 2011 using original photographs to replicate missing elements. Like other houses in Madison, this cottage originally had a detached kitchen; it was joined to the building during the recent rehabilitation.

A volume on Georgia architecture would be incomplete without a feature on the ubiquitous shotgun house. This typology is defined by its floor plan rather than by its architectural form and detailing. The shotgun house is a narrow building composed of two bays, normally a door and a window, and three to five rooms arranged front to back without a hallway. It takes its name from the notion that a shotgun could be fired through the front door and the projectile would pass through each succeeding room.

The shotgun house was widely popular from the 1870s through the first quarter of the twentieth century, typically housing working-class citizens in both rural and urban settings. The mill villages of Georgia were particularly common places for a concentration of this folk-housing type. Shotgun houses are widespread in Georgia—found in Augusta, Brunswick, Columbus, Macon, and many other places. Interestingly, they are uncommon in Savannah, where the wooden row house persisted into the late nineteenth century.

The houses at 313, 315, and 317 West 8th Street in Columbus are excellent examples of the type. These three display the usual arrangement of a front door

Shotgun houses, Columbus

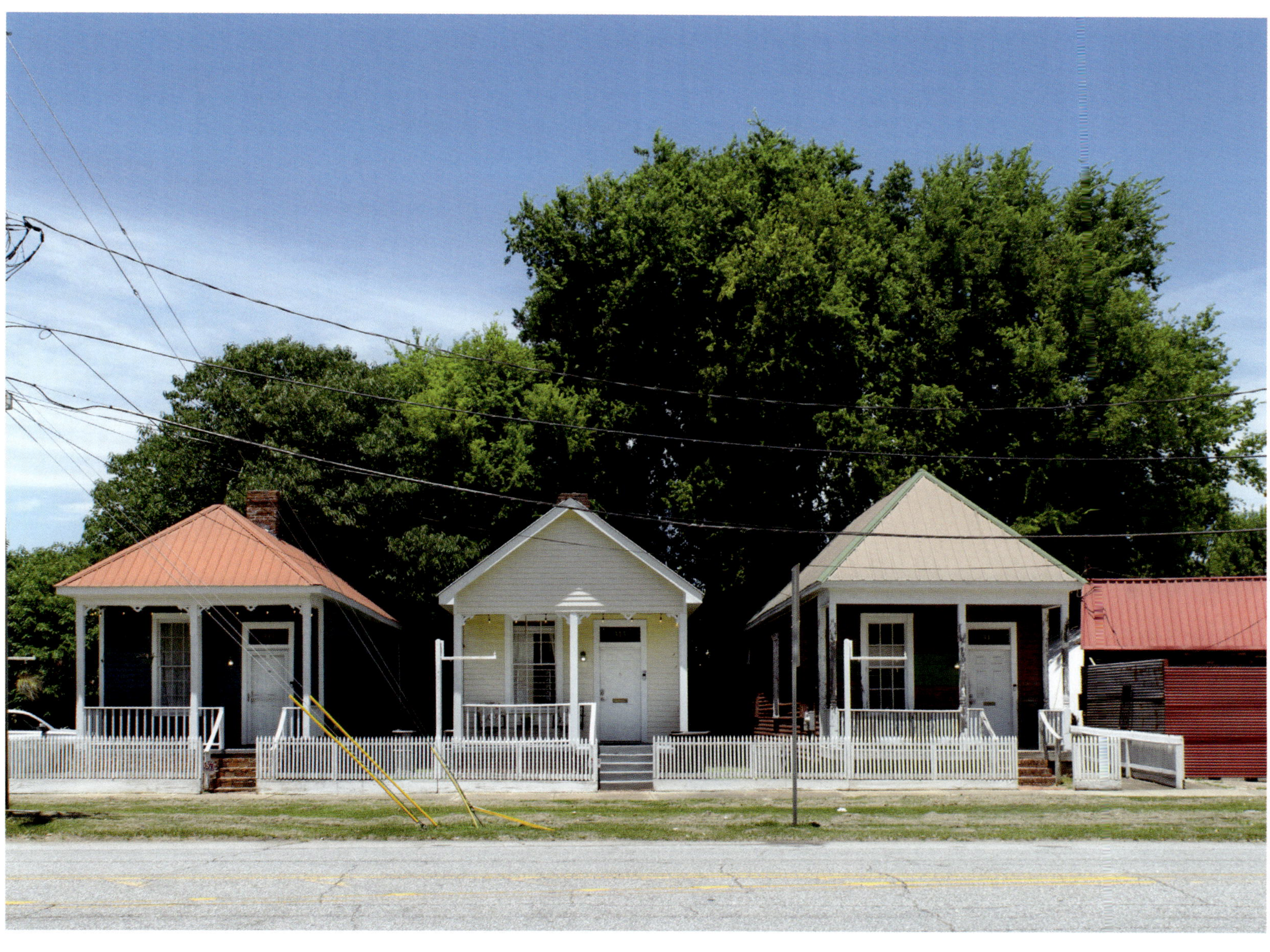

Trust Revolving Fund and Walmart Work Together to Save Three Historic Houses

The Miller House built in 1905, was one of three historic buildings saved by the Georgia Trust Revolving Fund in 2010. Three adjacent structures had been purchased by the Walmart Corporation to provide for a buffer strip required by the City of Forsyth before approval could be granted for construction of a new superstore. Activist preservationists in Forsyth opposed the proposed development and voiced their concerns directly to the Walmart Corporation and the Georgia Trust. Trust staff contacted the Walmart real estate department and proposed that the corporation donate the three houses and the estimated demolition costs of $50,000 to the Trust. The Trust asserted that their conservation easements would ensure that the buffer strip would be maintained in perpetuity. The Walmart Corporation agreed to this transaction, and the Trust was fortunate to sell all three historic buildings to local preservationists Veronica and Percell Kelley, who completed award-winning rehabilitations of these structures.

The Miller House illustrates the gable-ell type of Folk Victorian cottage that was common throughout Georgia in the nineteenth century. This type features intersecting gable or gable and hipped roofs that give the building an L shape.

This preservation victory is an example of how progressive real estate techniques can be utilized to serve the interests of private enterprise, economic development for Georgia's small cities, and the preservation of heritage.

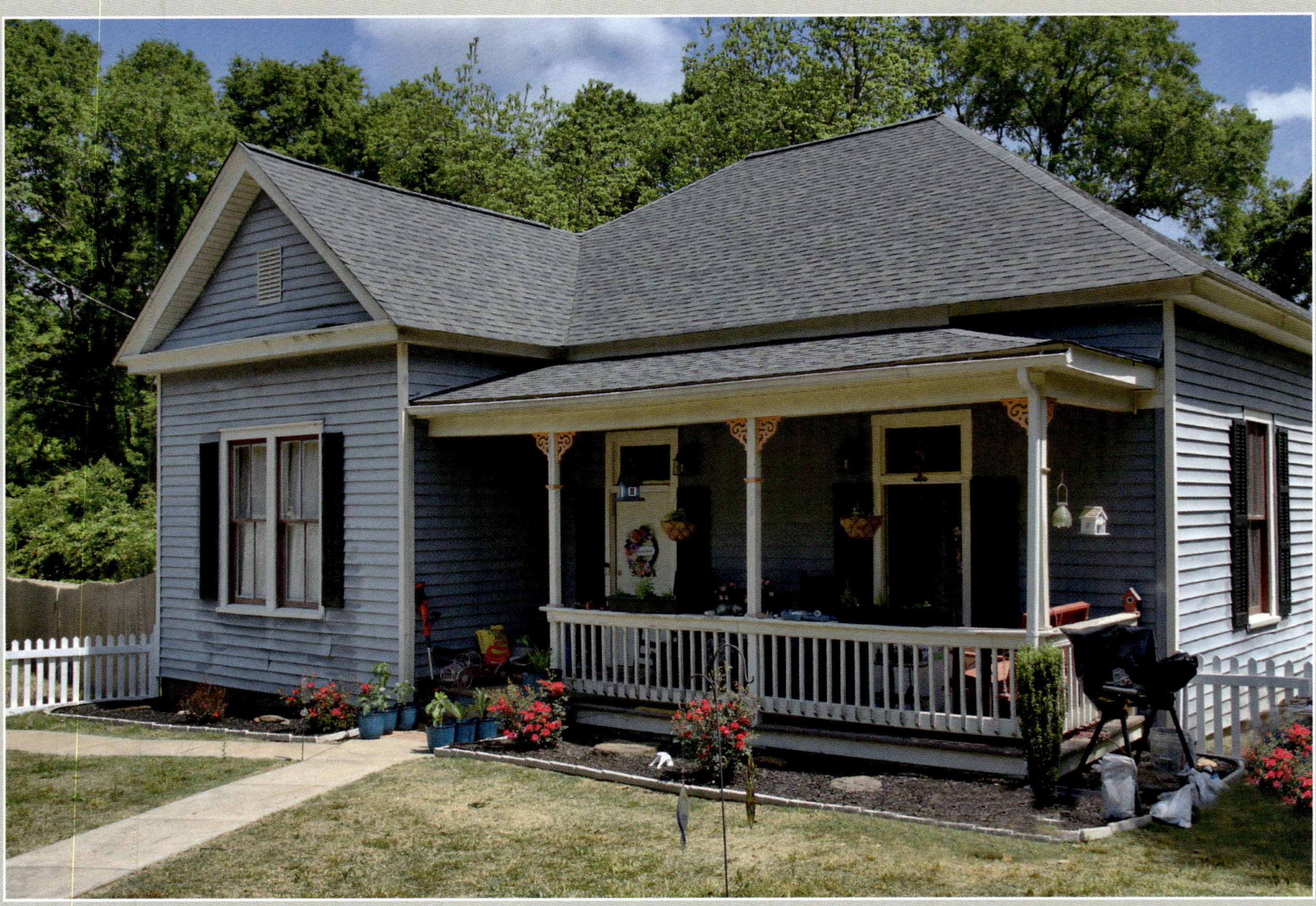

Miller House, Forsyth

and single double-hung window in the front facade. Two of the houses have a hipped roof while the central one displays the more common gable-end roof. Wood siding, as shown in these examples, is the normal exterior sheathing. These houses have simple Victorian decoration on their porch columns; this differs from examples displaying neoclassical detailing and many showing no architectural ornament at all.

There is an academic debate about the origins of the shotgun house. Some folklorists and architectural historians theorize that the form has African roots and migrated to Haiti and then to the American South; however, others believe the narrow form originated with the effort to maximize the number of buildings on expensive urban lots. The shotgun house form also enabled occupants to construct additions easily by simply extending the roofline toward the rear and adding rooms as a family grew.

Whatever its origin, the shotgun house is a character defining feature of the Georgia landscape. When preserved, it can offer affordable and adaptable housing to current and future generations.

It is fortunate that Georgians have embraced Victorian architecture and have worked diligently to preserve the landmarks and neighborhoods where these buildings are found. There are now significant concentrations of National Register–listed late-nineteenth-century buildings in Athens, Americus, Augusta, Columbus, Dalton, Madison, Rome, Savannah, Washington, and many other cities. This was not always the case; during the early days of the preservation movement Victorian architecture was not always valued and in some instances was even scoffed at. In many ways the early advocates of Victorian architecture can be compared to today's admirers of midcentury and modern architecture who are leading the cause of preservation into the future.

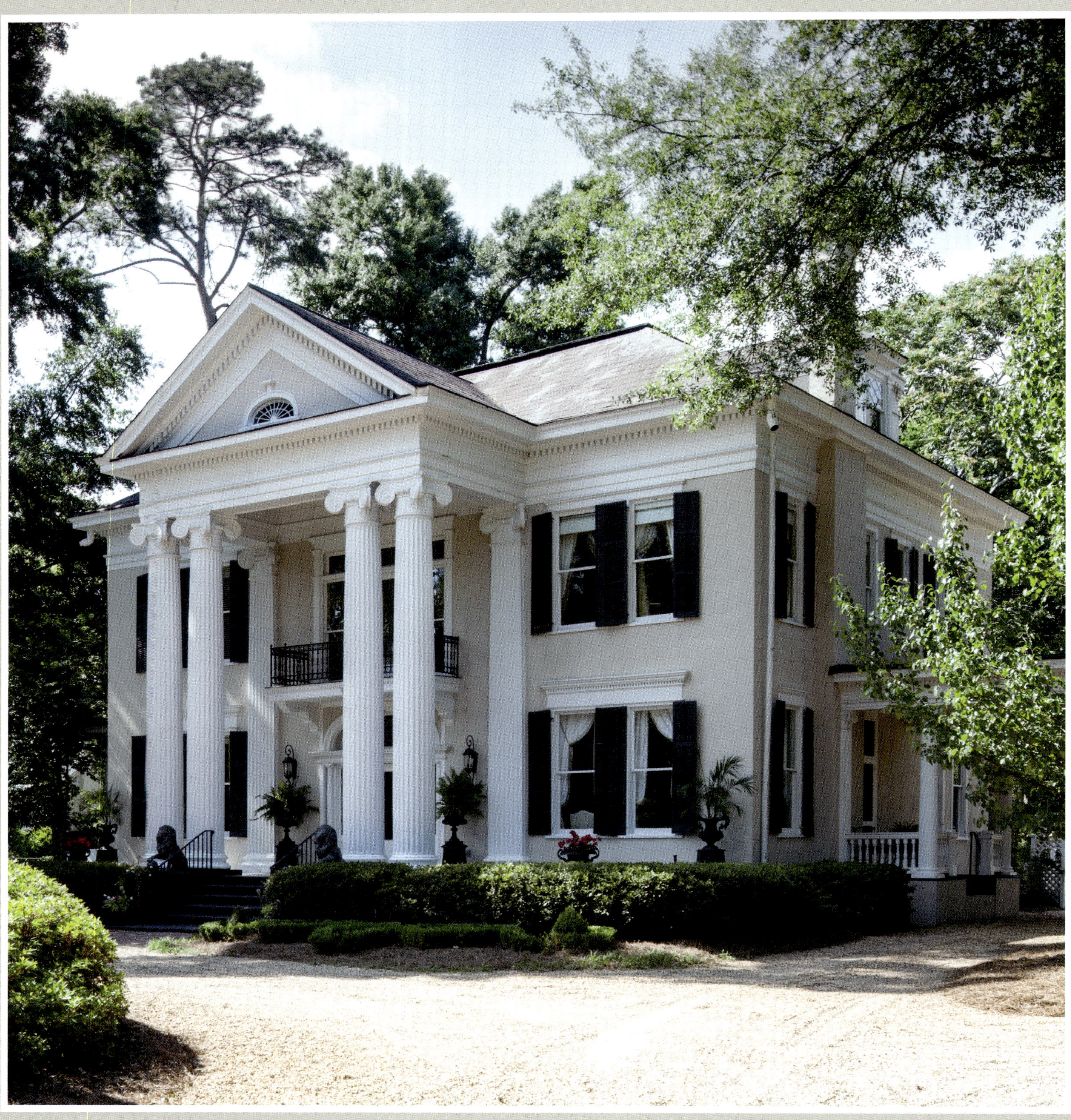

IV. Twentieth-Century Neoclassicism and Colonial Revival

MARK C. MCDONALD

At the turn of the twentieth century, white Georgians, especially those living in cities, had many reasons to feel confident. The difficult period of Reconstruction had passed, and the economy was recovering from the panic of 1893 and the ensuing economic depression that had persisted through the 1890s. The 1895 Cotton States Exposition, staged in what is now Atlanta's Piedmont Park, attempted to project a progressive future for Georgia and the south by displaying innovations in agriculture and technology. Booker T. Washington's speech advocating the "Atlanta Compromise," although controversial, even offered a possible solution to the area's longstanding racial problems.

Cotton prices rose, and the crop continued to be important for Georgia's farmers. Industrialization began to take hold, and during the early 1900s hundreds of textile mills relocated to the South from Northeast. These textile mills transformed the cities of Columbus, Augusta, Atlanta, and Macon but also had major impact on smaller cities such as Canton, Dalton, Griffin, LaGrange, Rome, West Point, and others.

Expansion of Georgia's industrial base was accompanied by the growth of the state's railroad network and a major shift in the population of its urban centers. Atlanta outpaced Augusta, Columbus, and Savannah as its population grew from 65,593 in 1890 to 302,288 by 1940.

As Georgians prospered and painful recollections of the Reconstruction period subsided, nostalgia for America's and Georgia's early history increased dramatically. This was by no means solely a Georgia phenomenon. The Daughters of the American Revolution, the National Society of the Colonial Dames, the Colonial Dames of America, and the United Daughters of the Confederacy were created in this period. Edith Wharton and Ogden Codman published *The Decoration of Houses* in 1897. This important work advocated a rejection of the prevailing Victorian aesthetic of heavy curtains, upholstered and overstuffed furniture, patterned wallpaper and carpets, and other expressions of the age. This pivotal work had an especially significant impact on America's burgeoning middle class.

Facing: Martin House, Augusta

Wharton and Codman's work assimilated for the popular culture what prominent Northeastern architectural firms had begun to advocate as early as the mid-1870s. The New York firm of McKim, Mead and White was the most influential group of architects of this movement. Charles McKim undertook a scholarly exploration of New England's colonial architecture and decorative arts in 1874 and by the early 1880s the firm's work began to lay out the possibilities for a transition from the asymmetrical, heavily ornamented Eastlake and Queen Anne styles to a simpler, symmetrical style of neoclassicism that McKim had become enamored of during his education at the Ecole des Beaux-Arts in Paris.

The pioneering work by the firm and its principals began with remodeling colonial houses, progressed to the design of new houses, and fully matured in its iconic commissions such as the Brooklyn Museum (1895), New York Public Library (1902), and Pennsylvania Station (1910), among many others. This firm's work was to have a profound impact on American and Georgia architecture of the twentieth century.

Before the information age, arts, culture, and technology were greatly influenced by international, national, and regional expositions that were staged to exhibit the latest innovations and promote business interests. These expositions gave the public its first knowledge of the latest trends of the day, including architectural fashions and innovations. The most famous of these is, of course, the Crystal Palace Exhibition of 1851 in London. Six million visitors witnessed thirteen thousand displays of technological innovations, decorative arts, scientific wonders, and other curiosities, in addition to the magnificence of Joseph Paxton's iron and glass architectural masterpiece.

In 1876, to celebrate the one-hundredth anniversary of American independence, Philadelphia hosted the Philadelphia Centennial International Exposition. This ambitious event featured industries that were transforming America from an agricultural and rural economy into a manufacturing, urban one. A highlight was the demonstration of the telephone by Alexander Graham Bell.

Paradoxically, the exposition also celebrated the colonial history of the young nation and fostered nostalgia for its past. One small but influential exhibit was the "Colonial Kitchen," which featured American antique furniture, domestic equipment such as a spinning wheel, and other period appointments.

A prominent building was Memorial Hall, designed by the Bavarian émigré architect Henry J. Schwartzman. This structure is an early example of the Beaux Arts style of architecture; it later became the Philadelphia Museum of Art and now serves as the Please Touch Museum.

A number of American cities staged expositions in the coming years, including Augusta, Georgia, which in 1888 hosted the Augusta National Exposition. It ran only for a few weeks but attracted enough attention to Augusta that similar events were hosted in the city in 1891 and 1893. The Augusta Expositions also served boosters' efforts to attract Northern seasonal inhabitants, especially to the Summerville community.

One of America's early festivals of this kind was the World's Columbian Exposition of 1893. Although it got off to an inauspicious start, with organizational complications delaying its opening until 401 years after the so-called discovery of America by Christopher Columbus, this exposition turned out to be an enormous success, attracting twenty million visitors.

Although the displays in Chicago were influential in many ways and included the first widespread demonstration of electrical lighting, its profoundest impact was to be on the development of architecture in the United States. Many of our country's finest architects designed buildings for the White City, as it came to be called because of the white plaster of paris exterior finish of the temporary structures.

The plan of the Columbian Exposition was designed by Daniel Burnham and Frederick Law Olmsted, and it followed the principles of the City Beautiful movement that was to dominate American urban planning in future years. McKim, Mead and White; Richard Morris Hunt; Peabody and Stearns; and many other architects designed grand buildings in the Neoclassical style for the site on Lake Michigan. The dissenter was the firm of Sullivan and Adler, whose contrasting Transportation Building looked forward to the Modernist movement and stimulated debate for decades to come.

In any event, the Columbian Exposition set a tone for American architecture and was praised by many critics as having a civilizing effect on American cities. This American New World would not look to the future or to its own Indigenous forms but to the past and to Europe to express its ambitions, culture, and architectural aesthetic.

Decidedly smaller in scope was Atlanta's 1895 Cotton States Exposition, whose plan developed by Bradford Gilbert was greatly influenced by the Columbian Exposition. Present-day Piedmont Park was the site of the Exposition and retains much of the original plan, including the 11.5-acre lake. Many of the Cotton States Exposition's buildings were Victorian in feeling. Perhaps the most interesting building on the site was the Women's Building, designed by Philadelphia's first female architect, Elise Mercur, in the Neoclassical style. Eight hundred thousand people attended the Cotton States Exposition, which helped launch Atlanta as the center of the New South.

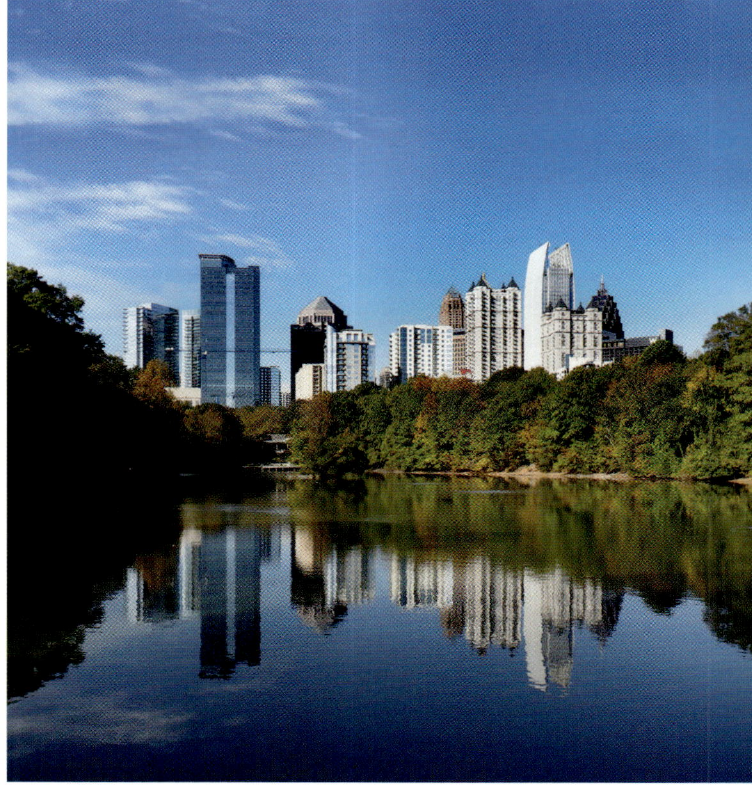

Piedmont Park, Atlanta, with midtown skyline

Georgia proved to be fertile for the development of a varied and sophisticated expression of the Colonial Revival, Beaux Arts, and Neoclassical forms of architecture. Savannah and Augusta had rich architectural heritages and were able to build upon this legacy by attracting Northern transplants and winter residents who attracted trained architects from the Northeast. Thomasville also became a haven for wealthy Northerners who built magnificent hunting plantations in these styles during the early twentieth century. Macon, Columbus, and many smaller cities that benefited from the expansion of the textile industry have impressive collections of these revivalist styles as well.

Atlanta, due to its enormous growth and prosperity—much of it spawned by the success of the Coca-Cola Company, the presence of Agnes Scott, Clark, Emory, Georgia Tech, Morris Brown, Morehouse, Spelman, and other educational institutions, and of course the real estate boom—provided an ideal environment for this architectural expression. The Colonial Revival and Neoclassical styles provided an optimal way for newly successful tycoons, professionals, and other prosperous citizens to demonstrate their wealth and taste in their homes and places of business.

Another key factor in the status of Atlanta in the early twentieth century's Neoclassical and Colonial Revival movements was the establishment there of the W. E. Browne Decorating Company in 1910 by W. E. Browne, Adolph Neubauer, Frank J. Graham, and Lewis Parker. For over seventy-five years, Browne Decorating Company was a leading supplier of decorative ornament, draperies, furnishings, et cetera, in the process defining an aesthetic for generations of architects, designers, and consumers. One of its employees, David R. Byers, a noted architectural and decorative arts consultant, served for over forty years and consulted on many prestigious Georgia and national projects.

The presence of Browne Decorating, the talent of David Byers, and the work of trained architects whose buildings are featured in this chapter are important. However, the building industry was so robust in the early twentieth century that hundreds of buildings in the Neoclassical and Colonial Revival styles were built without noted architects, or without architects at all. The expanded building industry responded to demand from the growing upper middle class. Architectural draftsmen and skilled builders, utilizing trade publications and readily available architectural millwork supplies, created an inventory of buildings that were comparable in quality to many of the architect-designed buildings that influenced them. The contributions of these factors and craftsmen, although not featured here, should not be taken for granted.

Neoclassical

Neoclassical buildings are characterized by adherence to symmetry. The front entrance is most frequently centered in the facade and windows are organized into regularly spaced bays on either side. The building is normally dominated by a portico that spans the full height of the facade. The entablature of the portico is supported by classical columns, most often with Ionic or Corinthian capitals. This portico can have a gable end, a slight hipped roof, or sometimes a semicircular bow in its entablature. Neoclassical buildings can be faced with stone, brick (with or without stucco) or, less commonly, wood clapboard siding. The portico may also have a balustrade above its roof edge, although this is less common. Neoclassical buildings have restrained ornament that differentiates them from Beaux Arts buildings, which commonly have elaborate iron railings, floral motifs, garlands, shields or other decorative treatments on their wall surfaces.

Houses from the first quarter of the twentieth century have endured particularly well, due to their ever-popular design qualities and because they were built well and of quality materials. Heart-pine lumber for framing, siding, and flooring was still readily available in the South, and with improved transportation and mass production, brick was less expensive than it had been before the turn of the century. Houses were designed with electrical wiring, modern plumbing, and central heating systems. Many also incorporated the automobile in their site planning and featured garages and porte cocheres. For these reasons, early twentieth-century Neoclassical and Colonial Revival homes remain quite popular today, and a great number of neighborhoods across Georgia are in a remarkable state of preservation.

It stands to reason that the earliest Neoclassical buildings in Georgia would be public buildings. After all, the budget for public buildings is frequently large enough and the building program complex enough to allow the hiring of trained architects, who were commonly brought in from outside the state. In addition, public buildings were traditionally designed in the Neoclassical forms and the style of the influential U.S. Capitol in Washington. The classical idiom was also associated with buildings that were meant to express democratic ideals and inspire confidence in our governmental institutions. Southerners, in particular, who had so wholeheartedly embraced the Greek Revival style for public buildings, places of worship, and homes were inclined to accept the new Neoclassical forms introduced by the architects who trained at the Ecole des Beaux-Arts in Paris.

One of Georgia's earliest Neoclassical buildings is also one of its most prominent. Construction of the Georgia State Capitol building was complete in March 1889 and came in slightly under its budget of $1 million. Chicago architects

Georgia State Capitol, Atlanta

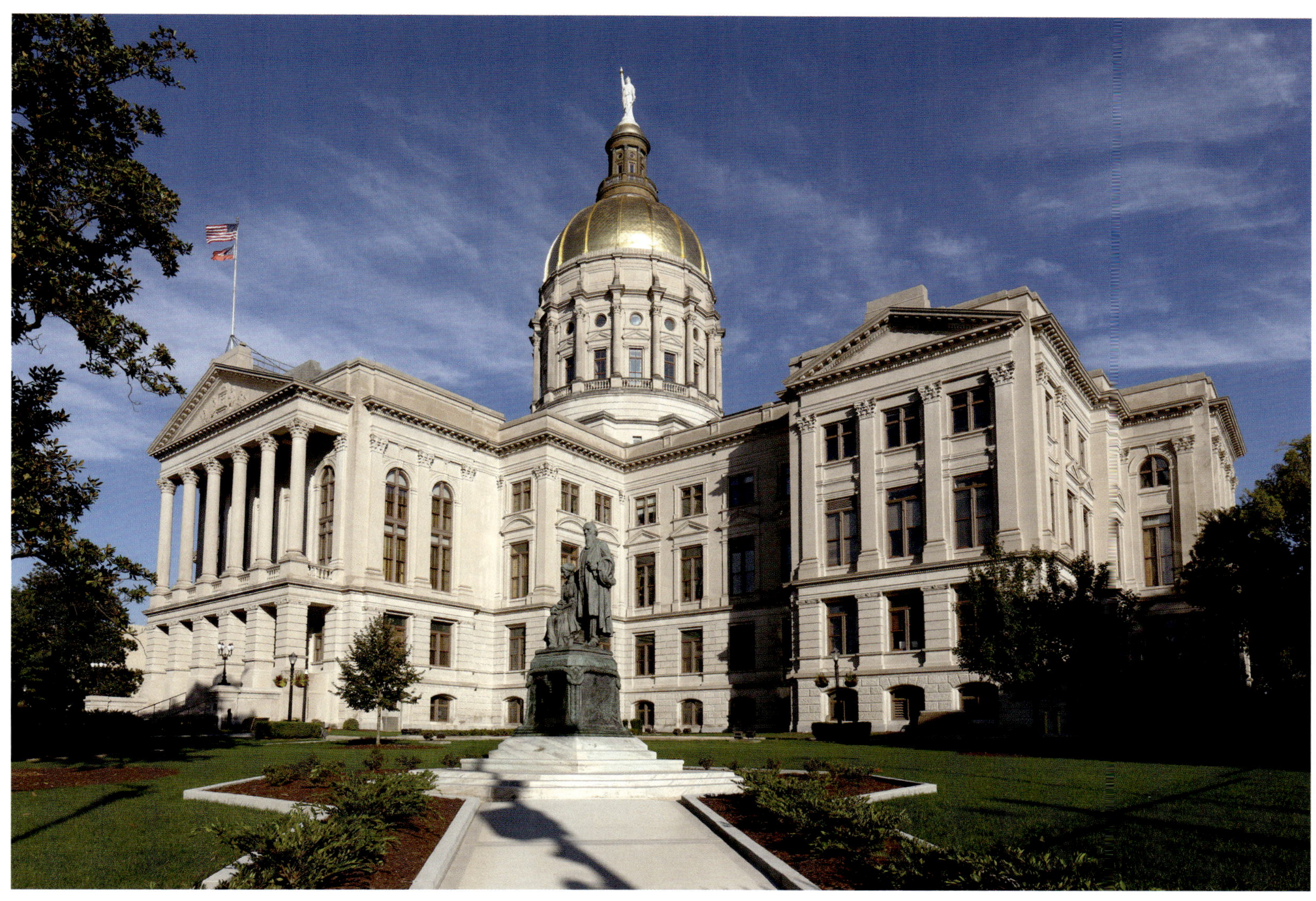

Franklin Pierce Burnham and Willoughby J. Edbrooke won a national design competition for the commission, and the firm delivered a building worthy of Chicago's reputation for architectural excellence. Both Burnham and Edbrooke went on to participate in the design of buildings for the World's Columbian Exposition in 1893.

The original intent for the Capitol building was that all materials used in construction would be products of Georgia. Although the pink marble used extensively in the interior is from Etowah, and the Georgia-made bricks were recycled from the old Atlanta city hall for budgetary reasons, the elegant limestone exterior came from Indiana. The building's famous Dahlonega-mined gold dome was not installed until 1958. Its original dome was covered by an alloy of lead and tin.

The Capitol building, true to its grounding in Neoclassicism, presents a high degree of symmetry. Its main facade, facing Washington Avenue, features a projecting portico composed of six Corinthian columns that rest on square stone pillars. Sculpted in relief in its stone pediment is Georgia's coat of arms.

The four-story portico is flanked on both sides by lengthy wings terminated by three-bay projecting corners that feature handsome yet restrained gable ends. The drum of the tall dome is a well-proportioned Renaissance Revival design featuring windows capped with triangular pedimented hoods topped by round oculi alternating with engaged columns. A statue of Miss Freedom crowns the top of the building.

The interior is as striking as the edifice's exterior. The magnificent central rotunda is flanked to the north and south by wings each containing grand staircases rising in a three-story atrium illuminated by clerestory windows. Paint colors and decorative details were meticulously returned to their original state during a 1997 restoration.

It is astounding that, unlike many historic state capitol buildings, the Georgia State Capitol still retains most of its original functions as the offices of the governor, lieutenant governor, secretary of state, and chambers and committee rooms of the Georgia General Assembly. When it was originally constructed, the Capitol was the tallest structure in Atlanta. Now surrounded by skyscrapers, the Capitol building, by virtue of its prominent site on a hill and its tall dome, continues to be a highly visible symbol of Georgia's status as a leader of the New South. It was designated as a National Historic Landmark in 1973.

The Neoclassical United States Penitentiary in Atlanta boldly demonstrates the prominence given to quality architectural design in the early twentieth century by the federal government. Completed in January 1902, the Atlanta federal prison was designed by the influential Saint Louis, Missouri, firm of Eames and Young. It was built for an occupancy of three thousand inmates, which made it the largest federal correctional facility of its time.

Thomas Crane Young was educated at Washington University in Saint Louis and studied at the Ecole des Beaux-Arts in Paris for two years in the early 1880s. His partner, William Sylvester Eames, studied at the Saint Louis School of

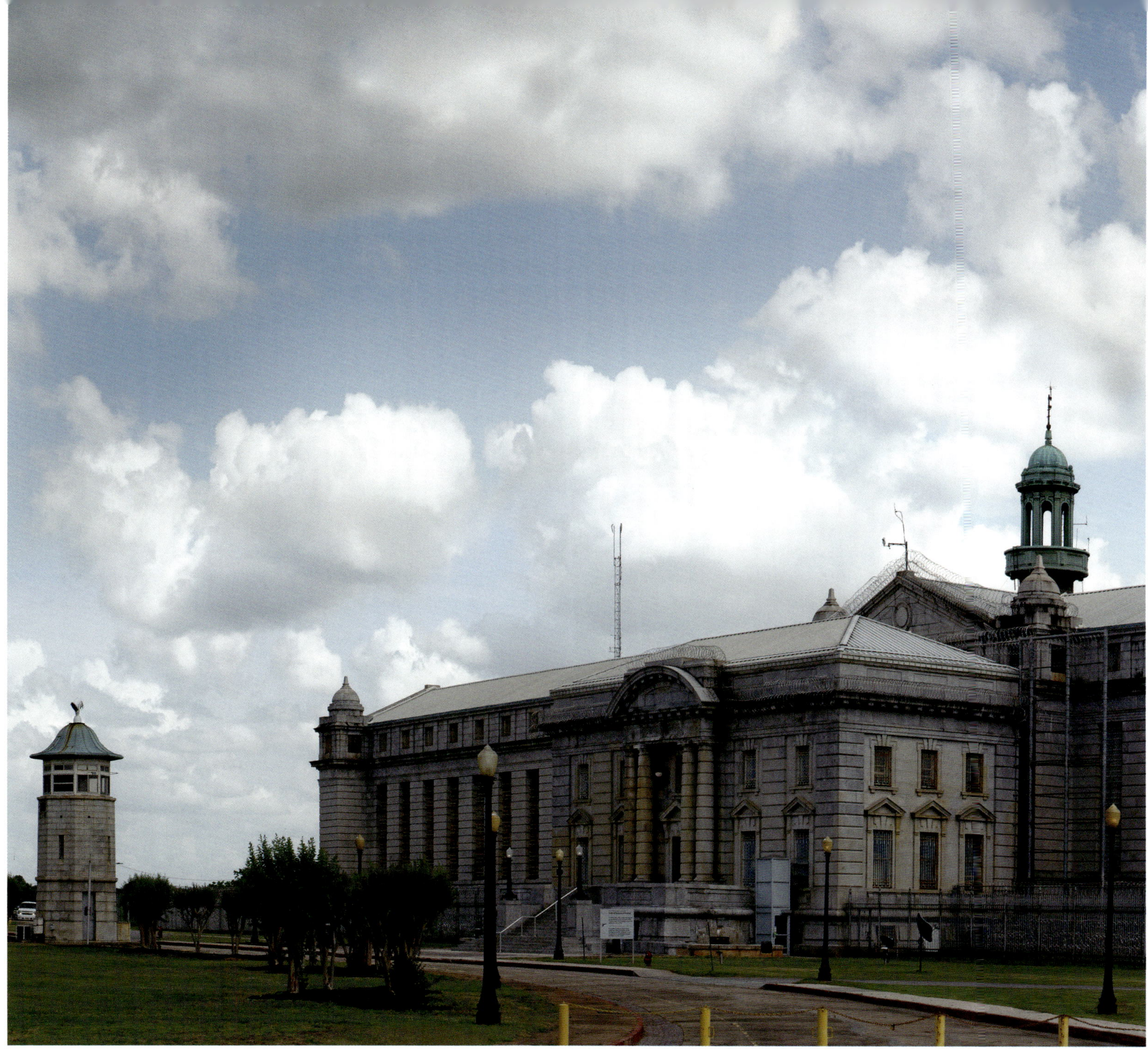

United States Penitentiary, Atlan a

Fine Arts and in 1904–5 was elected president of the American Institute of Architects, a quite prominent position in the emerging profession.

Authorized in 1899 by President William McKinley, the United States Penitentiary in Atlanta was the product of the Three Prisons Act of 1891. Eames and Young were commissioned to design the institutions in Atlanta and Leavenworth, Kansas. Both Atlanta and Leavenworth were built in the Neoclassical style and constructed of solid granite.

The Atlanta penitentiary was designed to be secure, and it certainly looks so; however, its massive scale is expertly broken down into components that manage to give it a semblance of human scale. Its front facade features a classically proportioned projecting front edifice composed of five bays resting on a *piano nobile*. Surrounding its front entrance is a colossal portico with pairs of banded Doric columns and a segmental arched engaged pediment.

Sitting well back from the projecting centerpiece is a multistory, massive cell block that is accented by a gabled stone portico at its roofline terminating with four small stone domes at the corners. A copper-clad tower with arched openings and dome rises high above the top of this cell block. Behind this lengthy stone cell block is a labyrinth of red-brick buildings that house the various functions of an extensive prison complex. These buildings, while contrasting with the front facade, are quite handsome in their own right. A massive concrete wall surrounds the prison campus, which contains a multitude of additional structures.

The Atlanta penitentiary has a fascinating history including the incarceration of many notable figures in American history. Organized crime characters such as Al Capone and Whitey Bolger did time here. Political prisoners who were incarcerated in Atlanta include Eugene V. Debs, who was convicted of sedition for his protest of the draft during World War I, and African American civil rights leader Marcus Garvey, who was convicted of mail fraud.

It is certainly a testament to sound building that a structure that has served its purpose for over a hundred years and whose stability is put to the test 365 days a year is still in operation. Most Georgians are likely unaware of the interesting history of this architectural wonder in southeast Atlanta.

The Lattimore House was built by Harry Hays Lattimore, one of the developers of the Ardsley Park subdivision of Savannah, in 1910. It was designed by Percy Sudgen, born in Halifax, England, and trained in Britain in engineering and architecture. His extensive work in Savannah is distinguished by the design of several school buildings.

One of the finest houses in Ardsley Park, the Lattimore House is two-story and symmetrically composed and features a colossal portico with four fluted Corinthian columns. It has wide tripartite windows on either side of the arched front entrance, and on the ground floor are two bay windows that project out onto the balustrade front porches. Built of cream-colored brick, this is one of the earliest Neoclassical buildings in Georgia, and it set the tone for one of the state's most significant early suburbs.

Ardsley Park is a planned neighborhood based directly on Oglethorpe's 1733 plan for Savannah and features large, lush, landscaped squares. However, in Ardsley Park the squares are offset from the main thoroughfare streets in deference to the introduction of the automobile. The neighborhood was also serviced by electric trolleys that connected it to downtown. It remains relatively intact today and is a highly desirable place to reside.

By 1850, Augustans began to build elegant homes on a hill outside of Augusta that came to be known as Summerville. Outbreaks of malaria in 1810 and 1820 created a desire to escape to more healthful environments, and this community began to thrive. It was incorporated as a city in 1861. The area later became a resort community, and Northeastern seasonal visitors added to the architectural diversity of Summerville well into the 1920s. It was annexed by the City of Augusta and has continued to flourish as a full-time residential community.

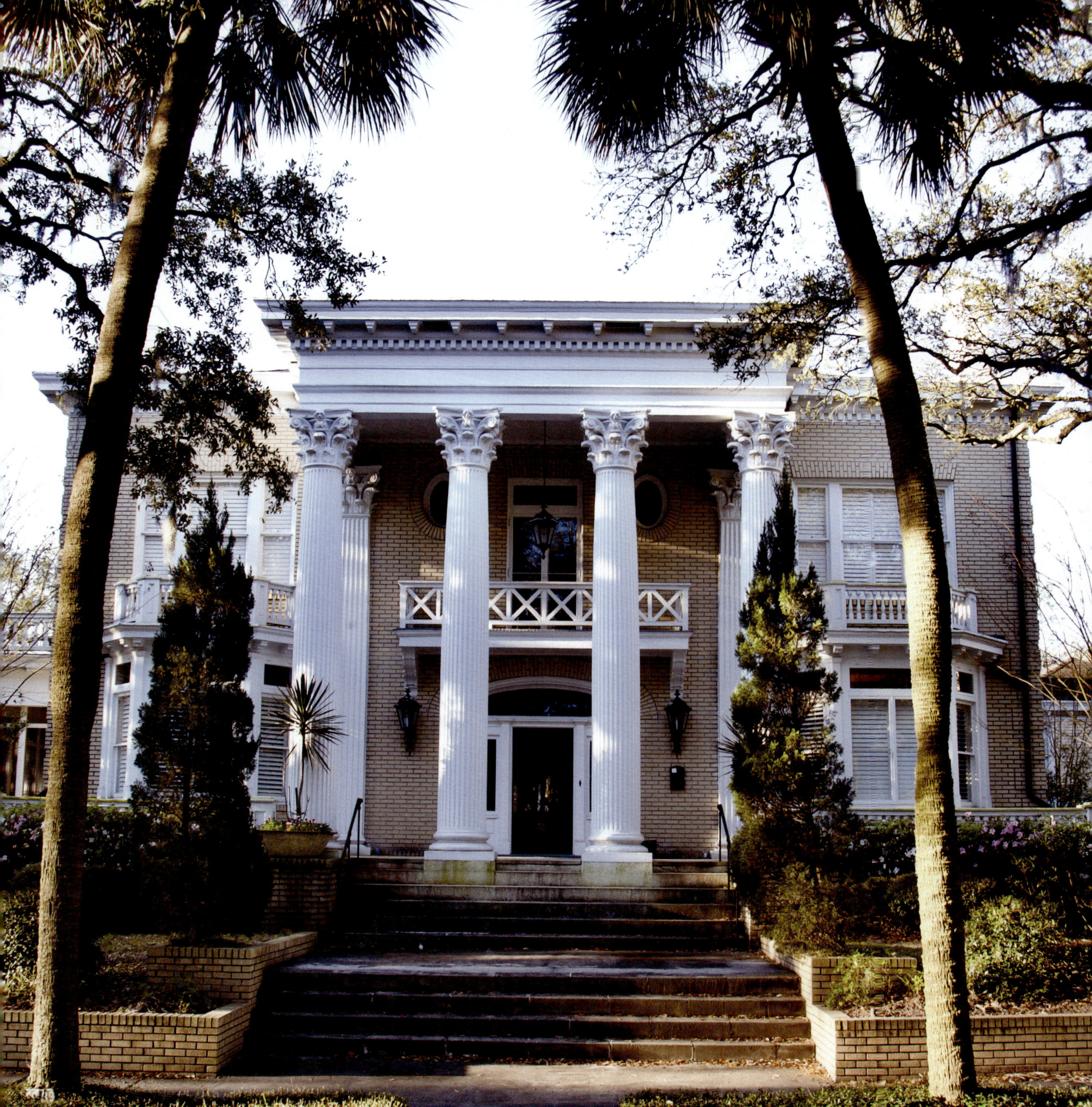

Lattimore House, Savannah

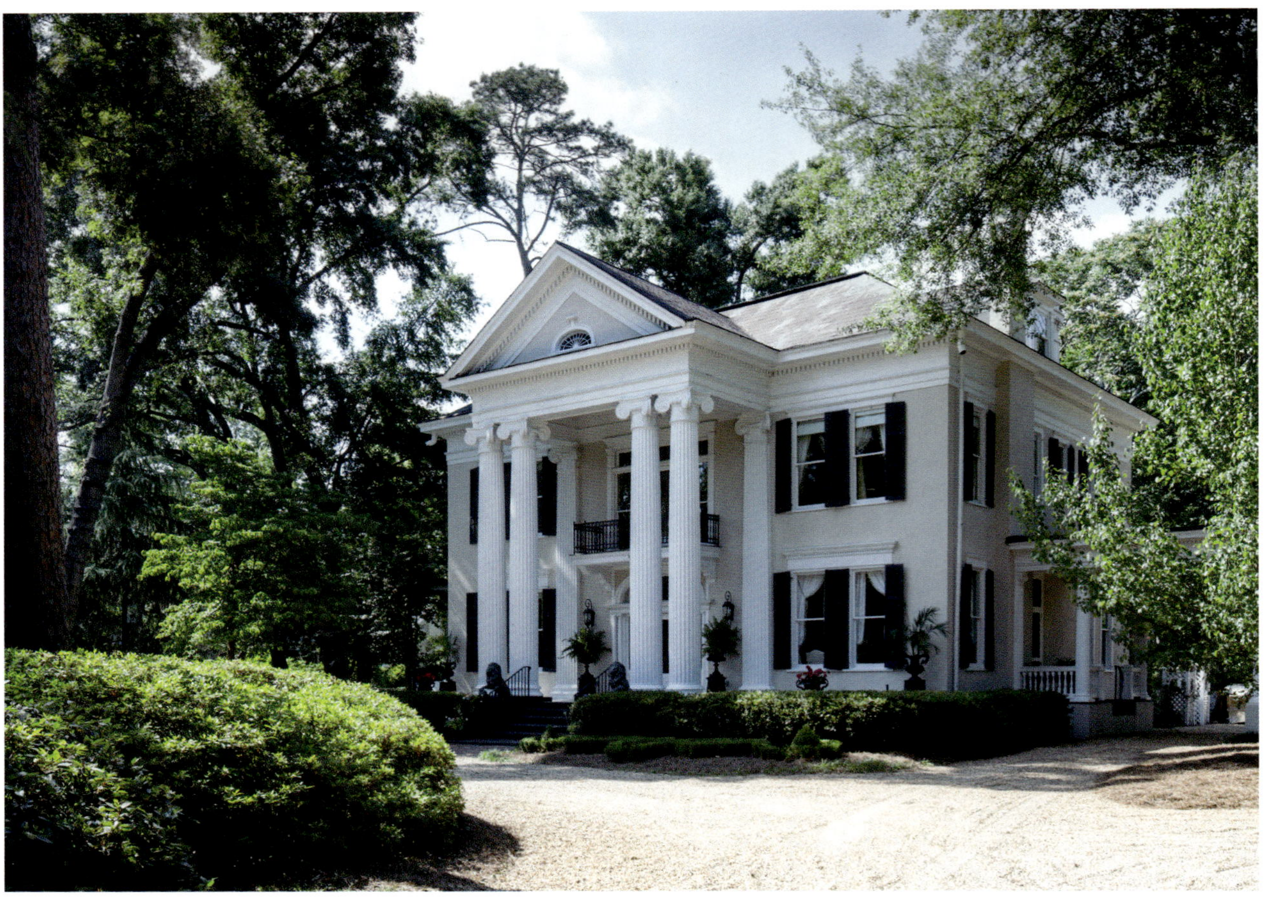

Martin House, Augusta

An early Neoclassical building in Summerville from circa 1910 is the Martin House. This handsome building is more directly descended from the Greek Revival architecture of antebellum Georgia. It, too, features a colossal portico with pairs of columns in the Ionic order and a triangular pediment. This pediment is accented with a fanlight. Under the portico at the second-floor level is a doorway with sidelights and an elegant balcony with decorative ironwork. At the ground floor, the entrance features an arched opening and fanlight. On either side of the front door are pairs of windows with blinds that are repeated at the second level. Unfortunately, the designer of this painted masonry house is unknown.

The Martin House has connections to several notable figures in Georgia history. Louise Martin, daughter of Mr. and Mrs. William Martin, who built the house, married Dr. Hervey Cleckley, a noted psychiatrist. Dr. Cleckley and his coauthor Dr. Corbett Thompson were the first to document the psychiatric condition known as multiple personality disorder. Their work is the basis of the film *The Three Faces of Eve*.

In 1919, William Marcellus Howard purchased the house. Howard served six terms in Congress, from 1897 to 1911, was on the board of regents of the Smithsonian Institution, was appointed to the United States Tariff Board by President William Howard Taft, and served as a trustee of the Carnegie Endowment for International Peace. In 1913, Howard courageously took on the case of Leo Frank who had been convicted of the rape and murder of Mary Phagan at Atlanta's National Pencil Company. Howard was successful in persuading Governor John

Slaton to commute Frank's death sentence. In what is one of the most infamous cases in Georgia history, Frank was lynched by an anti-Semitic mob in Marietta. William M. Howard resided in the house until his death in 1932.

There are few stories in Georgia history more interesting than that of Alonzo Franklin Herndon. He was born enslaved in 1858 and, upon Emancipation, moved to Atlanta, where he eventually established a chain of barber shops. His success in that industry allowed him to establish the Atlanta Life Insurance Company in 1905, which he led to great success, as it became the largest African American–owned insurance company in the United States.

In 1910, Herndon and his wife, Adrienne McNeil, began construction of their large home in the Vine City neighborhood of Atlanta, near the colleges that offered diplomas to the growing African American middle class. Adrienne Herndon was born in 1869 in Savannah and was a college instructor, activist, and professional actress who performed under the name Anne DuBignon.

The design of the Herndon House reflects the sophistication of this talented couple. The house was designed by Adrienne Herndon and was almost entirely built with African American labor. It is Neoclassical with Beaux Arts influences. The brick structure features a colossal portico with a trio of "Temple of the Winds" columns supporting a portico with dentil moldings crowned by larger modillions. The Beaux Arts influence is expressed by the Neoclassical balustrade which runs along the border of the portico and the main facade of the house. The facade features large arched opening at the ground floor with pairs of windows in the outer bays of the second floor and a doorway with transom

Herndon House, Atlanta

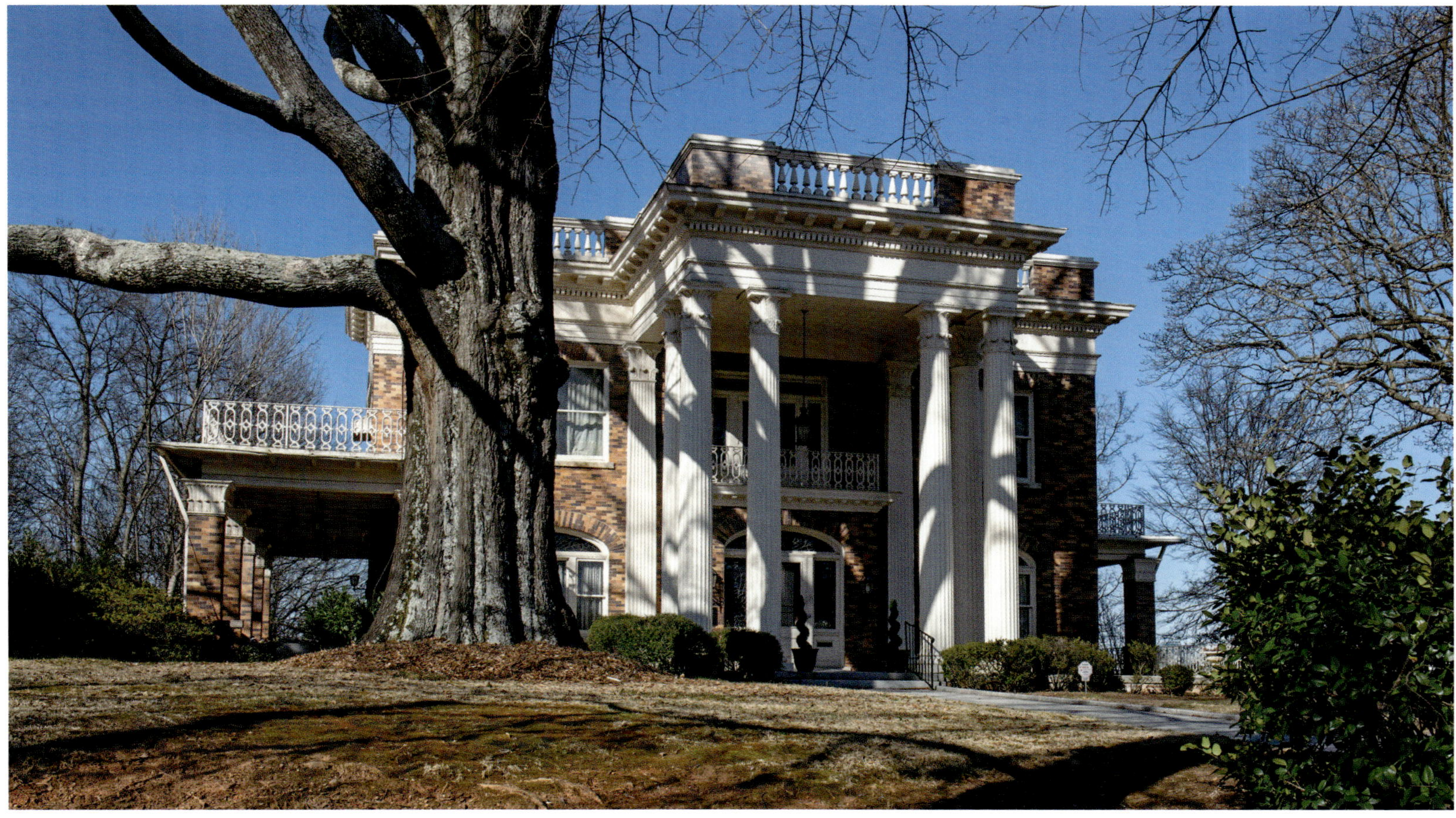

and sidelights in the central bay of the second floor. A cast-iron balcony hangs under this second-floor doorway.

The Herndon House is operated as a house museum by the Alonzo F. and Norris B. Herndon Foundation whose mission is to advance the Herndon legacy to educate, mentor and equip the next generation of entrepreneurs. The existence of such a grand house in the Deep South in 1910 is a testament to the ingenuity and work ethic of the Herndons and the advanced African American culture of Atlanta in the early twentieth century. The house is listed as a National Historic Landmark.

Beaux Arts

The Beaux Arts style derives its name from the Ecole des Beaux-Arts in Paris, the late nineteenth century's leading school for drawing, painting, sculpture, and architecture. The architecture program was quite selective in its admissions and demanding in its instruction. Noted American architects who studied at the Ecole des Beaux-Arts were Richard Morris Hunt, Henry Hobson Richardson, Charles McKim and Georgia's Neel Reid, among many others.

The architectural style associated with the school is an elaborate Neoclassicism, symmetrical and formal, but with great freedom of application of Neoclassical details and exuberant decoration. The style is typified by distinct groupings of columns on a facade, rather than strict adherence to the proportion and even spacing required by Neoclassical traditions. The integration of art is common, as, for example, in classical statuary embedded in a facade and in grand, richly adorned interior spaces. The style is frequently grandiose and used particularly for institutional buildings and mansions of the wealthy.

A great example of the Beaux Arts mansion for a wealthy businessman is Callan Castle, the Atlanta home of Asa Griggs Candler. Callan Castle is in reality a transitional building possessing echoes of the Victorian period, with asymmetrical massing especially evident in its Queen Anne–style rounded porch. Its portico, however, shows the influence of the elaborate Beaux Arts style. A trio of fluted Ionic columns on each end support an entablature that has a garland and wreath emblazoned on its surface. An oversized Palladian arch dominates its pediment. The cornice of the portico is adorned by well-crafted modillions. Under the portico are a pair of arched openings at the ground floor separated by slender arched windows and floor-length casement windows that open onto balconies on the second level.

Wings recessed from the portico, one of which is one story and the other two stories, retain the asymmetrical massing from the late nineteenth century. A one-story granite porte cochere stands farther back to the left of the house.

The architect for Callan Castle was George Murphy, who practiced in Atlanta until 1926. Murphy was born in Oxford County, Maine, in 1850 and appears to have been self-trained. He was fortunate to have developed a relationship with Asa Candler, for he also designed the Atlanta landmark Candler Building and other buildings for the Coca-Cola tycoon's various business enterprises.

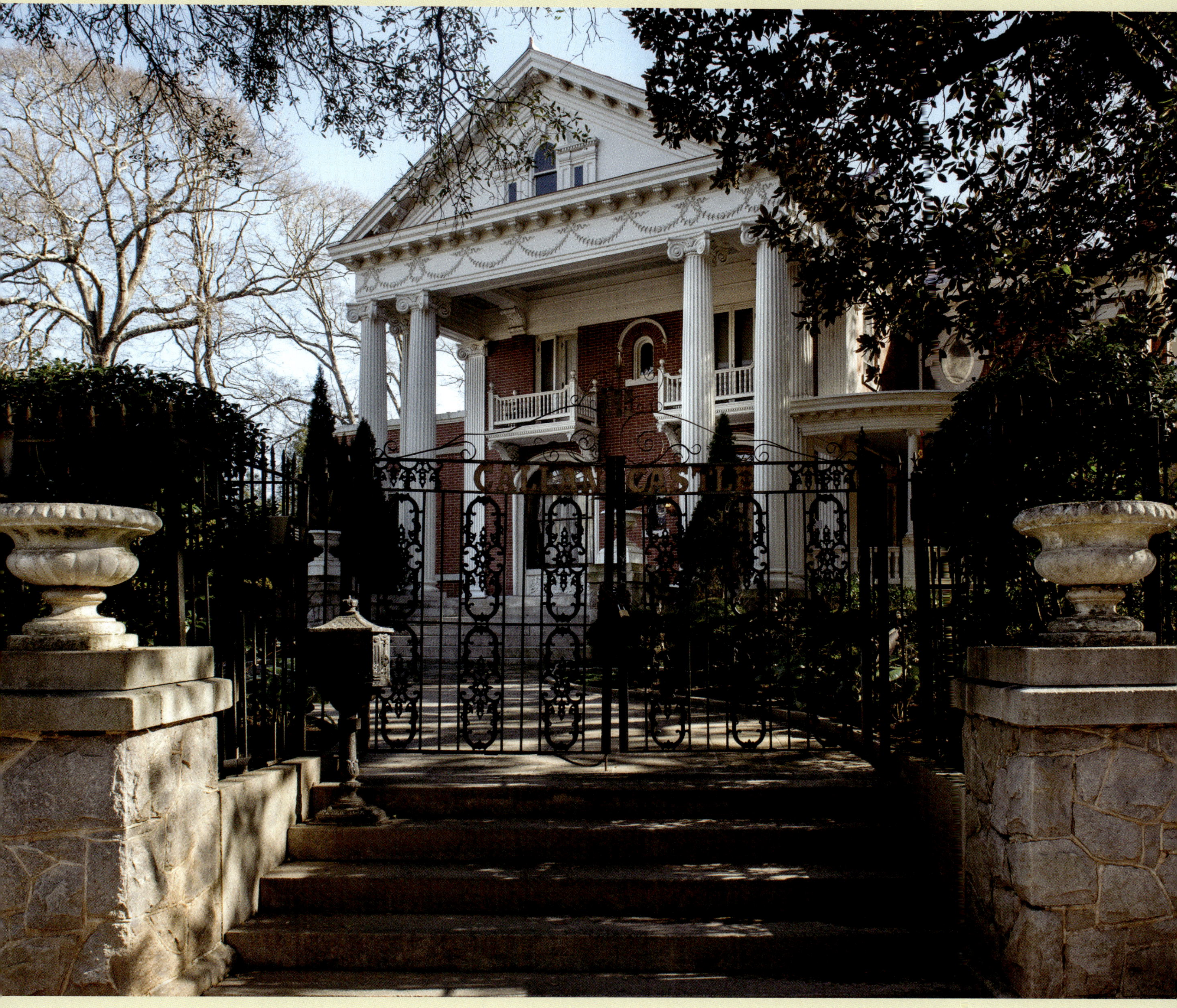

Callan Castle, Atlanta

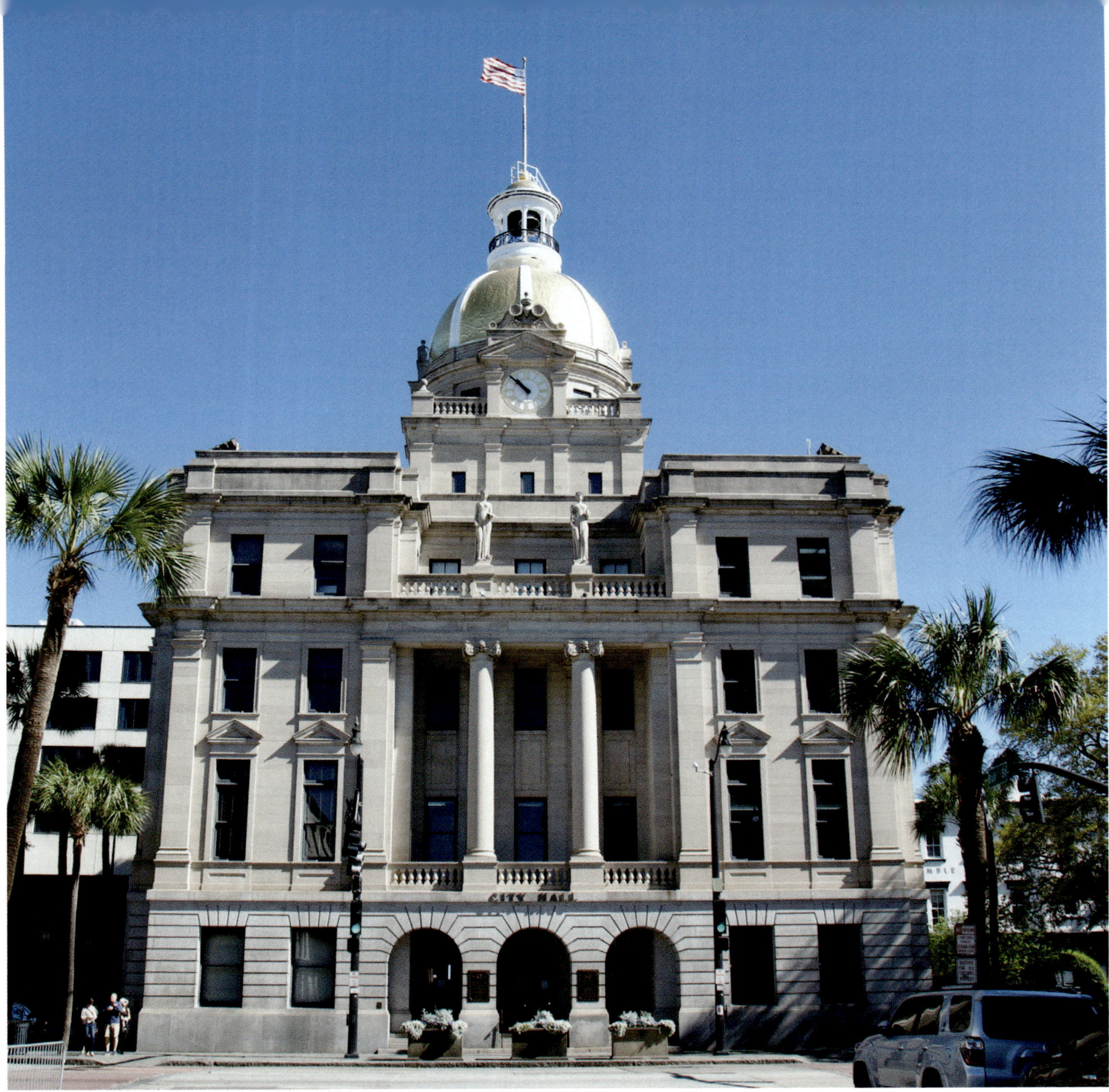

Savannah City Hall, Savannah

Savannah's City Hall of 1904–5, designed by Hyman W. Witcover, is a fine example of the Beaux Arts style. The building sits on a raised base of rusticated stone featuring three round arches. An inset Ionic portico dominates the second and third story, with classical statuary rising above the two central columns. Finally, a gold dome set above a clock tower crowns the seat of Savannah's city government. The building is sited at the terminus of Bull Street, which is the central spine of Savannah. The integration of architecture and urban planning was also a hallmark of the Beaux Arts style. This site may have been predetermined, since Savannah's earlier market house and city hall occupied this exact place.

City Hall's site is both symbolic and visually stunning. It relates to the Savannah River to the north, the reason for Savannah's existence, in direct alignment with the Bull Street squares with their notable monuments and with Forsyth Park and its iconic cast-iron fountain. Few cities in America can claim such an elegant composition within their urban plan.

Hyman W. Witcover was born in Darlington, South Carolina, and moved to Savannah in 1888 at the age of sixteen to work as a draftsman for Savannah architect Alfred Eichberg. Witcover went on to design a great number of Savannah buildings including the Bull Street Library and the Scottish Rite Temple.

The Nicholas Block House in Macon was built in 1905 and designed by architect Alexander Blair III. Blair was the son of an English-born and -trained architect, Alexander Blair II. Blair III designed the Grand Opera House in Macon, eight Georgia county courthouses, and many other notable buildings. His design for the Block House features an Italianate-style masonry block form with characteristic wide overhanging eaves supported unconventionally with oversized brackets paired with exposed rafter tails. Also unusual is the house's recessed center section, which features and arched doorway on the ground floor and large oval window set within a cartouche on the second level.

Arched windows are set within ornate arched window hoods with exaggerated voussoirs. Pairs of double-hung windows sit directly above these elaborate ground-floor windows. This entire composition sits upon a terrace enclosed by a stone balustrade. The projecting porch has massive brick piers that with characteristically Beaux Arts flair are embellished with stone cartouches.

Nicholas Block House, Macon

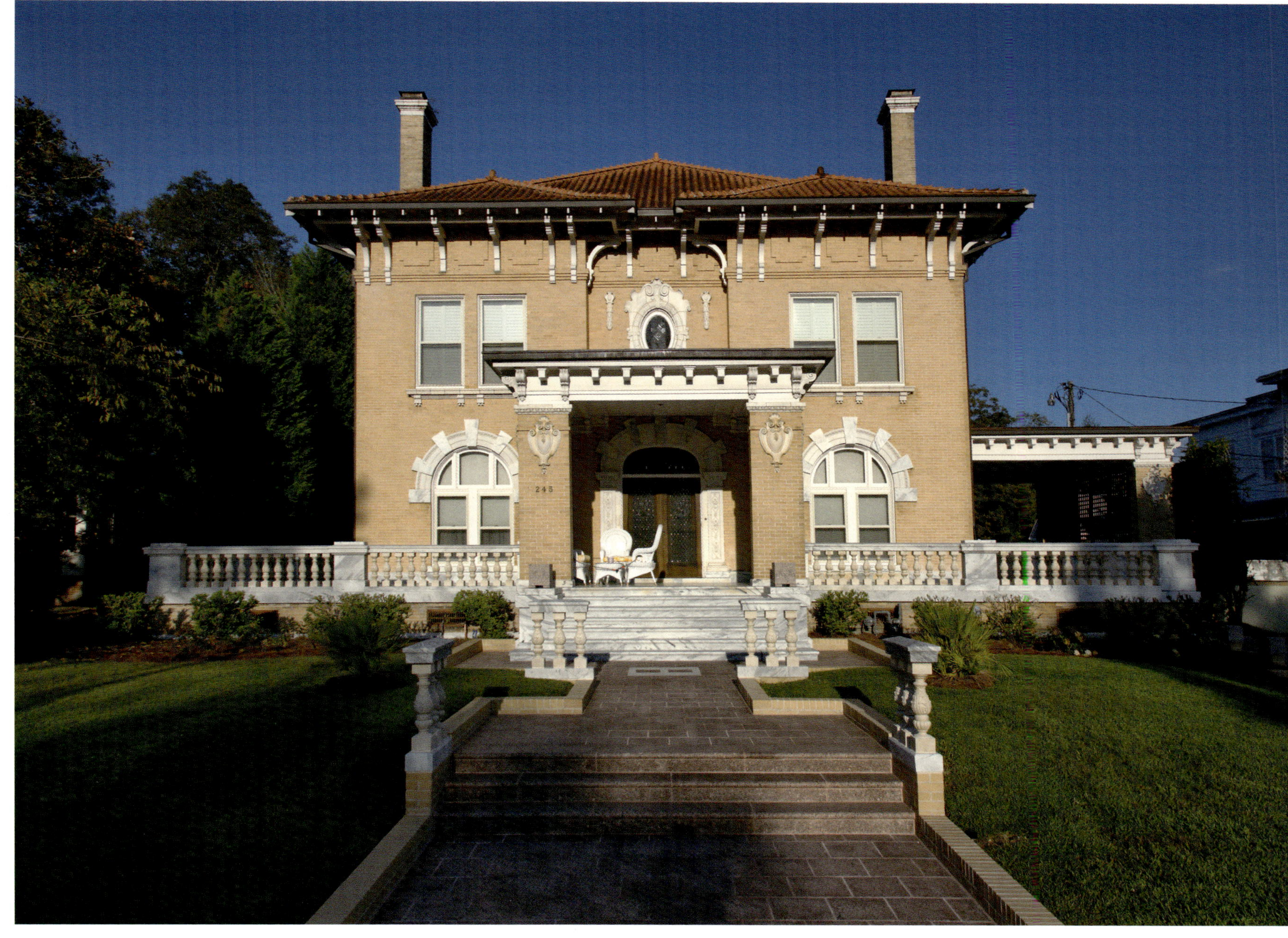

The Block House is located in the Macon Historic District in the College Hill neighborhood. This neighborhood contains some of Georgia's finest architecture, including two National Historic Landmarks, the Johnston-Felton-Hay House and the Raines-Carmichael House.

Architect Neel Reid is best known for the elegant Colonial Revival and Neoclassical houses he designed in Atlanta and other Georgia cities. Reid was born in Troup County in 1885 but moved to Macon, where he apprenticed with noted architect Curran Ellis before moving to Atlanta to work under Willis Denny, who was the architect of Rhodes Hall, presently headquarters of the Georgia Trust for Historic Preservation, and other buildings in Atlanta. Reid studied architecture in New York City at Columbia University (1905–7) and traveled extensively in Europe, where he studied briefly at the Ecole des Beaux-Arts in Paris.

In 1916, Reid received a commission to design the Southern Railway Brookwood Station, which fortunately is still in use today as Atlanta's Amtrak station. Reid's work is exemplified by classical proportions and restraint in ornament. His design for the Brookwood Station is a good example of his approach. The station is a red-brick Beaux Arts building composed of three bays, each featuring a classically composed Palladian arch infilled with cast-iron window and door casings. These bays are divided by four engaged Doric pillars that have a limestone cornice emblazoned with the words "Peachtree Southern RY Station." Unlike other Beaux Arts buildings, there is no ornament or decoration on the flat wall surfaces of the exterior.

This building, a favorite of many Atlantans, is one of the last remnants of Atlanta's once enormous inventory of railroad architecture. It too is endangered, because during the last twenty years there have been a number of proposals to move Amtrak service to other locations in the city. It is true that Brookwood Station is cramped for space by the I-85/I-75 connector bridge and that there is very limited automobile access and parking. If Amtrak relocates to another site, it is hoped that this charming part of the Southern Railway story can be adapted to another use.

Colonial Revival

The Colonial Revival style of architecture was the most popular form of building, especially for domestic architecture, in the United States during the early twentieth century. The style began in the late nineteenth century with the work of Charles McKim and the firm of McKim, Mead and White when they began to simplify Victorian buildings and move toward the adaption of New England–style colonial buildings for their Gilded Age clientele. After the turn of the century, when prosperity arrived in Georgia's cities and towns, Colonial Revival became the style of choice for Georgians who had accumulated wealth.

Buildings constructed in the Colonial Revival style display a great deal of variety. After all, period Colonial American buildings were quite different, depending

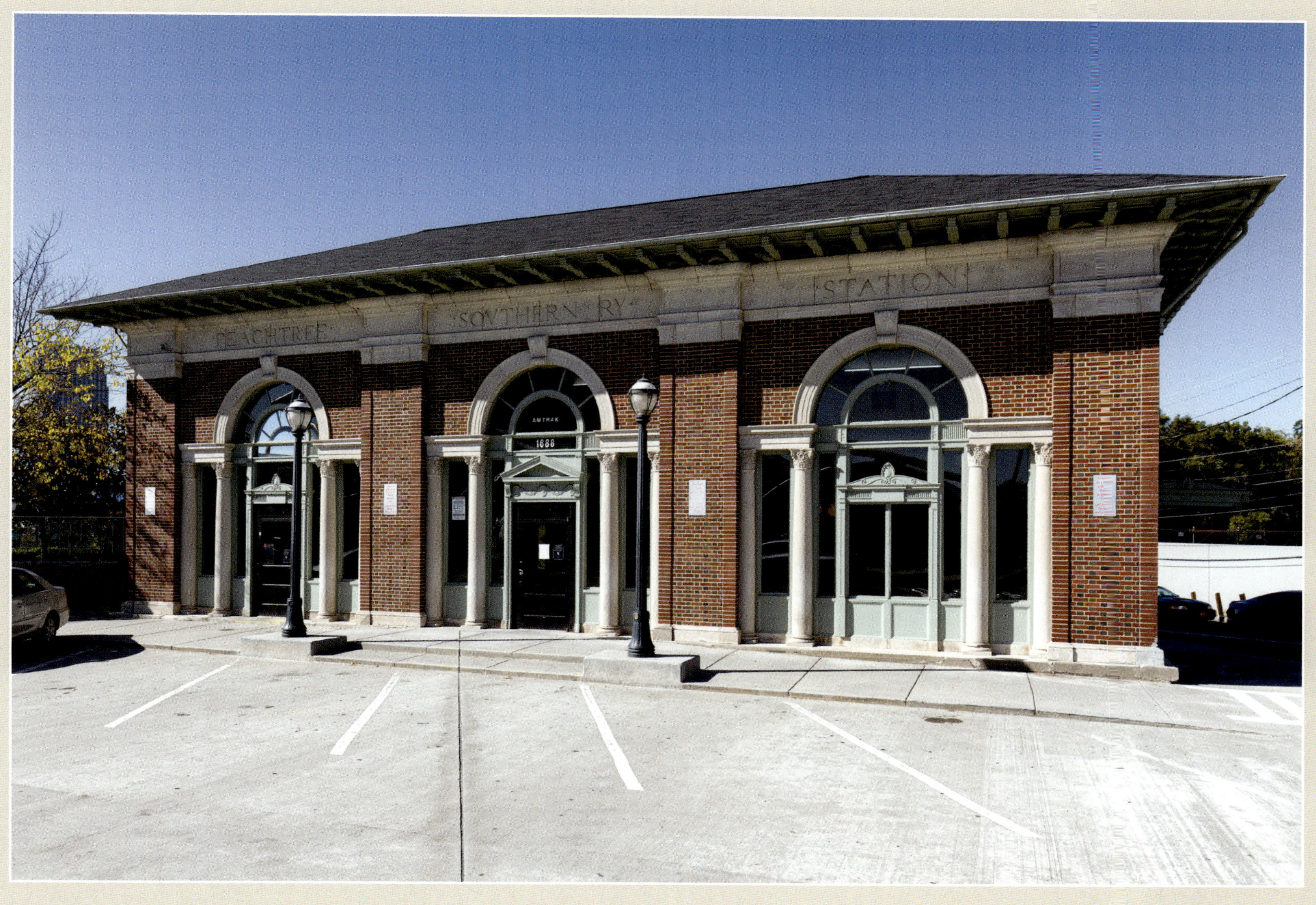

Southern Railway, Brookwood Station, Atlanta

on their location and the period in which they were built. There is a great deal of difference between a seventeenth-century New England house that might feature a gambrel roof, or a Tidewater Virginia brick house, and a Charleston single house with a piazza running down one side of the building. Accordingly, Colonial Revival houses take their inspiration from a variety of sources and, in fact, often take architectural details from several different models and blend them into one composition.

Colonial Revival houses nevertheless share certain characteristics. Normally, they are symmetrical, with the door centered in the front facade. They feature multipane, double-hung wooden windows and, if they include a portico, have classically detailed columns. The front door frequently has either a transom or a fanlight. The Colonial Revival house can be one story or multistory, have a gable or hip roof, and be faced with wood clapboard or brick veneer.

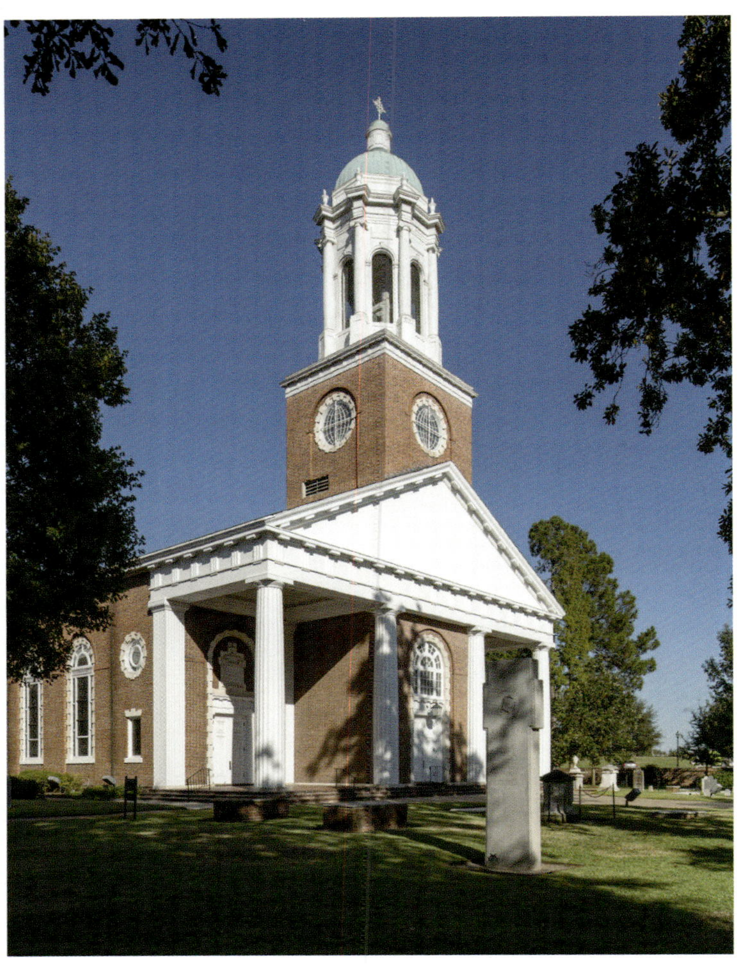

Saint Paul's Church, Augusta

One building that stays close to its inspiration is Saint Paul's Episcopal Church in Augusta. The present building was constructed in 1917–18 and is based upon an 1820 Federal-style church that burned in the Great Augusta Fire of 1916. The architect, Henry Ten Eyck Wendell, planned and supervised the construction as a faithful expansion of the original building.

Saint Paul's is a two-story brick basilica plan with a front portico that features four Doric columns. A handsome tower rises from the middle bay of the portico and extends above the roof, where it is crowned with a Neoclassical lantern. The brick tower features large round windows, with tracery, on its sides. The side facades feature arched windows that extend down the walls that frame the nave. The interior is true to the Colonial Revival spirit, with a series of arches, classically inspired detailing, and restrained colors. It departs from period colonial buildings in its use of colored leaded glass windows.

Henry Ten Eyck Wendell committed suicide in 1917 before the completion of the church reconstruction. He was born in 1859 in Waterford, New York, studied in the architecture program at Cornell University, and travelled to Europe in 1888 to further his knowledge of classically inspired buildings. He worked in many places in the United States, including various towns in New York State, Washington, D.C., and Denver, Colorado. During his sojourn in Denver, he designed the Colorado and Washington State buildings for the World's Columbian Exposition in Chicago in 1893.

Wendell had relocated to Augusta by 1908, undoubtedly due to commissions there, and he soon became the leading architect of the city. He designed a great number of prominent homes there and several institutional buildings as well. His outstanding work displays originality, finely crafted details, and an excellent sense of scale and proportion. His architectural legacy deserves greater appreciation in Georgia.

Another clear architectural homage is the James Dickey House on West Paces Ferry Road in the Buckhead section of Atlanta. This large white clapboard residence was designed by Neel Reid in 1915–17 on what was then 405 acres of land. The colossal portico supported by eight slender columns with Doric capitals was clearly inspired by George Washington's iconic Mount Vernon, which sits overlooking the Potomac River in Virginia. Mount Vernon also features eight columns, although they are expressed as square pillars. Reid's Dickey House is substantially larger than Washington's home and accomplishes this by the use of recessed, extended two-story wings on either side of the central block. The wing to the east features three round-headed arched floor-length windows, while the western wing has three bays of double-hung windows.

The 405 acres on which the house was built were later subdivided, and many of the grand estate houses of Buckhead are built on the original land purchased by James Dickey Sr. The Mount Vernon–inspired Dickey House now sits on a remaining two acres, and it clearly set the tone for Colonial Revival houses not only in Buckhead but also in many of the other developing, prosperous suburbs of Atlanta.

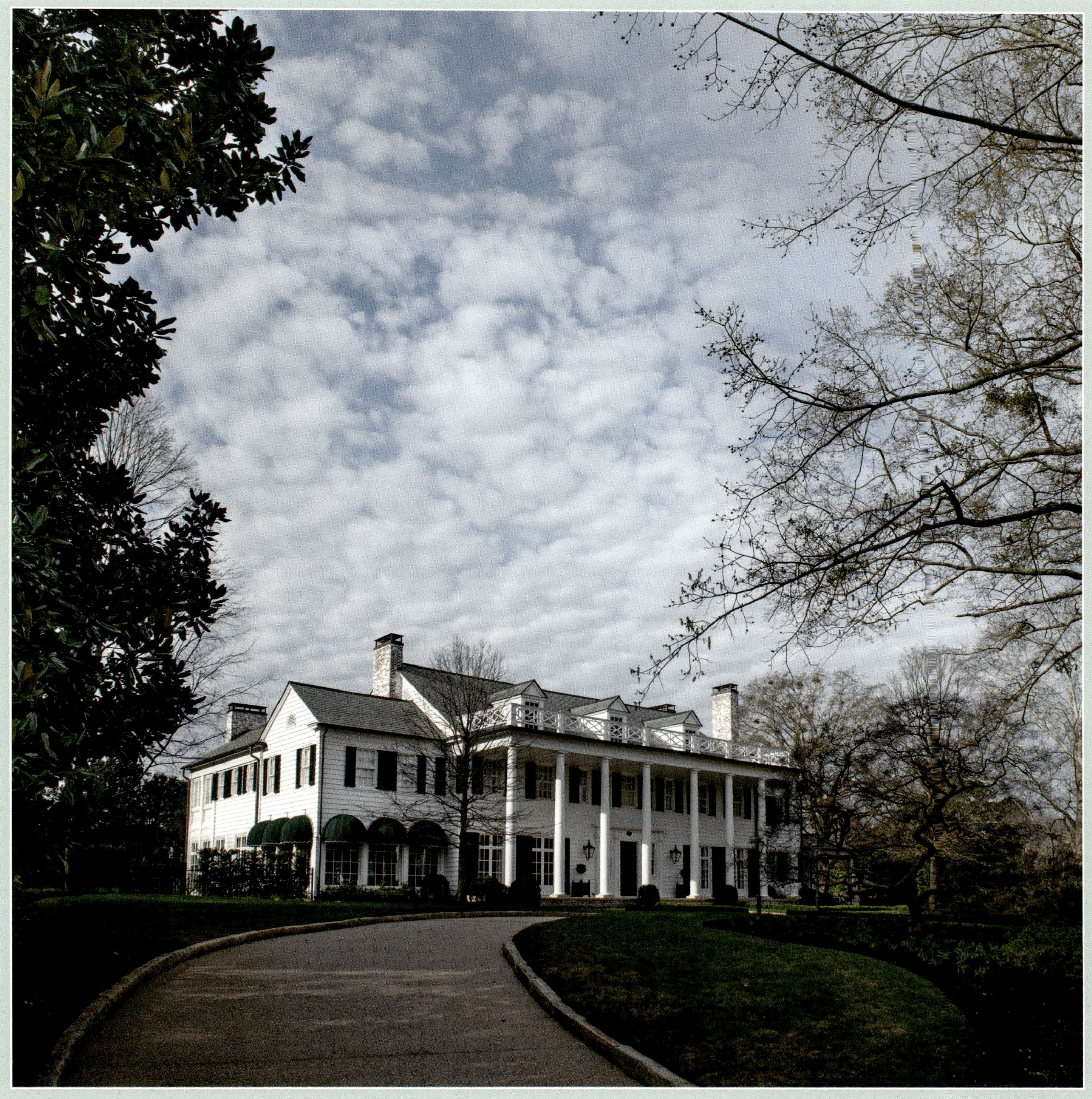

James Dickey House, Atlanta

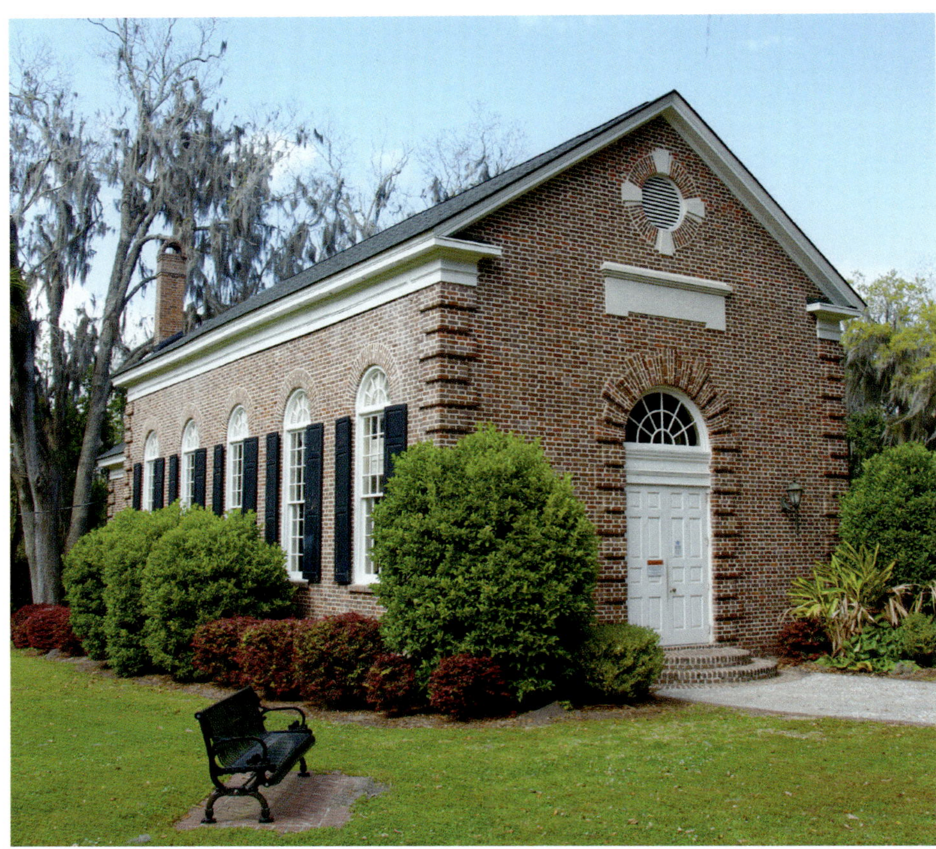

Whitefield Chapel, Bethesda Academy, Savannah

The Whitefield Chapel at the Bethesda Home for Boys, now known as Bethesda Academy, near Savannah, a scholarly interpretation of a small colonial parish church, was designed by Charleston architect Albert Simons. Simons was born in 1890 and completed degrees in architecture at the University of Pennsylvania. After graduation, he studied architecture at the Atelier Hebrard in Paris. After World War I, Simons returned to Charleston, where he played a key role in the Charleston renaissance, in part by helping to create the first local historic district zoning ordinance in the United States.

The Whitefield Chapel is located at the historic Bethesda Home for Boys, which was founded in 1740 by Rev. George Whitfield and claims to be the oldest continually operating childcare institution in the country. The National Society of the Colonial Dames commissioned the chapel in 1918. However, construction was postponed because of World War I, and the building was not completed until 1925.

The chapel is a simple building composed of handmade brick and features a single bay in its main facade consisting of an arched doorway containing a fanlight and surrounded by prominent brick voussoirs. Above this doorway is a stone lintel with a round vent in the gable end, also with pronounced voussoirs, this time expressed in stone. The interior features five arched double-hung windows on each side of the nave, a herringbone brick floor, and heart-pine pews. A small apse with a colored round-headed leaded glass window sits behind the altar. Simplicity of design combined with high-quality architectural details and materials make this one of Georgia's best Colonial Revival buildings, if also one of its least known.

An uncommon but highly successful application of the Colonial Revival style is seen in the Reid House apartments that sit on Peachtree Street in Midtown Atlanta. Reid House was constructed in 1924 and designed by architect Philip T. Shutze of the architectural firm of Hentz, Reid and Adler. This ten-story building is inspired by English Georgian architecture and features a central gable-end parapet defined by stone quoining that spans the entire ten-story composition. Stone finials sit at the corners and peak of this gabled parapet. Projecting rounded bays expressed in stone sit at the third and fourth levels of the facade, which helps to break up the mass and create a human scale for this multistory building. There are two entrances at ground level, each of which feature a round-headed arch and elegant wrought-iron work, also arched, which frames both entranceways. These wrought-iron ornaments have lanterns and are reminiscent of the Regency style seen in London and Bath, England. Blessed by a prime location in Midtown Atlanta across the street from the Woodruff Arts Center, Reid House was converted to condominiums in 1975. The building was listed on the National Register of Historic Places in 1979.

Reid House, Atlanta

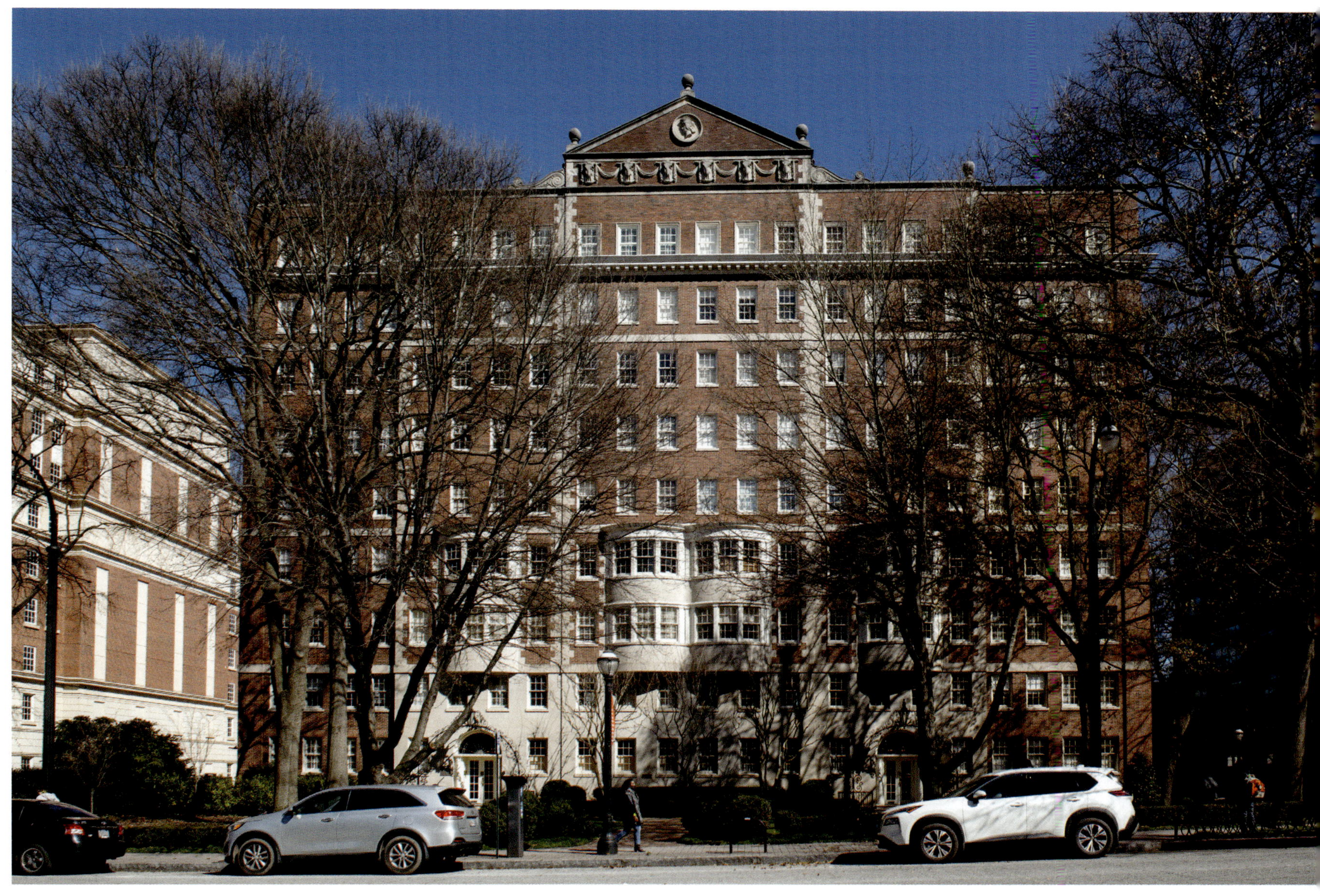

Philip Trammell Shutze was born in 1890, graduated from Georgia Tech in 1912, and received a bachelor of architecture degree from Columbia University in 1913. He was awarded a Rome Prize in 1915 and spent several years in Europe recording in detail Classical and Renaissance buildings. He became a partner of Hentz, Adler and Shutze in 1927. Shutze went on to design some of Georgia's finest Neoclassical, Colonial Revival, and Italian Renaissance Revival buildings, but he also forayed into Art Moderne architecture. His work extended beyond architecture to interior design and landscape architecture, and he was an avid collector of decorative-arts pieces, many now on display the Atlanta History Center.

Tudor Revival

The early twentieth century also produced an architectural revivalist style that was expressed not only in estate homes but also in smaller, middle-class houses in neighborhoods across Georgia. The Tudor Revival style was popular from around the turn of the century until the outbreak of World War II.

It is sometime called "stockbroker Tudor" for its popularity with individuals who had achieved rapid financial success. Its most visible characteristic is decorative half-timbering, especially on the second floor and gable ends. Front-facing gables are also a dominant feature of the Tudor Revival style, frequently on one side of the building. Indeed, this style is one of the few revivalist styles of the twentieth century that abandons adherence to symmetry.

Tudor Revival houses are usually constructed of a mix of materials. Brick, stone, or stucco can be used for the first floor, while false wood timbering with stucco infill is common above the ground floor. Windows are frequently varied in sizes and shapes and commonly have multiple panes, often with diamond shape muntins.

Callanwolde may be Georgia's most prominent Tudor Revival mansion. It was built between 1917 and 1921 for Charles Howard Candler, son of Asa Griggs Candler, and was designed by architect Henry Hornbostle of New York. Asymmetrical but balanced, its front facade has a stucco ground floor, while the upper story-and-a-half features elaborate half-timbering. Two front-facing gables dominate the facade, the one to the right has a projecting bay with a crenellated parapet, further adding to its English medieval appearance. Tudor arches are expressed in a wing off the front terrace and in the wide front doorway.

Located on Briarcliff Road in Atlanta, Callanwolde is part of a 12-acre estate that has period outbuildings and extensive gardens. The Candler family continued to occupy the home until 1959, when it was donated to Emory University, which sold it to the First Christian Church. The church leased it, and it began to deteriorate. Eventually the church sold the building to DeKalb County, whose efforts were led by the Druid Hills Civic Association and later by the Callanwolde Foundation. The estate is now operated as a fine arts, community, and cultural center and site for special events. It is an excellent example of historic preservation in action, combining architectural conservation with community outreach.

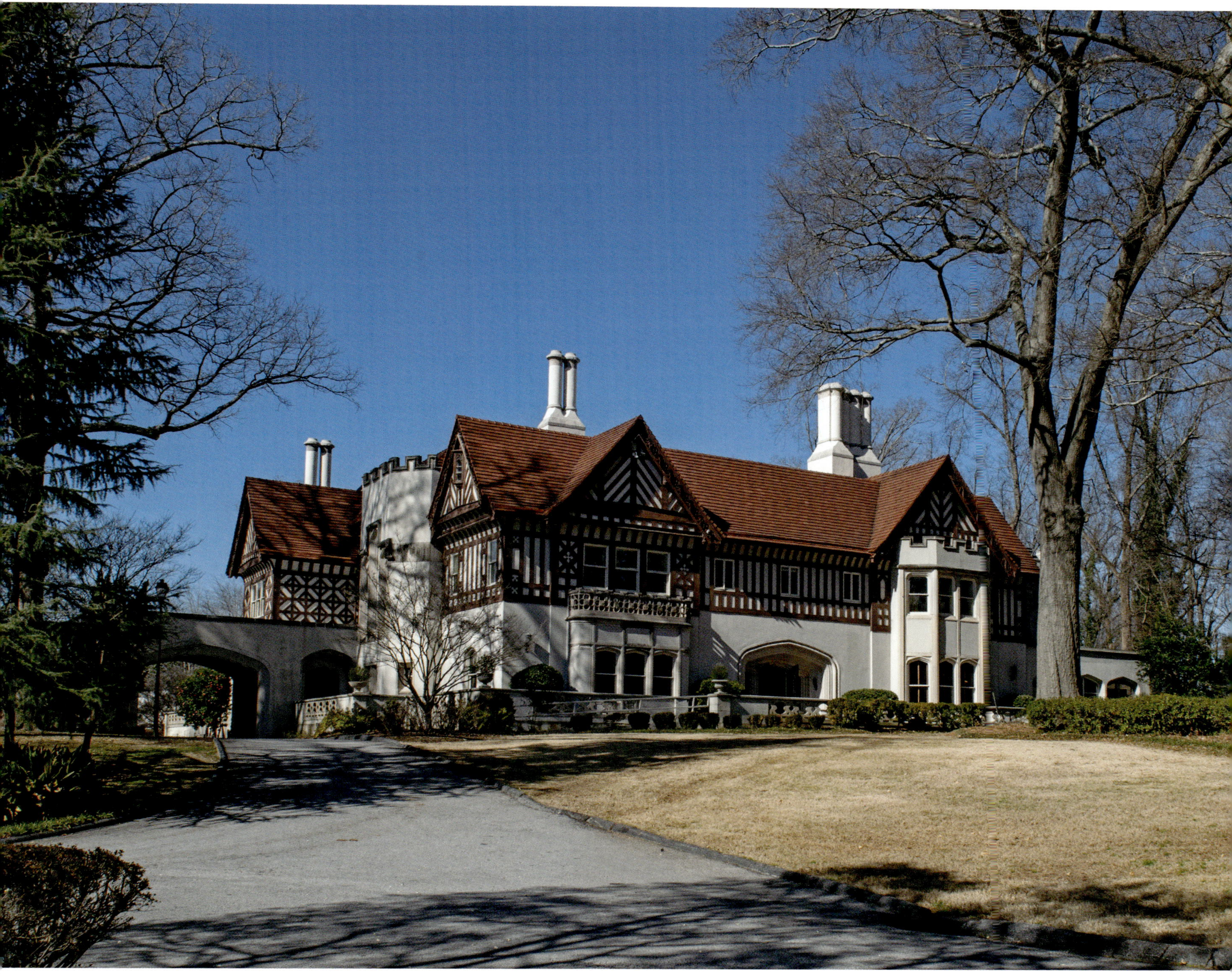

Callanwolde, Atlanta

In its architect, Henry Hornbostle, Callanwolde is another example of Georgia attracting a nationally significant designer to contribute to its built environment. Hornbostle was born in Brooklyn, New York, in 1867 and attended Columbia University and the Ecole des Beaux-Arts. He specialized in academic architecture and worked extensively at Carnegie-Mellon University in Pittsburgh, Northwestern in Evanston, Illinois, and Emory University, where he developed its master plan. He also designed several public works projects, including the famous Williamsburg Bridge that spans the East River connecting Manhattan to Brooklyn.

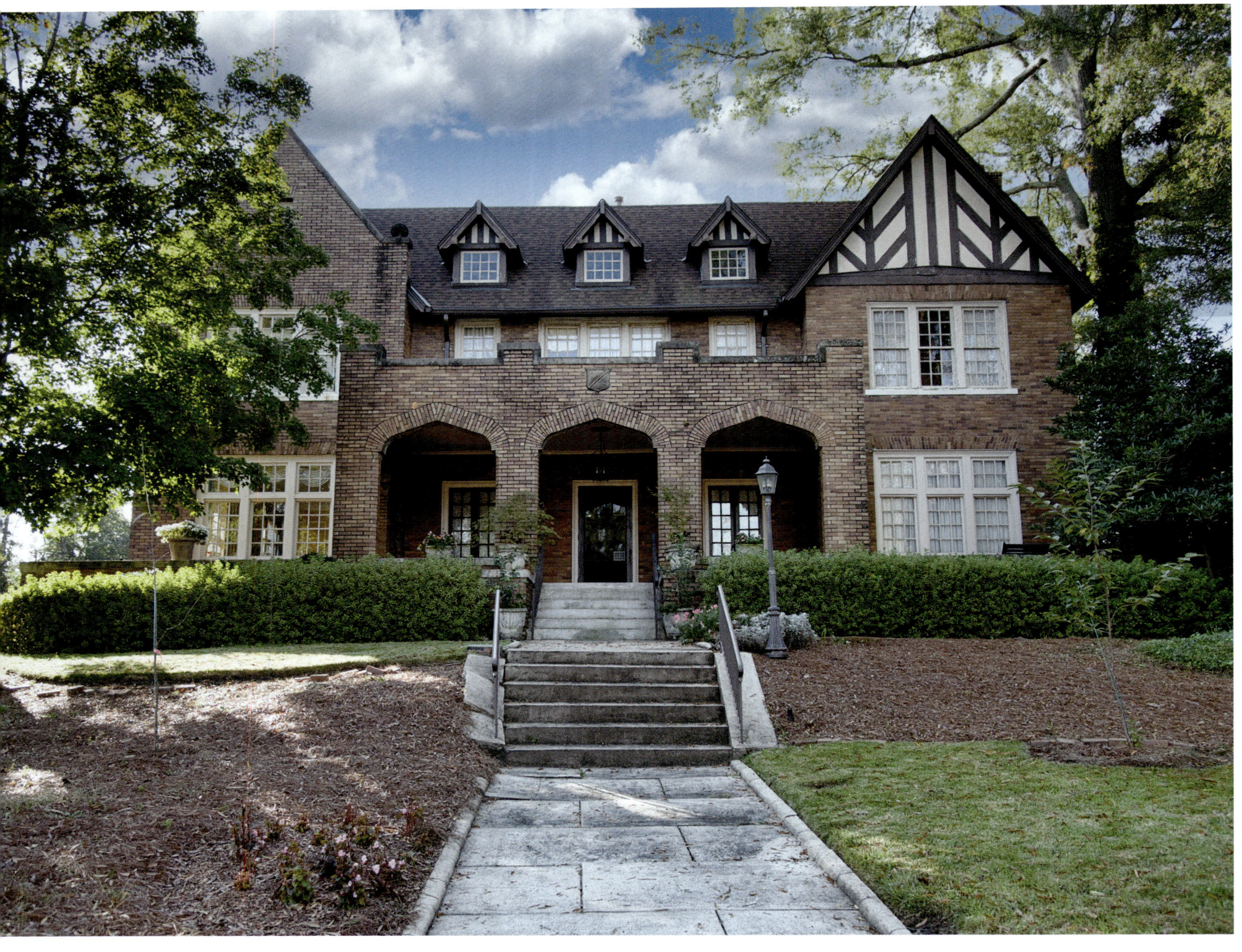

Joseph Neel House, Macon

The Joseph Neel House on College Street in Macon was designed in 1910 by Neel Reid. It is one of Reid's first commissions, and a personal one, as Neel was a close family friend and the architect's namesake. The house is an excellent example of Tudor Revival, featuring half-timbering on its prominent gable on the right of the facade and on three smaller dormer windows. The large gable on the left side of the facade lacks timbering, which creates the asymmetrical appearance often found in Tudor Revival houses. A three-bay projecting front porch with Tudor arches dominates the ground floor. Tripartite windows are found on both levels of the front-facing gable ends. The Federated Garden Clubs of Macon own and operate the Neel House, making it another example of successful historic preservation accomplished by women of Georgia who have done so much for the movement.

Musical Heritage of the Allman Brothers Preserves Tudor Revival "Big House"

A Tudor Revival house in Macon that tells an entirely different kind of story: From 1970 to 1973, founding members of the internationally famous Southern rock group the Allman Brothers Band lived in a Tudor Revival mansion on Vineville Avenue, paying the sum of $225 per month in rent. The band wrote some of their most notable songs in the house and recorded them at nearby Capricorn Records studios.

Built in the 1920s, this house features twin half-timbered gables on the second and attic levels of its front facade, which rests on a brick base that features double casement style windows. A projecting porch with stylized Tudor arches adorns the ground level. The porch has a parapet stucco wall with crenellations and a triangular stepped gable end in the center.

The Allman Brothers Band referred to this rather dilapidated rental property as "The Big House," and it is currently operated as a much-visited and successful museum by the Big House Foundation. The museum is dedicated to showcasing the rich musical heritage of Macon and telling the story of the Allman Brothers Band through interesting displays, period rooms, and the world's largest collection of Allmans memorabilia. This creative reuse of this notable house represents a new frontier in the field of preservation.

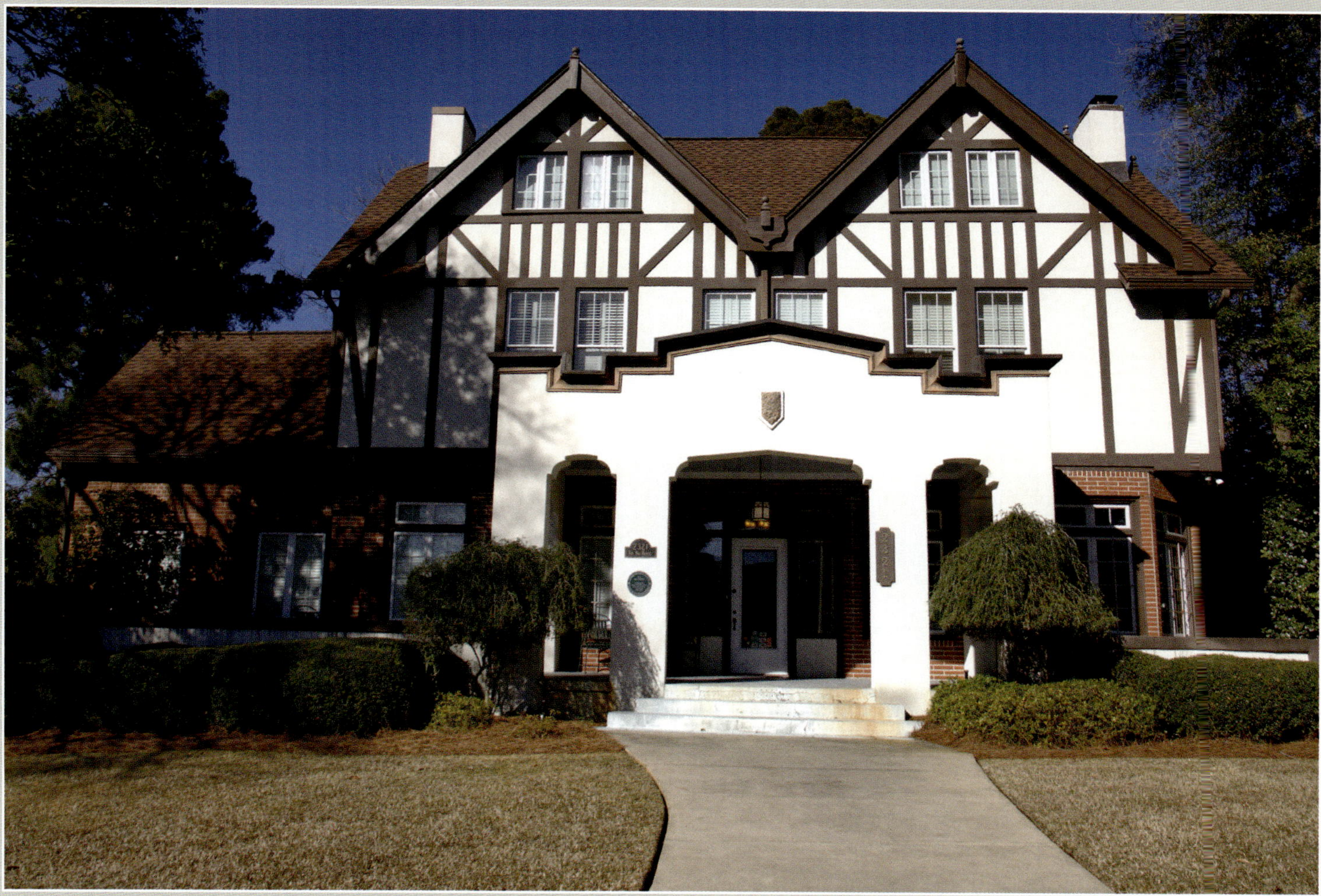

The Big House, Macon

The Tudor Revival style was also applied to hundreds of smaller houses in the developing early twentieth-century suburbs across Georgia. There are many variations of the style, some of which feature little or no half-timbering but express the style by the use of steeply pitched projecting gable ends, brick and/or stone, and multipaned windows. The vernacular application of the Tudor Revival enlivens many of these 1920s-era neighborhoods, adding to their architectural diversity.

Mediterranean Revival and Mission

The early twentieth century produced both a rich variety of architectural styles and the resources that enabled them to flourish. The prosperity of Georgia's cities created fertile ground for the development of the revivalist styles inspired by the late Italian and Spanish Renaissance. Buildings constructed in these styles require large budgets and therefore occur less often than their Neoclassical and Colonial Revival counterparts. Georgia architects and their patrons produced examples that stand at the forefront of quality in the United States.

The Italian Renaissance Revival building is normally inspired by Italian prototypes and includes direct quotations from their architectural features. These buildings usually have fairly flat hipped roofs, plain wall surfaces composed of stone or stucco, eaves ornamented with brackets, and arched windows on the ground floor with simpler windows on upper stories. Classically inspired buildings are commonly symmetrical, while those based on country villas may be asymmetrical.

Most Italian Renaissance Revival edifices were designed by trained architects, many of whom had traveled to Italy as part of their formal or informal education. Many of these architects kept detailed sketchbooks that exhibit the designs and details they admired. It is important to note that most of the buildings of this style are truly based on the late Renaissance, Mannerist, or Baroque examples, not the Renaissance buildings of Alberti, Brunelleschi, or Michelangelo.

Henry Ten Eyck Wendell of Augusta was one of the first residential architects in Georgia to explore the possibilities of this style. His work in Summerville shows his design talent in this style as well as others.

The lovely home known as Breetholm on Milledge Road in Summerville was built in 1901 and is a simple example of the style. This is a building whose mass is symmetrical but whose architectural detailing is varied. It has a projecting front-hipped gable with a diamond-shaped window in alignment with the arched front door and second floor balcony under a simplified window. The facade is enlivened by an elegant large tripartite window that is offset from the first and second floor. Like so many Renaissance Revival buildings it is stucco and features a ceramic tile roof.

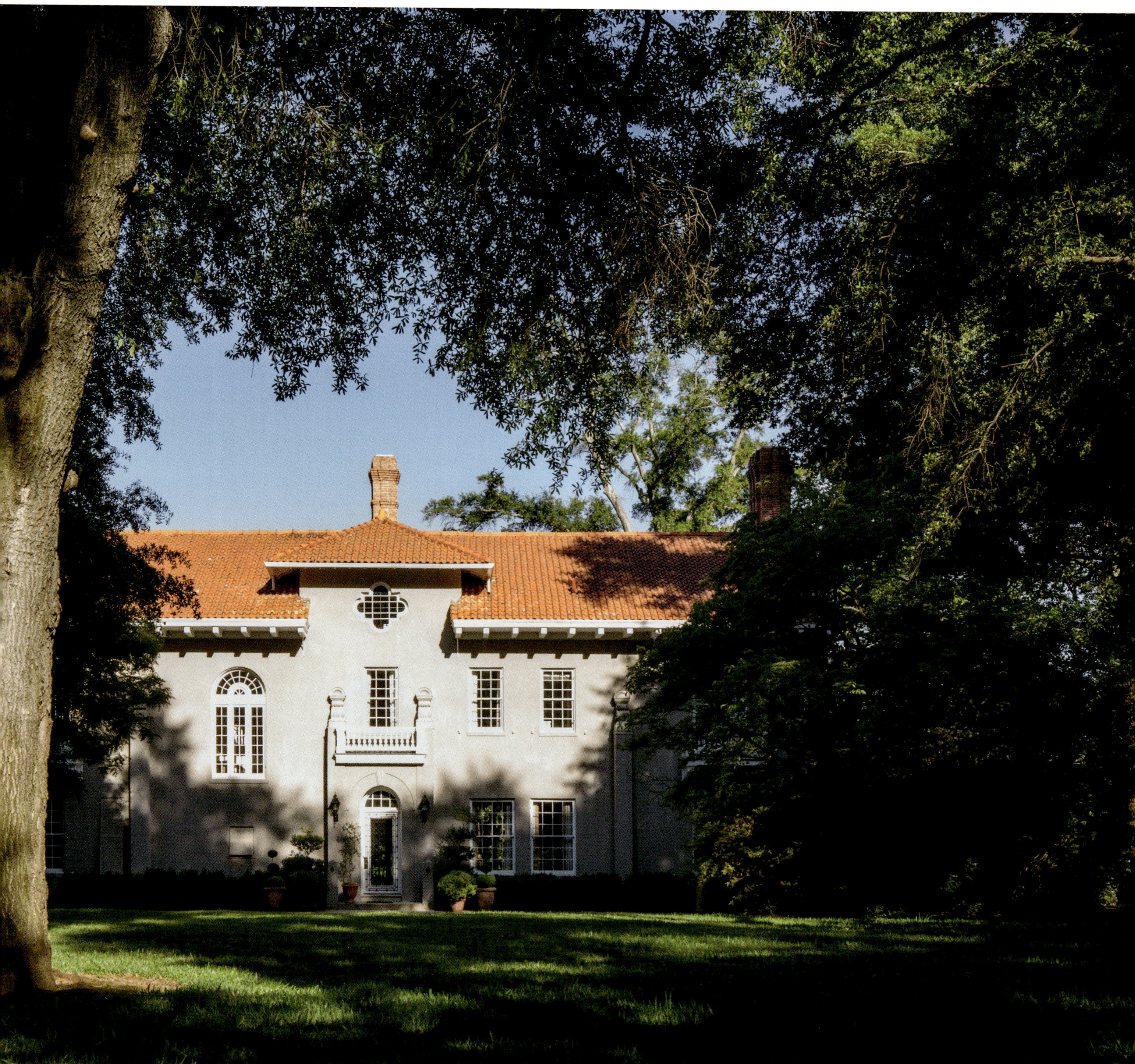

Breetholm, Augusta

On the same road is Wendell's building from 1911, the William B. White House. This house is strictly symmetrical. Again, it is composed of stucco and features a red ceramic-tile hipped roof whose eaves are supported by brackets. The center bay is clearly dominant, with an elaborate set of casement windows with flanking sets of engaged columns and a pronounced balcony on the second floor. A smaller entry door with narrow windows set in the stucco wall sits beneath this balcony on its ground floor.

The facade is divided into five bays on the second floor, with simple windows flanking the elaborate central bay. The ground floor has only thee bays, with pairs of windows inset into arches on either side of the front door. The house sits elegantly on a terrace which is bordered by a classically designed balustrade. This balustrade is repeated and incorporated into the house's beautiful landscape.

William B. White House, Augusta

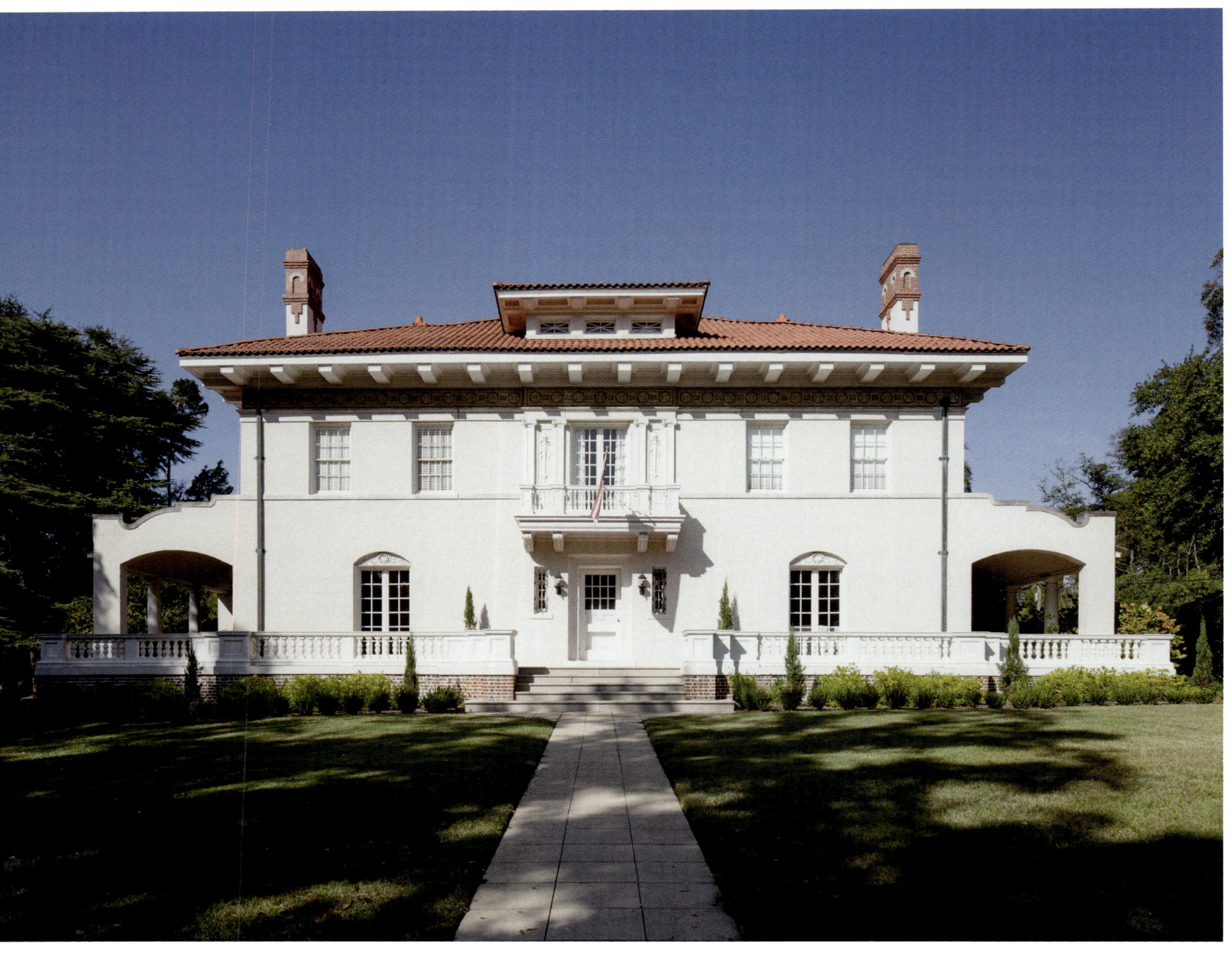

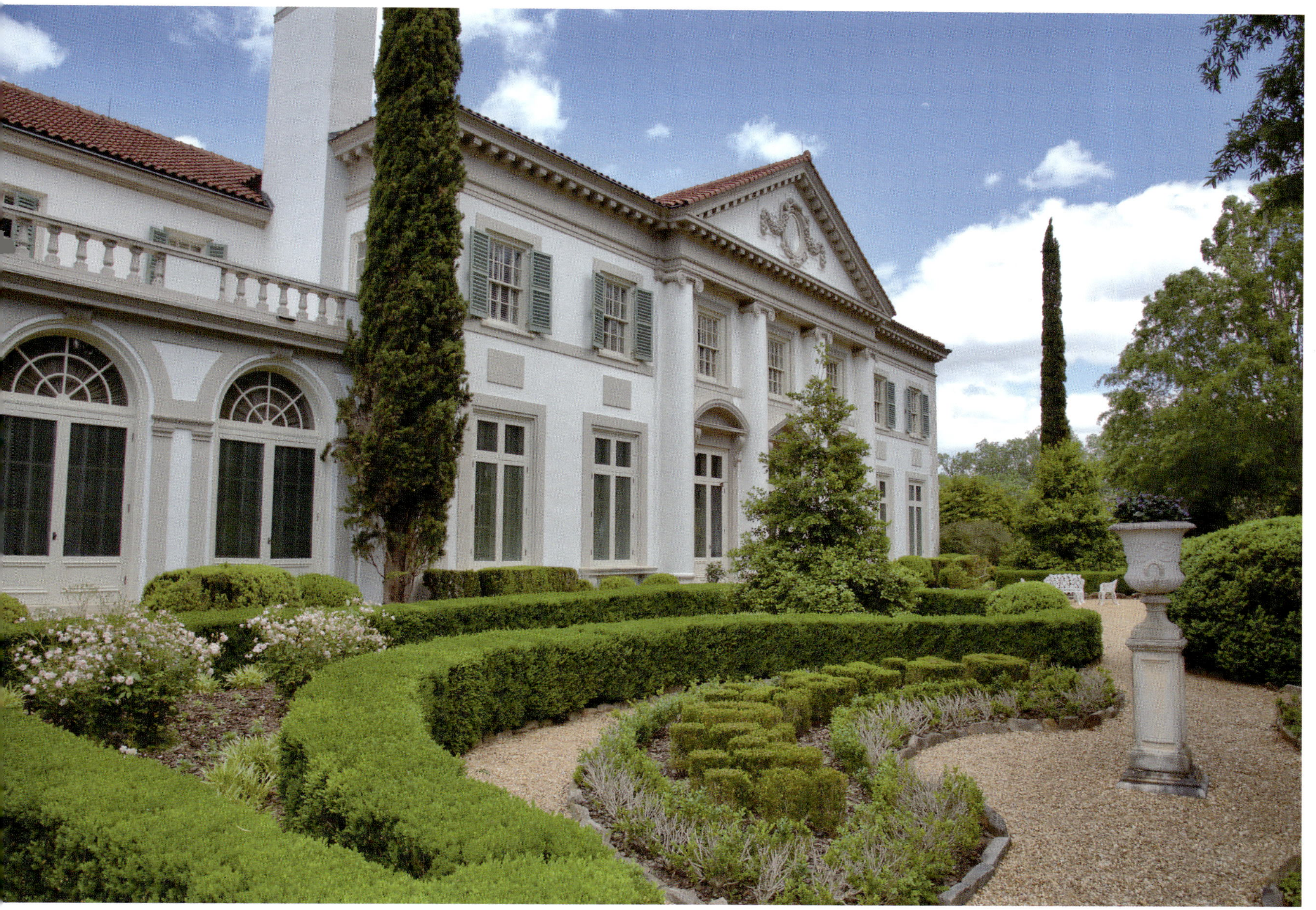

Hills and Dales, LaGrange

Neel Reid's Hills and Dales in LaGrange, from 1916, has rightly been described as a work of English Palladianism. The grand house has beautifully executed ornamental details applied to a Neoclassical composition reminiscent of the late eighteenth-century designs of Lord Burlington.

The main block of the house is composed of seven bays; the central four bays are given over to an engaged portico of four columns with Ionic capitals. The central doorway has a triangular window hood; doors on either side have segmental arched hoods. An oval window with sculpted garlands adorns the pediment framed by heavy dentil molding. Finally, the facade features heavy quoins on its corners. On one side of the main block is a projecting half-circle portico, again in the Ionic order, while an extensive wing set back from the main facade projects from the other side.

This magnificent house is sited within the extensive historic Ferrell Gardens, which were first planted in the 1840s. To the gardens Reid added statuary, fountains, outbuildings, and other improvements. The result is an architecture and landscape absolutely integrated with the west Georgia terrain.

Hills and Dales' builders were Fuller and Ida Callaway, and they were devoted to the creation and care of this magnificent estate. At Ida's death in 1936 the house was acquired by their son Fuller Jr., and in 1998 it became the property of the Fuller B. Callaway Foundation, which has opened the house and grounds to the public.

Reid's business partner Philip Shutze, who had studied and traveled extensively in Italy, was not to be outdone. In the 1920s Shutze designed a series of estates that borrow heavily from Italian Renaissance, Mannerist, and Baroque buildings.

Completed in 1922, Shutze's Calhoun House in the Buckhead neighborhood of Atlanta is an early work taking inspiration from Italian villas to create a single composition. This house, also known as Trygveson, is based on Villa Cuzzano in Verona, Villa Gori in Sienna, and Villa Spada in Rome. Its garden facade has a dynamic three-bay, three-and-a-half-story projecting block with broken pediment and urns adorning its roofline.

Calhoun House, Atlanta

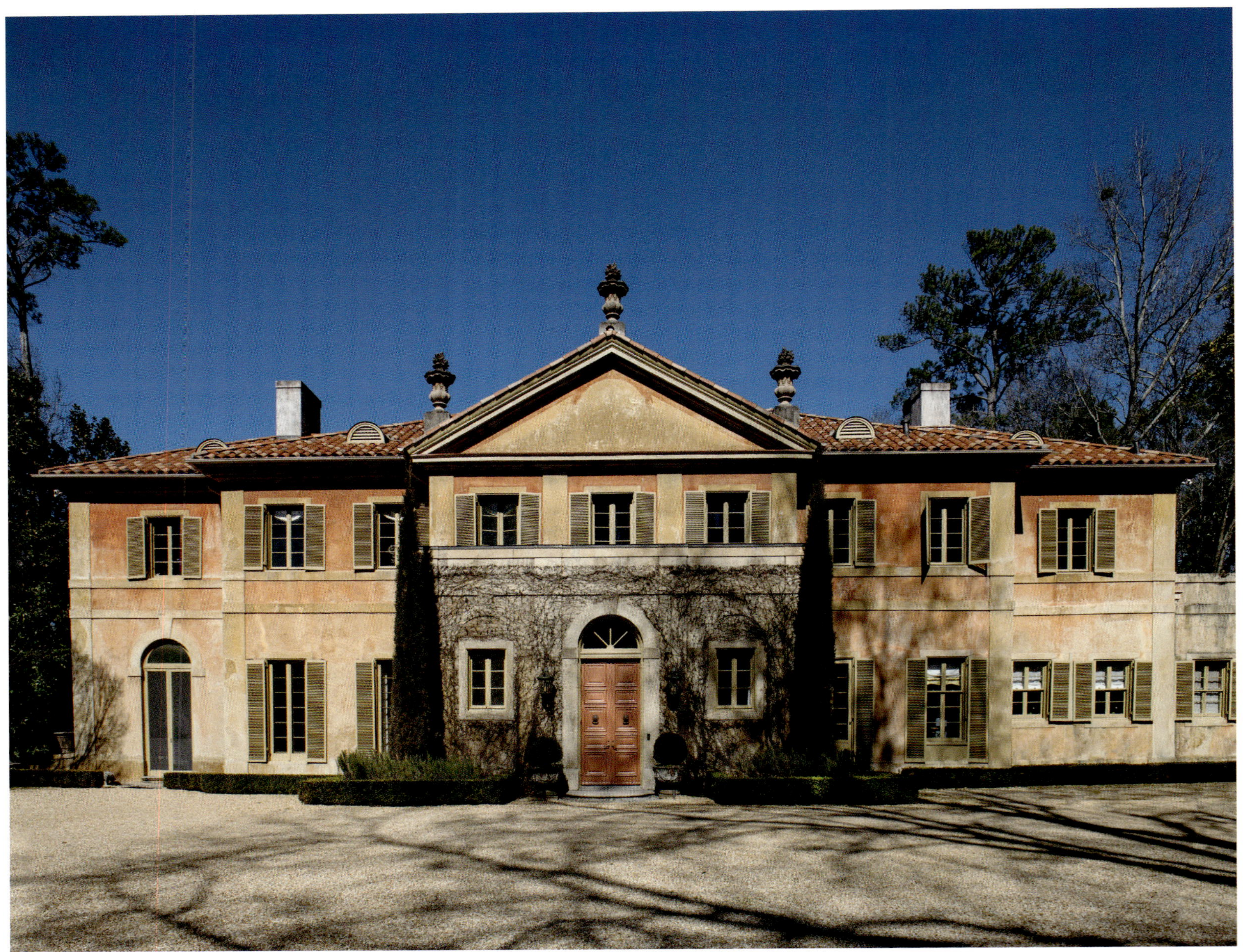

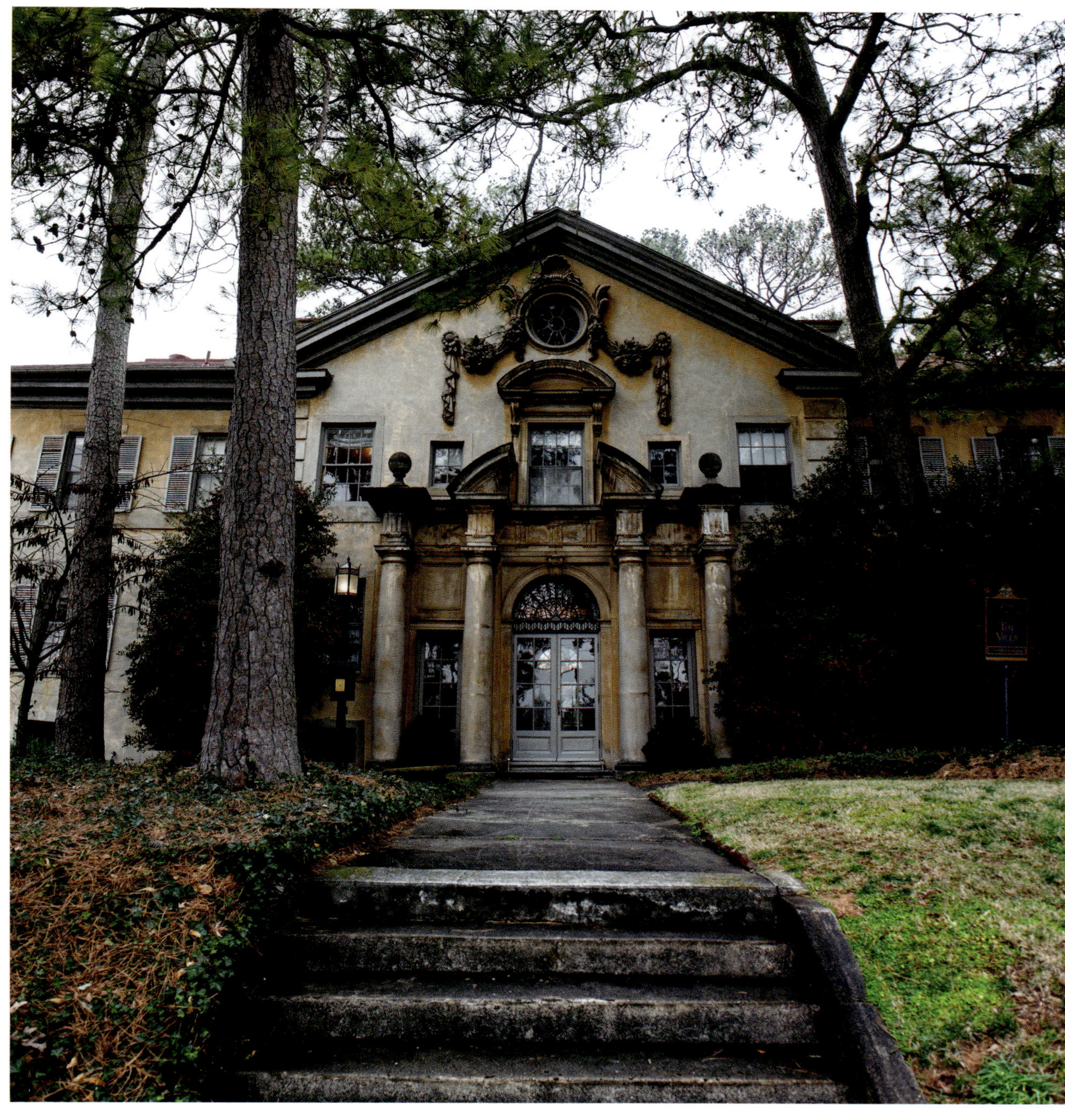

The Villa, Atlanta

A building in Ansley Park in Atlanta called the Villa demonstrates Shutze's ability to utilize this style in a multiunit apartment complex. Originally called Italian Villa, it was built in 1926 and modeled after a portion of the facade of the Chiesa di Santa Cecilia in Trastevere in Rome. The main facade of this building is dominated by a central gable whose central bay is a strong composition of an engaged portico with unfluted Doric columns supporting an entablature with triglyph and metope capped with a segmental arch. As in the Villa Albicini in Macon, Shutze places a window within this arch. This window has an elaborate segmental arch hood, and rising above this second-floor window is a round window festooned with an elaborate garland. As in other Shutze buildings, a faux patinated paint finish is utilized to give the building an instant antique quality. The building was converted to condominiums and now has twenty-five units.

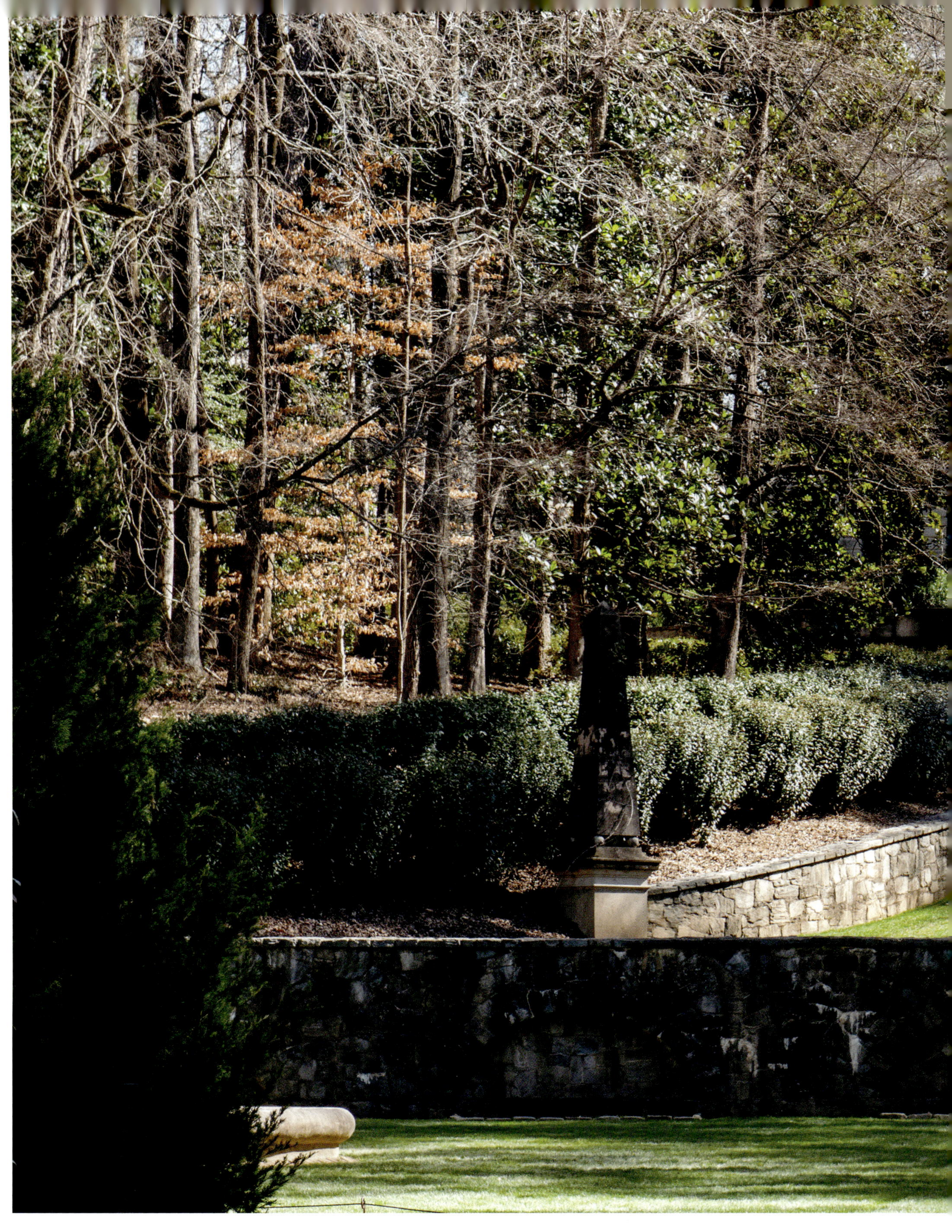

Due in part to its dramatic landscape, which faces Andrews Drive in Atlanta, the Swan House is Shutze's best-known work. The house was built in 1928 by Edward and Emily Inman and presents a sophisticated integration of architecture and landscape. Its west facade is sited at the top of a hill, for which Shutze designed a system of terraces accented with staircases, beautifully detailed retaining walls, fountains, and obelisks.

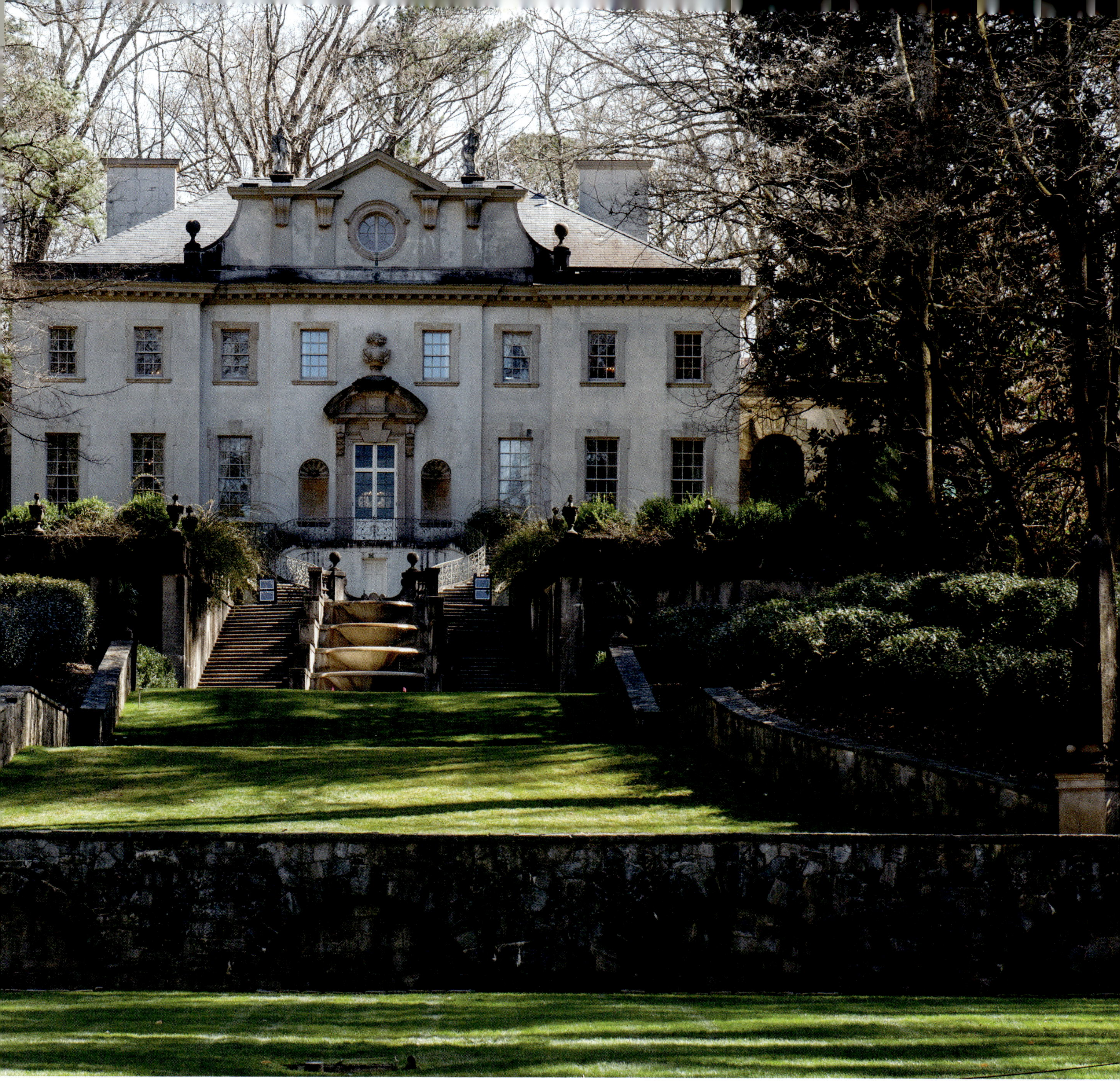

Swan House, Atlanta

The west facade is a two-and-a-half-story nine-bay stucco composition. It has a hipped roof with a segmented pediment resting on scroll brackets and a round window in its frieze. Sculptural figures and finials adorn this dominant feature. The central doorway also features a segmental arch topped by a large urn that rises between a pair of windows on the second floor. A pair of niches with shell motifs flank the central door.

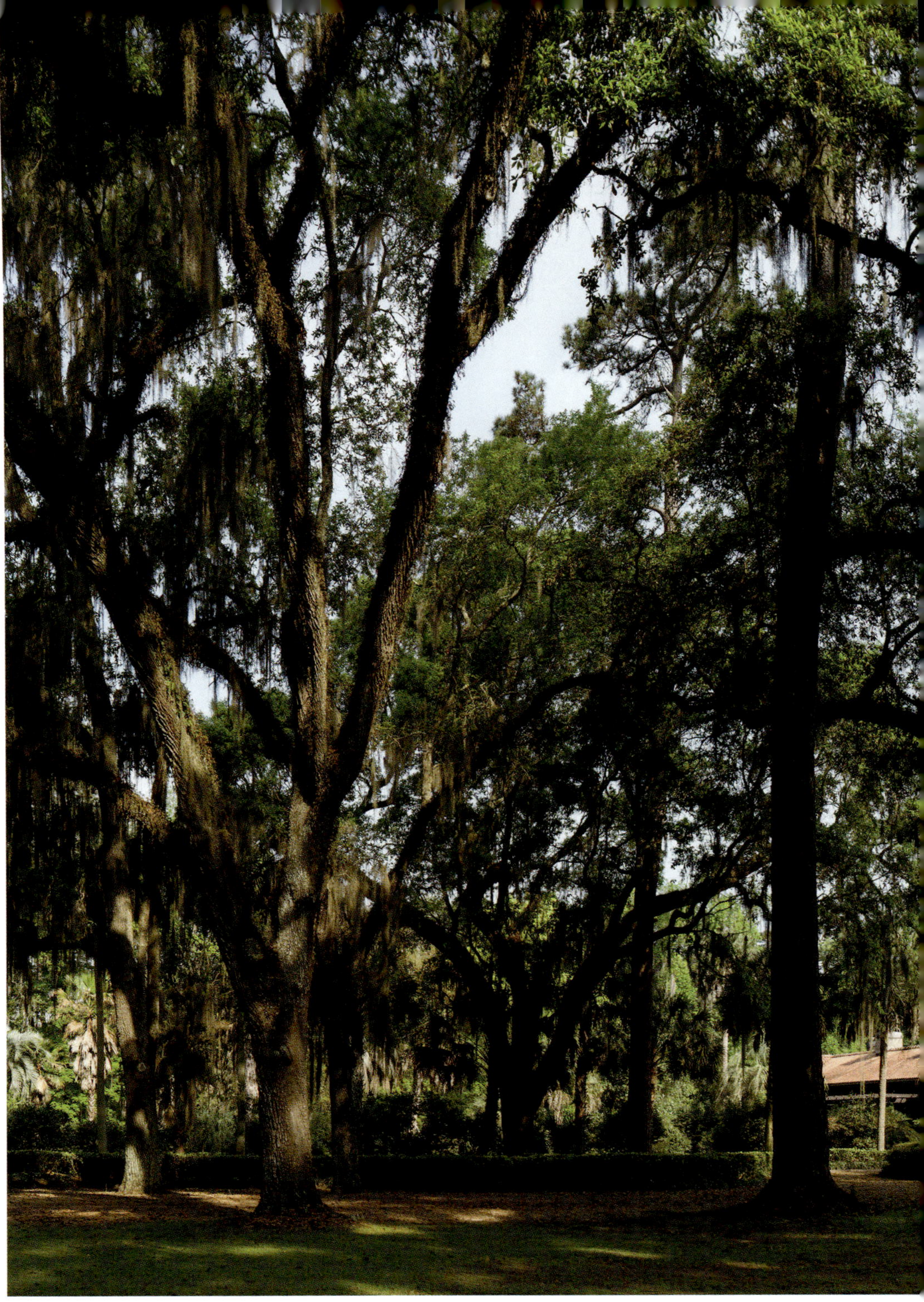

The less well-known east facade is more Neoclassical, lacking Baroque flourishes. It also has nine bays, and the central three are given to a two-story pediment in the Doric order. The entablature has beautifully executed triglyph and metope. Under its portico is a large central doorway with a segmental arch pediment, surrounded by heavy quoins. As on the west facade, a pair of niches flank the doorway, this time with urns topped by triangular pediments. As with most of Shutze's creations, craftsmanship is fundamental to the success of the designs. The Swan House seems to be flawlessly executed, and it is faithfully maintained by the Atlanta History Center, which has owned the site since 1966.

Shutze was a master designer, had an excellent sense of scale and proportion, and was a devoted scholar. He was also prolific, and designed residential buildings, hospitals, churches, banks, and office buildings. He died in 1982 at the age of ninety-one, leaving behind a tremendous architectural legacy.

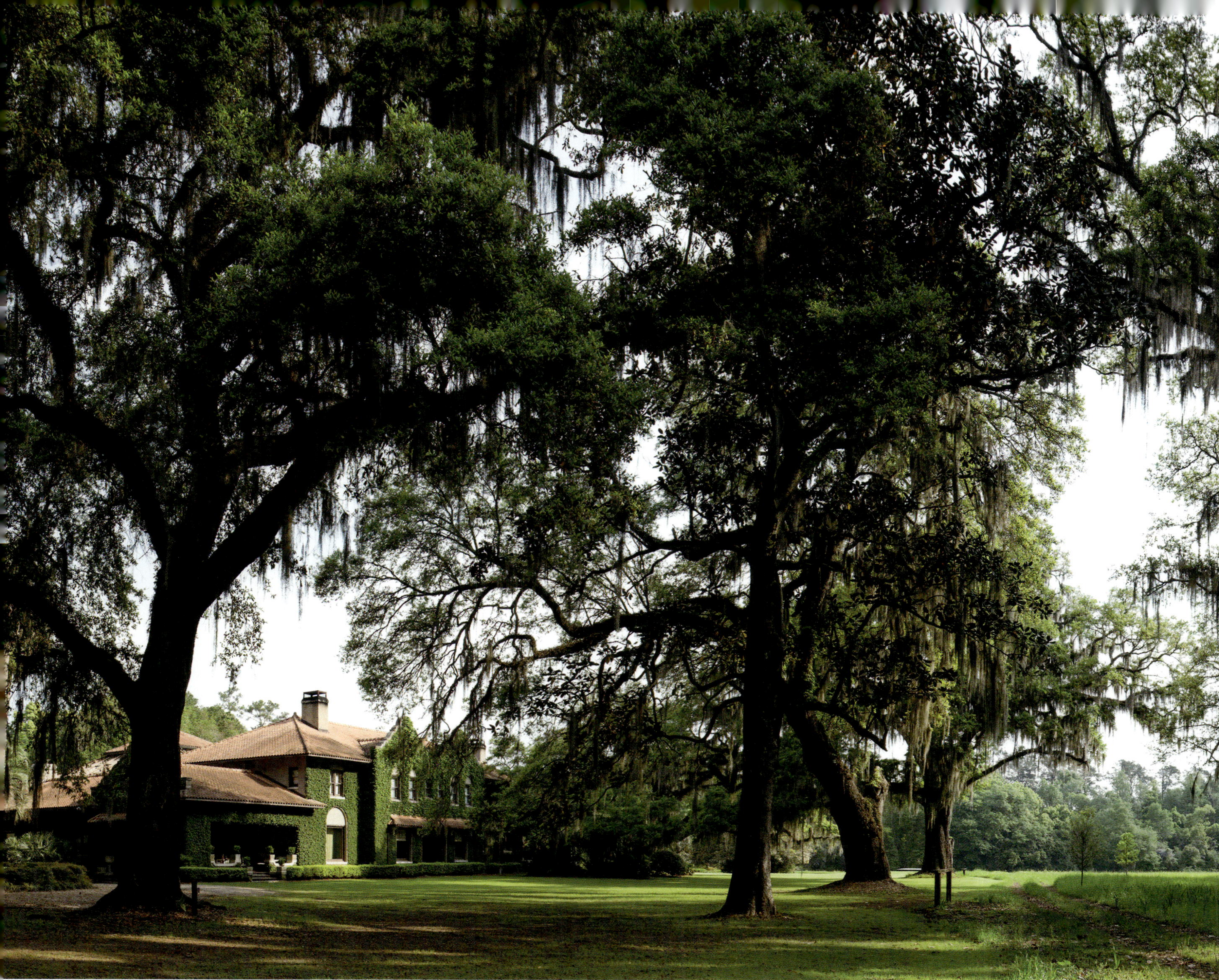

Millpond Plantation, Thomasville

Built in a completely different style, but every bit as brilliant and impressive, is Millpond, outside of Thomasville. Millpond was once a 10,000-acre hunting estate and takes its name from an extant still pond that served a nineteenth-century gristmill. The estate consists of a main house and numerous outbuildings and extensive gardens that surround the main house on three sides.

The main house, completed in 1905, was designed by the well-known firm of Hubbell and Benes of Cleveland, Ohio. It is a fine example of Spanish Mission Revival architecture and is highly original in its design. The principals of the firm were Benjamin Hubbell and Dominic Benes, who were responsible for a great number of prominent buildings in Cleveland, including the Cleveland Museum of Art, the Cleveland *Plain Dealer* headquarters, the Wade Memorial Building, and the West Side Market.

The extensive landscape was the work of Warren Manning of Boston. Manning was the son of a nursery owner, attended Harvard University, and was later employed by the legendary Frederick Law Olmsted. Under Olmsted, Manning worked on influential projects such as the World's Columbian Exposition and George Vanderbilt's Biltmore Estate in Asheville, North Carolina. Manning was a proponent of what he called the "wild garden" approach to landscape architecture, which emphasized the use of native plants in groupings and careful pruning and thinning to produce a manicured but natural appearance. His work at Millpond is a testament to this discipline and remains today a beautiful landscape that contrasts with while complementing the wild pine forest of Thomas County, Georgia.

Set within this landscape is the Millpond main house, which was pioneering for bringing nature indoors. The house's most prominent feature is its 10,000-square-foot courtyard covered by a steel-and-glass pyramid that can be opened and closed as weather allows. All of the first-floor rooms open onto this architecturally dynamic space whose center is a soothing pool surrounded by lush plants.

The main house occupies 38,000 square feet and has eleven bedrooms, ten and a half baths, elegant parlors, dining rooms, a billiard parlor, and a library. The extensive period kitchen is still intact. The house features a red tile roof and projecting gables in the Spanish Mission Revival style. In fact, its plan resembles that of an American Spanish mission with a church rising above other buildings in the complex but joined with a series of walls that create a courtyard. In the case of Millpond, that courtyard has been covered with a revolutionary pyramidal skylight. Most of the house is one story, although there is a large central section on one side that is two stories in height and features twin curvilinear stepped Mission gable ends. The house is finished in stucco but is covered in climbing vine that serves to further unify the house with its environment. There is also a corner porch with a fireplace that faces the landscape.

Millpond Plantation is a masterpiece of landscape design and architecture. It is also a testament to its builder, Jeptha W. Wade of Cleveland, Ohio, whose architectural taste and inheritance enabled the construction of this estate. Wade's grandfather, also named Jeptha Wade, was one of the founders of the Western Union Telegraph Company.

Craftsman

Another important architectural trend emerged in the early twentieth century that in many ways cut against the grain of the Colonial Revival and Neoclassical movements. The Craftsman style, also known as Bungalow or California Bungalow, was immensely popular from the early 1900s into the early years of the Great Depression. Although the Craftsman style emphasizes a lack of adherence to traditional architectural forms, it shares the values of nostalgia and romanticism with Colonial Revival and Neoclassism.

Irene Sargent and Gustav Stickley, both of Syracuse, New York, published the first issue of *The Craftsman* magazine in October 1901. This publication was highly influential on design in the United States, introducing readers to the ideas of the English thinkers William Morris and John Ruskin. Their design philosophies emphasized structural expression in design, honest materials, and most of all, quality of craftsmanship in the manufacture of furniture and the other decorative arts. There were crosscurrents in the larger design profession of the times, especially in the work of Louis Sullivan and his pupil Frank Lloyd Wright.

The style reached its zenith in the work of the architectural partnership of brothers Charles Sumner Greene and Henry Mather Greene. Greene and Greene, both educated at the Massachusetts Institute of Technology, settled in Pasadena, California, where they established their architectural practice in 1894. Their designs in Pasadena represent the height of achievement in the emerging Arts and Crafts movement and featured custom joinery, bespoke lighting fixtures, and hand-woven textiles, as well as the low-pitched roofs, wide overhanging eaves, exposed rafter tails, and structural honesty that defined Craftsman-style buildings for the next quarter century.

In reality, the Craftsman movement created a building form and set of ideals rather than merely a style, for as it developed in the United States it created multiple variations. There were Craftsman buildings that show decorative touches influenced by Greene and Greene; many that continued to use Neoclassical detailing; Mission-style examples; English-cottage variants; some in the Tudor Revival with half-timbering; and even buildings that borrowed details from Asia. Most Craftsman buildings are simple, yet consistent in their use of the low sloped roof, exposed rafters, wide overhanging eaves, and a prominent front porch frequently supported by tapered square columns that rest on square masonry knee-high piers. A mixed interplay of wood siding, shingles, and stone or brick is commonly employed for exterior materials.

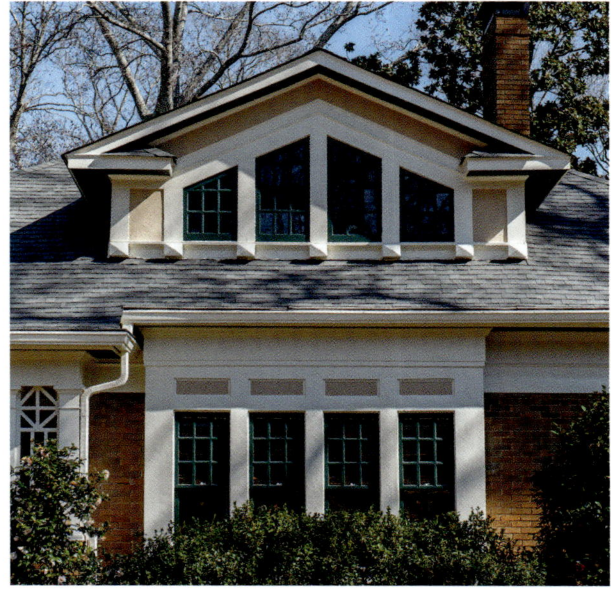

310 Adams Street, Decatur, dormer detail

The proliferation of Craftsman houses was due in large measure to the abundance of house-plan books and catalogs that flooded the market after 1900 and the innovation of kit houses. In 1906 the Aladdin Company of Bay City, Michigan, began to offer kit houses for sale and shipment to consumers. These kits included a set of plans and precut lumber, millwork, cabinetry, and everything else necessary to construct a house. In 1908, Sears, Roebuck and Company entered this business as well, employing its considerable marketing powers in this emerging industry.

One of the architects who contributed to the popularity of Craftsman-style houses was Leila Ross Wilburn. Wilburn was born in Macon, Georgia, in 1885, the daughter of parents who were promoters of female higher education and supported her desire to become an architect. After attending Agnes Scott Institute, Wilburn received private lessons in architectural drafting and accepted a position with B. R. Padgett and Sons, an Atlanta architectural and construction firm, and she later established her own practice. In 1914 Wilburn authored *Southern Homes and Bungalows* which featured designs for eighty-two houses, many of which were constructed in Georgia, with a high concentration in Decatur and Atlanta. This book featured Colonial Revival and Neoclassical houses, but Craftsman-style houses in particular. In 1920 Wilburn became one of the first two women to be licensed to practice architecture in Georgia. During her long career, which lasted until her death in 1967, she published nine different plan books and was responsible for the design of hundreds of houses all over the southeastern United States.

Wilburn's houses are concentrated in the MAK Historic District in Decatur, Georgia, where there are twenty-one homes that have been documented as her designs. The wood clapboard house at 208 Kings Highway is featured in *Southern Homes and Bungalows*. It is a classic Craftsman-style house, with its strong projecting gable with commodious inset porch. A louvered lunette that rests on a bracketed shelf dominates the gable end, which itself rests on piers that show a strong Asian influence. A tripartite window and an entryway with sidelights complete this handsome composition.

Another house in the MAK District is 310 Adams Street. This is one of Wilburn's most distinguished designs. This home is constructed in brick veneer and has a lovely inset porch located in the left of the facade. The entrance is to the side of the porch, and a large dormer dominates the roofline. This dormer has very sophisticated fenestration composed of four windows that together follow the triangular form of the dormer. A projecting bay window directly under the dormer is also composed of four windows, with panels above each sash. The double porch columns have inset decoration in the Arts and Crafts style.

The State of Georgia's native architects and builders, together with design talent brought in from out of state, created some of the nation's finest revivalist buildings of the early twentieth century. While industrialization created the financial resources to build these landmarks, these individuals chose to create buildings that for the most part looked back on European and American history, to a time that they may have romanticized as simpler and more bucolic than their present. Although this may have been a nostalgic stance, their legacies endure for future generations to enjoy and to contemplate our complicated history.

National economic prosperity in the first quarter of the twentieth century and the absence of a federal income tax until 1913 certainly played a key role in enabling the construction of the grand-scale architecture discussed in this chapter. Likewise, the 1929 stock-market crash certainly provided a bookend to the real estate boom and the excesses of the jazz age. Architecture never exists in a vacuum.

While many of the landmark buildings of the early twentieth century have been preserved, notable revivalist structures have been lost. Future generations will be deprived of P. Thornton Marye's Terminal Station in Atlanta, Frank Milburn's Southern Railway Stations in Atlanta and Savannah, and Samuel Cooper's Tudor Revival Glenridge Hall. The last, an enormous estate house located in Sandy Springs, was demolished in 2015, inspiring in us all a deeper commitment to preserve our historic buildings of the period.

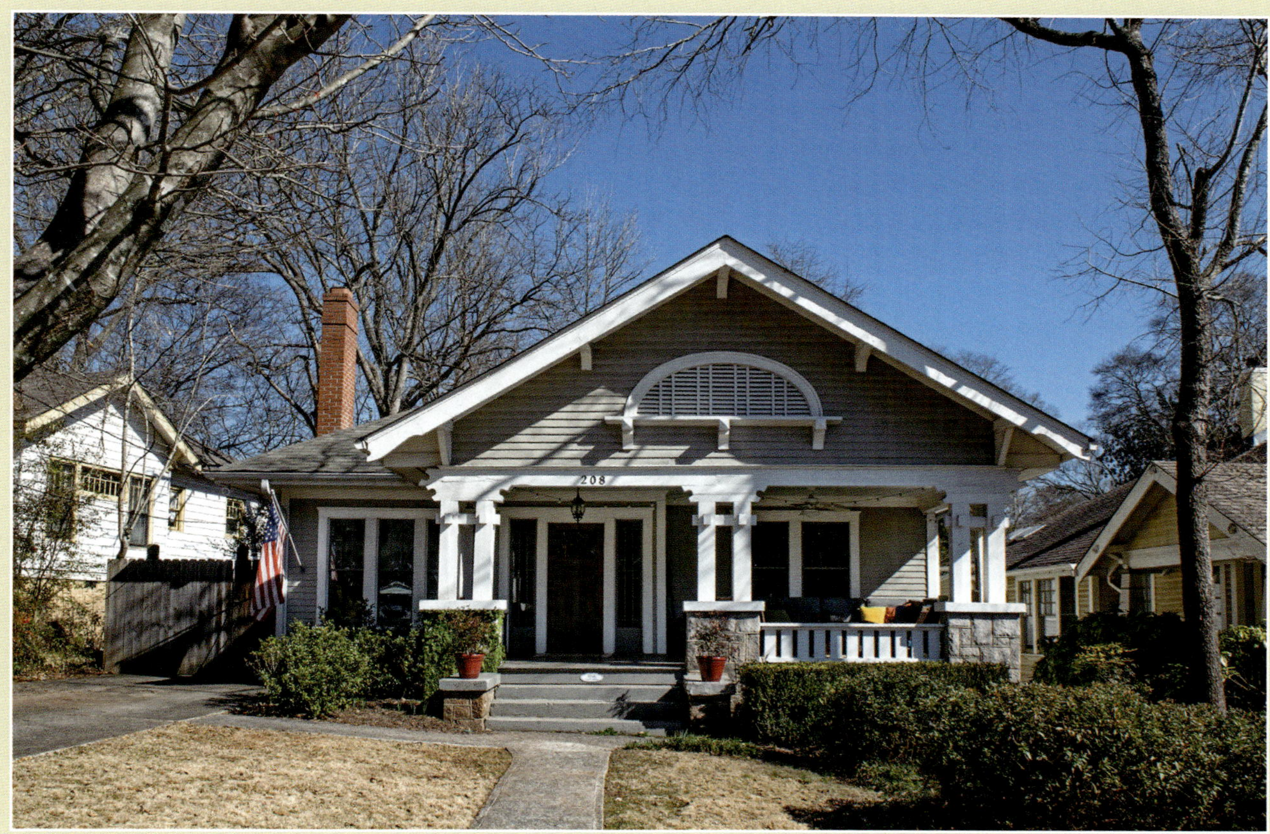

208 Kings Highway, Decatur

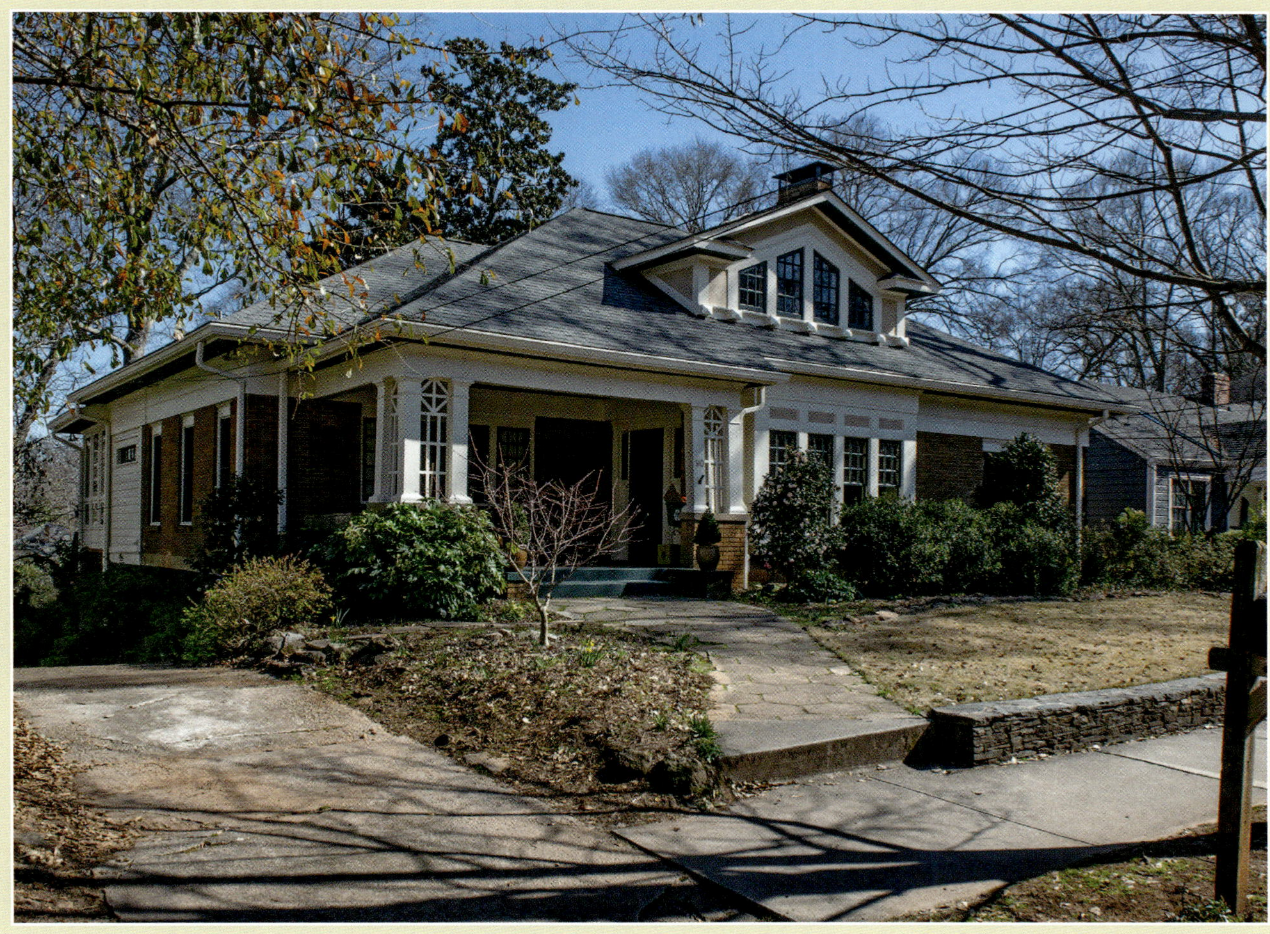

310 Adams Street, Decatur

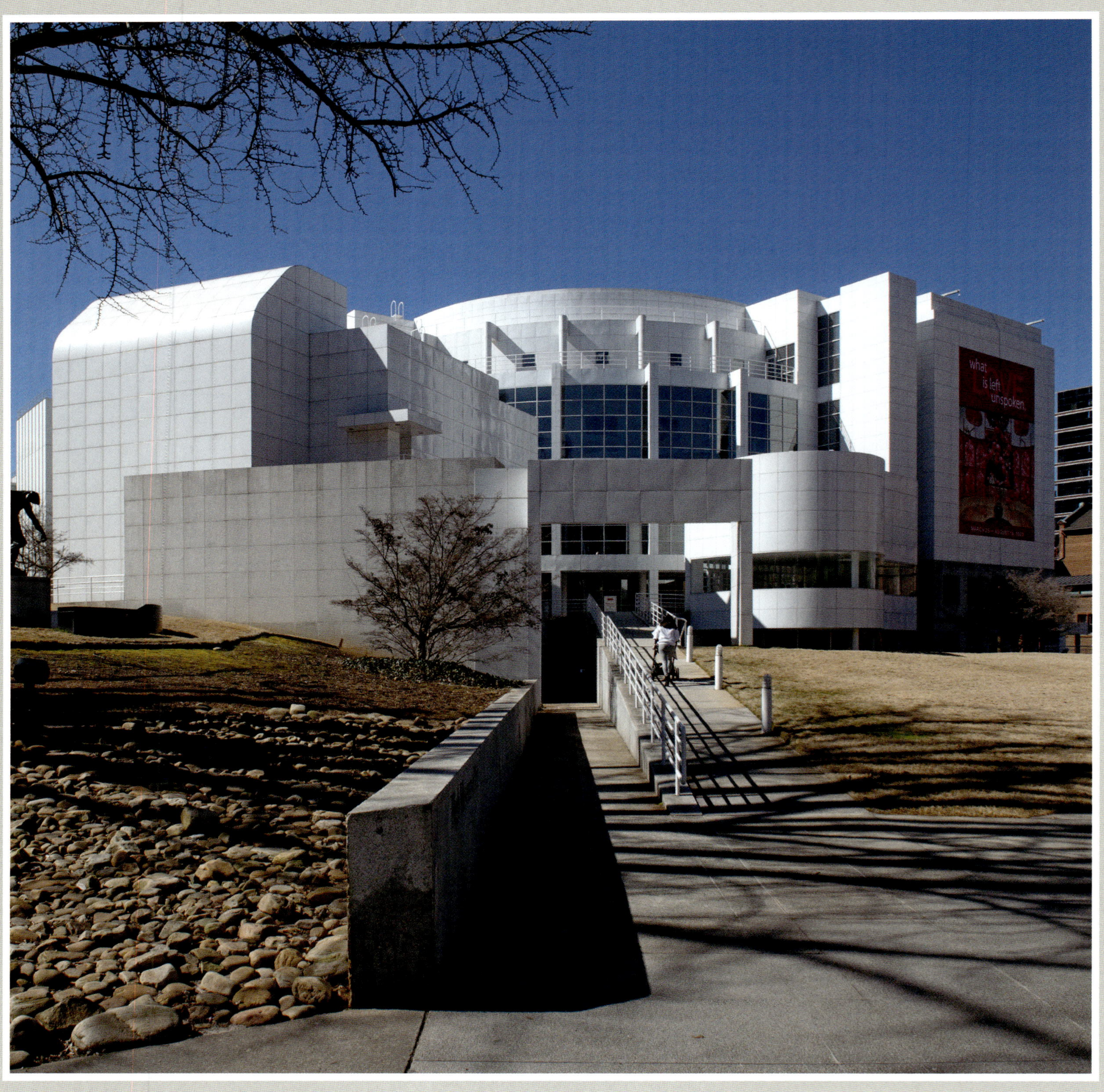
what
is left
unspoken.

V. Twentieth-Century Georgia Architecture

ROBIN B. WILLIAMS

The architecture of Georgia, like that of other parts of the country, experienced dramatic changes during the twentieth century. The introduction of radical new technologies transformed how buildings were built and illuminated and how people moved around. Electricity, elevators, steel-frame construction, reinforced concrete, and even telephones contributed to the development of skyscrapers, as did the growth of corporations and capitalism, with Atlanta the leading city in the New South. The automobile had arguably the largest effect, prompting the introduction of new building types that catered to the needs of drivers and facilitating the dramatic spreading out of cities with ever-expanding suburbs that accommodated changing lifestyles while also reinforcing patterns of racial segregation. Throughout the century, architects grappled with how best to express modernity. By the 1960s Georgia emerged as a place of architectural innovation and a destination for internationally significant designers.

Early Skyscrapers

After their introduction in New York and Chicago in the 1870s and 1880s, skyscrapers made their appearance in Georgia's cities beginning in the 1890s. The tall building quickly became synonymous with modernity. Erected in 1892, the eight-story Equitable Building in Atlanta was the state's first skyscraper, designed by the prominent Chicago firm of Burnham and Root, which had completed the world's first steel-frame skyscraper, the Rand McNally Building in Chicago, just two years earlier. Made of "fireproof" construction (a transitional combination of load bearing exterior brick and terra-cotta walls and an internal steel frame), the Equitable Building inaugurated an increasingly vertical downtown around the Five Points section of the city.

Facing: High Museum, Atlanta

Savannah witnessed the construction of its first skyscraper just three years later, in 1895, with the six-story Citizens Bank (now Propes Hall of Savannah College of Art and Design), designed by Swedish-born Atlanta-based architect Gottfried L. Norrman, whose office was in the Equitable Building. He incorporated new skyscraper technology into the Savannah building: an internal steel

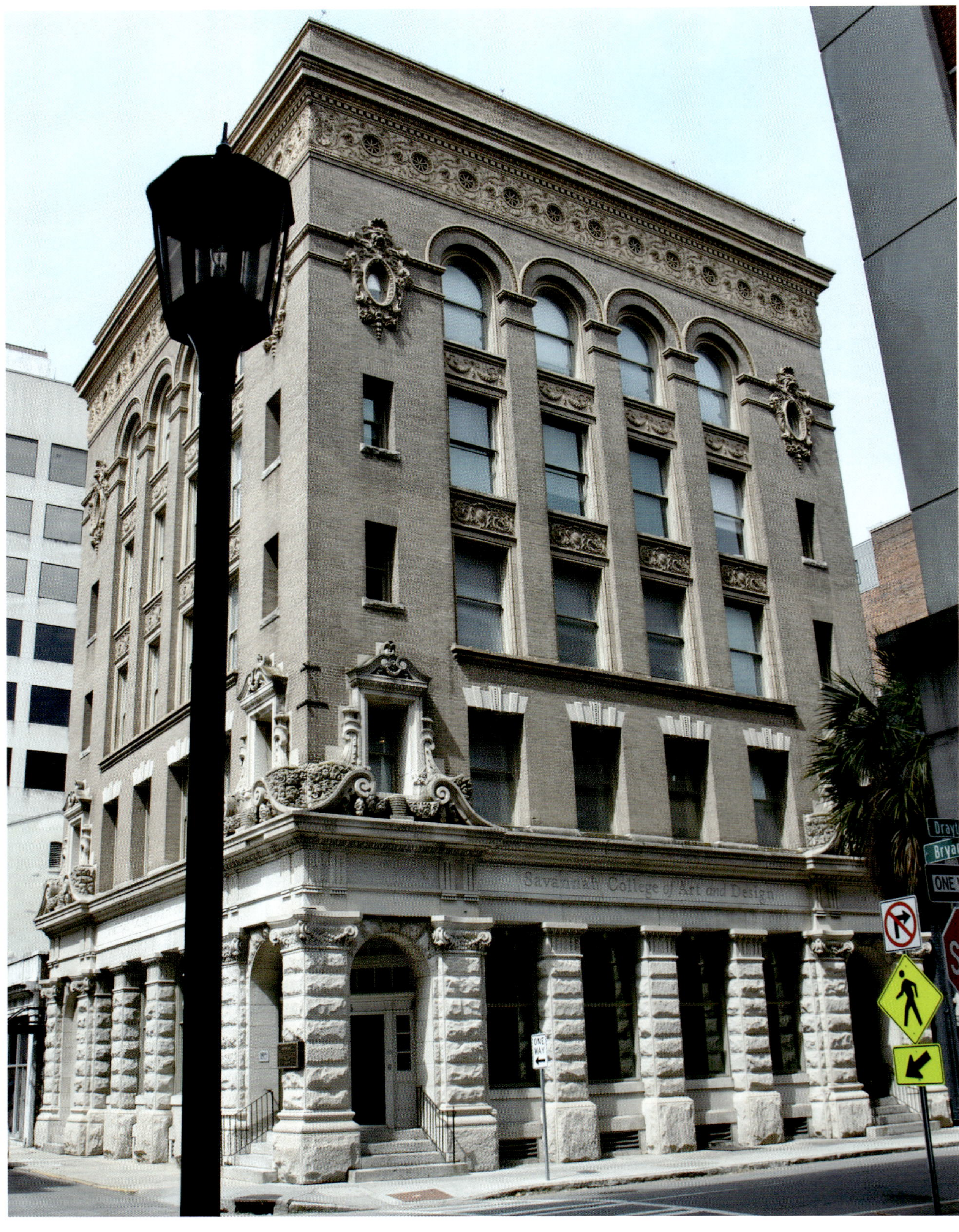

Citizens Bank, now Propes Hall of Savannah College of Art and Design, Savannah

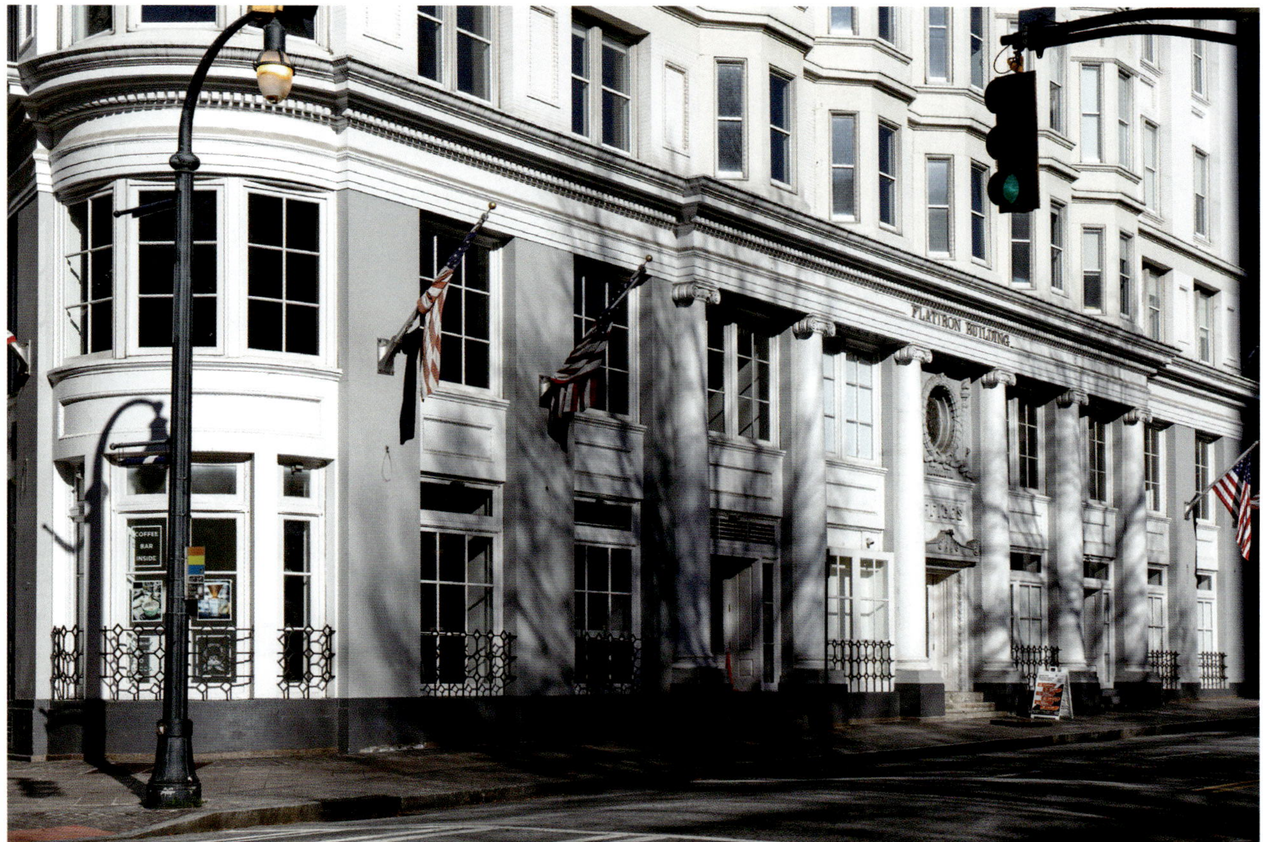

Flatiron Building, Atlanta

frame, fireproof terra-cotta walls and floors, and an elevator. But also like its Atlanta predecessor, the Citizens Bank has traditional load-bearing outer walls that nonetheless express verticality. Although its six stories barely qualify it as a skyscraper, the building rises to 74 feet, which towered over its original neighbors. The demolition of the Equitable Building in 1971 left the Savannah building as the oldest extant skyscraper in the state. The push for verticality soon spread to other Georgia cities. In 1908 the state saw its first reinforced concrete office building erected, the seven-story Southern Mutual Insurance Company Building, the first skyscraper in Athens. The skyscraper form arrived in Macon in 1911 with the American Federal Building, in Dublin in 1913 with the First National Bank (A. Ten Eyck Brown, architect), and in Augusta in 1912–14 with the Chronicle (later Marion) Building, designed by G. Lloyd Preacher.

As one of the fastest growing cities in the South at the dawn of the twentieth century, Atlanta naturally became the state's leading skyscraper city, with many of the earliest clustered around the Five Points area of downtown. The Flatiron Building (originally the English-American Building), erected in 1897, quickly became a symbol of the city, with the irregular site dictating its narrow triangular form, which accentuated the vertical thrust of its 11 stories. It was designed by Bradford Gilbert, the pioneering architect of the Tower Building, the first all-metal (cast-iron) framed building in New York (1888–90). The Flatiron Building follows the conventional tripartite composition for early skyscrapers defined by Chicago architect Louis Sullivan, who argued that tall office buildings should be like a column, with a base, shaft, and capital. A sense of verticality is strengthened by the use of continuous projecting bays that animate the side elevations above the second floor with an undulating rhythm—a signature design strategy of Burnham and Root, who would use it on their later Flatiron Building in New York of 1901, the fame of which inspired the Atlanta version to adopt the same name by 1920.

The skyscraper form challenged architectural firms to address rapidly evolving building technologies and changing client needs. Bruce and Morgan, Atlanta's most successful architectural firm at the turn of the century, reflected the dramatic impact of this new frontier. A partnership formed in 1882, the firm focused on civic buildings during the 1880s and early 1890s in Queen Anne, Second Empire, and Gothic Revival styles popular in the Victorian period. By the late 1890s, under the leadership of principal Thomas H. Morgan, the firm added skyscrapers to their portfolio. Typical of all early skyscrapers in Georgia, their Prudential (now Grant) Building of 1898 and Empire Building of 1898–1901, both in Atlanta, showcased the influence of the Chicago School, with straightforward boxy massing and regular fenestration framed by a grid of vertical piers and recessed horizontal spandrels reflecting the steel frame within. Originally, the first three floors of the Empire Building had the vertical piers separated by broad expanses of glass, to serve various retail functions.

In 1929 the Empire Building became the headquarters of the Citizens and Southern National Bank, which commissioned architect Philip Shutze of the firm Hentz, Adler and Shutze to redesign its first three stories. On the exterior, he replaced the expanses of glass with the seemingly solid, load-bearing walls of an Italian palazzo (evoking the Renaissance origins of banking). The richly sculptural quoining blocks, pronounced arch voussoirs, and the exaggerated scale of the voluted keystones draw more specifically from Italian Mannerism. Above, Shutze seamlessly expanded the building's Marietta Street facade from five bays to seven, revealed by the asymmetrical location of bays with central piers. The magnificent banking hall, which runs the full 204-foot length of the building, draws its inspiration instead from the interior of the ancient Pantheon, a building Shutze had measured while at the American Academy in Rome, with its monumental Corinthian columns and pilasters and the marble floor of alternating circles and squares.

The skyscraper form spread to other building types, notably hotels, apartment buildings, department stores, and government buildings. In Atlanta, the Piedmont Hotel (1903; demolished) was an early example, quickly followed by the Imperial, the Ansley, the Majestic, the Winecoff (now Ellis), and the Georgian Terrace, the last two designed by the prolific and versatile New York architect William L. Stoddart in 1911 and 1912, respectively. Stoddart's reputation spread to other cities in Georgia, where he was commissioned to design the 10-story Hotel Savannah in Savannah (1912; now the First City Club), whose upper "capital" section of a conventional tripartite skyscraper he enlivened with colorful

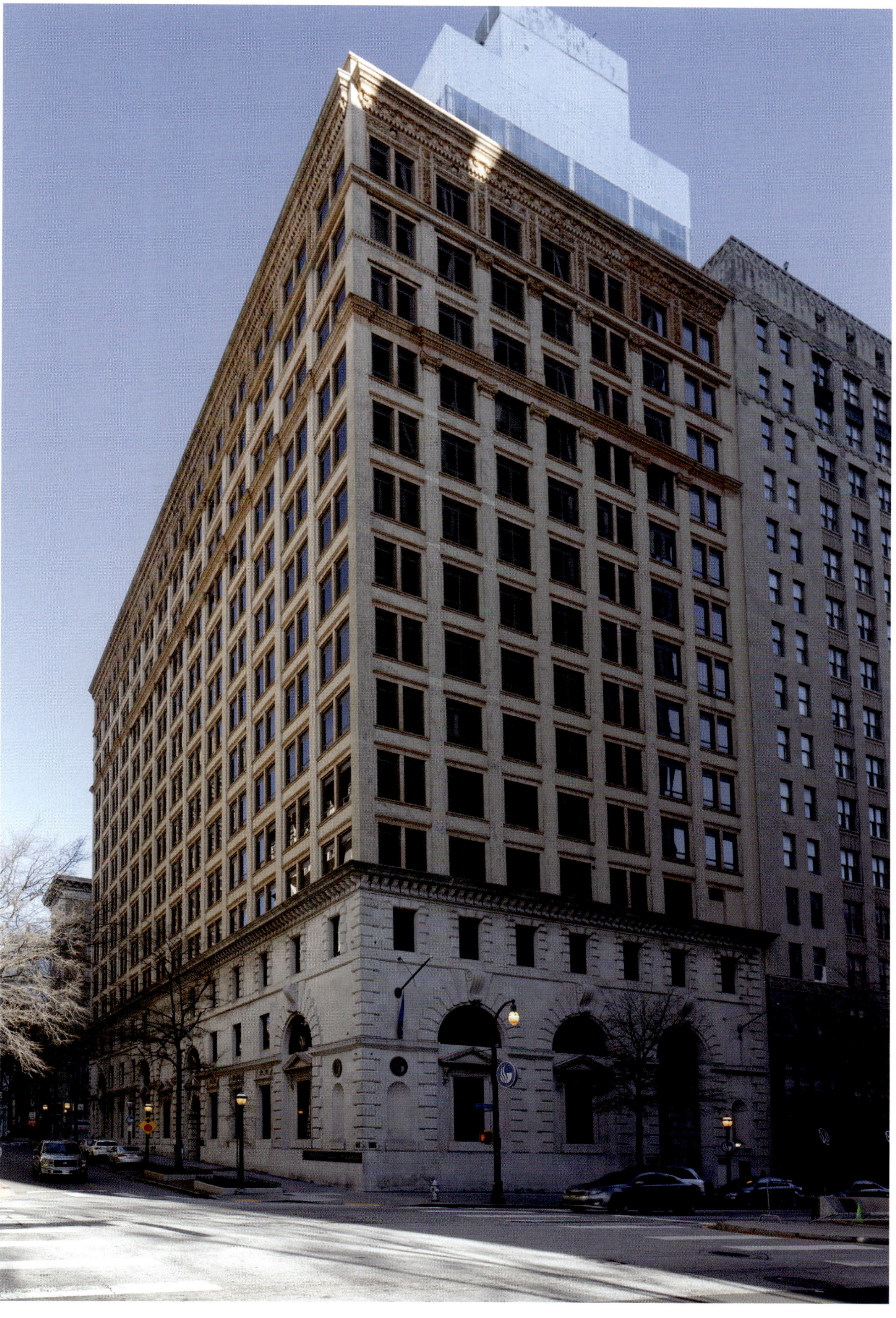

Empire Building,
Atlanta

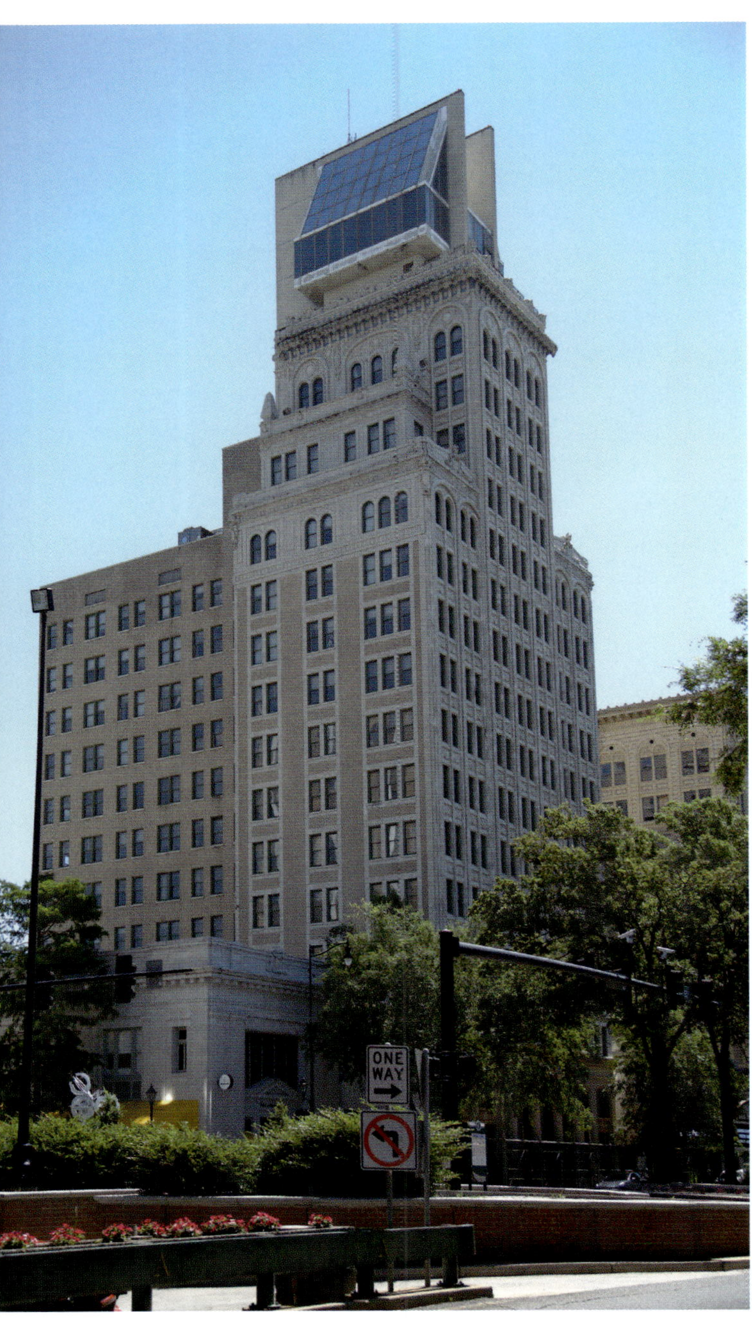

Lamar Building, Augusta

terra-cotta. A year later he designed the Lamar Building in Augusta, his most ambitious work in Georgia. Its completion was delayed until 1918 by the highly destructive fire of 1916 that damaged the incomplete structure along with many other buildings in Augusta. Unlike other tall buildings in the state at the time, the 17-story building evokes a New York form of skyscraper, its stepped massing similar to the recently completed Woolworth Building, with its taller central section capped by a hipped roof crown above the richly sculpted cornice. Vertical piers, expressed as bundled shafts, enhance the impression of height. The Lamar Building remains the tallest in Augusta.

Industrial Buildings

Innovations in construction technology also revolutionized factory architecture, with the introduction of reinforced concrete in the early twentieth century replacing load-bearing brick exteriors and heavy post-and-lintel timber frame interior structures. The Ford Motor Company Assembly Plant (now Ford Factory Lofts; 1914–15) and the Sears and Roebuck Building (now Ponce City Market; 1926)—neighboring buildings on Ponce de Leon Avenue in Atlanta—vividly illustrate its impact. They joined several other heavy industrial facilities located along a Southern Railway line (now part of the BeltLine) that symbolized Atlanta's growing importance as a regional commercial and industrial center.

In 1911 the Ford Motor Company introduced the concept of a national network of branch assembly plants, which doubled as regional offices and showrooms, to cut down on shipping costs of their wildly popular Model T and provide more immediate service to customers. Atlanta received one of the twenty-eight plants established between 1912 and 1915, the company having opened its first sales office there in 1907. Designed by John Graham Sr., Ford's supervising architect, the branch plants reflected their dual function as factory and showroom by combining the large expanses of windows made possible by their reinforced concrete construction with a restrained classical veneer on their most visible facades. In Atlanta, both the north facade fronting Ponce de Leon Avenue and the west side facing the city beyond were articulated with simple red-brick piers and off-white terra-cotta details, including the shallow segmental arches along the top of the building. On the inside, unadorned reinforced concrete floor slabs and cylindrical columns with mushroom capitals (for weight distribution, not aesthetics) reflect the standard factory construction methods of the period. The building served as the headquarters of Ford's Southeastern operations from 1915 to 1942.

Immediately west of the Ford plant, on the other side of the railway line, stands the former Sears, Roebuck and Company Mail-Order Warehouse and Retail Store, an enormous commercial building erected in 1926. Sears had established their highly successful mail-order business in 1894 in Chicago, expanding to retail operations across the country in 1925. The Atlanta facility, opened in 1926, was among the largest stores that Sears built during the 1920s and was designed

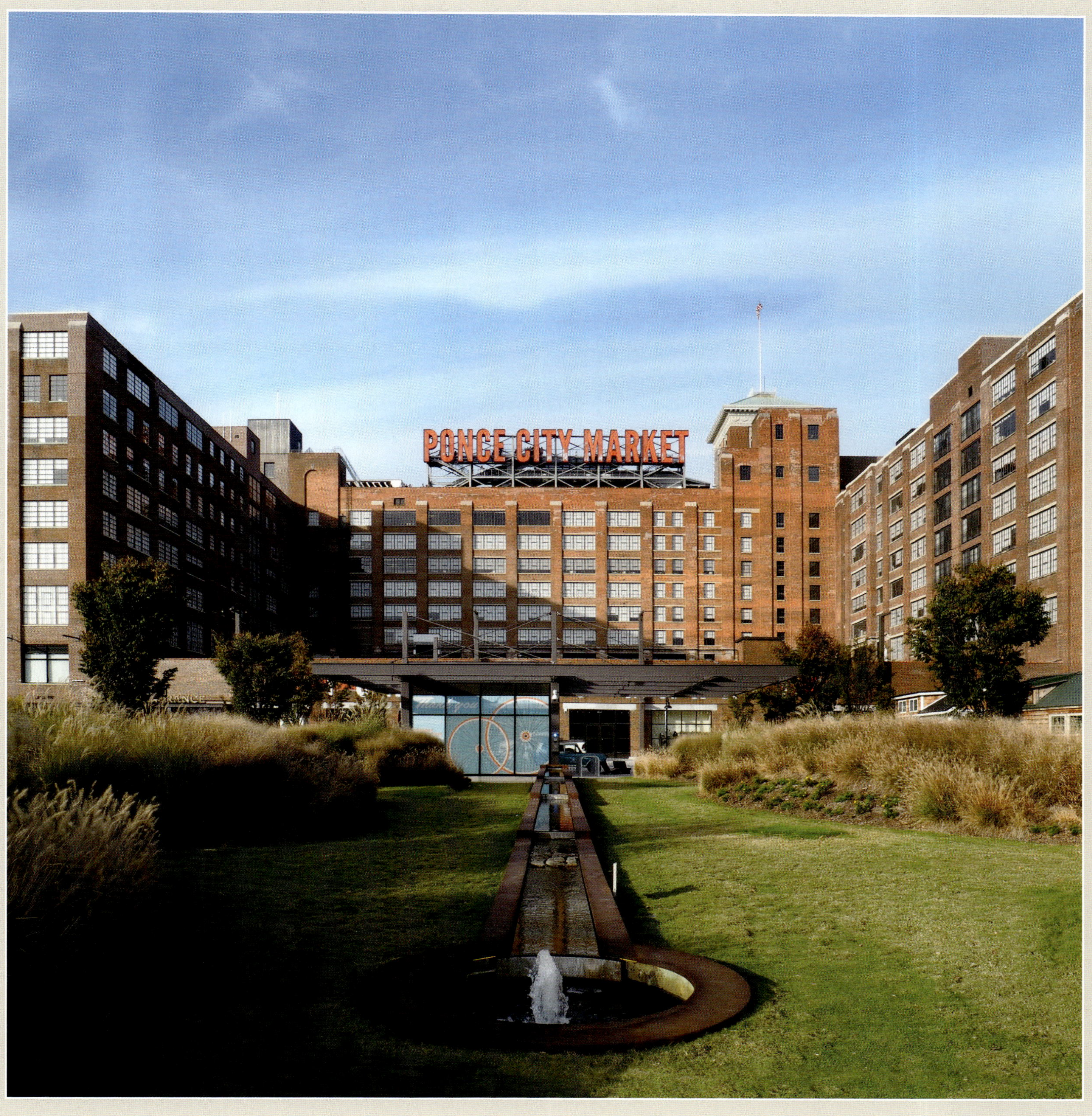

Sears and Roebuck Building, Atlanta

by Nimmons & Company, the Chicago firm responsible for all of the Sears facilities at the time. The Atlanta Sears building employed the same reinforced concrete construction technology as the Ford plant, but on a much larger scale. The building's monumental Ponce de Leon Avenue facade rises nine stories above a basement and reflects its Chicago School lineage with grids of vertical piers and recessed spandrels that frame the large sets of triple windows. Slightly projecting end pavilions crowned with stepped parapets break up the facade's great breadth, while a nearly central projecting tower rises an additional four stories and showcases the building's only ornament, Renaissance Revival–style arched windows near the top and entry arches. The Atlanta store was so successful that the front was extended westward in 1932 and rear expansions added in 1948, 1966, and 1971. By the late 1970s, however, the shift of retail to suburban shopping malls signaled a gradual decline in the facility's use by Sears, which sold it to the City of Atlanta in 1990. Underutilized, it was purchased in 2011 by Jamestown Properties, which transformed the building into a vast shopping and dining emporium called Ponce City Market, whose success has blossomed with the opening of the adjacent BeltLine.

Segregation

A defining reality of Southern cities, including those in Georgia, was racial segregation. The policy of "separate but equal" normally translated to considerably inferior facilities or separate entrances for African Americans, the traces of which have largely disappeared. In a few instances, however, quite remarkable buildings designed exclusively for use by Blacks exploited architectural style to underscore racial distinctions. An early example is the so-called Carnegie Library in Savannah of 1914, one of two libraries in the city to receive a Carnegie grant. The Colored Library Association of Savannah, established in 1906, received $13,000 in 1913, one of only two grants for libraries for African Americans in Georgia. By comparison, the main branch on Bull Street, originally called the Savannah Public Library, received $75,000, the second-largest grant awarded to the state (after Atlanta's main Carnegie library). In 1914 the Colored Library Association hired Julien de Bruyn Kops, the City of Savannah's superintendent of architecture. Calls for hiring a Black architect came too late to change the designer. The overall massing evokes an Egyptian temple, with its over-scaled, tapering pylon-like piers flanking the central staircase and the prominent cavetto cornice with its simple concave profile. Yet the materiality of textured red and black bricks and sandstone detailing reflects Arts and Crafts traditions. The brooding effect of this highly unusual design purposefully contrasted with the conventional Beaux Arts Classical language of other Carnegie libraries, including that on Bull Street. Inside, more Art Nouveau in character are the staggered sets of vertical linear ornament adorning the undulating main doorframe and the regularly spaced piers with stylized rosette capitals. Opened in 1915, the library fostered the educational enrichment of Pulitzer Prize–winning author James Alan McPherson and U.S. Supreme Court associate justice Clarence Thomas,

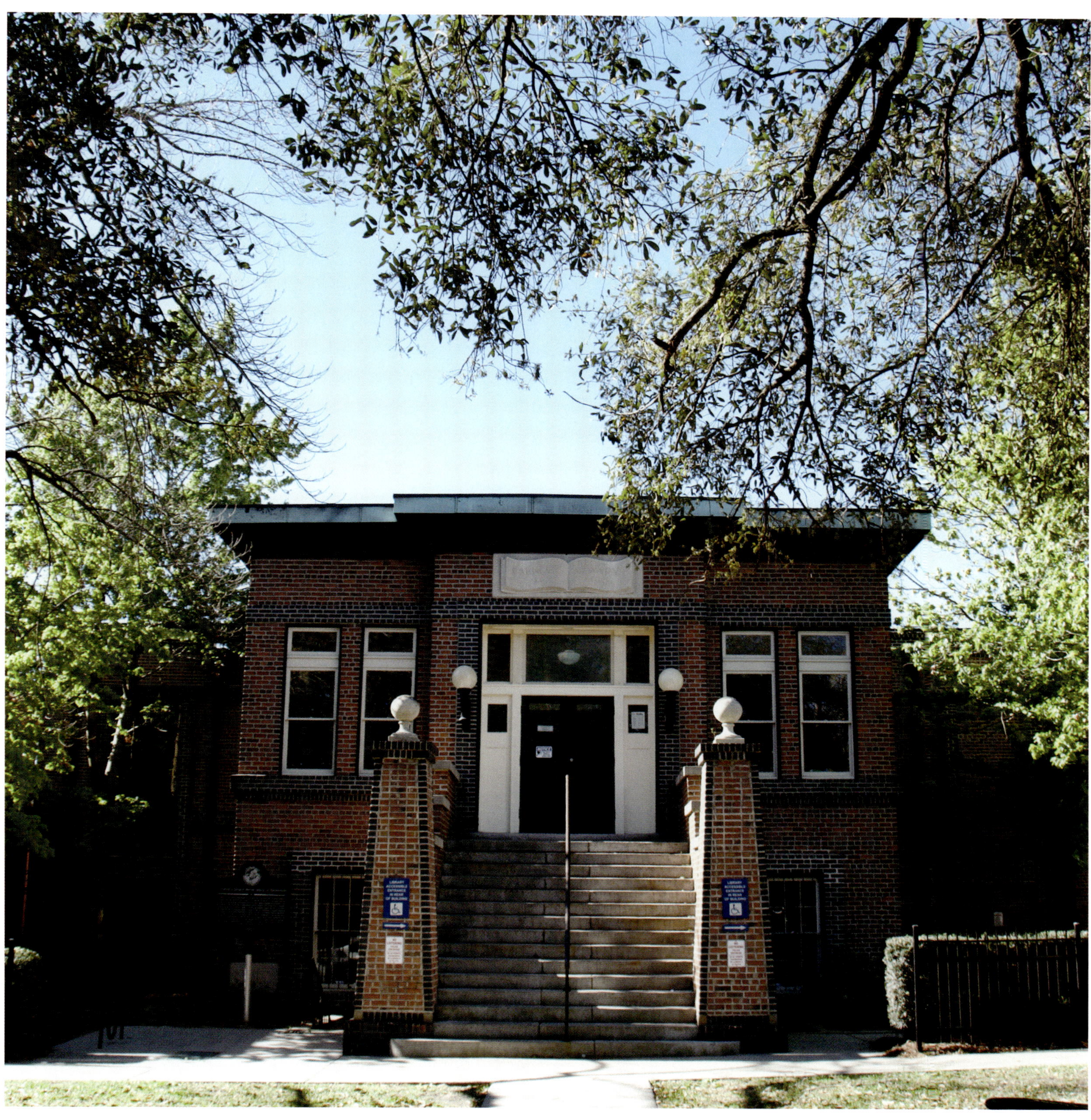

among many others. Closed in 1997, it was saved from demolition in 2001 by local and national efforts, which facilitated its respectful expansion and reopening in 2004. Also notable is the Booker T. Washington High School, the first Black public high school erected in Atlanta. It resulted from political pressure from the Black community to be included in the city's school-improvement program funded by a 1921 bond issue.

Carnegie Library, Savannah

Automobility

The emergence of automobiles around 1900, whether electric or gas powered, brought about a range of new building types, including dealerships, garages, and gas stations. The new transportation technology was promoted to a broader public though automobile exhibitions, beginning in New York in 1900. Just six years later Atlanta hosted the first in the Southeast, attracting 150,000 spectators over a seven-day period. In 1908 Savannah began hosting international road races, putting it at the epicenter of auto racing for the next three years. Lobbied aggressively by the Savannah Automobile Club, Mayor George W. Tiedemann, and Governor Hoke Smith, the Automobile Club of America selected Savannah over much larger cities vying to host the first American Grand Prix. The 400-mile race took place in November 1908 on a nearly 20-mile course and attracted automakers from around the world. Later called the Great Savannah Races, the Grand Prix returned to Savannah in 1910 and 1911 and was joined in 1911 by the rival Vanderbilt Cup.

Savannah retains the oldest automobile-related buildings in the state. A remarkable survivor is the T. A. Bryson Automobile Garage from 1904, which served as a Packard Motor Car Company showroom on the first floor and a 75-car garage on the second and third, accessed via an elevator. It is the oldest such showroom in the South. Its location facing Chippewa Square, one of

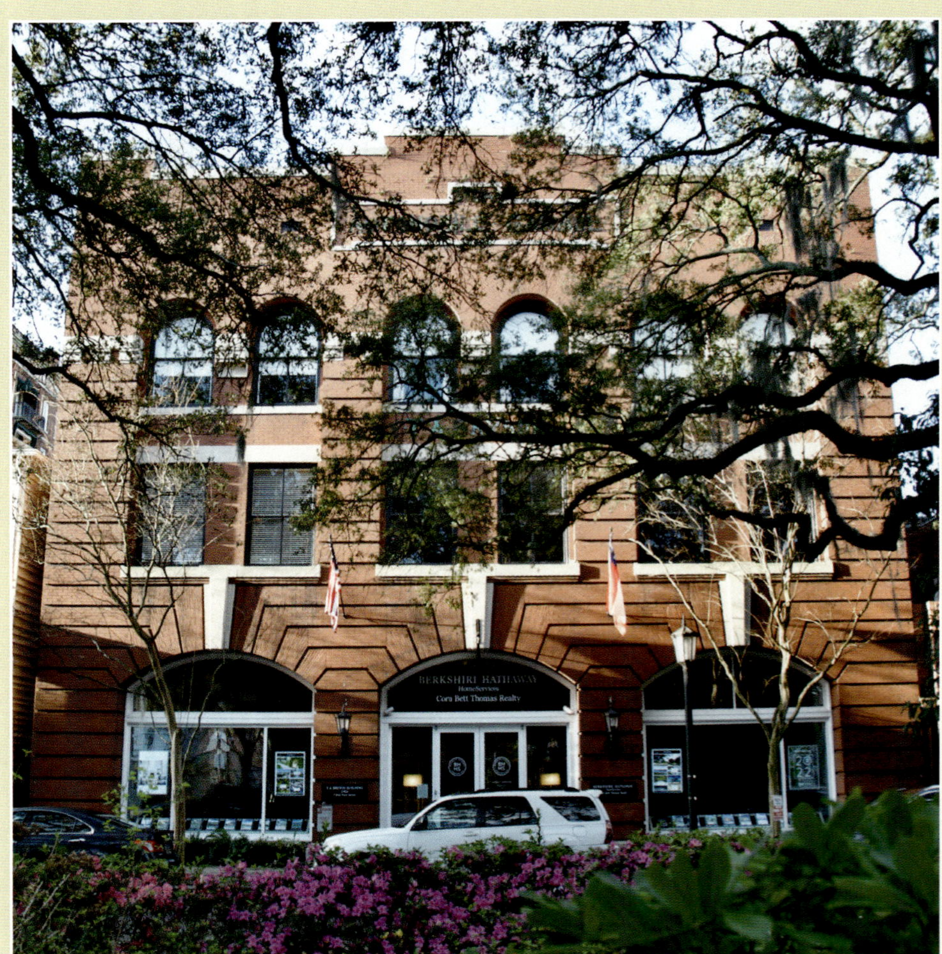

Bryson Automobile Garage, Savannah

the prestigious central squares on Bull Street, helped symbolize how owning a Packard was a mark of wealth and status. Stylistic detailing reflects the red-brick building's dual functions: elegant Renaissance Revival details on the first floor—gentle segmental arches (the middle one providing car access), exaggerated keystones, and deep channeling—and above, muscular Romanesque Revival piers and paired round arches. The surviving Art Nouveau–style original copper signage lettering conveyed fashionability.

Two of the oldest surviving gas stations in Georgia stand a few blocks apart in downtown Savannah and reflect the effort to incorporate this new building type into the dense urban fabric of a city center. Erected in 1920, the station attached to Blum Dimmit Company Autos (now Parker's Market) was designed by Savannah architect Arthur F. Comer in the Mediterranean Revival style with a dramatic terra-cotta tile roof, a rarity in Savannah. Just as they do today, gas pumps occupied the three arches fronting Drayton Street, while the larger openings on the south and north sides provide off-street vehicle access. Farther north on Drayton stands a former Standard Oil station erected in 1924. The elegant two-story building resembles a diminutive Renaissance palazzo, with the pumps similarly located in the front arches. Drive-through access was carved out of the cubic building mass, allowing for office space above. Several towns in Georgia preserve Pure Oil stations from circa 1930 with their distinctive Tudor cottage appearance defined by a steep side-gable roof, end chimney, and front gable

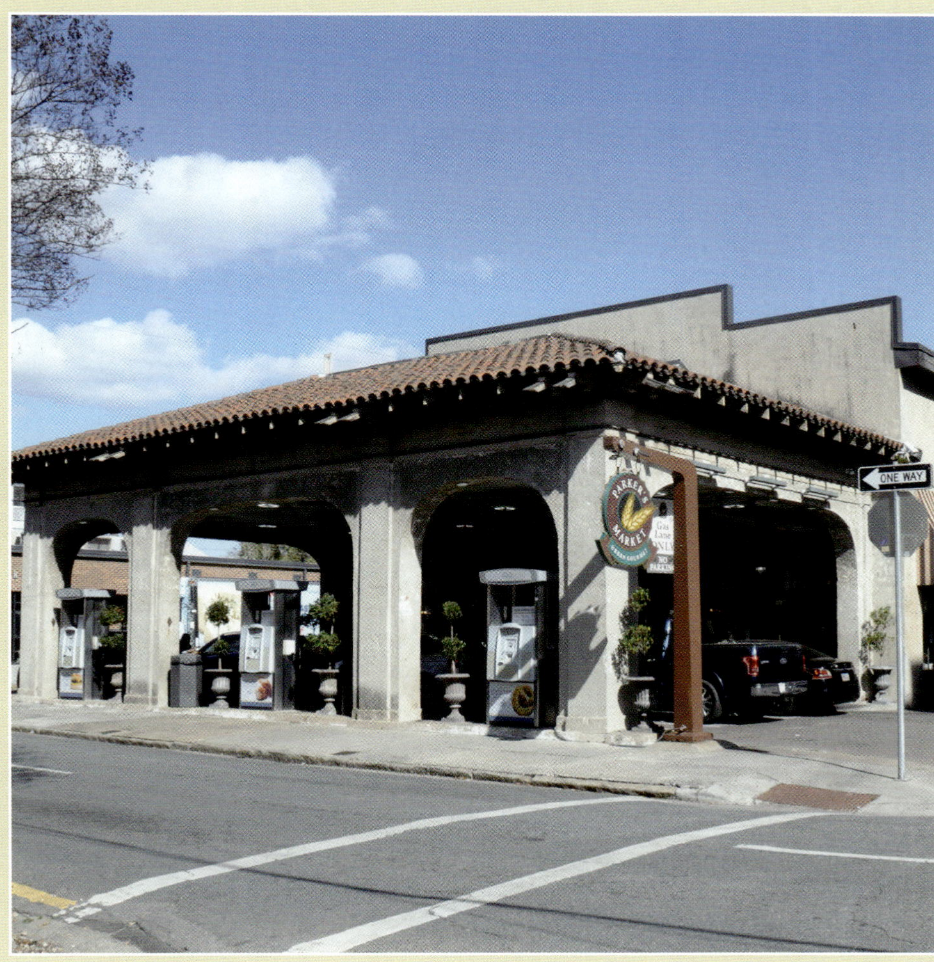

Standard Oil Station, Savannah

canopy. Often such stations were extended to include a repair garage. A beautifully restored Sinclair Gasoline station in Cumming, also circa 1930, follows the same composition but in a Spanish Colonial style.

The traditional styling of early gas stations reflected a desire to have such service buildings blend into the built landscape and convey a sense of assurance and familiarity. But automobiles offered a sense of escape and an opportunity to experience something new, and so a quality of the exotic, most commonly associated with cinemas, also characterized some automotive buildings. A fine example is the United Motor Services Building (now the Peachtree-Pine Building), originally one of about eighty car dealerships in Atlanta. Designed in 1921 by local architect A. Ten Eyck Brown, the broad two-story building presents an eye-catching array of colorful decorative motifs drawn from different historical traditions. A continuous glazed terra-cotta band with a blue and white Greek key alternating with small red and yellow squares and periodic red rosettes frames the sets of windows divided by the blue and yellow spandrel panels (each emblazoned with a red rosette) and monumental, vaguely medieval, faceted polygonal columns with colorful capitals. While sedate brown bricks provide a calming outer frame, their upper section spanning the building and crossing the top of the side facade displays a diaper or diamond pattern likewise drawn from medieval sources.

United Motor Services Building, Atlanta

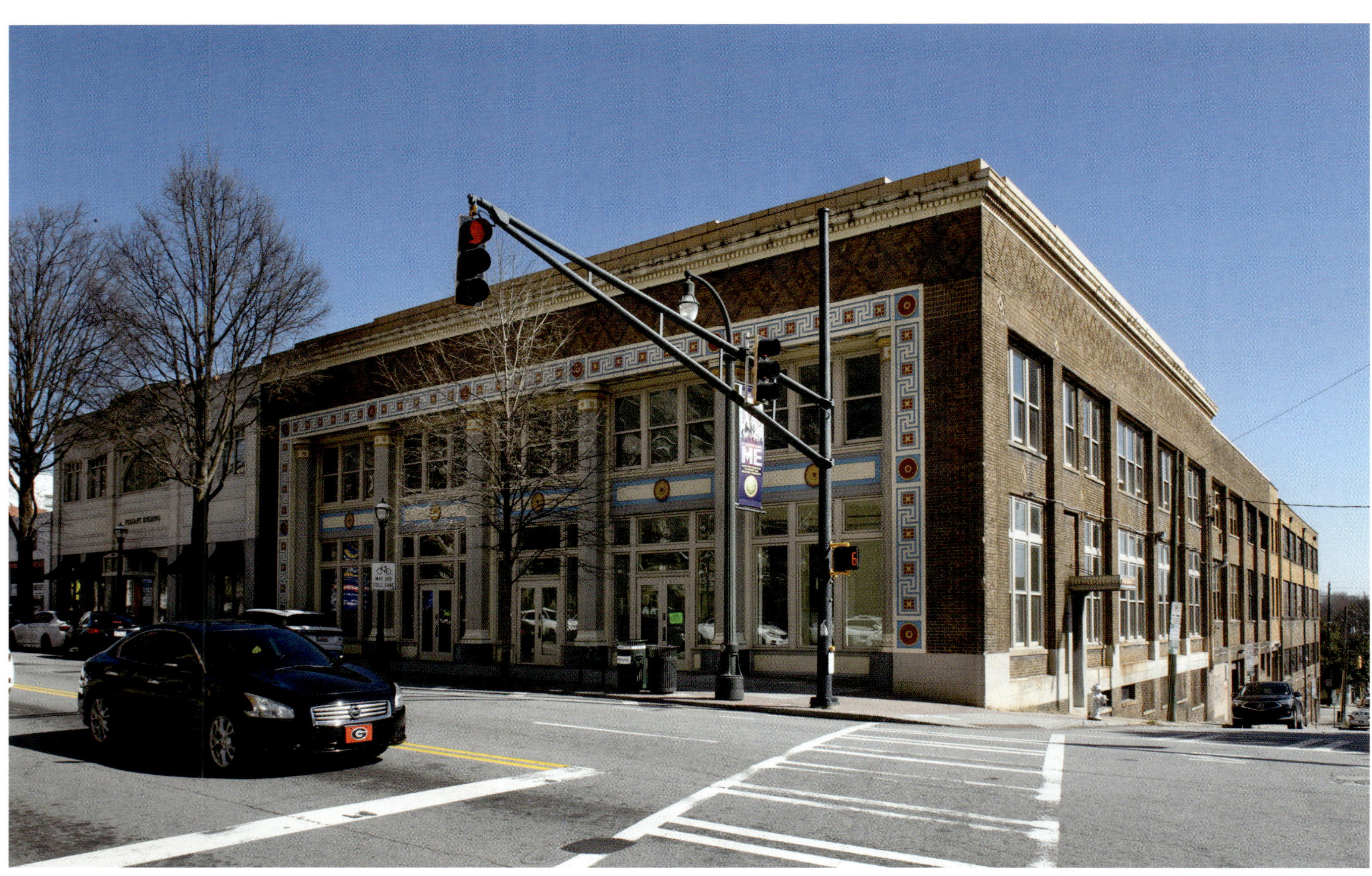

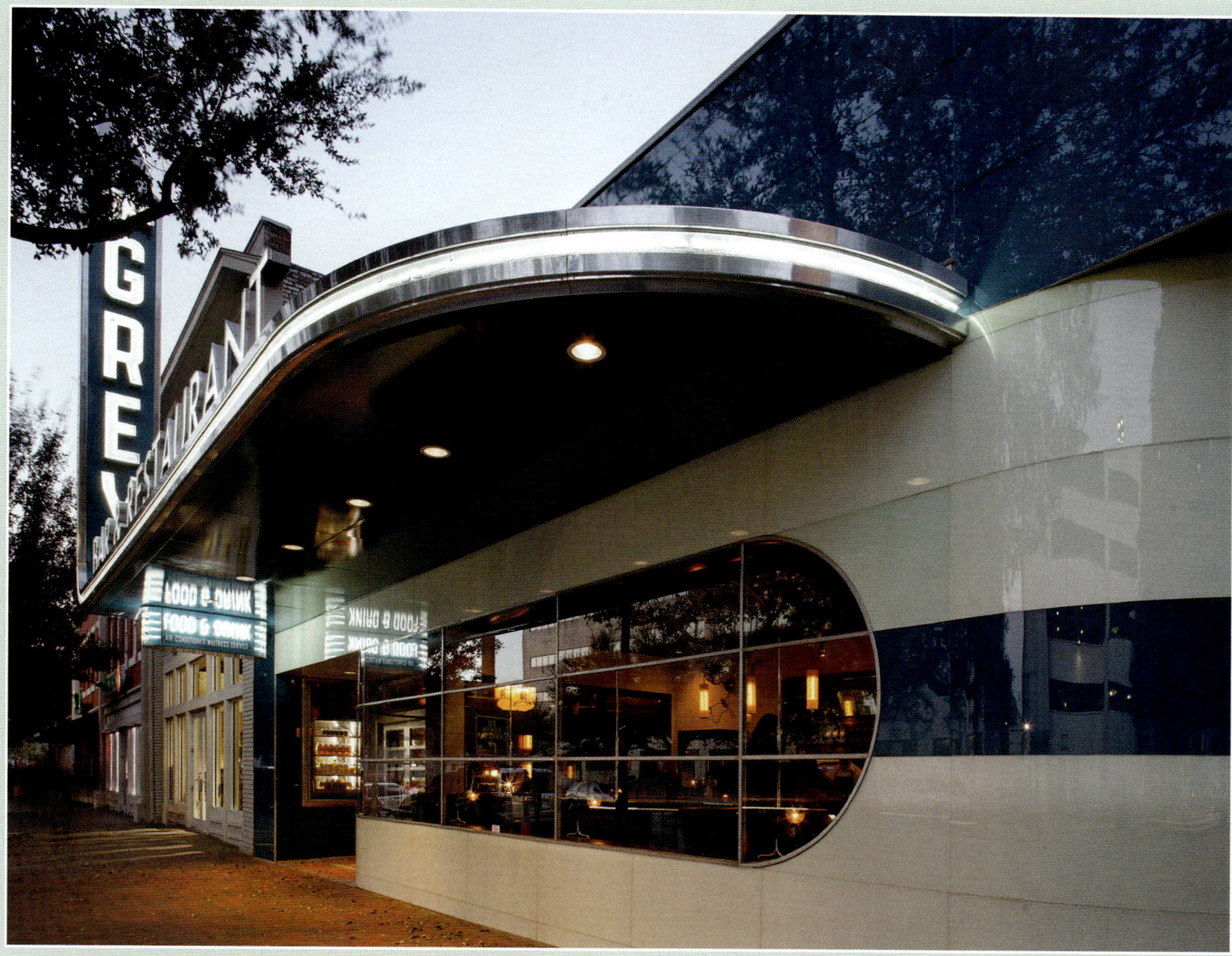

Greyhound Bus Station, Savannah

Art Moderne

By the late 1930s the association of automobility with modernity and movement found its visual language in the widely popular Art Moderne (or Streamline Moderne) style. Combining the geometric simplicity and abstraction of the budding Modernist movement with the rounded corners and sleek linear quality of streamlined vehicles—buses, trailers, locomotives, airships, and airplanes—the style was popular for any building type associated with travel. The Greyhound Bus Station (now The Grey Bar and Restaurant) in Savannah, erected 1937–38, vividly illustrates this pattern. One of several stations designed by architect George D. Brown for Greyhound, the mid-block building balances the rounded corner of the bus entrance at one end with the upward curvature of the projecting canopy into a blade sign at the other end. The facade was clad in blue and white Vitrolite panels (now replicated with rear-painted glass) while aluminum frames a continuous window ending in a bold curve—both evoking the shiny surfaces of freshly painted vehicles.

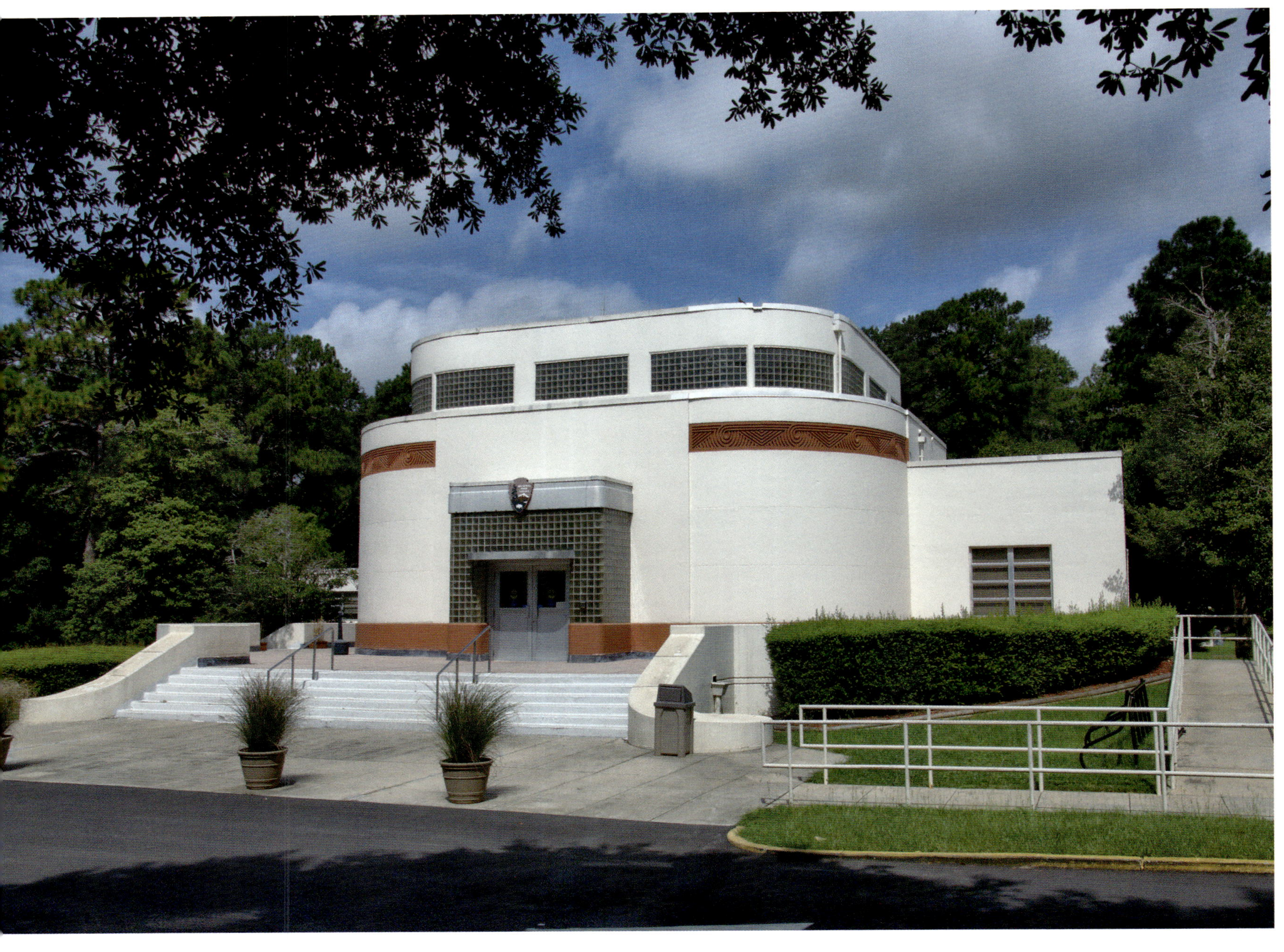

Ocmulgee National Monument Visitors Center, Macon

An unusual example of the Art Moderne style is the Ocmulgee National Monument Visitor Center near Macon. It is highly significant for being the National Park Service's first departure from its two standard visitor center stylistic formulas—the rustic form (often called "parkitecture") and a European-derived style. Supervising Park Service architect James T. Swanson Jr. deemed these options inappropriate for this important Native American archeological site. Designed in 1938 with construction beginning a year later by the Civilian Conservation Corps under the Works Progress Administration, completion of the reinforced concrete building was delayed by World War II until 1951. The visitor center showcases the overall simplicity, stepped profile, white color, rounded corners, smooth surfaces, and glass-block windows characteristic of the style. An incised terra-cotta-colored decorative frieze near the top of the main building mass references patterns found on the Creek Indian pottery excavated at the site.

Art Moderne was most popular for movie theaters in Georgia. In many cities and towns across the state, the theater is a focal point of the community, with fine examples being the Earl and Rachel Smith Strand Theatre (1935) in Marietta, the President Theatre (1935) in Manchester, the Zebulon Theatre (1936) in Cairo, the Tift Theatre (1937) in Tifton, the Ritz Theatre (1939) in Toccoa, the Elbert Theater (1940) in Elberton, the Colquitt County Theatre (1943) in Moultrie, and the Weis (now SCAD) Theatre (1946) and Savannah Theatre (1948–50) in Savannah. Particularly impressive and beautifully restored is the Miller Theatre in Augusta, designed in 1940 by Jacksonville-based theater architect Roy Benjamin. Commissioned by Frank Miller, a leading purveyor of entertainment in Augusta, the theater originally seated 1,600. The prominent semicircular marquee and the narrow facade above, simply adorned by thin projecting ribs that flank three vertical grooves, only hint at the drama within. The interior balances broad gestures with fine details. The freestanding octagonal ticket booth and sets of brushed aluminum doors with circular cutouts and ornate transoms lead to the surprisingly long lobby, with its geometrically patterned terrazzo floor and gently arched ceiling with recessed lighting. Situated at the rear of the block (where land is cheaper), the auditorium has bands of horizontal panels, and flanking the stage are a pair of large murals depicting stylized nude dancing figures. After closing in 1984, the theater was vacant for decades before reopening in 2017 following an award-winning nearly $25 million restoration.

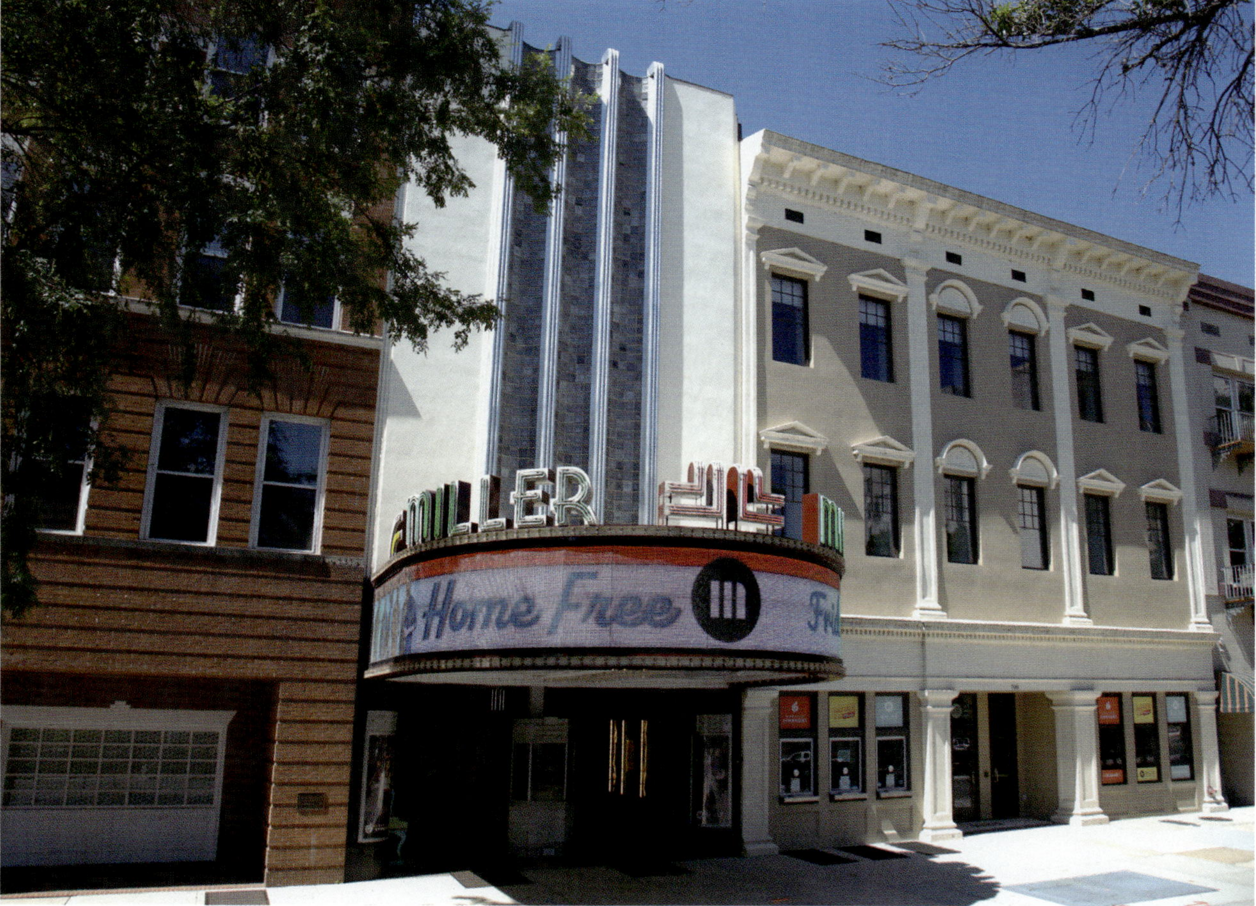

Miller Theatre, Augusta

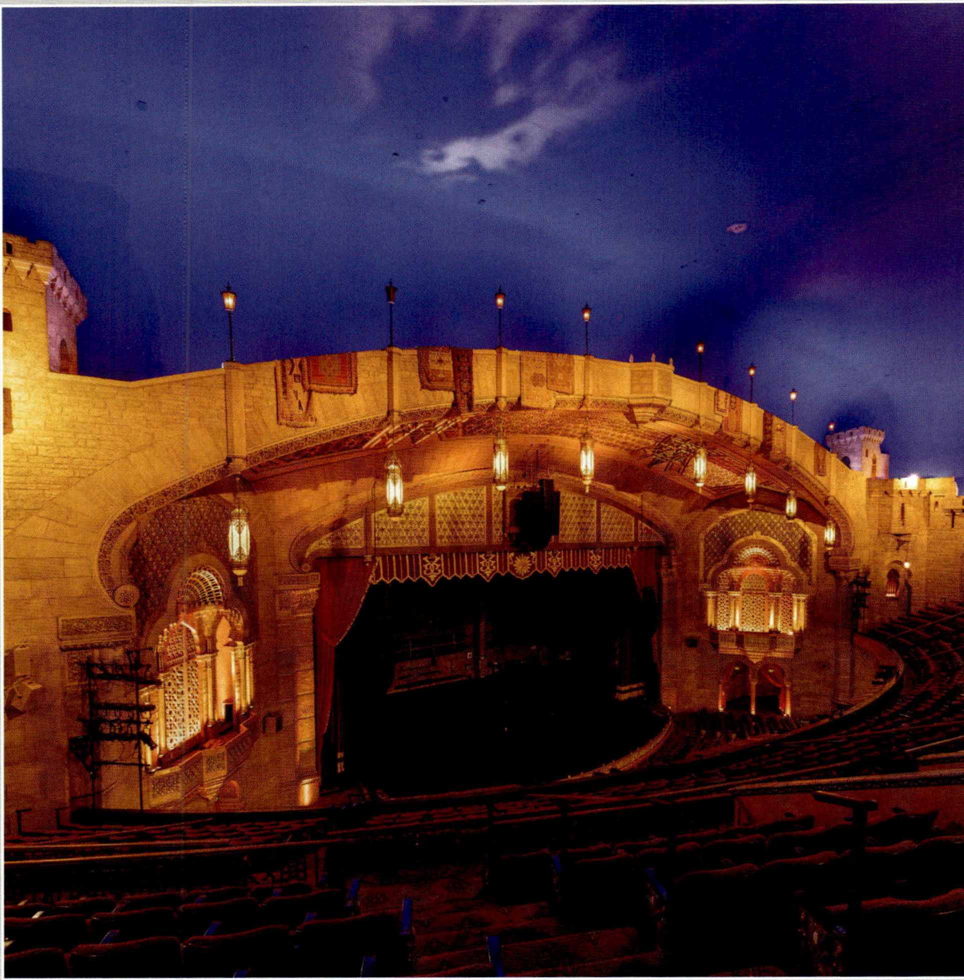

Fox Theatre interior, Atlanta

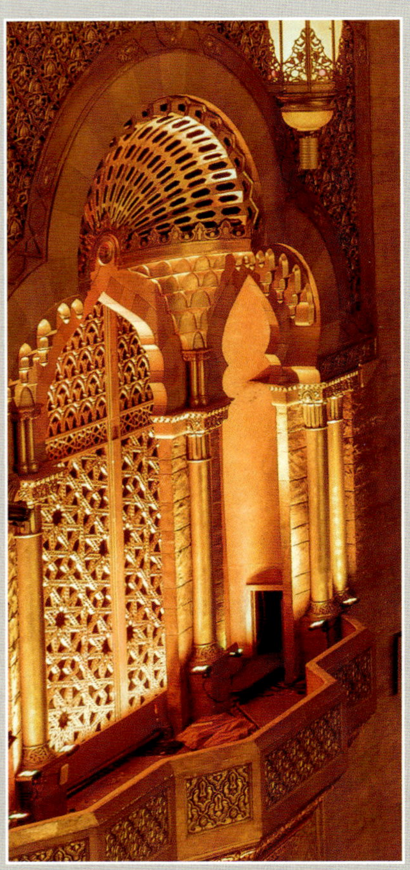

The Fox Theatre Legend Lives On, Thanks to 1970s Atlanta Preservation Victory

Few movie palaces—the largest, most opulent and exotic of theaters—survive in Georgia. The Lucas in Savannah and the Fox in Atlanta are the foremost extant examples. The Lucas, opened in 1921 and designed by Richmond architect Claude K. Howell, exemplifies the classical type of theater, with its combination Spanish Baroque exterior and extravagant Adamesque interior. With 1,700 seats, it was the flagship of the forty theaters owned in the South by Savannah-born theater developer Arthur Lucas and the only one named after him. Far grander is the atmospheric Fox, designed by leading Atlanta architectural firm Marye, Alger and Vinour and opened in 1929 after three years of construction. The building owes its eclectic and exotic style combining Islamic and Egyptian features to its original planned function as the Yaarab Temple, headquarters for Atlanta's Shriners organization. Faced with financial difficulties, the fraternal society leased the facility to film magnate William Fox, founder of the Fox Film Corporation, who made it the "Southern jewel" in his crown of five great theaters (along with those in Saint Louis, Detroit, Brooklyn, and San Francisco), while sharing use of the facility with the Shriners.

The exterior of the Fox displays a blend of exotic architectural features, with its striped masonry, Moorish horseshoe arches, pierced screens, minarets, and onion domes. Inside, principal designer Ollivier Vinour created an atmospheric theater evoking the outdoor courtyard of an Arab town enclosed by castellated walls and a large tent-like canopy above the balcony, leaving the ceiling in between to appear as the night sky, with stars and moving clouds, their appearance achieved with various mechanical and electrical devices. The interior also includes a ballroom and lounges in an Egyptian style. Threatened with demolition in 1974, the Fox became Atlanta's first major preservation campaign led by the nonprofit group Atlanta Landmarks, which raised sufficient funds to purchase the building. A similar campaign saved the Lucas, which closed in 1976 and after a $13 million restoration reopened in 2000.

Art Deco

While closely related to Art Moderne, Art Deco had an earlier and quite separate stylistic expression that had little to do with movement and automobility. Instead, it combined a modernized or stripped classicism with dramatic angular or stylized vegetal decorative motifs drawn from a wide range of exotic sources. There are relatively few examples of this phase of Art Deco in Georgia, with most being in Atlanta. And compared to the large-scale flamboyant expressions of Art Deco on buildings in other major cities, those in Atlanta are much more modest and restrained.

The Southern Bell and Telephone Company (now AT&T) Building, begun in 1928 and designed by Marye, Alger and Vinour, possesses the boldest use of the style in the city, but mainly around the entrance. Reflecting the design possibilities within the Art Deco style, the eclectic and exotic ornament includes vertical stripes of low-relief vegetal motifs and stylized Romanesque engaged capitals that support a corbelled arch and keystone evocative of Mayan architecture. Flanking the arch, implied piers with incised vertical lines sprout figural sculptures representing modern workers, the male (line repairman) holding tools and the female (operator) with a telephone. The celebration of workers on the exterior was matched by amenities inside to improve the quality of the workplace: air filtration, sound-dampening in the operators' room, showers, a cafeteria, and medical facilities. To either side of the entrance, pairs of stylized eagles similarly grow out of the linear ornament. Planned as a 25-story skyscraper, construction only reached the sixth floor before being suspended due to the Depression; construction resumed in the late 1940s and reached 14 stories. More conventional and quite rich Art Deco ornament appeared on a pair of tall buildings designed by Pringle and Smith, the leading firm in this style, the William-Oliver Building (1929–30) and the W. W. Orr Building (1930).

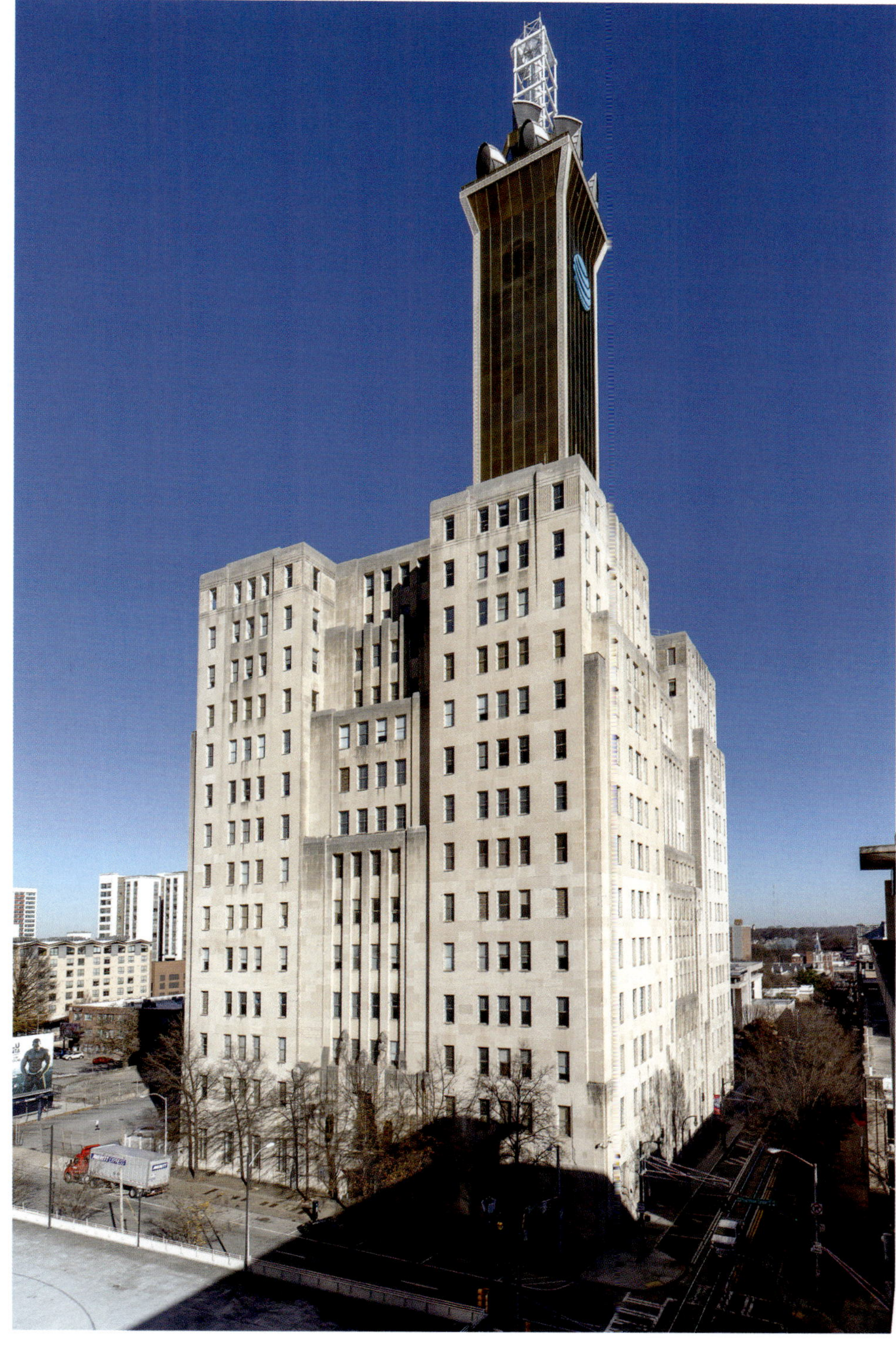

Southern Bell Building, Atlanta

The Globe Shoe Company in Savannah, designed in 1929 by local architects Levy and Clarke, is the most exuberant retail use of Art Deco in the state of Georgia. A colorful fluted classical molding outlines the first two stories, inside which a double-height recessed entry with boldly angled display windows, enlivened with floral-pattern etching across the top, originally framed a recessed etched-glass mural of stylized shoppers above a further recessed angled ceiling emblazoned with Native American sunburst and diamond motifs. Regrettably, the second floor was altered by removal of the mural, which was replaced in the 1950s with a grid of translucent glass panels more in keeping with Art Moderne. The third story is set off with a broad sunburst panel, above which a series of fluted vertical and horizontal moldings matching those below outline three sets of glass blocks (which replaced elongated casement windows in the 1950s).

During the 1930s, classical architecture, especially for government buildings, was "modernized" by having most traditional decorative details removed, leading to a simplified style most often called Stripped Classical, but also Modern Classic. Beyond becoming more abstract, sometimes the style was combined with Art Deco in terms of massing and details. This is the case for the Federal Post Office Building (now Martin Luther King Jr. Federal Building) in Atlanta, a Works Progress Administration–funded project designed by local architect A. Ten Eyck Brown and completed in 1933. Its location next to Terminal Station

Globe Shoe Company, Savannah

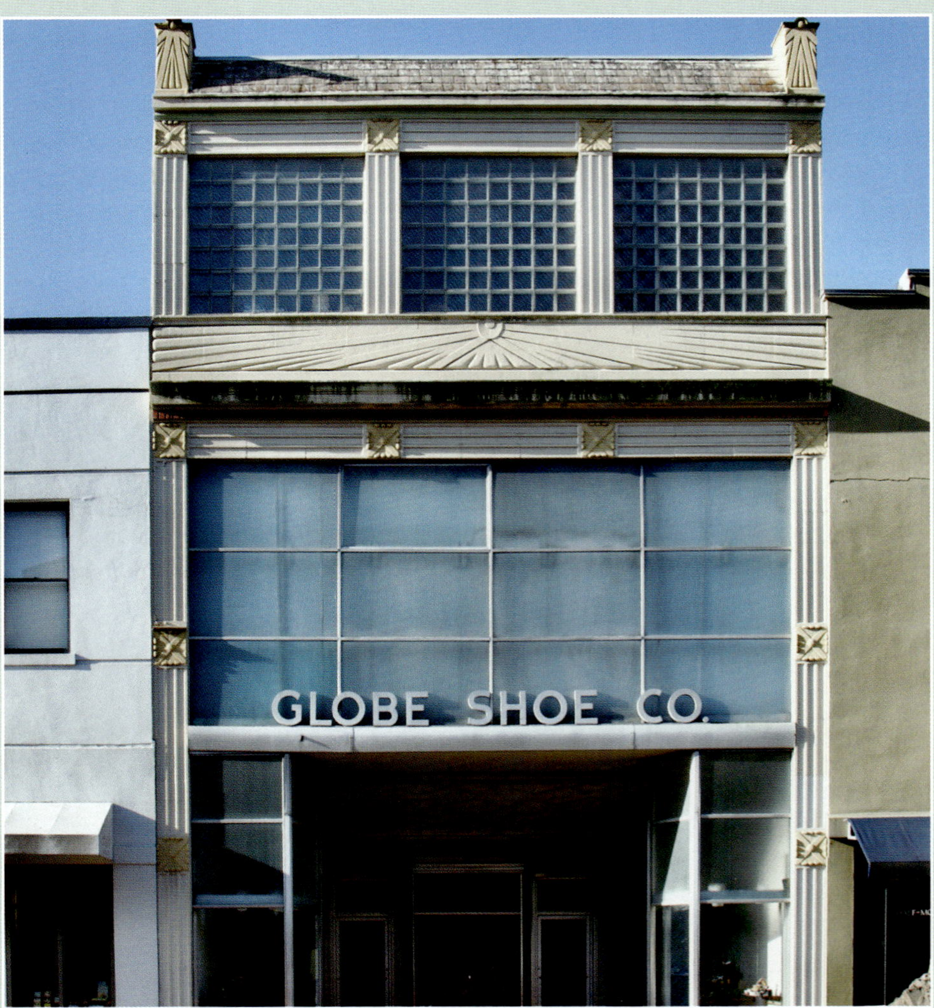

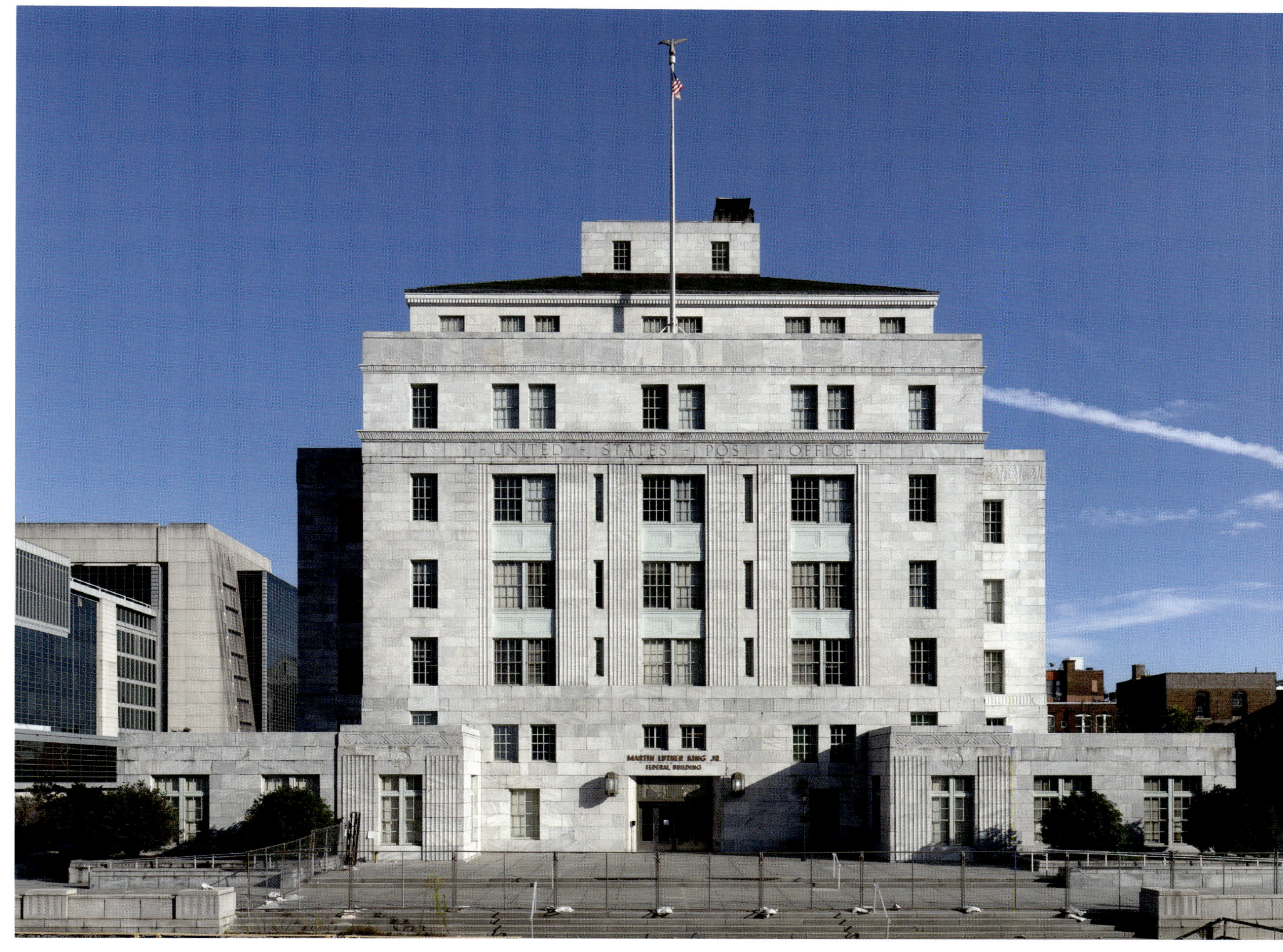

Martin Luther King Jr. Federal Building, Atlanta

allowed for the easy movement of mail via a tunnel. The monumental building combines the symmetry, broad staircases, and position set back from the street of classical public buildings but is shorn of the usual columns and cornices. Instead, its Art Deco stepped profile and crisp modern angular geometry give the building a muscular confidence. Upon closer inspection, the varied veining patterns of the marble cladding animate the surface, while pairs of shallow fluting, suggestive of classical pilasters but without bases or capitals (another Art Deco trait), adorn the area around the slightly recessed entrance, where the bronze materiality provides the only note of color. Above the doors a quartet of grills with vibrant sunburst motifs supports a decorative panel depicting bound fasces (a favorite motif in the 1930s in both the United States, where it represented the Republic, and Italy, where it symbolized fascism) and a highly stylized pair of eagles flanking a shield with stars and stripes, all set against another sunburst effect.

International Style

The Modernist movement in architecture emerged in Europe in the 1920s as a repudiation of the perceived corruption of traditional society and its artistic forms. Characterized by abstract geometry, the use of modern materials—glass, steel, and concrete—an emphasis on function and an avoidance of surface ornament, Modernist architecture was promoted by design publications, especially those by Le Corbusier, and by the Bauhaus, a radical design school in Dessau, Germany. It earned the label International Style from the inaugural architecture exhibition held at the Museum of Modern Art in New York in 1932. The arrival of architects from Europe during the 1930s, notably Walter Gropius and Ludwig Mies van der Rohe (both former directors of the Bauhaus), who joined the Harvard Graduate School of Design and the Armour (later Illinois) Institute of Technology, respectively, helped popularize the style in the United States.

Georgia Tech's Department of Architecture was instrumental in embracing and spreading the International Style in the state. In 1939 architecture professor Paul Heffernan was made chief designer of the Georgia Tech Campus expansion plans. Although his first building, Hinman Research Hall, built in 1939, reveals a transitional combination of Art Moderne and European Modernism, his postwar buildings fully embraced the Modern style. The Architecture Building

Peachtree-Seventh Building, Atlanta

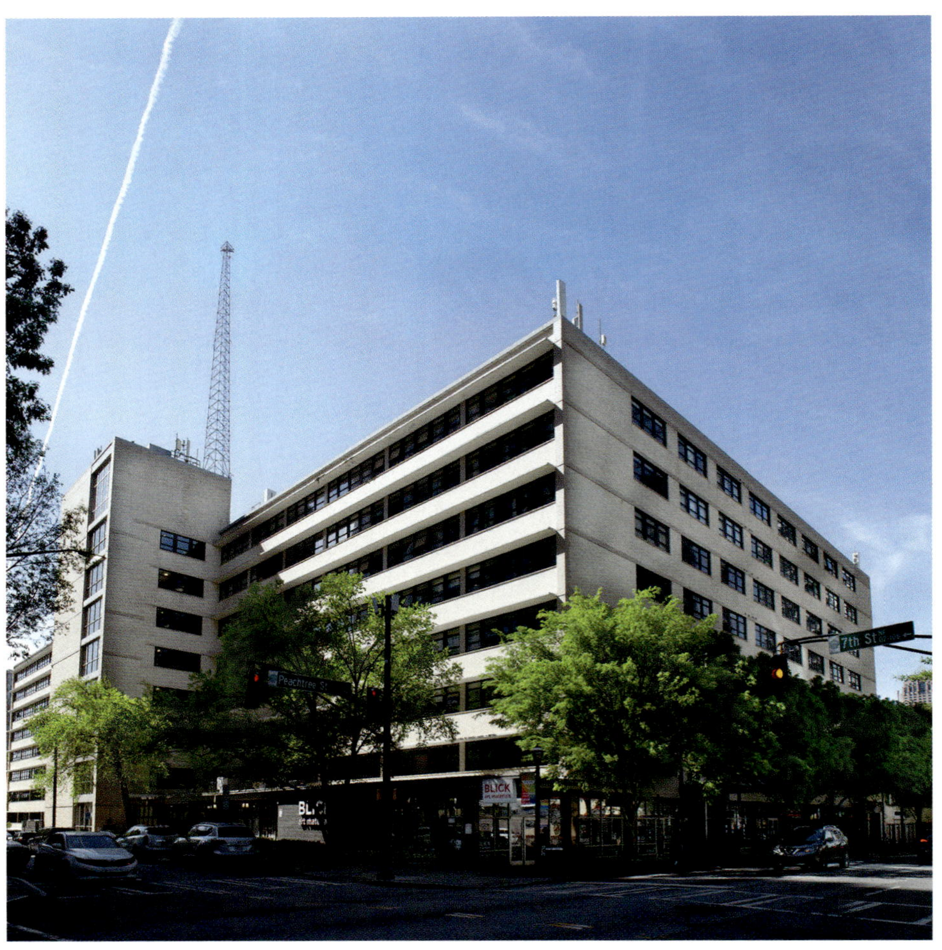

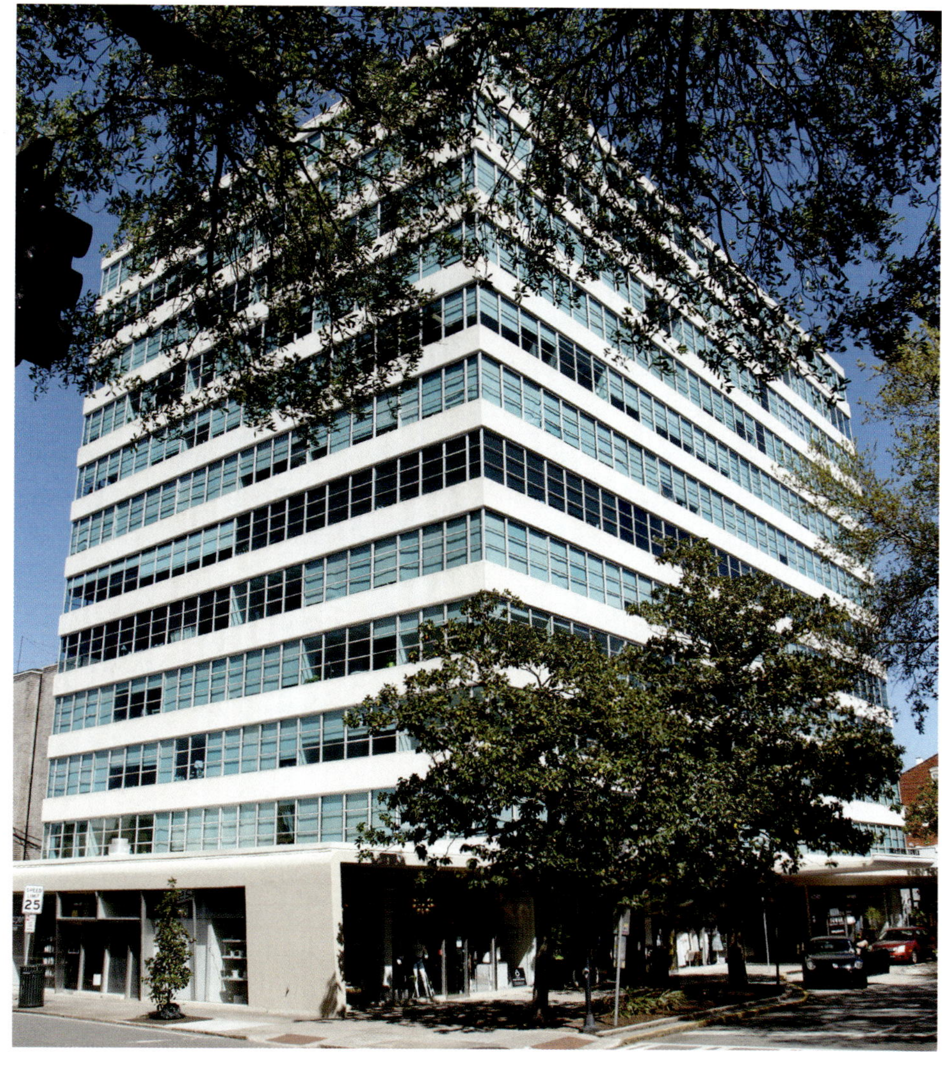

Drayton Tower, Savannah

(1950–52), codesigned with J. Hubert Gailey and Harold Bush Brown, showcases a Bauhaus influence with its dynamic asymmetrical composition and its play of vertical and horizontal planes of different materials and colors. A similar Bauhaus spirit infuses the Peachtree-Seventh Building (ca. 1949–51; now the Peachtree Lofts), a substantial eight-story air-conditioned office building designed by Cecil Alexander and Bernard Rothschild. The impressive horizontality of its long Seventh Street elevation, emphasized by the bands of windows sheltered by short concrete canopies (or *brises soleils*) that extend from the buff brick cladding, is counteracted by the bold vertical thrust of the projecting off-center stair and elevator tower, with a column of windows revealing the cantilevered concrete staircases within—a direct nod to the early twentieth-century buildings by Walter Gropius.

Arguably the boldest International Style building erected in Georgia during the immediate postwar years is the Drayton Arms Apartments (now Drayton Tower) in Savannah. Designed in 1949 by local architects Cletus Bergen and son William Bergen, who had recently received his architecture degree at Georgia Tech, the building was funded by the Federal Housing Administration to provide affordable efficiency apartments for veterans upon its completion in 1951.

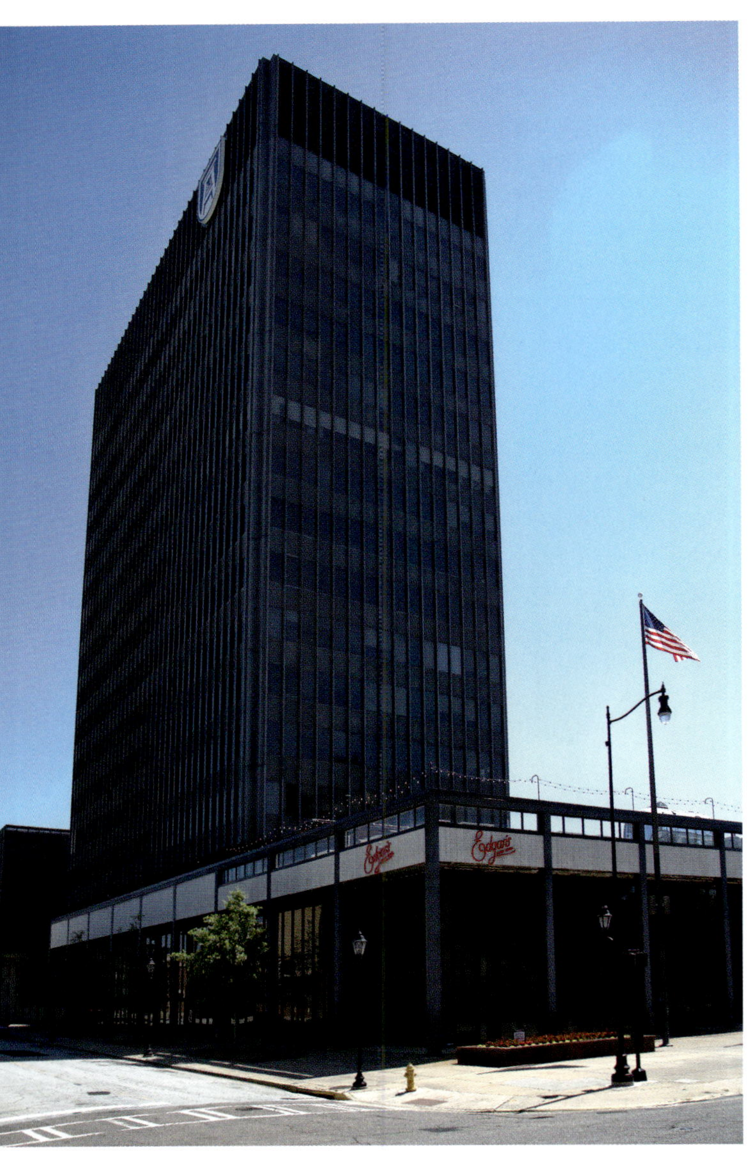

Georgia Railroad Bank Building, Augusta

The broad, ground-floor concrete podium housing shops reflects expressionist tendencies in Modernism, with its angled sides and dramatically cantilevered entrance canopy. Rising 11 stories above the podium, the building's pure cubic form displays a curtain wall of alternating bands of limestone panels and uninterrupted ribbon windows (possibly the first in Georgia), a characteristic of Le Corbusier's early works, that wrap around all four sides, made possible by the reinforced concrete structure. The pioneering green-tinted Solex "heat-absorbing" windows were produced by the Pittsburgh Plate Glass Company, which used Drayton Arms in their 1951 national advertising campaign promoting the product. Drayton Arms was also the first air-conditioned apartment building in Georgia.

In the 1950s Mies van der Rohe designed a series of high rises, notably the Lake Shore Drive Apartments in Chicago and the Seagram Building in New York, that popularized the boxy, black skyscraper clad in steel I-beams and dark-tinted windows. It spawned an abundant progeny of copies, derivatives, and variations, many by the prolific New York architecture firm of Skidmore, Owings & Merrill, including their 32-story Equitable Building in downtown Atlanta, completed in 1968. The recent replacement of the original signs, due to a change in building ownership, highlights the challenge of reconciling building preservation with corporate identity. A more intriguing black steel-and-glass Miesian variant stands out in Augusta, the Georgia Railroad Bank Building (now Augusta University Building), designed by local architect Robert McCreary and completed in 1967. The narrow 17-story tower is strongly derivative of Mies's vocabulary, with its vertical steel ribs and dark-tinted windows. But instead of standing free, the tower rises from a broader double-height podium, defined by freestanding black piers, a "frieze" of stone panels and recessed walls of glass. Even more unusual is the integration of a parking garage at the rear, connected via a skywalk, with its dark, louvered panels echoing the skin of the tower, which displays a creative and sensitive interpretation of the minimalist style. The tower here has also seen a succession of sign changes at the top of its facades.

Postwar Modernist Houses

The postwar years saw dramatic changes to residential architecture, as social values shifted toward a greater emphasis on privacy, a more relaxed lifestyle, and a desire to escape from the real or perceived problems of the city. Another factor motivating families to move to the suburbs was the goal of owning a detached house, a tangible symbol of social and economic success. Ranch houses became wildly popular following World War II with the development of low-density, car-oriented suburbs across the continent. Influenced by Cliff May's California ranch houses of the early 1930s and Frank Lloyd Wright's Usonian houses of the late 1930s, a ranch house is typically a wide, asymmetrical, ground-hugging, one-story house with large horizontal windows and (depending on the style) a very low pitch or flat roof.

The form arrived in Georgia in 1941, mainly in the minimal traditional style, with examples in Atlanta, Cordele, and Rome. A year later, Ellamae Ellis League, one of the first licensed female architects in Georgia, introduced the ranch form to Macon. Her equally pioneering daughter, Jean League Newton, who trained at Harvard's Graduate School of Design under Walter Gropius, designed the city's first Modernist ranch house, the Joseph and Mary Jane League House, in 1950. Commissioned by her brother and his wife, the unusual, rotated H-shape house is a study in graduated privacy, with the kitchen and living room at the front of the house (an innovative placement for a kitchen at the time), with elongated clerestory windows set high in the front facade of both rooms. The living room and adjacent dining room form an open L that extends into the middle section of the H with floor-to-ceiling windows overlooking an intimate courtyard hidden from public view. The opposite courtyard, accessible from the kitchen and the carport, functions as a utility yard. The rear and most private section of the house has four bedrooms in a row overlooking (and three directly accessing) the expansive and even more private backyard. It was the first ranch house in Georgia individually listed on the National Register of Historic Places.

Despite segregation, ranch houses became equally appealing to African Americans, who in most cases occupied houses originally built for whites. The Collier Heights neighborhood in Atlanta was unique in being developed, beginning in 1954, both by and for the city's growing Black middle class, and it became home to many prominent members of the Black community. Trained at Hampton University, architect Joseph W. Robinson (the first African American in Georgia

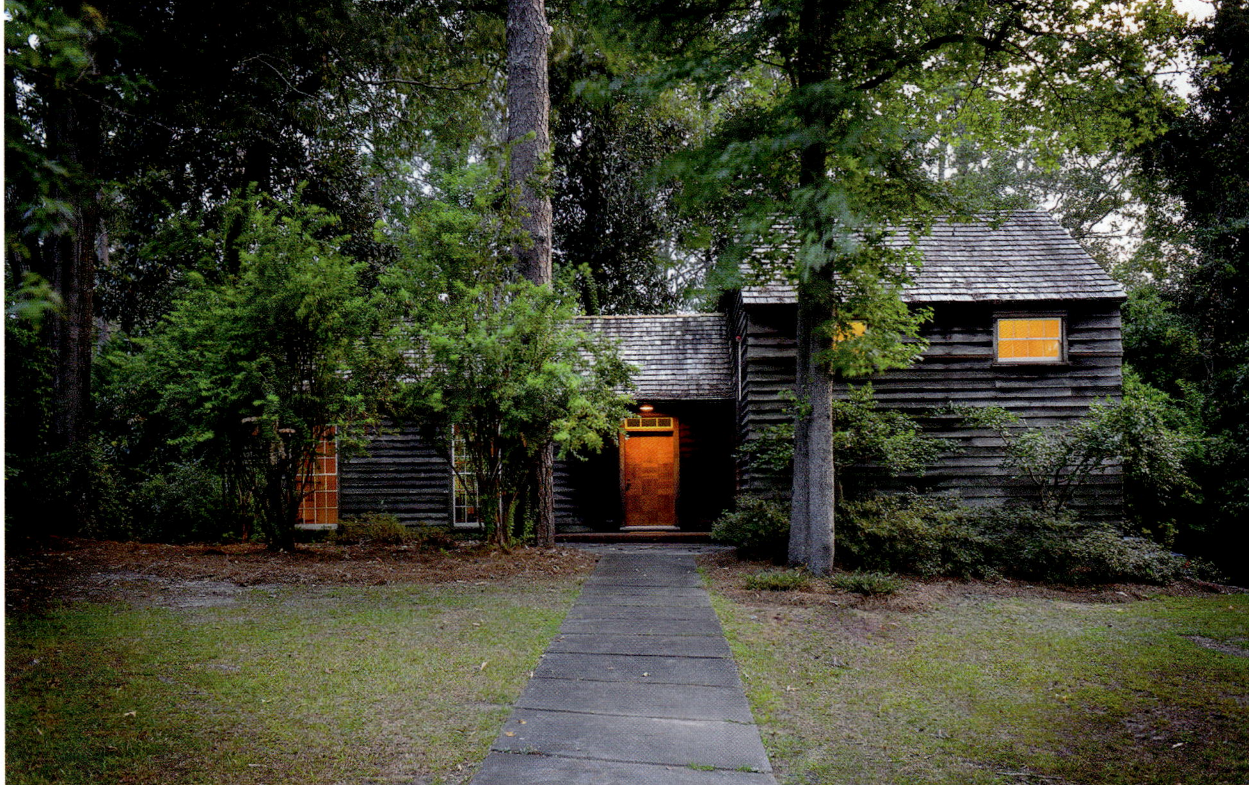

League House, Macon

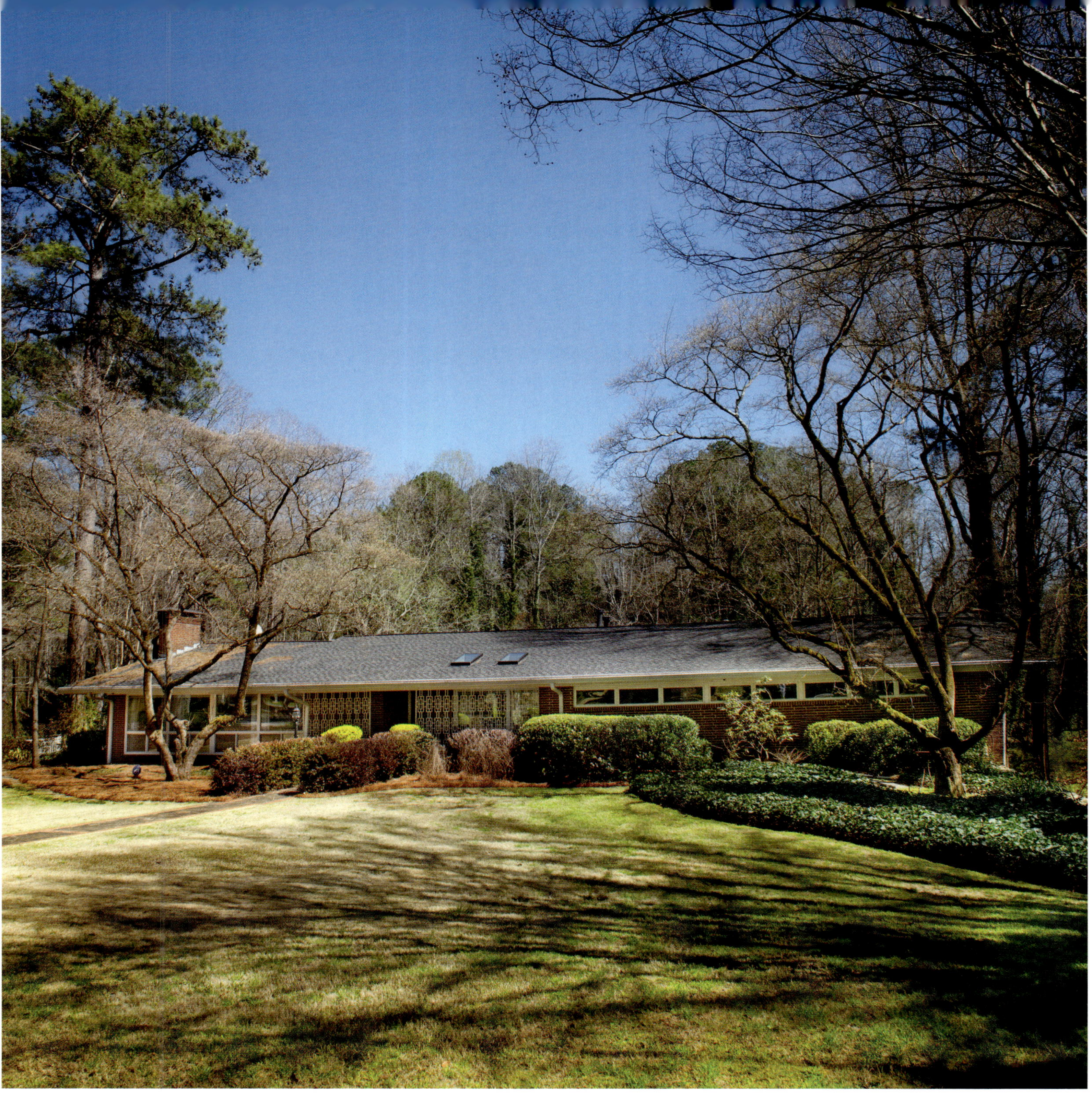

Herman Russell House, Atlanta

made a fellow of the American Institute of Architects) authored its most notable houses. The Herman Russell House is representative. Designed in 1963 for the prominent Atlanta businessman and first Black member of the Atlanta Chamber of Commerce, the large house appears as a conventional ranch from the front, with the only notable feature of its broad, low facade being the intricate veil-like metal screen enclosing the front porch. Erected on a steep slope, most of the house's enormous 8,761-square-foot area is situated on the lower rear level. With Blacks unable to patronize restaurants and hotel ballrooms in downtown Atlanta, the house included a substantial recreation room and indoor pool for entertaining. Elaborate recreation rooms were a hallmark of Robinson's designs and the only notable architectural feature distinguishing these houses from ranches in other areas.

The postwar embrace of Modernism also resulted in some boldly sculptural, expressionistic houses, including the circular Cecil and Hermione Alexander House in Atlanta, designed in 1956–57 by architect Cecil Alexander as his own family's residence. Organized around a central atrium covered by an accordion (or pleated) reinforced concrete roof, half of the circle, including the atrium, forms an open plan with floor-to-ceiling windows providing extensive views of the natural landscapes beyond. The other half of the circle comprises wedge-shaped bedrooms. Alexander's house was featured on the cover of *Life* magazine in 1957, in an article entitled "Tomorrow's Life Today." In 2008, it received an award for excellence in rehabilitation from the Georgia Trust.

Alexander House, Atlanta

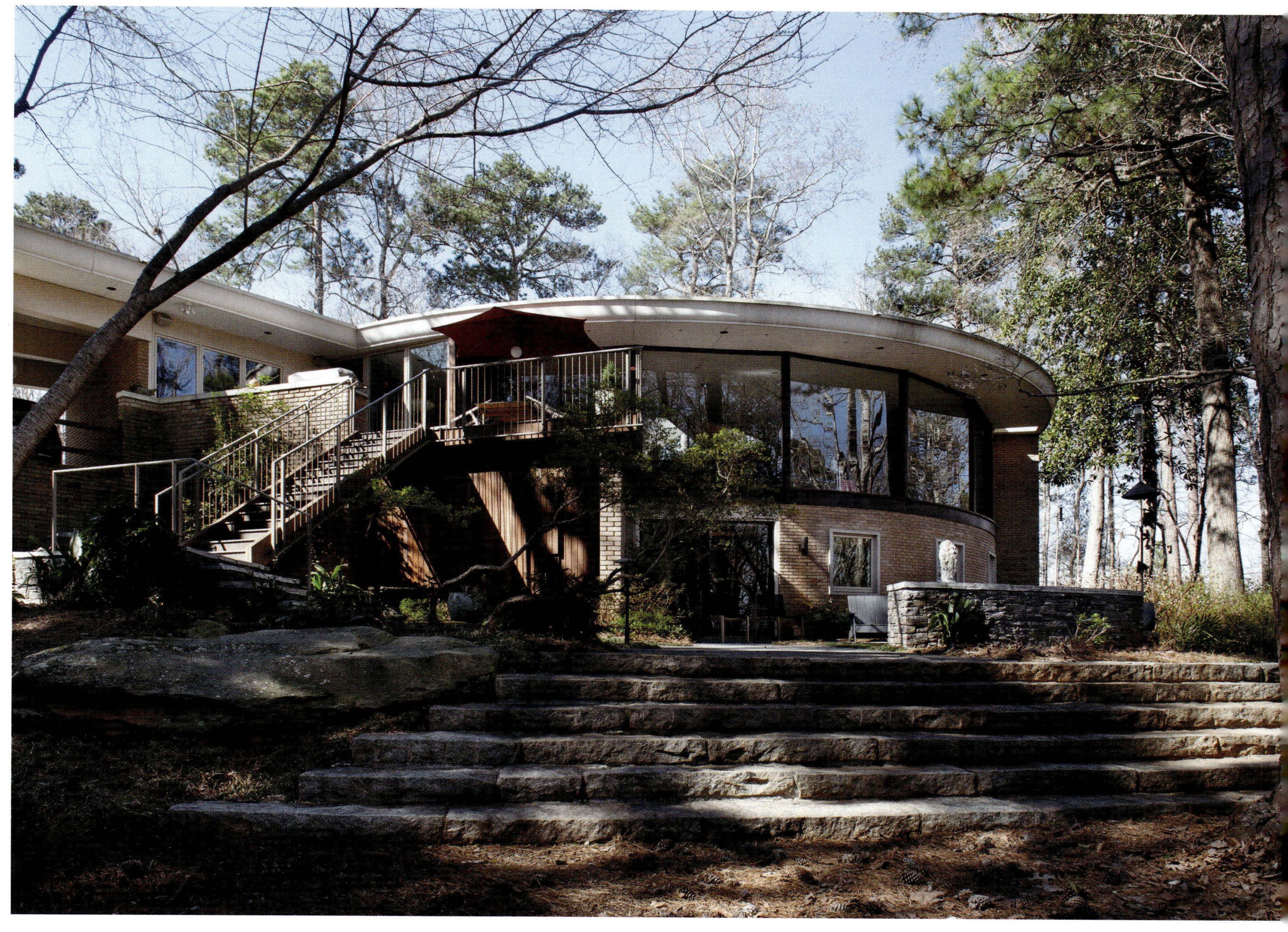

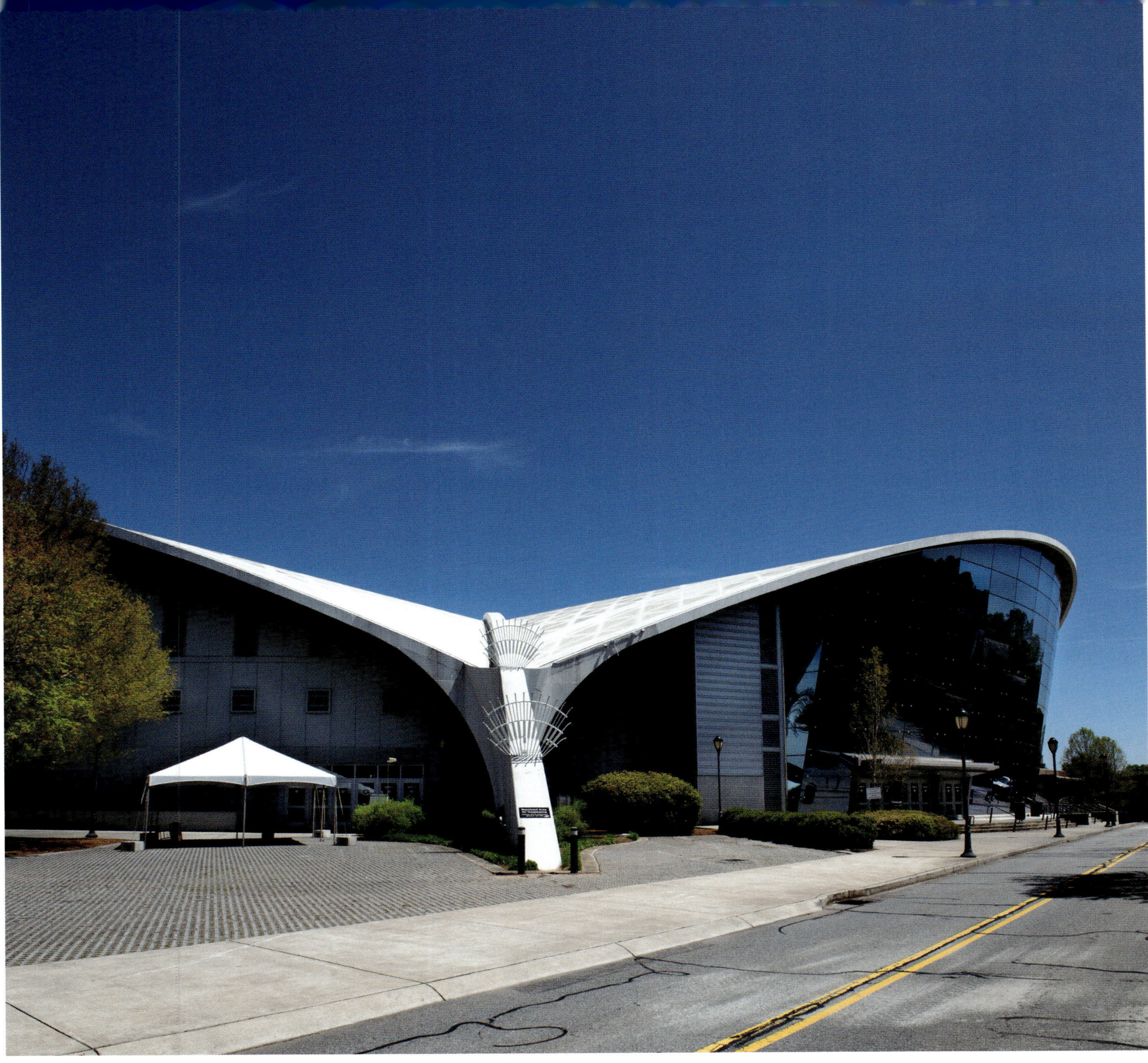

Stegeman Coliseum, Athens

Googie and Roadside Architecture

"Googie" architecture exploited the dramatic structural and sculptural possibilities of reinforced and precast concrete, usually in conjunction with automobility. Further influencing designers was the growing popularity of "space age" and "atomic age" designs that conveyed a powerful sense of excitement for the future. With eye-catching, extravagant designs and bold signage, the style served any car-oriented building type, particularly when involving a drive-through use. Atlanta once possessed many dramatic examples of Googie architecture, but most have succumbed to the city's own success and redevelopment. An exception is the later modifications of the Varsity restaurant in Atlanta that featured colorful angular signage and a large, freestanding canopy for car service, all influenced by the popularity of this style in the 1950s and 1960s.

The Georgia (now Stegeman) Coliseum on the University of Georgia campus in Athens demonstrates the bold structural possibilities of reinforced concrete. Erected in 1963–64 as a 10,523-seat multipurpose arena, the structure features a column-free interior made possible by two parabolic arched supports, each spanning 384 feet, that cross at right angles to form an X. They support the arched roof shells in each quadrant, reinforced on the underside by ribbed (or waffle) slab construction. The roof, completed first, overhangs the round building beneath on three sides. The work owes a clear debt to Eero Saarinen and his innovative Gateway Arch in Saint Louis and TWA Terminal at JFK Airport in New York, among other works. The moldable nature of concrete inspired other dramatically sculptural buildings, such as the round library wing attached to the otherwise conventional brick Decatur High School designed by Bothwell & Nash in 1965.

To capture the growing popularity of auto-tourism during the 1950s, Governor Ernest Vandiver created a new Tourist Division in the Georgia Department of Commerce. One of its initiatives was the creation of welcome centers on principal roadways near the state's borders, beginning with the Georgia Welcome Center in Sylvania (1961–62), located less than a mile west of the South Carolina border on Highway 301, a popular route prior to the construction of Interstate 95. Designed by Statesboro architect Edwin C. Eckles, the one-story building comprises an undulating roof of five precast concrete vaults forming shallow arches that run from front to back, the middle three of which cover the building, the outer ones covering sheltered patios. The three restrooms on the west side were originally designated as men's, women's, and "colored" (now simply an extra restroom). The L-shaped lobby and lounge with a display area retains the original aluminum chandeliers and terrazzo floors.

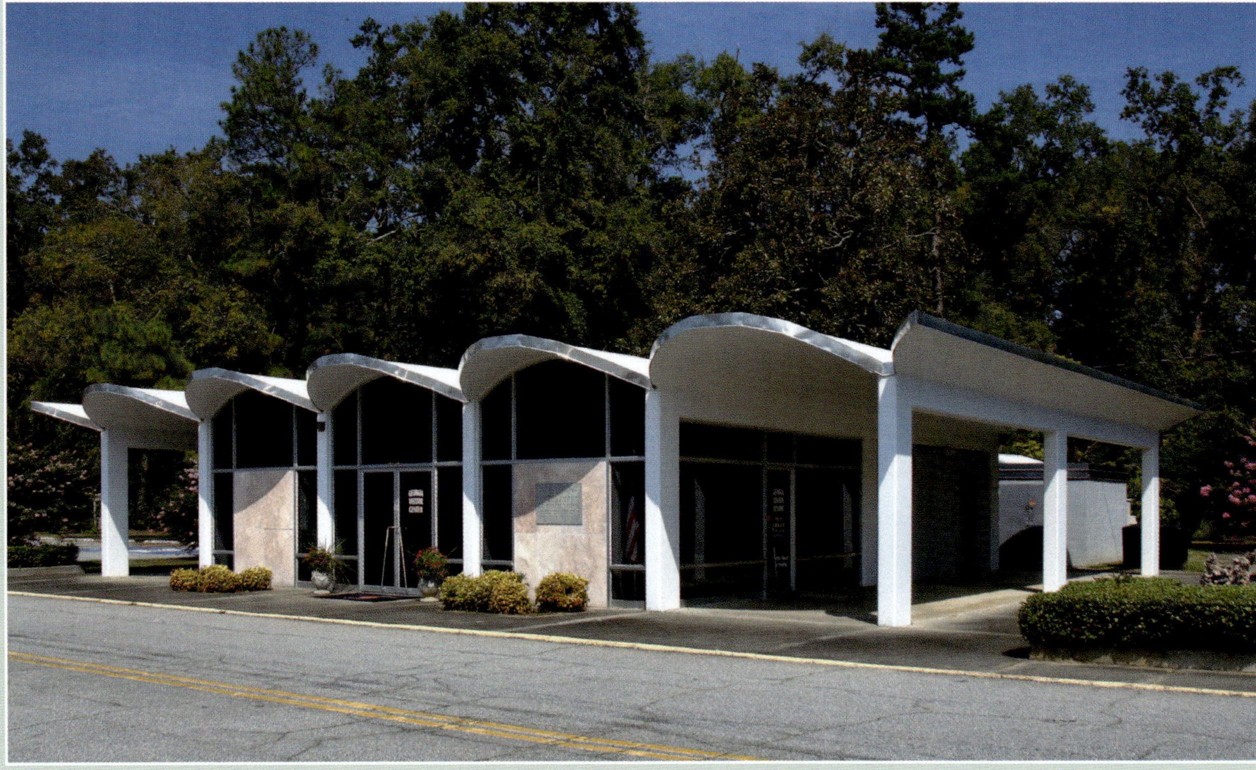

Georgia Welcome Center, Sylvania

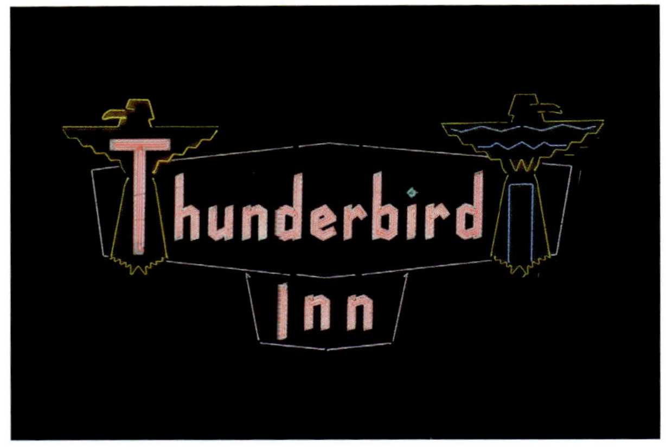

Thunderbird Inn, Savannah

With eye-catching signage to attract automobile travelers, motels (motor hotels) appeared along highways at the entrances to many cities across the state. Most disappeared as interstate highways changed travel routes and generic hotel-motel chains appeared to cater to travelers' desire for predictability. A rare survivor, and winner of recent preservation awards, is the Thunderbird Inn in Savannah, designed in 1964 by local architect John Knox Stacy. Located at the foot of the Talmadge Bridge (1954; replaced 1991) that carries Highway 17 over the Savannah River near downtown Savannah, the motel broadcasts its presence with a tall, colorful, enameled metal and neon sign oriented to the bridge. Wrapping around a parking lot, the two-story L-shaped motel has red, yellow, and seafoam-green panels and doors that heighten its visual allure. Hollow concrete block screens support the continuous outdoor corridor accessing the second-floor rooms. The hotel office adds to the drama with a boldly cantilevered canopy that tapers to a sharp edge.

Alternative Modernisms: Expressionism, Brutalism, and New Formalism

Throughout the twentieth century, alternative approaches to Modernism coexisted with the geometric and minimalist forms that became dominant worldwide by the 1950s. Instead of the apparent weightlessness of sleek glass and steel volumes, concrete allowed architects to explore expressive shapes and monumental qualities better suited to a range of building types not well served by the look of corporate boxes. By the 1960s, Georgia began experiencing a greater level of architectural and urban significance with the pioneering work of John Portman at Peachtree Center in Atlanta and the state's ability to attract leading architects to design projects.

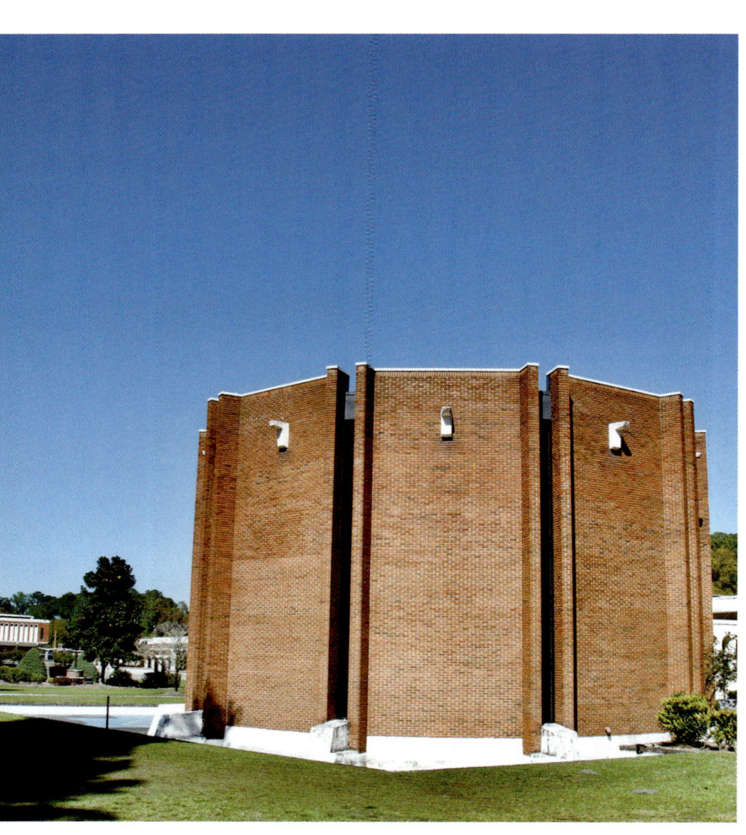

Benedictine Military School, Savannah

A rare example of a complete Modern campus preserving both buildings and landscapes in their original form, Benedictine Military School and Priory in Savannah is one of the most significant ensembles of Modern architecture in Georgia. Designed in 1962 by Georgia Tech–trained architect Juan Bertotto in collaboration with Thomas, Driscoll and Hutton, the complex combines the sculptural shapes and bold cantilevered concrete structures of expressionism with the emerging interest in abstracted round arch forms of New Formalism. The campus comprises five buildings arranged around three sides of a quadrangle with a shady walkway canopy of repeated "butterfly" prestressed concrete arches on concrete piers defining the fourth. The sculptural focal point, the ten-sided centrally planned brick and concrete priory chapel, rises from a pool of water in a manner similar to Eero Saarinen's cylindrical brick Kresge Chapel at Massachusetts Institute of Technology, completed in 1956. Inside, forceful concrete piers rise up to form a radial pattern evocative of Gothic ribbed vaulting above the centrally located altar.

Most postwar houses of worship aimed to strike a balance between traditional architectural forms that communicate their religious function—particularly front-facing gables, large windows, and steeples—and Modernism through an avoidance of explicit historicizing ornament. Druid Hills Church of Christ (1949–50), designed by local architect Norman F. Stambaugh, and architect Carol M. Smith's Mount Zion Second Baptist Church (1955–56), both in Atlanta, are representative early examples. Of the more than forty houses of worship the pioneering Modernist Pietro Belluschi designed across the United States, the relatively modest yet remarkable Covenant Presbyterian Church (1967–72) in Albany is the only one in Georgia. Although he is most famous for his International Style office buildings, Belluschi was one of the leading Modernist designers of religious architecture. Short sections of fieldstone support dark-stained rough-sawn pine walls that fill the gable ends of the cruciform, A-frame church designed to accommodate 480 worshippers. Its steep slate roofs descend close to the ground. The dark interior of exposed laminated beams and oiled cedar ceiling is illuminated by four tall, narrow stained-glass windows, one in each gable, that rise the full 42-foot height and continue overhead to form a cruciform skylight in the roof ridges—a captivating solution Belluschi was exploring on a larger scale in concrete at his Saint Mary's Roman Catholic Cathedral in San Francisco (1963–70).

Covenant Presbyterian Church, Albany

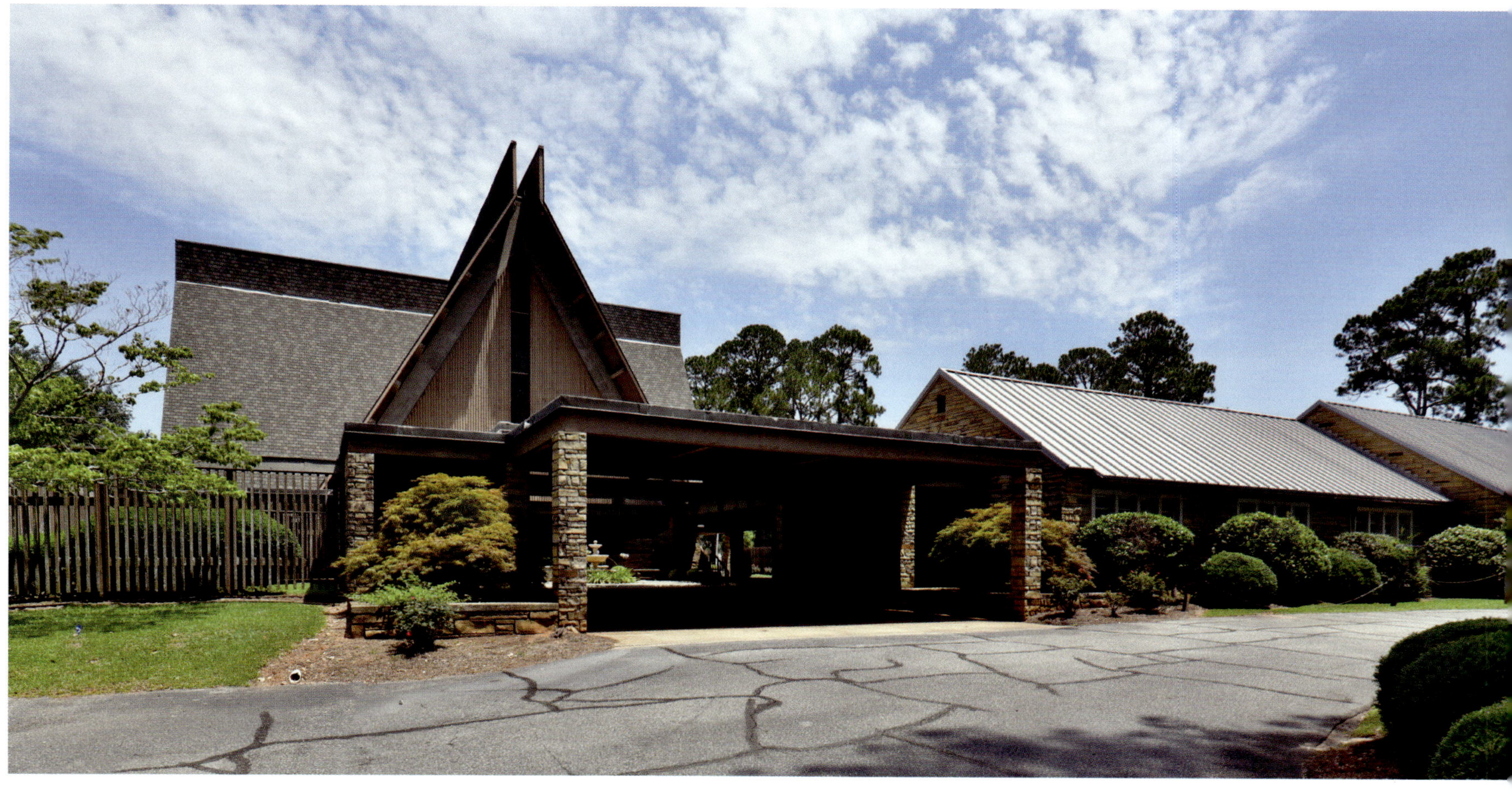

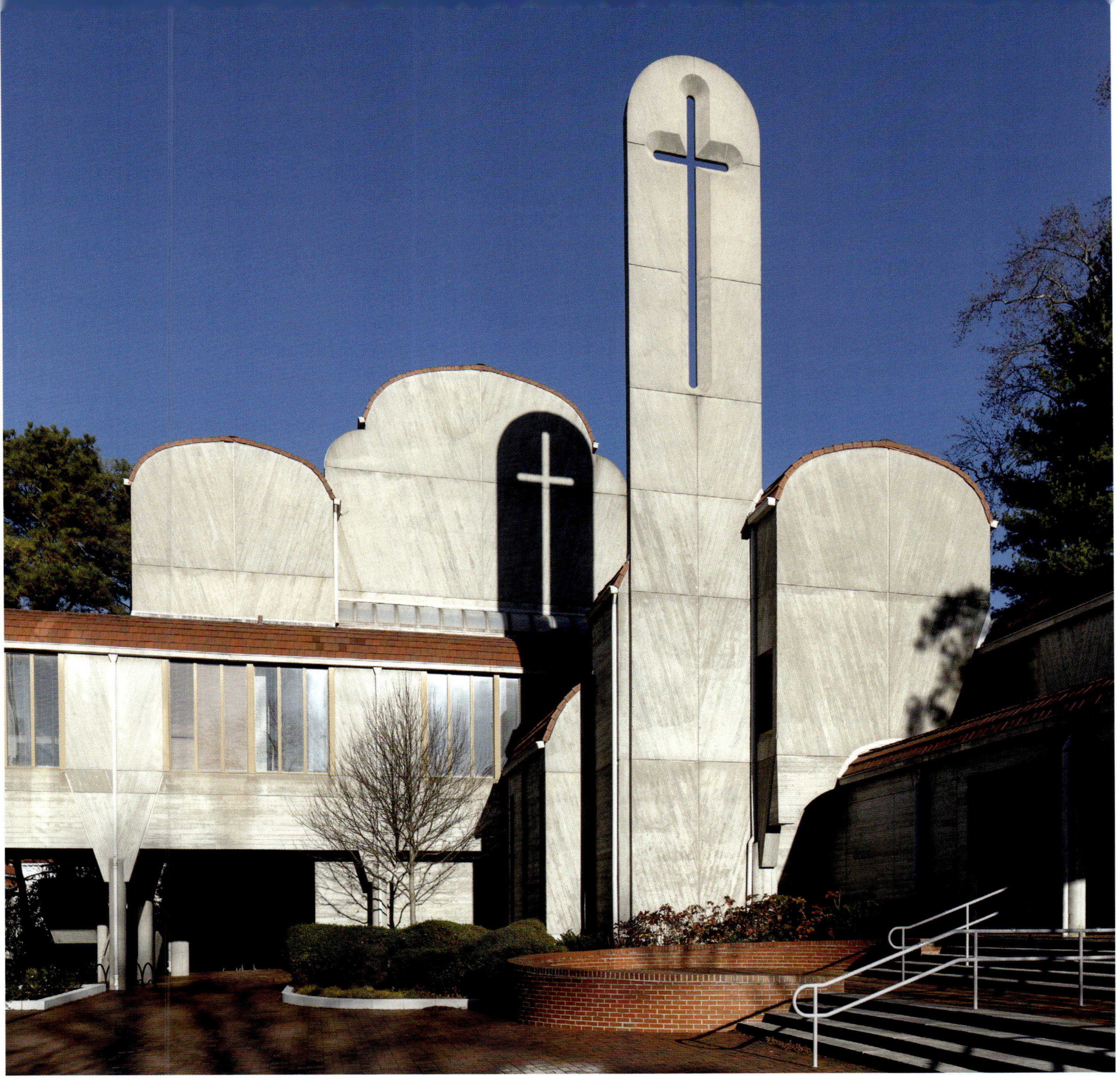

Cannon Chapel, Emory University, Atlanta

Another leading Modernist from out of state, Paul Rudolph, authored the impressive Cannon Chapel on the Emory University campus in Atlanta, part of the Candler School of Theology, from which the architect's father was one of the first graduates. Completed in 1981, the interfaith chapel employs the Brutalist technique, innovated by Le Corbusier in the 1950s, of exposed raw concrete imprinted with the image of rough formwork boards, but with a delicacy and refinement far removed from the bulkiness of Rudolph's earlier works, such as the Yale School of Architecture, for which he is most famous. The chapel deftly straddles an awkward sloping site and sensitively relates to its varied context. Connecting via a bridge to the main campus quadrangle, the chapel's concrete walls harmonize with its mottled grey marble classical buildings, their red tile roofs repeated on the chapel. Facing a lower-level and less formal courtyard, the chapel's main entrance introduces the sets of parallel elongated arched components, reminiscent of Louis Kahn's recent Kimbell Museum of Art, that form the structure, but with perpendicular vaulted elements added, such as the ramp. The entrance facade showcases three main arches, with the larger central one rising higher, giving a sense of the sanctuary space within, while a tall, narrow slab of concrete, perforated with a cross-shaped aperture, forms a tower. Inside, exposed concrete corner piers carry long concrete beams spanning the sanctuary from front to back, which support sets of the arched wooden ceilings. The warm-toned wood used generously throughout the interior softens and humanizes the stark coolness of the extensive exposed concrete.

The development of Peachtree Center in Atlanta as a market and convention complex created a model for multipurpose developments worldwide. Beginning with the Merchandise Mart (now AmericasMart Atlanta) in 1961, John Portman, as both architect and developer, aimed to bring commercial activity back into downtown. This massive 22-story wholesale trade center contained in a low-budget structure features a simple and rather foreboding exterior of concrete piers, narrow windows, and broad textured concrete panels. On adjacent blocks he later added the Gift Mart (1968) and Apparel Mart (1979), connected via multiple skybridges, a signature Portman feature. Begun in 1965, his multibuilding Peachtree Center, comprising seven office towers ranging from 25 to 35 stories tall, uses slightly varied precast concrete panels with tall, narrow, fixed-pane tinted windows set within beveled frames—a Formalist vocabulary that rejected the glassy Miesian aesthetic. The ensemble of high rises drew inspiration from the multibuilding Rockefeller Center in New York by using a consistent exterior cladding and an open sunken courtyard between the buildings, around which shops were clustered.

The centerpiece of the Peachtree Center and its most significant building authored by Portman was the Regency Hyatt House (now Hyatt Regency Hotel) in 1967, whose atrium forever changed hotel architecture. With 800 rooms, it was the first major hotel to be built in downtown Atlanta since the 1920s. The exterior harmonizes with other buildings in the complex through the use of precast concrete, but now horizontally organized as projecting balconies with the vertical openings in the concrete railings mimicking the windows on the office buildings. Set back from Peachtree Street, a generous forecourt with a gently arched canopy welcomes cars and pedestrians. The purposely low entrance canopy and vestibule intensify the drama of entering the spectacular full-height atrium within. Lined by the projecting concrete balconies of hotel rooms, the enormous atrium evokes an urban plaza paved in a European-style fan-shaped pattern, with a "sidewalk" cafe at the base and a 120-foot-tall wire sculpture, *Flora Raris*, by Richard Lipphold providing a sense of scale. The five glass-enclosed elevator cabs, widely imitated for many building types, allow guests to experience the atrium in the thrilling manner of an amusement park ride while ascending to their room or

Hyatt Regency Hotel, Atlanta

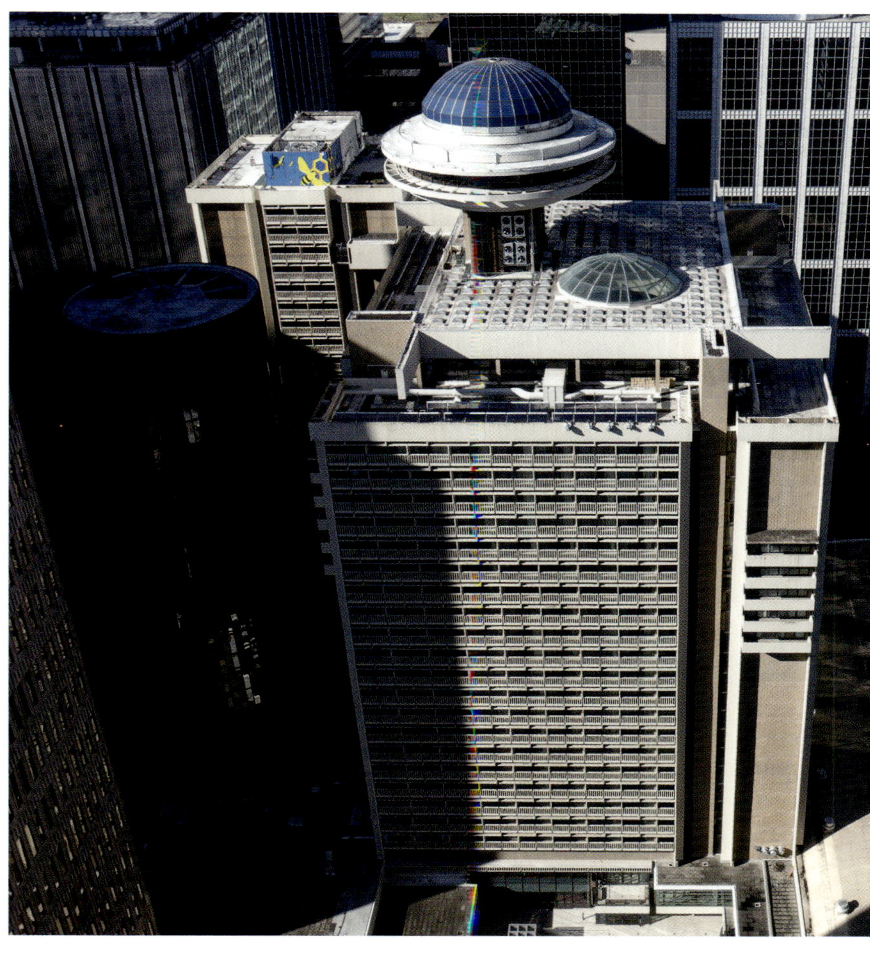

to the spaceship-like domed rotating Polaris restaurant on the roof. The hotel was so successful that additions were soon added—a 200-room cylindrical Late Modernist glass tower in 1971 (imitated at a larger scale in 1976 by Portman for his 73-story, 1,100-room, Westin Peachtree Plaza Hotel down the street) and a 350-room tower in 1983 matching the original exterior.

Atlanta Central Library (now the Atlanta-Fulton County Public Library) showcased the monumentality and architectural gravitas of Brutalism more powerfully than any other building in the state. The last work by the former Bauhaus instructor and influential Modernist Marcel Breuer, who designed it with Hamilton P. Smith in 1969. Construction was delayed by funding disputes until 1977, and it was completed in 1980, a year before Breuer's death. Similar to his Whitney Museum of Art in New York, the Atlanta library creates a sense of monumentality with its top-heavy composition of boldly cantilevered large masses and expanses of seemingly thick blank walls pierced by only a few large openings. Typical of Brutalism, of which this is a late example, the exterior walls are sheathed in large precast concrete panels, but with the unusual use of mechanically cut diagonal striations to animate the surface with subtle texture. Dominated by a monumental concrete staircase, the interior was designed to house one million volumes and accommodate one thousand users. Recent renovations have added more windows to the lower parts of the facade to make the building more inviting, but such changes threaten to diminish the building's historic integrity.

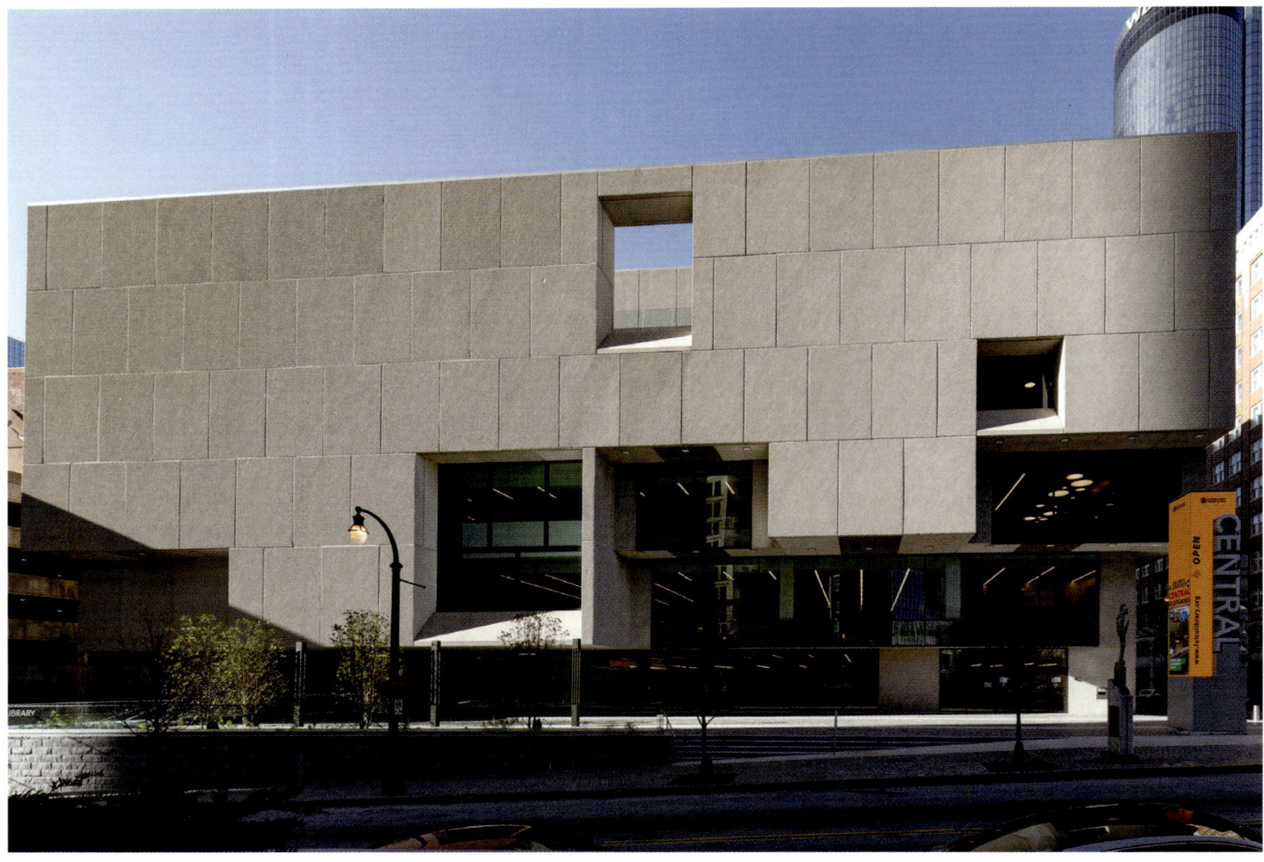

Atlanta Central Library, Atlanta

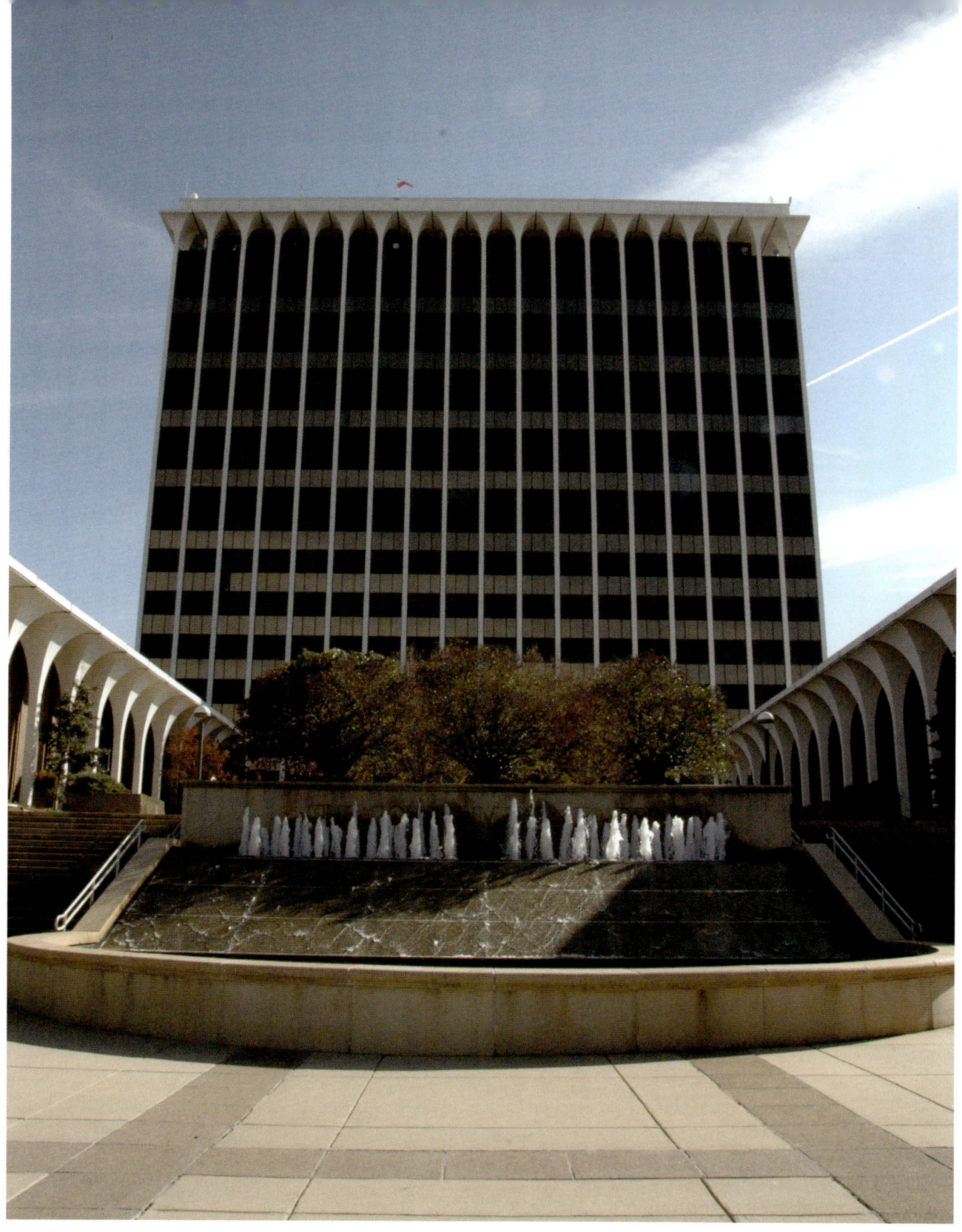

Columbus Government Center, Columbus

New Formalism offered another design strategy for achieving a sense of monumentality, particularly for civic buildings, mostly by referencing the classical tradition more directly, but in a stylized, modernistic way. The Columbus Consolidated Government Center (1971–73), designed by architect Edward Neal, vividly reflects this trend as a monumental multibuilding ensemble. Housing the merged city and county governments, the symmetrical three-building composition wrapping around a rectangular plaza accessed by a grand staircase recalls the layout of the Lincoln Center in New York, the most noted work in this style. In Columbus, abstracted white concrete piers merge to form a rounded arcade and cornice on each building that stands out against darker adjacent materials. Lacking broader appreciation, New Formalist buildings have not fared well in terms of preservation, and the fate of the Columbus buildings remains undecided.

The monumental, almost temple-like Citizen's Federal Savings and Loan Bank (now Synovus Bank) in Rome is the state's finest New Formalist building. Its assured confidence may owe to its designer, William F. Cann, being one of the principals (and in the mid-1960s, president) of the Saint Louis–based Bank Building & Equipment Corporation, which called itself "America's financial design center." Designed in 1974, it was among the company's last works. Monumental, tapering precast concrete columns with flared bases carry angled cross-shaped beams, forming freestanding porticos on the front and back and engaged on the sides, giving the impression of a colonnade wrapping around the whole building like an ancient peripteral temple. The outer bays on each facade have rough slate panels between the columns, contrasting the sleek bays of dark tinted glass in the middle. The colonnade supports a projecting solid parapet that reads as a massive abstract cornice, above which rises an attic story with major and minor window dividers aligned with the columns below.

Citizen's Federal Savings and Loan, Rome

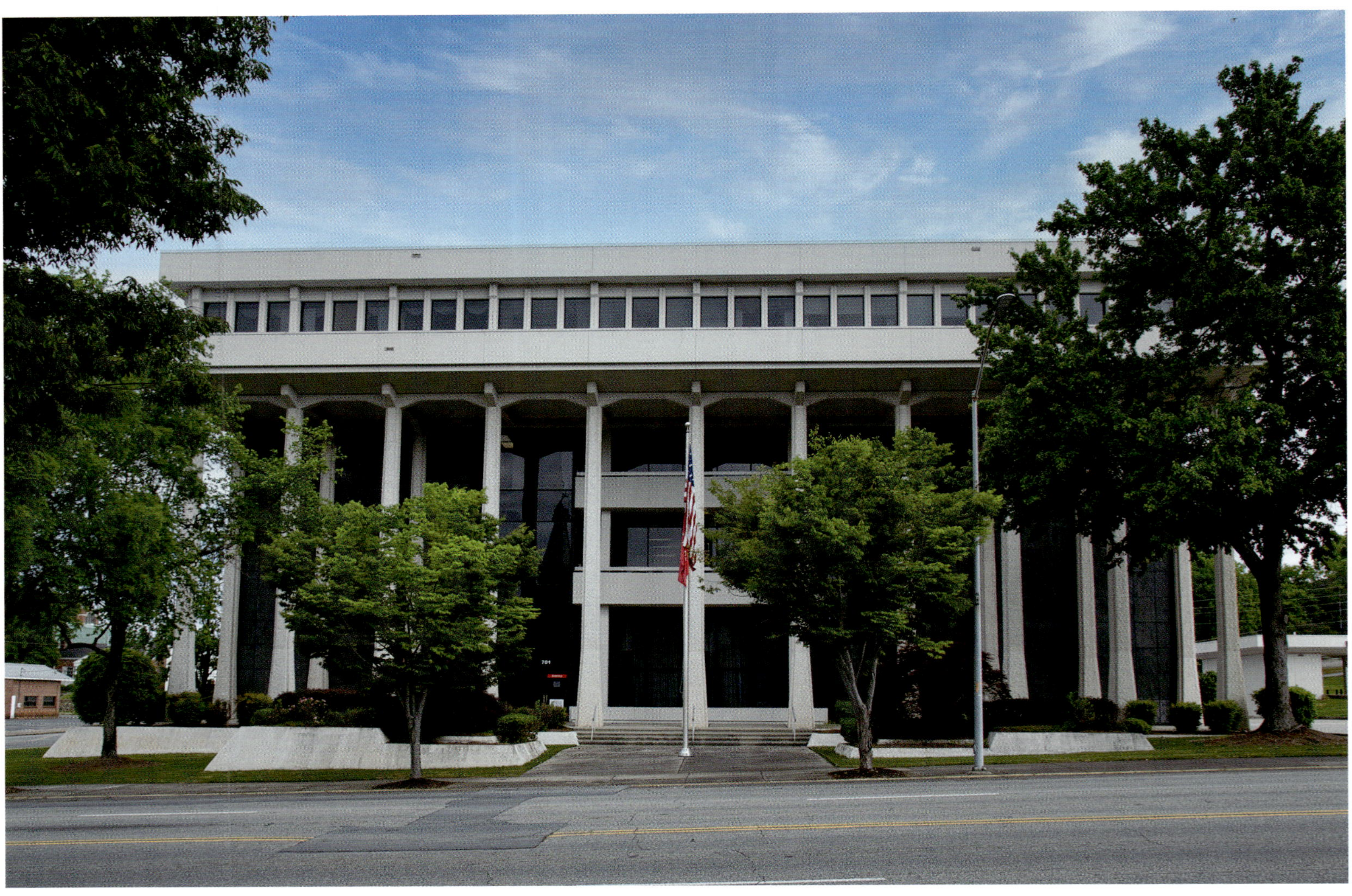

Late Modernism

While Brutalism and New Formalism critiqued and even subverted the Modernist ideals and materiality of the International Style, Late Modernism represented a continued commitment, but with more varied shapes and spaces and little concern for the theoretical underpinnings of the Modernist movement. A visual characteristic of Late Modernism is an emphasis on consistent harmonious and usually smooth surfaces, allowing a focus on the exploration of shape. Portman's cylindrical glass towers, the 1971 Hyatt Regency Hotel addition, and the Westin Peachtree Plaza Hotel in 1976, vividly illustrate this trait. During the 1970s and 1980s, the number of internationally prominent architects completing work in Georgia continued to grow.

Having begun his career with the Gulf Oil Building in Atlanta in 1949–50 (fragments of which survive on site), I. M. Pei returned to Georgia in 1973 to author the most radically designed and situated addition to a historic building in the state. R. Eugene Holley, owner of the Lamar Building in Augusta, commissioned Pei to add a penthouse to the venerable landmark. Completed in 1976, it is shockingly out of scale with the delicately proportioned building below. A recessed base provides access to an outdoor observation area on the old roof. Above, a one-story glass box extends outward on three sides, supporting a quasi pyramid of glass, the sloping sides rising another two stories before abutting two rectangular concrete slabs. Inside, the tall open interior was susceptible to heat gain. This work may be Pei's first completed exploration of the glass pyramid form, also used at the East Wing of the National Gallery in Washington completed two years later, that would define his most famous work, the Louvre Pyramid (1983–89). Meanwhile, in Savannah, fellow pioneering Modernist Pietro Belluschi consulted on the sleek 10-story 1975 addition to the east side of the historic 15-story Savannah Bank Building (1911; Mowbray and Uffinger). Clad in large sheets of limestone, the building's regular pattern of large single-pane tinted windows carefully aligns with the fenestration of the older building.

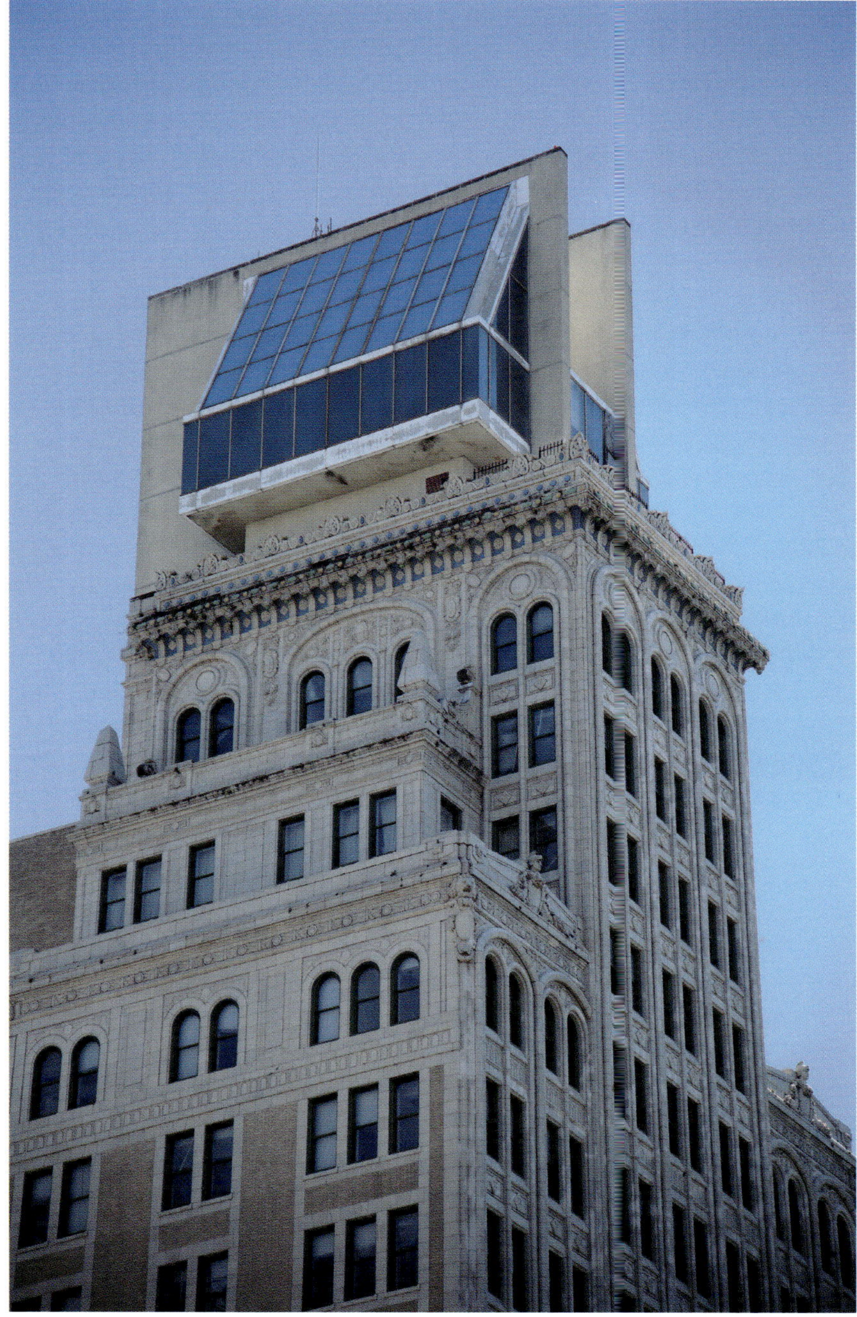

Lamar Building Penthouse, Augusta

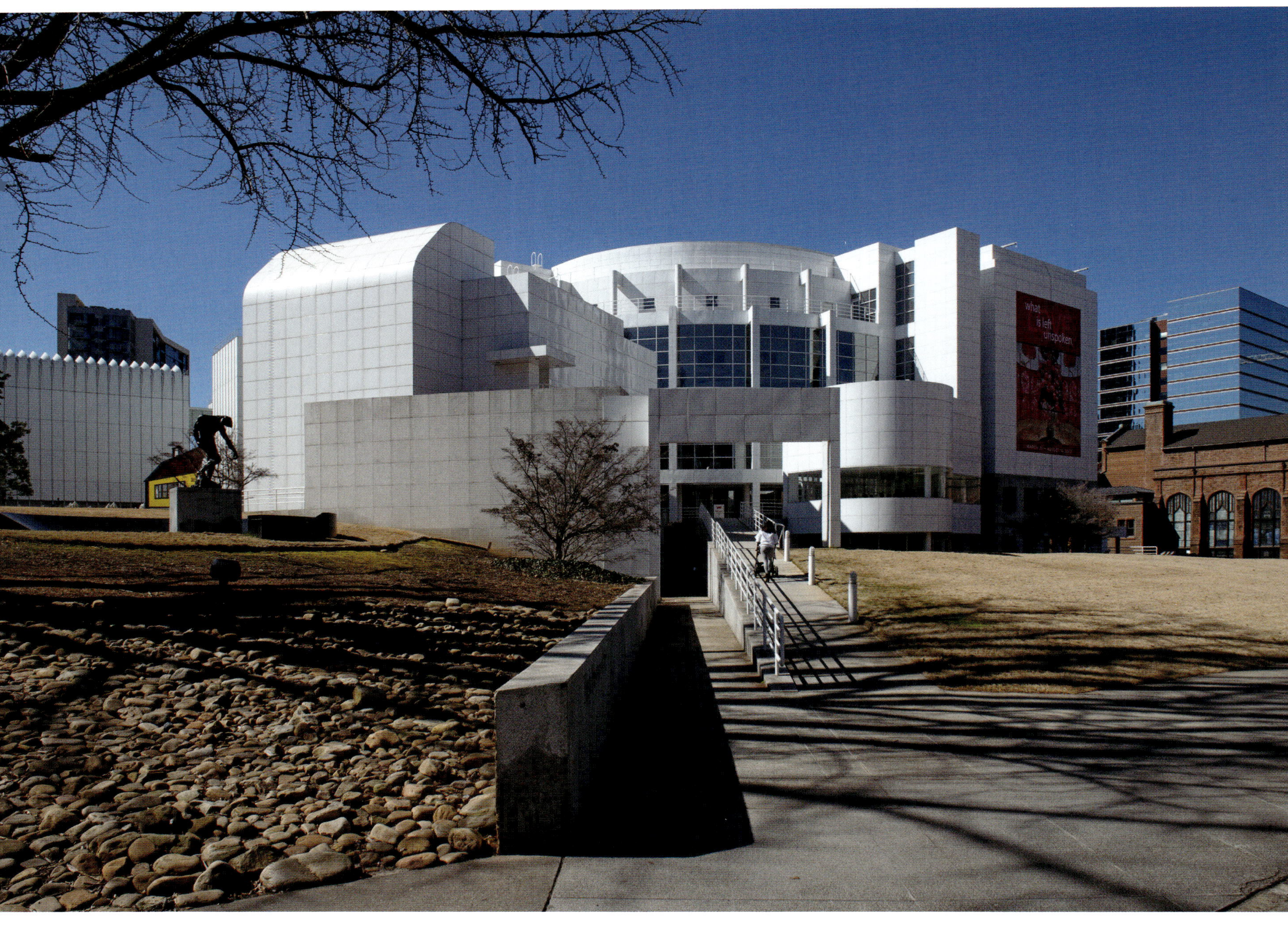

High Museum, Meier and Piano Buildings, Atlanta

The late twentieth century witnessed the emergence of the art museum as the building type with greatest place-making power, a potential unleashed by Frank Lloyd Wright's innovative and highly sculptural Guggenheim Museum in New York (1947–59) as a work of art in its own right. Beginning in the 1980s, art museums designed by prominent architects grew in stature and boldness of design, with the High Museum of Art in Atlanta (1980–83), designed by Richard Meier, being among the first. It is the most celebrated and recognizable landmark of Modern architecture in Georgia. Set well back from Peachtree Street, a processional ramp leads to the uniquely shaped and unapologetically modern building. Meier's design is an homage to early Modernism, beginning with its pristine white cladding of porcelain enameled tiles mimicking the white exteriors of early International Style buildings. The ticket-lobby pavilion to the right of the ramp references Le Corbusier's signature ribbon window and abstract "pilotis" columns, while its undulating shape is reminiscent of Alvar Aalto's Paimio (Finland) Sanatorium reception pavilion. At the center, the projecting angular fins radiating from the semicircular facade evoke Le Corbusier's unbuilt design for the League of Nations building. Despite its complexity, a rational logic guides the composition, with the theater rising to the left, the lobby atrium in the middle, and galleries at right. Inside, ramps line the curving edge of the quarter circle–shaped atrium leading to the various galleries that form an L wrapping around the space. Both the ramps and the radiating ribs in the skylight above reference Wright's Guggenheim atrium. In 2000–2005, Renzo Piano authored a respectful expansion of Meier's building, doubling the museum's size and adding a mid-block piazza linking the High with the neighboring Woodruff Arts Center. A new museum entrance from the piazza, leading into a tall, spacious lobby, has replaced the more dramatic original entry.

Savannah joined the art museum building craze that followed the 1997 opening of Frank Gehry's famed Guggenheim Museum in Bilbao, Spain. In 1998 the Telfair Museum of Art, the oldest art museum in the South (established 1883), selected Moshe Safdie from among five internationally recognized architectural firms invited to submit ideas for a new building. The resulting Jepson Center for the Arts, completed in 2006 and located on a site near but separate from the Telfair, illustrates the continued vitality of Late Modernism. In contrast to most art museums, like the High, that push their sculptural massing outward on an open site, the Jepson respects the city's historic grid, shifting the sculptural drama

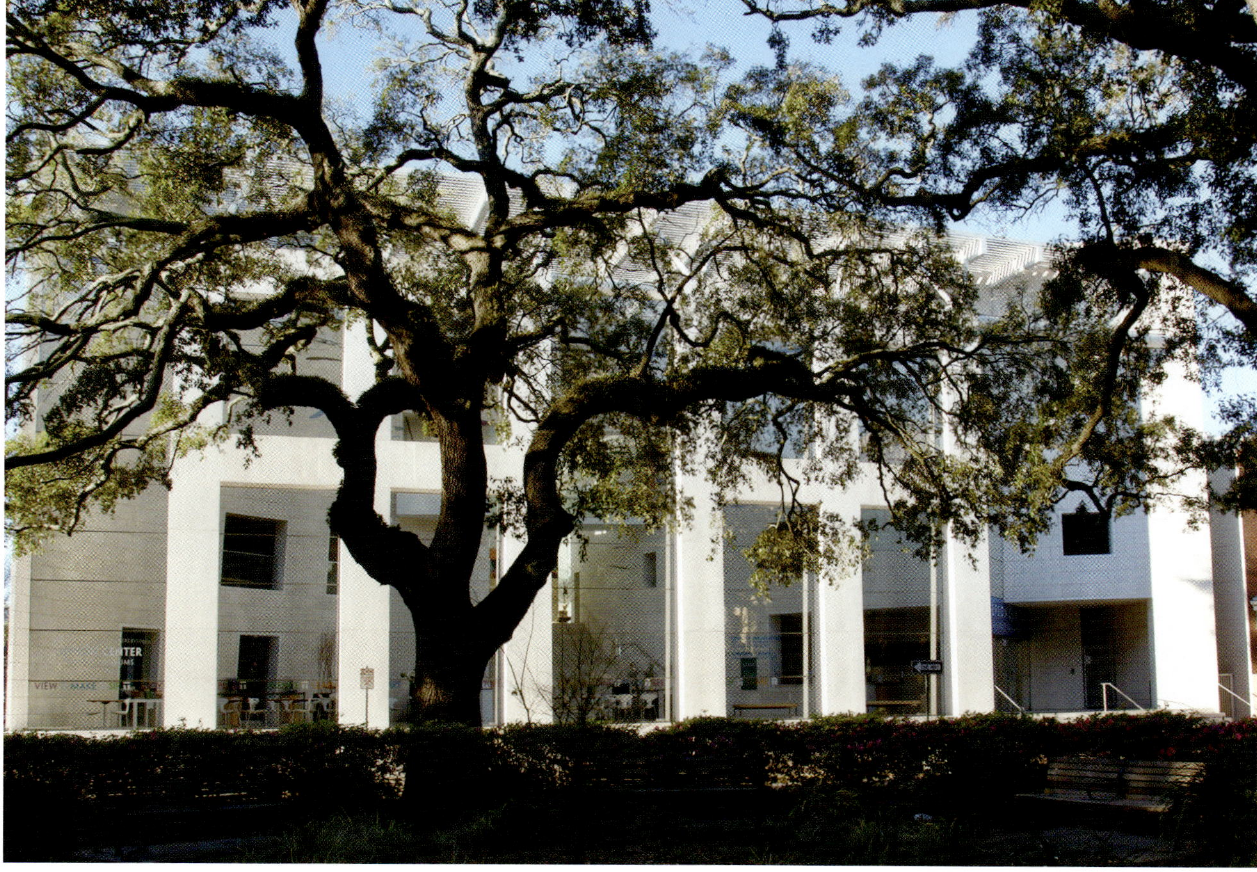

Jepson Center, Savannah

to the interior. Straddling parts of two city blocks, the building frames a grand staircase that cleverly disguises the connecting bridge that narrows between the opposing large convex masses of galleries and offices. Both the flat exterior and curving interior walls are clad with light-colored Portuguese limestone, while the louvered ceiling casts dynamic shadows on the various interior surfaces, further animating the spaces. Local opposition to completely glass north and south facades resulted in the addition of the rectangular concrete structures, which evoke the scale of nearby buildings and provide a tangible sense of enclosure for the light-filled atrium facing Telfair Square. Large exterior steps beneath these frames provide seating for pedestrians taking in the city's famed urbanism.

Postmodernism

Disillusionment with the universalizing tendencies and anonymous qualities of the International Style and its Modernist variants inspired incisive critiques beginning in the early 1960s. The designs of Louis Kahn illustrated how embracing the timeless qualities of classical architecture and a sense of solid monumentality could be combined with Modernism. More outspoken in his repudiation of Modernism was Robert Venturi, who responded to Mies van der Rohe's famous aphorism "Less is more" with the retort "Less is a bore." His designs championed a sense of surprise (what he called contradiction), complexity, individuality, and a connection to history. His 1973 book, *Learning from Las Vegas*, coauthored with Denise Scott Brown and Steven Izenour, drew attention to popular culture as a source of inspiration, to the value of applied ornament on buildings, and to the merits of architectural symbolism. Beginning in the 1960s, Postmodernism referenced the past and a sense of context in ways that ranged from earnest to whimsical.

Possibly the first manifestation of Postmodernism in Georgia, the Lominack House in downtown Savannah was designed in 1973 by local architect Jerry Lominack for himself and his wife. Among the first new houses erected in downtown Savannah since the 1920s, it was forced to sit back from the street by suburban-oriented zoning codes, thus deviating from the pattern of sidewalk-hugging row houses around it. The use of abstracted traditional forms—cylindrical and rectangular masses and numerous diagonal wall-ends evoking gables that frame small sections of steeply sloping standing-seam copper roofs—represents an attempt, typical of Postmodern architecture, to create a sense of place. The Lawrence P. Klamon House in Atlanta, designed in 1985 by Kemp Mooney of the firm Surber, Barber and Mooney, illustrates the Postmodern love of exaggeration, with its over-scaled Palladian arch entry and inflated arched dormer window. In Atlanta, the Postmodern style mostly impacted skyscrapers, with Philip Johnson and John Burgee's One Atlantic Center (colloquially, the IBM Tower; 1985–87) being both the first and the most successful example, its sober Gothic exterior and playfully and colorfully classical lobby reflecting the sense of contradiction espoused by Robert Venturi.

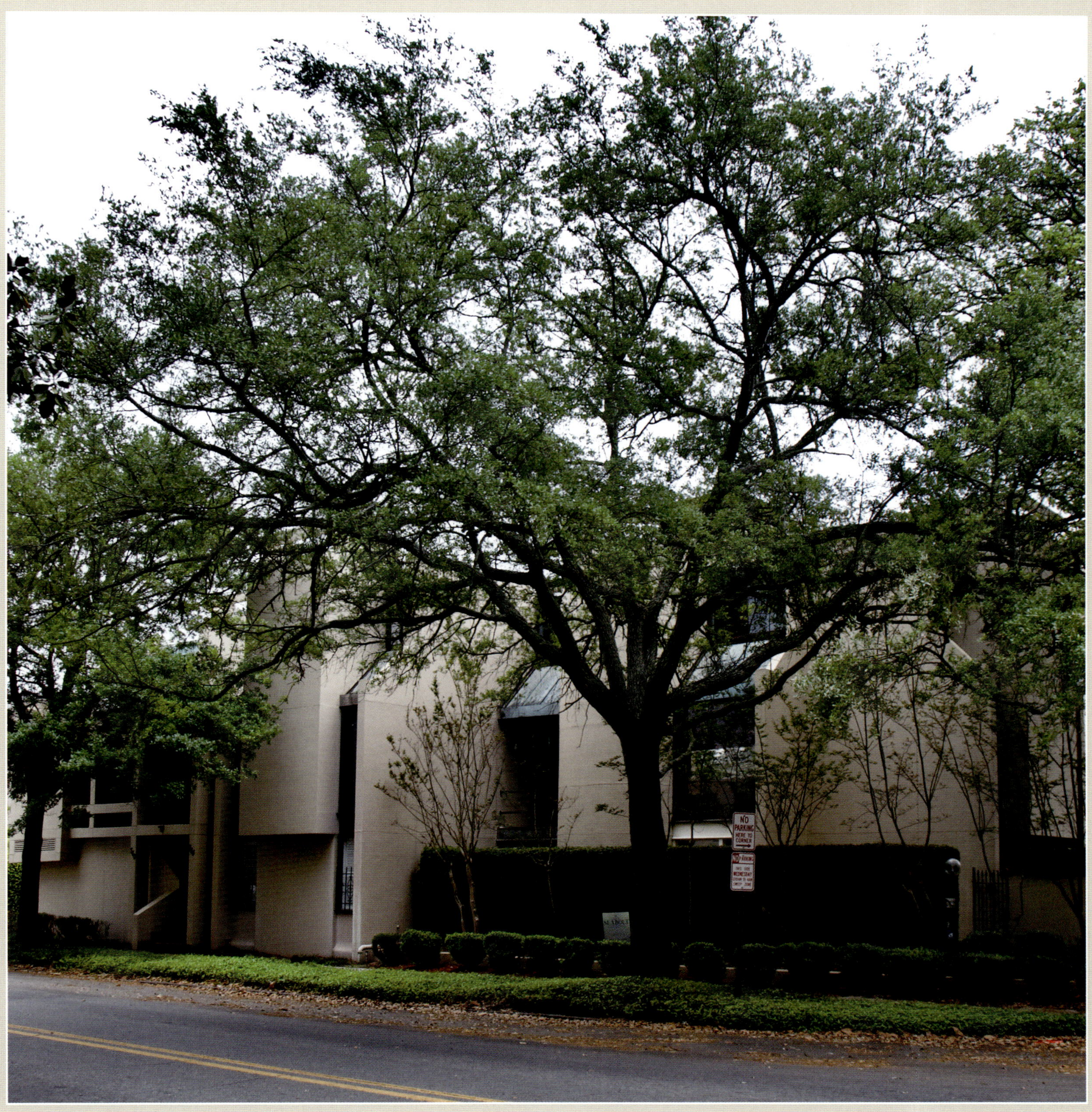

Lominack House, Savannah

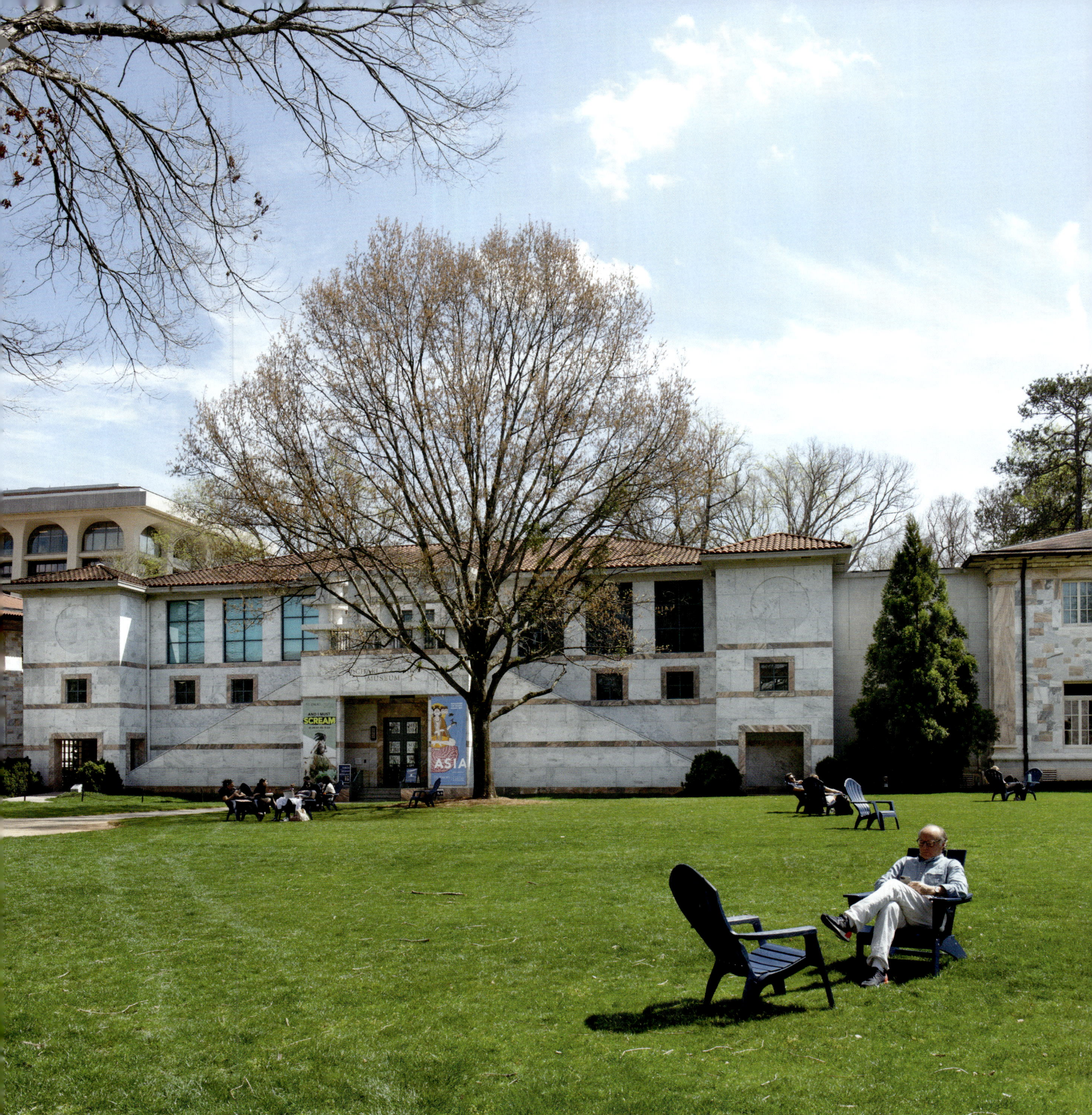

Carlos Museum, Emory University, Atlanta

Shortly after completing his controversial and iconic Portland Building in Portland, Oregon, leading Postmodern architect Michael Graves was commissioned in 1984 to adapt the Lamar Law School, one of the venerable Renaissance style buildings on the Emory University quadrangle, into facilities for the fine art and archeology departments and the newly established Michael C. Carlos Museum. His highly sensitive remodeling of the building's interior included simplified classical forms, strategic use of color, and stenciling of ancient floor plans related to the artifacts on display. Based on its success, Emory commissioned Graves in 1993 to author an expansion, an infill project occupying the only vacant part of the quadrangle, which guided the height, massing, and grey and peach marble materiality of the new building. Its projecting main entrance pavilion is flanked by the triangular outline of staircases evoking a classical pediment, leading to a balcony above the entrance. A vaguely Egyptian set of abstracted columns divided by three horizontal stone lintels defines the balcony and, along with the heavily framed square windows, signals the building's Postmodern vintage. The entrance is aligned with the ramp leading to the Cannon Chapel across the quadrangle, forming a strong cross axis that enhances the space's classical character. The balcony frame is echoed on the rear facade atop a simpler entrance pavilion pierced by a dramatic triangular opening in front of the door.

Responses to Postmodernism: Deconstructivism and Neotraditionalism

By the late 1980s Postmodernism evolved into other design approaches that furthered the goal of achieving a sense of place. Deconstructivism replaced historical references with various forms of expressionism, in which architects explore the complex relationships of a building with its site by fragmenting the traditional composition of a building. The movement ranged from the theoretically charged works of Peter Eisenman to the visual drama of undulating metallic shapes with Frank Gehry. This movement has had little impact on Georgia, with the designs of Scogin, Elam, and Bray, being rare examples. Their branch libraries are particularly notable, including the Clayton County Headquarters Library in Jonesboro (completed 1988), Carol Cobb Turner Branch Library in Morrow (completed 1991), and, most celebrated, their Buckhead Branch Library in Atlanta, completed in 1989. The fragmenting of forms is most concentrated at the entry, evoking the energy and dynamism of the rapidly changing suburban area. Angled planes of various shapes provide shelter for both cars and pedestrians and weave between metal frameworks suggestive of incomplete construction. Inside, a low entrance opens above the circulation desk with a large circular skylight in the ceiling exposing the building's steel frame and brightening this important node. Beyond, the building calms in a manner well suited to the perusing of shelves. At the far end of the building, in the tradition of Beaux Arts processional planning, is the serene reading area set in front of a large window wall providing plenty of light and views of the city.

Neotraditionalism, related to Postmodernism but with a sincere and unironic embrace of traditional architectural styles and forms, saw its most vocal advocates among New Classical architects who found their voices in the 1960s, with Allan Greenberg emerging as one of the movement's American leaders. While most examples of Neotraditionalism are residential, Greenberg's The News Building in Athens (1988–92) vividly illustrates its possibilities for a commercial building. Unapologetically historicist in character, the building nonetheless takes some liberties with the baseless Greek Doric order by removing its fluting. Greenberg uses ornament on the facade sparingly and strategically, with the antefixes on the pediment prominently giving the building a Greek silhouette—appropriate in a city named Athens. Inside, by contrast, vibrant colors adorn the various classical details in the column-filled atrium.

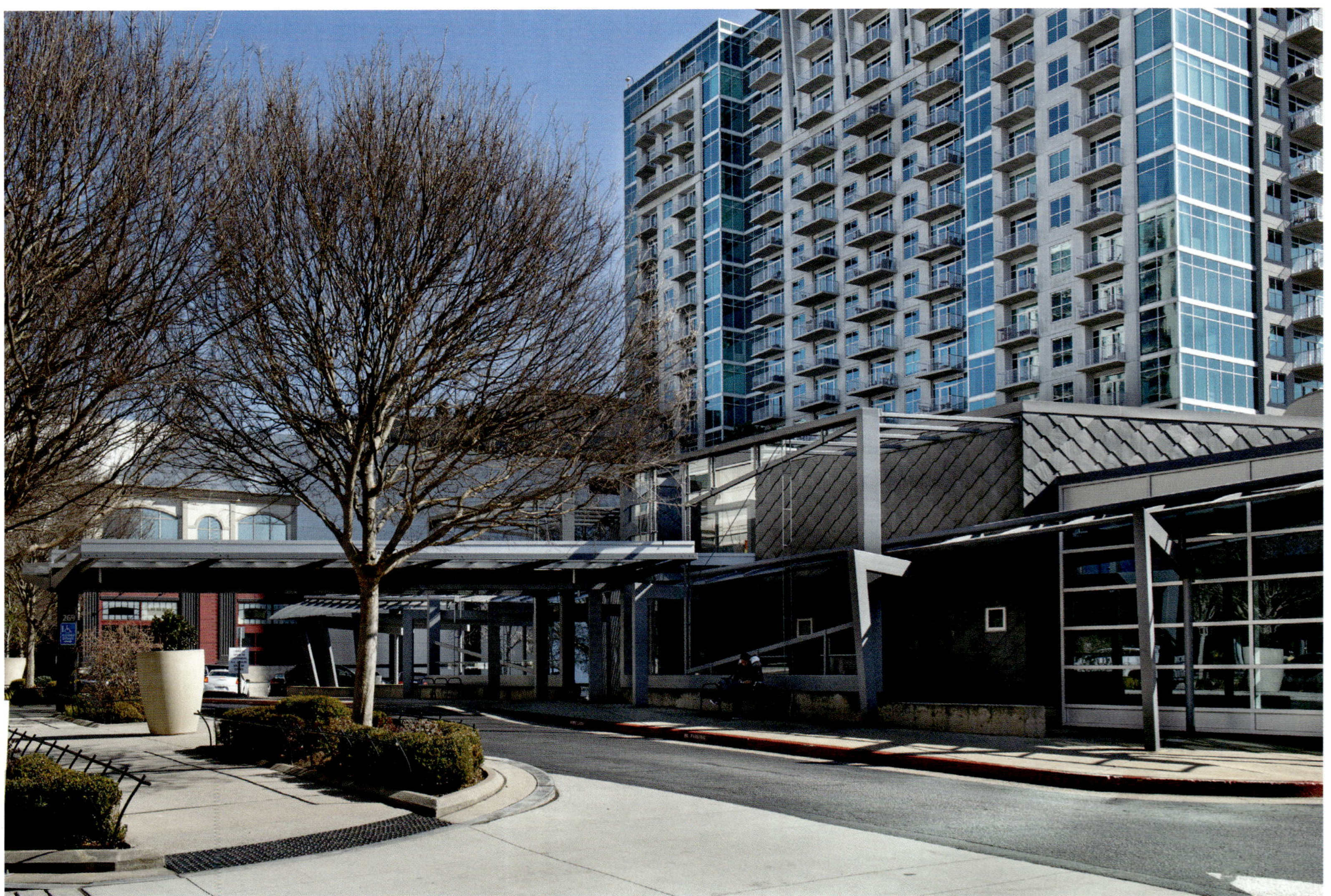

Buckhead Branch Library, Atlanta

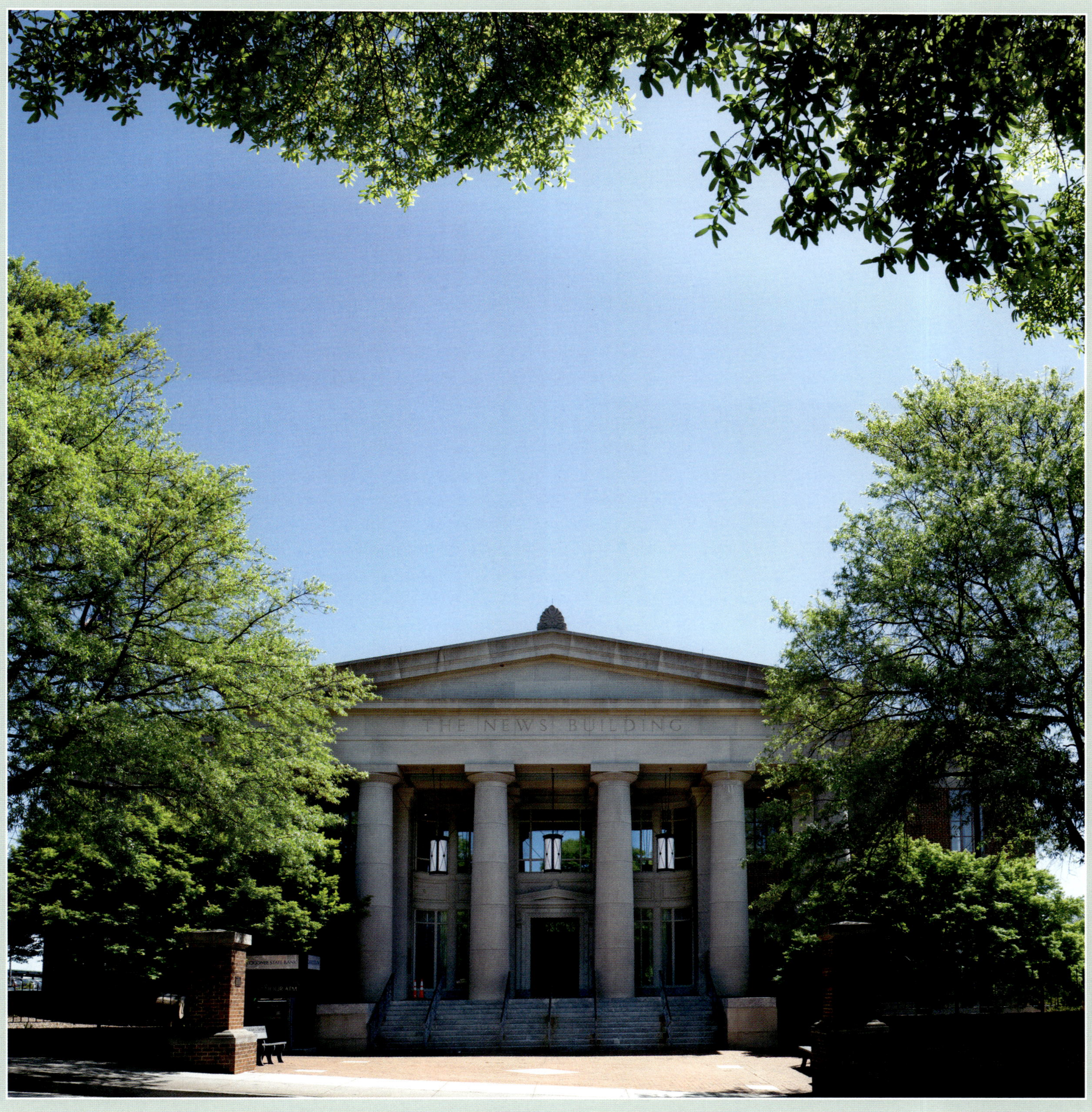

The News Building, Athens

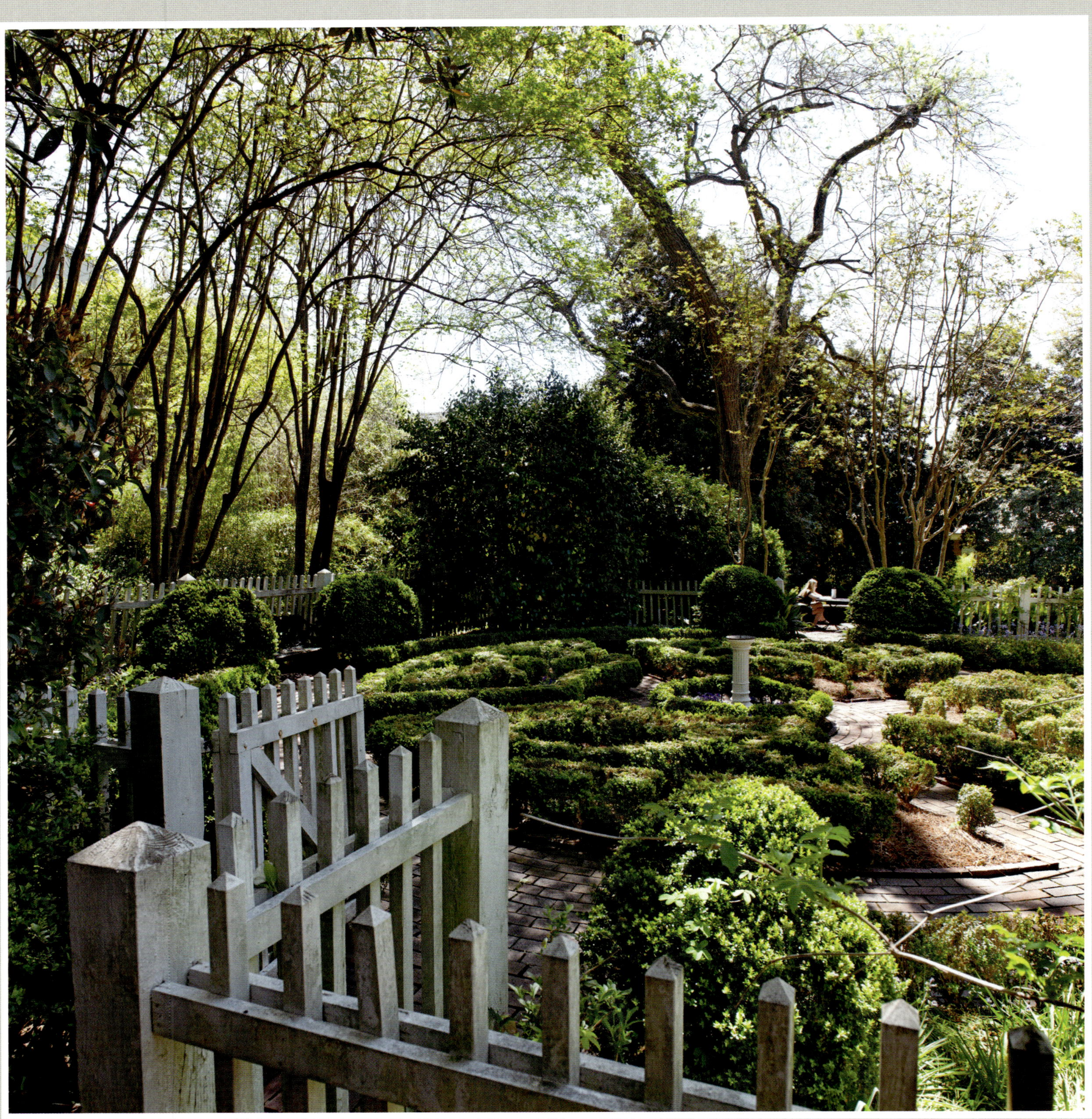

VI. Georgia's Historic Landscapes

SPENCER TUNNELL

GEORGIA, THE THIRTEENTH COLONY, founded in part to protect South Carolina from the feared predation of the Spanish, boasts a long and storied history of notable developments in the fields of landscape architecture, urban planning, and agricultural landscapes.

Georgia's horticultural heritage, springing from the travels of William Bartram and, before him, Hernando de Soto, shook the Old World with newly "discovered" flowers and plants, long known to Indigenous peoples of Georgia but mysterious and exotic to those in Britain and on the Continent.

Historians of cultural landscapes have broken the field into component parts:

- designed landscapes
- ethnographic landscapes
- historic sites
- vernacular landscapes

There is substantial overlap of these categories. For example, there are historic sites that are important designed landscapes. There are vernacular landscapes that include ethnographic components as well as historic sites. The bulk of the landscapes included herein are of a variety of scales and uses, with many reasons for inclusion. In each essay, there is a description of the landscape itself, a brief overview of its history, and a discussion of its significance. The preservation of the landscapes and gardens that follow may well include a pattern of urban development, as with the squares of Savannah, but beauty often has as much to do with the persistence and preservation of these important places as age or any other criteria.

The predominant category of landscapes treated here are designed landscapes. This is in part because Georgia began its colonial existence as the utopian dream of a social reformer. Despite the present association of Georgia, Atlanta, and the word "sprawl," this term did not apply to the state from its inception. Georgia

Facing: Founders' Memorial Garden, University of Georgia, Athens

did not surpass a population of five million until well after 1960. The Atlanta metropolitan region accounts for over seven million today. Our landscape heritage in this, the largest state east of the Mississippi, is of designed and carefully planned coastal cities as well as carefully constructed and stewarded plantations and farms. This continued following the Civil War, with carefully designed and crafted suburbs, parks, and estates.

The Savannah Plan

The Savannah Plan

The very name "Savannah" conjures images in most everyone's mind. Of all U.S. cities, it has been hailed as the best planned. It has been celebrated as a city whose plan has never been bettered, and with regret that it has not been replicated. Its tree-lined avenues and regular pattern of squares enveloped by moss-draped trees charm residents and visitors alike. Of all Savannah's attractions, the most beloved are its squares.

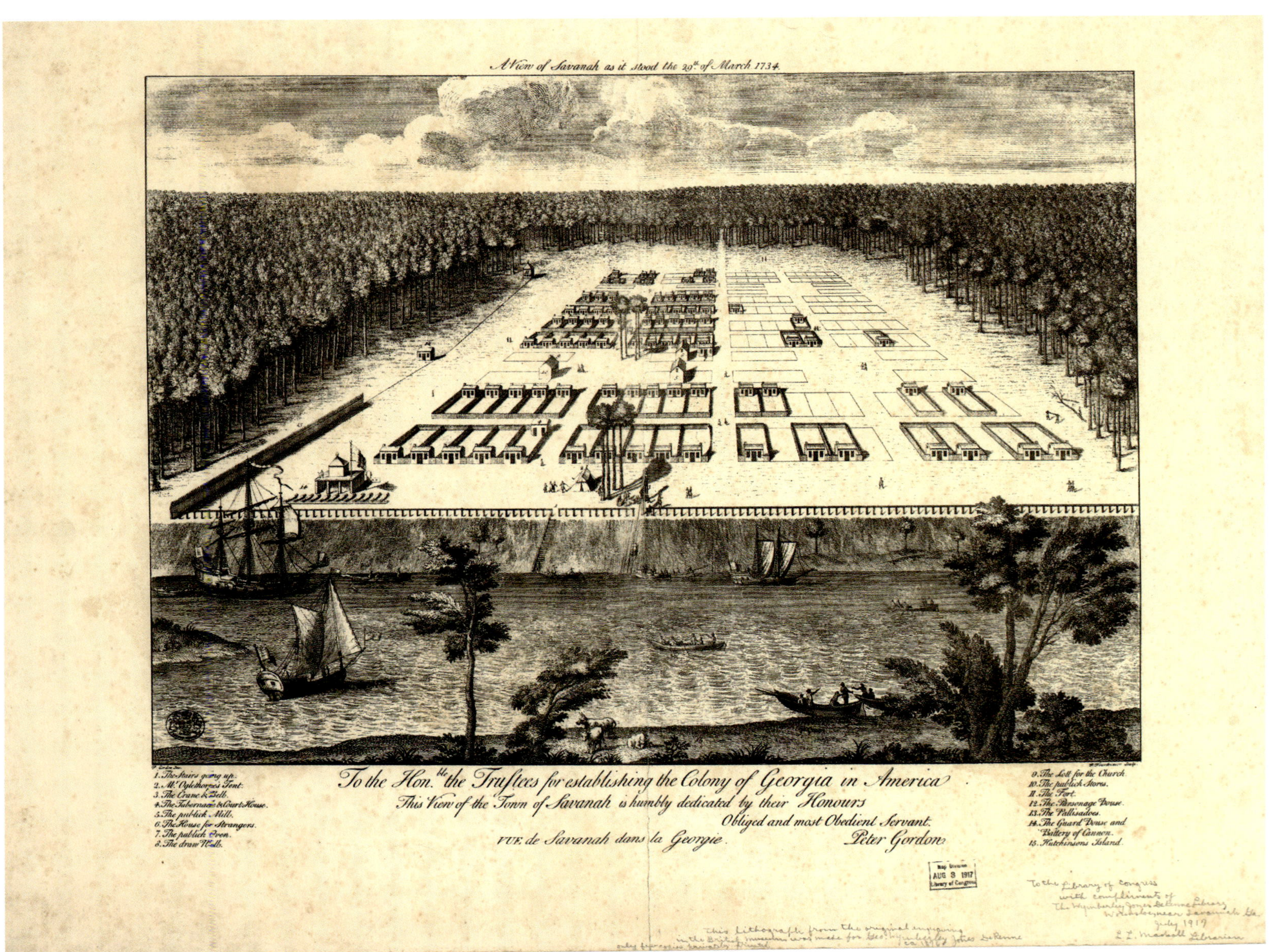

Two generations after the 1666 fire that devastated London, General James Oglethorpe was out to plan not just a new city, but a utopian community in the New World. With the modest start of a grid of four squares in 1734, the city plan had grown to include twenty-four squares by 1855. Though Oglethorpe left little evidence of his inspiration, Philadelphia had been founded in 1682 and featured a rational grid of streets and four public squares, and tracings of elements within the various plans for rebuilding central London after the fire appear in Oglethorpe's work, particularly in the plan by Richard Newcourt, which featured fifty-five square units that are the most reminiscent of Savannah's system of wards.

Oglethorpe's utopian dream of an egalitarian community free of enslaved peoples would not survive, but the power and beauty of his plan has continued to inspire replication since its inception. The initial squares were used for a variety of purposes, including the marshalling of local militia, but through 1855 the popularity of Oglethorpe's ward system was recognized, honored, and respected. Except for Philadelphia, which offers but four squares, no other colonial town shows the thoughtful and enlightened planning exhibited by Savannah, much less the breadth of vision of twenty-four squares.

Each ward contained a central square, forty lots for the construction of dwelling units to the north and south, and four trust lots to the east and west that were reserved for communal uses such as churches, civic buildings, and the like. A street grid system separated these tracts and included lanes to the rear of the dwellings. These lanes have proved remarkably resilient and are today utilized for utility lines, trash collection, access, and other uses, thereby reducing these elements in the streetscape.

Oglethorpe's vision was of a sustainable community, essential for an outpost as remote as Savannah. Each settler was offered a city lot as well as 5 acres for a garden and an additional 40 acres outside of town. The Civil War put a halt to further expansion of the plan, and the rhythm of Oglethorpe's vision was varied as the city rebounded after that war. During the Depression, male civic leaders proposed paving the city squares and extending streets through them to make traffic flow more easily. Presumably, this "improvement" would address the financial calamity. Women of the community stood firm and led the fight to preserve the squares, and many were renovated by landscape architect Georges Bignault. Further work was done on five of the squares by Clermont Lee, the first woman licensed to practice landscape architecture in Georgia.

Many urban planners of renown would affirm the observation of Edmund Bacon in his book *The Design of Cities*: "It is amazing that a colony, struggling against the most elemental problems of survival in a wilderness, should be able to produce a plan so exalted that it remains as one of the finest diagrams for city organization and growth in existence."

Forsyth Park

Forsyth Park occupies 30 acres of Savannah's historic district and represents a decided and visceral break with the traditional rhythm of squares in this planned city. The park is generally flat, characterized by large live oaks, an important fountain, and broad open fields to either side of a central axis or pedestrian promenade.

Forsyth Park is the last park built in the South prior to the Civil War, and it completed, in some ways, the vision that Oglethorpe held for the city he founded, as it fulfilled the function of a city commons that he had conceived. Whereas the relatively small squares held as their focus the wards they served, the city lacked a large park, a communal gathering place. While the commons—land held in common by the citizens of a community for general purposes or for grazing—was a well-established tradition in the North, except for the squares established by Oglethorpe or the central green of Williamsburg, commonly held land of any size was an unusual feature in a Southern city.

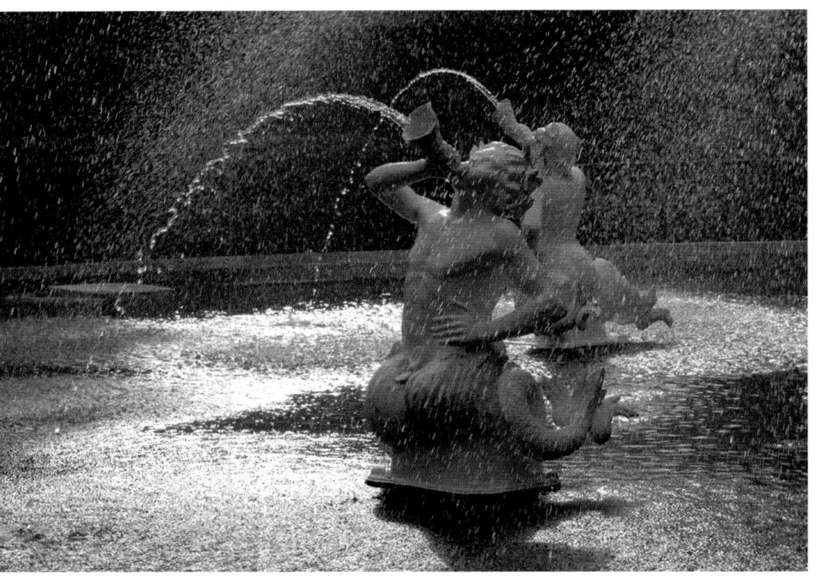

Forsyth Park, Savannah

The earliest part of Forsyth Park was conceived in the early 1840s by scholar, linguist, and sometime diplomat William Hodgson. The park was initially only 10 acres, the size of an entire traditional Savannah ward. In 1851 the park was expanded by the addition of approximately 20 acres and named in honor of Georgia governor John Forsyth. The cast-iron fountain was paid for by donations from Savannahians, who were urged to contribute to make their city more cosmopolitan. The fountain is, in fact, a piece that was not custom designed but a casting by Janes, Beebe, and Company, with other castings from Poughkeepsie, New York; Madison, Indiana; and, oddly, Cuzco, Peru. There is a fitting link to the Peruvian installation, as Hodgson served the United States as a diplomat negotiating relations with the then new Peru-Bolivian Confederation.

The initial design was by Bavarian landscape gardener William Bischoff. Bischoff was the royal court gardener at the Nymphenburg Palace when he came to visit his daughter in Savannah. The designs at Nymphenburg reflect a geometrical precision reminiscent of André Le Nôtre's Versailles but also his later work for Marie Antoinette in Le Petit Hammeau, the English-garden section of the palace grounds. Bischoff remained in and around Savannah for some years and returned to Germany after the outbreak of the Civil War in 1861.

Over its 180-year history, Forsyth Park has retained its place of honor and dignity in Savannah. It relates strongly to the grid pattern of the city while breaking with its historic design pattern and signaling the birth of a new city, a postwar city. Forsyth Park retains the essential components of the great urban parks of the world. That it was conceived and built in Savannah prior to a Civil War that would upend its city's economy is testament to the place the park already held in the hearts and minds of the citizens of Savannah and the role it plays in one of America's best planned and most livable cities.

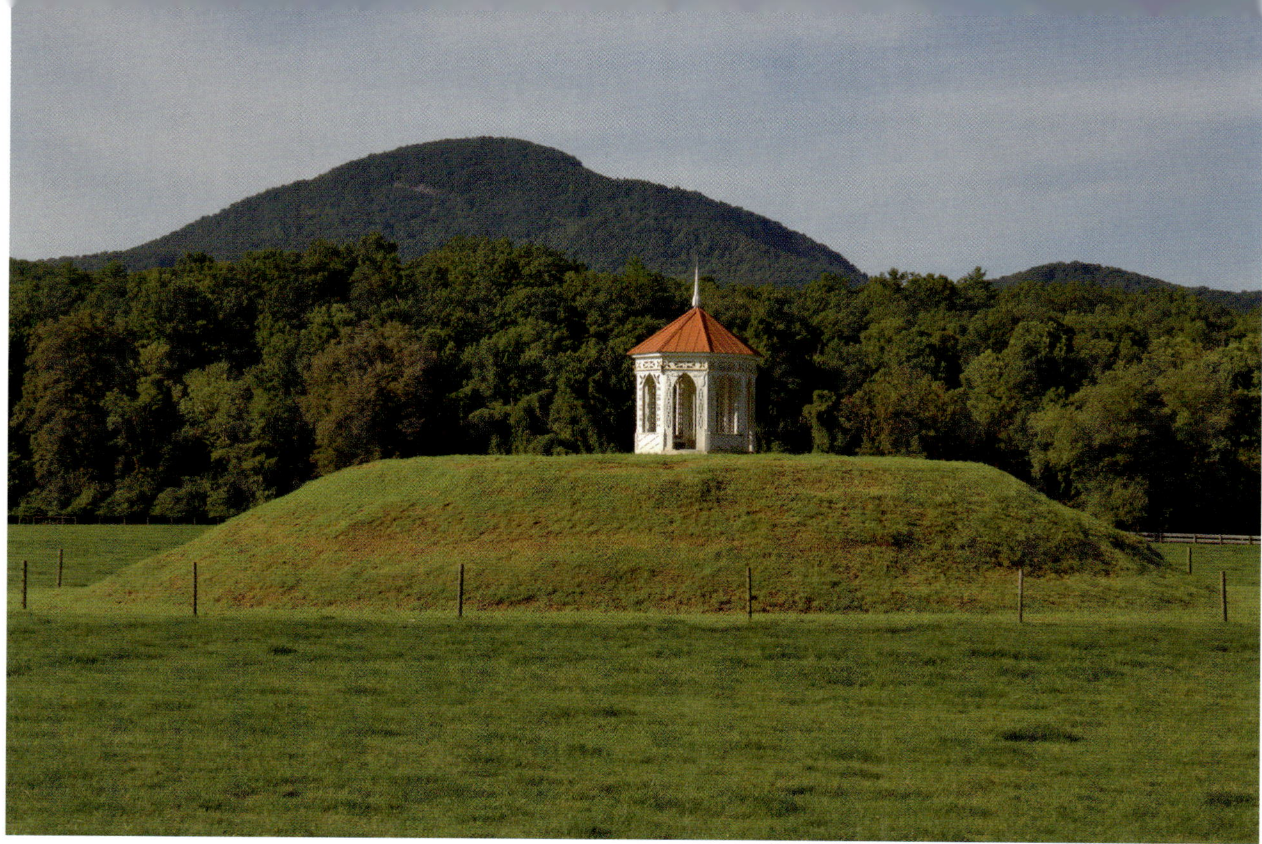

Sautee-Nacoochee Valley Landscape

Sautee-Nacoochee Valley

Georgia is one of the most rapidly developing states in the nation. In a state that for so long was associated with the "rural," the preservation of agricultural land for any purpose at all would have been considered . . . quaint! Other parts of the country, because of their scarcity of open space, have seemed to lead the way in this type of landscape preservation.

The Sautee-Nacoochee Valley is an area of largely undeveloped agricultural land comprising approximately 10 square miles in North Georgia listed in the National Register of Historic Places and recognized for its archeological, architectural, and scenic resources. The area defined as the most significant lies beneath the 1,400 feet elevation contour along the river valleys. A preservation study and subsequent scenic easements adopted in the early 1980s have assisted with the preservation of the appearance of the valleys and the all-important sense of place.

At the Sautee-Nacoochee Valley the entire context for these rural properties has been addressed holistically, and an effort has been made to acquire easements *before* the escalation of property values would have made such a process all but impossible. The gentle beauty of the Sautee-Nacoochee Valley is much as it has been for the past one hundred years and, because of the forward-thinking actions of the community, it is likely to remain so for the next hundred years and beyond.

The Sautee-Nacoochee Valley has been important since long before the first contact the Indigenous peoples had with settlers of European descent. The valley was first used by animal populations in their migratory routes from the Piedmont and Coastal Plain to the grasslands of present-day Tennessee and Kentucky; Indigenous populations followed these animal migratory routes, and they established such communities as Little Chota in the area.

By 1828 gold had been discovered, though extraction methods were crude and inefficient. Canals were dug to facilitate the transport of ore. Hydraulic mining was underway by 1858. By the end of the nineteenth century, the area in the foothills of the Appalachians fostered summer homes of the wealthy from the coastal areas. The timber industry had been established in the region from the early nineteenth century, but by the twentieth century any remaining stands of virgin timber had been removed. The slowdown of economic activity during the Great Depression hit the valley as it did the rest of the nation. During this period, rural electrification came to the area, and early and important archeological surveys were made.

Threats to the preservation of the rural and scenic character of the valley were first noted as Helen was reworked as an ersatz Alpine village in 1970. Unicoi State Park, in the county, was an important and carefully designed facility developed as the recreational aspects of the area were coming into focus. Moves to preserve the character of the valley were championed by local landowners, and local son and landscape architect Allen Stovall prepared the plan, which was largely adopted, to assist with purchase of scenic easements to preserve the rural character of the Valley.

Olmsted Linear Park–Druid Hills

Atlanta's Druid Hills neighborhood is home to a roadway and park designed by the father of American landscape architecture, and it is a miracle indeed that more than 120 years after construction, this road and 45-acre park are a place that its designer would still recognize.

The Olmsted Linear Park is the central organizing feature of the last residential suburban design of Frederick Law Olmsted Sr., and it represents the historic rehabilitation of seven park segments designed and planned by Olmsted and his firm between 1892 and 1905. Six of the park segments have a pastoral feeling—greensward, shrub borders, and shade trees—while one is largely a hardwood forest on steeply sloping terrain.

Atlanta engineer and entrepreneur Joel Hurt (1850–1927) assembled the roughly 1,400 acres that became Druid Hills between 1890 and 1892. Hurt engaged Olmsted in what became the last residential subdivision designed by the father of American landscape architecture. Olmsted's vision of large lots on the principal roadway flew in the face of conventional wisdom, which held that a greater number of smaller lots would generate more revenue. Olmsted maintained that larger lots along the principal thoroughfare would attract the high net-worth individuals who would solidify the popularity of the subdivision and ensure the sale of other, smaller lots. Hurt was concerned about the amount of land removed from the saleable acreage as well as the cost to develop that land into parks.

The financial panic of 1893 slowed design to a stop. The layout and grading drawings for Ponce de Leon Avenue that would shape the grades for the parkland and guide the layout for the electric railroad incorporated into the edge

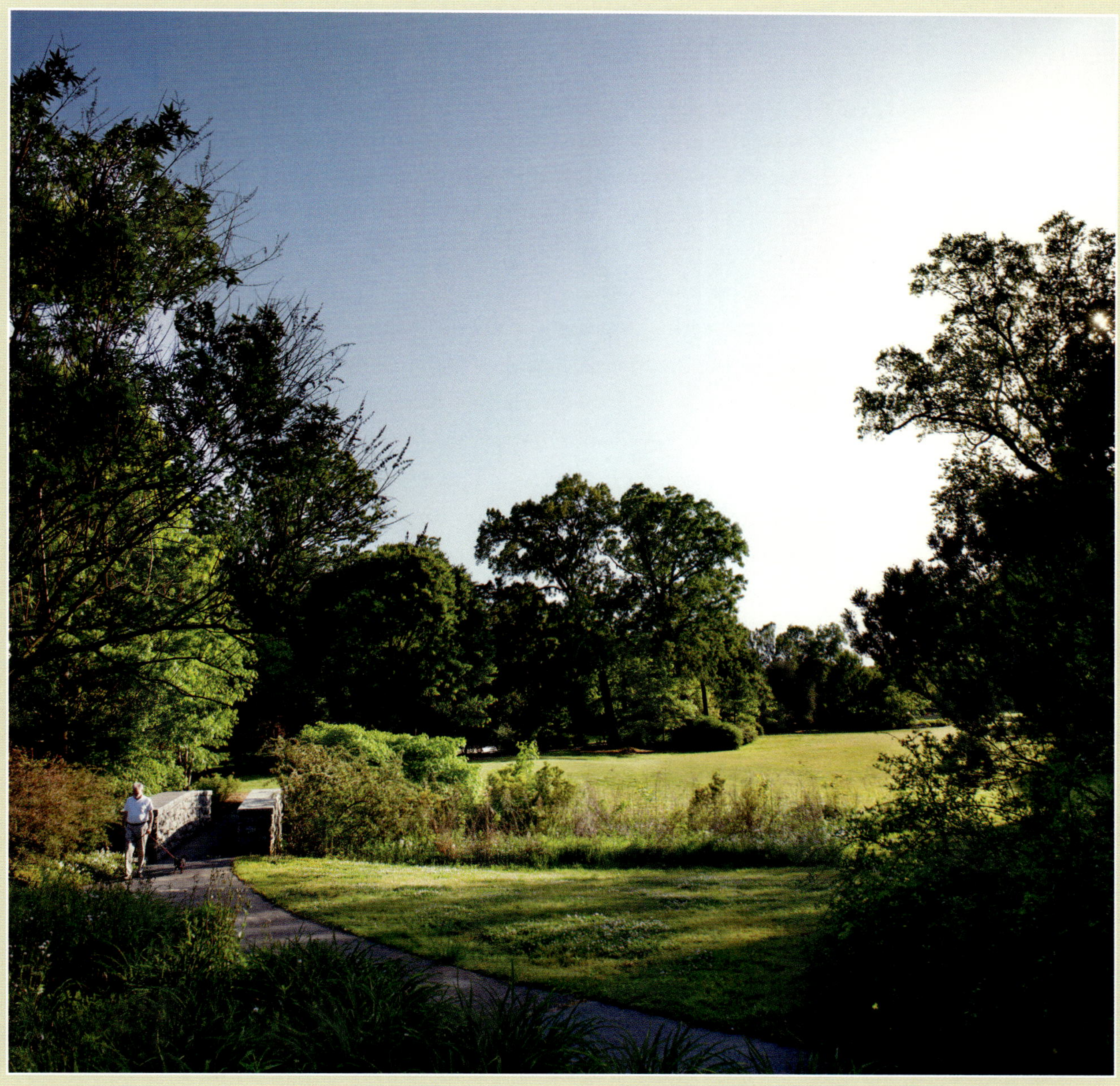

Olmsted Linear Park,
Druid Hills, Atlanta

of the park were all prepared and waiting for the right time for construction to move forward. By 1901, after Olmsted had retired, construction was underway for the roadways. In 1908, Hurt sold the entire property to Asa Candler for $500,000, the largest real estate transaction in Georgia's history at that time. Candler continued with the Olmsted plan, implementing much of it with the engineer on the ground who had been working with the Olmsted firm.

A highway planned by the Georgia Department of Transportation connecting Stone Mountain to downtown Atlanta threatened to demolish the woodland park (25-acre Deepdene Park) and defile other park segments. Speculation about such a dark future limited the amount residents would spend on their property for improvements, and upkeep and neglect began to show. The highway design changed over the years, but its continued presence on the state's drawing boards represented a very real threat for over twenty-five years. Even today, with the highway dream now gone, threats to the park and historic road remain, with whispers of widened roads or roundabouts, the latter an element not unknown in Olmsted designed communities, but never considered a part of this design. In 1975, the park and parkway were listed in the National Register of Historic Places. The neighborhood and park received the protection of the Atlanta Urban Design Commission's Historic Atlanta zoning and a similar designation from unincorporated DeKalb County, providing a measure of protection from design changes that could adversely affect the park.

Neighborhood activists worked persistently and doggedly for the defeat of the proposed highway and for the ultimate compromise that created Freedom Park and the Presidential Parkway. With that constant threat eliminated, work on the park began in 1995 with a master plan for its rehabilitation. Implementation began in 1998. The Georgia Trust awarded the park rehabilitation its Marguerite Williams Award for Excellence in Preservation in 2012. The path system Olmsted envisioned, along with plantings of trees and shrubs to help direct views and frame vistas, has been realized, and now new generations are living with and loving this park at the very heart of an important historic neighborhood.

At Druid Hills, the integration of the electric railroad into the parkland was unusual; most trolleys were built in the middle of travel lanes of streets. This improvement represented Olmsted's theory of "the separation of ways"—modes of travel given their own space. The Druid Hills development was designed for the wealthy to live outside the city proper, but within the design was the recognition that Atlanta and the region would grow, and the 22-acre forest preserved by Olmsted's design in 1892 would remain as part of the lungs of the city. Olmsted, first and perhaps foremost, was a social reformer, and the park designed for this suburb continues to function to the community's benefit over a century since it was first constructed.

Piedmont Park

A park of great significance must be many things to many people, and this aptly describes Piedmont Park. Visited by at least three presidents, not including sometime local resident Jimmy Carter, Piedmont Park—together with its progenitor the Cotton States Exposition—has seen many of Atlanta's most significant historical events. Piedmont Park has become what the exposition founders, Frederick Law Olmsted, and many others had hoped it would be: a place where all citizens of Atlanta, and indeed, the world, could come together for recreation in nature.

The 185-acre Piedmont Park in Midtown Atlanta has been the centerpiece of Atlanta's cultural life since its inception. With highpoints offering commanding views of downtown and the low-lying land of Clear Creek, the park is characterized by Olmstedian open spaces, copses of umbrageous shade trees, the lake Clara Meer, sport fields, and recreational facilities. Its location, blocks from Peachtree Street and MARTA public transportation, has added to its popularity. As the Midtown business and residential districts have grown, so too have Piedmont Park's popularity and importance to the city and the region.

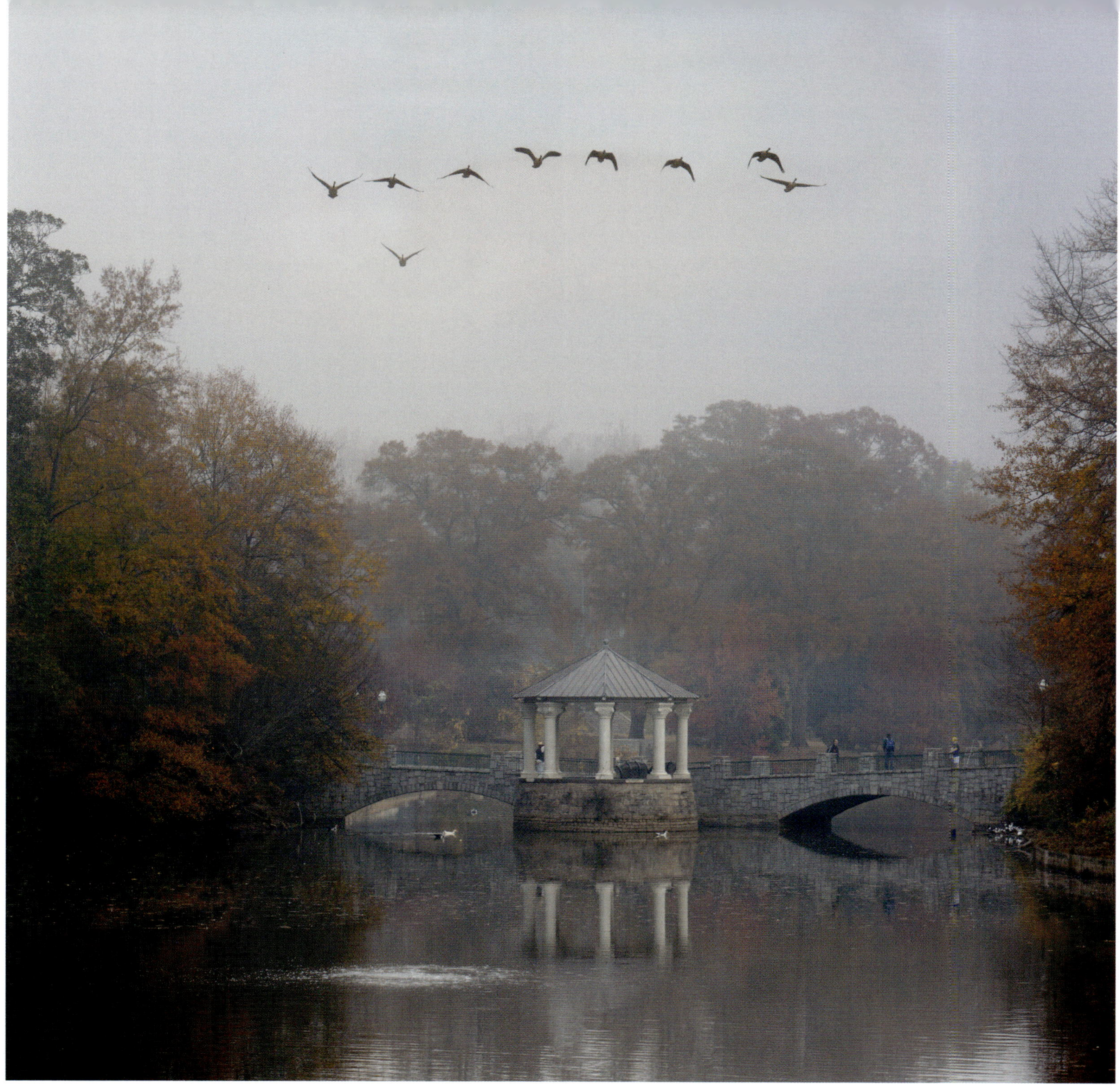

Piedmont Park, Atlanta

Piedmont Park's history as a public open space began with several fairs and exhibitions sponsored and promoted by members of the Gentlemen's Driving Club, now known as the Piedmont Driving Club. The first of these took place in October 1887. Fifty thousand people were present to witness a speech given by President Grover Cleveland. The fair was a financial success, and the organizers, all club members, began planning their next, more ambitious event: the Cotton States and International Exposition of 1895. The exposition was enormously popular and had an impact far beyond Atlanta. The controversial "Atlanta Compromise" on race relations grew out of a speech Booker T. Washington delivered at the exposition on September 18, 1895. Over 800,000 people attended during the ninety-day run— a huge success for a city whose population was only about 90,000.

The popular success of the fair did not assure financial success, and some of the promoters sought to sell the grounds for industrial use. The bulk of the exposition buildings and attractions had been temporary structures and did not survive long after it closed. Three stockholders bought up the company stock and held it until 1904, when the city finally purchased the land for Piedmont Park for $90,000. The Olmsted Brothers firm developed a master plan that modified the fairgrounds into a public park inspired by the Olmstedian vision of carefully crafted open spaces, curvilinear walks and drives, and up-to-the-minute engineering subordinated to the pictorial composition. Many aspects of this plan have been implemented slowly, over time, and remain—the paved pedestrian circulation system being the most obvious. Other elements have been built in ways the Olmsted Brothers could never have imagined, such as the Modernist Noguchi Playground, created in 1976 by the Noguchi Foundation and the High Museum of Art.

Since the beginning of the twentieth century, Piedmont Park has continued to deepen its hold on the local imagination and consciousness. Whether hosting the Atlanta Crackers baseball team from 1902 to 1904, offering the city's first public golf course (nine holes), or presenting the Atlanta Dogwood Festival (established 1933), the Atlanta Arts Festival (1954–96), or free concerts by the Allman Brothers and other rockers in the early 1970s, Piedmont Park has continued to thrive and respond to cultural changes. Integrated in the early 1960s, the park has hosted Atlanta Gay Pride and since 1978 has been the site of the finish line for the Peachtree Road Race, the largest 10K in the world with over fifty thousand participants.

In 1979 it was clear that a new master plan for Piedmont Park was badly needed. Prepared by landscape architectural firm Laubman and Reed, the plan's major accomplishment was the removal of automobile traffic from within the park boundaries. During this same period, the Atlanta Botanical Garden established its headquarters in a trailer in a maintenance area of Piedmont Park. The garden now comprises about 30 acres of land once within Piedmont Park. Its Fuqua Conservatory commands a prominent view of the park from the site once occupied by the Cotton States Exposition's United States Government building.

Yet another master plan was commissioned by the Piedmont Park Conservancy from design firm Tunnell-Spangler. Olmsted specialist Charles Beveridge was a member of the team. The goal of the master plan was the restoration of the park. The golf course was eliminated, and the open ditch for storm water was finally relocated to underground pipes along with other infrastructure, allowing for the creation of a meadow finally worthy of Olmsted's expectations.

In 2007–8, the Atlanta Botanical Garden and the Piedmont Park Conservancy announced plans to build a multistory parking deck to address the needs for their popular destinations. A land swap, controversial in some quarters, allowed for this new construction and improved access to the northernmost remote corner of the park. The subsequent addition of approximately 50 acres allows for the continued enhancement of the park and its environment.

The Augusta Canal

The preservation of the Augusta Canal provides the city with an important industrial working landscape. The canal is an approximately 13-mile-long waterway paralleling the Savannah River through suburban and downtown Augusta. It is said to be the only canal in the United States in continuous use for its original purposes of providing power, transport, and municipal water. Though many other canals are longer and better known, and though the canal has seen its roles shift and change, it remains an important component of the cityscape of Augusta and the region.

The initial 8.5 miles of the Augusta Canal were constructed between 1845 and 1846 and reached from the head gate structure near the falls on the Savannah River into downtown Augusta. Because of the canal's multiple uses for power, water, and transportation, it was one of the few successful industrial canals in the South. With a dream that Augusta would one day be "the Lowell [Massachusetts] of the South," Henry Cumming was the force behind this ambitious construction project. Soon after the initial construction, a sawmill, a gristmill, and the Augusta Factory (textiles) were completed.

With this significant industrial operation in place, Augusta was economically well positioned for the Civil War. Along the canal, the only permanent structure built by the Confederate States of America was the Powder Works. Much of this complex was demolished after the Civil War, with the brick reused for Sibley Mills. The Powder Works chimney, with its obelisk-like presence, punctuates this canal-side landscape.

Augusta Canal, Augusta

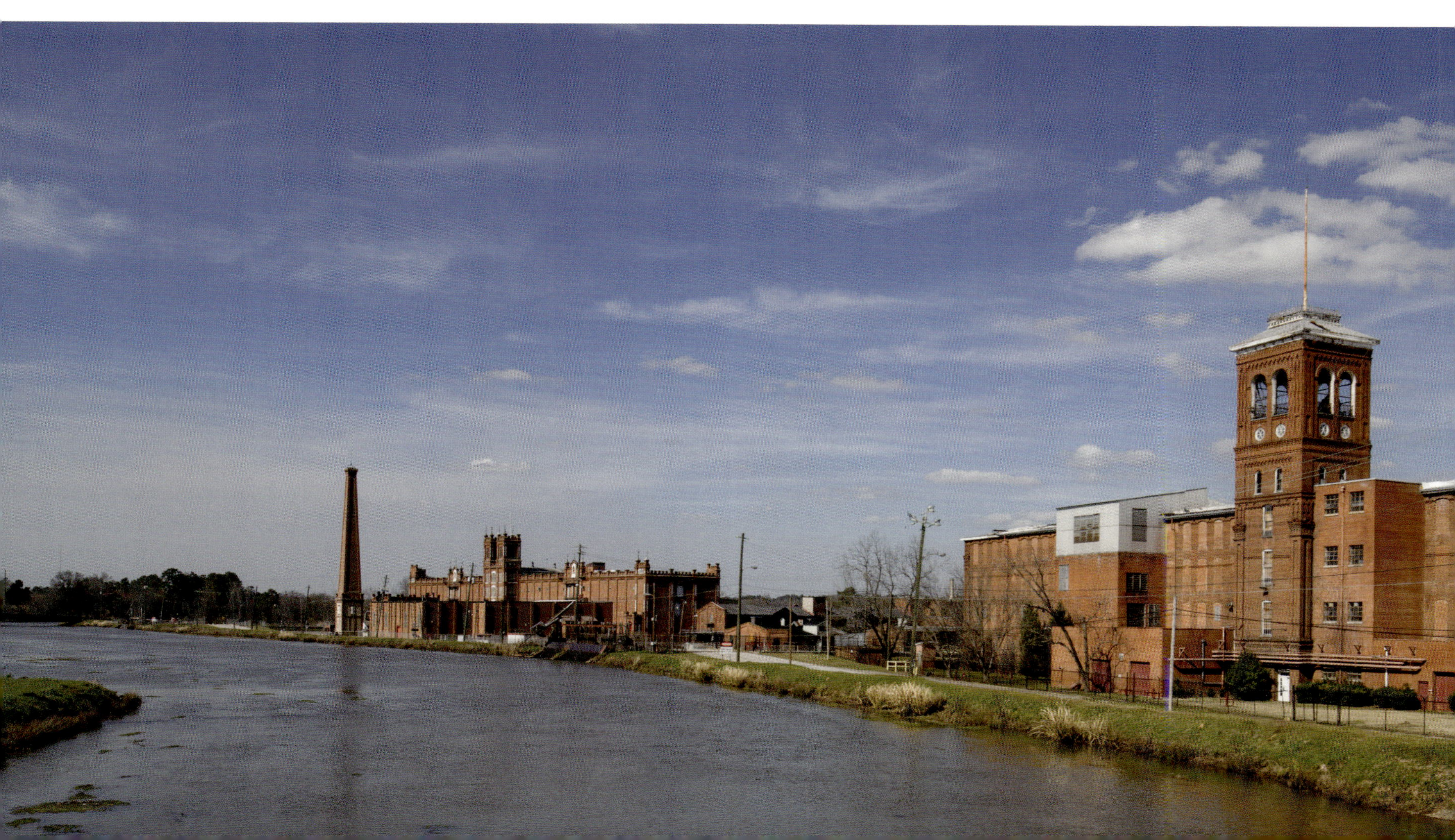

The canal continued to provide its "big three" (water, transportation, and power generation) to Augusta after the Civil War, and it allowed the city to prosper even while other Southern cities stumbled in a new world and new economy. By 1875 the canal was enlarged, and larger new factories built. In the 1890s a new water-pumping station was built along the midcanal area; it is still in use today. Flooding was a perennial problem and finally had to be addressed. The Federal Works Progress Administration made repairs and improvements to the canal in the early 1930s.

By mid-twentieth century the canal had fallen on hard times. Other means to generate electricity were in place, and the textile industry had shifted to other areas. The canal was considered as a route for a major highway, which would have led to it being drained, filled, and paved over. The canal would have been erased as a resource that could live again, as it does today.

The Historic Augusta Canal and Industrial District was listed as a National Historic Landmark in 1977 and named a National Heritage Area in 1996, the first area in Georgia to be so named. The Enterprise Mill along the canal has been opened as an interpretive center; boat tours are offered on the canal; and once-abandoned mills have been converted to offices and residential lofts. And still, after 175 years of continual service, the canal is the principal source of drinking water for the city.

Oak Hill at Berry College

The gardens at Oak Hill and at House o' Dreams are excellent examples of the "Country Place" era of landscape design so prevalent in the early decades of the twentieth century. The gardens were commissioned and built by one of the most influential women in Georgia history, Martha Berry, founder and benefactor of Berry College. The landscape architect for these gardens was Robert Cridland, an influential designer and writer who traveled in the South extensively. A 1932 Garden Club of America Annual Meeting program held in Atlanta listed Cridland as the designer of six of the thirty-eight listed gardens, twice the number of any other landscape architect represented. Cridland had worked for about ten years in the Atlanta area and was one of the best-known landscape architects in the region at the time Berry was modifying the property for her use and developing the college campus. Cridland's writing about landscape design was enormously influential, and he was working for Frederick Vanderbilt at his estate at Hyde Park, New York, while he was also working with Berry. At that time there were few professionally trained landscape architects with full-time design practices in the Southeast.

The gardens at Oak Hill and House o' Dreams are the personal gardens designed and built for Martha Berry between 1927 and 1932. In addition to investing substantial amounts of her own money, Berry was successful in reaching out to and securing donations from Andrew Carnegie, Emily Vanderbilt Hammond, Henry Ford, President Theodore Roosevelt, and Ellen Wilson, Georgia native and first wife of President Woodrow Wilson.

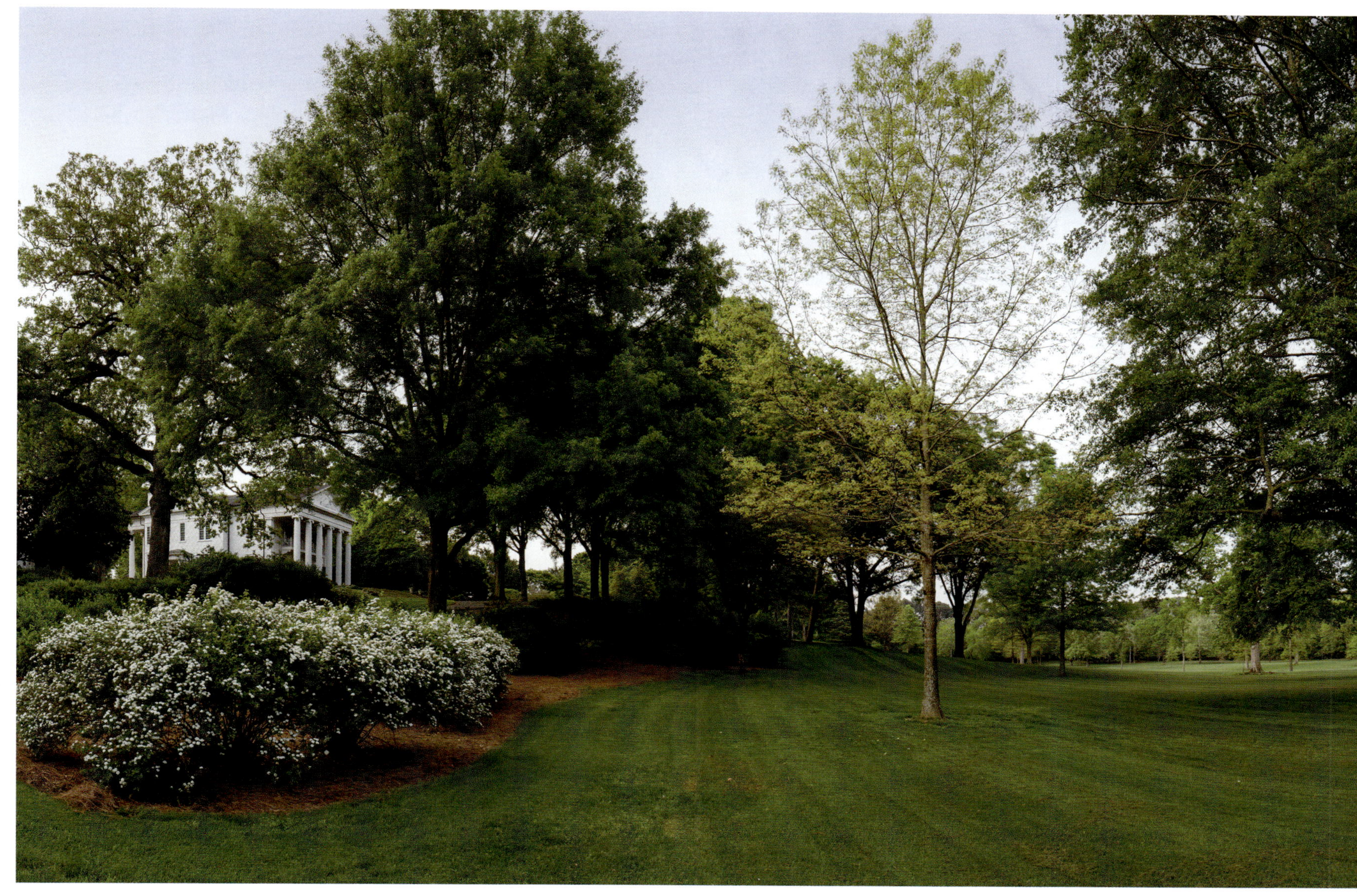

Oak Hill at Berry College, Rome

The Oak Hill complex consists of the 1847 Greek Revival house and the extensive gardens that complement the house. The gardens include a rectangular formal garden, the Goldfish Garden, the Sundial Garden, and the Sunken Garden. Together, these form a significant complement to the house and enhance the estate feeling of this 170-acre property. The House o' Dreams is a retreat created for Martha Berry on a nearby mountaintop within the 30,000-acre campus. This rustic board and batten cabin has a small formal garden built as a complement to that structure. The view of the surrounding valleys and distant mountain peaks in Alabama, Tennessee, and North Carolina makes for an astonishing setting and a welcome counterpoint to the Greek Revival formality of Oak Hill.

In 1923, the House o' Dreams and its garden were constructed for Berry at the pinnacle of Lavender Mountain. The house and garden were an audition, in a way, for the more extensive work that was to come at the Oak Hill complex. Oak Hill had been substantially rebuilt by Thomas Berry (1821–87) following a fire in 1884. Martha Berry bought the property from her siblings in 1927 and deeded it to the Berry Schools, the forerunner of today's Berry College, which she founded in 1902.

The Founders' Memorial Garden

Since its completion in 1946, Founders' Memorial Garden at the University of Georgia has served as an adjunct classroom and studio for the one of the largest and most well-regarded landscape architecture programs in the nation. The garden of 2.5 acres was designed by Hubert Bond Owens in 1939 and has been a central component of the life of the school since it was completed. In serving the first garden club in the United States and as many as fifteen thousand students of landscape architecture over the past seventy-five years, Owens has served the general public of the nation as well.

Founders' Memorial Garden is a series of garden spaces on the north campus of the university. It consists of four primary spaces: a cobblestone entry court, an arboretum of naturalistic plantings, a boxwood parterre garden, and a lawn framed by perennial borders within a serpentine walled enclosure. The Lumpkin House, a two-story brick structure with outbuildings, sits roughly in the center of the complex.

The garden's multiple rooms illustrate different responses to the challenges a designer faces. The parterre garden, rendered in the Colonial Revival style, is designed to complement the 1857 original residence and outbuildings; an outdoor courtyard easily accommodates larger events. The serpentine walled garden offers a large lawn appropriate for weddings or informal gatherings such as the well-attended football pregame parties. The informal arboretum offers spaces for quiet contemplation and relaxation.

Founders' Memorial Garden, University of Georgia, Athens

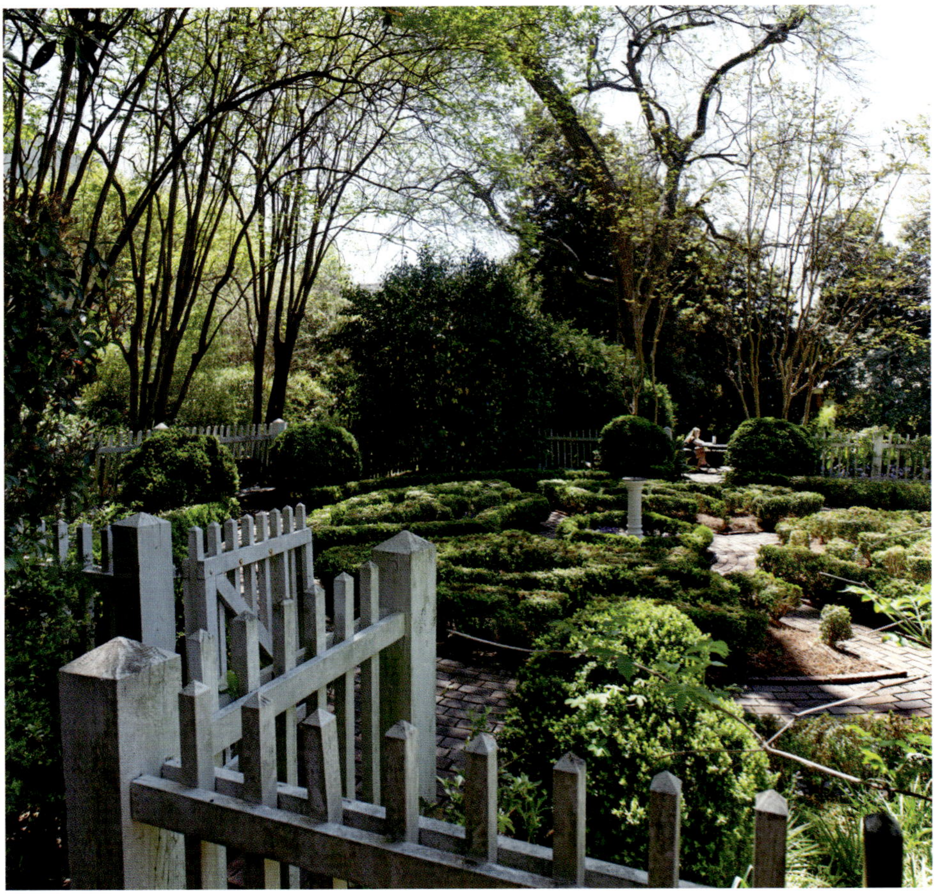

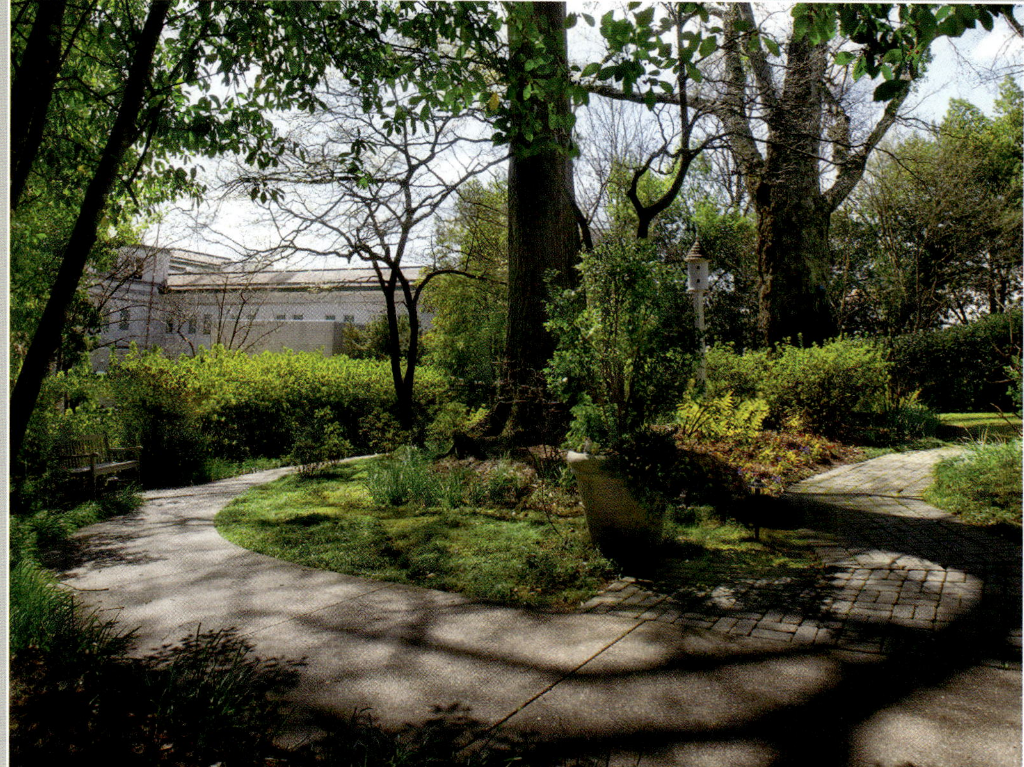

Egleston Hospital Garden, Emory University, Atlanta

Historic Garden Survives Demolition of Its Building

This exceptional garden was designed by Edward Daugherty in 1959 and survived the demolition of Egleston Children's Hospital. It is one of the first and most important midcentury gardens in the South. Daugherty, a Harvard-trained landscape architect, was raised in Atlanta. His design flowed from the principal spaces of the hospital and provided a south-facing outdoor space intended to afford patients and their families the opportunity to be outside the hospital environment: to take in the feeling of the sun and the breeze on skin, the fragrance of blooming plants—to return to humanity from the sterility and fear often associated with hospitalization and medical treatment. The organic forms, in plan view, are reminiscent of Matisse cut-outs from the 1950s. Daugherty reinterpreted a very conservative, traditional design from the 1920s at the first Egleston Hospital. The new hospital and garden were remade in the vibrant spirit of postwar United States for a vibrant postwar Cherokee Garden Club and Atlanta. The result has been a garden whose beauty and simplicity have served for over sixty years, an exceptional record for any garden. Daugherty was awarded the ASLA Design Medal in 2010, the highest award granted by the American Society of Landscape Architects.

The Children's Healthcare of Atlanta Garden is a quarter acre space built in 1959 along with the then-new Egleston Hospital building near the Emory University campus. The garden features organic, curvilinear paths and plantings ranging from mature shade trees to bulbs and groundcovers with open lawns.

The garden was designed to recall the original garden at the 1928 hospital building that was dedicated to Dorothy Blalock Black in 1932. When the new building was announced, Daugherty was engaged as the landscape architect and a garden was deemed an important part of the program for design and construction. The garden was designed along midcentury Modernist lines to complement the new, state-of-the-art hospital building designed by Abreu and Robeson. The maintenance of the garden had been championed by the Cherokee Garden Club since the original dedication, and this devotion continued with the 1959 building and change of site.

In 1998, Egleston Hospital merged with Scottish Rite and became Children's Healthcare of Atlanta. In 2008–9 the Abreu and Robeson building was demolished and a new structure built to the east, but this remarkable garden has survived. As of this writing, Children's Healthcare of Atlanta has announced it will be vacating the building, whereupon it will return to the stewardship of Emory University.

Hofwyl-Broadfield Plantation

Owned by one family continuously for over 160 years, the house at Hofwyl-Broadfield is an example of the Plantation Plain style. Situated on a bluff above the marshes of the Glynn and Altamaha Rivers, the plantation house gave the owners or the owners' agent, a good vantage to survey the brutal work that was the cultivation of rice in the South.

The Hofwyl-Broadfield Plantation is now a state park created from the property left to Georgia by the fifth generation of the family that grew rice on the banks of the Altamaha River from 1806 until 1913. The property, with its nearly 2,000 acres of land and marsh, includes the 1850 plantation house and outbuildings, expansive live oak groves around the house, and the rice fields themselves, as well as some of the features built to sustain rice production. On the property are live oaks between five hundred and eight hundred years old.

In 1913 the property was converted to dairy farming. This provided a profitable income to the owners and workers alike. As development in the surrounding county increased and Interstate 95 was built nearby, the last family member desired to assure the preservation of the property for posterity. Over one hundred years since rice was last grown in the marshes of Hofwyl-Broadfield, evidence of the rice fields is clear from aerial photographs and satellite images—a testament to the quality of construction achieved by the enslaved people. The enslaved West Africans brought with them techniques from their homelands, and the traces of their work and great sacrifice are still visible at Hofwyl-Broadfield. The descendants of the longtime owner preserved the property by leaving it to the Nature Conservancy. Through this group, it was entrusted to the State of

Hofwyl-Broadfield Plantation

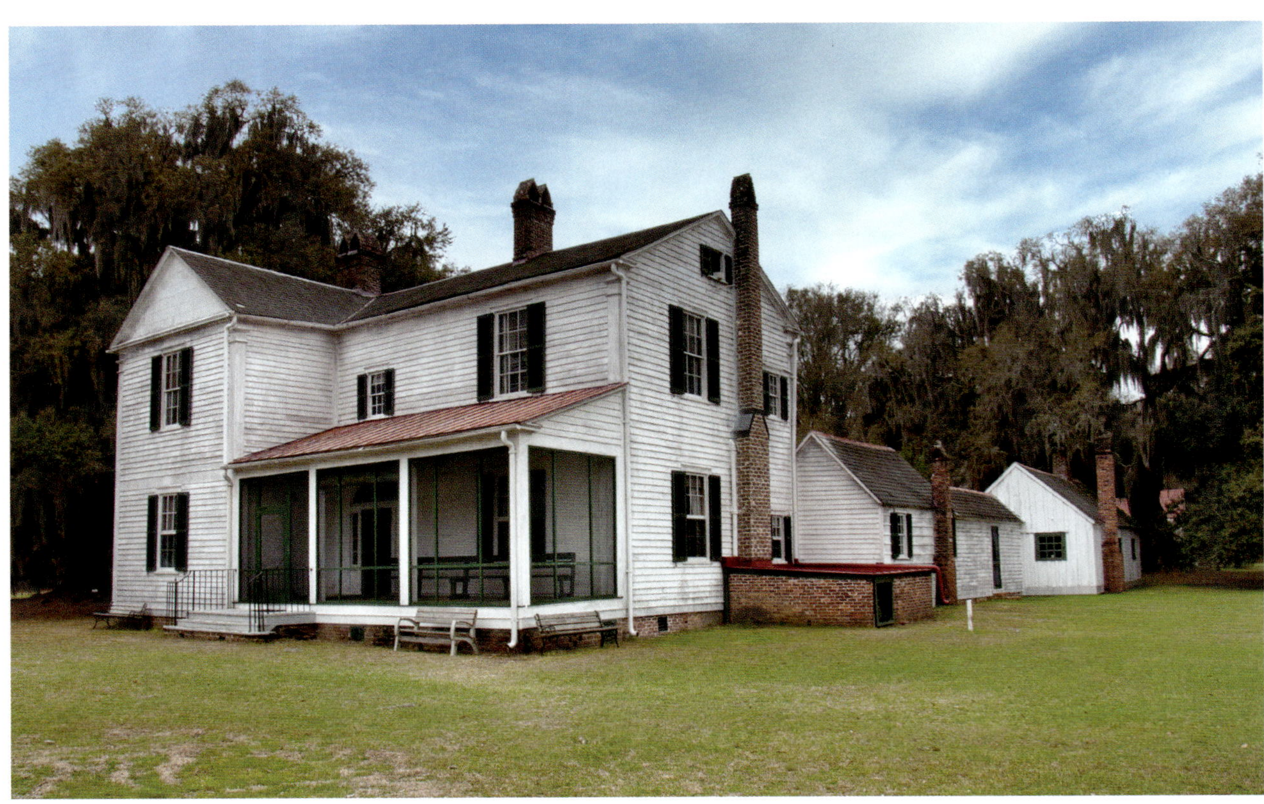

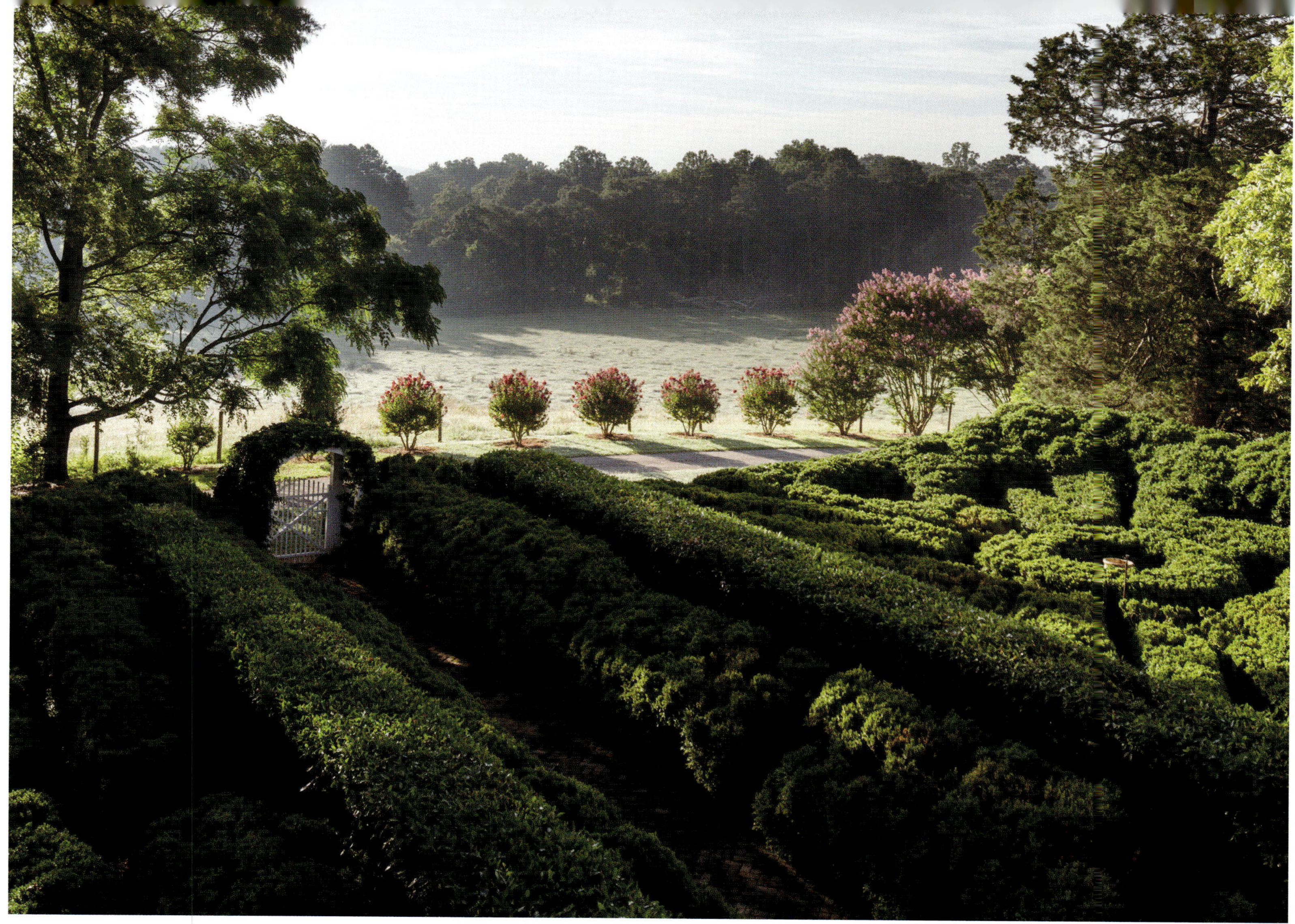

Valley View, Cartersville

Georgia. The long and bitter harvest of rice in Georgia, a part of our history often forgotten, is visible and most tangible at Hofwyl-Broadfield in the sacrifice of the people who worked the fields that lay in such contrast to the Spanish moss that drapes in great festoons from the ancient live oaks. Hofwyl-Broadfield casts a spell all its own.

Valley View

Valley View is the 250-acre farm and former plantation overlooking the Etowah River Valley in Bartow (formerly Cass) County in northwest Georgia. In the foreground of the house is a boxwood parterre garden, divided into halves by a walk along a central axis that aligns and connects the front door and central hall with the view of the valley that gave the place its name.

These gardens have been given the names of Sun and Moon. The Sun Garden, appropriately, lies to the south of the original brick herringbone walk. This garden is rendered in English boxwood and forms a circle with a diameter of about 10 feet, with radiating "rays" extending to the edges of its surrounding square perimeter. This garden is 50 feet square and contains eight outer triangular or trapezoidal beds formed by the represented sun's rays. The Moon Garden is likewise 50 feet square with a central circle 10 feet in diameter. The outer form, however, depicts a broader circle with six radiating rays. Four semitriangular beds account for the negative space between the larger circle and the containing square. The Sun Garden contains more rays and thus shines more brightly than the more composed and less dynamic Moon Garden. Less dynamic perhaps, but no less lovely.

Family records suggest that the house and garden were built after 1840, when James Sproull, originally of Abbeville, South Carolina, purchased the property from his brother-in-law, Wade Cothran. Cothran was a pioneer settler of Rome, Georgia. The initial land tract included 2,000 acres. The house and garden were built by enslaved persons who most likely came with the Sproulls from South Carolina. The house was built between 1840 and 1848 and features Greek Revival elements that were probably added after the main structure built but before the outbreak of the Civil War in 1861. The garden was built contemporaneously with the house and has been in continuous use by the Sproull family and their descendants since construction.

As federal troops neared Valley View during the Atlanta campaign of 1864, the family fled to Alabama, leaving the place in the watchful care of a German cabinetmaker who was a family employee. As with many other large farming operations, the family was able to keep the property intact and continue farming by switching from forced labor to other forms of agriculture. The expansive views from the portico of Valley View enhance one of Georgia's most important cultural landscapes and are testament to the careful stewardship of the family who owns the property. The family has donated a conservation easement to the Mountain Conservation Trust of Georgia.

Ferrell Gardens, Hills and Dales

The extraordinary garden begun by Sarah Ferrell inspired architect Neel Reid to design a villa worthy of Tuscany in the hot mid-Georgia sun. That these gardens were already 70 years old when the house was built for the Callaway family over 100 years ago adds to the magic and mystery that is Ferrell Gardens at Hills and Dales. That Ferrell Gardens has survived for 180 years is simply astonishing. Exceptional design of the gardens, with elements of Christian iconography and plants from the Holy Land, make it a museum for horticulturalists. The gardens inspired the architects Neel Reid and Hal Hentz to build their first Italian-inspired composition and set in motion an exploration of things Italian in relation to the landscape of Georgia that Reid and Philip Shutze would revisit and exploit to great effect. The house recalls Charles Platt's design for Timberline at Bryn Mawr, Pennsylvania, from 1907, though Reid's integration of the house and garden sets his design apart even from Platt's subtle mastery.

Ferrell Gardens at Hills and Dales is an elaborate collection of terraced gardens built in 1840 by Sarah Coleman Ferrell. The gardens have been owned by only two families in their entire existence. They formed the planted foreground to a house built by the Ferrells known as the Terraces, for the various levels sculpted into the land that sloped down to and away from the street outside of LaGrange, Georgia, not long after the town became the seat of Troup County.

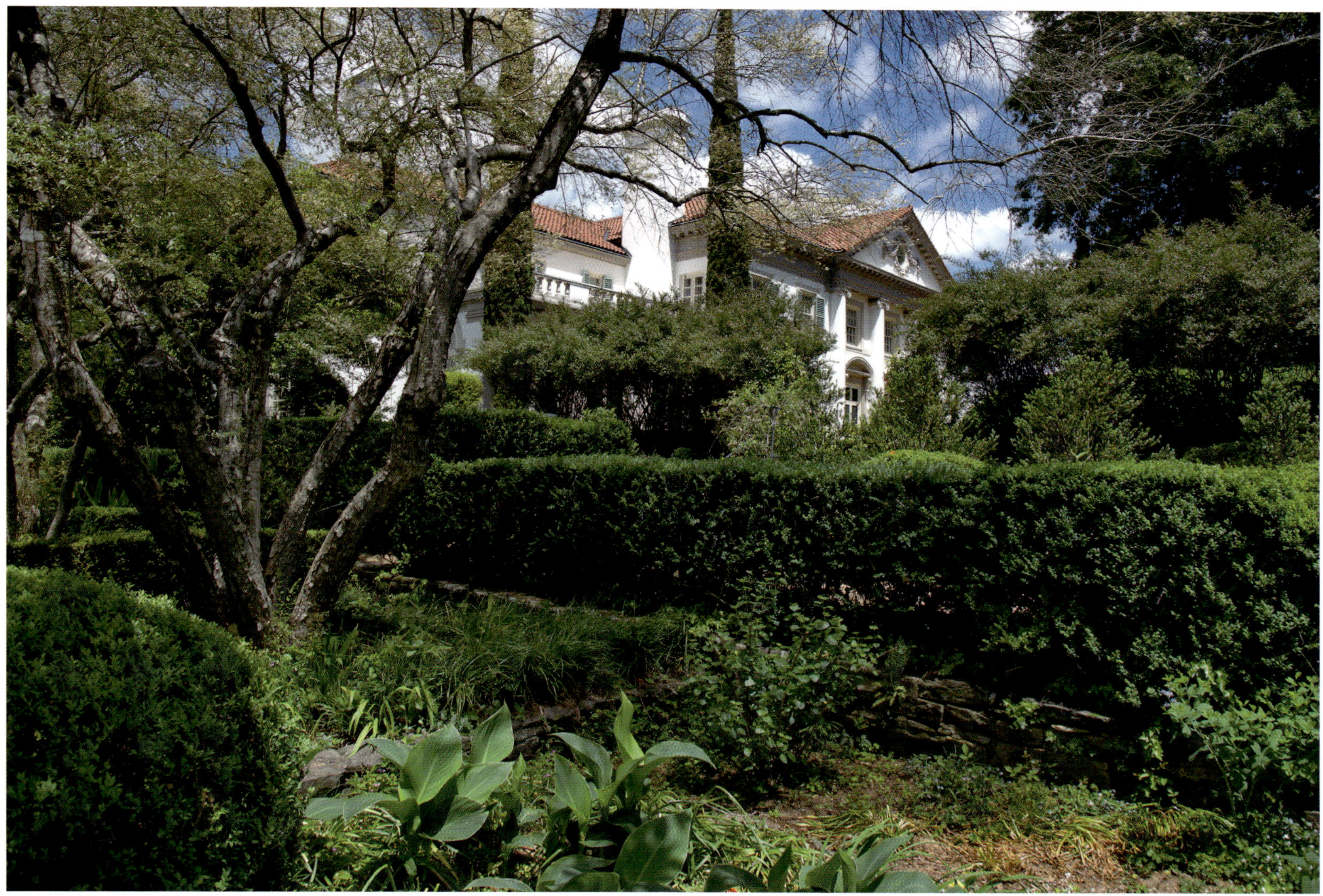

Ferrell Gardens, Hills and Dales, LaGrange

Boxwood forms an important horticultural component to the garden, and this adaptable evergreen is used to delineate paths and borders as well as embellish a strongly Christian iconographical program important to the original designer-builder. The garden follows five principal levels as it steps down the hillside, the largest near the 1917 house designed by the Atlanta architectural firm of Hentz, Reid, and Adler. The house and garden complex form a 5-acre component of a 2,500-acre property now owned by the Fuller Callaway Foundation.

Following the completion of the garden on the uppermost terrace, the Sunken Garden, West Garden, and Rose Garden were added, all by 1861. The gardens enjoyed a long period of repose after the Civil War, retaining and gaining reputation as a garden to visit, even a garden of pilgrimage. Among the modest embellishments made during this period was the planting of a memorial grove of seven pine trees in memory of a relation who died at the Battle of Seven Pines in Virginia in the spring of 1862. Perhaps a more poignant memorial would have been a grove in memory of one of the immediate family's own sons, Palman Ernest Ferrell, who died September 30, 1861, at Portsmouth, Virginia. The seven pines in the grove are surrounded by poplars. Perhaps both son and relation are honored in this planting.

The present Italian Renaissance–inspired "villa" by Hentz and Reid was designed and built between 1914 and 1916. The Callaways nurtured the place with love, care, and discretion, making few changes. Besides replacing the house, they added a fountain along the central axis of the garden and added mottoes "written" in boxwood—"St. Callaway" and "Ora Pro Mi"—to complement mottoes from Sarah's designs such as "God" and "God is Love."

The family passed the property to son Fuller Callaway Jr. and his wife Alice. When Alice died in 1998, the house, gardens, and 35 acres of the total property were left to the Callaway Foundation. The foundation continues the tradition begun by Sarah Ferrell and the Callaways of opening the property to the public. A visitors' interpretive center was constructed in 2004.

Woodlands, Barnsley Gardens

There is no greater example of romance and ruins in Georgia than Barnsley Gardens in Adairsville in former Cherokee territory. Godfrey Barnsley, of Derbyshire, England, arrived in Savannah in 1824, at eighteen years of age. In about 1833, he purchased 4,000 acres near Adairsville and began construction of his house and garden, in a manner heavily influenced by the writings of Andrew Jackson Downing (1815–52). He and his family moved to the site, on a hill overlooking a broad valley, in 1841. Legend has it that a Cherokee who was assisting Barnsley warned him not to build on that site, as it was sacred to the Cherokee. Undeterred, Barnsley continued his work, which included the main house with two outbuildings and a substantial garden of English boxwood in the foreground. The horticultural tasks were undertaken by Barnsley's Irish head gardener, John Connally. P. J. Berckman is credited with providing much of the rare plant material for the property in 1859.

The family sustained multiple losses of life from disease in the nineteenth century, which created the superstition of a curse on the property. In 1906 a tornado struck the house and Barnsley's granddaughter chose not to rebuild but to move into an outbuilding instead. In 1942 the property was sold out of the family and became a dairy farm. But the truly dark years were the early 1950s to the 1980s when Barnsely's dream was very nearly lost entirely and the property sat largely abandoned and forgotten.

The garden at Barnsley Gardens is an exceptional example of an antebellum parterre garden executed in boxwood. It lies in the foreground of the ruins of the Barnsley house, called Woodlands. The site chosen for the construction of the house, cursed or not, is prominent in the landscape, and the house and garden were inspired by the domestic design principles espoused by the foremost tastemaker of the day, Andrew Jackson Downing. The house and garden complex is an example of a domestic "villa" as popularized by Downing, and from 1841, through the Civil War, and until the death of Godfrey Barnsley, construction, refinement, and planting continued, with plants shipped from nurseries in Philadelphia and Augusta.

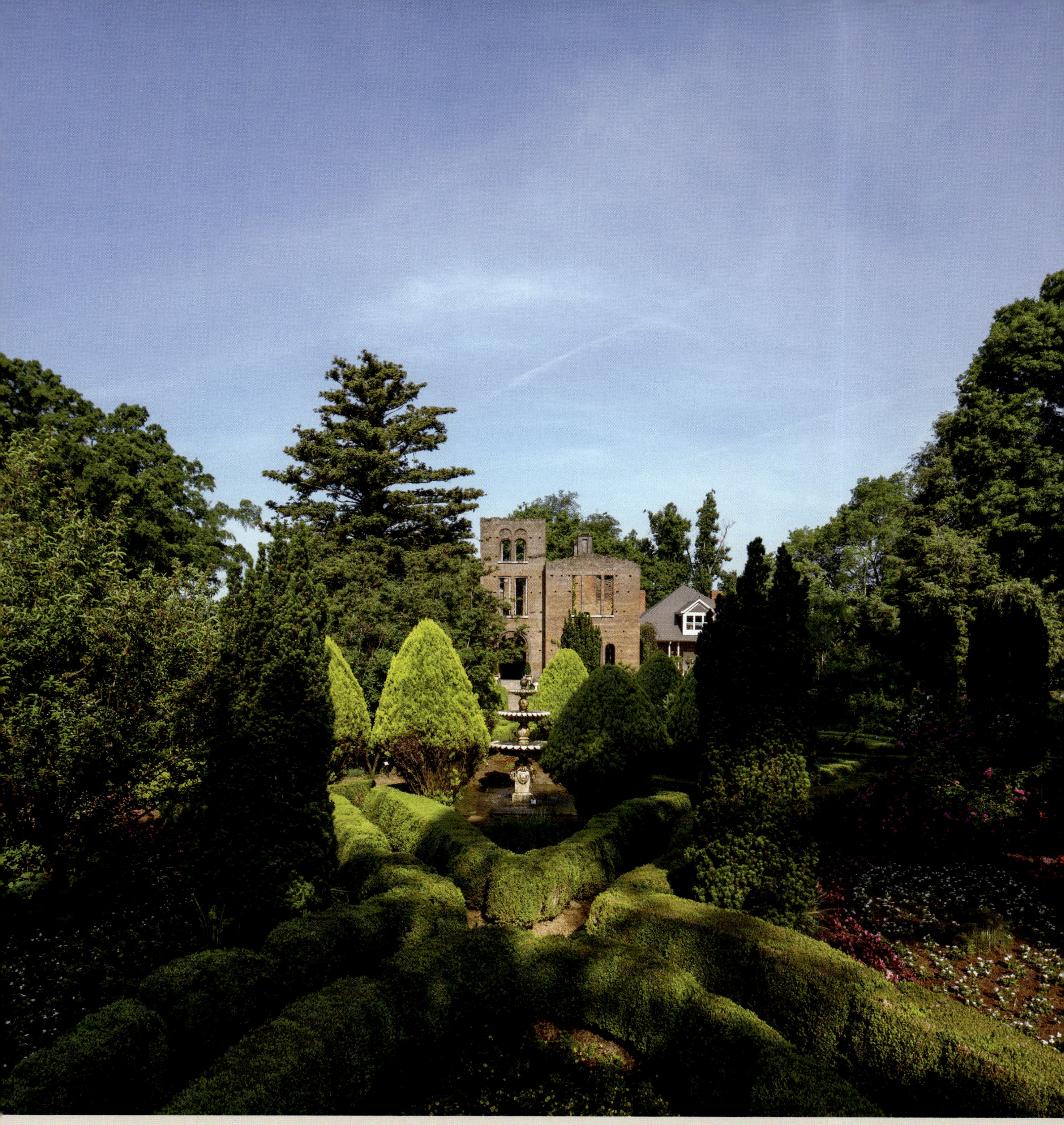

Woodlands, Barnsley Gardens, Adairsville

Even in its ruined state, the romance and beauty were undiminished, and in the luster of time, even enhanced. The estate was sold to become a golf and spa resort, and the developer used the ruined house as the backdrop for the restoration of the garden. The garden was almost as much a restoration as a preservation, as much of the parterre was visible but overgrown. Neglect is sometimes benign indeed. The garden, with its magic and mystery, was nearly wholly lost, but it now continues and confronts its second hundred years, restored and beloved, a remarkable horticultural and cultural survivor and a splendid ruin of immense interest and importance.

Millpond Plantation

Millpond Plantation is an exceptional hunting preserve of a type that was common in southwest Georgia in the late nineteenth and early twentieth centuries. It exemplifies the best land planning and landscape design available in the United States. Warren Manning (1860–1938), a second-generation landscape architect and a protégé of Frederick Law Olmsted Sr., prepared the master plan, land planning, and estate layout for much of the plantation, and they remain much as originally conceived. Among Manning's more important projects are Gwinn (Cleveland, Ohio), the Pinehurst Resort (Pinehurst, North Carolina), and Stan Hywet Hall (Akron, Ohio). That Millpond has survived for nearly one hundred years is remarkable given the important societal change during the period. The survival of this landscape is due in part to the remoteness of the site and the long tradition of hunting in the vicinity of Thomasville, dating from the late nineteenth century.

The entrance drive winds through dense forest, passes by a guest house, and wraps around the gardens on the northwest and southwest side of the house before ending at an arrival court near the eccentrically located main entrance at the south corner of the house. The central and by far most dramatic feature of the house is the 100-foot-square glass-roofed atrium. The principal rooms of the house open onto this unique feature, made more practical, if it can so be called, by being retractable. Wide lawns open to the southeast side of the house, which features enormous plate-glass windows in the living and dining rooms that offer riveting views of lawn and pine forests beyond. It was in this direction that the millpond once lay.

To the northeast of the main house is a large service court. A tunnel under the house allowed access for gardeners to reach the atrium garden without having to walk through the main cloistered walk surrounding the sunken garden while burdened with all the clobber necessary to support such a tropical paradise. To the northwest and southwest are two remarkable gardens. The northwest garden is half a long oval, divided into four quadrants. It is centered on the billiard room. The garden originally featured camellias, though plantings have been substantially simplified. The axial garden extending from a cross hall between bedrooms on the southeast side of the house is an elongated rectangle that features

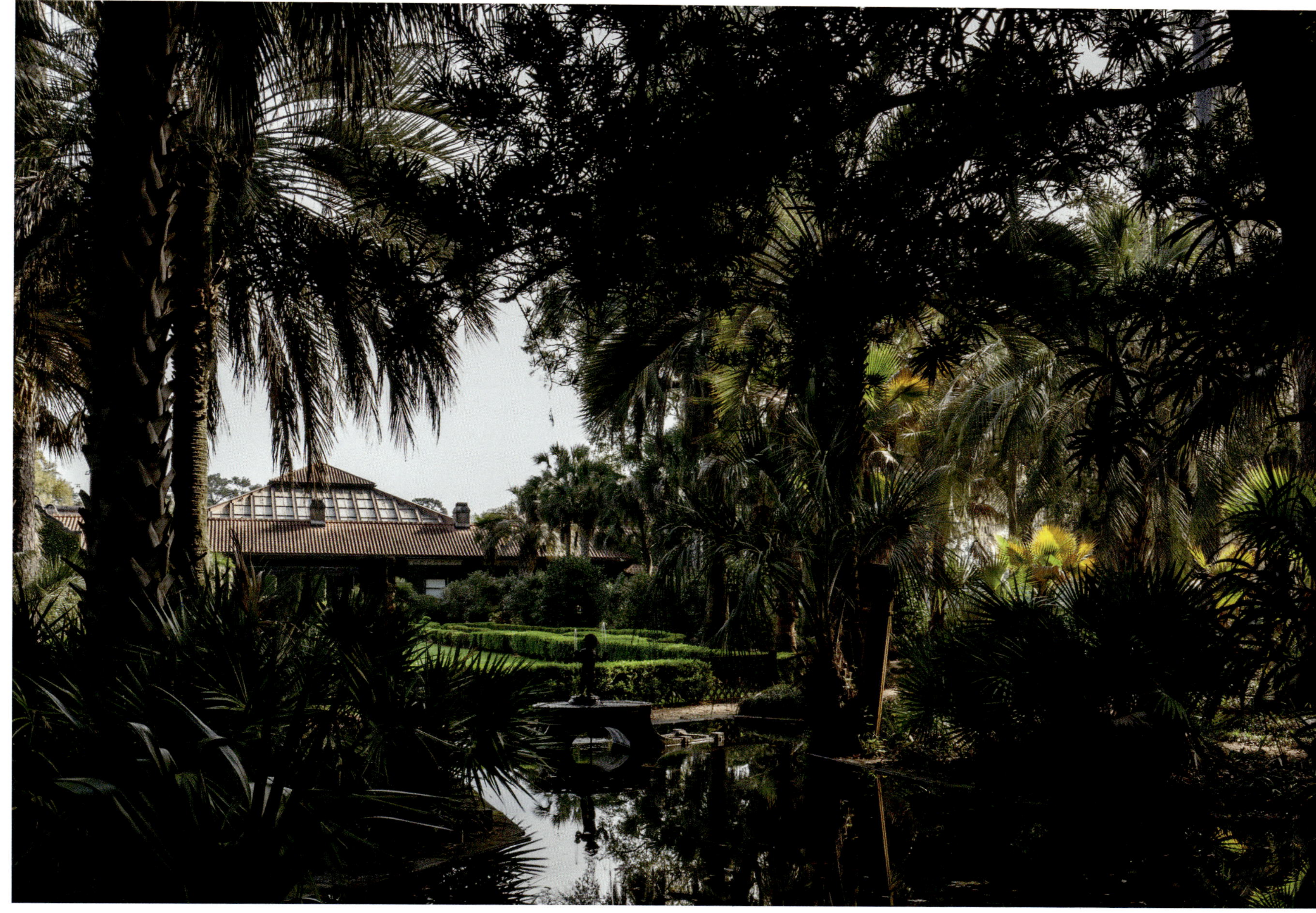

Millpond Plantation, Thomasville

palms of many types. The driveway lies beyond it. An arbor that once featured roses extends along a walk, repeating the geometry of the southeast garden.

During Jeptha Wade's ownership of Millpond, the holdings grew to 10,000 acres. The main house was built between 1903 and 1905, with the complex finished in 1910. After Wade's death in 1926, Millpond was owned by a trust for the benefit of its builder's three children. Upon their deaths, the property was purchased by the builder's grandchildren. The property was divided into three parts, and today Millpond is comprised of 7,000 acres.

The plantings in the gardens around the main house have been simplified to a certain extent over the years, yet the patterns laid out by Manning and the paths and the overall circulation of roads and drives over the property remain true. The property lies on the suburban edge of Thomasville and development pressures seem to be in balance with the long history of land preservation and quail hunting in Thomas County.

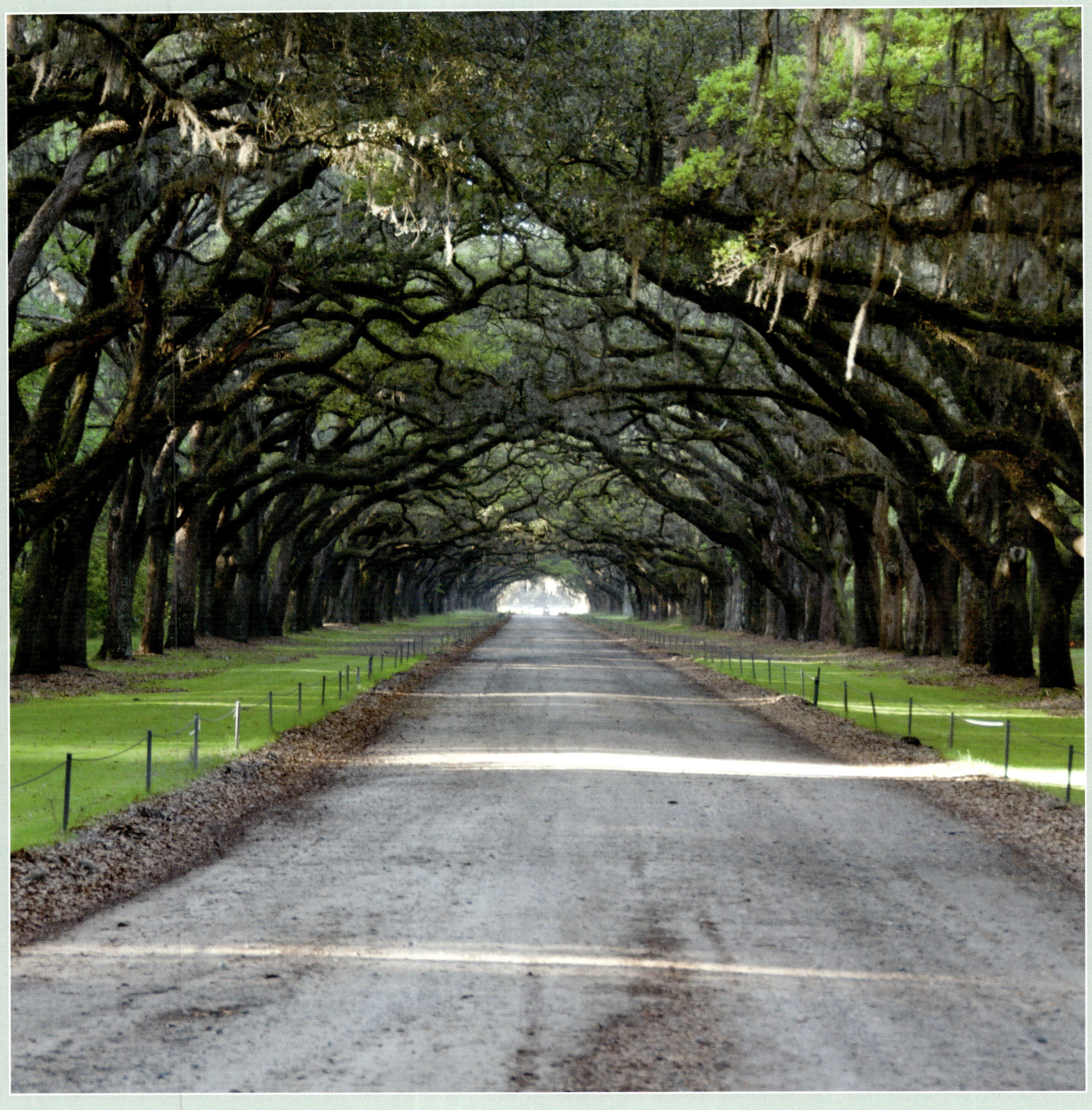

Wormsloe Allée, Savannah

The Wormsloe Allée

Considered a French tradition, the planting of an allée was often used to mark the birth of the next generation. The survival of the trees requires the cultural and horticultural agreement that their existence continues to serve a purpose and, further, that their care can be justified and perpetuated. The live oak can live to upwards of one thousand years, the longest-lived tree species east of the Mississippi. This most robust Georgia native tree has been lovingly cared for at Wormsloe State Park at Isle of Hope, near Savannah.

Though the allée at Wormsloe is but 130 years old, it commemorates the 287 years Noble Jones, his descendants, and farm workers have worked this land and seen it through revolution, war, depression, and enormous societal change. A remarkable survivor and an eloquent witness to the history of a people on this land.

The Wormsloe Allée is a nearly two-mile-long lane of live oak trees planted in 1891 to commemorate the birth of the sixth generation of the Noble Jones family. Over four hundred trees constitute the allée, spaced approximately 35 feet apart and 70 feet across the lane; the allée has been allowed to mature with plenty of space between the trees, enabling them to attain magnificent mature form.

Noble Jones, the founder of Wormsloe, served many important roles in the new colony of Georgia. He established his plantation seven miles from Savannah on the Isle of Hope on 800 acres he received as a land grant in 1756. The land remained in this family until it was transferred to the State of Georgia as a state park in 1973.

Jones cultivated exotic plants on the property, a fact noted by plant explorer William Bartram, and he sought properties inland for revenue-generating crops. In the antebellum period, Jones's great grandson (George Frederick Tilghman Jones, aka G.W. J. DeRenne) added to the original acreage with cotton, a principal crop farmed by enslaved peoples. In 1847, DeRenne began publishing books related to the history and literary traditions of Georgia. In 1927, the property was opened to the public as Wormsloe Gardens. The bulk of the property was transferred to the Wormsloe Foundation in 1961, and then to the Nature Conservancy in 1972, and finally to the State of Georgia in 1973.

The family continues to own and control the historic house site and approximately 50 acres surrounding it. The parterre garden at the house is intriguing, and it also features a live oak canopy. The State of Georgia operates the historic ruin of the house and fort built by Noble Jones. The Wormsloe Institute for Environmental History operates from a site on the property and is composed of an interdisciplinary group of ecologists, geographers, landscape architects, historic preservationists, archaeologists, historians, foresters, and more who share a common goal of conserving, documenting, and studying the human and natural history of the property and the surrounding region.

Currently, the ninth generation of descendants live on the Wormsloe property originally occupied in 1734 and granted by King George II to Noble Jones in 1756. That it is still largely intact and in continuous ownership by the original family is remarkable in our country.

Woodhaven, Grounds of the Georgia Governor's Mansion

The grounds of the Georgia Governor's Mansion are the important 18 acres that remain from the estate called Woodhaven, built between 1904 and 1911 by Robert Maddox (1870–1965) and his wife Laura Baxter Maddox. The grounds retain the sunken garden crafted by Laura Maddox with "a man and a mule." The Maddox house was demolished to make way for the 24,000-square-foot Governor's Mansion, though the basic circulation of drives that traversed the property was retained as it functioned well as laid out. The Maddox's tennis court was retained as well, as were an arbor walk and sheltered woodland paths that feature plants native to Georgia.

Edward Daugherty, FASLA, was engaged along with architect Tom Bradbury to work on the commission to create the first governor's residence designed for the purpose since the Old Governor's Mansion in Milledgeville was abandoned after serving the state from 1839 to 1868. It was Daugherty more than anyone, who urged the preservation of the gardens, which had been opened to the public on several occasions.

Daugherty was a strong advocate for all that he could preserve, and he was largely successful. His design for the west garden included a perennial border detailed by Daugherty's then-employee Dan Franklin. Daugherty was awarded the Design Medal in 2010 by the American Society of Landscape Architects, its highest honor. That the landscape at Woodhaven survived speaks to the importance of this notable garden to the people of Georgia and their historical memory. In President Jimmy Carter's endorsement of Daugherty for the Design Medal, he stated, "The mansion was built on the site of an historic Atlanta estate, and Mr. Daugherty met the challenge of accommodating the construction of the new mansion while preserving the beautiful grounds of the original estate."

On the grounds were four statues representing the four seasons, dating from the seventeenth century, that Maddox gave the state; they have been removed in recent years. Also now gone are the colonnade and arbors that once embraced the original tennis court. A chain-link fence presently encircles the tennis court.

The garden planting, expected to be retained and restored by Ben Fortson, Georgia's secretary of state in 1962, was substantially simplified by Daugherty. The bold terraced landform created by Laura Baxter Maddox remains. Two gardens Daugherty designed on the east and west side of the mansion have been significantly changed, and for most of the last fifty-three years, the landscape has been maintained by prisoners in the state penal system. A tornado in March 1975 cleared many of the majestic oaks that gave the site its original name of Woodhaven. The oak grove has not been replanted, and a vast expanse of zoysia lawn sweeps down to West Paces Ferry Road.

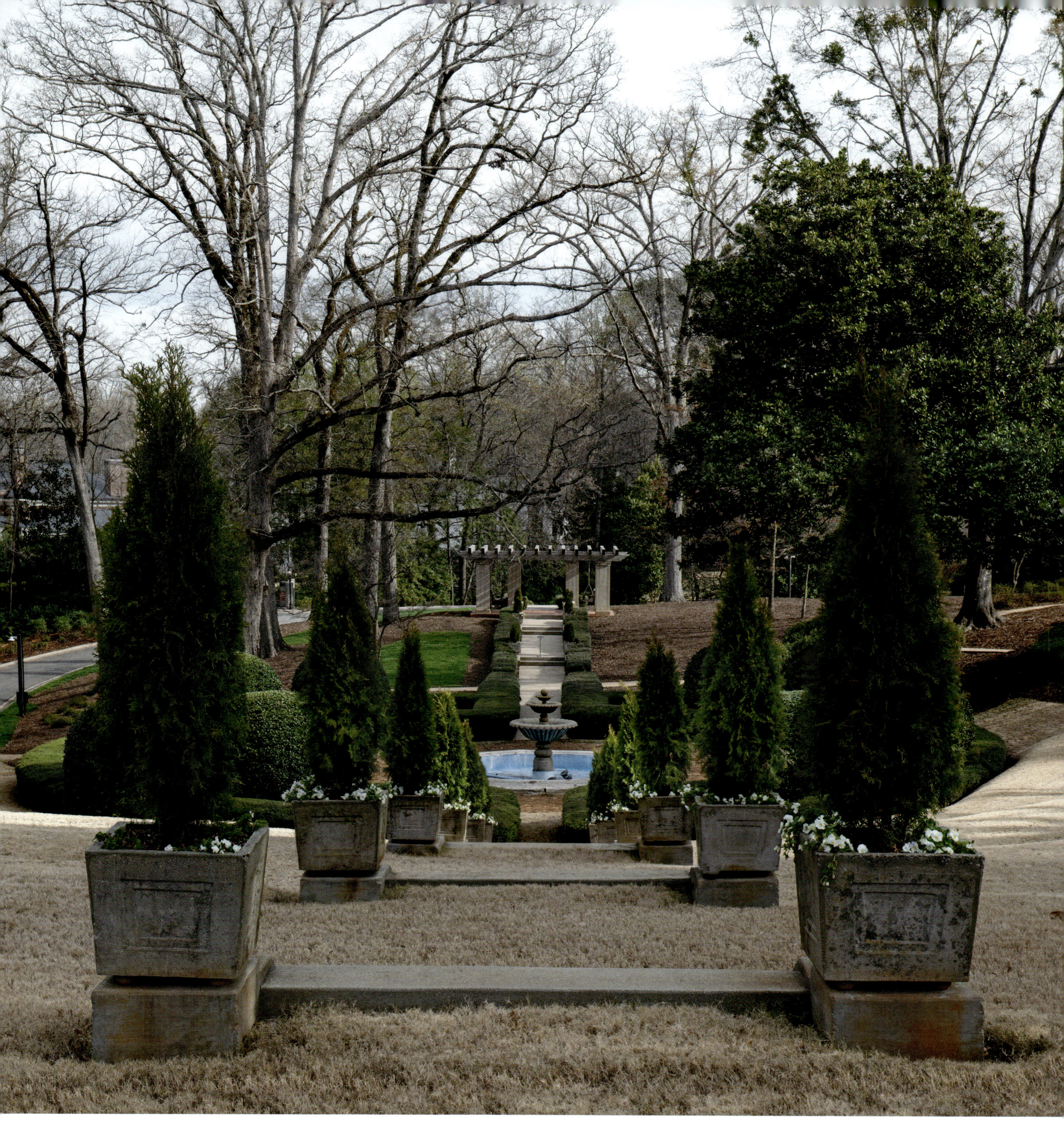

Woodhaven, grounds of Georgia Governor's Mansion, Atlanta

Broadlands

Broadlands is one of a few sites in Atlanta where the sense of place and space is close to the original intent of the builder and where the vistas retain the feeling of one hundred years ago. Broadlands is an exceptional property recalling the very essence of what the estate era of Buckhead was all about, creating a mythic setting for family and friends in a style befitting the owners' sense of self. At Broadlands, that original dream of Hugh Richardson and Josephine Inman Richardson, their architect, and the anonymous landscape genius is still very much discernable.

Hugh Richardson began acquiring property on Paces Ferry Road (now West Paces Ferry Road) after 1915. The Richardson property that would be called

Broadlands, Atlanta

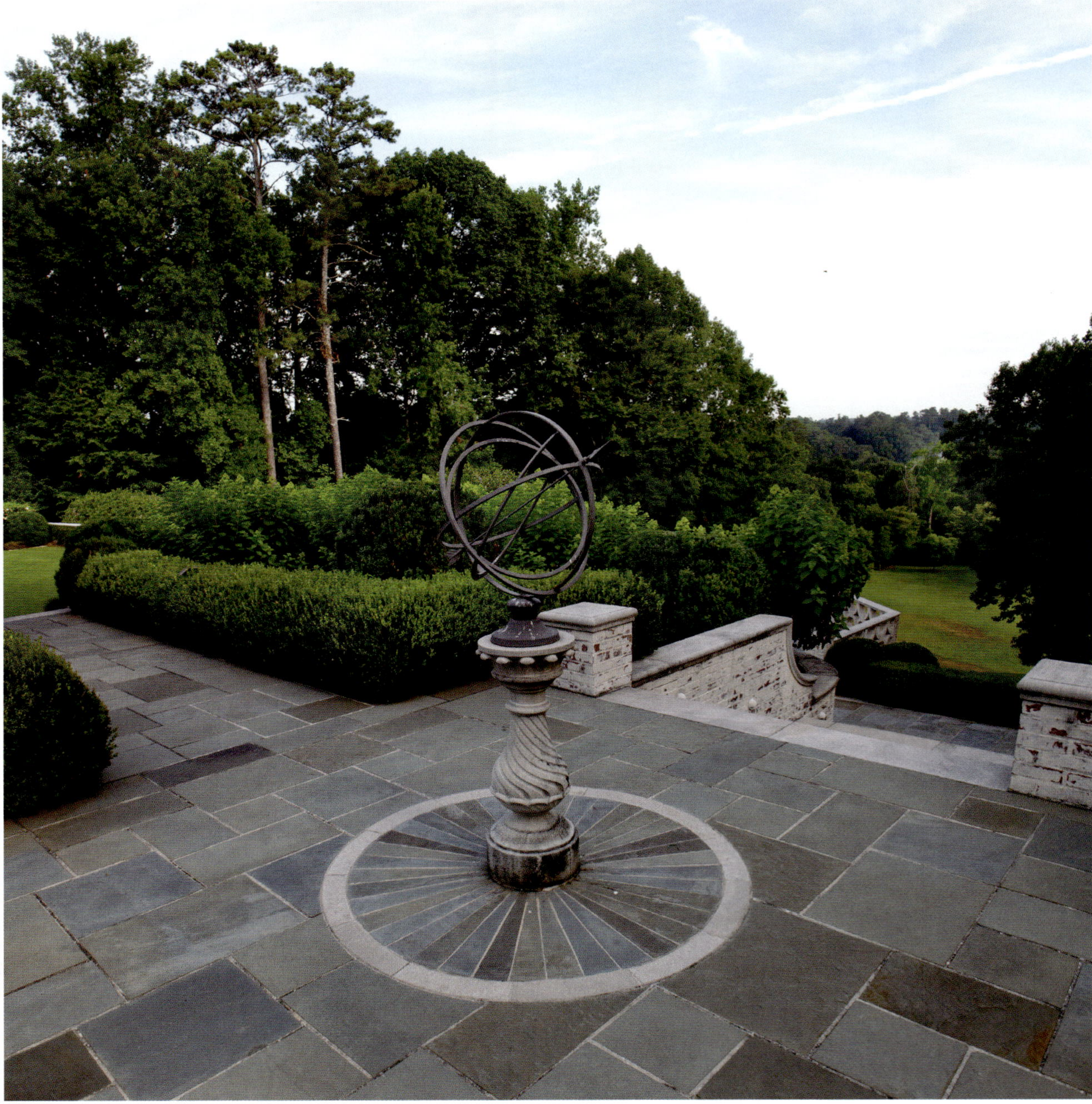

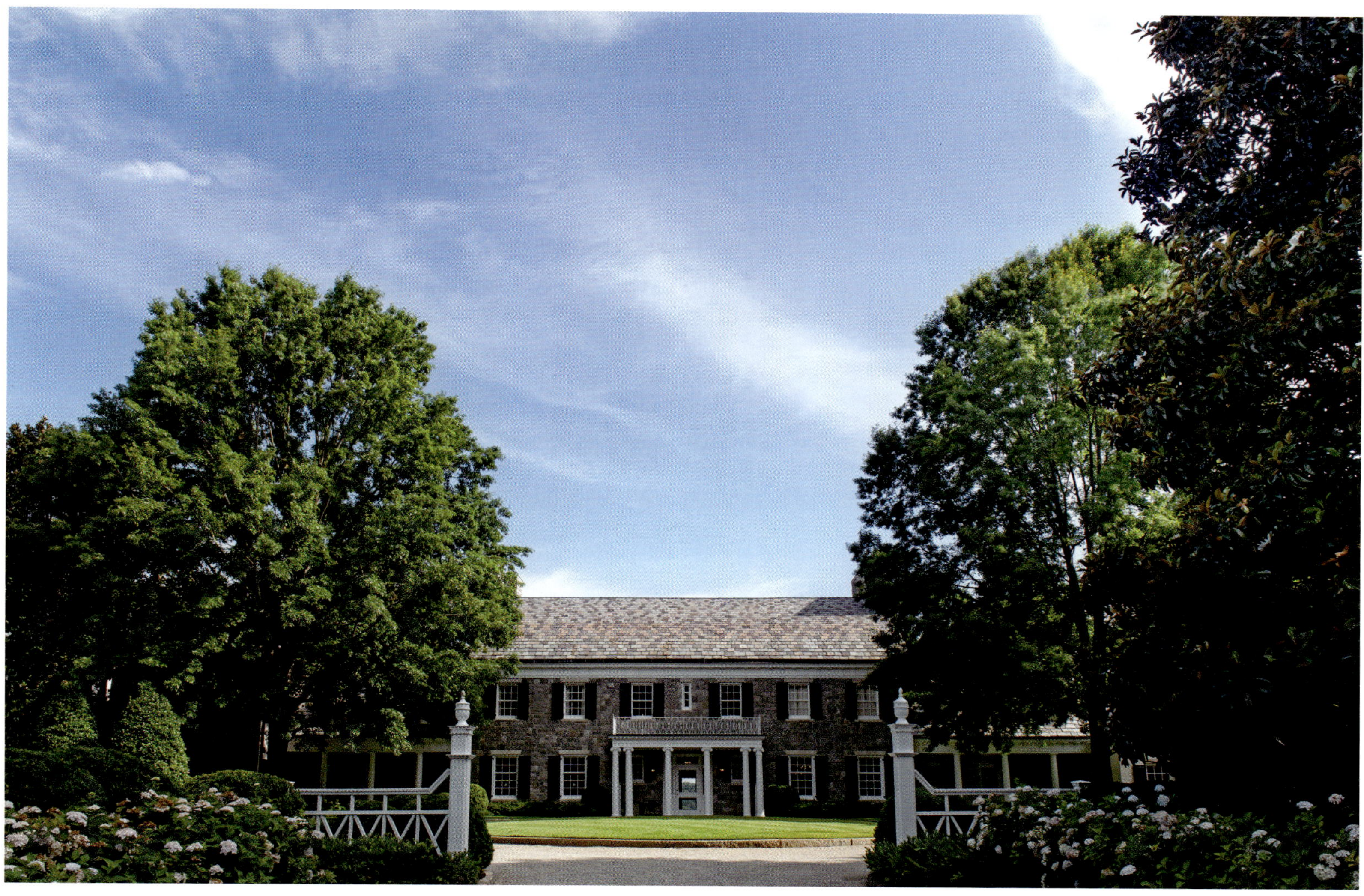

Broadlands, Atlanta

Broadlands included at one time almost 200 acres. During this period Richardson selected fellow Princeton graduate Aymar Embury II to be his architect. The house was a rendering of a colonial manse from Pennsylvania's Brandywine Valley, with a simple porch over the front door and two subordinate wings, one containing the music room (or ballroom), the other a balancing service wing. On the north face, a two-story "piazza," or porch, overlooked the broad acreage of bottom land that inspired the name of the estate and that Richardson was intent on farming. One of the hills was selected for the main house, another prominent hill to the south and west would become the site of another Embury house, for Richardson's son.

Changes were made to the landscape quickly, with a center stair piercing the uppermost wall that had created a balcony-like overlook of the garden below and the open fields and hills beyond. The beauty of the setting is not compromised by this change or later changes by the current owners, who added a pool on a lower level. This later addition, happily, is not visible from the main house.

A broodmare barn was built across Nancy Creek from the main property, and a long, low barn was built at the base of the high hill where the main house was located. The barn was placed so that it was not visible from the main house but added to the pastoral beauty of the property when viewed through the woods along Northside Drive.

The remaining 25-acre estate still includes its magnificent hilltop and the valley floor below and retains the rubble wall that once described the entire street perimeter of the property. Remnants of this subtle landscape feature, quarried on site, are one of the longer lasting imprimaturs of the Richardson era in the Buckhead section of Atlanta.

Swan House

The design for the Swan House and grounds represents the exuberant high point of the Country Place era in Atlanta just prior to the Great Depression. The estate of Emily and Edward Inman, commonly known as Swan House, is the originally 26-acre grounds that is the setting for one of the most important Renaissance Revival houses in the United States. The architectural expression of the house, created by Atlanta architect Philip Shutze, was continued into the surrounding grounds in a series of terraces and sloping lawns featuring a five-tiered cascading fountain and ending in an oval lawn at the lowest level, where two quatrefoil fountains mark the foci of the lowest ellipse. A boxwood garden was situated axially from a large loggia-like screen porch. The entrance drive, ascending the hill from Andrews Drive, winds through the forest and arrives at an oval entrance courtyard at the side of the house away from the street.

As exuberant as Shutze's design was, it also, ironically, is restrained in its use of planted borders and extensive cultivated beds. Instead, Shutze used architectural forms to expand the presence of the house across and through the landscape, while maintaining a relatively simple palate of plant materials: lawn, evergreen shrubs, and trees contrasting with lush forest. The preservation of this remarkable place was led by devoted fans of Shutze and relations of the Inmans. Shutze's site plan placed the house toward the rear of the property, allowing for a broad terrace in front of the house and the elaborate articulation of the ground plane into five levels. The most dynamic component of this composition is the five-tiered petal-shaped fountain set within the splayed double staircase that descends more than 15 feet. Shutze's inspirations for this cascading water element is the fountain cascade at the Villa Corsini in Rome and a similar element within the Diego Suarez and F. Burrell Hoffman masterpiece Villa Vizcaya in Miami, Florida.

Shutze called the boxwood garden off the screened porch, his "green garden in the Italian Style." It is contained on two sides by rustic granite walls. The south wall is more elaborately treated, with an arrangement of free-standing Ionic columns framing an eagle with wings spread. This column arrangement was modeled on a similar arrangement Shutze saw and studied at the Boboli Gardens in Florence. The garden was restored in 1996, after extensive archeological investigation revealed the original crushed limestone gravel that had been buried by layers of granite dust.

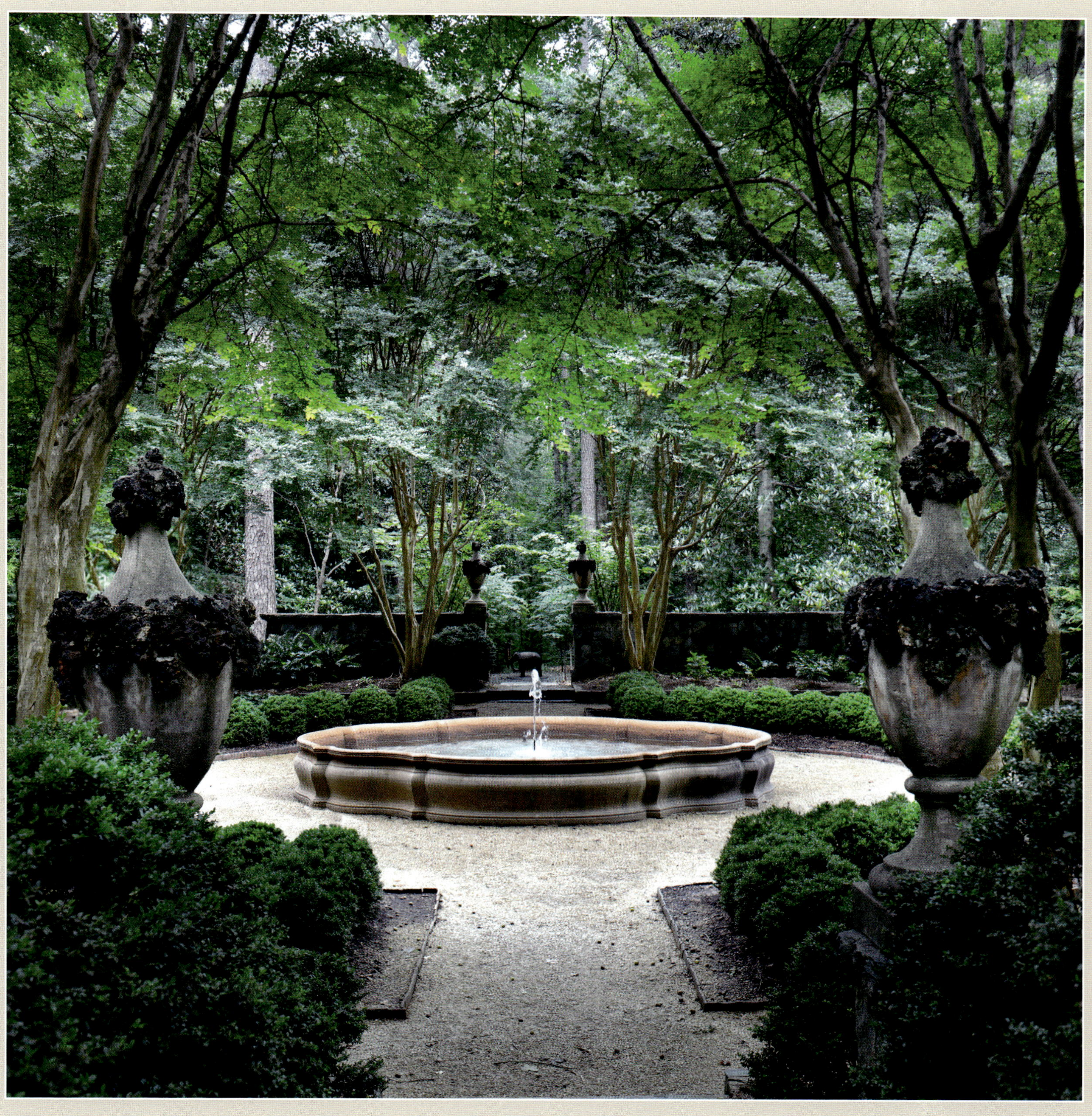

Swan House, Atlanta

The Goodrum Estate

The Goodrum House and Garden represent one of Philip Shutze's most complete creative and holistic design compositions. Shutze simply considered this one of his favorite projects and felt strongly enough about the work to nominate it for an award with the Architectural League of New York. It received their Merit Award in 1931, no small praise, as this group rarely recognized architectural achievement from other regions, especially the South. Shutze exercised enormous creative freedom with this project, and he was able to extend his stylistic expression beyond the walls of the house to include interior murals and furnishings, gardens, perimeter walls and fences, and a number of outbuildings. There is exceptional stylistic integrity in this Regency composition rendered in the Federal Revival style. With the Goodrum house and garden, Shutze was able to fulfill his artistic vision: the comprehensive villa, a cohesive connection between house, garden, and interior.

Goodrum Estate, Atlanta

Shutze designed the house and garden for Mrs. James J. Goodrum, a wealthy widow, in 1928. Construction began in 1929. Goodrum purchased the double

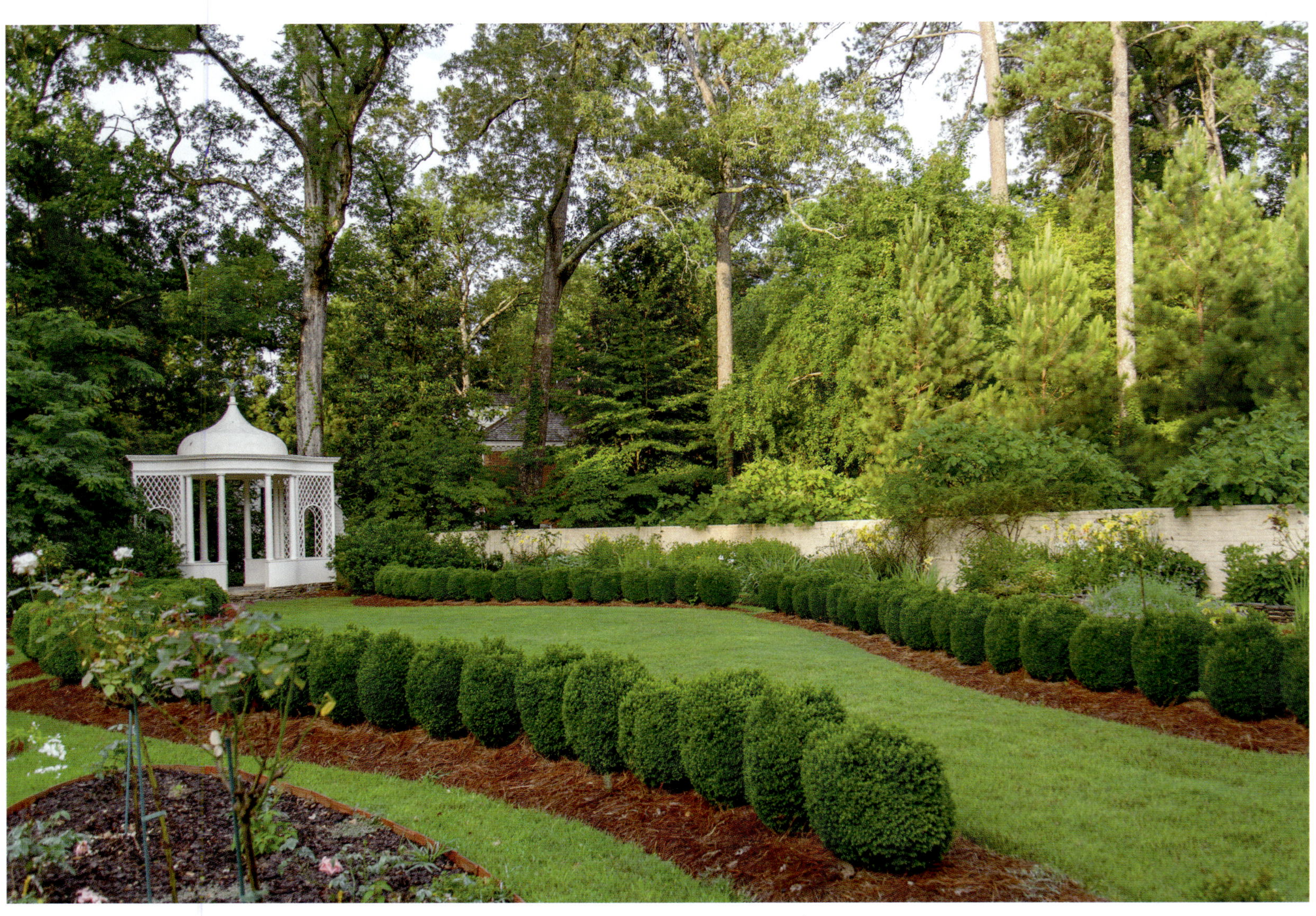

corner lot at the intersection of Habersham Road, Arden Road, and West Paces Ferry Road, in a section of Buckhead where properties ranged from 25 to 250 acres and fox hunting was popular. Shutze's design for the house was decidedly feminine and understated—far from the Baroque exuberance of his nearby earlier designs.

Conceived as a whole, it nonetheless was realized over a number of years: an estate landscape comprising four primary garden rooms that included a small garden modeled on an Italian garden theater, a formal lawn and perennial border behind the house, a serpentine walled garden featuring boxwoods, perennials, and roses; and a boxwood maze depicting the monogram of the builder. The maze was demolished after World War II, as the effects of the postwar labor shortage as well as other societal changes were unfolding.

About 1960 the property was sold to Mary Rushton, the owner of a doll company, who had loved the house for many years. During this period, few other changes were made to the garden. In 1982, Rushton sold to a developer who utilized Atlanta's current zoning regulations to divide the property into seven lots. Construction on these lots has had an adverse impact on the landscape.

In 2009, the Watson-Brown Foundation purchased the property, intent on restoring the house and grounds to the period of significance. The project took five years to complete. An enormous part of the restoration has been the work on the remaining garden spaces. The Italian garden theater on the east side of the property has been restored, removing damage caused by a Decorator's Show House event. The rear lawn has replaced the paved patio installed by the Abreus. The serpentine garden has been restored as has the boxwood maze.

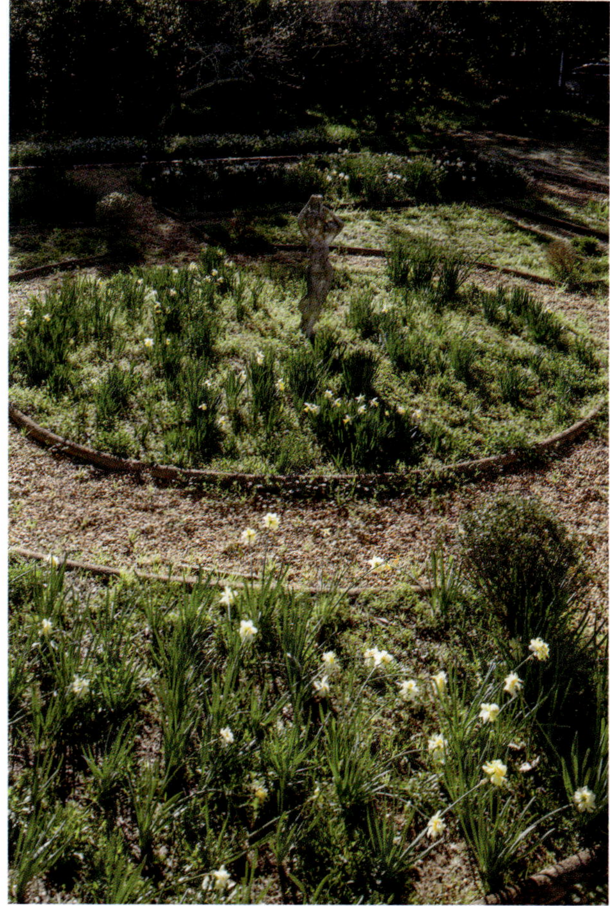

Carnes-Howard-Thomas-Chafee Garden, Summerville, Augusta

The Carnes-Howard-Thomas-Chafee Garden

The Carnes-Howard-Thomas-Chafee Garden is a survivor of two hundred years of social, environmental, and economic change and speaks to the persistence and continuity that is possible in a long-lived cultural landscape. Its traditional garden form is adaptable and workable, with beds narrow enough to be worked from two sides easily. The repetition of forms in the garden creates consistency, and the great number of beds and their symmetrical placement allows ample opportunity for diversity and exploration, even play. The surrounding landscape has been much changed, but successive generations of gardeners have taken on the responsibility of caring for this legacy garden, each providing individuality to the story of this place.

The Carnes-Chafee Garden is a residential landscape composed of seventeen planting beds set within the south-facing lawn of an eighteenth-century cottage in Summerville in suburban Augusta. The flower beds, approximately three feet wide and of varying lengths, are separated by gravel paths that vary in width from 30 to 48 inches. The outer beds are rectangular, but the center bed is circular, surrounded by four beds whose square outlines have been clipped to encase the center circle. The garden sits within a nearly symmetrical area of approximately

3,000 square feet. The form is a traditional one passed down through six owners over two hundred years. The garden has been known largely for its spring bulb display.

The story-and-a-half house adjacent to the garden is a wood-frame cottage on a high basement that dates from the last quarter of the eighteenth century. The kitchen was in a separate building, as was customary, to protect the principal residence from fire. The kitchen structure still stands, though it no longer serves its original purpose. The house was built on "the Hill," which rises above the flood plain of the Savannah River, offering residents relief from the oppressive heat and humidity near the river.

Boxwood (Kolb-Pou-Newton, Madison)

The gardens at Boxwood in Madison are remarkable survivors of 170 years of economic boom and bust, Civil War, Reconstruction, Depression, world war, and the civil rights movement. The longtime stewardship of this property, house, and gardens by the Newton family, who acquired the property in 1905 and maintain it to this day, is remarkable. The design of one of the gardens alone would be special; that the house was double sided, facing two streets and that each facade featured its own unique and exquisite garden is delightful. The house and gardens form a cohesive and beautifully integrated composition that speaks with the soft accents of the nineteenth century, nurtured and coaxed along with exemplary stewardship. Few efforts have been undertaken to improve this garden, to make it somehow more fashionable, and attempts to accommodate contemporary uses have been modest and limited to where the least amount of damage would be done.

Boxwood is an historic house and garden on a through lot in the historic district of Madison. The lot fronts on Academy Street and Old Post Road, one block from South Main Street. Between the two principal street facades and Academy Street and Old Post Road lie two intricate boxwood parterre gardens, each approximately 100 feet square. The patterns of each garden are composed primarily of English boxwood, accented with a variety of evergreen and deciduous flowering shrubs as well as herbaceous perennials.

The designs for each are intricate and unique. A long axis runs through both gardens and the central hall of the main house. Each garden is composed of two long rectangles parallel to their sidewalk and street: two long subdivided rectangular sections along the central walk and axis and two, generally square components close to each of the two street facades of the house. The long middle rectangles are further subdivided into subordinate units: on Academy Street, the rectangle is divided into a central oval and four embracing rectangles with their central edge clipped to receive their central oval; along the Old Post Road frontage these long rectangles are divided into eight portions—four square corner beds and then a Saint Andrew's cross divides the remaining space into trapezoids with three straight edges and two that come to a point near the center of

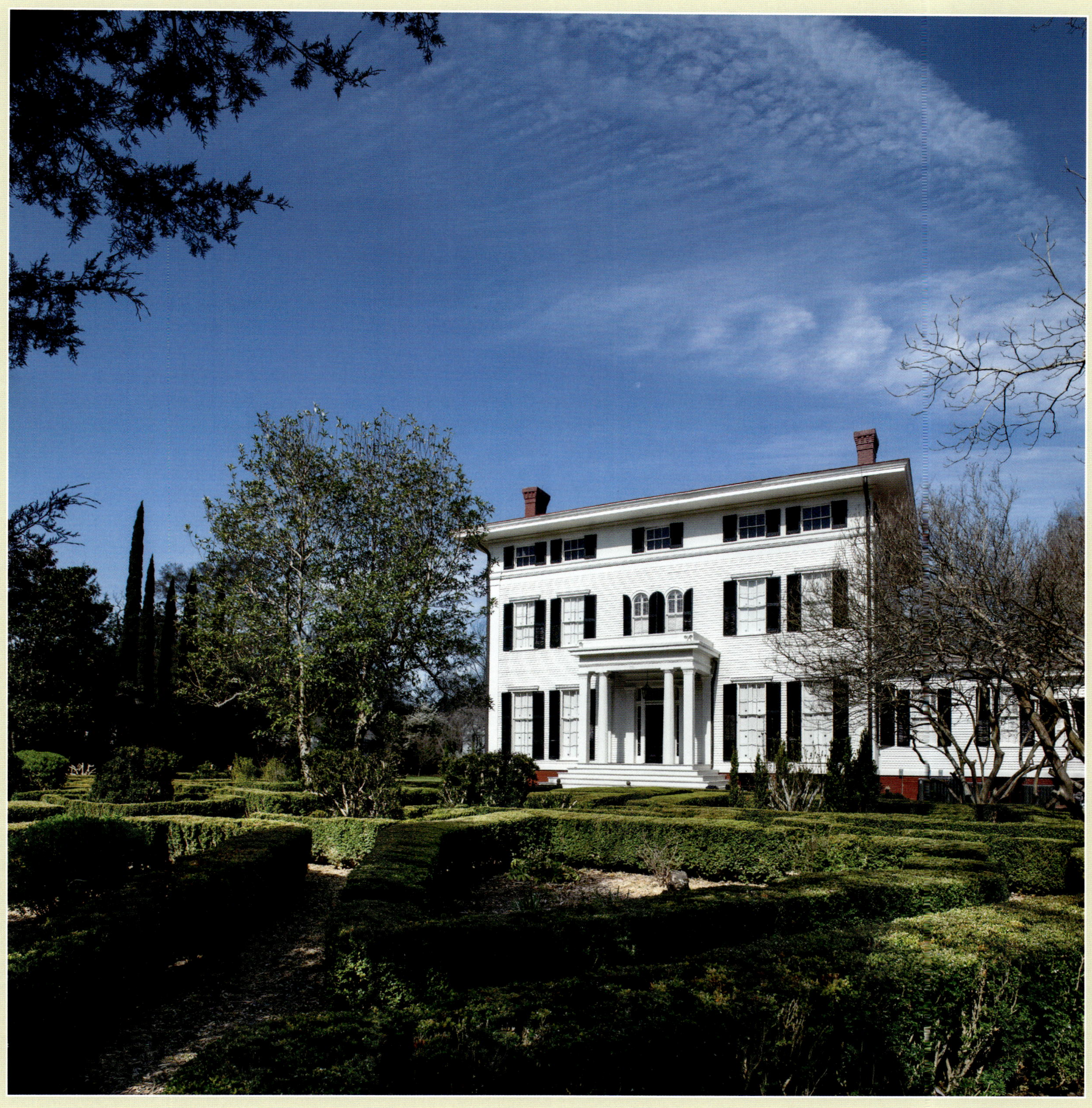

Boxwood, Madison

the bed. The final square components closest to the house form two matching quincunxes: those at the Academy facade feature an inverted diamond as a central element with four matching quarter circles that form the four corners of the figure; on the Old Post Road side these square gardens are quincunxes once again, but with a simple square as the central feature and four L-shaped beds creating the four surrounding corners. There is regularity in the overall arrangement of the garden and great variety and playfulness in the articulation of the geometry used.

Within this boxwood formwork, a variety of planting strategies have been explored over the long history of the garden. The Newtons carefully rooted boxwood cuttings from the original plants present when they purchased the property so that replacement boxwood have been at the ready when the inevitable happens and a boxwood dies and a space must be filled in.

The Kolb-Pou-Newton House was built in 1850 by Wildes Kolb at a time when cotton cultivation in Georgia was approaching a pre–Civil War peak of 701,000 bales annually. Kolb was said to be the richest man in town prior to the outbreak of the war. The house itself was unusual in that it reflected the high style of the Italianate, popularized by Alexander Jackson Davis (1803–92) through his pattern books. The double parterre gardens, reflecting the geometric pattern gardens of the era, were built contemporaneously with the house and are lovingly maintained by a third generation of the Newton family.

Owens-Thomas House Garden

The garden at the Owens-Thomas House is one of the best examples of a Colonial Revival garden designed by Clermont Huger Lee, the first woman licensed by the State of Georgia in the practice of landscape architecture. Though the garden, from 1954, is not an accurate depiction of the use of the space during the period of interpretation for the house, it has acquired significance of its own for its design excellence and as a signature work of an important landscape architect. Lee was raised in Savannah and studied landscape architecture at Smith College. She returned to her native city and worked for her entire career to preserve, protect, and celebrate the historic landscapes of this colonial city. Her work restoring and adapting the city's squares is important nationally. Her designs for the Owens-Thomas House, the Juliette Gordon Low House, and the Andrew Low House, among others, were carefully crafted and thoughtfully tailored, always with an eye to historically correct geometries and forms and authentic plant choices. That her much beloved work at the Juliette Gordon Low House was destroyed by the Girl Scouts of America in 2020 adds poignancy and power to the presence of this important remaining design and garden. This surviving design for a simple, formal parterre garden that seeks to complement an historic house museum without overshadowing it is one of the best-preserved examples of her work.

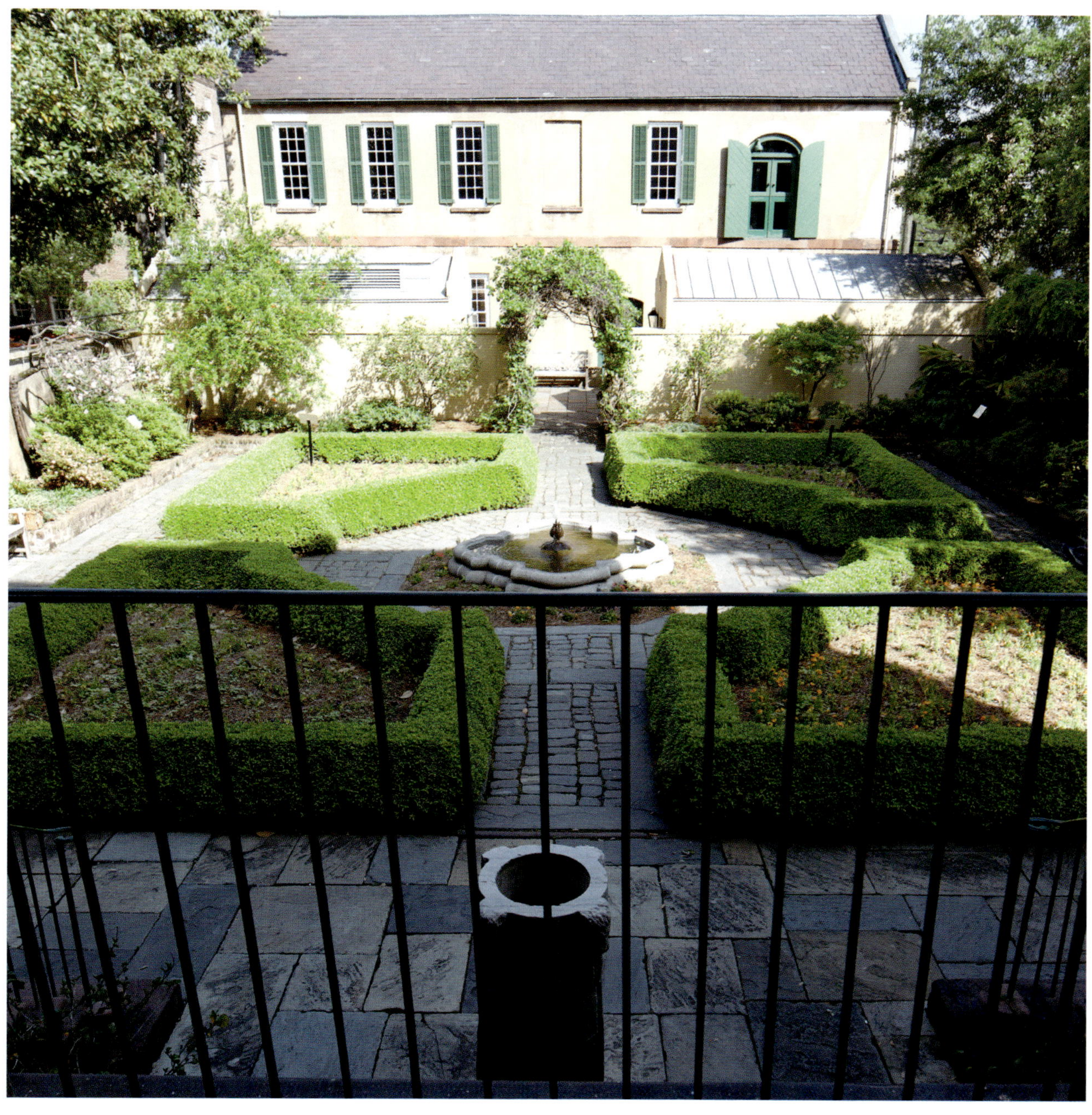

Owens-Thomas House garden, Savannah

The garden space was historically used as a service yard where laundry was hung out to air and dry, carpets were beaten and cleaned, some livestock was raised, and some herbs or vegetables grown. During the earliest period, the garden space was far from a decorative feature but rather was reserved for utilitarian purposes. Over time, as various aspects of domestic life became more mechanized, the space changed in appearance, though never with a garden of any pretension to thoughtful, considered design. The current design was developed by Lee as a complement to the conversion of the house into a museum. The garden is designed in a style appropriate to the period and reflects the growing interest in historicism popularized by the restoration of Colonial Williamsburg, Monticello, and the gardens at the University of Virginia.

Paradise Gardens

Paradise Gardens, the four-acre site of the home place and outsider-art installation created by artist Howard Finster near Summerville, Georgia, is perhaps, the apotheosis of the roadside tourist attractions that dotted the South during the early and mid-twentieth century. Finster was inspired by roadside attractions and so-called "museums" he had experienced as a young boy and propelled to "make sacred art" by visions that began as early as age three. True to his vision, Finster created art out of everything and anything he touched; nothing was off limits to his creative drive.

Finster called his creation the Plant Farm Museum; it was dubbed Paradise Gardens in an article by *Esquire* magazine in 1975. The garden features a series of structures cum sculptures, such as the Bible House, the Mirror House, the Hubcap Tower, the Bicycle Tower, the Machine Gun Nest, and the five-story Folk Art Chapel, the largest structure by far on the property. A winding path connects the structures; found objects ranging from necklaces and cutlery to mosaic tiles are embedded in the concrete walks. The site is listed in the National Register of Historic Places and includes sixteen contributing buildings, drainage canals, and a wheelchair ramp installed to accommodate disabled visitors—one of the last structures added to the site, in 1994.

Howard Finster was born in Valley Head, Alabama, in 1915. His school career was brief; by sixth grade he had left school, and by age sixteen he had begun to preach. He became a full-time Baptist minister in 1941 at the Rock Bridge Baptist Church, later serving at the Mount Carmel Baptist Church in Fort Payne, Alabama. Finster and his family moved to Trion, Georgia, in 1941, where he began doing odd jobs—carpentry, repairing bicycles, producing "family picture" clocks. In Trion he started building his first garden. After his move to Pennville, near Summerville, Finster began the realization of his vision of the Garden of Eden, building on swampy land that he added to over the years until he had assembled the current four-acre tract. To reduce the swampiness, Finster excavated soil from the basement of the small house on the property and used it as fill to separate the dry land from the water, a technique familiar to the one-time minister from Isaiah 40:4: "Every valley shall be raised." Finster created canals to further drain the property. The canals were given names of books of the bible and the land he created was planted with flowers and vegetables. His garden grew lush due to the abundance of water on site.

In 1976 he had another in his long series of visions, this one commanded him in a message from God to "make sacred art." Some sources suggest that the direction was "paint sacred art." Either way, his understanding of art was not limited to works on canvas, for his own work became three- dimensional and occupiable as he expanded the realm of what was generally regarded as art. This new vision only added volume and velocity; he was told to create five thousand works of art, a task he completed before Christmas 1985. His work from this period is numbered, and he continued painting long after he had achieved the goal laid out in his vision.

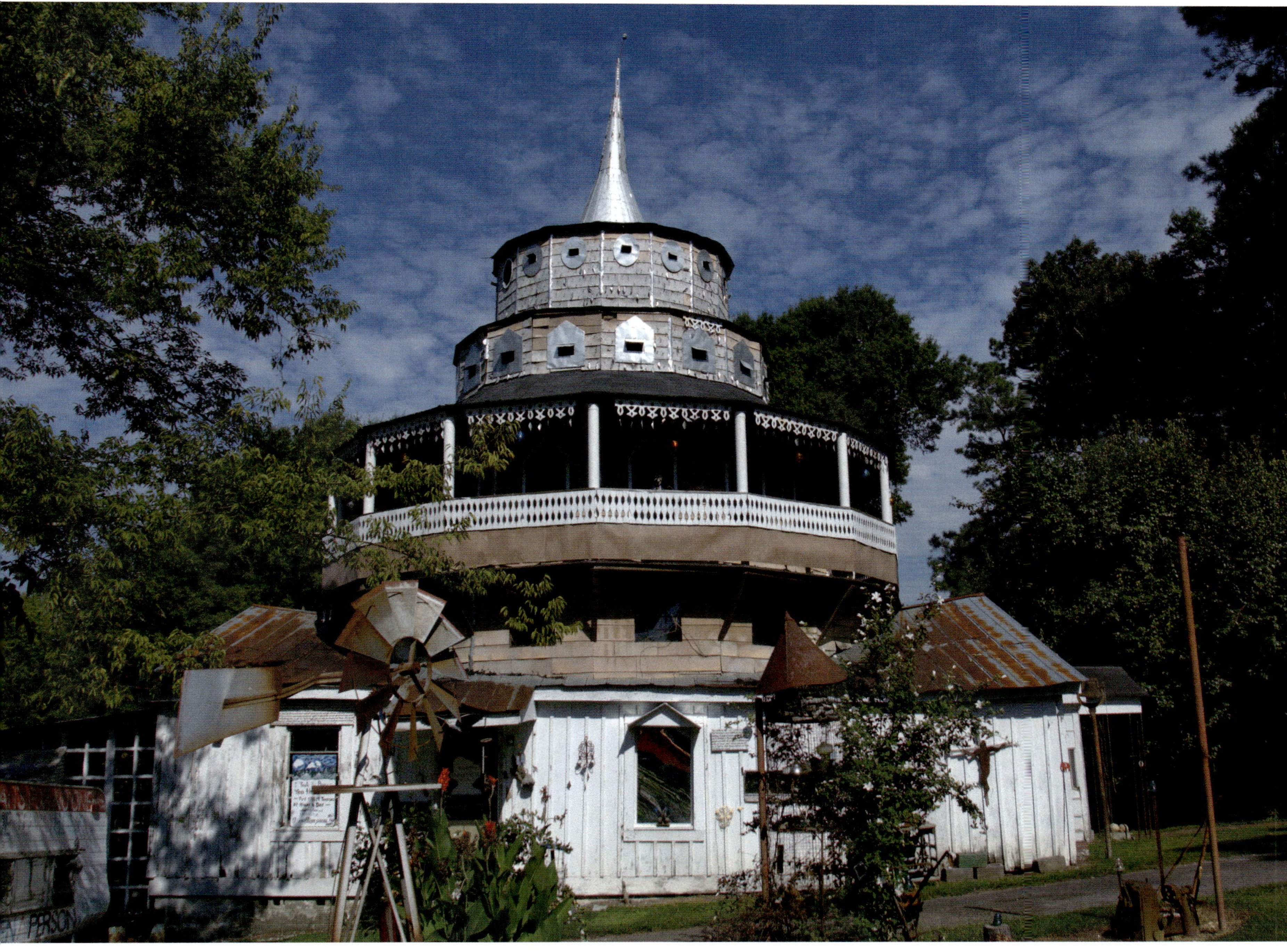

Paradise Gardens, Summerville

Finster's first major exposure was as part of a traveling exhibit of regional folk artists. In 1982, he was awarded a grant from the National Endowment of the Arts—a first for a self-taught artist. With his appeal broadening, Finster's work appeared on the cover of albums produced by popular bands such as Talking Heads and R.E.M.

Finster lived at Paradise Gardens for thirty-three years, from the time of his purchase of the property through 1994, when at age seventy-eight he moved to Summerville. After his death in 2001, the property quickly began to deteriorate. Chattooga County purchased the site, and the nonprofit Paradise Garden Foundation signed a fifty-year lease with the county with a mission "to preserve, maintain and showcase Rev. Howard Finster's visionary artistic site."

Pasaquan

Pasaquan, a seven-acre internationally known art environment outside of Buena Vista, in Marion County, was created by Eddie Owens Martin (1908–86), also known as "Saint EOM." Eddie Owens Martin's visionary art was in the service of a new religion, as opposed to the "old time religion" of Finster's Baptist heritage. Saint EOM was the founder and primary proponent of this religion, which fused elements of Native American, Precolumbian, Mexican, and other religious traditions. Martin was an outsider operating on an entirely different wavelength than the rest of the art world, guided by his inner, received visions. That he responded faithfully to these visions is clear.

The site contains six primary buildings that include an original farmhouse dating from 1885, painted concrete walls, and painted concrete structures. Initial walls constructed of wood decayed over time and were lost. Later walls of concrete remain and are decorated with images inspired by religious visions and use of psychedelics and marijuana. Many of the paintings depict mandalas, what Martin referred to as "cosmic mirrors." In addition to the principal farmhouse, other buildings and structures contribute to this National Register listed property: the Kiva, garage, Pagoda, and Studio (as enumerated in the Register listing).

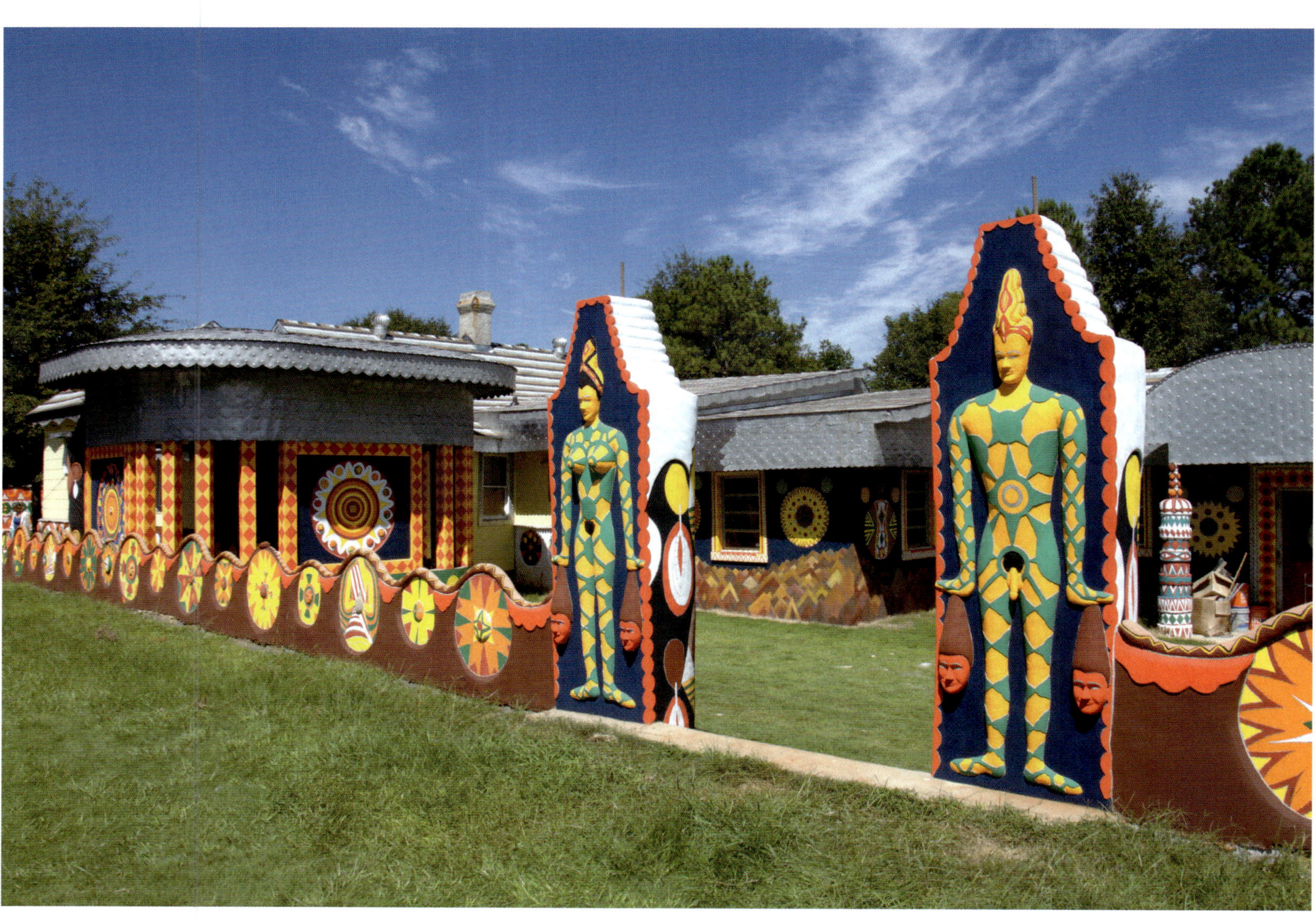

Pasaquan, Buena Vista

Martin is said to have been born at "the stroke of midnight on July 4, 1908," in Glen Alta, near Buena Vista. His father was abusive, and Martin escaped him not long after he completed all the schooling that the community offered at the time. At age fourteen, he wandered itinerantly about South Georgia and Florida before making his way to New York City. Martin's New York sojourn lasted from 1922 until 1957 with nearly yearly trips south after his father's death in 1929. Martin would somewhat grudgingly return home to help harvest the crops, but he knew his destiny lay elsewhere.

In 1935 Martin had a very strong vision while sick with pneumonia. The giant of his vision told him that "he could live, if he would follow the god's spirit." Martin had a longtime interest in the occult and mysticism; he had even been a fortune teller in New York, among many other occupations. He became a student of ancient cultures and was able to pursue these interests at the Metropolitan Museum of Art, the New York Public Library at 42nd Street, and the Museum of Natural History. One way or another, images from ancient cultures were permeating his consciousness. He began to believe that his hair and beard were his "antenna to the spirit world"; he believed that hair "keeps you in contact with the planets." By 1937, another vision, this time auditory, revealed to him that he would be "the start of somethin' new." He would be Saint EOM and a Pasaquoyan, "the first one in the world."

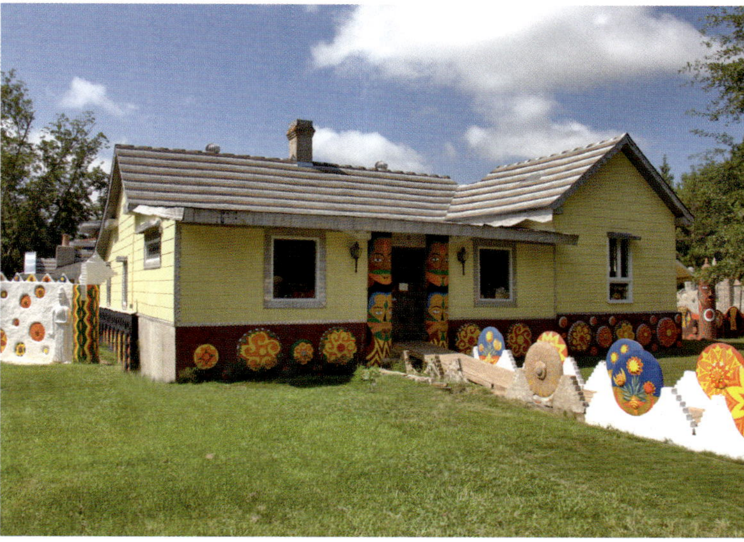

Pasaquan, Buena Vista

Martin's mother died in 1950, and he began more frequent visits to Georgia. Between 1950 and 1957 he began hauling rocks around the property for a reason that then escaped him. In 1957, Martin began construction of his artistic environment called Pasaquan. He could visualize what he wanted built and the symbols to be employed, and he knew them to be "very weird." His spirit guides would direct him on the specifics of each construction, though he often altered the dimensions given. Though many see a psychedelic aspect to the work, Martin did not use LSD, but he was a habitué of marijuana. Various helpers or assistants came in and out of Martin's orbit during the early 1960s, helping him craft various new constructions, though it was not until after he traveled to Mexico that these new constructions were painted. It was Martin's special zeal, understanding, and appreciation of the spirit world that gave the place its zing.

In declining health in the early 1980s, Martin committed suicide, leaving his property, quizzically, to the Marion County Historical Society. In 1987, the society offered Pasaquan to the Bradley Museum in Columbus; the museum politely declined. Undaunted, the Marion County Historical Society created the Pasaquan Preservation Society and recruited a qualified chairperson who became the society's first director. What money Saint EOM had could not be used immediately since the artist had never paid either state or federal income taxes and had never received a social security number. Several grants were secured in the first year to secure and stabilize the property. In 2006 the Georgia Trust for Historic Preservation named Pasaquan one of the year's Places in Peril. In 2014, the Kohler Foundation and Columbus State University joined together to protect and preserve the unique place that Eddie Owens Martin, Saint EOM, created.

SELECTED BIBLIOGRAPHY

Aiken, Charles S. *The Cotton Plantation South Since the Civil War*. Baltimore: Johns Hopkins University Press, 1998.

Barfield, James E. *Historic Macon: An Illustrated History*. San Diego, Calif.: Historical Publishing Network, 2007.

———. *Living Macon Style*. Macon, GA: Henchard Press, 2004.

Bonner, James C. *Milledgeville: Georgia's Antebellum Capital*. Athens: University of Georgia Press, 1978.

Bishir, Catherine. *North Carolina Architecture*. Raleigh: Historic Preservation Foundation of North Carolina, 1990.

Bonner, Judith H., and Estill Curtis Pennington, eds. *Art & Architecture*. Vol. 21 of *The New Encyclopedia of Southern Culture*. Chapel Hill: University of North Carolina Press, 2013.

Bowsher, Alice Meriwether. *Alabama Architecture: Looking at Building and Place*. Tuscaloosa: University of Alabama Press; Alabama Architectural Foundation, 2001.

Bryan, William D. "Taming the Wild Side of Bonaventure." *Southern Cultures* 23, no. 2 (2017).

Caldwell, Wilbur W. *The Courthouse and the Depot: The Architecture of Hope in an Age of Despair*. Macon, Ga.: Mercer University Press, 2001.

Calloway, Stephen, and Elizabeth Cromley, eds. *The Elements of Style*. New York: Simon and Schuster, 1991.

Cloues, Richard. "House Types." In *New Georgia Encyclopedia*. https://www.georgiaencyclopedia.org/articles/arts-culture/house-types.

Cobb, James C. *Georgia Odyssey: A Short History of the State*. Athens: University of Georgia Press, 2008.

Coleman, Kenneth, ed. *A History of Georgia*. Athens: University of Georgia Press, 1977.

Cooney, Lorraine M., and Hattie C. Rainwater. *Garden History of Georgia, 1733–1933*. Atlanta: Peachtree Garden Club, 1933.

Cothran, James R. *Gardens and Historic Plants of the Antebellum South*. Columbia: University of South Carolina Press, 2003.

Cox, James A. D. *Savannah Tour of Homes and Gardens*. Savannah, Ga.: Christ Church and Historic Savannah Foundation, 1996.

Craig, Robert M. *The Architecture of Francis Palmer Smith, Atlanta's Scholar Architect*. Athens: University of Georgia Press, 2012.

Davis, Lonnie J. "Creek Indian Land Cessions" (brochure). Ocmulgee National Monument, National Park Service.

Davis, Robert S. "The First Golden Age of Georgia Industry, 1828–1860." *Georgia Historical Quarterly* 72, no. 4 (1988).

Davis, Robert S. *Cotton, Fire & Dreams: The Robert Finley Iron Works and Heavy Industry in Macon, Georgia, 1839–1912*. Macon, Ga.: Mercer University Press, 1998.

Dennison, Watson W. *Cultivating Race: The Expansion Slavery in Georgia, 1750–1860*. Lexington: University Press of Kentucky, 2015.

Dowling, Elizabeth Meredith. *American Classicist: The Architecture of Philip Trammell Shutze*. New York: Rizzoli, 1989.

Ehle, John. *Trail of Tears: The Rise and Fall of the Cherokee Nation*. New York: Anchor Books, 1988.

Ellis, Clifton, and Rebecca Ginsburg, eds. *Cabin, Quarter, Plantation: Architecture and Landscapes of North American Slavery*. New Haven, Conn.: Yale University Press, 2010.

Gagnon, Michael J. "Antebellum Industrialization." In *New Georgia Encyclopedia*. https://www.georgiaencyclopedia.org/articles/history-archaeology/antebellum-industrialization/.

Gigantino, Jim. "Land Lottery System." In *New Georgia Encyclopedia*. https://www.georgiaencyclopedia.org/articles/history-archaeology/land-lottery-system/.

Gamble, Robert. *The Alabama Catalogue: Historic American Buildings Survey and a Guide to the Early Architecture of the State*. Tuscaloosa: University of Alabama Press, 1987.

Garvey, James W., and Lee Ann Caldwell. *Augusta*. Augusta, Ga.: Historic Augusta, 2018.

Goldberger, Paul, and Robert M. Craig. *John Portman: Art and Architecture*. Atlanta: High Museum of Art; Athens: University of Georgia Press, 2009.

Gournay, Isabelle. *AIA Guide to the Architecture of Atlanta*. Athens: University of Georgia Press, 1993.

Handlin, David P. *American Architecture*. London: Thames and Hudson, 1985

Harris, Cyril M. *Illustrated Dictionary of Historic Architecture*. New York: Dover, 1977.

Heeb, Mark. *A Field Guide to Historic House Types in Oglethorpe County, Georgia*. Lexington, Ga.: Historic Oglethorpe County Inc., 2004.

Herrington, Philip Mills. "Forgotten Plantation Architecture of Burke County, Georgia." MHP thesis, University of Georgia, 2003.

Hynds, Ernest. *Antebellum Athens and Clarke County, Georgia*. Athens: University of Georgia Press, 1974.

Inscoe, John C. "Georgia in 1860." In *New Georgia Encyclopedia*. https://www.georgiaencyclopedia.org/articles/history-archaeology/georgia-in-1860/.

Jeane, D. Gregory, and Douglas Clare Purcell, eds. *The Architectural Legacy of the Lower Chattahoochee Valley in Alabama and Georgia*. Tuscaloosa: University of Alabama Press, 1976.

Jones, Charles Colcock, Jr. *The Dead Towns of Georgia*. Cherokee Publishing Company, 1974. Originally published 1878.

Jones, Carmie M., ed. *Historic Savannah: A Survey of Significant Buildings in the Historic Districts of Savannah, Georgia*. 3rd ed. Savannah, Ga.: Historic Savannah Foundation, 2005.

Justice, George. *Courthouses of Georgia*. Athens: University of Georgia Press, 2014.

Kersey, Terrence Lee. "Upcountry Yeomanry in Antebellum Georgia: A Comparative Analysis." PhD diss., Georgia State University, 2017.

Lane, Mills. *Architecture of the Old South: Georgia*. Savannah, Ga.: Beehive Press, 1996.

———. *Savannah Revisited: History and Architecture*. Savannah, Ga.: Beehive Press, 1994.

Lawrence, John, Julie Turner, Glenda Major, Clark Johnson, Kaye Minchew, and Randall Allen. *Travels through Troup County: A Guide to its Architecture and History*. Troup County, Ga.: Troup County Historical Society, 1996.

Lewis, David F. *A Tour Through Time: An Architectural Guidebook to the Houses of Macon, Georgia*. Macon, Ga.: Historic Macon Foundation, 2010.

Linley, John. *Architecture of Middle Georgia: The Oconee Area*. Athens: University of Georgia Press, 1972.

———. *The Georgia Catalog, Historic American Buildings Survey: A History of the Architecture of the State*. Athens: University of Georgia Press, 1982.

Lounsbury, Carl R., ed. *An Illustrated Glossary of Early Southern Architecture and Landscape*. Charlottesville: University Press of Virginia, 1994.

Marrs, Aaron, C. *Railroads in the Old South: Pursuing Progress in a Slave Society*. Baltimore, Md.: Johns Hopkins University Press, 2009.

Martin, John H. *Columbus, Geo. From Its Selection as a "Trading Town" in 1827 to Its Partial Destruction by Wilson's Raid, 1865*. Thomas Gilbert, publisher, 1874.

McAlester, Virginia Savage. *A Field Guide to American Houses*. New York: Knopf, 2015.

Mears & Co. *The Columbus Directory for 1859–60, Containing the Names of Inhabitants, a Business Directory, Street Directory, and an Appendix of Much Useful Information*. Sun Book and Job Printing Office, 1859.

———. *The Macon Directory for 1860, Containing the Names of the Inhabitants, a Business Directory and an Appendix of Much Useful Information*. Andrews' Book and Job Printing Office, 1860.

Meyers, Christopher C., and David Williams. *Georgia: A Brief History*. Macon, Ga.: Mercer University Press, 2012.

Middle Georgia Historical Society. *Macon: An Architectural Historical Guide*. Macon, Ga.: Middle Georgia Historical Society, 1996.

Mitchell, William Robert, Jr. *The Architecture of William Frank McCall, Jr, FAIA: A Complete Designer in the Classical Tradition*. Savannah, Ga.: Golden Coast Publishing, 1985.

———. *Classic Savannah*. Savannah, Ga.: Golden Coast Publishing, 1991.

———. *Edward Vason Jones, 1909–1980: Architect, Connoisseur and Collector*. Savannah, Ga.: Golden Coast Publishing, 1995.

———. *J. Neel Reid, Architect of Hentz, Reid and Adler and the Georgia School of Classicists*. Savannah, Ga.: Golden Coast Publishing; Georgia Trust for Historic Preservation, 1997.

———. *Landmark Homes of Georgia*. Savannah, Ga.: Golden Coast Publishing, 1982.

———. *Madison: A Classic Southern Town*. Savannah, Ga.: Golden Coast Publishing, 2009.

———. *Thomasville: History, Homes and Southern Hospitality*. Thomasville, Ga.: Thomas County Historical Society and Thomasville Landmarks, 2014.

Moore, John Hebron. "Cotton Breeding in the Old South." *Agricultural History* 30, no. 3 (1956): 95–104.

Morrison, Mary L., ed. *Historic Savannah: A Survey of Significant Buildings in the Historic and Victorian Districts of Savannah, Georgia*. 2nd ed. Savannah, Ga.: Historic Savannah Foundation and Junior League of Savannah, 1979.

Nichols, Frederick D. *The Architecture of Georgia*. Savannah, Ga.: Beehive Press, 1976.

Peebles, Virginia T., and Elizabeth K. Barker. *This Place Matters: Columbus, Georgia*. Columbus, Ga.: Historic Columbus, 2016.

Perkerson, Medora Field. *White Columns in Georgia*. New York: Bonanza Books, 1952.

Reinberger, Mark. "Research Notes: Using Dendrochronology to Date First-Period Houses in the Georgia Backcountry." *Buildings & Landscapes: Journal of the Vernacular Architecture Forum* 27, no. 1 (2020): 65–77.

Rogers, William W. *Ante-Bellum Thomas County, 1825–1861*. Tallahassee: Florida State University, 1963.

Roth, Leland M., and Amanda C. Roth Clark. *American Architecture: A History*. Second Edition. Boulder, Colo.: Westview Press, 2016.

Rozier, John. *The Houses of Hancock, 1785–1865*. Atlanta: Georgia Trust for Historic Preservation, 1996.

Scott, Thomas A., ed. "Slavery in Antebellum Georgia." In *Cornerstones of Georgia History: Documents That Formed the State*, 63–76. Athens: University of Georgia Press, 1995.

Scully, Vincent. *American Architecture and Urbanism*. New York: Henry Holt, 1969.

Seals, Sonny, and George S. Hart. *Historic Rural Churches of Georgia*. Athens: University of Georgia Press, 2016.

Sears, Joan Nyles. *The First One Hundred Years of Town Planning in Georgia*. Cherokee Publishing Company, 1979.

Sullivan, Buddy. *Georgia: A State History*. Charleston, S.C.: Arcadia Publishing, 2003.

Thomas, Frances T. *A Portrait of Historic Athens and Clarke County*. Athens: University of Georgia Press, 1992.

Toledano, Roulhac. *The National Trust Guide to Savannah*. New York: Wiley, 1997.

Turner, Rhett. *Georgia County Courthouses: The Architecture of Living Monuments*. Portland, Ore.: Graphic Arts Books, 2013.

Vlach, John Michael. *Back of the Big House: The Architecture of Plantation Slavery*. Chapel Hill: University of North Carolina Press, 1993.

Wheeler, Kenneth H. *Modern Cronies: Southern Industrialism from Gold Rush to Convict Labor, 1829–1894*. Athens: University of Georgia Press, 2021.

Williams, Robin B. *Buildings of Savannah*. Charlottesville: University of Virginia Press, 2016.

Williford, William Bailey. *The Glory of Covington*. Atlanta: Cherokee Publishing Company, 1973.

Wilson, Richard Guy. *The Colonial Revival House*. New York: Abrams, 2004.

Worthington, Michael J., and Jane I. Seiter. "The Tree-Ring Dating of Ten Vernacular Buildings in Northeastern Georgia." Unpublished report. Baltimore, Md.: Oxford Tree-Ring Laboratory, 2018.

Young, Jeffrey Robert. "Slavery in Antebellum Georgia." In *New Georgia Encyclopedia* https://www.georgiaencyclopedia.org/articles/history-archaeology/slavery-in-antebellum-georgia/.

CONTRIBUTORS

Carl I. Gable has BA and JD degrees from Harvard University. He has authored and co-authored several publications, including *Palladian Days: Finding a New Life in a Venetian Country House; Villa Cornaro in the Enlightenment: Adapting a Palladian Villa to Eighteenth-Century Ideals;* and *Murano Magic: Complete Guide to Venetian Glass, Its History and Artists.* Gable is a former president of the Center for Palladian Studies in America and founding editor of its journal, *Palladiana.*

Carmie Jones McDonald has a master's of historic preservation and another in architectural history from the Savannah College of Art & Design, where she served as the valedictorian of her class. She authored *A Place Set Apart: The Architectural History of Montreat, NC* and was the editor for the third edition of *Historic Savannah.* She was formerly head of restoration for the Fox Theatre, served as an architectural historian for Ray, Ellis & LaBrie Consulting, and is a graduate of the Candler School of Theology at Emory University.

Mark C. McDonald is a graduate of Emory University and the University of Georgia School of Law. He has served as CEO of the Historic Salisbury Foundation, the Mobile Historic Development Commission, Historic Savannah Foundation, and the Georgia Trust for Historic Preservation. He is the author of a number of academic articles and was the principal author of the third edition of *Historic Savannah,* published in 2005. He has served as a book reviewer for the *Mobile Press Register, Georgia Historical Quarterly,* and University of Georgia Press.

Joseph Smith is a graduate of the Yale School of Architecture and the founding partner of Hall Smith Office, an architecture firm based in Madison, Georgia, that specializes in residential and commercial preservation projects as well as new infill construction within historic districts. Smith's work includes rehabilitation design of historic buildings, with special emphasis on vernacular and utilitarian architecture. In addition to his professional practice and teaching responsibilities, Smith serves as the vice-chair of the Madison Historic Preservation Commission and is a frequent speaker at HPC training sessions throughout the state.

Spencer Tunnell is a graduate of the University of Virginia, where he earned a master's in landscape architecture and architectural history. He formed Tunnell & Tunnell Landscape Architecture in 1988 and has received numerous awards for his preservation projects, including Olmsted Linear Parks, the Biltmore in Atlanta, and Boxwood Garden at Atlanta Historic Center. The firm has been recognized for its work by Atlanta Urban Design Commission, Georgia Trust, Atlanta History Center, and Atlanta City Council.

Robin B. Williams, Ph.D., has chaired the Architectural History Department at Savannah College of Art and Design since its creation in 1995. He is an educator who seeks to broaden awareness of how the built environment, past and present, shapes our lives, by reaching diverse audiences and pushing the boundaries of architectural history. Williams has authored many publications, including *Buildings of Savannah.* He has been involved with many other boards and organizations, including the Georgia National Register Review Board, the City of Savannah's Historic District Board of Review and currently serves on that city's Historic Preservation Commission

PHOTO CREDITS

Brian Brown
Jerusalem Lutheran Church, Thomas Ansley House, George Walton House, Midway Congregational Church, John David Mongin House, Charles Oddingsells House, Bowdre-Rees-Knox House, Shoulderbone Plantation & Outbuildings, Vann House, The Cedars, Nutwood, Raines-Miller-Carmichael House, Madison Presbyterian Church, Johnston-Felton-Hay House, Slate House, Zion Church, The Old Georgia State Capitol, Old Governor's Mansion, Bank of Columbus, Fort Pulaski National Monument, Hatcher-Grover-Schwarz House, Hancock County Courthouse, Lapham-Patterson House, Hill Harris House, Augusta Cotton Exchange, Jekyll Island Club, Baldwin Neely House, Windsor Hotel, Sacred Heart Catholic Church, King-Tisdell Cottage, Miller House, Nicholas Block House, Joseph Neel House, The Big House, Hills and Dales, Lamar Building, Ocmulgee Visitor Center, Miller Theatre, Georgia Railroad Bank, Georgia Welcome Center, Thunderbird Inn, Columbus Government Center, Citizens Federal S&L, Lamar Building Penthouse, Forsyth Park Fountain Detail, Sautee Nacoochee Valley Landscape, Hofwyl-Broadfield Plantation, Ferrell Gardens Hills and Dales, Paradise Gardens, Pasaquan

Walter Elliott
Ellamae Ellis League House

Richard Leo Johnson
Greyhound Bus Station

Diane Kirkland
Rhodes Hall Staircase, Demosthenian Hall, UGA North Campus Chapel, Parrott-Soucy House, Wrens Nest, Peters House, MLK Home, Stone Hall, Oglethorpe Courthouse, Rhodes Hall, McLeroy House, U.S. Penitentiary, Herndon House, Callan Castle, James Dickey House, Reid House, Callanwolde, Calhoun House, The Villa, Swan House, Wilburn House Kings Highway, Wilburn House Adams Street, Sears Building, United Motor Services, Peachtree Lofts, Herman Russell House, Cecil Alexander House, Stegeman Coliseum, High Museum, Carlos Museum, Buckhead Library, The News Building, Olmsted Linear Park, Piedmont Park, Founders Memorial Garden, Egleston Garden, Woodhaven Governor's Mansion, Broadlands Landscape, Broadlands Entry Court, Swan House Landscape, Boxwood Landscape

Kevin Lamb
Cedar Grove Plantation

James R. Lockhart
Ezekiel Harris House, Nicholas Ware House, Enterprise Mill, Martin House, St. Paul's Episcopal Church, Breetholme, William B. White House, Augusta Canal and Mills, Carnes-Chafee Garden. All courtesy of Historic Augusta Foundation.

Millpond Plantation, Oak Hill at Berry College, Valley View, Woodlands Barsnely Gardens, Millpond Plantation Landscape

Carmie Jones McDonald
Dinglewood, Columbus Shotgun Houses

Charlie Miller
Georgia State Capitol, Brookwood Station, Flatiron Building, Empire Building, Fox Theatre Interior, Southern Bell Building, MLK Jr. Federal Building, Cannon Chapel, Hyatt Regency Hotel, Atlanta Central Library

Bob Semsch
Goodrum Estate Landscape

Todd Stone
Covenant Presbyterian Church

John M. Tatum
Wild Heron Plantation, Christian Camphor House, James Habersham Jr. House, George B. Spencer House, John Berrien House, Hampton Lillibridge House, William Scarborough House, First African Baptist Church, Green-Meldrim House, Central of Georgia Railway Buildings, Hamilton-Turner House, Smithfield Cottage, McMillan Row Houses, Savannah Volunteer Guards Armory, Lattimore House, Savannah City Hall, Whitefield Chapel, Citizens Bank, Carnegie Library, Bryson Auto Garage, Standard Oil Building, Globe Shoe, Drayton Tower, Benedictine School, Jepson Building, Lominack House, Wormsloe Allée, Owens-Thomas House Garden

INDEX

Page numbers in italics refer to images.